C000070440

Andalucía
& Southern
Spain

routard

Managing editor: Liz Coghill
English translation: Penny Langton
Editorial: Deborah Taylor, Hilary Hughes

Additional research and assistance:
Michael Hutchinson, Sofi Mogensen, Kate
Williams, Michael Summers
Index: Dorothy Frame

Series director: Philippe Gloaguen
Series creators: Philippe Gloaguen, Michel
Duval
Chief editor: Pierre Josse
Assistant chief editor: Benoît Lucchini
Coordination director: Florence
Charmetant

Editorial team: Yves Couprie, Olivier Page,
Véronique de Chardon, Amanda Keravel,
Isabelle Al Subaihi, Anne-Caroline Dumas,
Carole Bordes, Bénédicte Bazaille, André
Poncelet, Jérôme de Gubernatis, Marie
Burin des Roziers and Thierry Brouard.

Our guides provide independent advice. The authors and compilers do not accept any remuneration for the inclusion of addresses in this guide. Please note that we cannot accept any responsibility for any loss, injury or inconvenience sustained by anyone as a result of any information or advice contained in this guide.

Feedback
We have done our best to ensure the accuracy of the information contained in this guide. However, addresses, phone numbers, opening times etc. do invariably change from time to time, so if you find a discrepancy please do let us know and help us update the guides. As prices may change so may other circumstances – a restaurant may change hands or the standard of service at a hotel may deteriorate since our researchers made their visit. Again, we do our best to ensure information is accurate, but if you notice any discrepancy, please let us know. You can contact us at: hachetteuk@orionbooks.co.uk or write to us at Cassell & Co, address below.

Price guide
Because of rapid inflation in many countries, it is impossible to give an accurate indication of prices in hotels and restaurants. Prices can change enormously from one year to the next. As a result we have adopted a system of categories for the prices in the guides: 'Budget', 'Moderate', 'Chic' and 'Très Chic' (in the guides to France), otherwise 'Expensive' and 'Splash Out' in the others.

Distributed in the United States of America by Sterling Publishing Co., Inc.
387 Park Avenue South, New York, NY 10016-8810.

A CIP catalogue for this book is available from the British Library.

ISBN 1 84202 028 5

Typeset at The Spartan Press Ltd, Lymington, Hants.
Printed and bound by Aubin, France. E-mail: sales@aubin-imprimeur.fr

Cover design by Emmanuel Le Vallois (Hachette Livre) and Paul Cooper.
Cover photo © Images Colour Library. Back cover photo © Richard Turpin/Aspect Picture Library.

Cassell & Co, Wellington House, 125 Strand, London WC2R 0BB

Andalucía & Southern Spain

The ultimate
food, drink and
accommodation guide

HACHETTE

Contents

THE VALENCIA REGION 355

Just Exactly Who or What is a Routard?

You are. Yes, you! The fact that you are reading this book means that you are a Routard. You are probably still none the wiser, so to explain we will take you back to the origin of the guides. Routard was the brainchild of a Frenchman named Philippe Gloaguen, who compiled the first guide some 25 years ago with his friend Michel Duval. They simply could not find the kind of guide book they wanted and so the solution was clear – they would just have to write it themselves. When it came to naming the guide, Philippe came up with the term Routard, which at the time did not exist as a bona fide word – at least, not in conventional dictionary terms. Today, if you look the word up in a French-English dictionary you will find that it means 'traveller' or 'globetrotter' – so there you have it, that's what you are!

From this humble beginning has grown a vast collection of some 100 titles to destinations all over the world. Routard is now the bestselling guide book series in France. The guides have been translated into five different languages, so keep an eye out for fellow Routard readers on your travels.

What exactly do the guides do?
The short answer is that they provide all the information you need to enable you to have a successful holiday or trip. Routards' great strength however, lies in their listings. The guides provide comprehensive listings for accommodation, eating and drinking – ranging from campsites and youth hostels through to four star hotels – and from bars, clubs and greasy spoons to tearooms, cafés and restaurants. Each entry is accompanied by a detailed and frank appraisal of the address, rather like a friend coming back from holiday who is recommending all the good places to go (or even the places to avoid!). The guides aim to help you find the best addresses and the best value for money within your price range, whilst giving you invaluable insider advice at the same time.

Anything else?
Routard also provides oceans of practical advice on how to get along in the country or city you are visiting plus an insight into the character and customs of the people. How do you negotiate your way around the transport system? Will you offend if you bare your knees in the temple? And so on. In addition, you will find plenty of sightseeing information, backed up by historical and cultural detail, interesting facts and figures, addresses and opening times. The humanitarian aspect is also of great importance, with the guides commenting freely and often pithily, and most titles contain a section on human rights.

Routard are truly useful guides that are convivial, irreverent, down-to-earth and honest. We very much hope you enjoy them and that they will serve you well during your stay.

Happy travelling.

Map List

Colour Maps

Symbols Used in the Guide

Please note that not all the symbols below appear in every guide.

- ■ Useful addresses
- 🚩 Tourist office
- ✉ Post office
- ☎ Telephone
- 🚆 Railway station
- 🚌 Bus station
- 🚕 Shared taxi
- 🚊 Tram
- River transport
- Sea transport
- ✈ Airport
- 🛏 Where to stay

- ✗ Where to eat
- 🍷 Where to go for a drink
- ♪ Where to listen to music
- 🍦 Where to go for an ice-cream
- ★ To see
- 🛍 Shopping
- ● 'Other'
- 🅿 Parking
- ✗ Castle
- ⁂ Ruins

- Diving site
- Shelter
- 🏕 Camp site
- ▲ Peak
- ● Site
- ○ Town
- ⋈ Hill
- Abbey, chapel
- Lookout
- Beach
- Lighthouse

Getting There

By Air

FROM BRITAIN

Round-the-clock flights leave Britain for destinations in Andalucía and southern Spain, as well as for Madrid and Barcelona. **British Airways** flies from Heathrow and Gatwick to Málaga, Seville and Granada. **Iberia** flies from Heathrow to Málaga and Seville and via Madrid to Almería, Granada and Jerez. Iberia also flies from Manchester, via Barcelona, to Málaga and Seville. Other scheduled airlines flying to southern Spain include **buzz**, from Stansted to Jerez, **easyJet** from Luton and Liverpool to Málaga and **Go** from Stansted to Málaga and Alicante. **bmi british midland** flies from Edinburgh, Glasgow and East Midlands to Málaga. There are also numerous charter flights, sold by high-street travel agents, from Britain, mostly to the Costa del Sol.

Standard return flights to Madrid or Málaga on scheduled airlines cost from £200. There's a lot of competition, thanks to the low-cost airlines, and prices can go as low as £60 for a return. Expect to pay from £140 for a return charter flight. The most expensive time to fly to Spain is usually during July and August, but there's every chance of bargain fares, even in the height of summer. The flight time from London to Madrid or Málaga is approximately 2 hours. The travel pages of the weekend broadsheet newspapers, teletext, websites such as www.cheapflights.com, www.expedia.com and www.lastminute.com are good starting points for finding package and air ticket bargains.

Ensure that any airline or travel agent is ABTA endorsed. Contact the **Air Travel Advisory Bureau** for information on airlines and prices.

✪ Avro: (charter flights) Vantage House, 1 Weir Road, Wimbledon SW19 8UX. ☎ (0870) 036-0114. Website: www.avro.com

✪ bmi british midland: Donington Hall, Castle Donington, Derby DE74 2SB. ☎ (0870) 607-0555. Website: www.flybmi.com

✪ British Airways: Waterside, PO Box 365, Harmondsworth UB7 OGB. ☎ (0845) 773-3377. Website: www.britishairways.com

✪ buzz: Endeavour House, Stansted Airport CM24 1RS. ☎ (0870)-240-7070. Website: www.buzzaway.com

✪ easyJet: easyLand, London Luton Airport, Luton LU2 9LS. ☎ (0870) 6000-000. Website: www.easyjet.com

✪ Go: Enterprise House, Stansted Airport CM24 1SB. ☎ (0870) 607-6543. Website: www.go-fly.com

✪ Iberia: Iberia House, 10 Hammersmith Broadway, London W6 7AL. ☎ (0845) 601-2854. Website: www.iberia.com

✪ Air Travel Advisory Bureau: Columbus House, 28 Charles Square, London N1 6HT. ☎ (020) 7635-5000. Website: www.atab.co.uk

TRAVEL AGENTS

■ **Airline Network**: (discount flights by phone only) ☎ (0870) 241-0019. Website: www.netflights.com

■ **Bridge the World**: (discount flights and packages) 47 Chalk Farm Road, London NW1 8AJ. ☎ (0870) 444-7474. Website: www.bridgetheworld.com

■ **Flightbookers**: (discount flights and packages) 177–178 Tottenham Court Road, London W1P OLX. ☎ (0870) 010-7000. Website: www.ebookers.com

■ **STA Travel**: (students and those under 26) 86 Old Brompton Road, London SW7 3LQ. ☎ (020) 7851-4132. Website: www.statravel.co.uk

■ **Thomas Cook**: (flights and packages) Branches nationwide. ☎ (0990) 666-222. Website: www.thomascook.co.uk

■ **Trailfinders**: (discounts and specialist itineraries) 215 Kensington High Street, London W8 6BD. ☎ (020) 7937-1234. Website: www.trailfinders.com

■ **USIT Campus Travel**: (students and those under 26) 52 Grosvenor Gardens, London SW1 OAG. ☎ (0870) 240-1010. Website: www.usitcampus.co.uk

Specialist Travel Agents

The following is a selection of British companies that specialize in arranging travel to Andalucía and southern Spain.

■ **Andalucían Adventures**: (walking, painting and cultural tours) Washpool, Horsley GL6 OPP. ☎ (01453) 832583. Website: www.andalucianadventures.co.uk

■ **Ramblers Holidays**: Box 43, Welwyn Garden City AL8 6PQ. ☎ (01707) 331133. Website: www.ramblersholidays.co.uk

■ **Real Ronda**: (villas and hotels in Serannia de Ronda) 19 Bucklands View, Nailsea BS48 4TZ. ☎ (01275) 859699. Website: www.real-ronda.com

■ **Simply Spain**: (city breaks, hotels, rentals) Kings House, Wood Street, Kingston-upon-Thames KT1 1SG. ☎ (020) 8541-2208. Website: www.simply-travel.com

■ **Spanish Affair**: (villas, packages, itineraries) 5–7 Humbolt Road, London W6 8QH. ☎ (020) 7385-8127. Website: www.spanishaffair.com

FROM IRELAND

Iberia flies daily to Barcelona, and to Madrid via Barcelona. Iberia can sell you a flight connection, from either Madrid or Barcelona, to any airport in Spain. **bmi british midland** flies regularly from Dublin to Málaga, and weekly from Belfast to Málaga. **Aer Lingus** flies from Dublin to Barcelona, via London, in summer only. There are also frequent charter flights, sold by high-street travel agents, from Dublin and Belfast to the Costa del Sol.

Flight time from Dublin or Belfast to Spain is just over 2 hours.

Scheduled flights from Dublin to Barcelona, Madrid or Málaga start at around IR£220 in low season, and can exceed IR£300 during July and August. To fly on to another airport in Spain from Madrid or Barcelona, add about IR£95. Charter return flights start at IR£200.

⊕Aer Lingus: 40–41 Upper O'Connell Street, Dublin 1. ☎ (01) 886-8888. Website: www.flyaerlingus.com

⊕bmi british midland: Belfast International Airport, Belfast BT29 4AB. ☎ (0870) 607-0555. Dublin Airport, Dublin 1. ☎ (01) 407 3036. Website: www.flybmi.com

⊕Iberia: 54 Dawson Street, Dublin 2. ☎ (01) 407-3018. Website: www.iberia.com

TRAVEL AGENTS

■ **American Express Travel**: 116 Grafton Street, Dublin 2. ☎ (01) 677-2874.

■ **Budget Travel**: 134 Lower Baggot Street, Dublin 2. ☎ (01) 661-3122.

■ **Budget Travel Shops**: 63 Main Street, Finglas 11, Dublin. ☎ (01) 834-0637.

■ **Thomas Cook**: 11 Donegall Place, Belfast BT1 6ET. ☎ (01232) 554-455. 118 Grafton Street, Dublin. ☎ (01) 677-1721. Website: www.thomascook.com

■ **Trailfinders**: 4–5 Dawson Street, Dublin 2. ☎ (01) 677-7888. Website: www.trailfinders.com

■ **USIT NOW**: 19–21 Aston Quay, O'Donnell Bridge, Dublin. ☎ (01) 602-1700. 13B Fountain Centre, College Street, Belfast BT61 6ET. ☎ (01232) 324-4073. Website: www.usitnow.ie

Specialist Travel Agents

■ **Exodus**: (adventure travel) Colette Pearson Travel, 64 South William Street, Dublin 2. ☎ (01) 677-1029. Email: cptravel@indigo.ie. Website: www.exodus.co.uk

Contact the British branch of the Spanish Tourist Office for further information. Most travel agents in Britain can also arrange travel to Spain for you. For more details, *see* 'Travel Agents in Britain'.

FROM THE UNITED STATES

American Airlines, **Delta**, **Iberia** and **US Airways** fly non-stop from the United States to Madrid. Iberia flies direct from New York, Miami and Chicago to Madrid and Barcelona, with connections to Málaga and Seville. Most other flights to Madrid leave from New York, Miami and Washington, but American Airlines flies from Dallas Fort Worth, Delta flies from Atlanta and

US Airways flies from Philadelphia. European airlines such as **Air France**, **British Airways**, **KLM** and **Sabena** also fly to Madrid, usually via other airports.

Many apex flights to Madrid will throw in a free flight to Málaga or Seville. Otherwise, Andalucía is a quick flight or train journey from Madrid.

If you buy a return transatlantic flight with Iberia, you might consider the **Iberia Visit Spain Airpass**. The airpass, which must be purchased before you leave, is good for four flights within Spain. It costs from US$260 (US$350 to include the Canaries).

Flight time from New York to Madrid is from 7 hours. Journey time from the west coast is from 9 hours.

Fares start at around US$650 for a return to Madrid from New York. Return fares from the west coast start at around US$750. Prices are highest in summer and during the winter holiday season, but the further in advance you book, the cheaper the fare, whenever you plan to depart. The cheapest apex (advance purchase excursion) fares must be booked at least 21 days in advance and involve a stay of at least seven days and no longer than one month. For the lowest apex or other fares, consult your travel agent and keep an eye on the airlines' websites, as these are often where the deals are posted first. The *LA Times*, *San Francisco Chronicle*, *New York Times* and *Chicago Tribune* publish travel sections full of advertisements for flight and package bargains. It's also worth investigating internet travel sites such as www.lowestfare.com, www.priceline.com, www.previewtravel.com, www.travelocity.com and www.expedia.com. Travel clubs, which offer discounts on travel services for an annual fee, are worth looking into.

Always ensure that any travel agent is endorsed by ASTA, or is a member of USTOA.

✪ Air Europa: (charter airline to Spain) 1001 Avenue of the Americas, Eighth Floor, New York, New York 10018. ☎ 1-888-238-7672. Website: www.air-europa.com

✪ Air France: 125 West 55th Street, New York, New York 10019. ☎ 1-800-237-2747. Website: www.airfrance.com

✪ American Airlines: 4200 Amon Carter, PD 2400, Fort Worth, Texas. ☎ 1-800-433-7300. Website: www.aa.com

✪ British Airways: 72 Astoria Boulevard, Jackson Heights, New York, New York 11370. ☎ 1-800-545-7644. Website: www.britishairways.com

✪ Delta Airlines: PO Box 20980, Atlanta, Georgia 30320. ☎ 1-800-221-1212. Website: www.delta.com

✪ Iberia: 333 North Michigan Avenue, Suite 2131, Chicago, Illinois 60601. ☎ 1-800-772-4642. Website: www.iberia.com

✪ KLM/Northwest Airlines: 100 East 42nd Street, Second Floor, New York, New York 10017. ☎ 1-800-447-4747. Website: www.nwa.com

✪ Sabena: Sabena Swiss Center, 608 Fifth Avenue, New York, New York 10020. ☎ 1-800-221-4740. Website: www.sabena.com

✪ US Airways: 10 Eyck Plaza, 40 North Pearl Street, Albany, New York 12207. ☎ 1-800-428-432. Website: www.usairways.com

TRAVEL AGENTS

■ **Air Courier Association**: 191 University Boulevard, Suite 300, Denver, Colorado 80206. ☎ (303) 278-8810 or 1-800-282-1202. Website: www.air-courier.org

■ **Last Minute Travel Club**: (standby deals) 132 Brookline Avenue, Boston, Massachusetts 02215. ☎ 1-800-LAST MIN.

■ **STA Travel**: (students and those under 26. Branches nationwide) 48 East 11th Street, New York, New York 10003. ☎ 1-800-781-4040. Website: www.statravel.com

■ **USIT (Council Travel) USA**: (students and those under 26. Over 60 branches nationwide) 931 Westwood Boulevard, Westwood, Los Angeles, California 90024. ☎ 1-800-226-8624. Website: www.counciltravel.com

Specialist Travel Agents

The following are just a selection of the United States travel agents that specialize in travel to southern Spain.

■ **Europe Express**: (general) 19021 120th Avenue, Suite 102, North East, Bothell, Washington 98011. ☎ 1-800-426-3615. Website: www.europe express.com

■ **Epiculinary**: (cookery tours to southern Spain) 321 East Washington Avenue, Lake Bluff, Illinois 60044. ☎ 1-888-380-9010. Website: www. epiculinary.com

■ **Eurobike**: (biking and walking tours) PO Box 990, DeKalb, Illinois 60115. ☎ 1-800-321-6060. Website: www.eurobike.com

■ **Headwater**: (activity and tours) 1312 18th Street North West, Suite 401, Washington, DC 20036. ☎ 1-800-567-6386. Website: www.headwater-breakaway.com

FROM CANADA

Iberia flies direct to Madrid from Montréal three times a week. European airlines, such as **Air France**, **British Airways** and **KLM**, fly regularly to Madrid, usually via other European cities. **Air Canada** also flies from Montréal and Toronto to Madrid, via other cities.

Flight time is from 9 hours and increases with stops. Return fares from Montréal or Toronto to Madrid start at around CAN$900, increasing to over CAN$1500 during holiday periods, particularly in July and August.

For scheduled deals, search the weekly travel sections of the broadsheets, check internet sites such as www.dial-a-flight.com and ring round discount travel agents. Cheaper tickets might be available to destinations such as London, Paris or Frankfurt, from where Spain is a quick flight or a straightforward overland journey. Alternatively, if you live close to the border, it might be worth travelling to an airport in the United States, such as New

York, and flying from there to Madrid. For more details, *see* 'Getting There by Air from the United States'.

✚ Air Canada: Royal York Hotel, 100 Front Street, West Arcade Level, Toronto M5K 1GD. ☎ 1-888-247-2262. Website: www.aircanada.ca

✚ Air France: 151 Bloor Street West, Suite 810, Toronto. ☎ 1-800-667-2747. Website: www.airfrance.ca

✚ British Airways: 4120 Yonge Street, Suite 100, Toronto M2P 2B8. ☎ 1-800-AIRWAYS or 1-800-247-9297. Website: www.britishairways.com

✚ Iberia: Toronto Pearson International Airport, Toronto L5P 1B2. ☎ 1-800-772-4642. Website: www.iberia.com

✚ KLM/Northwest: Toronto Pearson International Airport, Toronto L5P 1B2. ☎ 1-800-374-7747. Website: www.klm.com/www.nwa.com

TRAVEL AGENTS

■ **Collacutt Travel**: (general travel services) The Bayview Village Centre, 2901 Bayview Avenue, Toronto M2K 1E6. ☎ 1-888-225-9811. Website: www.collacutt-travel.com

■ **New Frontiers/Nouvelles Frontières**: 1001 Sherbrook Street East, Suite 720, Montréal H21 1L3. ☎ (514) 526-8444.

■ **Sears Travel**: (general services. 81 offices throughout Canada) ☎ 1-888-884-2539. Website: www.sears.ca

■ **Travel Cuts**: (student travel organization. Branches countrywide) 187 College Street, Toronto M5T 1P7. ☎ (416) 979-2406 or 1-800-667-2887. Website: www.travelcuts.com

■ **Travel House**: (tours, packages, discount travel. Branches countrywide) 1491 Yonge Street, Suite 401, Toronto M4T 1ZR. ☎ (416) 925-6322. Website: www.travel-house.com

Many United States travel agents will also organize travel for Canadian travellers.

Specialist Travel Agents

The following are just a selection of the Canadian travel agents that specialize in travel to southern Spain.

■ **Butterfield and Robinson**: (general) 70 Bond Street, Toronto M5B 1X3. ☎ (416) 864-1354. Website: www.butterfieldandrobinson.com

■ **Contiki**: (tours for under 35s) 355 Eglinton Avenue East, Toronto M4P 1M5. ☎ (416) 932-9449. Website: www.contiki.com

■ **Heart of Spain**: (cultural tours) 140 Dupont Street, Toronto M5R 1V2. ☎ 1-800-848-8163. Website: www.totaltravelservice.com

FROM AUSTRALIA AND NEW ZEALAND

There are no direct flights from Australia or New Zealand to Spain. European airlines such as **British Airways** and **KLM** fly regularly to Madrid and Barcelona, from Sydney and Melbourne, via other European cities.

Qantas flies daily from Sydney, Melbourne and Auckland to London and then to Madrid. **JAL Japan Airlines and Singapore Airlines** fly daily to Madrid and Barcelona from Sydney and Melbourne and regularly to Madrid from Auckland. **Thai Airways** flies three times a week from Sydney and Melbourne to Madrid via Bangkok. Flying via South America is worth looking into, with airlines such as **Aerolineas Argentinas** sometimes offering competitive prices.

Journey time to Spain from Sydney or Melbourne starts at around 19 hours, but can increase to over 25 hours, depending on departure airport and stops made. Journey time from Auckland is from around 25 hours.

Return fares to Spain from Australia begin at around AUD$1600 in low season, rising to AUD$2200 in high season. Low season fares from New Zealand begin at NZ$2200 and increase to over NZ$2800 in high season. Fares are highest for departures in summer and during the winter holiday. Early booking will reduce the price of your ticket, whenever your date of departure.

For those with the time, round-the-world tickets, offering up to six free stops, are frequently only slightly more expensive than standard return fares.

✪ **Aerolineas Argentinas**: 189 Kent Street, Level Four, Sydney 2000. ☎ (02) 9252-5150. 135 Albert Street, Level 15, Auckland 1. ☎ (09) 379-3675. Website: www.aerolineas.com

✪ **British Airways**: Chifley Square, 70 Hunter Street, Sydney 2000. ☎ (02) 9258-3300. Auckland International Airport, Auckland 1. ☎ (09) 356-8690. Website: www.britishairways.com

✪ **JAL Japan Airlines**: Darling Park, Level 14, 201 Sussex Street, Sydney 2000. ☎ (02) 9272-1111. Westpac Tower, 12th Floor, 120 Albert Street, Auckland 1. ☎ (09) 379-9906. Website: www.jal.com

✪ **KLM**: 115 Pitt Street, Level 13, Sydney 2000. ☎ (02) 9922-1555. Salvation Army Building, Second Floor, 369 Queen Street, Auckland 1. ☎ (09) 309-1782. Website: www.klm.com

✪ **Qantas**: Qantas Centre, 203 Coward Street, Mascot, Sydney 2020. ☎ 13-12-11 or (02) 9691-3636. 191 Queen Street, Auckland 1. ☎ (09) 357-8900 or 0800-808-967. Website: www.qantas.com

✪ **Singapore Airlines**: Singapore Airlines House, 17–19 Bridge Street, Sydney 2000. ☎ (02) 9350-0100. West Plaza Building, Tenth Floor, Corner Albert and Fanshawe Streets, Auckland 1. ☎ 0800-808-909. Website: www.singaporeair.com

✪ **Thai Airways**: 75–77 Pitt Street, Sydney 2000. ☎ (02) 9251-1922. Kensington Swan Building, First Floor, 22 Fanshawe Street, Auckland 1. ☎ (09) 377-0268. Website: www.thaiair.com

GETTING THERE

TRAVEL AGENTS

■ **Flight Centres**: 33 Berry Street, Level 13, North Sydney 2060. ☎ (02) 924-2422. 205 Queen Street, Auckland 1. ☎ (09) 309-6171. ☎ 1-1300-131-600 for nearest branch.

■ **STA Travel**: 855 George Street, Sydney 2000. ☎ (02) 9212-1255 (72 branches). 90 Cashel Street, Christchurch. ☎ (03) 379-9098 (13 branches). Website: www.statravel.com.au

■ **Thomas Cook**: 175 Pitt Street, Sydney 2000 ☎ 1-300-728-748 (branches nationwide) 96 Anzac Avenue, Auckland. ☎ 0800-500-600 (branches nationwide).

■ **Trailfinders**: 91 Elizabeth Street, Brisbane, Queensland 4000. ☎ (07) 3229-0887. Website: www.trailfinders.com.au

Specialist Travel Agents

The following is just a selection of the travel agents in Australia and New Zealand that specialize in travel to southern Spain.

■ **Adventure World**: 73 Walker Street, North Sydney. ☎ (02) 9956-7766. 101 Great South Road, Remuera, Auckland 1. ☎ (09) 524-5118. Website: www.adventureworld.net.au

■ **European Travel Office**: 133 Castlereagh Street, Sydney 2000. ☎ (02) 9627-7727. 407 Great South Road, Penrose, Auckland 1. ☎ (09) 525-3074.

■ **Ibertours**: 84 William Street, First Floor, Melbourne 3000. ☎ (03) 9670-8388. Website: www.ibertours.com

■ **IB Tours**: 47 New Canterbury Road, Suite Two, Petersham, Sydney 2049. ☎ (02) 9650-6722. Website: www.ib-tours.com.au

■ **Peregrine Adventures**: 38 York Street, Fifth Floor, Sydney 2000. ☎ (612) 9290-2770. Website: www.peregrine.net.au

■ **Top Deck**: 123 Clarence Street, Level Two, Sydney 2000. ☎ 1-300-656-566. Email: topdeck@deckers.com.au

FROM SOUTH AFRICA

Air France, **British Airways** and **Iberia** fly to Madrid from Johannesburg, usually stopping at least once en route. **South African Airways** flies to major cities in Europe, such as Frankfurt, Hamburg, London and Paris, from where Spain is a quick flight or straightforward overland trip.

Flight time is from 10 hours and increases with stopovers.

Prices for a standard return to Spain begin at around R5000, but can increase to over R20000. Prices increase for departures in summer, the winter holiday period and at weekends. The cheapest tickets on international flights from South Africa book up quickly. The further in advance you book, the more chance you have of getting the cheapest fares.

✪ **Air France**: Oxford Manor, First Floor, Oxford Road, Ilovo 2196. ☎ (0860) 340-340. Website: www.airfrance.com

✪ **British Airways**: Grovesnor Court, 195 Grovesnor Corner, Rosebank, Johannesburg 2196. ☎ 0860-011-747 or (011) 441-8600. Website: www.britishairways.com

✪ **Iberia**: Sandown House, Second Floor, Norwich Park Phase Two, Corner South Street and Norwich Close, Sandton, Johannesburg 2146. ☎ (011) 884-6122. Website: www.iberia.com

✪ **South African Airways**: Airways Park, Jones Road, Johannesburg International Airport, Johannesburg 1627. ☎ (011) 978-1763. Website: www.saa.co.za

TRAVEL AGENTS

■ **STA Travel**: Leslie Social Sciences Building, Level Three, University of Cape Town, Rondebosch 7700, Cape Town. ☎ (021) 685-1808. Website: www.statravel.co.za

■ **USIT Adventures**: Rondebosch Shopping Centre, Rondebosch Main Road, Rondebosch, Cape Town. ☎ (021) 685-2226. Website: www.usit campus.co.uk

By Train

FROM BRITAIN

You must change trains in Paris to get from Britain to Spain. 25 daily direct high-speed **Eurostar** trains leave London Waterloo for Paris Gare du Nord. You can join 15 of these trains to Paris at Ashford, Kent. From Paris Gare d'Austerlitz, one train leaves for Madrid in early evening and a sleeper departs at 10.24pm. The high-speed AVE train from Madrid takes just 2 hours 30 minutes to reach Seville. Slower and cheaper trains from Madrid to Seville take over 5 hours. Direct trains also leave Madrid for Almería, Granada and Málaga, and destinations in Valencia and Murcia.

Total journey time from London to Seville is around 24 hours, if you travel to Paris by Eurostar. This increases to about 30 hours if you travel by ferry and slower rail services.

An all-inclusive ticket from London to Málaga, Seville or Granada should cost from around £220. For rail travel to Spain, it's best to contact a travel agent such as **USIT Campus** (*see* 'Travel Agents in Britain') or **Rail Europe** for assistance. They can get you the cheapest tickets, particularly on Eurostar.

🚆 **Eurostar**: (London Waterloo–Paris Gare du Nord), Waterloo International Terminal, London, SE1 (Waterloo tube). Also: Eurostar Ticket Office, 102–104 Victoria Street, London SW1 5JL. ☎ (0990) 186-186 (7am–10pm). Website: www.eurostar.co.uk

🚆 **International Rail**: Chase House, Gilbert Street, Ropley SO24 9BY. ☎ (01962) 773646. Email: info@international-rail.co.uk. Website: www.international-rail.co.uk

🚄 **Rail Europe**: Travel Centre, 179 Piccadilly, London W1J 9BA. ☎ (0870) 584-8848. Website: www.raileurope.co.uk

InterRail Travel

European citizens can travel to Spain by train on the **InterRail** system. Travellers can buy an all-country pass (26 countries) or a 'zone pass' for a group of countries. Spain is zoned with Portugal and Morocco. A 22-day pass for travel in one zone costs around £230, or £170 for travellers under 26. A month-long pass for any two zones costs £280, or £160 for travellers under 26. The all-country pass costs £350, or £260 for those under 26, for one month.

Pass holders are entitled to discounts on ferry services across the Channel and between Spain and Morocco, but must pay supplements for travel by Eurostar, or other high-speed trains. Contact travel agents such as STA and Campus for assistance in buying InterRail tickets (*see* 'Travel Agents in Britain'). For further information on rail travel within Europe, contact **Rail Europe** or **International Rail**.

Train Travel in Europe for North American citizens

Eurail passes offer unlimited train travel through 17 European countries. The pass must be bought before leaving for Europe. Fares are dependent on the length of time that you plan to travel. Contact **Rail Europe** for more details.

🚄 **Rail Europe**: 226 Westchester Avenue, White Plains, New York, New York 10604. ☎ 1-800-438-7345. Website: www.eurail.com

FROM IRELAND

Passengers should travel by ferry and train to London, then from London to Paris, from where direct trains head frequently to Madrid and further south. A **Virgin Trains** service meets the ferry from Dublin at Holyhead and travels to London Euston in 3 hours 30 minutes. 25 daily **Eurostar** trains leave London Waterloo for Paris.

The Continental Rail Desk of **Iarnrodd Éireann** in Dublin can arrange journeys in Europe for you. For more details on travelling by train from Britain to Spain, *see* 'Getting There by Train from Britain'.

⛴ **Irish Ferries**: (Dublin–Holyhead) 2–4 Merrion Row, Dublin 2. ☎ (01) 638-3333. Enquiries from Northern Ireland: ☎ (01) 661-0511. Website: www. irishferries.ie

⛴ **Stena Line**: (Dublin Port–Holyhead) Charter House, Park Street, Ashford TN24 8EX. ☎ (01) 204-7700. Website: www.stenaline.co.uk

🚄 **Iarnrodd Éireann**: (Continental Rail Desk) 35 Lower Abbey Street, Dublin 1. ☎ (01) 677-1871.

🚄 **Virgin Trains**: (Holyhead–London Euston) ☎ (0345) 222-333. Website: www.virgintrains.co.uk

By Sea

FROM BRITAIN

Brittany Ferries sails twice a week, between mid-March and mid-November, from Plymouth to Santander, on the north coast of Spain. Journey time is 24 hours. Fares start at around £150 return for a foot passenger, £450 with a car. **P&O Portsmouth Ferries** sails twice a week, all year round, from Portsmouth to Bilbao. Journey time is about 35 hours from England and 30 hours return from Bilbao. Fares start at around £200 return, £400 with a car.

The ferry to Spain avoids the high tolls on French autoroutes, but if you prefer a shorter sea journey, **P&O Stena Line**, **Sea France** and **Hoverspeed** sail regularly to Calais from Dover. Brittany Ferries also sails to Roscoff, Cherbourg, St Malo and Caen.

Brittany Ferries: Customer Services, Millbay, Plymouth PL1 3EW. ☎ (0870) 556-1600. Website: www.brittany-ferries.co.uk

Hoverspeed: International Hoverport, Marine Parade, Dover CT17 9TG. ☎ (0870) 240-8070. Website: www.hoverspeed.co.uk

P&O Stena Line: Channel House, Channel View Road, Dover CT17 9TJ. ☎ (0870) 600-0600. Website: www.posl.com

P&O Portsmouth Ferries: Peninsular House, Wharf Road, Portsmouth PO2 8TA. ☎ (02392) 301000. Website: www.poportsmouth.com

SeaFrance: Eastern Docks, Dover CT16 1JA. ☎ (0990) 711-711. Website: www.seafrance.com

FROM IRELAND

There are no direct ferries from Ireland to Spain. The regular **Brittany Ferries** service from Cork to Roscoff, in northern France, is the best way to avoid travelling through Britain. Other convenient services are **Irish Ferries** from Rosslare to Cherbourg and **Stena Line** from Rosslare to Fishguard. If you would prefer to travel through Spain from Britain, *see* 'Getting There by Sea from Britain'.

Brittany Ferries: (Cork–Roscoff) Customer Services, Millbay, Plymouth PL1 3EW. ☎ (0870) 556-1600. Website: www.brittany-ferries.co.uk

Irish Ferries: (Rosslare–Cherbourg) 2–4 Merrion Row, Dublin 2. ☎ (01) 638-3333. Enquiries from Northern Ireland: ☎ (01) 661-0511. Website: www.irishferries.ie

Stena Line: (Rosslare–Fishguard) Charter House, Park Street, Ashford TN24 8EX. ☎ (01) 204-7700. Website: www.stenaline.co.uk

By Car

FROM BRITAIN

Your best bet is to take the **Portsmouth Ferries** service from Portsmouth to Bilbao, or the **Brittany Ferries** service from Plymouth to Santander. For more about ferries between Britain and Spain, *see* 'Getting There by Sea from Britain'.

If you would prefer not to travel by sea, **Eurotunnel** trains transport cars and their passengers under the Channel to Calais Coquelles in about 35 minutes. Trains depart roughly every 30 minutes during the day and hourly at night.

Expect to pay at least £200 for a return ticket on Eurotunnel including a car and passengers. Advance booking can sometimes reduce prices and is recommended for travel between June and August.

To drive in Spain, ensure that you have your driving licence, vehicle registration document and insurance. Speed limits are 30 mph (50kph) in built-up areas, 50–60mph (90–100kph) outside them and 75mph (120kph) on motorways. Seatbelts are compulsory and you must carry a warning triangle and a basic first aid kit. Contact the AA for further information and advice on driving routes.

Most motorways in Andalucía are toll-free. One *autopista* (toll motorway) connects Seville and Cádiz. You don't pay until you leave the *autopista*, depending on how far you've travelled, so be careful not to lose the ticket that you buy when joining the motorway. You must be 21 to hire a car in Spain.

🚞 **Eurotunnel**: (Folkestone–Calais), Customer Service Centre, Junction 12 of the M20, PO Box 300, Folkestone CT19 4DQ. ☎ (0870) 535-3535. 24-hour recorded information: ☎ (0891) 555-566. Website: www.eurotunnel. co.uk

■ **AA UK**: Norfolk House, Priestley Road, Basingstoke RG24 9NY. ☎ (0870) 500-600. Website: www.theaa.com

By Coach

FROM BRITAIN

Travelling by coach from London to southern Spain is gruelling. Journey times can be long, up to 35 hours, with stops of 5 to 7 hours in Paris, and a tiring final stretch on local buses.

There are two daily **Eurolines** buses from London Victoria to Madrid, via Paris. Journey time is about 26 hours. In summer, there are five weekly buses from London Victoria to Barcelona (24 hours) and three weekly buses to Alicante (32 hours) and to San Sebastian (21 hours). Daily buses leave Madrid for all cities in southern Spain.

One way fares start at around £80 to Madrid and return fares start at around £140, with concessions of about £10 to £15 on these prices for those under 26 or over 60.

Eurolines: (London Victoria–Madrid), Eurolines Travel Shops, 52 Grosvenor Gardens, London SW1W OAG. (Victoria tube). ☎ (0990) 143-219. Website: www.gobycoach.com

FROM IRELAND

Travelling from Ireland to Spain by coach is no picnic. The Irish bus service **Bus Éireann** runs regular buses from Dublin to London Victoria coach station. These services connect with **Eurolines** buses that leave London Victoria coach station for Spain, via France. Journey time from Dublin to Madrid is well over 30 hours, with lengthy waits in London and Paris. From Belfast, your best bet is to travel first to London, and then board a coach bound for Madrid at London Victoria. Eurolines departs from Belfast to London Victoria twice a day. For more details, *see* 'Getting There by Coach from Britain'.

Bus Éireann: Central Bus Station (Busaras), Store Street, Dublin 1. ☎ (01) 830-2222. Website: www.buseireann.ie

General Information

ACCOMMODATION

YOUTH HOSTELS

The Andalucían Youth Hostel Network (*Red de Albergues Juveniles de Andalucía*) consists of around 20 youth hostels and campsites, which are open all year round in Andalucía (Seville, Córdoba, Granada, Huelva, Cádiz, Málaga, Almería and Jaén). The hostels are usually staffed by students and are generally well maintained. The majority of youth hostels provide meals – breakfast, half board or full board. It is a good idea to reserve your place in advance between April and September as group bookings can take up all the beds at a hostel.

You must be an Youth Hostel member to stay in a hostel; make sure you have your membership card with you as you need to produce it to book a bed. If you are not a member, you can buy your membership on the spot from any hostel. The cost of membership varies depending on your age – 3 if you are under 26 and 6 if you are over. Traditional YHA cards are also valid. (*see* 'Getting There').

Depending on where the hostels and campsites are located, the year divides more or less into three seasons – low-season, high-season and very low season, when special offers are available. In major towns like Córdoba, Granada and Seville, the hostels almost always charge high-season tariffs, which often means that they are not the most economical option. If you are travelling with someone else, it sometimes costs less to go to a small hotel in the centre of town. Youth hostels work out cheaper than other forms of accommodation if you are either travelling alone or in a large group.

A major disadvantage to youth hostels is that most of them are located quite a distance from the town centre and some have fairly strict rules as well as curfews.

Booking Guidelines

– People of any age can stay in a youth hostel, you simply need to be a member.

– The **Youth Hostel Association (YHA)** for England and Wales publishes useful directories: the *YHA Accommodation Guide* (free to members), which details hostels in England and Wales, and the *Hostelling International Guide Books* (£8.50 each), which give information on Europe and the Mediterranean (volume one), and Africa, the Americas, Asia and the Pacific (volume two). These can be bought using credit/debit cards direct from the YHA.

– An international YHA card costs £12.50 for adults for a year and is valid in 62 countries and entitles you to stay in any of the 6,000 youth hostels all over the world. Opening times vary according to the country and the hostel. The **International Youth Hostel Federation (IYHF)** will issue the card. They also produce guidebooks to hostels overseas and run an international booking network from the same number.

– YHA members can book their beds abroad online through the **International Booking Network (IBN)**. A small booking fee of £3 guarantees you a bed in over 300 key hostels overseas. You can reserve beds in shared dormitories for up to nine people, for a maximum of six nights, up to six months in advance. You pay for everything in pounds sterling before leaving Britain and in exchange you get a receipt, which you present on arrival at the hostel. Three days' notice is needed for cancelling bookings, and the cost will be refunded in full minus a small administration fee (about £3.50–£5).

■ **Inturjoven**: central booking office, Miño 24, 41011 Seville. Open 9.30am–2pm and 5–7.30pm. ☎ (95) 427-70-87. Fax: (95) 427-74-62. Website: www.inturjoven.com

■ **YHA (Youth Hostel Association)**: Trevelyan House, Dimple Road, Matlock, Derbyshire DE4 3YH. ☎ (0870) 870-8808. Fax: (01727) 844126. Email: customerservices@yha.org.uk. Website: www.yha.org.uk

■ **IYHF (International Youth Hostel Federation)**: First Floor, Fountain House, Parkway, Welwyn Garden City, Herts AL1 6JH. ☎ (01707) 324170. Email: iyhf@iyhf.org. Website: www.iyhf.org. ■ For online booking with the **IBN (International Booking Network)** see www.hostelbooking.com

■ **Ireland**: www.irelandyha.org

■ **Northern Ireland** : www.hini.org.uk

■ **Scotland**: www.syha.org.uk

■ **USA**: www.hiayh.org

■ **Canada**: www.hostellingintl.ca

■ **Australia**: www.yha.com.au

■ **New Zealand**: www.yha.co.nz

CAMPING

Camping on public beaches is tolerated in theory as there are no private beaches in Spain. But take special care in the Tarifa region, as boats regularly try to put illegal immigrants ashore along this part of the coastline. Here, the Guardia Civil often patrol the area in helicopters and carry out occasional searches. If you want to camp on private property ask permission from the owners first.

Compared with youth hostels, official campsites are a far better option, they are fairly reasonably priced and have none of the restrictions of the hostels. Sites are categorized by the government and prices are fixed accordingly. By law, prices and categories must be clearly displayed at the entrances to all sites.

Spanish campsites are numerous and provide a variety of facilities including small shops (some even have hairdressing and beauty salons), swimming pools, tennis courts and children's play areas. There is also often on-site entertainment in the form of discos and restaurants. The only real problem is with sites near large towns which tend to be in unattractive locations and are usually fairly noisy. This problem is exacerbated at weekends when the Spaniards arrive – they seem to have at least one television per family and tend to go to bed very late, so take your ear plugs if you want to get some sleep.

Make sure you take some strong tent-pegs and a good mallet – the ground in this part of Spain is very dry and often incredibly hard (particularly in Seville).

VENTAS

Travellers have been eating and sleeping in *ventas* since Don Quixote's time. *Ventas* are simply country houses that, like inns, are set beside *caminos reales* (old thoroughfares and roads) where, in the past, travellers would stop to eat and sometimes spend the night. These establishments exist all over Andalucía and are a throwback to a time when road travel was the only way to get about. With the advent of the railways in the 19th century the *venta*, which by definition was located some distance from towns and cities, often in arid and hostile country, became sidelined.

Ventas are less popular than they used to be because the accommodation they offer is pretty basic. Consequently, when it comes to ordering food, you won't get a menu to read, and there probably won't be any set opening hours. However, they do have their own specialities, which can be anything from homemade bread, *rabo de toro* (oxtail) and local farm (*cortijo*) produce to homemade *morcilla* (black pudding), *jabugo casero* (home-cured ham) and *manteca colorada*, a special butter. During the hunting season *ventas* are great for game, with rabbit stew, marinated hare, golden partridge cooked in *fino*, cognac and gin, mutton *caldereta* (stew) likely to be on the menu.

If you want to stay in a *venta* choose one in the most out-of-the-way village you can – if possible more than 20 kilometres (12 miles) from popular tourist resorts. There will probably be a few basic tables outside and canteen-style crockery and cutlery. If just you want to eat at one, go for lunch as many *ventas* are closed for food in the evening.

In small villages, you will often find a local musician playing the guitar and singing flamenco songs for the pleasure of the owner and customers of the *ventas*. Some of the greatest Spanish singers have started their careers singing for free in a *venta*. This was the case with Terremoto, Pería and Algeçiras. Even the great Camarón started off this way.

HOTELS

There are many different types of hotel available in Spain, many of which are family-run boarding houses and bars offering rooms to let. This accommodation is offered under a variety of names and for a range of prices. The cheapest are the **fondas**, rooms offered by bars and small restaurants. Next on the price scale are the **Casas de huéspedes** (guest houses), **hospedajes** and **pensiones**, which offer similar accommodation. And finally, there are **hostales** and **residencias**. While the prices differ, there is not a lot to choose between these various establishments, which can usually be identified by the sign that they display: F (for *fonda*), CH (for *casa de huéspedes*) and so on. What the sign does not do is tell you the quality of the establishment. There are excellent *fondas* that have been completely refurbished by scrupulous owners but at the other end of the scale there are the tatty old *hostales* with nothing but fly-papers to welcome you at reception. If you can, visit the establishment before you book.

Whatever the case, these cheaper places are convenient for travellers who arrive without pre-booked accommodation and who are less concerned with comfort than with price. They are rarely recommended by the tourist offices because they don't meet stringent health and safety requirements, but are generally fine for a short stop-over.

Some of these boarding houses may be willing to offer a lower price in exchange for not issuing a receipt. This allows the hotelier to avoid paying IVA (seven per cent tax added to the price).

At the top of the range are the **hoteles**, which are rated by star, one being the lowest and five the highest. Try to arrive early to ensure that you get a room and ask to see it before handing over your passport at reception. Bear in mind that the prices displayed at reception and in the rooms can vary according to whether it is high, mid or low season.

If you want a single room, ask for a *habitación individual*; for a double ask for a *habitación doble*; and if you want a double bed, specify a *cama de matrimonio*.

Note that, as a rule, the prices shown do not include the additional 7 per cent tax (IVA), which will be added to your bill when you leave.

If you want to see a wider range of accommodation than that listed in this guide, you can get the *Ministerio de Transportes, Turismo y Comunicaciones* (Ministry of Transport, Tourism and Communication) guide to hotels called the *Guía de Hoteles Oficial de España*. It includes a short description of each establishment, prices and its classification. However, you need to understand Spanish to benefit from the descriptions. Alternatively, the Tourist Office also has a list of hotels and other accommodation which includes the most up to date prices.

Finally, it is worth noting that boarding houses in Spain offer bed but not breakfast. This is not usually a problem though, as it is easy, and often much pleasanter, to find a local café or bar serving breakfast.

THE *PARADORES*

The *paradores* are a network of exceptional, top of the range hotels set in superbly restored and refitted castles, manors, palaces, convents or monasteries. There are a few modern *paradores* but these are distinguished by the fact that they are set in unique locations. The facilities at these establishments are second to none and the service is superb as staff are trained to a high standard.

Prices vary according to category but, as a rule, they are all fairly expensive. On average, a double room costs 122€, although unlike the boarding houses, breakfast is included. In general, prices are lower at weekends and during low season.

Even if you can't afford to spend the night in a *parador*, you can still enjoy the locations and buildings by eating in their restaurants. The menus are reasonably priced given the high quality of the cuisine and the surroundings. It is, though, essential to book in advance during summer and at the weekends – and if you want to eat at any of the really popular ones, such as the *paradores* in Granada, you sometimes need to book as much as six months ahead.

Official website: www.parador.es

UK: Keytel International 402 Edgware Road London W2 1ED. ☎ and fax (020) 7616-0300. Email: paradors@keytel.co.uk

USA: Marketing Ahead, 433 Fifth Avenue, New York, 10016. ☎ (212) 686-9213. Fax: (212) 686-0271. Toll free: 0800-2231356. Email: mahrep@aol.com

– **PTB Hotels**, 19710 Ventura Boulevard, Suite 210, Woodland Hills, California 91364. ☎ (818) 884-1984. Fax: (818) 884-4075. Toll free: 0800-6341188. Email: info@paradors.com

– **PTB Miami**, 100 N. Biscayne Boulevard, Suite 604, Miami, FL 33132. ☎ (305) 371-8057. Fax: 1-305-3587003. Email: outptbxmia@aol.com

Australia: Ibertours Travel Level, 1–84 William Street, Melbourne, Victoria 3000. ☎ (061) 3-9670-8388. Fax: (061) 3-9760-8588. Email: ibertours@big pond.com

South Africa: Value Spain, 300/2 Jubilee Drive, Blackheath 2195, PO BOX 1900, Cresta 21118. ☎ (02711) 476-4404. Fax (02711) 476-4463.

APARTMENTS AND VILLAS

RAAR, Red Andaluza de Alojamientos Rurales (Andalucían Network of Rural Accommodation): Apartado 2035, E04080 Almería. ☎ (95) 026-50-18. Fax: (95) 027-04-31. This owners' association offers a number of houses, apartments and hotels for a range of budgets and in a number of locations. Brochures are available on request.

PROBLEMS AND COMPLAINTS

Hotels, bars, restaurants and taxis all have a *libro de quejas* (complaints book) overseen by the local authorities and aimed at quashing fraud and bad practice. In the event of any dispute, ask for this document and you will often find that the problem is miraculously resolved.

BOOKING ROOMS BY POST

If you want to reserve accommodation by post, you need to use the postcode beside the name of the town or village where you want to stay, as given in this guide. You can find them:

– next to the name of the town or village in places where there is only a single postcode, e.g. Seville (41000).

– within the listing for the individual hotel when there are several postal districts in the same town. (We also give the general postcode for the town in the general heading for the town.)

No postcodes are given for towns where there is no accommodation available.

BUDGET

Over the last few years prices have soared in Spain – and Andalucía is no exception. Gone are the days of bargain hotels and huge meals for a few pesetas. As well as general rises in the cost of food and accommodation, the differences between high, mid and low season prices have got much greater throughout the region making cheap summer breaks a thing of the past.

In places such as Seville, Granada and Córdoba, prices shoot up during the major fiestas and accommodation is at a premium in Semana Santa (Easter week) and during the Feria. In general, spring and autumn are classed as mid-season in Seville and Granada, while summer is priced as low season due to the heat and the fact that everyone wants to get out of the cities and be near the beach. Being further inland, Córdoba's high season is in spring and like Seville and Granada, prices are lower in summer because of the lure of the coast. Granada's high season is extended because it is closer to the beaches and resorts of the coast. Except for the major towns and cities inland, the high season prices only apply during Semana Santa and Christmas.

Needless to say, it is high season throughout the summer along the coast, where prices rise and fall in line with the water temperature.

Despite these broad guidelines, prices everywhere can fluctuate enormously over a short period depending on local fiestas, public holidays and other similar events so it is a good idea to check before you go to avoid any nasty surprises.

To help you gauge the cost of food and accommodation, the listings in this book are grouped into categories based on the cost of a double room. The range of prices for each category is given below. It is important to check whether tax (IVA) is included in the price or not. This is rarely the case, and a seven per cent tax is generally added when you come to pay the bill.

ACCOMMODATION

– **Budget**: 15–30€, often with a shared shower on the landing.

– **Moderate**: 30–42€

– **Expensive**: 42–72€

– **Splash Out**: over 72€

FOOD

Needless to say, food is available across the full range of prices almost everywhere you go. Having said that, you can no longer expect to enjoy fantastic meals for next to nothing, as you could a few years ago. The price of eating out in Spain is now in line with similar restaurants in Europe. Having said that, if you choose your tapas carefully you can still enjoy a tasty meal on a shoestring budget.

The price ranges below are calculated on the basis of a meal for one person.

– **Budget**: 9€ and under

– **Moderate**: 9–24€

– **Expensive**: over 24€

At lunchtime, the majority of restaurants offer set menus, particularly in the big tourist towns. The only advantage of this option is the price, so don't expect top-notch cuisine.

CLIMATE

The Andalucían climate is characterized by mild winters on the coast and rather colder ones inland. The summers, though, are universally dry and sunny and last from May to October. Rain is unusual in southeastern Spain but in spring it can get chilly in the evening.

The best time to go to Andalucía and southern Spain is either the spring or autumn. At these times of year the temperature is pleasant and you have the added bonus of avoiding the crowds of sunseeking holidaymakers. What-

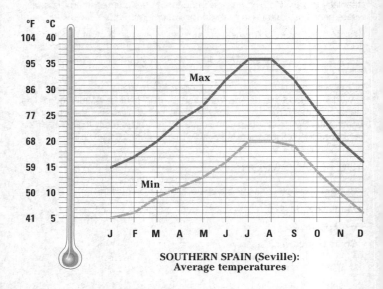

SOUTHERN SPAIN (Seville):
Average temperatures

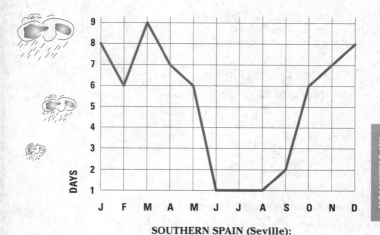

SOUTHERN SPAIN (Seville):
Number of rainy days

ever time of year you are travelling, make sure you check the dates of any fiestas and *ferias*, in advance, particularly around Easter time.

COMMUNICATIONS

POST

Post offices in large cities do not close at midday and may have longer opening hours than those in towns. As there is usually only one post office in each town, queues can be long. If you only want stamps, you can buy them at any *tabac*, most of which are identifiable by their brown and yellow signs. The mail system in Spain is fairly efficient and outgoing letters and postcards usually take five to seven days to other European countries and seven to ten days to the USA. Spanish post boxes are yellow.

Each town has its own postcode; this is indicated next to the town name in the guide, e.g. TARIFA 11380.

Incoming mail can be sent to you in Spain **poste restante** (*Lista de Correos*). Surnames should be underlined and written in capitals and addressed to: Lista de Correos, town name, province. Take your passport along when collecting and ask for mail to be checked under all of your names. They could be filed under first or middle names if your surname has not been hightlighted.

Post office opening times: 8am–12pm and 5–7.30pm

TELEPHONE

To make telephone calls you can either use a public phone or a phone in a bar. At the time of going to press phones take 5, 25, 50 and 100 ptas coins

(Euro denominations have not yet been given). Some take higher denominations. For international calls in a booth, you'll probably need to put in 200 ptas to ensure a connection.

Telephone Dialling Codes

International Dialling Codes to Spain

– From the UK:	00 34
– From the Republic of Ireland:	00 34
– From the USA:	011 34
– From Canada:	011 34
– From Australia:	0011 34
– From New Zealand:	00 34
– From South Africa:	09 34

International Dialling Codes from Spain

– To the UK:	00 44
– To the Republic of Ireland:	00 353
– To the USA:	00 1
– To Canada:	00 1
– To Australia:	00 61
– To New Zealand:	00 64
– To South Africa:	00 27

Phone Cards

Telephones that take phone cards (*tarjetas*) are easy to find everywhere you go. You can buy phone cards from newspaper kiosks. Some are priced at 1,000 ptas (6€) and others at 2,000 ptas (12€).

International calls can be made from phone booths marked *teléfono international*. Alternatively, you can use a Locutorio or Teléfonica office where you pay after your call. Here, you can also make reverse charge calls. Expect to queue at a Teléfonica at cheap rate times. Cheap rate is after 10pm on week days, after 2pm on Saturdays and all day Sunday.

Other Useful Numbers

Directory Enquiries	☎ 1003
European International Operator	☎ 1008
Non-European International Operator	☎ 1005

Reverse Charge Calls

Find a Teléfonica and arrange to make a reverse charge call. You could also call the operator and ask for a reverse charge call to be requested. Hotels may make arrangements for you as well, but expect to pay well over the odds for the privilege. Although you'll queue at Teléfonica offices, at least you can get your call on the cheapest rate.

GENERAL INFORMATION

CONVERSION TABLES

Men's sizes

Shirts

UK	USA	EUROPE
14	14	36
14¹/₂	14¹/₂	37
15	15	38
15¹/₂	15¹/₂	39
16	16	41
16¹/₂	16¹/₂	42
17	17	43
17¹/₂	17¹/₂	44
18	18	46

Suits

UK	USA	EUROPE
36	36	46
38	38	48
40	40	50
42	42	52
44	44	54
46	46	56

Shoes

UK	USA	EUROPE
8	9	42
9	10	43
10	11	44
11	12	46
12	13	47

Women's sizes

Shirts/dresses

UK	USA	EUROPE
8	6	36
10	8	38
12	10	40
14	12	42
16	14	44
18	16	46
20	18	48

Sweaters

UK	USA	EUROPE
8	6	44
10	8	46
12	10	48
14	12	50
16	14	52
18	16	54
20	18	56

Shoes

UK	USA	EUROPE
3	5	36
4	6	37
5	7	38
6	8	39
7	9	40
8	10	42

Temperature

- To convert °C to °F, multiply by 1.8 and add 32.
- To convert °F to °C, subtract 32 and multiply by 5/9 (0.55). 0°C=32°F

US weights and measures

1 centimetre	0.39 inches	1 inch	2.54 centimetres
1 metre	3.28 feet	1 foot	0.30 metres
1 metre	1.09 yards	1 yard	0.91 metres
1 kilometre	0.62 miles	1 mile	1.61 kilometres
1 hectare	2.47 acres	1 acre	0.40 hectares
1 litre	1.76 pints	1 pint	0.57 litres
1 litre	0.26 gallons	1 gallon	3.79 litres
1 gram	0.035 ounces	1 ounce	28.35 grams
1 kilogram	2.2 pounds	1 pound	0.45 kilograms

GENERAL INFORMATION

DANGERS AND ANNOYANCES

Like all tourist hot-spots, Andalucía has its fair share of pick-pockets, car-thieves, con-men and the like. So as always, it pays to take sensible precautions.

Thefts from cars are particularly common in Seville and Córdoba so try to use car-parks with attendants and don't leave anything in sight on the seats or the back shelf to tempt a thief. Foreign cars often have their windows smashed for the sake of little more than a few books.

If you have a hire car, try leaving a Spanish newspaper in a prominent position – would-be thieves might be fooled into thinking you're a local. If you do get your window smashed, look under 'Useful Addresses' for details of garages that provide a window replacement service.

To deter car crime, some towns have set up 'car-sitter' schemes. This can be a good and inexpensive option under the official schemes; the price of the service is printed on the attendant's ticket. Don't agree to let just anyone mind your car, though, especially if they do not offer you an official ticket. If you do agree to someone unofficially minding your car, make sure you pay them when you return and not before you go – for obvious reasons.

TIME-SHARE FRAUDS

On the Costa del Sol, from Marbella to Málaga, seemingly friendly young people may often engage you in conversation and then try to persuade you to come and meet real estate and time-share agents. Their techniques range from charming to aggressive but in most cases any deal you are offered is some sort of a con and you are best to steer well clear. The only way of avoiding an embarrassing situation is to ignore them completely.

ELECTRICITY

The standard electric current throughout Spain is 220V or 225V (although occasionally it is 125V); most European appliances should work as long as you have an adaptor for European-style two-pin plugs. North Americans will need this plus a transformer.

EMBASSIES AND CONSULATES

SPANISH EMBASSIES OVERSEAS

Great Britain: Consulado General de España, 20 Draycott Place, London SW3 2RZ. ☎ (020) 7589-8989. Email: conspalon@mail.mae.es

Republic of Ireland: Spanish Embassy, 17a Merlyn Park, Ballsbridge, Dublin 4. ☎ (01) 269-1640

USA: Spanish Embassy, 2375 Pennsylvania Avenue NW, Washington DC 20037. ☎ (202) 728-2340. Fax: (202) 833-5670. Website: www.spainemb.org

Canada: Spanish Embassy, 74 Stanley Avenue, Ottawa, Ontario K1M 1P4. ☎ (613) 747-2252. Fax: (613) 744-1224. Email: spain@DocuWeb.ca. Website: www.DocuWeb.ca/SpainInCanada

Australia: Spanish Embassy, 15 Arkana Street, Yarralumla, ACT 2600. ☎ (02) 6273-3555. Fax: (02) 6273-3918. Email: embespau@mail.mae.es. Website: www.embaspain.com

South Africa: Spanish Embassy, 169 Pine Street, Arcadia, Pretoria 0083, Pretoria. ☎ (12) 344-38-75. Fax: (12) 343-48-91

OVERSEAS EMBASSIES IN SPAIN

Great Britain: British Embassy, calle de Fernando el Santo 16, 28010 Madrid. ☎ (917) 00-82-00. Email: webmaster@ukinspain.com. Website: www.ukinspain.com

Ireland: Embassy of Ireland, Ireland House, Paseo de la Castellana 46, 28046 Madrid. ☎ (915) 76-35-00. Fax: (914) 35-16-77. Email: irlmad@ibm.net

USA: Embassy of the Unites States of America, calle Serrano 75, 28006 Madrid. ☎ (915) 87-22-00. Website: www.embusa.es

Canada: Canadian Embassy, Núñez de Balboa 35, 28001 Madrid. ☎ (914) 23-32-50. Fax: (914) 23-32-51. Email: mdrid@dfait-maeci.gc.ca. Website: www.canada-es.org

Australia: Australian Embassy, Pza Descubridor Diego de Ordás 3, 28003 Madrid. ☎ (914) 41-60-25. Fax (914) 42-53-62. Website: www.emb australia.es

New Zealand: New Zealand Embassy: 3rd floor, Plaza de La Lealtad 2, 28014 Madrid. ☎ (915) 23-02-26. Fax: (915) 23-01-71

South Africa: South African Embassy, Edificio Lista, Calle de Claudio Coello 91–6, 28006 Madrid. ☎ (914) 36-37-80. Fax: (915) 77-74-14. Email: embassy@sudafrica.com. Website: www.sudafrica.com

EMERGENCY CONTACT NUMBERS

Fire, Police, Ambulance: ☎ 091

ENTRY REQUIREMENTS

EU citizens and Swedish and Icelandic nationals only need a valid identity card to enter Spain for up to 90 days. British nationals must use their passports as they have no ID card. Nationals of the USA, Australia, New Zealand and Canada can also enter the country for 90 days on their passports.

For stays over 90 days, EU, Swedish and Icelandic citizens can apply for a residence permit (*permisio de residencia*) once they are in Spain. This permit is valid for one year and you can extend the residence permit for up to five years. To apply for this permit, go to the *Oficina de Extranjeros* in the main cities or police stations. You will need to prove that you have enough money to support yourself without working (around 30 a day). You can do this either with a contract of employment, a Spanish bank account or records of your foreign exchange transactions.

US citizens are only permitted to apply for one 90 day extension but need to show proof of funds as above. Other nationalities will need to get a special visa from a Spanish consulate before leaving for Spain.

FESTIVALS

In Spain it seems that almost no excuse is needed to hold a fiesta – almost any reason will do. Of course saints' days call for one – but then there are the other (much more obscure) contenders: bulls, donkeys and even snails. Fiestas are a magical experience and it's definitely worth planning your holiday to coincide with at least one, although make sure you check the dates as they change slightly from year to year depending on the religious calendar. Some of the major fiestas are spectacular, like the *Feria de Abril* in Seville, the *Fiesta de los Patios Córdobeses* (Festival of the Patios) in Córdoba, and the pilgrimage in honour of *Nuestra Señora del Rocío* (*Our Lady of the Dew*) in the province of Huelva. Semana Santa (Easter) is celebrated practically everywhere and includes impressive processions with huge statues paraded through the streets.

The origin of many fiestas is religious. In the past, the Catholic authorities sensibly adopted pagan festivals as their own and in contrast with the Protestantism of northern Europe, did little to sever the ties with the old commemorations and rituals. Under Franco's repressive regime enthusiasm for fiestas, was paradoxically, stronger. Indeed, his regime had little effect in terms of de-Christianizing the peninsula, which simply serves to prove that neither dictators nor dogmas can alter the attachment of a people to their traditions and the desire to celebrate.

The dates of fiestas and *ferias* can vary from year to year, often being celebrated on the nearest weekend to the date in question. It is worth checking for exact dates if you wish to see one of these celebrations. Key holidays and fiestas include:

– **Moors and Christians**, traditional festival, (February 2–5) Bocairente, Valencia

– **Cádiz Carnival**, (February)

– **Carnival**, throughout Spain (27 February)

– **Semana Santa**, Easter week, celebrations throughout Spain (March/April)

– **La Feria de Abril**, Seville, lasts one week (April/May, two weeks after Semana Santa)

– **Moors and Christians**, Alcoy, Alicante (late April)

– **Cruces de Mayo**, Granada (3 May)

– **Jerez Horse Fair**, Jerez de la Montera (early May)

- **Festival de los Patios Córdobeses**, Córdoba (early–mid-May)
- **Festival of the Courtyards** and **May Fair**, Córdoba (May)
- **Romería del Rocío**, traditional pilgrimage to El Rocío, Huelva (May/June)
- **San Bernabe Fair, Marbella**, (always around 11 June)
- **San Juán Festival**, Javea, Alicante (mid-June)
- **Sea Festival**, Fuengirola, Málaga (16 July)
- **Santander International Festival,** throughout Spain (August)
- **La Tomatina**, (popular festival), Buñol, Valencia (25 August)
- **Moors and Christians**, Benidorm (end September)
- **Fuengirola Fair**, (early to mid-October)
- **Benidorm Festival**, (November)
- **The Verdiales**, pop music festival, Málaga (28 December)

FOOD AND DRINK

With the exception of well-known tourist resorts, mealtimes tend to be quite late in Spain. Breakfast is taken between 8 and 11am, lunch from 1.30 to 4pm and dinner from around 9 to 11pm (when it's cooler).

IVA (VAT) is added to the bill at the standard rate of 7 per cent, but up to 12 per cent in some chic restaurants and bread (*pan*) is charged as an extra in many places.

In principle, restaurants are required to display a *menú del día* (menu of the day), or, if they don't display it, to offer it. This is not always the case, though.

In tapas bars, depending on how hungry you are or whether you just want to try out a number of the specialities, you can ask for *un pincho* (a small portion) *una tapa* (also a small portion), *una media ración* (half a portion) or *una ración* (a full portion). If you are going to eat in bars, it is worth knowing that *sandwich* means a toasted sandwich, *bocadillo* is a filled roll and *tostada* is toast.

NATIONAL CULINARY SPECIALITIES

– *La paella*: this famous Spanish rice dish is made with chicken, lean pork, ham, prawns, peas, garlic, onions, spices and saffron. Paella originated in Valencia in the 19th century in the Albufera area, a lagoon near the city. A true peasant dish, the fishermen made use of the wide variety of locally available meat and fish, such as eel and rabbit, as well as the produce from the *huertas* (market gardens), including green beans, peas and artichokes to make paella. Saffron, extracted from the dried stigma of purple crocuses, gives the paella its golden yellow colour. It requires some time to prepare and is traditionally cooked in the open air in a *paellera*, a large pan placed on a tripod over the wood pruned from the vines. When the fire gets going, the rice begins to cook, becoming impregnated with the flavours of the ingredients and producing the delicious *soccarat* – a crisp brown crust around the edge of the pan. Watch out for cheap, quickly-prepared rice dishes (*arroz*) that are not a patch on a real paella.

– *La tortilla*: a thick omelette that usually includes potatoes (*patatas*), mixed herbs and sometimes chorizo, tomatoes, cubes of bacon, peas, or, more unusually, crayfish tails. It can be served hot or cold.

– *El cocido* (chick-pea stew): a main course that is served everywhere in a variety of guises.

– People with a sweet tooth should make a point of trying **churros** (doughnut sticks) and **buñuelos** (a larger version of churros). These are probably the tastiest types of pastry on offer in Spain and are divine with their traditional accompaniment of thick hot chocolate. Other sweets are mostly milk and egg based.

– **Leche frita** (a sweet, set custard that is allowed to cool in a large shallow dish before being cut into large squares, fried in oil and sprinkled with sugar), **tocino del cielo** (made with egg yolk and syrup), **natillas** (a thick custard that is flavoured with either cinnamon or lemon), **arroz con leche** (rice pudding) and **torrijas** (french toast).

ANDALUCÍAN SPECIALITIES

A few years ago, Andalucían cuisine was notorious for being rich but greasy. Now, though, gourmet cooking is being taken seriously and there is plenty of high-class cuisine available. You only have to look at the number of dishes on offer in tapas bars to see how much variety there is in the region's cuisine. These days the ubiquitous olive oil is used with a lighter hand, producing food that is rich and flavoursome but not too heavy.

Starters

– *Gazpacho*: this Andalucían speciality has now become popular in restaurants all over Europe. *Gazpacho* is a cold soup made from raw vegetables (tomatoes, peppers, onions, cucumbers, garlic, olive oil, vinegar and bread). Particularly delicious when served very well chilled. It is often accompanied by side dishes of croutons, diced tomato, cucumber and onion that can be added to the basic soup at the table.

– *Salmorejo*: another cold soup that is mainly found in Córdoba – it is thicker than *gazpacho* and not usually served as highly chilled. It is often served with finely chopped hard-boiled egg.

– *Ajo blanco*: this variation on the classic *gazpacho* is white in colour, its main ingredient being garlic. Texture and flavour are added with ground almonds, lemon juice, olive oil and bread.

– *Jamón*: one of Andalucía's greatest specialities is mountain ham; it is sweated in summer and dried in the open air in winter. There are two main varieties, the most common is *jamón Serrano*, which comes from common pink pigs (*patas blancas*) and is produced all over Spain. The hams are dried in the cold air of the Alpujarras mountains (near Granada) for a year. These hams are available everywhere you go and are the least expensive of the speciality hams. While it is delicious, this ham can't compete with the delicious *jamón Ibérico*. This ham comes from the black pigs (*patas negras*) that live in the Guadalquivir valley between Córdoba and Huelva. The hams are dried in the Trevélez area for two years. Like fine wines, these hams have recently obtained the right to an equivalent of the *appellation contrôlée*, a label guaranteeing their quality and origin. This ham has a wonderful flavour and a beautiful texture, but it comes at a price – it is three times as expensive as ordinary *serrano*. The best of the best of these hams is *jabugo*. It too comes from *patas negras* (black pigs) but these lucky creatures are raised on a special diet of acorns that give their meat greater depth of flavour.

Fish

– Fish is common in restaurants and bars on the coast. It is usually fried and served with a sauce; its freshness makes it a real treat. Dishes to try include fresh tuna with tomato, cuttlefish with broad beans, fresh anchovies and bass cooked in salt (*lubina al sal*). Bream is also cooked like this. The fish is placed on a large bed of salt which helps retain its flavour without, surprisingly, making it taste too salty.

– *Calamar a la plancha* (grilled squid): not specific to the region but this is one of the best places for it.

– *Fish cooked in wine*: a variety of fish is served with white wine, spices, tomatoes and onion. A simple but tasty classic.

– *Fried fish mix*: a bit of everything – the fish is diced and fried. If the fish or the squid is fresh, this recipe is a winner. In some ports, you can find little stalls which specialize in fried fresh fish. They wrap it in paper so that you can eat it in the street. Cheap and delicious.

Meat

– *Rabo de toro*: oxtail served with a meaty gravy is a very tasty but not very filling dish as the oxtail has a lot of bone. It is mostly found in and around Córdoba.

– *Riñones al jerez*: kidneys in sherry. This is a simple but delicious dish that is well worth trying – the sherry adds a subtle sweetness to the grilled kidneys.

– *Morcilla*: Spanish black pudding, it is very good but fattier than its English cousin.

– *Cordero lechal*: suckling lamb. It's not found everywhere but if you come across it it's definitely worth trying.

Cheese

Not usually eaten with a meal but more often as a tapa. Some of the aged cheeses are particularly good. There are also some good goat and sheep cheeses (particularly in Ronda).

Desserts

Andalucía has many desserts that are specific to the region, so as well as trying national dishes like spice cakes, baked custard tarts and many kinds of deep-fried dough cakes (similar to doughnuts), make sure you try *mantecados*, which are a bit like lardy cakes but without the currants, and *cabello de ángel*, a lemon syrup cake. Also worth a mention is *turrón*, a speciality of Alicante that is based on eggs and almonds and is similar to nougat.

WHERE TO EAT

– **Tapas bars** and ***ventas*** (country bars and restaurants) vary enormously in Spain, ranging from modern bars to quick-stop cafés. Whatever form they come in, though, you can be sure of lots of atmosphere and an unmissable opportunity to try the local specialities. For more on tapas bars and *ventas* see 'Background'.

– ***Parador* restaurants**: considered quite rightly as luxury establishments by the hotel business, *paradores* often prove to be surprisingly affordable, especially considering their gourmet menus. If you're looking for good food and restaurant service, you won't be disappointed if you go to a *parador*. Like all smart restaurants, you'll have proper table linen, good service and fine food. You'll find that portions are generous and that there will be a good choice of well-prepared local specialities on the menu. To add a touch of local flavour, the waiting staff are often kitted out in regional dress.

DRINK

The most popular drink in Spain is beer, (*cerveza* – pronounced '*cerbesa*' in Andalucía), and it is always served very cold. If you ask for a *cerveza*, you will get a bottle – a *quinto* (20 cl) or a *tercio* (33 cl). If you want a beer on tap, ask for *una caña* (25 cl), *un tubo* (33 cl), *un tanque* or *una jarra* (50 cl). A shandy is called *una clara*.

Horchata is a popular non-alcoholic drink originating from Valencia. It is made from *chufas* or tiger nuts (a plant related to papyrus that grows in the marshes of the Guadalquivir). It is tasty and refreshing with a consistency similar to a milkshake.

Almost everywhere you go you will be able to get a *granizado de limón*, a refreshing drink made with lemon juice, sugar and crushed ice. Another popular non-alcoholic drink is iced coffee, which is usually served with sugar over crushed ice.

Another popular and refreshing option in the summer is rosé wine mixed with lemonade. Ask for *casera* or *tinto de verano*.

Popular with young Spanish people is *calimocho*, an unpleasant-sounding mixture of red wine and Coca-Cola. You can make up your own mind about it.

The majority of wines produced and sold in Andalucía are white. If you prefer red, ask for *vino tinto*.

Andalucían Wines

Andalucía produces a lot of wines, many of which can be sampled in the tapas bars. Predictably, when you think of Andalucían wine, you think of sherry (*jerez*). Sherry got its name from the British when they began taking an interest in the wines produced in Jerez. At the time, the name of the town was spelt 'Xerez', pronounced 'Sherez', hence 'sherry'. The British influence has been so strong that the majority of the sherry-producing companies have British names to this day.

Jerez' is obviously produced in the region of Jerez de la Frontera but wines from Málaga are also getting a good name for themselves. Although less well-known, the Montilla-Moriles vineyard near Lucena, to the south of Córdoba, produces some interesting white wines.

Listed below are some of the wines that you will come across:

GENERAL INFORMATION

– **Wine from Jerez**: the region's wines are discussed at some length in the section devoted to this town. It is well worth visiting some of the impressive vineyards of Jerez. The world famous wine-making (and bull-rearing) Domecq family lives in this region, a fact which endows the local wine with a certain aristocratic superiority.

– **Wine from Málaga**: this sweet, fortified wine used to be known as 'ladies' wine' because in the past elderly English ladies apparently had a taste for it.

The vineyard covers just 500 hectares (1,236 acres), making it the smallest producer of wine in Andalucía. Two varieties of grape are used – the *muscatel* and the *pedro ximénez*. The wines are bottled after a careful ageing process based on the *solera* system where the young wine is mixed with an older wine, consequently doing away with a precise vintage, then aged in barrels. The result is a fine strong wine of around 16 per cent proof. Despite its sweetness it is popular on account of its pleasant smooth and rounded style.

– **Wine from Montilla-Moriles**: these are the wines from the Córdoba region near Lucena where the vines are planted among olive groves. The small town of Montilla produces a substantial part of the region's white wines, which are similar to those of Jerez. These include *fino*, *oloroso*, *amontillado* and *pedro ximénez*. The *pedro ximénez* wines are strong, sweet and full-bodied. The *solera* system, where young and old wines are mixed is also used here, although earthenware jars are used in place of barrels.

– **Vermut al grifo**: This literally means 'vermouth on tap' and it is mostly served in traditional bars or *bodegas*. Vermut al grifo is white wine blended with herbs. Usually (but not always), the wine has been heated during the blending process to aid the release of flavours. It is then mixed with sparkling water and poured directly from small casks, rather like pressurized beer. The style is light, refreshing and sparkling, and bears no resemblance to bottled vermouth. Make sure this drink is accompanied with lots of tapas as it's likely to go to your head very quickly!

HEALTH

If you are travelling from another EU country, collect an E111 form several weeks before you travel. They are usually available from main post offices in Britain. If you are in possession of this form you can claim back the cost of any medical expenses incurred while you are in Spain.

Inoculations: None for Spain, but polio and typhoid are recommended if you plan to combine your visit with a trip to North Africa. Check with your doctor before travelling for the latest information.

Farmacia: For minor ailments, visit a *farmacia*. They are listed in phone books or ask at your hotel. Pharmacists are very highly trained and can dispense many prescription drugs. Most pharmacists also speak English and will be able to offer advice on common ailments and how to alleviate the symptoms. Opening hours: 9–1pm and 4–7pm; some are open 24 hours and there is a rota of late opening and weekend pharmacies listed in the windows of those that are closed.

GENERAL INFORMATION

LANGUAGE

Andalucíans have one of the most distinctive Spanish accents as well as some notable pronunciation differences. If you speak Spanish, you will quickly notice some of these variations. For example, Andalucíans tend to leave off the final 's' from some words, and where as in Castilian Spanish the 'c' is normally pronounced as a soft 'th' before an 'i' or an 'e', it is pronounced as an 's' in Andalucía. The locals also have a habit of speaking in quick bursts and this means they have a tendency to miss out consonants in the middle of words. So – instead of '*Siga todo recto*', (continue straight on) you might well hear something like '*Si'a to'o re'to*'!

Some Common Vocabulary

yes	*sí*
no	*no*
good day	*buenos días*
hi	*hola*
good evening	*buenas tardes*
good night	*buenas noches*
today	*hoy*
yesterday	*ayer*
tomorrow	*mañana*
this morning	*esta mañana*
this evening	*esta noche*
goodbye	*adiós*
bye/see you later	*hasta luego*
please	*por favor*
thank you	*gracias*
thank you very much	*muchas gracias*
that's OK (as a response to thank you)	*de nada*
excuse me	*perdóneme*
sorry	*disculpe*
do you speak English	*¿habla inglés?*
what is your name	*¿cómo se llama?*
I don't understand	*no entiendo*
I don't know	*no sé*
how do you say that in Spanish?	*¿cómo se dice en castellano?*

GENERAL
INFORMATION

what time is it?	*¿qué hora es?*
I would like . . .	*quisiera . . .*
OK	*de acuerdo/vale*
stamp	*sello*
envelope	*sobre*
change	*cambio*
cash machine	*cajero automático/bancomat*
credit card	*tarjeta de crédito*
cheap	*barato*
expensive	*caro*

Accommodation

hotel	*hotel*
hostel	*albergue*
boarding house	*hostal, fonda, pensión*
garage	*garaje*
room	*habitación*
double room	*habitación de dos camas*
could you show it to me? (the room)	*¿me la puede enseñar, por favor?*
air-conditioning	*aire acondicionado*
bed	*cama*
double bed	*cama de matrimonio*
reservation	*reserva*
how much per day?	*¿cuánto por día?*
service included	*servicio incluido*
could you wake me at 8am?	*¿me puede despertar a las ocho?*
breakfast	*desayuno*
blanket	*manta*
pillow	*almohada*
towel	*toalla*
toilets	*servicios*
soap	*jabón*
bathroom	*cuarto de baño*
shower	*ducha*
I would like the bill	*quisiera la cuenta*
the courtyard	*el patio*
the garden	*el jardín*

Eating Out

lunch	*almuerzo*
dinner	*cena*
meal	*comida*
set-menu	*menú*
menu	*carta*
mutton	*carnero*
lamb	*cordero*
pork	*cerdo*
beef	*vaca*
ham	*jamón*
chicken	*pollo*

veal	*ternera*
loin of pork	*solomo*
chop	*chuleta*
roast	*asado*
grilled	*a la plancha*
fried	*frito*
fish	*pescado*
seafood	*mariscos*
starters	*entremeses*
eggs	*huevos*
omelette	*tortilla*
salad	*ensalada*
vegetables	*verduras*
dessert	*postre*
cheese	*queso*
ice-cream	*helado*
red wine	*vino tinto*
white wine	*vino blanco*
still/sparkling water	*agua sin gaz/con gaz*
beer, shandy	*cerveza, clara*
black coffee	*cafe solo*
coffee with milk	*cortado*
the bill	*la cuenta* (or *me cobras*)
waiter	*camarero*
plate	*plato*
glass (for water)	*vaso*
glass (for wine)	*copa*
knife	*cuchillo*
spoon	*cuchara*
fork	*tenedor*
serviette	*servilleta*
salt	*sal*
pepper	*pimienta*
mustard	*mostaza*
oil	*aceite*
vinegar	*vinagre*
butter	*mantequilla*
bread	*pan*
bottle	*botella*
I'm vegetarian	*soy vegetariano (for a man)/vegetariana (for a woman)*
market price	*precio s/m (según mercado)*

Driving

where does this road lead?	*¿a dónde va esta carretera?*
is this the road to . . . ?	*¿es ésta la carretera de . . . ?*
how many kilometres away?	*¿a cuántos kilómetros?*
to the right	*a mano derecha*
to the left	*a mano izquierda*
straight on	*todo recto*
I've broken down	*tengo una avería*

service station	*gasolinera*
unleaded	*sin plomo*
where is the water?	*¿dónde hay agua?*
on the bend	*a la vuelta*
far	*lejos*
further	*más lejos*
near	*cerca*
not allowed	*prohibido*
downhill slope	*bajada*
uphill slope	*cuesta*
bend	*curva*
works	*obras*
village	*pueblo*
traffic lights	*semáforo*

GENERAL INFORMATION

Landmarks

roundabout	*rotunda*
chapel	*capilla*
church	*iglesia*
(bus-)stop	*parada*
corner of the road	*esquina*
newspaper kiosk	*kiosko*
telephone cabin	*telefono público*
dead-end	*callejón*
tower	*torre*
warehouse	*almacén*
industrial estate	*polígono industrial*
market	*mercado*
meat market	*mercado de abastos*
square	*plaza*
walk/street	*paseo*

At the Station

station	*estación*
ticket	*billete*
what time does the train arrive at . . . ?	*¿a qué hora llega el tren a . . . ?*
where do I have to change	*¿dónde hay que cambiar?*
the next one	*el próximo*
the last one	*el último*
the first one	*el primero*
reduced price	*precio reducido*
single	*sencillo*
return	*ida y vuelta*
entrance	*entrada*
exit	*salida*
connection	*enlace, cambio*
ticket-office	*taquilla*
platform	*andén*
luggage	*bultos*

compartment	*compartimiento*
carriage	*coche*
sleeping-car	*litera*
ticket inspector	*revisor*

Time

day	*día*
week	*semana*
Monday	*lunes*
Tuesday	*martes*
Wednesday	*miércoles*
Thursday	*jueves*
Friday	*viernes*
Saturday	*sábado*
Sunday	*domingo*
morning	*mañana*
noon	*medio día*
afternoon	*tarde*
evening	*noche*
midnight	*media noche*
hour	*hora*
quarter	*cuarto*
half	*media*
minute	*minuto*
cloudy	*nuboso*
rain	*lluvia*
rain showers	*churrascos*
fog/mist	*niebla*

Figures

one	*uno, una*
two	*dos*
three	*tres*
four	*cuatro*
five	*cinco*
six	*seis*
seven	*siete*
eight	*ocho*
nine	*nueve*
ten	*diez*
eleven	*once*
twelve	*doce*
thirteen	*trece*
fourteen	*catorce*
fifteen	*quince*
sixteen	*diez y seis*
seventeen	*diez y siete*
eighteen	*diez y ocho*
nineteen	*diez y nueve*
twenty	*veinte*

fifty	*cincuenta*
one hundred	*ciento*
two hundred	*doscientos*
five hundred	*quinientos*
one thousand	*mil*

Pronunication: in Spanish, 'ñ' is pronounced like the 'gne' in 'lasagne' and the 'v' is pronounced more like a 'b'. Consequently, España is pronounced *Espagna*, Sevilla, *Sebilla*, Valencia, *Balencia*, etc.

Andalucían Glossary

– *Abbassides*: name given to the Arab caliphs descended from the Abu Abbas al-Saffah dynasty.

– *Alcaicería*: souk or bazaar selling luxury items such as raw silk.

– *Alcazaba*: a town enclosed by high ramparts. Not to be confused with *alcázar*.

– *Alcázar*: palace inhabited by kings or governors.

– *Almohades*: dynasty that reined during the Islamic occupation of much of Spain and the whole of North Africa from the middle of the 12th century to the middle of the 13th century.

– *Art of the Caliphate of Córdoba*: found in the art of the *Mezquita* (mosque). The Syrian influence was very strong in this area.

– *Azulejos*: earthenware tiles that covered the walls forming amazing geometric patterns. The predominant colours are blue, green, ochre and silver. The patterns are interlinked, often forming stars.

– *Churrigueresque*: exaggerated, ultra-ornamented baroque style. The name is taken from the family of architects and sculptors who were the main proponents of the style, the most outstanding of whom was José Benito Churriguera.

– *Flamboyant Gothic*: late gothic (particularly 15th century). The stone tracery is reminiscent of flames.

– *Mauresque*: name given to Muslim art used in Spain generally.

– *Mihrab*: a niche in a mosque, indicating the direction of Mecca. Generally vaulted and decorated with delicate motifs and calligraphed sacred texts.

– *Moriscos*: Muslims who remained in Spain after the Reconquest. The repression that they suffered forced them to take refuge in the Alpujarras mountains, before they were driven out of the country in 1609.

– *Mozarabic* (art): Christian art influenced by Muslim art during the Arab occupation, from the 10th century onwards.

– *Mozarabes*: name given to Christians during the Muslim occupation of Spain.

– *Mudéjar* (art): Muslim art applied to palaces and Christian buildings after the Reconquest. Muslim art very much lived on even after the Reconquest, often mixed with other styles, successfully or otherwise. The Catholic

Monarchs adored the luxurious style to which the caliphs and sultans were accustomed and endeavoured to decorate their own palaces in a similar fashion. The best example of this style is the Alcázar in Seville, dating from the 14th century. The Mudéjar style is most evident on the ceilings, walls and the area around doors.

– *Musulman* (art): the art of the various different Arab dynasties – Omeyades (9th–11th centuries), Almoravides (11th century), Almohades (12th century), Nasrides (13th–14th centuries).

– *Omeyades* or *Umayyades*: an Arab dynasty that ruled over part of Spain from the 8th century to the middle of the 11th. Founded by Mu'awiyya, a caliph in the 7th century.

– *Plateresque*: this refers to a style that is so ornamental and finely wrought that it resembles the work of gold- and silver-smiths. It became popular under the Catholic kings and was influenced mainly by the Gothic and Italian Renaissance styles. It is mainly used around the framework of doors and windows of both religious and civil buildings. Diego de Siloé is one of the most famous exponents of this craft.

MONEY

THE EURO

TIP From 28 February 2002, the euro (€) will be the sole currency accepted in Spain. Consequently, all prices in the current edition are given in euros.

At time of going to press, many of the establishments in our listings had not yet converted their prices to the new currency so readers should be aware that prices have been rounded up and down in the course of the conversion process.

The official peseta/euro conversion rate has been fixed at 166.386 ptas to one euro. The €/£ conversion rate stands at about 63p to 1€. Check the currency website **www.oanda.com** for up-to-date £/€ conversion rates.

1 euro = 166.386 ptas
1 euro = around 63p

As a general rule, **banks** are open Monday to Friday, 10am to 2pm. The majority offer currency exchange and charge commission. Commission can vary considerably from bank to bank. You will get a better deal if you avoid changing money in tourist hot-spots. The best and cheapest method is to purchase traveller's cheques before you go.

– Almost all towns and villages have cash machines – the main ones are Telebanco (distinguished by a yellow and blue sign), Servired (black with coloured arrows), Argentaria and Caja España, all of which take MasterCard and Visa. A commission is levied on the day the transaction is made.

CREDIT CARDS

Visa and Mastercard (Access), American Express credit cards, and Cirrus and Plus debit cards are accepted throughout Spain and if you know your PIN number, you can use ATMs to withdraw cash. American Express and Visa have reciprocal arrangements with Banco de Bilbao. Mastercard is not accepted as widely as the other major credit cards. Check with your bank about whether you will be able to withdraw cash from your normal current account using your bankers card.

If your credit card is lost or stolen call:

American Express	☎ (915) 72-03-03
Diners Club	☎ (915) 47-40-00
Mastercard	☎ (900) 97-12-31
Visa	☎ (900) 97-44-45

CASH AND TRAVELLER'S CHEQUES

You can go to almost any Spanish bank (*banco*) or savings bank (*cajas de ahorros*) to change money and traveller's cheques and you'll probably find a branch of at least one bank in every town except the smallest. Most branches will be able to change traveller's cheques, although beware the commission rates in the smaller ones as these can be high.

The largest banks are Banco Central Hispano (BCH) and Banco Bilbao Vizcaya. Both can quickly arrange cash advances on credit cards and will change traveller's cheques for a reasonable commission. Smaller banks can be slow and expensive on commission. For flexibility, and if you are going to be staying in small towns and villages, take a credit card or bankers card so you can withdraw cash from an ATM. Apart from the advantages of speed and despite the charge on withdrawing cash from credit cards (usually 1 per cent), it is still a cheaper and more flexible method of getting cash than using traveller's cheques.

However, whenever you travel, having a variety of means of getting cash is always useful. Remember to keep your credit cards, cash and traveller's cheques in separate places so if you lose one, you have still got something else to fall back on.

In tourist places you will find currency exchanges (*casas de cambio*) or you can look out for a department store called El Corte Inglés, all of which have exchanges. Their rates are competitive and the facility is available during normal shop opening hours.

Hotels will also offer exchange facilities, although the commission is often high.

Banking Hours

Monday to Friday, 9am–2pm, Saturday 9am–1pm (but not from June to September when banks are closed on Saturdays).

GENERAL INFORMATION

GENERAL
INFORMATION

Emergency Cash

If you do run into trouble and need to get money from overseas urgently, use the Western Union Money Transfer system, which is available through large banks and anywhere displaying the Western Union sign.

MUSEUMS, SITES AND OPENING HOURS

As a general rule, admission prices to places of interest in Spain are reasonable.

Museums and sites can be divided into three categories – the major sites all have fairly high admission charges (around 6€). Some of them offer free admission one day a week. On these days it is a good idea to arrive early as the sites become very busy and the queues can be long. The smaller museums have more affordable admission fees (between 1 and 4€). Many of them are free to citizens of the European Union (remember to take your passport or identity card). There are often student reductions, but again you need to show a student card. On the whole, prices are broadly comparable to others on the continent. While there are some free museums you may have to pay to get into some of the more famous churches.

> **TIP** Opening hours are notoriously fickle. The tourist office will say one thing and the notice outside a particular site another. You could arrive during an advertised opening time to find that yet another set of hours are actually being operated. The ones listed in this guide were accurate at the time of writing but are no more reliable than the information from the sources given above – municipal or regional authorities are given to changing them several times a season, often without warning.

PUBLIC HOLIDAYS

New Year's Day	January 1
Epiphany	January 6
Easter	March/April
Assumption	August 15
National Day	October 12
All Saints' Day	November 1
Constitution Day	December 6
Christmas Day	December 25

August is the month that most of Spain is on holiday. Large cities, such as Madrid, are semi-deserted as everyone escapes the heat. Don't be surprised if a number of restaurants, shops and museums close or operate erratic opening hours during the holiday season. If you are planning to travel without booking accommodation and transport, think again as you may be left stranded and disappointed.

SHOPPING

One of the hardest things for foreigners to get used to in Spain is the opening hours of shops. They tend to close for lunch at around 2pm. They open again at 5pm and close again at around 8 or 9pm.

Spain used to be famous for being cheap, but these days, as a fully fledged member of the EU, prices have risen in line with other European economies, bringing Spain's standard of living well into line with other EU countries.

Having said that, there are still some bargains to be found, including adults', and children's shoes, which are both high-quality and cheaper than in many countries in Europe, especially Britain. Leather clothes and accessories are also good value for money, as are silk goods.

It's worth looking out for locally and regionally produced goods as they are often cheap and well-made.

TIPPING

It is customary to tip in almost all bars and restaurants where table service is given. The usual amount is 10–15 per cent, although in the cheaper places less or no tip is expected. In more up-market places, a tax (IVA) of 7 per cent will be added to your bill. The price of the menu of the day (*menú del día*) usually includes a service charge, so check your bill before leaving a tip. Service charges and taxes are usually included in hotel bills, however, in addition, a tip should be left for the chambermaid and porters should be tipped per bag. Tip taxis 10–15 per cent when metered.

TOURIST OFFICES

Spanish National Tourist Office Website: www.tourspain.es

Great Britain: Spanish Tourist Office, 22–23 Manchester Square, London, W1M 5AP. ☎ (020) 7486-8077. Fax: (020) 7486-8034. Email: info.londres@ tourspain.es. Website: www.tourspain.co.uk

USA: Tourist Office of Spain, 845 North Michigan Avenue, Water Tower Place, Suite 915 East, Chicago, IL 60611. ☎ (312) 642-1992 or 944-0216. Fax: (312) 642-9817. Email: chicago@tourspain.es. Website: www.ok spain.org

– Tourist Office of Spain, 8383, Wilshire Boulevard, Suite 956, Beverly Hills, CA 90211. ☎ (323) 658-7188. Fax: (323) 658-1061. Email: losangeles@ tourspain.es. Website: www.okspain.org.

– Tourist Office of Spain, 1221 Brickell Avenue, Miami, FL 3313. ☎ (305) 358-1992. Fax: (305) 358-8223. Email: miami@tourspain.es. Website: www.okspain.org.

– Tourist Office of Spain, 666 Fifth Avenue, 35th Floor, New York, NY 10103. ☎ (212) 265-8822. Fax: (212) 265-8864. Email: oetny@tourspain.es. Website: www.okspain.org

GENERAL INFORMATION

Canada: Tourist Office of Spain, 2 Bloor Street West, Toronto, Ontario, M4W 3E2. ☎ (416) 961-3131. Fax: (416) 961-1992. Email: toronto@tour spain.es. Website: www.tourspain.toronto.on.ca

Australia and **New Zealand**: The Spanish National Tourist Office (SNTO), 1st Floor, 178 Collins Street, Melbourne, Victoria. ☎ (03) 9650-7377 or (1) 800-817-855.

TRANSPORTATION

CAR HIRE

Car hire is not too expensive in Spain and the major car hire companies such as Hertz, Avis and Europcar operate in most of the major towns and airports. Local companies can be cheaper though. The easiest way to book car hire in advance is by calling or visiting the websites of companies to compare prices and check that you can pick up and deliver the car back to the place of your choice. You'll need to book well in advance for car hire during the busy summer months.

Driving in Spain

The majority of service stations accept major credit cards (MasterCard, Visa, Diners Card, American Express). The speed limit on the motorway is 120 kilometres per hour (75 miles per hour). Despite appearances to the contrary, seatbelts are required by law so make sure you use them or risk a fine.

It is important to note that stop signs are not always marked by a white line on the road so remember to extra take care at these junctions. On the whole, driving can be quite tricky in the towns (particularly in Granada) as there not many signs and lots of one-way streets and at certain times, like just before lunchtime and at the end of siesta, things can get quite frantic.

Spain is no different to anywhere else when it comes to car crime so be sure to take precautions by parking somewhere that is patrolled and, of course, don't leave anything in sight inside the car (*see* 'Dangers and Annoyances').

A famous site along the sides of the Andalucían motorways are the enormous 13-metre-high metal cut-outs in the shape of bulls. These advertising boards for Osborne brandy were due to be withdrawn when the regulation banning advertising along motorways came into force. However, a committee of intellectuals, politicians and artists made such a fuss, declaring that it would mark the demise of a national symbol, that in 1994 the authorities gave way. Keep an eye out as several dozen of these proud-looking beasts still remain.

Roads and Tolls

The road network is generally good and often excellent. All the same, take special care if it rains, as the road surfaces can become very slippery, even on the motorways.

In Andalucía and the south in general, there are no tolls (except on the Cádiz–Seville and Málaga–Marbella sections) and the roads themselves are in excellent condition. The *autovías*, effectively four-lane motorways with a central reservation, are also free.

TRAINS

Rail Services

RENFE (Red Nacional de los Ferrocarriles de España – Spanish National Railway Network) operates a comprehensive but complex range of train services.

Cercanías	local commuter trains
Regionales	slow service that connects cities
Largo recorrido	long-distance express trains

The express services (*largo recorrido*) are priced according to speed and luxury. They range from *Diurno*, *Intercity* (IC), *Estrella* (signified by a star), *Talgo*, *Talgo Pendular* (Talgo P), *Talgo 200* (T200), and *Trenhotel*. Prices on the faster, more luxurious routes can be prohibitive. You need to book these and other high-speed services in advance.

There is also an increasing number of super-fast train services running from Madrid to Alicante (AVE – *Alta Velocidad Española*) and from Seville to Alicante (EuroMed). Also very expensive, these services are nevertheless comfortable and very fast.

If you are on a budget, you will need to work out alternative routes using the *Regionales*. As staff can be reluctant to spend the time helping to work out budget travel, you will need to call the rail information service on ☎ 91 (Spanish only) or check the website: www.renfe.es (English version available) in order to plan your journey.

Remember to check all the services available so you are familiar with all the options open to you in terms of time of travel and cost.

Some rail services are substituted with buses, known as rail buses. The journey costs the same but will leave from the bus station instead of the railway station. These rail buses run on indirect routes or at inconvenient times.

In addition to the normal windows for ticket sales, most stations also have a window marked *atención al cliente* (customer services) where staff are available to answer queries about ticket prices, departure times and services, such as sleeper cars. The standard of service is generally efficient and staff can often provide you with written details. Alternatively call ☎ (91) 328-9020 (Madrid), (95) 454-0303 (Seville), (95) 625-4301 (Cádiz) or use the 24-hour reservation number or the information number (*see* 'How to Book' below).

– **FEVE** (Ferrocarriles Españoles de Vias Estrechas – Spanish Narrow Gauge Railways): this is a provincial railway company that only offers one class of travel. Its network complements RENFE's network.

Tickets, Fares and Rail Cards

Rail Cards

InterRail cards are valid on the AVE with a 9€ supplement in tourist class. InterRail cards are generally accepted throughout the suburban train network as well as on inter-city trains (sometimes with a supplement). Advance reservations are obligatory.

Rail cards (InterRail and Eurail) are valid on all RENFE services except EuroMed. Supplements are payable on the fastest services. These can appear fairly random but if you reserve a seat in advance, you will know exactly what you'll be paying. It may also be worth paying an additional 3€ or so to get a large, computer generated ticket to prove you have paid the supplement and so avoid arguments with the ticket inspector on route.

If you are under 26 and plan to use the railways extensively in Spain, you can buy a budget ticket RENFE Tarjeta Explorerail. It can be bought in Spain from RENFE offices or travel agencies and used on all services except some high-speed trains. You can get second-class passes for 7- (114€), 15- (138€), or 30-day (180€) periods.

Other Passes

These may not include surcharges.

Britain/Ireland: Spanish EuroDomino Pass, available from Rail Europe, USIT Campus or selected travel agents. Passes are priced according to whether the traveller is over or under 26 for periods of three (£69–89), five (£106–132) or ten days (£182–227).

Australia/New Zealand: Spain Flexipass. Passes are issued for a specific number of days within a two-month period and can be either first or second class. They are priced accordingly: three days (A$250–320, NZ$300–385), five days (A$365–460, NZ$435–550) and ten days (A$625–795, NZ$750–1050).

North America: Spain Flexipass. Passes are issued for a specific number of days within a two-month period and can be either first or second class. Unlimited travel is available for three days in a two-month period for $150–195 (depending on class of travel). Seven additional days can be bought for $30–35 per day. Also available to North American travellers is the Rail 'n' Drive pass, which offers a combination of three days' rail travel and two days' car hire during a two-month period. These can be reserved through Rail Europe, 226 Westchester Avenue, White Plains, NY10604. ☎ 1-800-438-7245, www.raileurope.com and travel agents.

How to Book

Tickets for services other than *largo recorrido* and other high-speed trains can be bought on the day of travel. For all other services, you need to book in advance.

Advance booking is only available outside Spain in North America through VE Tours. ☎ 1-800 222-8383, fax (305) 477-4220. If you want to book in advance from any other country, use the website www.renfe.es or contact RENFE direct in Spain using the 24-hour telephone reservation service,

Distances between towns (in kilometres)

(F^RA = Frontera)	ALGECIRAS	ALICANTE	ALMERÍA	ARCOS DE LA F^RA	BARCELONA	BAEZA	CÁDIZ	CARMONA	CÓRDOBA	GIBRALTAR	GRAZALEMA	GRANADA	HUELVA	JAÉN	JEREZ DE LA F^RA	MADRID	MÁLAGA	MARBELLA	MOJÁCAR	RONDA	SEVILLE	TARIFA	ÚBEDA	VALENCIA	VEJER DE LA F^RA
ALGECIRAS	—	664	381	104	1222	389	127	227	354	21	119	287	315	342	119	740	156	91	398	97	200	27	399	706	81
ALICANTE	664	—	284	583	528	385	646	627	522	658	615	346	761	433	607	414	500	567	237	582	665	685	376	166	650
ALMERÍA	381	284	—	120	809	489	519	395	332	360	380	152	516	207	635	660	225	290	82	348	422	329	243	430	318
ARCOS DE LA F^RA	104	583	120	—	1316	489	152	109		21	48	275	197	321	60	662	180	143	515	85	125	116	500	362	114
BARCELONA	1222	528	809	1316	—	763	1316	1024	908	1201	1135	909	1140	804	1346	625	997	1131	727	1189	1046	1249	753	739	1303
BAEZA	389	385	489	489	763	—	418	152	142	368	360	102	349	47	508	342	233	298	336	328	255	416	10	387	470
CÁDIZ	127	646	519	152	1316	418	—	152	263	159	120	335	121	367	30	651	193	196	601	145	125	104	420	762	57
CARMONA	227	627	395	109	1024	152	152	—	116	262	126	121	121	220	108	490	193	133	490	133	27	145	262	629	170
CÓRDOBA	354	522	332		908	142	263	116	—	386	289	166	260	104	116	400	187	252	400	257	145	370	146	524	288
GIBRALTAR	21	658	360	21	1201	368	159	262	386	—	161	266	274	321	55	737	135	65	307	58	95	48		710	102
GRAZALEMA	119	615	380	48	1135	360	120	126	289	161	—	257	224	313	90	609	137		234	32	130	146		652	134
GRANADA	287	346	152	275	909	102	335	121	166	266	257	—		55	305	432	131	196	584	226	226	314		451	350
HUELVA	315	761	516	197	1140	349	121	121	260	274	224		—	336		584	240				94	312	406	763	258
JAÉN	342	433	207	321	804	47	367	220	104	321	313	55	336	—	360	335	186	251	289	281	81	369	57	435	394
JEREZ DE LA F^RA	119	607	635	60	1346	508	30	108	116	55	90	305		360	—	621	275	340	717	115	116	518		726	62
MADRID	740	414	660	662	625	342	651	490	400	737	609	432	584	335	621	—	544	609	742	658	544	737	332	352	683
MÁLAGA	156	500	225	180	997	233	193	193	187	135	137	131	240	186	275	544	—	65	307	95	220	183	308	582	237
MARBELLA	91	567	290	143	1131	298	196	133	252	65		196		251	340	609	65	—	372	58	285	118	346	626	172
MOJÁCAR	398	237	82	515	727	336	601	490	400	307	234	584		289	717	742	307	372	—	430	408	490	369	369	479
RONDA	97	582	348	85	1189	328	145	133	257	58	32	226		281	115	658	95	58	430	—	125	124	338	628	122
SEVILLE	200	665	422	125	1046	255	125	27	145	95	130	226	94	81	116	544	220	285	408	125	—	197	245	667	143
TARIFA	27	685	329	116	1249	416	104	145	370	48	146	314	312	369	116	737	183	118	490	124	197	—	426	727	54
ÚBEDA	399	376	243	500	753	10	420	262	146				406	57		332	308	346	369	338	245	426	—	378	480
VALENCIA	706	166	430	362	739	387	762	629	524	710	652	451	763	435	726	352	582	626	369	628	667	727	378	—	795
VEJER DE LA F^RA	81	650	318	114	1303	470	57	170	288	102	134	350	258	394	62	683	237	172	479	122	143	54	480	795	—

☎ (902) 24-02-02. Alternatively, buy your tickets at a travel agent or at the railway station on arrival, although travel will be subject to availability.

BUSES

There are numerous small bus companies operating along minor roads. Buses cost much the same as the trains but are much quicker and more regular. This is by far the best means of transport if you haven't got your own vehicle.

MOTORBIKES

This is a great way to see Spain. Motorbikes give you the freedom to stop almost anywhere to admire the view, especially along the scenic coastal roads. As with driving a car, be sure to take extra care if it rains as some of the smaller road surfaces aren't as good as those on major routes. It goes without saying that you shouldn't ride when wearing a rucksack and that you are required by law to wear a helmet at all times.

HITCH-HIKING

It is possible to hitch-hike across most of Spain, although it is easier along the coastal routes in Andalucía because there are more tourists here – hitching rides with locals is more difficult. In general, hitching is not considered safe and getting a ride on major routes can also be difficult. All in all, you are better off getting a bus or a train.

WEBSITES

Useful Sites to Try

www.espagne.infotourisme.com – the tourist office's official site.

www.elpais.es and **www.elmundo.es** – the sites of two major daily newspapers.

www.flamenco-world.com – a site in English and Spanish all about flamenco, including a few soundtracks.

www.toros.viadigital.com – for *aficionados* of bullfighting, an attractive site dedicated to the traditional art (in Spanish).

www.turAndalucia.com – an extensive, well-documented site about Andalucía, with good graphics and plenty of photographs. Lots of practical information, details of hotels, restaurants, festivals and shows as well as suggestions for themed itineraries based around flamenco, gastronomy, wine, and similar topics.

www.costadelsol.net – a mine of useful tourist information on the Costa del Sol. Excellent navigation with links to lots of other sites. Although there is a version in English, the links sometimes take you to pages that haven't been translated, this is especially true of information that has been posted up by the smaller towns.

www.costadelsol.sopde.es – unfortunately this site is only available in Spanish but it offers comprehensive information about the Costa del Sol and a search facility that covers everything from car-hire to casinos. It is especially useful if you want to find out about inland walks, so if you're a Spanish-speaker, check it out.

WORKING IN SPAIN

As long as you have the relevant passport and visa requirements to stay in the country longer than 90 days (*permiso de residencia – see* 'Entry Requirements/Passports and Visas') you can undertake voluntary work in Spain.

EU citizens should visit the EU's web site, which gives advice for those planning to live or work abroad. Website: http://citizens.EU.int/

If you want long-term paid work in Spain, unless you have applied for a job from home, the best option is to teach English in a language school. Formal qualifications (TEFL or ESL) will help a lot; if you turn up without having arranged anything in advance, you could end up just pounding the streets until you find a school that will take you on, which could take a while.

Informal language teaching, translation work and work requiring specific skills are also possibilities, as long as you can prove your ability and are prepared to work at finding a job. The Spanish Yellow Pages (*Paginas Amarillas*) and job agencies are good places to start your job search.

Possibilities for seasonal work in Spain include general hotel work, bartending and waiting, and working as an au pair. You will find it almost impossible to get work on the harvests.

Background

For the hundreds of thousands of holidaymakers who flock to this region every year, the main attractions of the Costa del Sol are the beaches and good weather. But the area also offers much of cultural interest and there is far more to the region than sun, sea and sand.

Although their origins and religious backgrounds are varied – including Moorish, Jewish, Catholic and gypsy – the local people have one or two key common characteristics – warm-heartedness and friendliness. It is difficult to pin down what it is that gives Andalucía its special quality, but perhaps it is its broad cultural mix. A mix that is evident in the clicking heels of the flamenco dancers, the virile stance of the bullfighters, the croutons in the divine *gazpacho* and the simple pots of brightly-coloured trailing geraniums on the windowsills of simple whitewashed houses.

Whatever your reason for visiting Andalucía, you'll find fascinating and colourful variety everywhere, from its landscapes, monuments and cuisine to its multifaceted cultural background and popular events; here, there is something for everyone.

VITAL STATISTICS

Area: 505,955 square kilometres (197,322 square miles)

Currency: the euro

Government: parliamentary monarchy

State: Kingdom. Spain is divided into 17 autonomous communities

Head of State: King Juan Carlos I, since 1975

Head of Government: José María Aznar, since May 1996

GEOGRAPHY

Geographical location: Andalucía extends across the whole of the southern area of Spain, and also includes two enclaves on the north coast of Morocco – Ceuta and Melilla. It is the biggest region in Spain.

Geography: vast plains inland, a string of beaches all along the coast and a high mountain chain, the Sierra Nevada, which includes Mount Mulhacén, the highest mountain in Spain at 3,482 metres (11,424 feet).

Climate: the highest temperatures in Spain, varying between 14°C (57°F) in January and 26°C (79°F) in August, with highs of up to 40°C (104°F).

Population: Seville (750,000), Málaga (528,079), Córdoba (315,948), Granada (242,000), Jaén (107,184), Almería (165,000), Cádiz (145,595) and Huelva (140,675), Valencia (746,683) and Alicante (274,577).

Economy: tourism, agriculture and farming.

THE ENVIRONMENT

There are no two ways about it, the coast of southern Spain has been ravaged on a huge scale by unscrupulous developers. Nevertheless, you can still find plenty of places that have escaped the concrete mixers – Mojácar, San José, Salobreña, Nerja, Mijas (in the mountains), old Marbella, Tarifa and Vejer de la Frontera (not far from the coast), to name but a few.

While most major towns have suffered from the addition of sprawling modern suburbs the majority still harbour their old quarters and these are definitely worth visiting. So, although you might be disappointed by first impressions, the old centres of towns such as Málaga and Cádiz will reward the effort taken to get to them.

Away from the coast it is easier to find places of interest and unspoilt landscapes to enjoy. So if you want to see the best of the region head inland to the mountainous region of Las Alpujarras, which lies between Almería and Granada, and meander through the traditional white-washed villages around Ronda and Jerez de la Frontera.

HISTORY

FROM THE BEGINNING TO THE VISIGOTHS

Rock paintings in the Altamira caves are evidence that man was present in the Iberian peninsula in the Palaeolithic period. According to ancient myth, the Iberians were a people who came from Africa and gradually mixed with the Celtic tribes living in the inland areas of the country, while the coastal zones were in the hands of the Greeks and Phoenicians. Then in 241 BC, a Carthaginian called Hamilcar Barca marched in and founded Barcelona right on Rome's doorstep, throwing down the gauntlet to the Empire and bringing Spain into conflict with the Romans: the Carthaginians threatened Rome and Pompeii was defying Caesar at the same time. This period of conflict produced some of the most important and well-known personalities in Rome's history, including Trojan, Hadrian and Seneca (Nero's tutor).

In spite of its mineral deposits, which gave it a certain amount of economic prosperity, the Iberian peninsula was peaceful compared to the upheavals in the Roman Empire. Christianity came to the region towards the end of the first century AD and became established by the fourth century. But peace was not to last. Spain, like the rest of Europe, was subject to barbarian invasions and in 409 the Vandals arrived. They were followed by the Alans and the Suevi, who settled in the region until the Visigoths – chased from Aquitaine by Clovis in 507 – withdrew to Languedoc and the north of Spain.

THE LOSS OF SPAIN

Internal disputes and persecutions (particularly aimed at the Jews) wea-kened the Christian Visigoth kingdom towards the end of the seventh century. At the Council of Toledo in 589, Reccared and later Receswinthe, commended a Christian education and baptism but banned the Passover and circumcision. He even went as far as the confiscation of goods from Jewish families and businesses. Unsurprisingly, some Jews, on seeing the Muslims arrive at Gibraltar and then on the beaches of Barbate, saw an opportunity to get rid of the Visigoths – besides, helping the Arabs had the added advantage of giving the Jews access to the Babylonian Talmudic schools of Sura and Pumbedita. Some Visigoths had already seen which way the wind was blowing and had taken refuge in North Africa, although this area had already been invaded by the Arabs who were driven by their zeal to spread Islam. It didn't take much to incite Tariq ibn Zyad to take an expeditionary force of 7,000 Berbers across the Straits of Gibraltar to Spain in 711. The Visigoth kingdom had become unpopular and had already begun to crumble when they arrived. Two years later the majority of Spain had been overrun and become an emirate of the Maghreb, dependant on the huge Arab empire and its caliph. For a long time, this period when Spain was part of the Arabic empire was not referred to in Spanish historical accounts, and the idea that three cultures (Christian, Muslim and Jew) could have coexisted was difficult to grasp. Some generations of scholars (notably in the 19th century) interpreted these events as divine punishment meted on the Visigoths for their many crimes.

AL-ANDALUS

Once on land, Tariq (or Tarik), riding on the victory that he had achieved over the Christians, pressed on to Toledo, which rapidly surrendered to him, before heading for Guadalajara. At the same time, another army headed off to take the rulers of Córdoba to task. A year later, General Musa ibn Nusayr, Tarik's military chief, disembarked with 18,000 foot soldiers, mostly of Arab origin, and, in a relatively short space of time, had added Medina Sidonia, Carmona, Seville and Mérida to his list of conquests. Like all good military chiefs he left his men on the ground and returned to make his report to headquarters in Damascus, the seat of the Umayyad caliphate. Two years later he went back to Spain and, in 714, he seized Zaragoza, Lérida, Soria, Oviedo and Gijón, conferring on his son the task of subjugating the Levant as far north as Narbonne. In less than five years, the Arab-Berbers, who represented only 3 percent of the population in Spain, brought ten million native inhabitants under their control. Two thirds of the Iberian Peninsula was in the hands of the Muslims who named it Al-Andalus.

Before long, though, problems arose between the Berbers, who were the first to arrive, the followers of the *haridji* (who claimed that all believers were equal in the eyes of Allah and should enjoy the same rights), and the Arabs. In 750, there was revolution in the palace at Damascus. Helped by non-Muslim Arabs and Shiites, al-Abbas 'dethroned' Marwan II. The Abassids then took power from the Umayyads and the seat of power was moved to Baghdad. In 756, Abd al-Rahman, the head of the Umayyads arrived in Almuñecar and had himself proclaimed emir. He made his headquarters in Córdoba and, although he still recognized the caliph, he took the view that as Baghdad was a long way away and that he could rely on the loyal support of the Umayyads who ruled the army, he was in an excellent position to continue the war and fill his coffers with the spoils. The successful rule of the

Muslims' was founded on the collection of tributes from Jews and Christians in exchange for a guarantee of freedom to worship.

During this period of Arab domination, Charlemagne, an ally of the Caliph of Baghdad, made an unsuccessful incursion into Spain, losing his son during his troop's withdrawal from the battle of Roncesvalles.

As well as this attempted invasion, there were many ups and downs and reversals of fortune, but the Umayyads managed to stay in power for 170 years. After such a long period of domination, Abd al-Rahman III cut all ties with Baghdad and proclaimed himself caliph of his own territories. Imposing his authority on all his tributary strongholds and towns, he managed to amass a huge fortune and build himself a splendid palace outside Córdoba. His rule of iron ensured a continuous period of power from 912 to 961. His successor, Hisam ibn abu Amir, better known as al-Mansur or Almanzor ('The Conqueror'), was a powerful minister and a warrior. He, in turn, ensured that the caliphate retained its authority for another 50 years. As time went on, the caliphate began to fall apart and broke up into mini-kingdoms known as *taifas*. Ethnic disagreements arose between the Berbers from northern Andalucía and the Arabs from the south, there were religious and military upheavals, and even the rugged nature of the peninsula worked against the creation of a united front against the Christians, whose mission it was to regain the territory and power they had lost.

THE *REYES DE TAIFAS*, ALMORÁVIDES, ALMOHADES AND CHRISTIANS

After the fall of the Umayyads, Al-Andalus began to disintegrate. From Granada to Denia, Almería to Zaragoza small-time local chiefs gained and retained power with the help of mercenaries. The politics of the *taifas* consisted of knowing how to handle their customers. The Christians negotiated their presence by means of the payment of tributes (*parias*). The *taifas* formed alliances with one another to protect themselves and to carry out raids on their neighbours and the Christians took advantage of their gains. It was in this context that Rodrigo Díaz de Vivar, more commonly known as el Cid (a name which probably came from the Arabic *Sidi* or *Caïd*) came to fame. Territorially, he was one of the most powerful princes of the time and he fully exploited the tribute system. In 1081, however, he was condemned to exile by the king. His response was to make it known throughout the region of Valencia that he and his men were available for hire by anyone, Christian or Muslim. Whatever has been said in praise in the *El Cantar del Mío Cid*, the fact remains that he was basically a mercenary and had both Muslims and Christians in his ranks. And there was no shortage of takers for the outcasts' services.

But gradually the situation became increasingly confused. So much so, that in 1086 the *taifas* sent out a cry for help to the Berbers, who had recently converted to Islam and who also controlled the gold routes in the Maghreb. On arrival, the Berbers' leader, Yusuf, found that the local rulers were incapable of organizing themselves and eventually he imposed his own authority, effectively annexing Andalucía to his Moroccan empire from 1090 to 1145. But once again, internal strife resulted in the fragmentation of power.

Meanwhile, the Christians were slowly but surely sharpening their knives, making plans and filling their coffers with Arab gold.

In 1125 the Almohades, fanatical Berbers from the Atlas Mountains, followed the example of the Almorávides before them – namely, they invaded and took control of the whole of Al-Andalus. But they were too late, because by now the die was cast, and this time it was in favour of the Christians.

SPAIN OF THREE CULTURES

How were Christians, Muslims and Jews, along with all the sub-categories of the three religions – *mudéjares* (Muslims living under Christian rule), *mozárabes* (Christians living under Arab rule), *moriscos* (Moslems converted to Christianity), and so on – able to live together for nearly six centuries? Did they live with each other or alongside each other? What were the relationships like between these believers who shared a religious history that they could not acknowledge?

They certainly didn't live together in total harmony, although they appeared to get along peacefully in the main. Each community restricted itself to its own particular area of town. As well as a Christian quarter, these areas included a Jewish quarter or *Aljama*, an *Alcázar* or commercial quarter with its souk and caravanserai, and a Muslim-Arab *Alcaicería* used for the exchange of luxury goods. The latter's medina was protected by high walls and was always situated in the *arrabales* (the suburbs surrounding a mosque) so that members of different ethnic groups could meet. Only Jews practised usury as money-lending was forbidden by Christians and Muslims. Christians usually included a paragraph in their town foundation charters or *fueros* relating to other religious groups. It is from these that we now know that, in some places, Jews had to wear a distinguishing sign on their clothing. By contrast, this was rarely the case for Arabs. All of these rules depended on local laws and, as is always the case, some rulers were more permissive, and less inclined to persecution, than others.

But by the turn of 14th century, trouble was beginning to brew again and with the spread of the Black Death the situation began to deteriorate further as persecution increased. The Catholic Monarchs were not particularly sympathetic and forced conversions increased, although this did not prevent some so-called converts from practising their own religion in secret.

However, before the deterioration in religious tolerance and during the golden age, the Córdoba mosque, enlarged on many occasions, provided a venue for men of different cultures to meet. Muslims, Jews and Christians worked side by side. Never before had astronomy, philosophy and medicine made such progress. The Jews' contribution to Christian life was significant – commerce and finance were in their hands, they excelled in medicine (they were the only people permitted by their faith to carry out human dissections), and made notable contributions to the fields of science and printing. In comparison, the Muslims or *mudéjares* made their biggest contribution in rural matters and did a wonderful job in the *huertas* (cottage gardens) of numerous towns; they were particularly adept at implementing methods of irrigation. Even today, you can still find the remains of a *noria* (water-wheel) or an *aljibe* (cistern) in the Andalucían countryside. To further learning, Alfonso X (the Sage), provided two Arabs with a scholarship so that they could compile the *Tablas Alfonsies*, one of the keystones of European astronomy.

During this period, Andalucía witnessed a period of intense scientific advancement, but there was a great deal of cultural and artistic activity too and the emirs and caliphs took advantage by filling their palaces with fineries from the orient. They also had harems and slaves. Local crafts also flourished, with weavers, goldsmiths and ceramicists all taking part in the building of the kingdom of Al-Andalus.

Academic life also thrived and towards the middle of the 12th century, the Mozárab and Jewish communities translated a multitude of ancient texts from Arabic into Latin. This is how the Christians discovered the writings of Aristotle.

THE *RECONQUISTA* (RECONQUEST)

Although Martel succeeded in stopping the Moors advancing into France, this did not signify the beginning of the Reconquest, and in 732 Córdoba still had little to fear from the French. The Reconquest is difficult to summarize as there were several factors that allowed the Christians to recover their territories. To start with it seemed as if all the Spanish sovereigns jointly conspired to marry off their daughters to the French nobility. This resulted in the French clergy taking a new interest in their Spanish neighbours and gradually Benedictine monks moved in to set up religious communities in the abbeys. Another key factor was that Alexander II was upset by the sacking of Santiago de Compostela by the Arabs in 997 and called for a crusade against the infidel. This lasted some hundred years, but eventually a chink was found in the Moorish armour and on 5 May 1085, Fernando, the first king of Castilla, seized Toledo. The news spread like wildfire throughout the Christian world. The counts of Barcelona and Cerdaña consequently built an alliance with Aragón and the religious military orders of Santiago, Calatrava and Alcántara were founded, both of which played an important role in the Reconquest itself. When these religious armies were not fighting, they were busy repopulating the conquered territories (even offering plots of land to ex-convicts). Despite a few setbacks, the tone was set and the Spanish sovereigns even received help from the Crusaders. Castilla took Córdoba in 1236 and Seville in 1248, while Aragón retook the Balearics, then Valencia (1238). From then on the Muslims were confined to the kingdom of Granada. The Reconquest was not achieved quickly or bloodlessly and throughout the long campaign Muslim military might often proved too much for the Christians. In 1195 at Alarcos, they suffered a devastating defeat, although they had moments of triumph, including at Las Navas de Tolosa in July 1212 when they reportedly killed sixty thousand Moors.

BIRTH OF AN EMPIRE

It was not until the marriage of Isabel of Castilla and Fernando II of Aragón in 1469 that the two kingdoms – which had expanded and asserted their authority over a large part of the peninsula – forgot their rivalries and began to work together to lay the foundations for a unified Spain.

By this time, Aragón had carved out its own maritime empire following the Reconquest of the Balearics. Conversely, under the leadership of Abu l-Hasan Ali (or Muley Hacén), the Moorish power base had continued to shrink until, by the end of the 15th century, all he had left was the kingdom of Granada. Isabel and Fernando then took Gibraltar, thus depriving the Moors of a rearguard base. One of Muley Hacén's sons, Boabdil, took refuge in Málaga and fell into the hands of the Christians who sent him back home, rather rubbing salt into Arabic wounds. The Arabs then sent emissaries to the sultans of Tlemcen, Fez and Egypt, but not one of them came to their aid. In truth, they had already realised that hope for the future of Al-Andalus was already dwindling.

In August 1491, Isabel had the camp of Santa Fé built near Granada and just nine months later, the Nasrid kingdom of Granada, incarcerated behind the city walls, was starved into surrender. The Catholic Monarchs and Boabdil signed a document called The Capitulation of Santa Fé, which was the final act of the *Reconquista*. There was bad news for the Christians though – the Turks had closed the Gibraltar straits, denying the Christians access to the silk route. An alternative route had to be found and in an appendix to the Capitulation the Catholic Monarchs agreed to a bizarre project proposed by a Genoese explorer by the name of Cristóbal Cólon; otherwise known as Christopher Columbus.

THE INQUISITION

The Catholic Monarchs witnessed not only the birth of a colonial empire (ratified by the treaty of Tordesillas signed on 7 June 1494 dividing all future territorial discoveries between Spain and Portugal), but also the bringing together of an institution that was to make the whole of Europe tremble – the Holy Inquisition.

As the big Spanish cities were liberated from Arab occupation, the Jews, who had been left more or less alone until then, were systematically persecuted. After the executions in Seville in 1391, the 'baptisms by blood' increased throughout Spain, forcing the Jews to convert or die. The Inquisition, under the leadership of Torquemada, was created to keep a close eye on these new 'Christians'. From 1485, he showed a rare degree of cruelty in the execution of his duties, and, even though the Catholic Monarchs and Pope Sixtus IV themselves considered his methods shocking, they nonetheless decreed that the Jews should be expelled from the Iberian peninsula on the 30 March 1492, three months after the fall of the kingdom of Granada.

OVER THE SEAS

The terror that the Inquisition inspired was such that Renaissance ideas had only a small impact on Spain. Besides, the discovery and exploration of new countries had seized the attention of the nation and a 'get rich quick' mentality took hold. As a result, a new breed of rough-and-ready, unscrupulous adventurers called the *conquistadores*, appeared. They embarked on remarkable overseas voyages with the single aim of finding treasure, knowing that the more riches they brought back to the Spanish court the more they would keep for themselves. The greediest even tried to escape the tutelage of Spain, carving out their own 'kingdoms' in the vast New World – hijacking convoys and disappearing back into the undergrowth with their booty. Piracy became commonplace and from the end of the 16th century onwards it was as if a free-for-all had been declared.

The administration of these new territories soon became a major concern for the Spanish crown, not to mention the problems arising from the over-exploitation of the indigenous population. In 1516, Bartolomé de Las Casas published an investigative report which concluded that the black slave trade would have to be intensified in order to safeguard these people. In 1523, Las Casas became a Dominican monk and proceeded to take on the role of champion of the Indian cause. But the pursuit of Eldorado had already taken its toll and when the *conquistadores* saw the wealth of the Aztec and Inca empires, their greed knew no bounds. Despite the *Novas Leyes* (new laws) passed in 1542 by Charles V, and drawn up in favour of the Indians, 10 years later Las Casas published a grim report entitled *Brief Account of the Destruction of the Indies* (the word 'America', which appeared for the first time in a letter to Metz in 1507, was not yet widely used).

BACKGROUND

CARLOS V

On 14 May 1516, the sole heir to the Catholic Monarchs, Carlos I (already master of the Netherlands and the Franche-Comté through his great grandfather, Carlos the Bold), acceded to the throne after having deposed his mother, Juana la Loca (Joanna the Mad). The union of the two kingdoms of Castilla and Aragón – which was still no more than a marital alliance – now became a political reality. In January 1519, on the death of his paternal grandfather Emperor Maximilian of Austria, Carlos I inherited Alsace, the Rhineland, Austria and the Tyrol. When he was elected Holy Roman Emperor six months later, he took the name Carlos V. No western ruler has ever equalled his power, and his master-plan was to create a hereditary monarchy for the whole empire. France, finding itself encircled, took a dim view of these ambitions, and Francis I – who had also wanted the title of Holy Roman Emperor – took every opportunity to obstruct him. But it was a previously unknown monk that dealt the Germanic Holy Roman Empire the fatal blow – Luther. His ideas single-handedly wrecked any notion of authority, whether it came from the Church or from the Emperor.

GREATNESS AND DECLINE

Discouraged, Carlos V abdicated in 1556 and retired to a monastery in Yuste, leaving Spain, the colonies and the Netherlands to his son Felipe II, and the rest of his empire to his brother. Around this time, the Iberian peninsula was experiencing a cultural boom (with El Greco's arrival in Toledo) and economic and military success (with the annexation of Portugal in 1580 and an influx of wealth from the two colonial empires). At the same time, Spain was acting as the champion of the Counter-Reformation and the protector of the Catholic faith (Teresa of Ávila drew up the Rule of the Carmelites in 1568). As well as these successes, it also experienced some bitter setbacks, notably with the rebellion of the Netherlands, where the Reformation had taken a strong hold; a rejection born of persecution.

Meanwhile, Spain made an attempt to punish Elizabeth I of England after the execution of Mary Stuart (the Catholic queen of Scotland), by sending a formidable fleet (the Invincible Armada), to teach the English a lesson on 18 June 1588. The aim was to transport an army, which had been amassed in Holland, across the Channel, but storms and English privateers cut them off and they were forced to retreat. These events marked the end of Spanish maritime supremacy.

In the years that followed, Spain lost its hold in Europe – the English under Drake took Cádiz in 1595 and the French recovered Picardy. And Spanish troops tried in vain to quell the separatist will of the Netherlands having been called to support the Germanic Holy Roman Emperor in crushing the rebellion of the German Protestant princes (1618–48); but it was wasted effort as the Treaty of Westphalia recognized the new state. Portugal regained its independence and recovered its colonial possessions and under Louis XIV, France retook Artois, Roussillon, Flanders and the Franche-Comté.

England installed itself on Gibraltar, never to give it up, thus acquiring a strategic base between the Atlantic and the Mediterranean. After the War of Succession and the treaties of Utrecht (1713) and Rastatt (1714), Spain lost the Netherlands, Naples, Sardinia and Sicily. Finally, after the Franco-Spanish defeat at Trafalgar (1805), Napoleon Bonaparte added to this list of disastrous losses by putting his brother Joseph on the Spanish throne in 1808 – to the detriment of Carlos IV and his son Fernando VII.

MOTHER COUNTRY AND COLONIES: NEW REALITIES

Thanks to the help of the English, Fernando VII regained his throne in 1813 with a constitution that was quite liberal for Spain. But inept politics, together with the impact of revolutionary ideas (the right to self-determination, for example), sparked off the disintegration of the Spanish empire, aided in 1815 by the Congress of Vienna, which abolished the black slave trade and set limits on slavery in general. In turn, Argentina (1816), Chile (1818), Mexico and Peru (1821), Colombia (1822), Bolivia (1825), Ecuador and Venezuela (1830) all proclaimed their independence from Spain. Deprived of the resources from its ex-colonies and drained by its efforts to retain them, Spain, already economically very impoverished, was badly prepared for the emerging industrial revolution and sank into political chaos. Despite an attempt at a republic between January 1873 and December 1874, these events served only to facilitate the establishment of a succession of dictatorial governments.

The relationship between Spain and its American colonies was very different to that of other European colonists. While other colonial powers genuinely wanted to settle in the New World and to build a new homeland with its own economy, the Spanish and Portuguese simply pillaged South and Central America, stripping them of their resources, with the principal aim of exploiting the continent's riches and enjoying greater financial status back home. Once independent, the old Spanish colonies were left in poverty ill-prepared to exploit their own resources. As for Spain, the huge loss of revenue left her with the enormous economic problem of financial reconstruction.

THE ADVENT OF FRANCO

The reign of Alfonso XIII, from 1902, did not improve the situation and, after numerous ministerial reshuffles, General Primo de Rivera took the initiative with a *coup d'état* in 1923. All the ingredients for a dictatorship were present – a dissolved parliament, no constitution and a single rule political party. All the same, social conflicts obliged Primo de Rivera to resign in 1930, and even the monarchy was challenged. Elections followed and the Socialists and Republicans had the majority on several occasions. From April 1931, some large cities proclaimed themselves republics, even though Alfonso XIII had not abdicated. Meanwhile strong anti-clerical feelings arose among the population leading, on occasion, to excesses of violence. New elections in February 1936 gave overwhelming victory to the *Frente Popular*, a coalition of left-wing parties. This time a republic was declared and a new wave of violence ended with the assassination of the monarchist minister Calvo Sotelo (13 July 1936), which served as an excuse for the outbreak of civil war.

THE CIVIL WAR

On 17 July 1936, the uprising began. It started with the garrisons stationed in Morocco (Ceuta and Melilla, which were still controlled by Spain) and, commanded by General Franco, it spread like wildfire to the west and north of Spain. It was a savage war with one atrocity after another, including the execution of Federico García Lorca, the obliteration of the town of Guernica and the targeting of civilian populations, setting in motion patterns of violence which were to be repeated everywhere during World War II. While the Republicans got little overt assistance from the major powers – apart from the USSR – the Nationalist troops received considerable support from Hitler and Mussolini.

On 26 January 1939, Barcelona – where the Republican government had taken refuge – fell into Franco's hands. Madrid followed on 28 March. Thousands of people crossed the Pyrenees, fleeing from an undesirable regime and the repression that would inevitably ensue. With the Civil War claiming a million lives in three years, Spain, deprived of its intellectual elite, suffered a succession of assassination attempts on its leader, a paralysed economy, and a non-existent cultural life, and sank little by little into a repressed torpor.

THE DEATH OF FRANCO: A NEW SPAIN

General Franco died on the 20 November 1975, almost 40 years after the military uprising of 1936. His death was as desired as it was feared. The pessimistic predicted another civil war but they did not take into account the ability of King Juan Carlos, the successor designated by Franco in 1969. He capably handled the transition, first by taking the oath before the Cortes on 22 November and then by calling upon a new man, Adolfo Suárez, to act as prime minister. Suárez succeeded in gaining approval, by means of a referendum, for a liberal project of institutional reform. In 1977, the Spanish communist party was given legal recognition, thanks to the authority and flexibility of Juan Carlos.

In the elections in June 1977, the *Unión de Centro Democrático* (Central Democratic Union) won and took government; the Socialist Party was next in line and the Communist Party next. The Francoist right-wing party was very much an also-ran. The parties representing the autonomous communities also made significant political gains. The process of democratization was felt, not just in politics, but in every sphere of Spanish life. In the Moncloa pact, which aimed to reduce purchasing power and limit inflation, the four main political parties showed a considerable degree of common sense. Gradually, all (or nearly all) the monuments raised to the glory of General Franco throughout Spain, were removed. The new authorities renamed thousands of roads, bridges and hospitals to remove his name and now Madrid has just one modest statue of Franco which is in the Ministry of Employment and is unnamed.

THE CONSTITUTION

The new constitution for a 'social and democratic' Spanish state was in fact a parliamentary monarchy. This model was submitted to the Spanish people by referendum and 88 per cent of the votes cast approved it, but the rate of abstentions was high (32 per cent, 56 per cent of which was in the Basque country). It came into effect on 29 December 1978 and finally put an end to the Francoist regime. The elections of 1982 confirmed victory for the Socialist Party and its leader, Felipe González. They were re-elected in 1986 and 1989. In 1996 the right-wing party, the Partido Popular (Popular Party) came to office, with José-María Aznar as its leader.

JUAN CARLOS

If there is one person who is loved by all Spaniards, it is Juan Carlos. Youthful and personable, he can sometimes be seen on the streets of Madrid riding a motorbike or driving his Mercedes. Juan Carlos is immensely popular despite the fact of his difficult heritage as the grandson of Alfonso XIII. Brought up outside Spain, the king was put on the throne by Franco himself. On the death of the dictator, Juan Carlos showed great courage, an iron will and a great diplomacy as well as supporting the prime minister in his task of democratization and liberalization. And he was quick to understand the advantages to Spain from the country opening its doors and becoming part of Europe.

However, it was during the attempted coup on 23 February 1981 that he really earned his place in the hearts of the Spanish people. Throughout that historic February night, Juan Carlos managed to dissuade the military one by one from participating in the coup. By denouncing the plot, he showed a composure and courage which the Spanish are unlikely to forget in a hurry.

At the same time, he further legitimized the role of the monarchy in the country. Since then, he has remained in the public eye, his photo appearing regularly in the papers. The old Nationalists have learned to respect him little by little while the young appreciate him for his easy-going attitude and his spirit of openness.

THE END OF THE 20TH CENTURY AND THE BEGINNING OF THE 21ST

Less than 20 years after the death of Franco, Spain has caught up with nearly a century of European progress. Not only has it been able to overcome its past (the aborted Francoist coup in February 1981), but it has been quick to take on its characteristic open, positive attitude once again. The fact that Barcelona hosted the Olympic Games in the summer 1992 and the Expo in Seville in the same year is a testament to the good will, encouragement and hope that Spain has managed to inspire. Most importantly, however, is the success with which it has overcome the trauma of the Franco years – which for a long time ostracized it and relegated it to a living symbol of fascist regimes. Spain is in the process of becoming a country to be reckoned with in the Europe of the future.

Preparation for Expo 92 brought about massive improvements to roads and monuments and cost the region of Andalucía a small fortune. But after the euphoria of the Expo and the fading of the dream of economic boom, the population has sunk under the burden of the region's debts and the problems of high unemployment.

Agriculture (predominantly wine and olives) and livestock-rearing are the principal resources of Andalucía, which has little industry. The region has actively been developing its tourist industry, although sometimes with devastating results. The Costa del Sol has, in places, been massively overdeveloped and many coastal towns and cities have lost much of their original character and natural beauty. Despite this, there are still areas that have been relatively untouched by huge hotel developments and the disadvantages of mass tourism. Away from the coast, southern Spain and Andalucía remain largely untouched, offering a great escape from the crowds that dominate the coastal regions.

With a commitment to the EU and the benefit of grants and other aid, Spain is continuing to rebuild. Recently, especially in the fields of fashion, art and culture, Spain has begun to emerge as an innovative and forward-looking country with an exciting and youthful generation eager to get on with building its future.

SOME SIGNIFICANT DATES

Neolithic period: Iberian tribes, probably from Africa, become established in the south and east of Spain.

202 BC: Roman occupation.

AD 484: the kingdom of the Visigoths spreads throughout Spain.

711: first Moorish invasions from North Africa.

BACKGROUND

756: the caliph of Damascus, architect of the expansion of Arab civilization in Spain, establishes himself in Córdoba.

1000–1500: Reconquest – the Christian states progressively retake possession of the territories lost to Islam.

1469: marriage of Fernando de Aragón and Isabel de Castilla. Union of the two long-time rival kingdoms.

1478–79: establishment of the Inquisition by Tomás de Torquemada.

1492: fall of the kingdom of Granada on 2 January. Discovery of America by Christopher Columbus on behalf of the Catholic Monarchs (Fernando V and Isabel I). Expulsion of the Jews to 'protect the religious unity of Spain' (about 200,000 Jews leave for North Africa, Italy and the Ottoman empire).

1512: Navarra absorbed by Castilla.

1516–56: reign of Charles V (Charles I of Spain), grandson of Isabel la Católica, over a huge empire, 'where the sun never sets', in both Europe and America.

1588: destruction of the Invincible Armada.

1656: *Las Meninas* and the family of Felipe IV painted by Velázquez.

1700: accession to the throne by Felipe V, grandson of Louis XIV, at the beginning of the War of Spanish Succession (1701–14). It ends with the loss of the Netherlands and the kingdom of Naples.

1808: Napoleon's brother, Joseph, is named king of Spain and is given the nickname 'Pepe Botella'. Madrid, occupied by French troops, revolts. Beginning of the War of Independence.

1813: victory of the Anglo-Portuguese army under Wellington, aided by the Spanish. Fernando VII regains the Spanish throne.

1814–33: disintegration of the Spanish empire in America.

1898: Cuban independence, the loss of Puerto Rico and the Philippines.

1902–31: reign of Alfonso XIII starts. It is marked by an economic revival and a dictatorial regime (1923–30) under Primo de Rivera.

1931: the Left takes control of the big towns as a result of the municipal elections and proclaims a republic. King Alfonso XIII abdicates.

1935: constitution of the *Frente Popular*, which unites unions and parties on the left.

1936: success for the *Frente Popular* in the February elections. The leader of the monarchist opposition, José Calvo Sotelo, is assassinated and troops on the north coast of Morocco are given the signal to revolt. Under General Franco, the revolt spreads rapidly. It is the beginning of the Civil War. It lasts for three years, and Franco's rule lasts for nearly 40.

1939: the Republican government withdraws to Barcelona but it is taken by the Nationalists. The Republican government then takes refuge in France. Madrid, the last point of Republican resistance, finally falls on 28 February.

1969: General Franco officially names Prince Juan Carlos, Alfonso XIII's grandson, as his successor.

1975: 20 November, death of Franco. 22 November, Juan Carlos becomes King of Spain.

1977: official recognition of the Spanish Communist Party.

1978: the new 'social and democratic' constitution is put in place.

1982: victory for the head of the PSOE (Spanish Socialist Workers' Party), Felipe González, who becomes prime minister.

1986: Spanish entry into the European Community. Legislative elections mean that Felipe González retains his absolute majority even though he loses a million votes.

1987: in the European, regional and communal elections, Felipe González's PSOE loses its absolute majority in the municipal councils of a number of major towns (including Madrid).

1989: slender majority for Felipe González's party. Spanish presidency of the EC.

1992: Expo 92 in Seville (April to October); Olympic Games in Barcelona (July).

1996: after 13 years in power, Felipe González is defeated by José María Aznar and the right-wing Partido Popular (Popular Party). The new prime minister negotiates the support of the Nationalists, particularly the Catalans under Jordi Pujol.

1997: in July, members of ETA, the Basque separatist organization, assassinate a young councillor in the town of Ermua in Vizcaya (one of the three provinces of the Basque Autonomous Community). Such hatred and disgust is aroused by ETA's actions that nearly two million people protest in the streets of Madrid and Bilbao. The political leaders of ETA go on trial in Madrid.

1997: marriage of the Infanta of Spain to a handball player in October.

1998: the Basque nationalist parties sign the 'Izarra' declaration, inspired by the Northern Ireland peace process, in September.

2000: in March Aznar's Partido Popular (PP) wins the legislative elections with 10.2 million votes and 183 ministers, seven more than is needed for an absolute majority. Andalucía does not escape the spread of the centre-right – four provinces out of eight bring home the PP (including Almería). The socialist Manuel Chaves, governor of the region since 1990, fails to obtain the majority he wanted and needed.

BACKGROUND

THE ECONOMY

Spain has an industrialized economy as well as a strong agricultural sector. Until 1975 when the country was under the rule of the Franco regime, the Spanish economy developed almost in isolation from the rest of Europe and the world. Its trade was protected from foreign competition by tight import controls and high taxes. It was during this period that Spain evolved from a predominantly agrarian economy to an industrial one. Spain joined the

European Community in 1986 and made the transition into a European economy fairly easily.

Despite the fact that Spain's traditional shipbuilding, steel and textile industries declined, Spain still achieved the highest average growth rate in the EU during the 1980s and returned a steady performance throughout the 1990s.

Despite the decline of older industries, manufacturing has experienced rapid expansion in chemicals, electronics, information technology and industrial design.

The structural weakness of the Spanish economy means that unemployment remains high. Other economic factors, like interest rates are within the limits that allowed Spain to join the European Monetary Union at the beginning of 1999.

The agricultural sector is strong, producing cereals, vegetables, citrus fruit, olive oil and wine. The fishing industry, although past its peak, is still one of the world's largest. Tourism is a major contributor of wealth to Spain.

THE PEOPLE

Andalucía's contrasting landscape of light and shade, of arid plateaux and fertile valleys, is also the cradle of an equally divergent culture. Like the landscape, Andalucían culture was born as a result of the exceptional symbiosis of Jewish, Muslim and Christian peoples. This powerful period of cooperation ended with the advent of the Inquisition in the 15th century, but its legacy lives on today.

Islam had a powerful influence throughout the whole of Spain for almost a thousand years, its people enjoying standards of scholarship, craftsmanship, art and philosophy unmatched elsewhere in Europe. But the Reconquest by the Christians, slowly began to encroach on Muslim life until it was violently brought to an end throwing Andalucía into decline as it succumbed to persecution, massacre and exile.

To grasp the essence of the Andalucían character, it is important to understand its rich, although often painful, history and its exciting cultural mix of Muslim, Jewish and Catholic influences. This history is on show everywhere you go in Andalucía. Extraordinary monuments, often in the amazing Mudéjar style, testify to the powerful Arab influence throughout the region. The Giralda in Seville, the Mezquita in Córdoba and the Alhambra in Granada are just a few other grandiose examples of Moorish architecture. But even in the towns you can sense a North African flavour in the white-washed walls of the houses with their window sills adorned with brightly coloured geraniums.

Another manifestation of the Andalucían spirit is a love of quality. This can be seen in regional products like sherry or *jerez* from the province of Cádiz. This famous wine has a world-wide reputation along with the bulls and horses from the area around Seville.

Andalucíans have a natural bent towards pleasure, especially in the simple things in life – wine, women and song, to coin a phrase. By comparison, the people of Castille attach much more importance to work, religion, discipline and politics. In Andalucía, what can be done today is gladly put off until tomorrow and a poet is held in much higher regard than a priest. The Andalucían attitude to life is out of step with the seriousness of the north – unlike their northern compatriots, Andalucíans take their time, dismiss accusations of chauvinism and seem to be happy to allow their children more freedom than the disciplined offspring of the north.

When they are not sitting in dreamy contemplation, Andalucíans enjoy a good festival, when they have a chance to express their passionate temperaments. You need to see the Semana Santa processions in Seville to understand even a little what the festive fervour is all about and what it is that gives these fiestas their almost pagan flavour. The *ferias* (fairs or carnivals) are great occasions for everyone to meet up and enjoy themselves. Since Franco's death, fiestas have been given a new lease of life with the young taking part, expressing their patriotic fervour and taking the chance to make the most of the time to visit *bodegas* (traditional wine bars) as part of their merrymaking.

In the last half century a revival of interest in traditional song and dance swept through Andalucía, with flamenco and song being used to express the pain, love and hope that epitomise the Andalucían heart.

HUMAN RIGHTS

Spain is currently facing significant problems of racism and racial violence. This is particularly an issue in Andalucía, where there is a relatively large immigrant community. There are frequent reports of attacks on immigrants and ethnic minorities, sometimes of an organized nature, and often encouraged by the rhetoric of right-wing politicians. There is systematic economic exploitation of the immigrant community, with the payment of very low wages, long working hours and legal limitations on the rights of foreign workers. That a large proportion of the immigrant population is illegal exacerbates these problems due to their even more vulnerable position.

The coast of southern Spain is a popular entry point for asylum seekers and illegal immigrants. The bodies resulting from failed attempts to cross the Mediterranean are regularly washed up on the beaches, and there is a distressing reluctance on the part of the authorities to deal with the problem; bodies are often left on the beaches for some time, and there is a lack of diligence in identifying them. There is also evidence of violence against immigrants and asylum seekers by the police and other official agencies, and of detention and subsequent deportation in very poor conditions. There have even been claims by ships' masters of requests by Spanish officials to carry illegal immigrants as cargo rather than passengers, a breach of international maritime law.

Human rights issues tied up with the Basque separatist terrorist organization ETA (Euskadi Ta Askatasuna) activities have spread beyond the Basque area of northern Spain to affect the whole country. While the ETA campaign of terrorism is in clear violation of the rights of its victims, there are also serious question marks over the official response. There are frequent allegations of police brutality against suspects. The UN Committee Against Torture found that the ability of the police to detain suspects incommunicado in detention for up to five days facilitated the ill-treatment and torture of suspects, and that there was an official tolerance of this with minimal punishments for officials who had abused suspects. Regrettably, the Spanish courts are prepared to accept statements made under duress as evidence, which both encourages and approves torture as an instrument of the legal system.

The Committee Against Torture found prison conditions in Spain to be poor, with overcrowding, and evidence of violence by both prisoners and prison officers. There was a suggestion that these problems appeared especially pronounced in the southern areas of Spain.

As is still the case in many Western European states, the position of women in Spanish, and especially southern Spanish society falls some way short of equality. There is considerable domestic violence, with low conviction rates. According to the UN, despite some recent improvements, the participation of women in the labour market remains amongst the lowest in Western Europe, and those women who do work are paid less than men. The same UN body was also critical of the limited involvement of women in public life, and suggested that efforts be made to encourage women to become involved in public decision-making processes, at both a national and a regional level. However, so far there is little evidence that this is happening.

IMMIGRATION

ANDALUCÍA: THE COVETED 'FRONT DOOR' TO EUROPE

The routes through Andalucía used by illegal immigrants entering Spain are well charted. Ironically, they largely follow the trading routes of the 18th-century slave traders who took Africans to America. Immigrants make their way to Algeria, and Morocco, travelling from as far a field as Dakar in Senegal, in order to cross the Straits of Gibraltar into Spain.

In the early 1990s, the Tangier Medina became a favourite jumping off point for people trying to get into Europe illegally. Those wishing to gain entry apparently needed to do little more than turn up at certain well-known cafés and organize their journey. Spanish and Moroccan authorities appeared to turn a blind eye to these practices allegedly so that cheap labour was available for the construction for the Olympic stadium in Barcelona and the exhibition centre for Expo 92 in Seville. The authorities were accused of having full knowledge of the unhindered influx of North Africans on the Ceuta–Algeciras ferry.

Today, it has become much more difficult to get into Spain illegally and attempts to cross illegally often end tragically either in death or in deportation. Non-government organizations have criticized the precarious position of children who have no identity papers or relatives to care for them. They sleep on the streets of Ceuta and are often arrested and driven back to the border. With nothing to lose, they sometimes cling to the axles of lorries being loaded onto the ferries or conceal themselves in containers in order to get back across the border. Although such desperate measures are becoming less common, there are plenty of people who are happy to make money out of smuggling immigrants. They charter flat-bottomed boats (the notorious *pateras*), because they can't be detected by coastguard radar and pack in as many men, women and children as they can. The majority of crossings run between Tangier and Tarifa, Ceuta and Algeciras and, for the very brave, Nador and Almería. The confluence of the Atlantic Ocean and the Mediterranean Sea makes the navigation of these boats very difficult and the Guardia Civil no longer bother to keep a record of how many sink. According to the Moroccan newspaper *Libération*, more than 3,500 illegal immigrants' bodies have washed up on the Andalucían coastline since the beginning of the 1990s. The majority of crossings take place at night during the summer months. Sometimes, the mafia who organize the journey deceive immigrants to the extent that they are dropped off on the coast of Morocco and don't even make it to Spain. Other alleged routes into Spain include riding on a fishing vessel, a practice that the authorities are accused of knowing about but ignoring, due to the fall in fish quotas. Spanish fishermen are said to bring across immigrants with hashish taped to their bodies. On arrival part of the drug consignment is handed over to the fishermen and the rest is given to the immigrant to help him or her through the first few months in Spain.

Another popular means of entering Spain involves getting over the wall that divides the enclave of Ceuta (a tiny piece of Spanish territory on the Morocco coast) from Morocco along an 8-kilometre (5-mile) border. The 3-metre (10-foot) high wall has recently been equipped with hi-tech sensors and heat-sensitive cameras. The Guardia Civil stand guard in their high look-out posts, aided by binoculars. Anyone caught trying to cross the frontier without the correct passport is immediately returned to the border. Anyone found with a forged passport is sent to the Calamocarro camp. Though originally built to house 500 people, it is now home to over 2,000 people. Some of its occupants are prepared to go to any lengths to get into Spain, including self-harming. They hope that a non-governmental organization will get permission for them to be sent to Europe for urgent medical attention. This is, though, ultimately self-defeating, as more and more Spanish hospitals are refusing to accept patients who have neither entry visas nor money.

In general, the people who do manage to get across the border into Spain already have friends or relatives to help them. And usually, the final destination of these immigrants is not Spain but France, Switzerland, Britain or Germany. Spain is simply a convenient stopping off place where they can put together a bit of money; if they are lucky they get taken on as casual labour during harvest time.

THE FUTURE

The richer countries of Europe are well aware of how easy it is for immigrants to cross their borders illegally. By the end of 1999, the Ceuta Guardia Civil had escorted around 33,000 would-be immigrants back across the border. A Spanish blockade will certainly not resolve the problem of immigration. As long as poorer people are attracted by the prospect of wealth and opportunity, illegal immigration will continue to be a problem. However, Spain has recently taken positive steps towards putting Spaniards and immigrants (whether legal or otherwise) on a more equal footing. New labour laws now recognize every individual's right to social security and union representation, so putting an end to sweatshop conditions and slave wages. And the country is also to take a fresh look at its immigration quotas and other related procedures as part of a first step towards dismantling the smuggling rackets and putting those who profit from the misery of others out of business.

TRADITION AND CUSTOMS

Spanish life has undergone considerable change in recent years which has resulted in many religious customs being adapted to suit modern ways of life, especially in large towns and cities, and particularly among women.

The predominant religions, in line with Spain's history, are Catholicism and Islam. However Christianity, and Catholicism in particular, is still the majority religion.

Unlike many other southern European countries, shaking hands (rather than kissing on the cheek) is the customary form of greeting in Spain. If invited to someone's home, take a small gift. Flowers are only sent for special celebrations, though, so take something like soap, an ornament or maybe a culinary delicacy.

Away from the tourist resorts, scanty bikinis and beachwear in general should only be worn on the beach or around the pool.

The Spanish are keen on smoking and it is widely accepted in public areas of all kinds.

CORRIDA – THE BULLFIGHT

It's seen by some as a barbaric ritual and by others as a sublime art, but whatever view you take, bullfighting has deep historical roots that are thought to go back to the Neolithic period when the Iberians first came to Spain. Evidence of this can be found in a granite cave near San Martin de Valdeiglesias, about 70 kilometres (45 miles) west of Madrid. Here, in what was once probably an Iberian shelter, there is a carving of a group of bulls called the Bulls of Guisand. For the Iberians, as for the Cretans, the bull was a god and was worshipped as such. The art of bull-baiting was a ceremony that involved fighting a wild bull before ritually sacrificing it. The victory of man over beast was obligatory endowing the man who took on the fight with strength and divine power.

Over the centuries the format of the bullfight has changed, but the social significance is the same, especially for the many *aficionados* of the ancient sport. In a Spanish *corrida* (bullfight) the bull is almost always killed, although very occasionally it may be spared. But to defend bullfighting on these grounds is misguided; the essential aim remains the death of the bull at the hands of the matador. As far as most Spaniards are concerned, bullfighting is an integral part of Spanish culture and, as such, needs no justification.

THE SOCIAL IMAGE OF THE BULLFIGHTER

For a long time bullfighters had a very negative image. Coming from underprivileged backgrounds, they were looked down upon because they were seen to be squandering their high earnings on big cars, flashy clothes and glamorous girls. In the past, they even had the dubious distinction of being dispossessed by Alfonso X and excommunicated by Pius XII. This negative attitude was, fortunately, balanced by having the support of the nobility who themselves fought bulls, although it was just for pleasure. Recently, things have changed, and bullfighters now manage their wealth like competent businessmen.

As a sport, bullfighting remains very much in the male domain and only one woman has stormed its ranks. In 1996, Cristina Sánchez a young woman from Madrid, earned her full colours as a matador. She proved to the male *aficionados* that a woman could enter the arena with as much courage as her male counterparts. The sport's detractors questioned whether this was really progress and intense pressure was brought to bear for her to quit. After the San Isidro festival in Madrid in 1999, she did in fact announce her retirement but by then she had spent three years as a matador and had proved her point.

Today, bullfighters are known as 'toreadors' but this name is a fabrication of the librettist of Bizet's opera Carmen, who made it up because he preferred it to '*torero*'. It's not a Spanish word at all.

WHAT YOU NEED TO KNOW

Bullfights, *corridas de toros*, take place during festivals, on public holidays and on Sundays in big towns in the summer. The majority of the fights are with *novilladas*, newcomers or novices. With *novilladas*, the *novillos* (bullocks) are less than four years old and the *novilleros* (young bullfighters) have not yet earned their full colours as matadors. Another difference is that there aren't any *picadores*, mounted members of the bullfighting team, at the event (*see below*). As they are still gaining experience, the *novilleros* are keen to impress the crowd with their skill and bravery making these fights real spectacles.

In the past, these young pretenders practiced their art in the village *capeas* – improvized bullfights that took place in public squares – but, although popular, they have gradually become less common. Maybe because formal bullfights are such big business these days.

Most major *plaza de toros* (bullrings) hold up to 25,000 spectators, although the size depends on the stadium, which is usually dependent on the size of the town hosting the event. Seat prices are based on how close spectators are to the action and whether or not they are in the shade (*sombra*) or in the full sun (*sol*). Traditionally, fights used to take place at 5pm when the sun was still high making the shade worth paying extra for, but these days, many of the big fights take place at 7 or 8pm when it is cooler. However the seats in the first row (*barreras*) and the boxes on the first level (*palcos*) are still sought after, although the stands (*gradas*) also offer good views of the fight.

THE RITUALS OF THE *CORRIDA*

If you want to attend a *corrida*, it is useful to understand the ancient rituals of the fight. Before the matador can enter the ring, a signal has to be given by the president of the *corrida* to allow the *paseo* (procession) of the *cuadrillas* (teams) into the ring. First in the ring are two mounted *alguaciles* (constables) who represent law and order in the ring and are responsible for seeing that the rules are obeyed. Then come the matadors or *espadas*, followed by their teams: the *peones* (bullfighter's assistants), the *picadores* on horseback, the *monosabios* (ring attendants) and finally the mule teams to remove the bull and dead horses.

The matadors, dressed in tight, flamboyant costumes embroidered with sequins, salute the president while one of the *alguaciles* asks permission to open the *toril* (pen). The matadors exchange their cloaks for *capas* (capes). These are also brightly coloured and are either pink lined with yellow cloth or blue lined with pink.

The bull comes out of the pen, adorned with *divisa*, a cascade of ribbons in the colours of its *ganadería* (pedigree) or breeder.

THE *SUERTES* (STAGES) OF THE BULLFIGHT

The First Tercio

During the first stage, the bullfighter makes a number of different moves or *pases* with his cape to goad the bull into charging him. There are a huge variety of choreographed moves that true *aficionados* understand and appreciate. The *larga* is a single-handed pass that drives the bull to follow the length of the cape's sweep. Another key move is the *verónica* where the bullfighter performs a two-handed sweep with the cape while standing directly in front of the bull. Following these taunting moves comes the start of the end for the bull and his opponent as the fight and the matador's performance is dependent on what happens next. At this point, the *picadores* drive their *suerte de varas* (lances) into the *morrillo* (the back of the bull's neck). The bull must take the three statutory lances (a condition of its eligibility for a reprieve, however notional that idea may be). The next stage is the *quite* when the matador draws the bull away from the *picador* to give it respite after receiving the lances. This leads into the second stage of the fight.

The Second Tercio: The *Banderillas*

The next phase depends on how badly injured the bull is after it has suffered the lances. It is now that the *torero* confronts the bull without his cape. Instead, he holds two long barbed batons called *banderillas*, which are decorated with brightly coloured paper. There are several different ways of executing this phase, depending on the bull and the position in which it is standing. The different manoeuvres used by the matador are the *suerte de banderillas al quebro de frente* (full frontal), *al relance*, *a toro corrido*, *al siesgo* (oblique), *a la media vuelta* (half-turn), *al cuarteo* (quarter circle), to name but a few.

The Third: *La Faena* (The Main Performance)

The *toreo de muleta* is the stage when the *muleta* (a piece of red cloth folded over a stick) is used to kill the bull. For the spectators, it is often the most attractive phase, as they wait impatiently for the bugle to give the signal for the bullfighters to begin their work.

There are many different *pases de muletas* that can be performed now. These include *redondos* (turns), *altos* (high moves), *de telón* (the curtain), *ayudados* (the two-handed move), *de frente* (a move in front of the bull), *molinetes* (pirouettes), *afarolados* (overhead flourishes) and *por la espalda* (the reverse move).

At the climax of the fight, and when the bull is at last exhausted, the matador stands still and summons the bull to him. This is called the *suerte de recibir*. But if the bull refuses to approach him, the bullfighter moves towards the bull and this is called the *volapié*. If both move towards each other at the same time, it is referred to as *a un tiempo*. The bullfighter aims to thrust his sword between the shoulders of the bull and straight into its heart. This final movement can be a deep thrust, short thrust, left-handed thrust, or long thrust and is named accordingly.

The *descabello* (coup de grâce) – is carried out when the bull is mortally wounded but is not dead (which is usually the case). To kill the bull instantly the matador uses a special sword (the *verduguillo*), which he thrusts into its back, severing its spinal column.

The Arrastre

This is the end of the bullfight when the mules drag the bull's corpse out of the ring. If the spectators are satisfied with the performance of the matador, they wave white handkerchiefs. If, on the other hand, they are not happy, there is a *bronca* (an uproar of whistling and shouting) – in Seville disapproval is expressed by silence.

BULLFIGHTING TERMS

– *Aficionados*: enthusiasts

– *Barrera*: barrier protecting the public from the arena

– *Bronca*: raucous expression of disapproval. Whistling, shouting, cushion-throwing, etc.

– *Cogida*: goring

– *Derechazo*: a pass with the muleta to the right

– *Descabello*: sword used to administer the coup de grâce

– *Estocada*: death thrust

– *Feria*: two week festivals during which the corridas are held

– *Montera*: headgear worn by the matador

– *Muleta*: red cloth used by the matador in the last *tercio*. The pink and yellow cape is used in the first two *tercios*

BACKGROUND

– *Pase de muerte*: the final pass before the death stroke

– *Plaza de toros*: bullring

– *Tempe*: the rhythm of movement between the bullfighter and the bull

– *Tercio*: each of the three phases of the bullfight

– *Recibir*: the moment of the kill when the matador is waiting for the bull to charge

– *Volapié*: the moment of the kill when the bullfighter approaches the bull and swivels away at the last minute

FLAMENCO

Towards the end of the 1980s, flamenco (gypsy folk song and dance) started to attract an audience outside its homeland and could be heard everywhere, from nightclubs to local radio stations. Even the brightly-coloured rustling dresses of the flamenco dancers were copied by the ready-to-wear market.

Flamenco is a traditional art that has been passed down through generations since the arrival of gypsies in Spain during the 15th century. On their nomadic journeys through India, North Africa and Europe – persecuted and looked down upon wherever they went – the gypsies drew on the songs they heard on their travels to create their own unique voice. From their wide repertoire of traditional songs they created the *Cante Jondo*, the most powerful form of flamenco, the heart-rending cry that comes from the very soul of the proud, independent gypsies. The first literary reference to flamenco dates back to 1750 in *The Book of the Triana Gypsies* by Jerónimo de Alba Diéguez. This contains a reference to a dance (*la Danza del Cascabel Gordo*) performed by a dozen gypsy virgins.

At the beginning of the 19th century, the effects of the Napoleonic War, the restoration of absolutism under Fernando VII and economic problems forced poverty-stricken rural dwellers to seek their fortune in the cities, leading to even greater suffering and hardship. At the same time, flamenco began to spring up in the bars (tablaos) of Andalucía, particularly those of the Triana district of Seville. This rich and colourful free form of song was used to express not only the hardship, misery and violence endured by the gypsies but a whole range of emotions including their pride.

By 1850, a fashion for cabaret had emerged in Spain and flamenco could be heard everywhere from Seville to Madrid. At the same time, sailors were returning with music from Cuba, Puerto Rico and Argentina – *milongas*, *colombianas*, *guajiras* – and these rhythms were gradually absorbed into flamenco.

By the end of the 19th century, flamenco was progressing from the bar to the theatre. Slowly it gained acceptance, revealing its capacity to express sadness, passion and melancholy to a whole new audience. The famous Valencian writer Vincente Blasco Ibáñez wrote at the time, 'We are a sad people, we have it in our blood. We cannot sing without sounding threatening or without crying, and the more our songs are mixed with sighs and anguished cries, the more beautiful they are'. But flamenco's reputation and, to some extent, its popularization came by way of an artistic elite who found in its melancholy music a fitting expression for their romantic feelings. New themes of love and patriotism, culture and pride in Andalucía were introduced. Among this group was García Lorca who staged the *Concurso de Cante Jondo* (a flamenco singing competition) in Granada in 1922. Since that time flamenco has developed in many different directions, from its purest form – a singer accompanied by the rhythm of a hammer beating on an anvil in imitation of a blacksmith at work – to the symphonic arrangements of songs by Spain's greatest flamenco singer of the 20th century, Camarón de la Isla (*see* 'Famous People'). Flamenco has four basic styles or *palos* which are played in the provinces of Cádiz, Seville, Málaga and Granada – the *soleares*, *siguiriyas*, *tangos* and *fandangos*. These styles are subdivided into a large number of variations and rhythms, many of which originate from specific areas, including *malagueñas* (from Málaga), *cartageneras* (from Cartagena), *granaínas* (from Granada), *rondeñas* (from Ronda), *alegrías*, *bulerías*, *cantiñas*, *rumbas*, *tientos*, and so on. An important feature of classic flamenco is the *duende*, or spirit of flamenco music. Impossible to explain and difficult to achieve, this intensely powerful and emotional communication with the audience sends shivers down the spine. Only the most gifted performers are able to touch their audience in such a way and the experience is unforgettable.

THE ARTISTS

Flamenco music has a huge number of popular and talented artists to its name. Two of the best interpreters of the art are Enrique Morente and the late Camarón de la Isla. Enrique Morente – considered to be the greatest living flamenco *cantador* – was born in 1942, and is known for his adaptations of García Lorca, San Juan de la Cruz and the work of other notable poets. Camarón de la Isla, born José Monge Cruz, began his career singing in the bars of Cádiz and Málaga. He and the guitarist Paco de Lucía began to explore new horizons together, pushing forward the boundaries of traditional flamenco performance. They introduced pop arrangements, making use of drums, electric bass and guitars. Mick Jagger, Miles Davis and Peter Gabriel are just a few of his famous admirers. His death at the age of 41, on 2 July 1992, deprived Spain of one of her most popular and gifted flamenco singers.

The duo of Lole y Manuel also enjoys enormous popularity in Spain. Lole Montoya grew up in Casablanca and Manuel Molina originally comes from Seville. Lole's pure, crystal-clear voice and Manuel's guitar-playing produce an explosive mixture of classical and popular sound. They were amongst the first to successfully introduce their own songs and music into the traditional flamenco repertoire.

Other outstanding flamenco artists include Terremoto (meaning earthquake, a reference to the effect caused by Fernando Fernández Monge's famously deep voice), Diego 'El Cabrillero', Luis de Córdoba, El Indio Gitano, La Niña de Los Peines, El Pele, Susi, Fernanda and Bernarda de Utrera, and La Perla de Cádiz. The top guitarists include Paco de Lucía (*see* 'Famous People'), Manolo Sanlúcar, Sabicas, Enrique de Melchor, Rafael Montoya, Ramon de Algeciras, Tomatito and the Carmona Habichuela brothers.

RECORDINGS

It is difficult to find good recordings of true flamenco outside Spain, almost as if the duende is incapable of crossing the Spanish border in digital form. If you are a flamenco fan, the best option is to visit a record shop while you are in Spain. One excellent label is *Fonomusic* (website: www.fonomusic.es) which has gathered together all the greats in its *Cultura Jonda* collection. Its catalogue of 20 or so records contains a number of good live sound recordings, made at ventas and fiestas, where you can sense the presence of the duende.

SPANISH GYPSIES

The most aristocratic and representative part of Andalucía is what I call the gypsy

Federico García Lorca

The popular image of gypsies portrays them as swarthy, ancient travellers with gold rings in their ears, the women draped in long shawls, leading fair-haired children by the hand and accompanied by scruffy animals. They are depicted as folk musicians, intoning their sadness in song, and as carrying silver daggers sullied with the blood of their vagabond crimes, suggesting a capacity for cruel flashes of defiance. Something about these nomads has always unnerved settled civilizations who have given gypsies countless names – tziganes, bohemians, travellers and Romanies being just a few. Persecuted and mocked, but always feared, the gypsies have always had travel and the desire to explore the open road in their blood. and their attitude to life is both the scorn and envy of Western sensibilities. Their mobility and their particular way of dressing are in strong contrast to settled habits and a stable way of life. But gypsies have an unnerving collective power and solidarity – and an even more disturbing sensuality. The importance of family is central to their identity and they have a strong sense of loyalty to their clan, as well as their own strict code of conduct.

THEIR ORIGINS

Scholars now believe that the gypsy (or Romany) language can be classed as neo-Indian, which would seem to confirm that the gypsies originated in the north of India.

It is believed that the gypsies left India between the 8th and 10th centuries, a notion that comes as something of a surprise as it was previously understood that gypsies came from Egypt. Indeed, the Spanish word for gypsy, *gitano*, comes from *Egipcio*, the Spanish for Egypt, and the first families to arrive in Catalonia in the 15th century were given the title 'Dukes of Little Egypt'. More radical theorists even believe that gypsies are survivors of Babylon. However, historians are agreed that the Roms (their own term for themselves – *rom* meaning 'man' in their language) would have left India in two separate groups – one moving inland and the other spreading around the coasts. They crossed Baluchistan, Persia, the Arabian and Syrian deserts and Egypt; and one group ended up in the Iberian peninsula.

The arrival of these peculiarly dressed nomads caused quite a stir in Spain. The men were draped in long multi-coloured blankets and the women wore oriental turbans mounted on wicker frames. In France, the Church was quick to judge them – and their penchant for magic – and consigned them directly to hell. In Spain, however, they were seen in a more favourable light and a gypsy count, Tomás de Egipcio, even enjoyed the favour of King and Queen Blanca of Navarra and enjoyed their support over a number of political incidents. Andalucía was under their spell and the Westerners were fascinated by these magnetic, nomadic, mysterious people. The men were admired for their equestrian skills, and people were drawn to gypsy dance and music; soon their travels began to be romanticized. This harmonious relationship continued until the 17th century when society turned against them.

INTEGRATION

When the gypsies arrived in the 15th century, Spain was going through a turbulent time. The year 1478 saw the start of the new Inquisition and 1492 marked the capture of Granada, the expulsion of the Jews and the discovery of the Americas. At the same time, the cordiality of the Spanish people towards the gypsies began to turn to suspicion. This was a period of rapid change and rampant intolerance and in 1499, the first law against the gypsies was passed. The Catholic Monarchs issued a warning – either work or leave the country. Isabel and Fernando thought it immoral for these people to be making a living from begging. In addition, religious pilgrimages were on the decline, meaning that the gypsies could no longer join the ranks of the faithful to wander as they pleased. In a very short space of time, they went from being mysterious, romantic nomads, to vagabonds.

In the mid-15th century, the Inquisition held a bloody sword over Spain. The Archbishop of Tarragona, following the French example, suddenly preached condemnation of the gypsies, and, in 1539, Carlos V reinforced that antipathy by signing a new anti-gypsy law. Any gypsy leading life as a vagabond or a beggar would be liable to six years in the galleys. In 1544, it was decided that any gypsy caught in the act of stealing would have his ears cut off. There was a flood of laws specifically aimed at the gypsies and in 1594, a plan was put forward to get rid of them altogether.

They were accused of all sorts of crimes including stealing children, fornicating, robbing churches and practising sorcery. It was also decided to separate the men from the women to prevent reproduction! Happily, this grotesque project was quickly abandoned (only to be resurrected three and a half centuries later when the Nazis carried out the systematic sterilization of the Tziganes).

In July 1611, the Council of State voted for the expulsion of the gypsies and in some places there was an attempt to ban their dances and costumes. However, the plan to expel them proved impossible and Spain decided as a last resort to absorb them slowly by a process of integration.

BACKGROUND

HISTORY REPEATS ITSELF

In 1748, the right to asylum ceased to recognize the gypsy people and, in 1749, the Bishop of Oviedo decided upon a campaign of complete eradication. He proposed a radical solution – penal servitude in perpetuity for all gypsies. Children from the age of 12, men and women were to be seized and put into labour camps. The plan was accepted, and, in the space of a single night, more than 10,000 gypsies were arrested and put into forced labour. Soon, however, landowners were angrily demanding the return of their workers, as many of them had become integrated and carried out essential work. Fernando VI conceded that the round-up had been a blunder and, amid general consternation, the 'honest' gypsies were finally released.

The gypsy problem was still not resolved and it was suggested that they should be sent to the Americas where they would interbreed with the natives and gradually disappear. A multitude of suggestions and plans was put forward but none proved practicable or effective.

On 19 September 1783, Spain passed a decree marking a radical change in its gypsy policy. The travellers were to send their children to school where they could be turned into good citizens and curbed of their hereditary wanderlust. And so Spain finally began to absorb the gypsies into their culture.

Despite the gypsies' rough ride through the highs and lows of Spanish history, for good or for bad, they finally found themselves established. But even today, they are still the object of the Guardia Civil's scrutiny. However, the current gypsy status varies according to the different provinces. Since the 18th century, more than 88 per cent have settled and become integrated in Spanish society, and particularly successfully in Andalucía where the gypsy community numbers around 300,000. Many have jobs, some in important positions. Often, thanks to bullfighting and flamenco, they have the opportunity to express their inherent virtuosity and passionate spirit. Unfortunately, many of them live in shanty towns and cramped conditions in the suburbs where they are exposed to the problems of unemployment and drugs. Forced into labouring and menial activities, such as shoe-shining and illicit street-vending, the gypsies have had to sacrifice their true identities and take on what amounts to a caricature of themselves. If they steal it is because they have no other way of feeding themselves, and, if they lie, it is to protect themselves.

The question has arisen over which is worse, the gypsy or the *payo* (non-gypsy). Manuel Martín from the national association for gypsy affairs asks, 'What can a *payo* expect from a gypsy? Basically, not a lot. Why? Because the *payo* has done so little for the gypsy over the course of five centuries? The *payo* had the power of life and death over the gypsy, he tortured him, and he made him pay dearly for being a gypsy. The gypsy problem was created by the non-gypsies and so it is for them to resolve it.'

In the eyes of 'pure-blooded' Spaniards, the gypsy is by turn admired and despised; they are referred to as *gitano* a term that is at the same time a compliment and an insult.

PATIOS – INNER COURTYARDS

It was the Romans who came up with the idea of building living quarters around a central courtyard, called a *patio*. The Arabs were quick to see the advantage of this arrangement giving residents the opportunity to enjoy fresh air and a degree of protection from the elements away from the eyes of curious passers-by. *Patios* had the added advantage of protecting people from heat and sunlight almost all day, except at midday when the sun is directly overhead. Spanish families have traditionally used the *patio* as a place to gather together and chat – catching up on news, shelling peas or simply enjoying a drink and a cigarette as the sun goes down. A riot of green plants often completely obscures the walls, while a charming central fountain provides the sound of cool trickling water in the background.

The *patios* in Córdoba are undoubtedly the most beautiful in Andalucía. They captivate their visitors with uneven cobbles, stunning decorative tiles that adorn the lower walls and at their entrances elegant wrought iron gates (*see* 'Festivals' under 'General Information').

TAPAS

A BRIEF HISTORY

There is some dispute about the origin of tapas. According to some they are of royal origin – allegedly a king ordered that drinking establishments were to serve a snack with every glass of wine in the interests of saving people from alcoholism. Others argue that their origins are the result of small plates being used to stop flies falling in the drinks. As the empty plates looked a little strange, olives were added to brighten them up. Whatever the reason, the origin of the word tapas lies in the verb *tapar*, meaning 'to cover up'.

In Andalucía, all popular bars offer tapas but do not always advertise them. If you want tapas but there are none on show ask, *¿De tapeo, que hay?* (What sort of tapas have you got?) and hope you understand the answer. In days gone by, the price of the tapas was included in the price of the drink. Nowadays, however, they are priced separately, with the exception of olives and pistachios both of which are sometimes served free with drinks.

IR DE TAPEO

Ir de tapeo (literally, 'going for tapas') is the Spanish equivalent of a pub crawl, only it's much more civilized. It involves going from bar to bar enjoying different tapas in each. Each bar, *mesón* (a traditional inn), *taberna taurina* (bullfighting bar) or *peña flamenca* (flamenco bar) will have its own speciality. In one it might be *morcilla* (a type of black pudding), in another *tortilla* (omelette), while almost all offer their own particular brand of *pescadito frito* (fried fish). You eat standing up and if there is sawdust on the floor, you should feel free to join the locals in dropping used napkins and prawn heads and tails onto the floor when you've finished. The tapas are often on display in a glass cabinet on the bar so you can point at what you want, otherwise there is sometimes a tapas menu. Order two or three dishes between a few of you to start with and then move on to the next place.

FAMOUS PEOPLE

CINEMA

Victoria Abril (born 1959): With her kooky features and deceivingly disingenuous appearance, she is a veteran of more than 80 Spanish, English and French films. As one of Almodóvar's muses she appeared in *Tie Me Up! Tie Me Down!*, *High Heels* and *Kika*. Her latest venture is an Icelandic comedy, *Reykjavik 101*, in which she plays a flamenco dancer.

Pedro Almodóvar (born 1951): one of the major forces in the *movida*, the irreverent cultural movement that emerged after the lifting of the repressive blanket cast over cinematography during the Franco regime. After a few short films, it was *Pepi, Luci, Bom and Other Girls on the Heap* (1980) that brought Almodóvar widespread public attention. He claims to be strongly influenced by Spanish cinema of the 1950s and film-makers such as Fernando Fernan Gomez. *Women on the Verge of a Nervous Breakdown* (1987) moved his work closer to mainstream cinema and he became a satirist of post-Francoist Spain, particularly the yuppie years of the government of Felipe González. Almodóvar's prolific and ultra-creative work in the 1980s and 1990s made him the undisputed master of Spanish film. In 1999, he received the award for best director at the Cannes Film Festival, as well as a BAFTA, Academy Award and Golden Globe for best foreign film for *All About My Mother* (*Todo Sobre Mi Madre*). The film was dedicated to all mothers but particularly his own who had died a few months before the film was released.

Antonio Banderas (born 1960): this internationally renowned sex symbol comes from Málaga, where he also went to drama school. He was one of Almodóvar's favourite actors and appeared in *Labyrinth of Passion*, *Matador* and *Women on the Verge of a Nervous Breakdown* amongst others. After his widely publicized marriage to Melanie Griffiths, he went on to forge a lucrative career for himself in the States. He has starred in a number of Hollywood blockbusters including *Philadelphia*, *Evita* and *Zorro* co-starring with Hollywood icons like Tom Hanks and Madonna.

Luis Buñuel (1900–83): a giant of Spanish cinema, Buñuel was in fact a naturalized Mexican. In 1925, he fled the Primo de Rivera dictatorship for France where he studied at the Academie du Cinéma in Paris. In 1928, he collaborated with Salvador Dalí on the making of his first film *Un Chien Andalou*, a surrealist manifesto that caused a massive scandal at the time. His left-wing sympathies forced him out of Spain and in 1946 he settled in Mexico. After a period of exile in the United States, he went back to Mexico and found himself at the forefront of film-making with such beautiful films as *The Young and the Damned* (*Los Olvidados*) where his surrealist precepts and moral stance are still very much in evidence. He finally returned to Europe, where he made some of his greatest films – *Belle de Jour* (1966) and *Tristana* (1970) with Catherine Deneuve. Two of his films, *The Discreet*

Charm of the Bourgeoisie (1972) and *That Obscure Object of Desire* (1977) with Carole Bouquet, both won him Oscars for Best Foreign Film.

Others include the actor/singer **Miguel Bose** – the son of bullfighter Dominguin and Italian actress Lucia Bose; the sublime **Penelope Cruz** who first received international acclaim for her role in *Jamón Jamón*, directed by José Juan Bigas Luna and, after appearing in a number of films by Almodóvar, finally conquered Hollywood with her role in *Captain Corelli's Mandolin*; **Rossi de Palma**, another of Almodóvar's favourites whose unusual physique has also inspired Jean-Paul Gaultier; **Marisa Paredes** and **Cecilia Roth,** the unforgettable heroines of *All About My Mother*; and, also, the film director **Carlos Saura**.

LITERATURE

Miguel de Cervantes Saavedra (1547–1616): Cervantes was born in Alcala de Henares (a suburb of Madrid) into a family of *conversos* (converted Jews). Although descended from an illustrious family, his father was a poor medical practitioner who was also completely deaf. As a child Miguel was effeminate and suffered from a dreadful stutter but was already proving himself to be a brilliant poet. At the age of 20, he moved to Rome to find employment as a servant to a cardinal. He then joined the papal army in the war against the Turks, losing the use of his left hand from a gun-shot wound in the battle of Lepanto in 1571. After being involved in a string of other battles, he was captured by the Turks and spent five years in prison in Algeria. His private life was a succession of scandals – he married for money, had a daughter who was allegedly not his and lived with his sisters who earned money by selling their favours. Frequently falling into debt, he was imprisoned on several occasions (like his father before him) and only found renown towards the end of his life with the publication of *Don Quixote*. Although this is his best-known work, he also wrote around 20 plays although only two are still performed today. Despite a life of penury and hardship, the father of the modern novel is today considered one of the greatest writers of all time.

Federico García Lorca: the life of the author of *Romancero Gitano* is detailed in the introduction to the city of Granada.

Eduardo Mendoza (born 1943): his novels are almost exclusively set in Barcelona and are a fine mix of humour and irony and intrigue, flavoured with elements of the Picaresque and Gothic. *The Truth About the Savolta Case*, focuses on the bourgeoisie and anarchists of the expanding regional capital in 1917. *City of Marvels* underlines the colossal fortunes of this Catalan city, while *The Year of the* Flood sees him railing against the Catalonia of the Franco years. As a lawyer in international law, Mendoza has also walked the corridors of power, accompanying Felipe González to the United States on the occasion of his meeting with Ronald Reagan.

Jorge Semprun (born 1923): born in Madrid, Semprum suffered the consequences of totalitarianism at a very early age. His family was exiled from Spain by Franco when he was only 14 years old. They started a new life in France where Semprun studied philosophy at the Sorbonne. Four years later, he joined the resistance movement and became a member of the

Spanish Communist Party before being arrested by the Gestapo and deported to Buchenwald in 1943. From then on, he worked tirelessly in politics while maintaining a parallel literary career. Having originally worked as a translator for UNESCO, he then achieved acclaim as a writer, winning various literary prizes including the Fémina in 1969 for his novel *La deuxième mort de Ramon Mercader*. Semprun also wrote screen plays. From 1988 to 1991, he was Minister of Culture in the Spanish government. Today he lives in Paris where he concentrates principally on his career as a writer.

MUSIC

Montserrat Caballé (born 1933): it was in a 1956 production of Puccini's opera *La Bohème* that Montserrat Caballé first came to the attention of opera lovers. Although her career got off to a slow start, her amazing vocal technique, the versatility of her range and her imposing presence opened up a wide variety of roles, from the romantic heroines to dramatic avengers of wrong-doings. She played Puccini's *Tosca*, Verdi's *Aida* and Richard Strauss's *Salomé* at the Vienna Opera in 1959. Her worldwide renown was jump-started in 1965, when she replaced Marylin Horne in *Lucrezia Borgia* at the Carnegie Hall, New York and in 1992 she achieved popular acclaim for her duet on the song *Barcelona* with Freddie Mercury.

Camarón de la Isla (1950–91): a massively popular flamenco singer who was so well-loved and admired in Spain that grandmothers would take their children to be touched by him in the belief that it would bring them luck. His collaboration with Paco de Lucía proved an important stepping stone in his career. He died tragically at the age of 41, leaving numerous Spaniards bereft.

Lola Flores (1923–95): a native of Jerez de la Frontera, Lola was the darling of popular flamenco music. When she died in 1995, she left her daughter, Lolita, to carry on the family tradition albeit in a much more commercial style.

Paco Ibáñez (born 1934): a Valencian singer who in 1967 was banned by the Franco regime. Taking refuge in France his songs cast a lucid eye over his native country and are a good point of reference for understanding the evolution of Spanish society over the years.

Julio Iglesias (born 1943): an undoubted favourite of women of a certain age throughout the Western world. In his campaign for world domination Julio has sung in seven different languages (including Japanese). It is obviously a winning formula as he holds the record for the highest number of albums sold worldwide. Aside from legendary hits like *To All the Girls I've Loved Before* and *Begin the Beguine*, the Latin lover has also performed duets with Diana Ross, the Beach Boys and the Pointer Sisters. His son, Enrique Iglesias is now following in the footsteps of his famous father.

Paco de Lucía (born 1947): along with Camarón de la Isla, he is generally recognized for bringing flamenco to a worldwide audience. This internationally renowned guitarist, a native of Cádiz, has played with numerous other luminaries from a wide range of musical disciplines (such as Al Di Meola and John McLaughlin), and has raised the flamenco guitar from the role of accompaniment to solo instrument.

ART

There are so many renowned Spanish artists that it is impossible to list them all here. Some of the most famous include the painters **El Greco**, **Velázquez**, **Goya**, **Zurbarán**, **Miró**, **Picasso**, **Dalí** and **Tapies**, and the architect **Gaudí**.

BULLFIGHTING

El Cordobés (real name Manuel Benítez Perez; born 1936): the major 20th century figure of the bullfighting world. Born in the province of Córdoba, El Cordobés started fighting in the private rings of the *fincas*, trying out young bulls. His lightning-quick movements soon brought him to the public's attention, and his original and audacious style had legions of classic bullfighting *aficionados* on the edge of their seats. His passes, such as the *salto de la rana* (the leap of the frog), nowadays form part of the standard repertoire of all young *toreros*. Since his retirement, another El Cordobés has been thrilling crowds in bullrings across Spain – his alleged son, Manuel Diaz, who, even if he is not of the same blood, has inherited his sense of spectacle and his great boldness.

El Juli (real name Julian Lopez; born 1981): Julian Lopez started attending the bullfighting school in Madrid at the age of 11 and was spotted 5 years later performing as a *novillero* (a novice bullfighter who fights bullocks) in Mexico. After a triumphant return to his native country, he performed in the arena at Nîmes in 1998 and confirmed his reputation in May 2000 at the San Isidro Feria, which is considered by all *aficionados* as the major event of the bullfighting calendar. By all accounts El Juli has enjoyed a meteoric rise – and this virtuoso is still only in his early 20s.

POLITICS

General Franco (1892–1975: lead a military coup in 1936 and ruled Spain until his death in 1975 when he nominated King Juan Carlos his successor. He was responsible for putting two million people in concentration camps – more any other leader in Spanish history. One victim was the writer Federico García Lorca.

Felipe González Márquez (born 1942): after being a long-term member the PSOE (the Spanish Socialist Workers' Party), González took over as its secretary general in 1974 and led the party to a landslide victory eight years later. He was the leader of Spain's first left-wing government since the Spanish Civil War and remained in power for 14 years. Although some complained that the 'workers' referred to in the party's name were increasingly ignored, his two seven-year terms resolutely propelled the country towards the future. During his time in power, Spain experienced progressive democratization, entry into NATO and the EU, the signing of the Maastricht Treaty, the instigation of a new criminal code, educational reform, the implementation of new infrastructures, the building of hospitals and the initiation of other major building programmes. After a narrow victory in the 1993 elections, he and his party were beaten three years later by the *Partido*

Popular (Popular Party). Since he resigned in 1997, he has been linked with a variety of scandals (all vigorously denied), such as the Filesa affair (hidden financing of the Socialist Party), the case of Luis Roldan (the ex-director of the Guardia Civil sentenced to 27 years in prison for having diverted two thousand million pesetas to various Swiss bank accounts), and the 'dirty war' against Basque terrorists, for which several members of his government were convicted in the 1980s.

José María Aznar (born 1953): the head of the *Partido Popular*, he became prime minister when González resigned as leader of the Socialist Party in 1997.

SPORT

Miguel Induráin (born 1964): Miguel Induráin Larraya, also known as 'Indu', was born in the tiny Navarran town of Villava and won his first cycle race at the age of 11, after which he never looked back. For a long time he struggled to escape from Delgado's shadow, only really proving himself a force to be reckoned with in 1990 on the extremely difficult ascent of Luz Ardiden. Being part of the Tour de France team sponsored by Banesto Bank, he has notched up enough victories to ensure himself a place in cycling history alongside names such as Anquetil, Merckx and Hinault. His five consecutive victories in the Tour de France, two in the Paris–Nice, two in the Giro d'Italie, the one-hour record achieved in 1994 and a gold medal at the 1996 Atlanta Olympic Games are all proof that his reputation has been fairly earned.

Pedro Delgado (born 1960): born in Segovia, Perico Delgado, a renowned cyclist between 1985 and 1990 has recently slipped into the shadow of Indu's name. Nevertheless he remains one of Spain's greatest cyclists. His first victory was in the Vuelta de España in 1985. When he first took part in the Tour de France in 1983, he proved himself to be excellent in the mountains, although inconsistent in the sprint finishes and this cost him victory. In 1984, he was hoping for a chance to put the situation right, but a fall left him with a broken collarbone. It wasn't until 1987 that it looked as if he would finally win the Tour de France. But his luck deserted him again as the Irishman, Stephen Roche drew ahead and robbed him by 40 seconds of the victory that would have seen him crowned champion. It was not until 1988 that he finally succeeded in carrying away both the yellow jersey and the winner's trophy. He still participates in the Tour de France today, but is no longer among the front-runners.

Carlos Sainz (born 1962): born in Madrid, he proved himself a genuine all-round sportsman while still young – twice Spanish squash champion, he has also taken part in ski championships, racket and ball sports, and golf. He was introduced to racing-driving at the wheel of a Toyota in 1988, before going on to successfully compete in the Acropolis race in Greece, the Thousand Lakes in Finland and the RAC Rally in Britain.

Arantxa Sanchez Vicario (born 1971): often called 'the bulldog of women's tennis' by sports journalists her career was rather inconsistent until her brother Emilio (once seeded in the top ten male tennis players) took over as her trainer and succeeded in getting her back on top form. She won the French Open at Roland-Garros in 1998 and 1989, the US Open in 1994, and was a semi-finalist at Wimbledon in 1996. To commemorate her success at the French Open, she named her two dogs, Roland and Garros.

BOOKS

Romancero Gitano (1928), by Federico García Lorca. In the troubled times of the 1930s in Spain, the gypsy was for García Lorca one of the last vestiges of a golden age of innocence. In this book, the poet draws on popular literary forms such as the romance, investing them with his own vision of the world. In these poems he invokes Andalucía, its landscapes, animals and flora to describes the essence of the Andalucían soul.

For Whom The Bell Tolls (1940), by Ernest Hemingway. A lyrical view of the Spanish Civil War from one of America's greatest writers. The book centres round a couple called Jordan and Maria and the ideas of a group of politically committed intellectuals in the 1930s.

Although these next works are not specifically about Andalucía, they are good reference points if you want to understand a bit more about Spain in general.

Toreros de Salón (1963), by Camilo José Cela. The author's most distinctive trait, aside from a biting irony, is restraint and his refusal to make value judgements. In a series of portraits he describes saloon bullfighters and their bulls. Winner of the 1989 Nobel Prize for Literature, he sees the saloon bullfighter in every one of us.

Don Quixote de la Manche (1605), by Miguel de Cervantes. A Picaresque novel that roams all over Spain following Don Quixote on his knightly adventures. A parody of the chivalric novels fashionable at the time, this is a classic – essential reading for anyone with a love for Spain and literature.

Lazarillo de Tormes, edited by Aubier-Flammarion. Written by an unknown author, *Lazarillo de Tormes* is a jewel in the crown of Spanish literature. This short and highly amusing book is known to have been published around 1554. The story is simple enough – a boy is handed over to a blind man at a young age to act as his servant. From the blind and cunning beggar, he passes into the hands of a stingy priest, then a scrawny riding master and a fortune teller. In the course of his apprenticeship the protagonist becomes a servant to everyone despite his strong desire to be his own master. Finally, however, through cunning and cynicism he manages to scramble out from the bottom of the pile. An amusing portrait of society at the time, and a record of a sombre century. This apparent autobiography opened the way to a Picaresque tradition that Cervantes was soon to assume as his own.

BACKGROUND

Andalucía

SEVILLE (SEVILLA) 41000   DIALLING CODE: 954

For maps of Seville, see the colour plate section.

Seville, the fourth largest city in Spain, is considered by many to be the heart and soul of Andalucía. In 1492 Christopher Colombus set sail from the city on his famous voyage to the Americas, and 500 years later, in 1992, the event was commemorated with Expo 92. Over the course of its long history, Seville has assembled a truly remarkable architectural heritage, of which the Giralda and the Alcázar are outstanding examples. It's a place that has succeeded more than any other city in Spain in reconciling a sense of history with the demands of the modern, so although it remains quintessentially Spanish it has a very cosmopolitan atmosphere. The inhabitants of Seville are gregarious, outgoing, and easy to talk to. They're also nocturnal – the *movida* which erupted on the scene with Spain's transition to democracy in the mid-seventies is still very much alive here. To understand this, you need look no further than Santa Cruz – by day a sleepy *barrio* of narrow cobbled streets and verdant patios, and by night (and weekends especially) a teeming labyrinth of tapas bars and wine shops.

Historically, Seville is a city with a mixture of Islamic and Christian heritages, and the Guadalquivir river is lined with monuments to both cultures. They're well worth seeing, of course, but what really makes Seville special is its people – so no visitor should miss the chance to abandon the river and strike into the centre of the city to explore the streets of the old town, peep into the patios and have a chat with the locals, who are amazingly friendly. Seville is not only a treat for the eyes but a tonic for the heart. It is also home to two of opera's greatest figures, Carmen, the seductive gypsy, and Figaro, the roguish barber.

Caution

Every tourist town has its downside and Seville is no exception. Bag-snatchers are a problem, while cars with foreign number plates are especially vulnerable to break-ins. Take sensible precautions – never leave valuables in your car, no matter where it's parked – thefts take place even when there's an attendant on duty. A new strategy employed by many petty thieves is to follow your car by scooter then smash a window and snatch your wallet or handbag while you wait at a red light. It seems that no matter how carefully you guard against thieves, they'll always come up with a new ploy to steal your valuables, so be vigilant.

The Tourist Seasons

As an inland city, Seville lives to a slightly different tourist calendar from the rest of Andalucía. High season is around Easter (March/April) and during the Feria in April, when prices double and rooms are hard to find. Low season is during the stiflingly hot months of July and August. The rest of spring and the autumn is somewhere between the two. So when planning your visit, be aware that prices can vary considerably from one period to another.

A Brief History

In ancient times Seville was occupied by the Phoenicians, Greeks and Carthaginians before being absorbed into the Roman Empire. Then in the eighth century came the Moors who, during their long sojourn, transformed the city into one of the architectural marvels of Europe. With the Christian occupation came renewed prosperity as many local families grew rich on the fabulous treasures of the newly-discovered Americas. They flaunted their wealth by building spectacularly opulent houses in a fusion of Christian and Moorish styles with their slick *azulejo* panels, gardens and cool, shady patios. These houses are now a source of delight for modern tourists, proving that Seville's charm is like a good wine; it gets better with age.

After the glories of the Discoveries came a decline and an outbreak of the plague that killed a large proportion of the city's population. Another low point in Seville's history came in 1936 when the army attacked the working class districts of the town in order to take control of the city. But present-day Seville holds its head high, and with good reason. Flamenco has never had a wider audience, and Andalucían chic has real meaning. The 1992 Expo may have come and gone, but the attractions of Seville continue to draw visitors by the million every year.

ORIENTATION

Driving in Seville is no easy business, especially on weekdays. It makes little sense either, as the most interesting parts of the city can only be seen on foot. When you begin to get footsore, jump in a cab – they're not expensive, and there are plenty of them.

Santa Cruz (C1-2, colour map II and colour map of Santa Cruz): the historic centre of the city, stretching beyond the cathedral in a maze of narrow streets and flower-decked balconies, richly-decorated facades and quiet, leafy patios.

Calle Sierpes (B1, colour map II): a long pedestrian street lined with small shops and stalls, and pavement cafés. It's always lively. The neighbouring streets are worth taking a detour to see.

– The banks of the Guadalquivir: popular with the locals for a Sunday promenade, about 15 minutes' walk from the centre of the old city. Across the river is modern Seville.

– Triana (A2, colour map II): on the right bank of the river, across from the old city, Triana only really comes to life at night. Behind the chic riverside houses is a working-class *barrio* which until recently was the capital of Andalucía's large gypsy community. In the last three decades modernization and property speculation have reduced parts of Triana to soulless anonymity, but much of its charm survives, as do the brightly-coloured tiles that decorate its houses. It's the best place to go for nightclubs where people dance the *sevillana* (an old folk dance) and salsa.

USEFUL ADDRESSES

Tourist Information

🄗 Tourist Office (A2, colour map of Santa Cruz and B2, colour map II): avenida de la Constitución 21B. ☎ 422-14-04. Email: ot-sevilla@turismo-andaluz.com. Open all year, Monday–Saturday 9am–7pm, Sunday and public holidays 10am–2pm. Ask for the free map of the city. You can also pick up a map of Andalucía and hotel brochures for the region. The staff are friendly and some speak English. There is a free monthly guide called *El Giraldillo* available in all tourist information offices as well as in most hotels and popular sightseeing spots – it is a mine of information on shows, exhibitions, *corridas*, museums, flamenco and other events in Seville. *El Giraldillo* is in Spanish; other useful events guides published in bilingual format (English and Spanish) are *Welcome Olé* and *The Tourist*. They're also free, but not as comprehensive.

🄗 Tourist Office (Centro de Información de Sevilla; A1, colour map II): on the corner of paseo de Cristóbal Colón and Puente de Isabel II. ☎ 450-56-00. Open all year, weekdays 8.30am–8.30pm; 8.30am–2pm Saturday and Sunday. Mainly information on Seville, though some literature on the surrounding region is also available.

Services

✉ Post Office (B2, colour map II): avenida de la Constitución 32. Open 8.30am–8.30pm (2pm Saturday). Closed Sunday.

Work Center (Cybercafé) (A2, **11** on the colour map of Santa Cruz): puerta de Jerez. ☎ (9021) 16-00-11. Open 7 days a week, 24 hours a day. Copy shop that also has 10 computers connected to the Internet (and three photocopiers) for less than 1€ for 10 minutes or 5€ for 60 minutes. There are also several cybercafés in calle Betis in the Triana district offering similar prices.

Banks and Bureaux de Change

– There are plenty of **banks** along avenida de la Constitución (A2, **4** on the colour map of Santa Cruz), especially near the tourist information office. All of them change money and all of them have cash machines.

■ **American Express** (B1, **2** on colour map II,): plaza Nueva, beside the Inglaterra hotel. ☎ 421-16-17. Open Monday–Friday, 9am–8pm, Saturday 10am–1pm. Closed Sunday.

Bike Hire

■ **Sevilla Mágica** (A2, **10** on the colour map of Santa Cruz): calle Miguel de Mañara 11. ☎ 56-38-38. Open all year – in spring and summer Monday–Saturday 10am–9pm, Sunday 11am–3pm; in winter 10am–3pm, 5–8pm (closed Sunday). Mountain bikes and touring models in excellent condition hired by the half or whole day (around 12€) or for longer. Themed circuits (such as Seville by night, churches and convents, Andalucían architecture,

(vertical text in left margin) SEVILLE

bars) are available. After a tour of the city on foot, a bike is an excellent way to discover Seville's less central attractions. You can also buy tickets for flamenco shows here.

Health

■ **Emergencies**: ☎ 061.

– **Hospitals**: the public hospitals provide free first-aid treatment to EU nationals holding the appropriate social security document (E111).

■ **Casa de Socorro Esperanza Macarena**: Maria Auxiliadora. ☎ 42-01-05.

■ **Hospital Universitario Virgen del Rocio**: avenida Siurot. ☎ 45-81-81.

■ **Chemists**: open weekdays 9.30am–8.30pm (most close at lunchtime) and Saturday morning. A rotation system ensures that at least one chemist is open throughout the night in Seville – all display a list of duty chemists. One very central chemist is Farmacía Iberica (B1, **9** on colour map II), calle Tetuan 4. ☎ 22-59-48.

Police

■ **Police**: ☎ 091 (emergencies). Police station (B3, **7** on colour map I).

■ **Lost property** (A1, colour map II): calle Almansa 21. ☎ 21-50-64.

Other Useful Addresses

■ **English-language newspapers**: these are easily found in the city-centre kiosks, especially calle Sierpes (the long pedestrian thoroughfare, B1, colour map II), and around plaza Nueva.

■ **Laundry** (B1, colour map II): Auto-servicio de lavanderia, calle Castelar 2. ☎ 21-05-35. Open 9.30am–1.30pm and 5–8.30pm. Closed Saturday afternoon and all day Sunday. It also has instructions in English. A welcome sight for all backpackers.

■ **Iberia Agency**: (off map II from D1): avenida Buhaira 8. ☎ 98-82-08.

TRANSPORTATION

🚂 **Santa Justa railway station** (off map I from D2-3): avenida Kansas City, in the east of the city. ☎ (902) 24-02-02 (information and reservations). A new station with services to all major Spanish cities and a left-luggage office.

🚌 **Bus stations**: Seville has two. Several companies operate from each terminus, although only one company serves any single destination. *See* 'Leaving Seville'.

➕ **Airport**: ☎ 44-90-00.

Getting Around the City

■ **Municipal buses**: not particularly useful if you are staying in the old town as they mainly serve Seville's outlying suburbs. There are, however, some 'circular' route buses, which follow a circuit round the city. These are useful for getting around the town or going to la Cartuja, the site of the Expo. The bus following the inner circuit is the C3 or C4 (depending on whether it is going clockwise or anti-clockwise), for the outer circuit you need the C1 or C2 (again, depending on your direction of travel). A map of the bus routes is available from the information kiosk in plaza Nueva and plaza de la Encarnación. You can buy single tickets on the buses themselves (around 1€) or from the kiosks at the beginning of the lines. *Bonobus* passes, which are valid for 10 trips, are available from the bus kiosks (around 3.5€ for direct journeys; around 4€ if you want to change – although you must catch the connecting bus within an hour).

■ **Taxis**: ☎ 67-55-55; 58-00-00; 62-22-22.

■ **City-centre car-parks**: parking in Seville can be very tricky. The best thing to do is leave your things at the hotel and your vehicle in an attendant-guarded car-park. The tourist information office has a list of car-parks in the city. These include calle Marqués de Paradas (A3, **8** on colour map I); plaza de la Concordia and plaza de la Encarnación (C3, colour map I) – all are open 24 hours a day and close to the centre.

When you park in the street, an official parking attendant (recognizable by their caps) will usually come over to sell you your parking ticket – at least it saves you walking to the ticket machine.

Buses To and From the Airport

Amarillos Tour operates a regular link between the city and the airport. Buses run from 6.45am until 10.30pm, with departures every 30 minutes. The journey costs around 2€. The first stop is at Santa Justa station and the terminus is at puerta Jerez, in front of Hotel Alfonso XIII (C2, colour map II). For the trip out to the airport, puerta Jerez is also the most central pick-up point. Departures run from 6.15am to 9.30pm. There are fewer buses at weekends and on public holidays.

WHERE TO STAY

For maps of Seville, see the colour plate section.

It is usually quite easy to find accommodation if you start early in the morning. However, finding somewhere to stay during Easter week or the Feria in April without having made a reservation means you run the risk of disappointment. The cost varies with the season, especially with deluxe hotels, whose prices have a tendency to rise sky high during Easter and the Feria. To complicate things further, each hotel seems to have its own interpretation of high and low season, so even at the same time of year prices can vary dramatically

On the map the town appears to sprawl for miles, but in fact the areas of interest are conveniently situated next to one another so the distances involved are not too great. Still, you may find yourself walking more than you expected, as it's easy to lose your bearings in the maze of streets in the city centre. Always make sure you've got a map (available from the Tourist Office) and don't hesitate to ask for directions in case of doubt.

If you have a car, get as close to your hotel as possible, drop off your luggage and park elsewhere.

Youth Hostel

🛏 **Albergue Juvenil Sevilla**: calle Isaac Peral 2, 41012 Seville. ☎ (955) 05-65-00. Fax: (955) 05-65-08. Website: www.inturjoven.com. In a street off avenida de la Palmera. To get there, take the No. 34 bus from the plaza Nueva and get off at calle Sor Gregaria de Santa Teresa. From April to October, it costs about 12€ per night for under 26s or 16€ for over 26s (with a YHA card). For the rest of the year it's around 2€ cheaper. The youth hostel is out to the south of the town centre, which is a bit of a drag, and for two people it doesn't work out much cheaper than a small *hostal*. On the other hand it's a good option when everywhere else is full, however, as it sleeps 300 people, with two or three beds per room. Reservations can be made by phone or fax. Furnishings are clean and functional. The hostel is situated in a green and spacious part of Seville, but it is a far cry from the charm of the *hostales* in the centre of town. There is a cafeteria and a small garden. You can eat here for about 4€.

☆–☆☆ Budget to Moderate

The best bet for cheap accommodation in Seville is a *hostal*. Don't be put off by the name – the *hostal* is really just a family-run hotel-cum-boarding house. Broadly speaking, if you've seen one you've seen them all – balconies overflowing with flowers, balmy courtyards, homely atmosphere and typical Andalucían charm – although cleanliness varies from place to place. The listings

place special emphasis on charm and hospitality, though the latter can be sometimes be difficult to gauge – bear in mind that the young lad who opens the door during the siesta period may not have quite the same attitude as his parents, whose livelihood depends on visitors like you.

🛏 **Hostal Bailén** (A3, **22** on colour map I): Bailén 75, 41001 Seville. ☎ 22-16-35. In a street parallel to calle Gravina, tucked away in a peaceful corner next to the Museo de Bellas Artes. A room with a bathroom costs around 30€ and around 24€ for one without. The friendly landlady welcomes you into what seems to be her living room. The rooms are centred around a little enclosed patio and are very clean. Some of them contain very beautiful *azulejos* (colourful ornamental tiles). The atmosphere is of a friendly family-run B&B. In the summer, a two-roomed apartment is also available.

🛏 **Pensión Cruces El Patio** (B1, **21** on the colour map of Santa Cruz): plaza de las Cruces 10, 41004 Seville. ☎ 22-96-33. Ideal *pensión* for budget travellers as the rooms are cheap – 36€ for a room with a bathroom, and 24€ without. There are also several small dormitories with five to seven beds, at 12€ per person. All centred round a patio filled with plants and birdcages. You can put your washing out to dry on the sunny second floor terrace. On the downside, the owners are not particularly welcoming and the housekeeping is a bit slack.

🛏 **Pensión San Pancrasio** (B1, **23** on the colour map of Santa Cruz):

plaza de las Cruces 9, 41004 Seville. ☎ 41-31-04. This is a small *pensión* at the end of an alley leading to plaza de los Cruces. Rooms with bathrooms cost 27€, and ones without 21€. It is quiet and peaceful with a welcoming family atmosphere.

☗ **Hostal Gravina** (A3, **25** on colour map I): calle Gravina 46, 41001 Seville. ☎ 21-64-14. Fax: 21-96-45. The rooms cost about 24€ and do not have showers. There is a public car-park with an attendant nearby, offering reduced rates for guests. The only drawback is that the street is often noisy.

☗ **Hostal Romero** (A3, **20** on colour map I): calle Gravina, 21, 41001 Seville. ☎ 21-13-53. The rooms are like monks' cells, but not depressingly so. They cost about 24€ without a bathroom and 30€ with. Unassuming and well kept. Friendly welcome.

☗ **Pensión Archeros** (B1, **41** on the colour map of Santa Cruz): calle Archeros 23, 41004 Seville. ☎ 41-84-65. It's pot luck with regard to the room size, and rather over priced at 30–48€. Pretty open patio with rather fussy architecture. Could do with a lick of paint. Very Latin atmosphere.

☗ **Hostal Bienvenido** (B1, **26** on the colour map of Santa Cruz): calle Archeros 14, 41004 Seville. ☎ 41-36-55. In a quiet pedestrian street. Rooms without bathrooms with the minimum of mod cons from 24 to 33€. The hallway is decorated with artificial flowers and old flamenco posters. The welcome given occasionally belies the name of the hotel.

☆☆ Moderate

☗ **Hostal Paris** (A3, **46** on colour map I): calle Pedro Mártir 14, 41001 Seville. ☎ 22-98-61. Fax: 21-96-45. Website: www.sol.com/hostal-paris. There is an underground car-park, for which there is a fee. About 42€ for a double room. All rooms have bathroom, air-conditioning and TV. Not especially charming, but quiet, light and comfortable. The owners are very welcoming.

☗ **Hostal-Residencia Lis II** (B3, **24** on colour map I): Olavides 5, 41001 Seville. ☎ 56-02-28. Website: www.sol.com/hostal-lisII. In an alleyway linking San Eloy and O'Donnell. Charming old house with vine-draped balconies overlooking an enclosed patio. Simple double rooms that are generally clean, for 72€ with a bathroom. Set in a lively part of town, so fairly noisy. Avoid the ground floor rooms. Perhaps a touch on the expensive side.

☗ **Hotel Zaida** (A3, **47** on colour map I): calle San Roque 26, 41001 Seville. ☎ 21-11-38. Fax: 21-88-10. Website: www.andalunet.com/zaida. A lovely house in the Mudéjar style of the 18th century. Comfortable air-conditioned rooms with bathroom, TV and telephone, all at about 42€, although some have better views than others. Some rooms have rather attractive cast-iron bow-windows. The reception area is in the pretty patio with its profusion of marble and stucco columns.

☗ **Hostal Sevilla** (B3, **30** on colour map I): calle Daoiz 5, 41003 Seville. ☎ 90-21-60. A charming hotel decorated in a simple, elegant manner, set in a square bordered with orange trees. Comfortable air-conditioned rooms, painted in white and grey-green with bathrooms for 36€. Pretty patio and a pleasant foyer with a TV.

☗ **Hostal Marco de la Giralda** (A1, **35** on the colour map of Santa Cruz): calle Abades 30, 41004 Seville. ☎ 22-83-24. In a lovely quiet little street, near the cathedral. A pleasant, clean *hostal*, albeit rather nondescript, with a patio. Rooms with a shower from 36€.

≜ Pensión Fabiola (B1, **28** on the colour map of Santa Cruz): calle Fabiola 16, 41004 Seville. ☎ 21-83-46. Right in the heart of the Santa Cruz area (although in a quiet street), offering rooms without bathrooms for 36€ and rooms with for 42–60€, all set around a patio. The rooms are clean, though sparsely furnished, and some are decorated with *azulejos*. Some rooms sleep three or four people.

≜ Hostal Córdoba (B1, **34** on the colour map of Santa Cruz): calle Farnesio 12, 41004 Seville. ☎ 22-74-98. Rooms without bathrooms are around 36€. Rooms with a bathroom are nicer, but are about 42€. Situated in a delightful little street in Santa Cruz opposite No. 10 calle Fabiola, with a picturesque view of the church tower of Santa Cruz.

≜ Hostal Monreal (A1, **32** on the colour map of Santa Cruz): calle Rodrigo Caro 8, 41004 Seville. ☎ 21-41-66. Ideally situated in the heart of the Santa Cruz area. Rooms with bathrooms are about 48€, and rooms without about 36€. The facade is delightful, with its little columns, statuettes and friezes. On a lively crossroads near the cathedral, which is busy well into the small hours. The rooms overlooking the street are not recommended if you like early nights. Ask to see several rooms as there is quite a variety – some have wonderful ceilings, others have bow-windows, and a few have balconies. In summer the rooms by the patio are stiflingly hot. The place isn't particularly clean and the welcome is a bit unpredictable – a pity as this could be a lovely place.

≜ Hostal Goya (B1, **33** on the colour map of Santa Cruz): calle Mateos Gago 31, 41004 Seville. ☎ 21-11-70. Fax: 56-29-88. Rooms with bathrooms from about 51€ and with shower only for about 45€. A strange combination of slightly Asian-influenced decor. The rooms

overlooking the road can be noisy. Nice and clean, but you don't always get a friendly welcome.

☆☆☆ Expensive

≜ Hotel La Rabida (B1, **37** on colour map II): calle Castelar 24, 41001 Seville. ☎ 22-09-60. Fax: 22-43-75. Email: hotel-rabida@sol.com. Double rooms cost 63€ from March to October and 56€ for the rest of the year. North of the bullring and a 5-minute walk from the cathedral. The large patio is all marble – rose-coloured marble on the walls, white marble for the floor and green marble columns. The rooms aren't particularly attractive, but they are quiet and comfortable and have a telephone, TV and bathroom. Good air-conditioning. Ask for a room in the old part of the hotel. Reasonably priced given the location and facilities.

≜ Hotel Simon (B2, **36** on colour map II): calle García de Vinuesa 19, 41001 Seville. ☎ 22-66-60. Fax: 56-22-41. Website: www.sol.com/hotel-simon. This old-fashioned but charming hotel is a mere 3-minute walk from the cathedral. Rooms cost from about 84€. Majestic patio with marble columns and a fountain. There are 17th- and 18th-century paintings in the corridors and some of the rooms are decorated with *azulejos*. Ask for a room on one of the upper floors. A good breakfast is served in the pleasant dining room. The street is fairly noisy at night.

≜ Patio de la Cartuja (B1, **43** on colour map I): calle Lumbreras 8–10, 41002 Seville. ☎ 90-02-00. Fax: 90-20-56. Paying car-park. A beautiful 18th-century building built around a spacious triangular patio and tastefully restored. This outlying hotel offers small, pleasantly decorated apartments from about 72€ with bathroom, small kitchen and living room (with a folding bed). Attractive prices for family groups, as it costs about 84€ for four people. The classic double rooms are slightly on the small side. You are best off asking for a room on one of the upper floors.

â **Hotel Maestranza** (B1, **45** on colour map II): calle Gamazo 12, 41001 Seville. ☎ 56-10-70 and 22-67-66. Fax: 21-44-04. Website: www.andalunet.com/maestranza. As comfortable a hotel as you'll find anywhere, and all the more attractive for its central location – it's located about 100 metres from the cathedral and the Santa Cruz district. The rooms are exactly as you would expect from this type of hotel, and cost about 63€ from May to the beginning of October, and about 57€ for the rest of the year (more for the week of the Feria).

☆☆☆☆ Splash Out

In this category of accommodation, prices vary significantly depending on season, religious festivals such as Easter and local events like the Feria. It is advisable to find out quite how much you'll be charged first, in order to avoid any nasty surprises.

â **Hotel Los Seises** (C1, **44** on colour map II): calle Segovias 6, 41004 Seville. ☎ 22-94-95. Fax: 22-43-34. In the heart of the Santa Cruz area, a stone's throw from the Giralda. A rather exceptional place as architects used the structure of an 18th-century building to make a modern, high-class hotel. Enjoy these luxurious surroundings, complete with a lovely little swimming pool and a bar, for just over 174€

in high season and 120€ in low season. All mod cons and friendly, professional staff. From the rooftop the hotel boasts an excellent view of the Giralda and the surrounding brown and ochre roofs.

â **Hostal Doña Maria** (A1, **38** on the colour map of Santa Cruz): Don Remondo 19, 4104 Seville. ☎ 22-49-90. Fax: 21-95-46. Website: www.hdmaria.com. In a quiet little street right by the cathedral. If you are lucky you may get one of the four bays in the hotel car-park, if not, parking is a bit of a pain. A cosy, stylish little hotel where each room has an individual touch – some of them have splendid Spanish baroque-style furniture. In high season a double costs about 162€ and 90€ or thereabouts for the rest of the year. There is a terrace on the roof with a small swimming pool (open from June to September) and a classic view of the Giralda. It's a shame that the welcome is not as friendly as you might expect from this sort of establishment.

â **Hotel Alfonso XIII** (B3, **39** on colour map II): San Fernando 2, 41001 Seville. ☎ 22-28-50. Fax: 21-60-33. This top luxury hotel does not come cheap at around 385€ per room, and 438€ over Easter and the Feria. It was built for the World Exposition of 1929 and is considered the most beautiful hotel in Andalucía. However the quality of service doesn't justify the high prices charged. If you can't afford to stay here, at least pop in to enjoy a drink in the wonderful setting of its enormous galleries.

WHERE TO STAY IN THE SURROUNDING AREA

Campsites

The campsites of Seville are nothing special, to say the least. They are listed here in order of preference, not by their proximity to the town centre. They can all be reached by bus, but it's not straightforward.

⛺ Villsom: located 12 kilometres (about 8 miles) south of town, in Dos Hermanas (postcode 41700), off the Cádiz road (N IV). ☎ and fax: 472-08-28. By car take the Dos Hermanas–Isla Menor exit, then turn right under the bridge. By bus – take one of the green and yellow buses operated by the Los Amarillos bus company from calle Palos de la Frontera (near the park surrounding the Plaza de España), with the destination 'Dos Hermanas'. If you tell the driver that you're going to the Villsom Campsite, he'll drop you off right outside. The campsite is open all year round. It costs about 3–4€ per person, including one car and a tent. In season, get there early as it fills up fast. It is quite noisy because the *autopista* (motorway) is nearby but it's still quieter than most of the others in the area. The site is pleasantly shady but the ground of beaten red earth is fairly hard, like a clay tennis court. The campsite is well maintained and has on-site security. The free swimming pool is nice enough and has a life-guard. There is a small shop, but it's quite pricey, so you might prefer to go to the supermarket that is a 5-minute walk away on the other side of the motorway. Other facilities include mini-golf, a bar and washing machines. On the whole, fairly clean. Payment in cash only. The staff are not especially friendly.

⛺ Camping-Motel Club de Campo: avenida de la Libertad 13, 41700 Dos Hermanas. ☎ 72-02-50. Located 8 kilometres (5 miles) to the south of Seville. Open all year round. By car, take the Cádiz road and exit at the sign for Dos Hermanas (SE 420). Continue on the road for about 5 kilometres (3 miles) towards Dos Hermanas – you'll see signs for the campsite just as you get into town. Prices are fairly low – just over 3€ per person, including a car and a tent. The campsite also has some double rooms for 48€ and there is a large swimming pool, a bar and a restaurant. There isn't a lot of shade on the campsite and the proximity of the railway line means it's not very quiet either, but the site itself is fairly pleasant and there's a bus service to Seville that leaves in the morning and returns at night, which is very handy.

⛺ Seville: Located 5 kilometres (3 miles) northeast of Seville, on the road to Córdoba. ☎ and fax: 51-43-79. This is the closest campsite to Seville. From the town centre, take bus No. 70 from near the plaza de España and then walk the remaining kilometre to the campsite. Otherwise, an easier option might be to take the shuttle bus from avenida Portugal next to the Citrone bar (close to the plaza de España) – it takes you straight to the campsite for less than 3€. The service runs throughout the day. By car, take the Brenes exit from the motorway. A pitch costs 3€ per person and per car, and 2–3€ for a tent. The campsite is squeezed between the motorway and the end of the airport runway. Although planes don't land or take off during the night it can be noisy during the day, and the planes create quite strong gusts of wind. All in all it would be hard to find a worse spot. Swimming pool (admission fee). Free showers. The site is fairly well maintained but rather depressing. Bungalows are also available for hire.

WHERE TO EAT

For maps of Seville, see the colour plate section.

Seville's cuisine is imaginative and varied. There are many restaurants in town, although you could just as easily take the cheaper option of doing the rounds of the delightful tapas bars. Many of the restaurants also have a bar where you can snack on tapas and a glass of wine, although you won't be able to do this in the more upmarket establishments.

☆ Budget

There aren't many cheap restaurants as the numerous tapas bars offer such an attractive alternative. As a general rule, avoid all-inclusive or set menus as they tend to be very average and rarely feature any of the regional specialities.

Throughout the Santa Cruz area there are sunny little squares filled with the tables and chairs of nearby restaurants. Enjoy the setting because although most of the restaurants have attractively-priced set menus, the food is, on the whole, rather disappointing.

✕ Mesón Los Gallegos (B3, **51** on colour map I): Capataz Rafael Franco 1. ☎ 21-40-11. In a street parallel to the plaza la Campana. Open every day lunchtime and evening. Offers a decent tourist menu for less than 10€. The tapas are between 1 and 2€. Friendly, fun atmosphere (the waiters shout the orders at the top of their voices), traditional dishes and ample portions. Large bowls of excellent *gazpacho*, a good prawn *tortilla* and a tasty *pulpo a la gallega* (Galician-style octopus).

✕ Bodega Paco Gongora (B1, **53** on colour map II): calle Padre Marchena 1. ☎ 21-41-39. Closed on Sunday in July and August. A satisfying meal costs around 12€. This quiet little *bodega* has three bulls' heads on the walls, which keep a close eye on customers. It also has the ubiquitous hams hanging overhead and a long wooden bar snaking down one side of the room. You can get a *ración* (serving) or *media ración* (half serving) of tapas for a reasonable price at the bar. Don't give in to the waiting staff who have a tendency to hurry you along, especially if you're not having a big meal, and take your time.

✕ Restaurante Las Escobas (A1, **52** on the colour map of Santa Cruz): calle Alvarez Quintero 62. ☎ 56-04-16. Open every day from noon to midnight. Expect to pay 9–12€ for the different set menus and 6–12€ for an à la carte dish. Decent food with some original dishes like cod in orange sauce. Eat at one of the tables outside or inside under an attractive coffered ceiling. The clientele are almost all tourists, but it's not bad for a restaurant situated only a stone's throw from the most visited monument in Seville.

☆☆ Moderate

✕ Enrique Becerra (B1, **54** on colour map II): calle Gamazo 2. ☎ 21-30-49. Open 1–5pm and 8pm–midnight. Closed on Sunday. Fairly close to the cathedral. The decor tries to evoke a cosy atmosphere, which doesn't quite work, but you can get good tapas for about 2€ a dish. *Medias raciónes*, like paella, *bacalao* (salted cod), *calamares con papas* (squid and potatoes), range from about 6€ but they won't be enough to fill you up. For a more traditional sit-down meal you should go to the restaurant area, often mentioned in the novels of the famous Spanish author Arturo Pérez-Reverte. Typical Spanish cuisine, but quite expensive.

✕ Restaurante Las Cuevas: (*See* 'Where to Eat Tapas and Have a Drink'.) In the Triana area.

✗ **La Primera del Puente** (B3, **85** on colour map II): calle Betis 66. ☎ 427-69-18. Right by the river. There's no set menu here, and simple dishes from the à la carte menu cost around 15€. A cool refuge that is especially pleasant in summer when the town centre is really stifling. Pretty, well-shaded terrace in tiers, with a view over the Guadalquivir and the Torre del Oro. Rather touristy.

✗ **Casa Robles** (B1, **56** on colour map II): calle Alvarez Quintero 58. ☎ 21-31-50 or 56-32-72. Meals for around 27€ in the restaurant and from 15€ in the bar. This place comprises a long room with a counter covered with tempting-looking tapas. The *alcaparras* (a cross between a caper and a miniature fig) that are served instead of olives as an aperitif are delicious, and you can also get mushrooms and unusual seafood tapas. Sit at the tables outside, or inside at the bar. The restaurant (on the first floor) specializes in fish and meat dishes.

✗ **Restaurante A. Donaire El Tenorio** (A1, **55** on the colour map of Santa Cruz): Mateos Gago 11.

☎ 21-40-30. Open every day except Sunday. There is a good lunchtime set menu for about 12€, served Monday to Friday. In the evening, the food reverts to classic Andalucían cuisine – perfect, beautifully prepared meals, all à la carte. There's no tapas bar here, it's a proper restaurant with all the trimmings, including cloth napkins and tablecloths, a cosy atmosphere, beautiful decor (engravings, paintings, drawings and photos of bullfighters) and to top it all they serve a mean *gazpacho*.

☆☆☆ Expensive

✗ **La Albahaca** (B1, **59** on the colour map of Santa Cruz): plaza de Santa Cruz 12. ☎ 22-07-14. Set menu from about 27€ at lunchtime, but you are probably better off opting for one of the exquisite à la carte dishes. Set in a charming little square, this is a really authentic, high-class restaurant. The cuisine is inspired by the finest traditional Andalucían and Basque cooking – the sea bream, *merluza* (hake) and pheasant are particularly recommended.

WHERE TO FIND THE BEST CAKES AND ICE-CREAM

For maps of Seville, see the colour plate section.

✗ **Confitería La Campana** (B3, **57** on colour map I): calle Sierpes 1. Open every day 10am–8pm. At the end of this pedestrian street (alongside several nice but pricey clothes shops) on the corner of plaza Campana. It has been here since 1885 and is much photographed due to its superb window display. There's a delightful tiled frieze of cherubs behind the counter. They do very good cakes. Over Easter, try the *torrijas* – deep-fried, crustless bread soaked in honey. A old pair of scales awaits you at the exit.

✗ **Confitería-bar Cáceres** (B1, **62** on the colour map of Santa

Cruz): calle San Jose, 24. *Desayuno* (breakfast) for less than 4. This place is handy if you're staying in one of the *pensiones* in Santa Cruz. Situated a short stroll from the little square of Santa Maria la Blanca, this is a good place to come for breakfast. Unlike the shop, the selection of food is enormous – cakes, Viennese pastries, cheese, jams, tapas and sandwiches are all on offer. The difficulty is choosing what type of breakfast to have, sweet or savoury (the *desayuno de la casa* allows you to have both). Customers tend to be young, mainly British tourists, however there are also some locals, dressed for work or in casual clothes. Prices are reasonable, but the staff are not overly friendly.

✖ **Convento de Santa Inés** (C3, **58** on colour map I): calle Maria Coronel 5. Open 9am–1pm and 4–7pm. Closed on Sunday and on religious holidays. Situated at the end of the courtyard under the arches. You have to ring the bell to get someone to serve you. The nuns pass you their little packages of cakes on a revolving tray and you hand over payment in the same way. It is designed so that the nuns have no eye contact with the customer, yet this does not prevent them from giving a friendly welcome. The sisters certainly know how to make a good cake – their *tortas de chocolate* are particularly delicious.

🍦 **Rayas** (C3, **61** on colour map I): Almirante Apocada 1. Open from noon to 1am. Closed in January. Delightful ice-cream parlour, with about 50 flavours on offer, some of which are divine. Amongst others, you should try the lemon sorbet with pieces of Genoese sponge, the *crema Sevillana* and the unforgettable *mascarpone* ice-cream.

WHERE TO EAT TAPAS AND HAVE A DRINK

For maps of Seville, see the colour plate section.

As you'll have realized by now, going out for tapas is a time-honoured Spanish custom. Most tapas bars have a whole display of delicious looking dishes to choose from, with a wide choice of house and daily specials. If you don't know the name of something, just point it out to the waiter. *Chorizo* (a kind of spicy salami) is always worth trying – it's nothing like the stuff you get in the supermarkets at home. Other recommendations include squid, *tortilla* (potato omelette), *bacalao* (salted codfish), anchovies, octopus salad, and *revueltos* (a kind of scrambled egg). Whatever you have, it's sure to be delicious.

Normally three or four tapas make up a meal and prices are usually displayed behind the bar, so you can keep an eye on what you are spending as you go along. Where prices aren't listed, make sure you don't get ripped off. The bill is often written in chalk on the bar. Prices are more or less the same everywhere, starting at the best part of 1€ for anchovies, *tortillas*, and *espinacas* (spinach), to about 8€ for a platter of cheese and ham. The best idea is to follow the good old tradition of bar-hopping, so you can try out the tapas at several places along the way. You're guaranteed a friendly, lively atmosphere, except during siesta time when all the bars are closed (between 3 and 7pm).

The Historic Centre

🍷 **Bodega Santa Cruz** (A1, **70** on the colour map of Santa Cruz): calle Rodrigo Caro 1. A stone's throw from Hostal Monreal, in the heart of the Santa Cruz area. Open every day until midnight. Better known by the name of Las Columnas, a reference to the pillars at the front. At weekends the delirious excitement of the crowd makes the journey to the bar a bit of an ordeal. For those brave enough to try, have some of the *tortillitas de bacalao* (salted cod omelette) or the *roquefort pringa*, a small toasted sandwich with roquefort, made as you wait. Then, like everyone else, try and make your way back out again, balancing your glass and sandwich, and eat it leaning against the parked cars in the street.

℟ Patio San Eloy (B3, **71** on colour map I): calle San Eloy 9. ☎ 22-11-48. Open every day. Here too, the atmosphere hots up at the busy times. Of course a lot of alcohol is consumed, while eating different types of small sandwiches (salmon, Roquefort) or *empanadas* (a type of pie), sitting on the attractive tiled steps or standing beneath the hams hanging from the ceiling. The decor is quite stunning. It feels more like an old hammam than a bar. To the right of the entrance is a small wine bar, which is more intimate than the upper part of the bar, and attracts a younger crowd.

℟ La Bodega (B3, **72** on colour map I): Fernan Caballero 6. ☎ 21-19-20. Closed on Sunday and for a fortnight in August. In a small street off San Eloy. Open from noon to 2pm. A tiny bar, which is very popular, very typical and extremely unassuming – it is rarely frequented by tourists. In the evening the regulars take their places under the harsh neon lights. The owner is very kind and will take the time to describe each tapa to you if you speak a bit of Spanish. Good cold beer, delicious tapas and *montaditos* (small sandwiches) with prawns, anchovies, cheese or salmon. There's also a very nice spicy *chorizo*.

℟ Bodeguita Antonio Romero II (B1, **95** on colour map II): calle Gamazo 16. ☎ 21-05-85. The customers crowd around the long bar to savour the excellent tapas, which are unusually inventive. Particularly worth trying is the succulent *bacalao en aceite* (cod in oil), and the *piripi al cerdo* (pork). Friendly atmosphere but not yet frequented by too many tourists. Go and enjoy it soon, before it gets overrun.

℟ Hijos de Morales (B2, **78** on colour map II): calle García de Vinuesa 11, on the corner of calle Cristóbal de Castillejo. Not far from the cathedral, in the direction of the river. Closed on Sunday. This is the oldest *bodega* in town – it's been here for nearly 150 years, and hasn't been painted for the last 50 or so. Find a seat in the room in the old wine cellar where the tapas menu is written on huge jug-shaped wine vats and the decor includes old barrels and peeling walls. The *vino* is very good and the general atmosphere makes you want to stay all day. Very popular with locals at lunchtime.

℟ Café-bar Las Teresas (B1, **89** on the colour map of Santa Cruz): calle Santa Teresa 2. ☎ 21-30-69. This place has it all – beams of sunlight, a marble and wooden bar, walls covered with yellowed posters, an old clock that has long since stopped ticking, hams slowly dripping grease – the epitome of a Spanish bar. However it is a bit of a tourist trap and it's probably best just to have a drink, rather than trying the tapas, as they are nothing special and there are plenty of other bars to see.

℟ El Rinconcillo (C3, **79** on colour map I): calle Gerona 42, on the corner of Alhondiga. ☎ 22-31-83. Behind Santa Catalina church. Open all day. Closed on Wednesday. Superb bar, opened in 1670, with hams hanging from the wooden ceiling, yellowing walls and ornamental *azulejos*. Try the delicious *espinacas con garbanzos* (spinach with chick peas). The *pavias de bacalao* (cod fritters) are also excellent. Have a quick look at the room on the right, with its remarkable display cabinet and painted ceiling, a legacy of the former grocers that was next door. The bar is frequented by a mixed bunch of tourists and locals.

℟ Bodega Extramaña (C1, **96** on colour map II): on the corner of calle Alfalfa and calle Candilejo. ☎ 41-70-60. A lovely friendly little *bodega* serving specialities of Extremadura

– a huge variety of ham including the famous *serrano*, as well as several delicious cheeses. A very popular establishment where all the food is wonderful.

☛ Cervecería Giralda (A1, **80** on the colour map of Santa Cruz): calle Mateos Gago 1. ☎ 22-74-35. Located to the north of the cathedral. Not to be confused with the restaurant of the same name on the corner of the street that is not nearly so nice. This place used to be a Moorish bath-house, and has been converted into a superb, stylish café-bar, with a few tables and chairs outside. With its pleasantly trendy atmosphere this is an ideal meeting place. On the whole a little bit more expensive than the other bars listed.

☛ Bar Garlochi (C1, **83** on colour map II): calle Boteros 26. Open from 10pm every night. A modern bar, richly decorated with an esoteric assortment of objects. Female busts have been carved out of the wooden pillars, there are wicker chairs, statuettes and drapes hanging from the walls. Quite a mixture of the rococo and the religious, with loud music creating a backdrop for the friendly, trendy crowd. Try the *agua de Sevilla*, a gorgeous cocktail consisting of cognac, Cointreau, whisky, pineapple juice, champagne and crème chantilly.

☛ Antigüedades (A1, **75** on the colour map of Santa Cruz): Argote de Molina 40. Only open in the evening, from 8.30pm to 3 or 4 in the morning. In a lively part of town, where there are also lots of small restaurants. Quite a young crowd. Cheap sangría.

☛ Cervecería Internacional (B1, **94** on colour map II): calle Gamazo 3. ☎ 21-17-17. Open every day except Wednesday, 2–4pm and 8pm–2am. A jolly, noisy venue, particularly popular with the younger crowd. It's best to go in the evenings. This is basically a beer palace, with more than 200 brands on offer, from a wide range of countries. There are also good-value tapas to go with your beer. Signs and mirrors decorate the walls.

☛ Horno San Buenaventura (B2, **77** on colour map II): on the corner of avenida de la Constitución and calle Vinuesa. Opposite the cathedral. ☎ 22-18-19. Open every day 7.30–11pm. This place isn't merely a tapas bar, it's a tea-room, a grocers, a patisserie and a takeaway. Set in a huge, immaculate space, everything is tastefully designed – from the hanging hams and the sparkling bottles to the beautiful dishes of food, tantalizing cakes and appetizing sandwiches. They even serve *gazpacho* by the glass here. Unsurprisingly, it's a bit more expensive than other places (it's quite popular as a venue for business lunches), but it's handy if you come out of the cathedral feeling a bit peckish.

☛ El Caserón (B3, **73** on colour map I): calle Javier Lasso de la Vega 9. Brick and wood decor, in a not-so-central part of town, but lively nevertheless. The waiting staff are friendly and you can perch on a stool and try a variety of reasonably priced pork tapas, kebabs and sandwiches of various sizes.

Other Places

In the evening, especially at the weekend, the area around plaza El Salvador (B-C1, on colour map II) fills with huge crowds of young people drawn to the string of bars on its streets. Perhaps here, more than anywhere else in Spain, the inhabitants have become accustomed to going out until late at night from a very young age. In fact, Seville has enjoyed the reputation of having the most lively nightlife in Europe since the 16th century. The places listed below all offer an excellent atmosphere and a good chance to enjoy the Spanish nightlife alongside the locals.

❢ **La Antigua Bodeguita** and **La Alicantina** (B1, **86** and **87** on colour map II): these are both in plaza El Salvador, by the church of the same name. They are both closed on Sunday. This is one of the prettiest parts of Seville, especially in the evening. Note that *La Alicantina* is closed on Wednesday and Thursday evening during the Feria. These bars don't have much in the way of *azulejos* (ornamental tiles), though people don't come for the decor but to drink cheap beer with their friends. Groups gather on the steps of the church and there is a real feeling of kinship and exuberance. In the small square, old people feed the pigeons and children play while their mothers stroll and chat.

❢ **Calle Perez Caldos** (C1, **88** on colour map II): a street lined with lots of bars. You shouldn't leave Seville without having spent at least one evening out and about round here.

Calle Adriano: in the evening at the weekend, this street becomes a meeting place for hundreds of young people with plastic bags full of bottles of alcohol, fizzy drinks, glasses, ice cream, peanuts, and before you know it the party begins. Propped up against old cars, with blaring radios, the street comes spontaneously to life, under the watchful eye of the police who make sure things don't get out of hand.

The Triana District

This is a pleasant and popular part of town, on the other side of the river to the main centre and, as yet, not too touristy. Triana has been a favourite haunt of Seville's youth for some time now. Although there's not much going on during the day, apart from on calle Betis which runs alongside the river, the area really comes into its own after nightfall.

❢ **Hostería Las Cuevas** (A3, **60** on colour map II): calle Virgen de las Huertas 1; on the corner of calle Paraiso. ☎ 27-80-42. Whatever you have, you'll be hard-pushed to get a bill higher than 12€. A really authentic place, where many of the locals (and quite a few businessmen at lunchtime) come for a good meal that won't break the bank. You can eat tapas at the bar or more substantial speciality dishes in the dining room or at the tables and chairs outside. Options on offer include *cola de toro* (oxtail), delicious aubergine fritters and *bacalao a la plancha* (chargrilled cod). The quality and freshness of the food is excellent especially at such a low price. From this point of view it is probably one of the best restaurants in Seville.

❢ **Cervecería Casa Cuesta** (A2, **84** on colour map II): Castilla 3. ☎ 33-33-37. In a street running parallel to the riverbank. An old bar off the tourist track with *azulejos* on the walls and marble tables. It's not worth coming to this part of town just to go to this restaurant, but if you're in the area it is a pleasant place to stop. Don't bother trying the tapas as they are not particularly interesting.

❢ All along calle Betis – the road that runs along the Guadalquivir river – there are lots of modern, trendy bars. The atmosphere varies from place to place, so just go with the flow.

♈ Casa Anselma, Bar Joaquim Arenas (off colour map II from A2): on the corner of calle Antillano Campos and No. 49 calle Pagès del Corro. You can't miss it – it's the amazing building completely covered with old *azulejos* (ornamental tiles). It's only open in the evening, from midnight onwards. Closed on Sunday. Decorated with all kinds of paraphernalia related to bullfighting, including mirrors and portraits. Some evenings musicians will strike up on the guitar, and before long everyone is dancing.

WHERE TO HEAR A CONCERT

♈ La Carbonería (C1, **76** on colour map II): calle Levíes 18. ☎ 21-44-60. Open every evening 8pm–4am. A free entry bar (a beer costs about 2€), this former charcoal factory has been converted into a concert hall and a collection of bars. It has a large hall with whitewashed walls and an amazing carved chimney. You can come here for a drink and a concert (phone for further information or look in the free newspaper *El Giraldillo*). There are usually four concerts an evening. At the back, there is an immense patio full of plants where you can get some fresh air and chat without shouting. A favourite haunt of both Spanish and foreign students, as well as families from Seville, at different times of the day or year. As with everywhere else in this city, the later it gets, the more animated the atmosphere becomes.

WHERE TO DANCE

> *Near the ramparts of Seville, at the house of my friend Lillas Pastia, I will dance Seguidillas, and drink manzanilla.*

From Bizet's *Carmen*

Seville has changed considerably since the time of *Carmen*, but many of the dance traditions depicted in the opera have stayed the same. People still dance flamenco, but even more, they dance the *sevillana*, a popular folk imitation of flamenco. They dance *sevillana* in the nightclubs in the Salado district accompanied by small local bands, which on occasion can be excellent. Watching the dancers it soon becomes apparent that the *sevillana* – and even more so the flamenco – is not an improvised dance. Couples perform the dance with grace and technical dexterity proving that the *sevillana* requires innate talent to be danced well. It is well worth going to see the locals in action (and joining in if you dare), particularly on a Friday or Saturday night when things get lively.

– **El Salsaya**: on the riverside, between the two Seville 92 bridges. Free entry. Lots of room to dance. Trendy decor.

– **Disco Terraza Verve**: in paseo Torneo, between the Barqueta bridge and the El Alamillo bridge. There are two dance floors – one playing house and techno, and the other catering for an older crowd with reggae, disco and rock.

WHERE TO HEAR FLAMENCO

The Andalucían soul is said to have two key characteristics – a sense of tragedy and a natural pride or nobility. And no art form manifests this more directly than flamenco, which is always performed straight from the heart. The sound and sight of flamenco, tinged as it is with joy, suffering and tragedy, is indescribably moving. There are several types of flamenco, each showing differing degrees of gravity and depth – the best is *Cante Jondo*, a style which few visitors have the privilege of experiencing – the shows put on for tourists are pale imitations. Even so, for the uninitiated, the rhythm of the guitars, the clapping hands, the swirling skirts and the wailing voices make for a very exciting spectacle. The *tablaos flamencos* are based on stories from folklore; there are two places where this is particularly worth seeing as the productions are still fairly authentic and are not just performed for the benefit of tourists.

Los Gallos (B1, **92** on the colour map of Santa Cruz): plaza de Santa Cruz 11. ☎ 21-69-81. Open every day 9pm–1.30am. Tickets cost 21€, and include drinks. There are two shows a night, at 9pm and 11.30pm, each lasting two hours. The good thing about this *tablao* is its intimacy, comfort and small stage, which allows the audience to see the artists at close quarters – important in helping to understand the emotions being portrayed and feel the power of the singing and dancing. Performed by a talented and energetic group of musicians and dancers. Advisable to book in advance.

El Arenal: calle Rodo 7. ☎ 21-64-92. Tickets cost about 25€ and include drinks. Not quite as nice as *Los Gallos*, but it's a good show in a smart venue. The first show starts at 9pm, and the second at 11pm.

SEMANA SANTA

Throughout Semana Santa (Easter Week), which starts on Palm Sunday, Seville is invaded by tourists, both Spanish and foreign. The atmosphere of penitence and devotion is contrasted by a show-time spirit, giving the entire event a unique and highly-charged atmosphere. It isn't clear how many people go for religious reasons and how many to enjoy the huge, heavy *pasos* (a series of floats bearing figures representing the Easter story) and admire the bizarre costumes worn by revellers. For non-believers the *pasos* is a carnival parade, a big media spectacle, albeit with a spiritual slant. But for the believer it is a time for fierce devotion to Christ and repentance for the sins of the past.

In preparation for Semana Santa, each of the different areas of the city, as well as the outlying towns and villages, form a local committee or community group known as a *cofradía*. At the *paseo*, the members of each *cofradía* form a slow procession, starting from their headquarters and parading around the streets of Seville, often for several hours, usually taking in plaza San Francisco, which is temporarily transformed into a vast stage set, like an enormous religious theatre. In long robes and pointed hats, the members of the *cofradía* assume the roles of penitents, walking solemnly behind an enormous wooden cross, while the *paso* follows slowly behind. *Pasos* are large, richly decorated floats, often in the baroque style, carried by about ten men. They are incredibly heavy and the bearers often stop to rest before handing the burden to others in their group. Watching these cortèges is a genuinely moving experience. On the *paso* there is always a statue of Christ on the cross or a weeping Virgin Mary. As it passes by, flamenco singers chant *saetas* – heart-rendingly poignant incantations of sorrow. Eventually everyone makes their way to the plaza San Francisco, where the party continues.

If you want to get a closer look at the *pasos* statues, you need to visit the churches of each *cofradía* where they are on display on the mornings of Maundy Thursday and Good Friday.

THE FERIA

The Feria takes place every year, two weeks after Semana Santa. It is held in the area between avenida Juan Pablo II and avenida Ramón de Carranza.

It was originally an enormous agricultural fair aimed at stimulating the local economy but over the years it has turned into a festival, and today it provides a stunning spectacle of colour, dancing, and traditional dress.

During the Feria beautiful Andalucían girls ride on horseback through the city in traditional flounced dresses (*flamencas*) accompanied by their menfolk who wear the customary short tailored jackets. Eminent local families and companies spend a fortune on entertaining in *casetas*. In these open wooden 'houses' people eat, drink and dance over the six days of the festival performing traditional *sevillanas* and *seguidillas* to the rhythmic sound of guitars, tambourines and castanets. Onlookers crowd into the entrances to get a better view of the festivities but unless you've got friends in high places, getting into any of these *casetas* will cost you a small fortune. There are, however, a number of public *casetas* where you can join in the fun, drinking and carousing until the early hours of the morning. And as well as the partying, the Feria is major occasion for bullfights, with a whole programme of events at the local bullring.

– For minor *corridas*, you can buy tickets at the bullring (plaza de Toros). But for more important fights, you will need to buy your tickets in advance at 'La Teatral' in calle Tetuan. Remember, though, that for these fights tickets will be more expensive.

– During the Feria most shops close at 2pm.

– The dates of the Feria vary by a few days each year, depending on when Easter falls – check with the Spanish Tourist Office before you leave for more details.

WHAT TO SEE

The opening hours given below are those provided by the venues themselves, although they are liable to change significantly at short notice, depending on the season, public holidays and the whims of the local authorities. The opening times stated here should be taken only as a guide. In the free monthly publication *El Giraldillo*, which you will find at almost any tourist attraction, you will find accurate information on current cultural events.

In the Old Part of Santa Cruz

★ **The Cathedral** (A1, on the colour map of Santa Cruz): open Monday to Saturday 11am–6pm and Sunday 2–7pm, including during services. ☎ 21-49-71. Admission is quite expensive – around 5€, with a reduced rate for students. It is free on Sunday. You will generally have to wait about 20 minutes to get in during the busy seasons. Try to get there between 3 and 4pm, as there are usually fewer people at this time of day. On the way in you will be given a map along with your ticket. Outside the cathedral you may get hassled by gypsies for money in exchange for a buttonhole which they will try and pin on you by force. Be firm with them. They are sometimes accompanied by pick-pockets who take advantage of the diversion to take your purse or wallet, so watch out.

Like many other Catholic buildings in the area, this one was built on the site of a mosque – in this case the Almohades mosque which was built in the 12th century. Only the Giralda and several old walls survive from this period. Following the Reconquest of Seville under the Catholic Monarchs, this vast cathedral was built on the foundations of the razed mosque.

The cathedral is absolutely massive – 130 metres (426 feet) long, 76 metres (249 feet) wide and rising some 56 metres (184 feet) above the ground. It is the third largest cathedral in the world after St Peter's in Rome and St Paul's in London, and the biggest of all Gothic cathedrals. There isn't enough room here to provide an exhaustive list of what to see in the cathedral – that would take another whole guidebook – but below there is a short summary of some of the main points of interest.

– First and foremost, is the rather solemn **Capilla Real** (Chapel Royal), built in the Renaissance style of the 16th century with richly ornamented stone-work. In the centre lies the tomb of Ferdinand III, the patron saint of the city. You can also see the tomb of Alfonso X the Wise, king of Castilla and León, who strived to unite Judaism, Christianity and Islam in the interests of world peace and the happiness of mankind. There hasn't been a kingdom since that has come so close to finding social harmony. Alfonso reigned at a time of great prosperity for Seville. How different the world would be today if his dream had been realized.

– The massive *retablo* of the **Capilla Mayor** is without doubt the supreme masterpiece of the cathedral. The carved wooden scenes extend for 200 metres (656 feet). In total there are 1,500 wooden figures, gleaming with gold leaf. More than two tonnes of gold were used to gild the 45 scenes from the life of Christ and the Virgin Mary, and the central Nativity scene. It's a work that required staggering wealth to create and today is still the largest altarpiece in the world. Of particular interest is the technique used by the artist to create a sense of perspective. The higher carved figures are much bigger than the lower ones with the result that the more distant, lofty figures appear more imposing.

– **El Coro** (the choir): beautiful Gothic pews.

– **Sacristía de Los Cálices**: there are several works by Goya and Murillo.

– **Sacristía Mayor**: amid the vast collection of reliquaries there is a silver monstrance weighing more than 300 kilograms.

– **Funeral monument of Christopher Columbus** (Cristóbal Colón in Spanish): the remains of Columbus, now housed in the right wing of the transept, are said to have been brought back from Havana, Cuba at the end of the 19th century. There is however some doubt that *his* remains were actually brought back and the real remains could still be somewhere in Cuba. Either way, the tomb is impressive. It is borne by four knights wearing costumes representing the four great kingdoms of Spain. The one on the right carries an oar, symbolizing the discovery of America, while another holds a cross representing the victory of Christianity. Close to the funeral monument, there is also a beautiful carved wooden organ, supported on pink marble columns.

★ **La Giralda** (A1 on the colour map of Santa Cruz): the same opening times as the cathedral. The beautiful simplicity of this former minaret dominates the Seville skyline and at around 98 metres (322 feet) in height it is even taller than the Cathedral. The fact that it was left standing after the Reconquest is evidence of the good will that existed between the Christians and Muslims in the 12th and 13th centuries. The elegance and grace of the square tower lies in the simple blocked symmetry of the brickwork and the later addition of a baroque bell tower by the Catholics. Obvious comparisons can be drawn between this monument and the Koutoubia of Marrakech, or the Hassan Tower in Rabat; all three dating from the Almohada era at the end of the 12th century.

The name *Giralda* is a corruption of *Giraldilla*, or weather vane, so-named in honour of bronze allegorical figure of Faith that revolves at the top of the tower. The weather vane turns with the slightest breath of wind – and at that height there is quite a lot of movement.

It's worth making the trek up the slopes and short flights of steps, that lead to the top of the tower, a pathway that was designed so that mounted guards could get to the top on horseback. From here, there is a superb panoramic view of Seville, with the outskirts of the city almost dissolving in the intense light. This is also a good vantage point from which to admire the fine cathedral vaults and to appreciate the shape of this vast edifice.

★ **El Patio de los Naranjos** (the Courtyard of the Orange Trees): next to the cathedral is a pretty courtyard from the original mosque. At its centre is a Moorish fountain for daily ablutions. On the main gateway, there is a splendid depiction of the biblical story of the merchants being evicted from the temple, while carved in the stone around the courtyard there are inscriptions from the Koran.

★ **Alcázar** (the Citadel) (A2, on the colour map of Santa Cruz): entrance in plaza del Triunfo. ☎ 50-23-23. Open Tuesday to Saturday 9.30am–7pm from April to September, and from 9.30am–5pm on Sunday and public holidays. From October to March it is open Tuesday to Saturday 9.30am–5pm, and on Sunday and public holidays 9.30am–1.30pm. It is closed on Monday. Admission is 4–5€ for adults, but is free for students, children under 16 and adults over 65. You can hire headphones at the entrance if you want an audio tour.

In its time, the Alcázar has been everything from a sumptuous Arab palace to a fortress (under the Almohades), but most of what can be seen today was built during the Christian period, after the Reconquest. It was Pedro III 'the Cruel' who commissioned the work in the Mudéjar style – a style developed during the period when the Moors were working under Christian rule. As time passed, successive illustrious occupants of the Alcázar made their mark on the building, often at the expense of the work of the previous owner, and usually in the popular architectural style of the time. This explains the mixture of Gothic, Hispano-Muslim and Mudéjar styles, not to mention many other less dominant styles. Christopher Columbus and Magellan came here to ask for funds for their voyages.

– **El Patio de León**: this was built a century later than the Alcázar and was originally a military barracks. On the right hand side is the court, which was built in the Mudéjar style. It was here that Pedro the Cruel had his brother executed after discovering he was having an affair with his wife.

– **La Sala de los Azulejos**: a room decorated with traditional brightly coloured tiles known as *azulejos* which are typical of Seville. They are arranged in complex geometrical patterns in Islamic style.

– **El Cuarto del Almirante** (the Admiral's room): dating from the beginning of the 16th century with a display of paintings from the 19th and 20th centuries. There is a particularly interesting picture of the World Exhibition of 1929.

– **La Sala de Audiencias** (Chapel of the Navigators): an extension of the previous room. It has a gilt wooden ceiling, and tapestried walls that are woven with the coats of arms of the Admirals of Castilla involved in the discovery of the Americas. The room is surrounded by silver friezes. One particularly interesting example dates from the 16th-century and depicts the Virgin of the Navigators – under her large cape, she shelters and protects Christopher Columbus, Ferdinand, Charles V, Amerigo Vespucci and several American Indians who were brought back from the journey. This was the very first picture of the conquest of the New World.

– **El Patio de Montana**: another fine example of the Mudéjar style with its typical octagonal pillars. The Spanish royal family lives on the upper floor whenever they come to Seville. The cornice is supported on some beautiful, foiled arches and marble columns. 'And the only conqueror is Allah', proclaims one of the inscriptions.

– **El Vestíbulo** (the Vestibule): the place where important visitors were received and relieved of any weapons they might have been carrying. This room was designed so that while visitors couldn't see inside the palace, so protecting family life, each guest or visitor could be welcomed in person. The colourful geometrical patterns which decorate the walls and pillars are extraordinarily varied and there is a remarkable inlaid door which leads to the patio de las Doncellas.

– **El Patio de las Doncellas** (Patio of the Maidens): this is the central nucleus of the building and it is decorated with the palace's most beautiful *azulejos* as well as finely-worked stucco panels in authentic Islamic style. Several of the friezes depict verses from the Koran. It is here that great receptions took place, notably meetings between princes and caliphs, sultans and kings. Sometimes young girls were offered as gifts. There is a wonderfully harmonious blend of the Mudéjar style with the Plateresque.

Above the doorway are the coats of arms of Castilla and León. There is a fountain in the middle of the patio and the floor is of white marble.

– **El Salón de Embajadores** (Salon of the Ambassadors): this is the political heart of the palace and one of the most beautifully decorated with multi-coloured stucco work, finely carved lintels and an extraordinary dome in the form of a *media naranja* (half-orange) as well as an intricately carved wooden doorway. In a time before electric light, architects had to use ingenious methods to exploit all sources of natural light. The use of tiny steel mirrors set into the ceiling is as fine an example of their ingenuity as you'll see. As the light streams through the arches it reflects off the white marble floor and onto the mirrored ceiling lighting up the whole room. However beautiful and subtle these innovations, it is still easy for the infinite richness of the *azulejos* to overshadow them. No two patterns are the same but the throne room is the most highly decorated with three arches on either side of the room and balconies above, supported by carved wooden dragons.

– **Salón del Techo** and **Las Habitaciones de los Infantes**: two more fantastically beautiful rooms that are typically overflowing with *azulejos*, multi-coloured *yeserías* (plasterwork), *artesonados* (panelled) ceilings, and ornately carved doorways.

– **Patio de las Muñecas** (the Doll's Court): attributed to Pedro the Cruel and dedicated to family life. It is so named because of the tiny doll-like faces that decorate the inside of the arches. The stucco is exquisitely ornate. There is a small courtyard surrounded by arcades. Some of the plasterwork has been copied from the Alhambra in Granada.

On the first floor:

– **Capella Palacio Carlos V** (the Chapel of Carlos V): climb up to the chapel to admire the beautiful *azulejos* decorated with motifs in the popular turquoise of the 16th century. Also some religious paintings.

– **El Palacio de Carlos V** (the Palace of Charles V): displaying some marvellous tapestries of the Conquest of Maghreb. Woven in silk from Granada, one of them illustrates the Battle of Tunis. The map of the world gives an interesting insight into how the world was understood to be arranged in the past – even Spain appears to be in the wrong place.

★ **Los Jardínes del Alcázar** (B1-2, on the colour map of Santa Cruz): it is nice to take a stroll in the gardens after you've looked round the Alcázar. They are open at the same times as the palace. Only the Arabs could have managed to create such a soothing mixture of running water and luscious planting. The pathways are made of brick and if you look closely some have small holes to allow excess water to drain away. Pedro the Cruel, who is said to have been a man who liked his practical jokes, often organized big parties in these gardens. He would get all the ladies to come into the gardens then open the sluice gates, so that their dresses would get sprayed with water. At the time there was an unusual custom that involved drinking the water from the basins the ladies had washed in. But one day, a guest refused to do so. The king was amazed at this until the courtier replied 'the reason for not trying the sauce, was for fear of liking it too much and starting to covet the partridge', which was an elegant way of saying something rather crude.

The cool, peaceful gardens are an excellent place to take refuge from the crowds and heat. With their narrow pathways weaving between fountains, orange trees and palms they provide a soothing place to relax before heading for the next attraction.

★ **Plaza de la Virgen de los Reyes**: a delightful square behind the cathedral. Take a look at the archiepiscopal palace with its wonderful baroque door.

★ **Santa Cruz** (C1-2, on colour map II, and on the colour map of Santa Cruz): this is probably the most attractive district in Seville. It was built on the foundations of the former Jewish quarter, squeezed in between the Alcázar and the cathedral. It is named after the cast iron cross in the plaza de Santa Cruz that dates from 1692. From the Alcázar head to the magnificent plaza de Doña Elvira. Then just wander around the maze of winding narrow streets. You'll come across small squares bounded by lines of orange trees, churches, stately homes, whitewashed houses and delightful patios. It offers a delightful and picturesque area for a walk at any time of day, although it is particularly lovely at dusk and is wonderfully peaceful in the afternoon, making it a good time to stick your head round some of the gates to admire the patios. At No. 4 calle Gúzman el Bueno there is a particularly fine example of a patio, where plants and sunlight combine to create the unique and intimate atmosphere that is the essence of the inner courtyard.

★ **La Casa Lonja** or **Archivo de Indias** (Archive of the Indies; A2, on the colour map of Santa Cruz): in the plaza del Triunfo, to the right of the Alcázar. ☎ 21-12-34. Only open between 10am and 1pm. Closed on Saturday and Sunday. Free entry. A 16th-century archive that houses some remarkable documents dating back to Columbus's time. There are thousands of records covering all aspects of life. Anyone with an interest in Central or South America will particularly enjoy looking at the 16th-century maps of Mexico, Cuzco and Lima. Also of interest are the 18th-century dictionaries, the travel diary of a governor of Mexico and accounts detailing ancient customs of the indigenous peoples. The signatures of some of the most famous explorers in the world can be seen here, including those of Magellan, Pizarro and Amerigo Vespucci. La Lonja also hosts relevant temporary exhibitions; check listings for details.

The Rest of the City

★ **Casa de Pilatos** (Pilate's House; C-D1, on colour map II): plaza de Pilatos 1. ☎ 422-52-98. Open every day 9am–6pm. You need two separate tickets to see the whole house, one for the lower and one for the upper part of the mansion – each costs around 3€. This is possibly the most dazzling stately home in Seville. It was built in the 16th century by the Marqués de Tarifa on his return from Jerusalem and is apparently in imitation of Pilate's house.

It is a wonderful example of the vitality of Mudéjar art. The main patio includes some amazing *azulejos* – each section having a different pattern and every corner of the square is inhabited by Greek and Roman statues. There are busts of Roman emperors that were brought all the way from Italy. The rooms around the patio are individually decorated and the doorways are all beautifully embellished with inlaid wood. In the room on the right, the walls

SEVILLE

are covered with beautiful *azulejos* embossed with plaster cast motifs and above it all is an amazing coffered wooden ceiling. The *Descanso de los Jueces* (Judges' Retiring Room) is also full of stucco work and also has some impressive *azulejos* as well as bearing the coats of arms of the Enríquez and Ribera families, who between them have owned the palace since the 15th century. At the back of the house is the *chapel de la flagelación* (the flagellation chapel) – which is thought to be the oldest part of the palace. The next room has a tiny fountain in the centre and a remarkable inlaid ceiling. This leads on to a small formal garden, dotted with Roman statues. Go back through the central patio and up the majestic stairway covered with mosaics and stop to admire the splendid cupola in the form of a bees' nest. To see the rest of the palace you have to be accompanied by a guide, although the upper floor is not as spectacular as the one on the ground despite having several vast and richly furnished rooms that are hung with paintings and tapestries.

★ **Parque María Luisa and the Plaza de España** (C-D3, on colour map II): once the grounds of the Palacio de San Telmo, these extensive gardens were redesigned in 1929 for the Ibero-American Fair by the French architect Forestier. It is a lovely place for a walk, especially in summer when the orange, palm and eucalyptus trees provide welcome shade from the sun. The Paseo de las Delicias, is lined with some extraordinary pavilions that were erected for the Exhibition. Hidden behind the palm trees, you can glimpse the sumptuous homes of some of Seville's most affluent families.

The grandiose and spacious Plaza de España, originally designed as the centrepiece of the fair, is a vast semicircular building of brick and *azulejos*, whose towers, archways and pinnacles encompass a boating lake ornamented with fountains and statues. It is a very popular landmark. At the weekend, thousands of Sevillians stroll round the plaza admiring the 58 panels of *azulejos*, each representing a different region of Spain. Some hire rowing boats while others linger on the elegant bridges that cross the water.

★ **Museo Arqueológico** (Archaeology Museum): in the María Luisa Park. This building was also built for the Exhibition. It is open on Tuesday 3–8pm, Wednesday to Saturday 9am–8pm, and Sunday and public holidays 9am–2pm. It is closed on Monday. The entrance is through the Paseo de las Delicias which follows the banks of the Guadalquivir, or by walking through the park. There is a large collection of Roman artefacts and Oriental gold work on display. The museum chronicles the lives of the many people who have lived in the area. Look out for the mosaics from the second and third centuries – some of which are from the Itálica site in the outskirts of Seville – and what is claimed to be the torso of Claudius, which is very expressive and dates from the first century AD.

★ **Museo de Artes y Costumbres Populares** (Museum of Folk Arts and Costumes): housed in the Mudéjar pavilion, opposite the Museum of Archaeology and operating the same opening times. Free entry for EU nationals. A magnificent building of brick towers and marble pillars. The contents, however, do not do justice to the grandeur of the building. There are examples of traditional costume (with some beautiful lacework), musical instruments, religious artefacts and furniture. The collection isn't massively interesting and sometimes things seem to be there just to fill the space.

★ **La Torre del Oro** (B2, on colour map II): on the river-bank. ☎ 22-24-19. Open Tuesday to Friday 10am–2pm and Saturday and Sunday 11am–2pm. It is closed on Monday and in August. Admission costs about 1€ and is free on Tuesday. It's name, literally 'the Tower of Gold', is somewhat misleading as it doesn't house any treasure. It was in fact built as a watchtower from which an enormous chain was suspended across the river to block the path of invading Christian ships. Its name is a reference to the golden *azulejos* that used to embellish it. There is a small naval museum which exhibits maritime engravings, sections of hulls, a few marine instruments and maps, but it is only moderately interesting.

★ **La Plaza de Toros** (the Bullring; A-B2, on colour map II): the entrance is in Paseo de Cristóbal Colón. ☎ 21-03-15. Open week days 10am–2pm and 3–7pm; also on Sunday when there is a *corrida* and during the Feria, 9.30am–7pm. You can only see the bullring if accompanied by a guide. There's a tour every 15 minutes which costs about 3€ and gives you the chance to stand inside the ring where so many great names have fought since 1761 when it was built.

The dominant colours of the ring are white and ochre representing the light of the sky and the red of the blood. It has a capacity of 14,000 and is slightly oval in shape, apparently because of an error by the architect; the original plan was lost some time during the 150 years it took to build the bullring. In the small museum, which is housed in the vaulted cellars beneath the terraces, there are copies of engravings that used to belong to Queen Eugenia. There is also information about *juego de cabezas y lancas*, a precursor to modern-day bullfighting, which was fashionable until the end of the 15th century. Other exhibits include portraits of bullfighters in costume. There are three things to look out for in particular – the stuffed head of the mother of the bull which killed Manolete in August 1947, the *Pink Cape* painted by Picasso and a drawing by Cocteau. If you're into bullfighting, it's probably quite an interesting museum, but it's not really worth seeing otherwise.

There are about 40 fights a year in Seville, usually taking place between Easter and October and mainly held on a Sunday. After more than 70 years without a fatal accident in the Seville bullring, there were two deaths in 1992 (the year of the Expo).

★ **Paseo de Cristóbal Colón**: this is the avenue along the bank of the Guadalquivir from the Torre del Oro. It makes a pleasant place for a stroll in the early evening.

★ **La Plaza del Salvador** (B1, on colour map II): this square is very busy at the weekend, with crowds of people sitting outside the cafés and in front of the baroque facade of the church (*see* 'Where to Eat Tapas and Where to Go for a Drink'). Not far from here is **calle Sierpes**, a long pedestrian street and the busiest shopping area in Seville; it gets very animated in the late afternoon. No. 39 has a beautifully tiled facade, and there's a great patisserie at No. 45.

★ **The Area Opposite the Cathedral** (B2, on colour map II): on the other side of avenida de la Constitución and not quite so touristy. This is a more working class area than Santa Cruz. Although it may lack the charm of the latter's whitewashed houses and sleepy little squares, the atmosphere here is slightly more authentic.

★ **El Museo de Bellas Artes** (Museum of Fine Arts; A3, on colour map I): plaza del Museo 9. ☎ 22-07-90. Open Tuesday 3–8pm, Wednesday to Saturday 9am–8pm, and Sunday 9am–3pm. It is closed on Monday and public holidays. Free admission for EU citizens.

Housed in a former 17th-century convent, the internal decor alone merits a visit. It consists of three patios and a cloister and has a collection of around 2,000 paintings, only half of which are on display at any one time. This is an excellent art gallery. It has examples of the work of a number of artistic schools including medieval Spanish art, the Manneristic period, European baroque, Sevillian art from the 18th and 19th centuries, Romantic art and paintings from the beginning of the 20th century. The medieval section has some real gems, including a 15th-century portrait of Christ and a stunning Madonna and Child. Passing through the former church, you can see works by Uceda and Murillo, displayed alongside beautiful frescoes in the arches and in the cupola. There are also a few canvasses by the fantastic Juan de Valdés Leal. In the 20th century section there are particularly outstanding works by Gonzalo Bilbao and Villegas Cordero. Upstairs are some beautiful 16th-century altarpieces (in room IV), as well as many works by Murillo and Zurbarán, and two magnificent pictures by Brueghel. One depicting Adam and Eve in the Garden of Eden, surrounded by the animals of the creation and very reminiscent of the work of Douannier Rousseau.

★ **La Basilica de la Macarena** (C1, on colour map I): open 9am–1pm and 5–9pm. This basilica is famous for its baroque statue of the Virgin of Macarena, the patron saint of Seville. The ceremony of carrying the statue out of the church takes place at midnight on Maundy Thursday and is one of the big events of Semana Santa. A small museum attached to the church contains many relics associated with the Macarena, as well as jewels and embroidered robes. The Puerta de la Macarena (Macarena gate) opposite the church was rebuilt in the 18th century from Arab ruins.

Towards the south lies the Macarena district, a quiet area scattered with beautiful churches (San Luis, San Marcos). It is pleasant area for walking and offers some respite from some of the busier, more touristy parts of town.

★ **Arts and Law Faculty**, previously the **Fábrica de Tabacos** (Tobacco Factory; C3, on colour map II): the entrance is opposite calle San Fernando 31, not far from the hotel Alfonso XIII. Closed on Sunday. It was previously a tobacco factory, built in the 18th century in a beautifully simple classical style. For a long time it was the second biggest construction in Spain after El Escorial. Thousands of girls used to work in this tobacco factory, including the fictional Carmen.

★ **Hospital de la Caridad** (Hospital of Charity; B2, on colour map II): calle Temprado 3. ☎ 22-32-32. Open Monday to Saturday 9am–1.30pm and 3.30–6.30pm. Admission costs between 2 and 3€.

The only part of this former hospice, with its beautiful multi-coloured baroque belltower, that is open to the public is the old baroque church, which contains a number of interesting pictures. In the courtyard there are several panels of *azulejos* depicting religious allegories (the Passion of Christ and the

Temptation in the Wilderness). The decoration of the church was paid for Don Miguel de Mañara, a 17th-century roué (and allegedly the inspiration for Don Juan), who felt the need to atone for his sins. Also thanks to his donations, both the hospital for the poor and the church were built. He is buried in the doorway of the church.

Don Miguel commissioned Valdés Leal and Murillo to paint subjects dear to his heart. This probably explains why Valdés Leal's two works, *Death* and *Vanity*, are imbued with such harsh and implacable realism (these paintings are around the nave, at the entrance). *Death* depicts the character of Death carrying a coffin and snuffing out the last light of life. *Vanity* shows a vain man being eaten by worms. In a completely different vein, Murillo painted the miracle of the feeding of the five thousand and the miracle of Moses and the waterfall, in which he has managed to capture a real feeling of joy. These four pictures summarize the contradictory feelings of joy and remorse being suffered by Don Miguel.

★ **The Triana District** (A2, on colour map II): apart from the section along the Guadalquivir, this area is of no particular historical or architectural interest. But it might be worth a visit at night to the bars and clubs where the local dance groups meet to dance the *sevillanas*; if you are lucky you might catch one of their performances. For a while now, Triana has enjoyed a reputation as one of the trendier parts of Seville (*see* 'Where to eat Tapas and Go for a Drink' in the Triana District) and is definitely a happening part of town.

Outside the City Centre

★ **La Cartuja**: located on the right bank of the Guadalquivir towards the east. ☎ 48-06-11. It's easy to get there on foot if you take the pasarela de la Cartuja (a footbridge) at the end of calle de Baños (A2, on colour map I). Open Tuesday to Saturday 10am–9pm and Sunday 10am–3pm. Free admission on Tuesday. There are guided tours from noon to 7pm in summer, and from noon to 5pm in winter. Admission costs about 2€. You receive a good English guide and map at the entrance.

This was the heart of the World Expo of 1992 and a symbolic landmark of the event. La Cartuja was formerly a Carthusian Monastery and was restored in 1986. Now, this is the only building from the old Expo site that is still standing. Surrounding the monastery are the pavilions and fixtures of the Expo buildings and sadly they have been left to fade and rust, fenced in by hundreds of metres of railings. So only a massive scrap-heap remains – very different from the original plans that promised a series of pavilions for use in years to come. Today, La Cartuja is open to visitors as is the Science and Technology Zone, although it is now an activity park. The Cartuja was founded at the end of the 14th century after someone had a vision of the Virgin Mary near the site in 1248. Over time the building has seen many upheavals the most striking of which was its transformation into a ceramics factory in 1841. Surprisingly, the high, bottle-shaped towers that are set around the church do not detract from it, but rather, bring a strange kind of harmony to the area. A high point in the church's history was a visit from Christopher Columbus – he first came here to prepare for his second voyage. It has also been claimed that his body was laid to rest in the crypt

SEVILLE

of the church for 30 years, although this is difficult to substantiate. Another major event was the invasion of the Napoleonic troops in 1810, although their visit didn't have the same glorious association as they evicted the Carthusian Monks.

In the main building you can visit the **Museo de Arte Contemporáneo** (Contemporary Art Museum), with its collection of 20th-century Spanish paintings, sculpture and ceramics. There is a great diversity of work here and regular temporary exhibitions. It's a nice place to wander round, especially as you can often find that you are almost the only visitor, even in the height of the tourist season.

★ **Isla Mágica**: a new theme park set around a lake and built on part of the old Expo 92 site. There are lots of buses here from the centre of town: C1, C2, C3, C4, 2, 13 and 14. ☎ (902) 16-17-16. Website: www.islamagica.es. Open every day, from mid-March to mid-September, 11am–9pm and 10pm–2am, from October it's only open at weekends. These opening hours are liable to change so it is always best to phone before setting out, especially if you are visiting out of season. Admission before 4pm is around 21€ for adults and 14€ for children, after 4pm the price is reduced to around 14€ for adults, and 11€ for children. You get a good detailed map as part of the admission fee, which is drawn in the style of a *Guía del explorador* (explorer's treasure map), which is the park's theme. It was also the theme of Expo 92, as it was built in celebration of the 500th anniversary of the discovery of the Americas. The Isla Mágica has six main zones, all covering 35 hectares and loosely connected by the exploration theme. Visitors enjoy fantasy visits to the Indies, America, the Amazon, pirate hideouts, the Fountain of Youth (for the under fives) and Eldorado. The park has the usual fairground attractions, boat trips, shows, films, shops, restaurants, themed scenery, pirates and more – parents will enjoy it just as much as their kids.

MARKETS

▣ Flea Market (B2, on colour map I): a small market is held on Alameda de Hercules every Thursday and Sunday from about 8am–1pm. Knick-knacks and all sorts of second-hand goods. Lots of little bits and pieces for sale, but the real attraction is the atmosphere and charm of the area. It's fairly peaceful and there is a pleasant collection of ochre facades and red brick houses with attractive balconies. Quite different from the bustling Santa Cruz area and well away from the hectic crowds of the city centre.

▣ Market: plaza del Duque. Held on Thursday, Friday and Saturday from 10am–9pm. Hippy-style stalls selling silver jewellery, exotic necklaces and T-shirts.

WHAT TO DO

– There are two **swimming pools** in Seville, but they are only open on Saturday and Sunday. One is in the north of the city. **Piscina Municipal de la Virgen de los Reyes** (off map I from C1), avenida Doctor Fedriani, ☎ 437-68-66; the other is a bit further out and is just past Santa Justa

Station, at the **Centro deportivo San Pablo** (D2, on map I), avenida Kansas City, ☎ 459-68-42.

– **Pedalo Hire** (B2-3, on colour map II): pedaloes can be hired from both banks of the Guadalquivir, just downstream from the Torre del Oro. It's a lovely way to idle away a few hours at the end of an afternoon. The current is very slow as Seville is only 10 metres (33 feet) above sea level. It's one of the prettiest parts of the river too, with the Torre del Oro, la plaza de Toros and other monuments providing the perfect backdrop to the river.

– **City Tour in a Double Decker Bus**: there are two companies offering this service, the originally named **Seville Tour** and **Tour por Sevilla**. They are both located at the foot of the Torre del Oro on Paseo de Cristóbal Colón. A ticket is valid for two days and you can hop on and off the bus at any one of the four stops. It costs about 4€. The whole circuit takes about 1 hour and 20 minutes. There's a bus every 30 minutes from 10am to 7pm (until midnight in summer). This is generally a more popular way of seeing the city with older visitors than younger as the music and commentary that is piped through the headphones leaves a lot to be desired. All the same, the route takes you by several of the most important sites and monuments. The fact that the ticket is valid for two days is handy, although it is a bit expensive.

SHOPPING AND SOUVENIRS

Pottery is the main thing worth buying in Seville. Calle Garcia de Vinuesa has some lovely pottery shops, as does calle Antillano Campos (A2, on colour map II), in the Triana area. There is a great variety of style and quality. Even if you don't buy anything, window-shopping is still a pleasure.

WHAT TO SEE OUTSIDE SEVILLE

★ **Itálica**: these Roman ruins are about 10 kilometres (6 miles) out of the city along the Mérida road. Open Tuesday to Saturday 9am–5.30pm (until 8pm in summer) and Sunday 10am–4pm (3pm in summer), but it's closed on Monday. Admission is free.

Little is known about old Hispalis (the Roman name for Seville) but it seems clear that several generations had made their mark even before the Romans arrived. An African called Scipion founded the area known as the 'old town' for his convalescing soldiers in 206 BC. The Roman Emperor Trajan was born here and his adopted son Hadrian, who came from Rome, built the 'new town'. This was the most beautiful part of the town and, since its discovery in 1781, archaeological digs have been ongoing.

If you look between the large paving stones in the streets that connect different parts of the town, you can catch glimpses of the amazingly sophisticated drainage system used at that time. There is also a crumbling amphitheatre, once one of the largest in the Roman Empire, with a capacity of 25,000. Another place of interest is the Planetarium which was decorated with some exceptional mosaics that were set in the shape of medallions to represent the planetary divinities. Apart from its obvious archaeological interest, a visit to Itálica is also a good opportunity for a pleasant stroll in attractive surroundings.

✕ If you want to have lunch after looking round the site, head for bar Juan-Luis in **Guillena**, about 10 kilometres (6 miles) north of Itálica. It is a simple bar in an ordinary village, but it serves up some good home cooking.

★ **El Rocío**: about 64 kilometres (40 miles) away from Seville in the Almonte direction, this village has a venerated image of the Virgin Mary, to which a pilgrimage is made every Pentecost. Gypsies and pilgrims in traditional dress converge on the area on horseback and in carriages. The atmosphere is fantastic during this event, although at other times of year the village is very peaceful.

LEAVING SEVILLE

By Train

🚂 **Santa Justa Station**: see 'Transport'. From here you can get to nearly all major Spanish cities. ☎ 454-02-02 (for information) and ☎ 54-03-03 (for reservations).

By Bus

There are two bus stations:

🚌 **Estación Prado de San Sebastián** (D3, on colour map II): calle Manuel Vasquez Sagastizabal. ☎ 41-71-11. Left-luggage facilities. Buses to Algeciras, Alicante, Almería, Arcos de la Frontera, Barcelona, Cádiz, Carmona, Córdoba, Granada, Jaén, Jerez de la Frontera, Málaga, Nerja, Ronda, Tarifa, Valencia.

– Bus Companies: **Comes** ☎ 41-68-58; **Bacoma** ☎ 441-46-60; **Amarillos** ☎ 41-52-01; **Alsina** ☎ 41-88-11; **Casal** ☎ 441-06-58.

🚌 **Estación Plaza de Armas** (A3, on colour map I): avenida Cristo de la Expiación. ☎ 90-80-40. For shorter journeys (Aracena and Huelva) and Portugal (Lisbon), but also for Madrid, Mérida and Almonte.

ARACENA 21200

About 89 kilometres (56 miles) northwest of Seville. Take the N630 for 35 kilometres (22 miles) then the N433 for 54 kilometres (35 miles). The second half of the route goes through luscious countryside and fields of olive groves.

Aracena is an attractive town built on steps cut into the hillside and crowned by the ruins of an ancient castle. Although the streets, like its inhabitants, seem a little sleepy it has a unique charm. The town's main attraction is the nearby caves, which make a popular tourist destination.

GETTING THERE

– A bus operated by the Casal company runs between Seville and Aracena twice a day (morning and afternoon), leaving from the plaza de Armas in Seville.

WHERE TO STAY AND EAT

♠ **Campsite**: about 5 kilometres (3 miles) east of the town, to the right if you're coming from Seville. In a good hillside location. Modern and clean with a swimming pool. Not too busy either, which is a bonus.
✕ There are a number of moderately priced restaurants in plaza San Pedro, a kilometre or so below the caves.
✕ Budget travellers may prefer to have tapas in the **Los Angeles** bar on calle San Pedro – the street leading up from plaza San Pedro towards the town centre.

WHAT TO SEE

★ **The Caves**: the route is clearly signposted as you come into the village. Admission charge. There are guided tours practically every hour from Monday to Friday, 10.30am–6pm; on Saturday and Sunday, they are every 30 minutes. Tours last one hour. The 1,500 metres (5,000 feet) of natural galleries are amazing – after a succession of narrow passageways you come out into a vast cavern full of magical stalactites and stalagmites. It's very impressive, but much like similar caves elsewhere. Unfortunately, you can't wander around on your own, you have to go with a group and most of the guides only speak Spanish. Several scenes from *King Solomon's Mines* and *Journey to the Centre of the Earth* were filmed here.

CARMONA 41410   DIALLING CODE: 954

About 38 kilometres (24 miles) east of Seville with 10 daily bus services from the city. Don't be put off by the ugliness of the outlying areas of the town. Beyond the ramparts is a superb little medieval citadel perched at an altitude of 430 metres (1,400 feet) and overlooking the surrounding plains. Over the last 5,000 years it has been inhabited by a variety of different tribes. What remains from their respective eras are several extraordinary churches and ancient monuments that seem to bring together every possible Andalucían style from Roman simplicity to delirious baroque and even some Oriental influences. Leave your car outside the ramparts and enjoy wandering round the maze of peaceful streets. When you get back to your car, stop at the ancient Roman cemetery on the way out of the town.

USEFUL ADDRESSES

🆗 **Tourist Information**: arco de la Puerta de Seville; under the arch of the large gateway into the town. It is well signposted as you come into the town. ☎ 19-09-55. Fax: 19-00-80. Open Monday to Saturday 10am–6pm and

Sunday 10am–3pm. Good information on the town with a clear map available; most of the staff speak English.

WHERE TO STAY

☆ Budget

♠ **Casa Carmelo**: right opposite the church of San Pedro. ☎ 14-05-72. Fairly comfortable.

☆☆ Moderate

♠ **Hostal San Pedro**: San Pedro 1. ☎ and fax: 14-16-06. A double air-conditioned room costs about 42€. Not exactly the cheapest place in town but clean and comfortable, although the owners are not particularly welcoming. Credit cards not accepted.

♠ **Pensión Comercio**: torre del Oro 56. ☎ 14-00-18. Inside the city walls. If you come in by the city gate from Seville, it's just on the left along the ramparts. About 48€ for a double room. Typical Andalucían house, with a lovely patio and terrace, facing the ramparts and the church of San Pedro. Air-conditioned rooms with or without en-suite bathrooms, but too expensive for the level of service provided by the unsmiling staff. There is a small restaurant where guests can eat.

☆☆☆☆ Splash Out

♠ **Parador Alcázar del Rey Don Pedro**: Located high up in the old part of the town, in the Alcázar. ☎ 14-10-10. Fax: 14-17-12. One of the most beautiful hotels in the parador chain. Set in a Moorish fortress converted into a house by Pedro the Cruel. The parador overlooks the plains and you can see for miles around from its lofty position. There are gardens, a restaurant and a swimming pool. Delightful, if slightly austere, it has been totally renovated. Annoyingly, the rooms can be very noisy as the car-park is usually jam-packed and is busy late at night and into the early hours of the morning. Consequently, you might prefer to just come for a drink on the flower-filled patio.

WHERE TO EAT

✗ **Bar Plaza**: on the corner of calle José Ramón de Oya and plaza San Fernando, the nucleus of the old town. Open every day. A small bar in the square (as the name suggests) serving excellent tapas including *pulpo a la gallega* (Galician-style octopus), delicious *espinacas* (spinach), *merluza* (hake) and on Sunday, *paella*.

✗ **La Almazara**: Santa Ana, 33. ☎ 19-00-76. Near the church of Santa Ana. Set menus from about 12€. A choice of tapas at the bar or good quality regional dishes in the restaurant.

WHAT TO SEE

★ **Streets and alleyways of the old town**: a lovely place to wander and admire the drooping palms and the charming old houses with their pretty balconies, ornamental *azulejos*, and ochre and salmon-pink facades. Several small cafés line the square. There is an old palace with a particularly ornate facade on one of the adjacent streets. Calle Martin Lopez leads to the vast, austere church of Santa Maria. Inside is a typically

Plateresque altarpiece. A short distance beyond the church is the convent of Santa Clara.

★ **El Alcázar de la Puerta de Sevilla**: the entrance is in the Tourist Office, and the Alcázar has the same opening times. Information brochure in English is available. The restored ruins of the former Alcázar with its stairways, terraces, turrets and wonderful views is a lovely place for a gentle stroll.

★ **The Church of San Pedro**: just outside the ramparts on calle San Pedro. Of special interest for its tower, which was fashioned after the Giralda in Seville. baroque interior.

★ **Ancient Roman Cemetery**: Situated at the entrance to the town, and well signposted. Open 9am–2pm and 4–6pm; open only in the morning on Sunday. An enormous Roman cemetery with more than 900 tombs dating from 200 BC to AD 300. Look out for the remains of the old amphitheatre, you can still get a rough impression of how it used to look.

CÓRDOBA 14000   DIALLING CODE: 957

Córdoba, like Granada, is a city with a history of different cultures fusing together, such as when the Moors, Jews and Catholics all peacefully lived here together in the past. This religious and cultural tolerance is manifested in much of the architecture – for example, the way in which the Judería, or Jewish quarter, nestles around the Great Mosque, la Mezquita. The Judería seems almost like a separate village even though it's set in the middle of a large town. Its narrow, winding streets are a great place for meandering around, admiring and enjoying the whitewashed walls and flower-filled patios as you go. The places of historic interest in Córdoba are all fairly close together so it's best to leave your car behind and explore on foot. If you enjoy walking, there are some lovely walks further out of the town along the banks of the Guadalquivir. Most of the good hotels and bars are concentrated in the town centre, though.

Like Seville, Córdoba has its share of bag-snatchers and thefts from cars, even if they are left in car-parks with security guards, and especially if they have foreign number plates. Take sensible precautions and don't leave anything of value in your car.

A Brief History

It is not clear why the Carthaginians, and then the Romans, founded a town in a place with such evident military vulnerabilities. Whatever the reason, the Moors were apparently seduced by the city, which they seized in the eighth century and made into the capital of their vast empire. At that time Córdoba's prosperity rivalled that of Constantinople and the city had more than 300 mosques. For almost three centuries, peace prevailed between the Muslim, Jewish and Catholic cultures. The Moorish influence is evident in every building that dates from this period. The caliphs and the emirs, all great lovers of art and learning, avoided any religious segregation and as a result artists and intellectuals from all over Europe flocked to Córdoba to enjoy the tolerance that allowed philosophers, historians, and scientists of different faiths to share their knowledge and ideas. Goldsmiths, tailors, potters and musicians were welcomed and cherished by sovereigns who appreciated beautiful craftsmanship.

However, this tolerance was partly maintained due to some stringent laws. These included a tax that all citizens had to pay to preserve their civil autonomy and be allowed to practice their faith. Slavery was legal, and citizens had to offer a share of their harvest to the notoriously cunning and irascible emirs. They were also expected to shower their rulers with gifts simply to maintain their freedom and prosperity.

The city reached its peak in the 10th century. At the time, Córdoba was the leading light of Europe. But soon family disputes began to rage between several of the emirs and this marked the beginning of a period of decadence. In 1212 the Moorish troops were wiped out by the monarchs of Aragón and Navarra, representing a fatal blow to Islam. The Moors were forced to retreat back across the Straits of Gibraltar. They made a tentative effort to return, but were rebuffed. In the centuries that followed the standard of life Córdoba had enjoyed under the caliphates began to deteriorate. The Catholics failed to show the Moors the same degree of tolerance they themselves had enjoyed under the Muslims and Córdoba neglected its agriculture, abandoning the ingenious systems of irrigation developed by the Moors.

Today, however, agriculture has experienced a resurgence and vast cultivated plains now once more surround around the city.

USEFUL ADDRESSES

Tourist Information

❶ Tourist Office (B3 on the map): calle Torrijos, 10. ☎ 47-12-35. Fax: 49-17-78. Email: otcordoba@andalucia.org. Opposite the Mezquita. Open Monday to Saturday 9.30am–6pm (8pm in summer), as well as Sunday morning. Information on the whole region of Andalucía as well as Córdoba. English-speaking staff.

❶ Tourist Office (A2-3 on the map): plaza Juda Levi, in the Convention Centre. ☎ and fax: 20-02-77. Email: turismo@aix.ayuncordoba.es. Open from Monday to Friday. A couple of minutes' walk to the west of the Mezquita. This office only provides information on Córdoba. English-speaking staff. Map of the town and opening times of the places of interest.

Services

✉ **Post Office** (B1 on the map): calle Cruz Conde 15. Open Monday to Friday 8.30am–8.30pm, and Saturday 9.30am–2pm. Closed Sunday.

Internet: at Hostal El Pilar del Potro (C3, **27** on map), you can get on line 24 hours a day at a cost of less than 1€ for 15 minutes (*see* 'Where to Stay').

Money

■ **Banks and Bureaux de Change**: most of the banks are on avenida Ronda de los Tejares (B1 on the map). They all have cash machines. The most central is the Caja Sur, opposite the Mezquita.

Police and Medical Assistance

■ **Police**: ☎ 091 (to report a theft) and ☎ 092.

■ **Police Station**: calle Doctor Fleming, on the corner of Conde Vallellano. ☎ 59-45-00.

■ **Lost Property**: ☎ 47-75-00.

■ **Hospital Reina Sofia**: avenida Menendez Pidal. ☎ 61-00-00. West of the town centre.

Transport

🚂 **RENFE** (off the map from B1): *see* 'Leaving Córdoba'.

🚌 **Bus Station** (off the map from B1): *see* 'Leaving Córdoba'.

■ **Taxis**: ☎ (957) 76-44-44.

■ **Car-parks**: You can visit Córdoba town centre on foot. There's a public car-park just down from the Mezquita (B3 on the map), on Amador de los Rios (pay and display). Note that thefts from cars are common so take sensible precautions and don't leave anything of value in your vehicle. There's also a multi-storey car-park, Edaco, on calle Conde de Rubledo (B1 on map) with 24-hour security. Other places to park near the centre are as follows – all along paseo de la Victoria and de la República Argentina, or on the other side of the river, where there are lots of spaces along avenida de la Confederación. Make sure you are legally parked otherwise you may well get clamped.

Cycle Hire

Córdoba La Llana en Bici (C3, **2** on the map): paseo de la Ribera 9. ☎ (957) 42-58-84. Website: www.cordobaenbici.com. Open every day 9am–2pm and 4–9pm (3–6pm in winter). You can hire mountain bikes by the hour (3–4€), for half a day or a whole day (about 14€). You can also take guided tours around the town and as far a field as Medina Azahara (about 21€). On Sunday there are trips to the nearby mountains. You are picked up by minibus in the morning and collected again in the evening. It costs about 36€, including breakfast and lunch. If you prefer to go off on your own, staff will happily advise you on the best places to go in Córdoba.

WHERE TO STAY

The hotels in the old part of town are definitely recommended. They are traditional and attractive, with beautiful cast iron grills protecting well-tended, flower-filled patios. The hotels near the stations are functional, somewhat characterless, but slightly cheaper. If you come by train, try and phone round the hotels in the town centre on the off-chance that there may be a vacancy, as they are certainly the better option.

CÓRDOBA TO GRANADA

☆ Budget

☗ **Albergue Juvenil** (Youth Hostel, B2-3, **10** on the map): plaza Juda Levi, 14003 Córdoba. ☎ 29-01-66. Fax: 29-05-00. Website: www. inturjoven.com. Two minutes' walk from the Mezquita, right next to the Tourist Office. Open all night and all year round. As in many other Andalucían towns, accommodation costs around 12€ a night between April and October if you are under 26 and 16€ if you are over (you need a YHA card). The rest of the year it's slightly cheaper. There are about 60 rooms sleeping two, three or four people, all with a bathroom and air-conditioning. It's modern and clean, and mixed-sex groups are allowed to share rooms. The staff are friendly and most speak a bit of English.

☗ **Martinez Rücker** (B3, **15** on the map): calle Martinez Rücker 14, 14003 Córdoba. ☎ 47-25-62. About 50 metres east of the Mezquita with a paying car-park. Double rooms from about 18€ in low season and from 24€ in high season. A lovely house with a gorgeous patio, pretty carved furniture and 19th-century paintings on the stairs. The owners are polite and the rooms basic, but pleasant. Rooms for three or five people work out very cheaply. Communal showers. Good value for money.

☗ **Hostal Internacional** (B2, **18** on the map): calle Juan de Mena 14, 14003 Córdoba. ☎ 47-83-49. Charming *pensión* located in a narrow pedestrian street a stone's throw from plaza de las Tendillas. Rooms cost 24–30€ depending on the facilities. There are also rooms that sleep three or four. The owners are very welcoming – something of a rarity in this touristy town.

☗ **Hostal Rey Heredia** (B2-3, **13** on the map): calle Rey Heredia 26, 14003 Córdoba. ☎ and fax: 47-41-82. Double rooms from 18 to 24€. Large Andalucían house with a rather cluttered patio. The rooms are basic, with high ceilings, electric fans and wash basins, and some have nice little balconies. There are three bathrooms on each floor, all spotlessly clean.

☗ **Hostal El Portillo** (B2, **12** on the map): calle Cabezas 2, 14003 Córdoba. ☎ and fax: 47-20-91. Near the Mezquita. Double rooms from 18€ with wash basin. An attractive establishment run by a polite, attentive owner. Note that the rooms overlooking the street are quite noisy and those over the patio are rather dark.

☗ **Hostal Los Arcos** (C2-3, **20** on the map): calle Romero Barros 14, 14003 Córdoba. ☎ 48-56-43. Fax: 48-60-11. Double rooms from about 21€ without bathrooms in low season and from 30€ with a bathroom in high season. Attractive reception area and nice rooms. Most of them overlook the patio or a quiet little street, which explains why it is so peaceful here. Good value for money. Ask to look at the rooms first as they aren't all the same size. Avoid room No. 6 which is next to the entrance so you can hear the doorbell ringing all night long. In the evenings there is a superb view of the Mezquita from the terrace.

☗ **Hostal Almanzor** (B3, **21** on the map): calle Cardenal González 10 (previously known as corregidor Luis de la Cerda), 14003 Córdoba. ☎ and fax: 48-54-00. A 5-minute walk from the Mezquita. Rooms start at about 30€, and most of them have bathrooms, TV and air-conditioning. There is a small surcharge for credit card payments so it's better to use cash. There's no patio, and the place doesn't have any special charm, but it's very comfortable and impeccably clean for such a reasonable price (which even includes parking). The owners are very sweet which makes it quite a good bet, despite the drawbacks.

â Hostal Trinidad (B3, **17** on the map): calle Cardenal González 58 (previously known as corregidor Luis de la Cerda), 14003 Córdoba. ☎ 48-79-05. A small *hostal* with only two rooms for around 23€ with a shared bathroom. Two small terraced courtyards and tidy, basic rooms. Not remotely deluxe but very peaceful.

â Hostal La Milagrosa (**16** on the map B2): calle Rey Heredia 12, 14003 Córdoba. ☎ 47-33-17. This *hostal* has an attractive white and ochre facade, and is situated in a relatively quiet street very near the Mezquita. Very clean rooms for 24–30€ depending on the facilities, set around a pleasant little patio full of artificial flowers and other decorations. Parking can be difficult.

☆☆ Moderate

â Hostal Seneca (B2, **14** on the map): Conde y Luque 7, 14003 Córdoba. ☎ and fax: 747-32-34. Closed for a fortnight in August and at Christmas. A nice little *hostal* run by a lovely French lady. A very clean, simple establishment with a friendly atmosphere, set around an attractive patio. Rooms with or without showers, between 30 and 39€ depending on season. Breakfast included. This is one of the nicest places to stay in this category in Córdoba.

â Hostal Maestre (C2, **19** on the map): calle Romero Barros 16, 14003 Córdoba. ☎ and fax: 47-53-95. Reasonably priced private parking. This *hostal* was recently completely redecorated and now offers good facilities for a reasonable price. Double rooms with bathroom and in theory air-conditioning from about

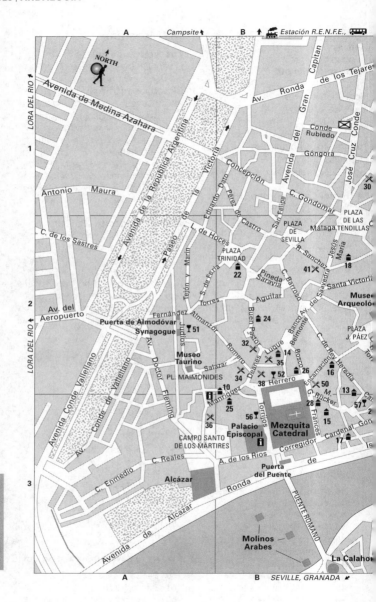

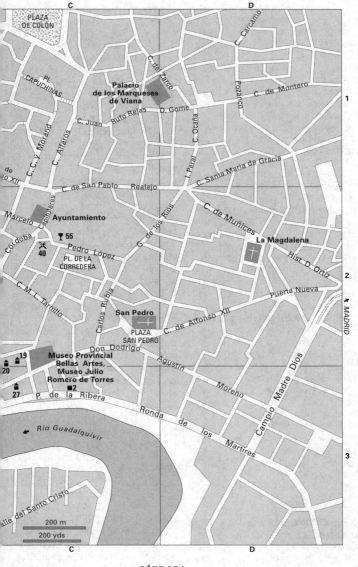

CÓRDOBA

24€ in low season, and from 33€ in high season. Not to be confused with the hotel of the same name next door, which is also very nice, but a bit more pricey. The same people run both places (they share the same telephone number). The interior is elegant with white tiling and ceramics everywhere, and spotlessly clean. There are also family apartments available from 48€.

🛎 **Hostal Luis de Gongora** (B2, **22** on the map): Horno de la Trinidad 7, 14003 Córdoba. ☎ 29-53-99. Fax: 729-55-99. Located on the edge of the Jewish Quarter next to the Escuela de Artes Aplicadas. Closed for a week in June and at Christmas. A classic, comfortable hotel, but lacking in charm and it doesn't have a patio. Double rooms with telephones and spotless bathrooms from about 30 to 36€ depending on the size of the room and the season. It is peaceful and the staff are polite.

🛎 **Hostal El Pilar del Potro** (C3, **27** on the map): calle Lucano 12, 14003 Córdoba. ☎ 49-29-66. This modern *hostal* maybe lacks the charm of those in the old part of town but nevertheless it is well situated, comfortable and relatively cheap, and all the rooms have air-conditioning and a bathroom. Double rooms from 30 to 42€ depending on season. For internet addicts there are three computers available for use for less than 1€ for 15 minutes.

☆☆☆ Expensive

🛎 **Hotel Mezquita** (B3, **28** on the map): plaza Santa Catalina 1, 14003 Córdoba. ☎ 47-55-85. Fax: 47-62-19. Situated opposite the main entrance to the Mezquita. Comfortable rooms with TV, telephone and air-conditioning, from 39 to 66€ depending on the season. There are some magnificent clocks and antique furniture in the lounge, and beautiful pictures in all the communal areas of the hotel. Reasonably priced given its luxurious surroundings and convenient location.

🛎 **Hotel González** (B3, **25** on the map): calle Manriquez 3, 14003 Córdoba. ☎ 47-98-19. Fax: 48-61-87. Located opposite the Tourist Office in plaza Juda Levi. A 16th-century town house that has been beautifully restored to house this pleasant hotel. Rooms from 42 to 69€. Despite being small and not particularly well sound-proofed, all the bedrooms have an en-suite bathroom, air-conditioning, TV and a telephone. The patio is beautiful and doubles up as a restaurant. The owners are welcoming and speak several languages.

🛎 **Hotel Marisa** (B2, **26** on the map): Cardenal Herrero 6, 14003 Córdoba. ☎ 47-31-42. Fax: 47-41-44. Opposite the Mezquita. Double rooms from 56 to 63€ depending on facilities and the season. Extremely well located, the rooms are nondescript but comfortable with a shower or bath. Slightly more expensive than the hotels listed previously and not quite as good. Rather a cold welcome.

🛎 **Hotel Albucasis** (B2, **24** on the map): calle Buen Pastor 11, 14003 Córdoba. ☎ and fax: 47-86-25. Closed in January. Paying car-park (about 12). A very pleasant new hotel (with bathrooms and air-conditioning), but rather characterless, tucked away in a quiet, pretty corner of the town. Double rooms from 54€ in low season, and 66€ in April, May and the summer months. Some of the rooms have a view of the Mezquita's tower.

WHERE TO STAY IN THE SURROUNDING AREA

Campsites

⚑ **Camping M. El Brillante**: avenida Brillante 50, 14012 Córdoba. ☎ 40-38-36. Fax: 28-21-65. About 2 kilometres (1 mile) north of the town, in the Villaviciosa direction. Bus Nos. 10 and 11 go every 10 minutes from in front of plaza de Colón, until 11pm. Bus No. 12 goes from the junction of José Cruz Conde and Ronda de los Tejares. By car, take a right from the plaza along viaducto El Nogal, cross the railway line, then follow Avenida Brillante and look out for the campsite on the right. It's well signposted. A pitch costs around 4€ for one adult, a car and a family-sized tent. There is a wall running around the perimeter of the campsite, which is shaded by eucalyptus trees. There are utility rooms with washing machines and there's a small shop. New toilet and shower blocks right next to the swimming pool, for which there is a small charge. The ground is hard, but the staff are friendly, although the best thing about this place is its proximity to the town.

⚑ **Camping Los Villares**: carretera Los Villares, 14811 Córdoba. ☎ 33-01-45. Located about 10 kilometres (6 miles) north of Córdoba. Not very easy to get to on public transport. By car, go along avenida Brillante, then follow the signs for Parque Forestal Los Villares. The site is right in the heart of a woodland park, so there is a huge amount of space and lots of shade. A pitch costs about 11€ for two people, one car and a tent. Decent bathrooms. The campsite is quite close the Andalucían fire service depot and in the height of summer, their

small planes and helicopters can make it noisy.

⚑ **La Campiña**: 14547 La Guijarrosa. Situated about 38 kilometres (24 miles) from Córdoba. ☎ and fax: 731-53-03. >From Córdoba, take the N IV, exit No. 424 (Aldea Quintana), continue to Aldea Quintana, then follow the road to Victoria and head in the direction of La Guijarrosa – it's about 2 kilometres (1 mile) out of the village. If you're coming from Seville, take the La Carlota exit and, before you get to La Carlota, turn right to La Guijarrosa. It's really too far to get to by bus. Open all year round. A pleasant, very well-maintained site in the middle of an olive grove. Pitches cost about 3€ per person, with one car and a tent. Friendly family welcome. It is very peaceful during the day. At night the cicadas start up, vying with the noise from the nearby disco. Swimming pool, bar, restaurant (good food and home baked bread) and a small shop.

⚑ **Carlos III**: 14100 La Carlota. About 28 kilometres (18 miles) from Córdoba. ☎ 30-03-38. Take the Carlota exit from the Madrid–Seville motorway. The campsite is set between a motorway and a major road. A pleasant, spacious site with a free swimming pool that is also open at night, a supermarket and a playground for the kids. A pitch costs at least 3€ for one adult, a car and a family-sized tent. There are also some bungalows, sleeping 2–6 people. Quite a sheltered site, but a bit noisy because of the proximity to the motorway. There is a bus every 2 hours to Córdoba – a journey of around 50 minutes.

WHERE TO EAT

There are lots of tourist traps in the centre of town so take a good look around before you decide where to go.

⌘ Budget

✕ **Mesón El Rey de las Tapas** (B2, **41** on the map): Rodriguez Sanchez 5. ☎ 48-56-92. Open 9.30am–4pm and 7.30pm–1am. The tapas here cost about 1€ and it's hard to find anywhere cheaper, but this is not reflected in the quality of the food. Not exactly central but a hundred per cent authentic and well off the beaten tourist track. There's nothing of olde worlde charm about this establishment – the TV has pride of place on the fridge and the lighting is harsh and bright. Uncomplicated, good value food. In the winter there's a barbecue in the small central patio.

✕ **La Fragua** (A3, **36** on the map): calle Tomás Conde, opposite No. 12, at the end of calleja del Arco. ☎ 48-45-72. Closed Saturday and Sunday evenings, as well as all day Monday. There's an unpretentious but filling set-menu from 6€. Credit cards are accepted. The interior is air-conditioned, and there are also some tables and chairs on the tiny patio. The à la carte menu offers a choice of typical dishes. The clientele is slightly touristy, but not overly so.

✕ **Taberna Casa Rafaé** (B2, **32** on the map): calle Deanes 4, on the corner of Buen Pastor. ☎ 29-90-08. Located to the northwest of the mosque. Open noon–4pm and 7–10.30pm. Closed on Tuesday. For about 6€ you can choose from a variety of tapas, *tortillas* and paella (although the latter is rather short on seafood). Tourists mix with locals to create a lively clamour. The welcome and the service both leave something to be desired.

✕ **Mesón Restaurante El Burlaero** (B2, **35** on the map): calleja de la Hoguera 5 (entrance from calle Deanes or Cespedes, behind the Mezquita). ☎ 47-27-19. There are two set-menus both costing about 12€, however neither is anything to write home about. You might be better choosing a meat dish from the à la carte menu. The tables are set out in a peaceful, sunny little square – the restaurant's real plus point. Lots of bullfighting paraphernalia at the bar. Not cheap for what you get.

⌘⌘ Moderate

✕ **Casa Pepe de la Judería** (B2, **34** on the map): calle Romero 1. ☎ 20-07-44. A meal costs around 15€ and you can either sit in the restaurant or at the tables outside. Right in the heart of the tourist area, you could walk by it a dozen times without even noticing its existence, but the Casa is a restaurant prized by the locals. You can sit at the bar or in one of the downstairs rooms and enjoy excellent tapas – aubergines fried in honey, fried chorizo, anchovies or hake and pepper salad. The *rabo de toro* (oxtail) is delicious. Note that it's more expensive if you sit at the tables outside.

✕ **Taberna Salinas** (C2, **40** on the map): Tundidores 3. ☎ 48-01-35. Open at lunchtime and in the evenings. Closed on Sunday and throughout August. For about 10€, you can have a tasty à la carte meal, in peaceful surroundings with excellent service. At the entrance there is a nice bar serving tapas. Decorated with barrels, photos, old pictures and all the other paraphernalia typical of a traditional Andalucían bar. The establishment was founded in 1879 and has a covered patio, and some nice rooms with a laid-back, elegant feel about them. The food lives up to expectations and is very much in line with the setting. There are some quite inventive dishes on offer, such as *naranjas picas con aceite y bacalao*, an unusual mixture of oranges and cod.

✕ **Taberna San Miguel** (B1, **30** on the map): plaza San Miguel 1. ☎ 47-83-28 and 47-01-66. Open noon–4pm and 8.30pm–midnight. Closed Sunday and in August. One of the most beautiful and characteristic restaurants in Córdoba, the Taberna San Miguel has been going since 1880. Expect to pay 12€ for an à la carte meal. There are several small rooms, each with a different theme. This is an authentic Andalucían bar complete with guitars, lanterns, ancient ornamental *azulejos*, barrels, mirrors, photos of bullfighters and in one of the rooms inscribed earthenware tiles.

☆☆☆ Expensive

✕ **El Caballo Rojo** (B2, **38** on the map): calle Cardenal Herrero 28. ☎ 47-53-75. This is one of the best restaurants in Córdoba – although the decor might look a bit flashy, the food is varied with both creative and traditional styles and the service is attentive. An à la carte meal costs 24–30€, otherwise the equally good set-menu is about 23€, (available lunchtime and evenings). All the old favourites appear on the menu, although many have been given a new twist. The atmosphere is cosy but elegant. The *gazpacho* is particularly delicious and is recommended when the weather is hot.

WHERE TO GO FOR A DRINK AND HAVE A SNACK

✕ **Bar Santos** (B2, **50** on the map): calle Magistral González Frances 3. In the street that runs along the east side of the Mezquita. Closed on Thursday. A funny little place, which you probably wouldn't think to visit had it not been recommended. Inside the decor is distinctly psuedo-Andalucían and the walls are smothered with yellowing photos of bullfighters. The place has a reputation for its *tortillas españolas* (Spanish omelettes), or you could have the famous fried chorizo. It's best to eat standing at the bar like everyone else, enjoying your tapas with a *cerveza* (beer).

🍷 **Bodega Guzman** (A2, **51** on the map): calle Judíos 7. Open at lunchtime and in the evening from 8pm. Closed Thursday. This *bodega* specializes in white wine. The decor is fairly typical with *azulejos*, a bull's head and photos of bullfighters. The wine is stored in racks at the back and you can go and have a look if the waiters aren't too busy. With pale neon lighting and a TV set, there's no concession to tourists here. Try the excellent *montilla* straight from the barrel. There are a few tapas to complement the wine.

🍷 **Cafétin Halal** (B3, **57** on the map): calle Rey de Heredia 28. ☎ 47-76-30. Open every day 5–8pm. There's a bit of a Moroccan feel to the place with its cushions, benches, rugs and copper plates. Somewhere to stop for mint tea and dates – popular with teenagers and 20-somethings.

🍦 **Croissantería-Heladería Queen** (B2, **52** on the map): calle Herrero 4. Don't expect anything picturesque and you won't be disappointed. This is a good breakfast spot as it happens to be opposite the Mezquita. The Viennese pastries are a bit on the expensive side though.

WHERE TO SEE FLAMENCO

♥ La Bulería (C2, **55** on the map): calle Pedro López 3. ☎ 48-38-39. Closed in December, January and February. Located on the outskirts of the old part of town. There's a show nearly every evening, starting about 10.30pm. Admission costs 10–11€, including drinks. Very cheap for a Flamenco show – fairly touristy, but professionally performed. The food is quite good.

♥ Tablao Cardenal (B3, **56** on the map): calle Torrijos 10. ☎ 48-33-20. Closed on Sunday and in January. Opposite the Mezquita. Good quality shows (which start around 10.30pm) for around 17€, performed by renowned artists. In the summer the show is even better as it takes place outside on the large, pleasant patio.

FIESTAS AND CULTURAL EVENTS

– **Fiesta de la Cruz**: starts at the beginning of May to celebrate spring. Precise dates vary from year to year.

– **Fiesta de los Patios**: in May. The town goes crazy every night. The patios are all decorated and the 31st is the big day for all those entered in the competition. The judging panel visits every patio, awarding points and commenting on what they see.

– **Feria**: held during the last week of May. A fabulous fiesta featuring the typical Andalucían ingredients of traditional dress, couples on horse-back, wine stalls, castanets and dancing. You can get tickets from the bullring or the Ronda de los Tejares. Note that some shops and museums close early in the afternoon for the whole Feria week.

– **Cata del Vino**: wine-tasting festival in May lasting several days. All the local vineyards submit their wines for tastings. The festival takes place on the avenida de America at the junction with Acera Guerrita.

WHAT TO SEE

Some museums and sites are free one day a week. These are listed below, but unfortunately the day seems to change from time to time so it's probably best to check with the tourist information office. As usual, the opening times listed here should only be used as guidelines.

★ **La Torre de la Calahorra** (on map B3): on the other side of the Roman bridge. ☎ 29-39-29. Fax: 720-66-77. From 1 May to 30 September, opening hours are 10am–2pm and 4.30–8.30pm; and for the rest of the year 10am–6pm. Admission costs 4–5€ including the slide show. This large Moorish tower houses a sort of museum dedicated to Islam. It was founded by Roger Garaudy, a revisionist who denied the existence of the Nazi gas chambers and has now converted to Islam. There is an audio tour available in a number of languages (English, French, Spanish and German) although it makes no reference to the history of the caliphate of Córdoba, of its grandeur in the ninth and tenth centuries and subsequent decline, and simply expounds Garaudy's religious beliefs, which can be moving or irritating depending on your sympathies.

★ **La Mezquita** (the Mosque-Cathedral; B3 on the map): ☎ 47-05-12. Open every day, 8.30am–7pm in summer (last ticket sold at 6.30pm), and 10am–7pm in winter. Tickets cost around 5€, although admission is free if you want to attend a service, usually held on a Sunday morning. If you're wearing a hat, it should be removed before you enter the building.

It was the growing number of Muslims in Córdoba who in 784 AD urged Abd al-Rahman I, the then leader of this independent emirate, to raze to the ground the church that was orginally on the site and build what was to be the biggest mosque in the Islamic world at that time.

Long before the Christians arrived in the area, the Romans had built a temple dedicated to Janus on the site. When the mosque was built, the Roman and the Visigoth temples that had stood there were destroyed and their stones used in its construction. The Mezquita was not just a place of worship but also a university and a court of law – even before the last stone was laid, the building was bustling with life, a great testament to the success of its creator, Abd al-Rahman II.

But the work was not over, and al-Rahman's successor extended the mosque, which was already too small, adding eight transversal naves. In the 10th century a further 12 were added. Not only is it the most interesting building in Córdoba, but probably in the whole of Andalucía, matched only by the Alhambra in Granada. Its forest of marble pillars is one of the most striking and unusual images in the history of architecture.

– **El Patio de los Naranjos** (Court of Oranges): entry to the Mezquita is via this courtyard. It was redesigned after the Reconquest as under the Muslims it contained only palm trees and three fountains for the performance of ritual ablutions before prayer. The patio you see today dates from a much later period. The orange trees are said to have been planted during the reign of the Catholic Queen Isabella because she was partial to marmalade, which is, of course made from bitter oranges. In spite of the slightly neglected air of the patio you can still make out the irrigation channels dug by the Moors.

– **The Interior**: if you only see one thing in Córdoba it must be the pillared interior of La Mezquita. Before the Reconquest there were more than 900 pillars but today only 856 remain. A real mark of the architect's genius is the way the ceiling height is almost doubled by a second row of arches, set above the first. This touch was almost certainly inspired by the designs of the ancient aqueducts scattered throughout Iberian peninsula.

The elegance and beauty of the red and white marble arches is stunning. It's easy to make out the ones that came from the ancient basilica because of their very fine carvings. Also, some columns are taller than others so they had to be sunk deeper into the floor of the building. One of these tall pillars comes from Egypt and dates from the reign of Amenophis IV. If you look closely you can see that some of the columns are at an angle – a result of the great Lisbon earthquake, whose tremors affected buildings as far a field as the Mezquita. It is easy to get confused and overawed by this labyrinth of beautiful pillars so give yourself plenty of time to admire the detail and sheer dimensions of the building. In one corner of the mosque the remains of the former basilica of St Vincent can still be seen.

– **The Mihrab and Maksura**: at the very heart of the mosque lies the Mihrab (the niche indicating the direction of Mecca) and the Maksura (the enclosure reserved for the caliph), the most sacred parts of the building. Only the caliph and his court had access to these areas and they represent the peak of Islamic 'baroque' – carvings, golden mosaics, arabesques and inscriptions from the Koran incorporated into marble panels using mosaics and gold-leaf. The faithful, who were obliged to bow down in prayer seven times a day have worn away the marble in places. The staggeringly beautiful cupola of the central sanctuary was cut from a single block of marble in the shape of a shell. The Byzantine mosaics with which it is decorated, consist of thousands of tiny gold, glass and ceramic tiles and were a gift of the 10th-century emperor of Constantinople. Running all the way round the Mihrab is a frieze in gold and blue, listing the 99 names of Allah. Above are the windows through which the women were allowed to see inside the mosque. On each side of the Mihrab, there is a plaster tree of life which symbolizes eternity, and an oil lamp stolen from the Berbers in the 11th century is suspended on a chain hanging from the cupola.

– **The Chapel of St Teresa**: to the left of the Mihrab. It is very strange to come across this Christian baroque chapel in these exotic surroundings. It contains the tomb of a cardinal as well as several paintings, though its main point of interest is a 17th-century ivory statue of Christ.

– **The Cathedral**: following the Reconquest of Córdoba, Carlos V gave permission for the central part of the mosque to be destroyed in order to construct a cathedral. When he next came to Córdoba he bitterly regretted his decision. 'If I had known', he said to the canons, 'what you were going to do, I would not have allowed it, you have destroyed something unique and built something commonplace.'

This 16th-century, Renaissance-style cathedral would probably have been perfectly acceptable had it been built somewhere else. Its strange, heavily worked transept and the multiple rounded ribs contrast too strongly with the serenity of the Islamic architecture. The choir is a mish-mash of all the styles of the period – Gothic, Renaissance, Plateresque and baroque. The transept is Gothic, the nave early baroque and the cupola High Renaissance. As for the columns, they are an indiscriminate mix but take a look at the beautiful pews that are carved from mahogany imported from Cuba, the pink marble altar and the two pulpits, one resting on a pink marble ox. Several of the surrounding chapels also have beautifully decorated altarpieces. The middle of the Mezquita is a strange place to build a cathedral but its existence may have prevented the destruction of the mosque in its entirety, which would have been a tragedy.

– **The Most Recent Section** (end of the 10th century) stands out because of its rows of identical, black marble columns. To make the new section harmonize with the older, the arches were made of stone then painted red to mimic brick work. Each column bears the signature of the Arab sculptor who created it, making an interesting detail. A display cabinet contains copies of the signatures of all the artists.

★ **El Alcázar** (A3 on the map): entrance in calle Caballerizas Reales. ☎ 42-01-51. Opening times in summer are 10am–2pm and 6–8pm, in winter, 10am–2pm and 4.30–6.30pm, on Sunday it is open 9.30am–3pm. Closed

Monday. Admission costs about 2€ during the week, with a discount for students and is free at weekends.

This fortress overlooking the Guadalquivir dates from the 14th century. Originally a palace, it was built by the Catholic Monarchs. It was later appropriated by the Inquisition, which used it as its headquarters for more than 300 years. It has no connection with the Alcázar of Seville. This building is much more unassuming, especially as so little remains today. Some of the stones (to the left of the entrance) may well be of archaeological significance and there are some interesting Roman mosaics on display that date from the time of Emperor Augustus. One of them has alternating geometrical motifs and another shows a depiction of Neptune. A remarkable third-century Roman tomb sits in one of the corridors but the site's main attraction is the view of the Guadalquivir from the ramparts. There is a particularly beautiful view of the Roman bridge – 240 metres (788 feet) in length – the construction of which is attributed to Emperor Augustus. The bridge, defended by the imposing crenellated, square tower on the other side of the river, is one of the reasons why Córdoba was able to expand as a town. The tower was built by the Moors who named it the **Tower of Calahorra**. Nowadays it houses the interesting **Town Museum** (*see above*). It is set in the **Gardens of the Alcázar**, which are lovely to wander around.

★ **La Judería** (A-B2 on the map): the former Jewish quarter is the oldest part of the town and surrounds the mosque. The Jewish community of Córdoba used to be the largest in the whole Iberian peninsula and greatly contributed to the prosperity of the town. Enjoy a stroll round the maze of small streets and alleyways, lined with opulent houses, convents and churches. The only physical evidence that this was the Jewish quarter is the synagogue.

– **The Synagogue** (A2 on the map): calle Judíos 20. Open 10am–2pm and 3.30–5.30pm; Sunday 10am–1.30pm. Closed Monday. This small synagogue used to be privately owned and dates from the beginning of the 14th century. It's the only one that remains from that period, other than the one in Toledo. The upper part is decorated with stucco displaying a mixture of Hebrew inscriptions and geometric patterns.

★ **La Casa Andalucía** (A2 on the map): calle Judíos 12. ☎ 29-06-42. Next to the synagogue. Opening times are 10.30am–8.30pm (6pm in winter). Admission costs about 2€. A superbly restored, 12th-century house – you can see the cellar (containing mosaics from the time of the caliphate), the patio and several other rooms. There are carpets, crockery, furniture and an interesting mock-up of the paper-making process – as Córdoba was the first town in Europe to make paper in the 10th century.

★ **La calle de las Flores**: a charming street not far from the cathedral leading to calle Velázquez Bosco. It is a delightful place to wander, and from a square at the end of the street admire the picturesque view of the cathedral's tower.

★ In the same vein, **calle Pedro Jimenez** is famous for being the shortest street in the town. It goes by the name of calle del Pañuelo (pocket handkerchief street) because of its size.

★ At the junction of calle Cardenal Herrero (on the north side of the Mezquita) and calle Magistral González Frances, at the top of a double flight of steps, sits the **Virgen de los Faroles** (Virgin of the Lamps). The statue is copied from a canvas by the brother of Julio Romero de Torres. The two women at the feet of the Virgin are allegories of sacred and profane love.

The Museums

★ **El Palacio de Viana** (C1 on the map): plaza Don Gome 2. ☎ 48-01-34. At the bottom of calle Enrique Redel. Note that it is only open 10am–2pm in summer, and 10am–1pm and 4–6pm in winter. It is closed on Saturday afternoon and on Sunday. Admission costs about 3€ and tickets can be bought for the patios only, or for the palace and the patios. This is a splendid building, especially if you like patios. The visit is split into two sections – you can either just wander through the 13 superb patios that surround the building or join a guided tour of the palace (in Spanish only). There is a huge variety of patios – some are vaulted, others have pools, gardens, flower beds, orange trees and beautiful wisteria. You get a leaflet in English with your ticket.

The palace itself dates from the 14th century, but it has been renovated several times, extensively in the 17th century. Most of the rooms on the tour are decorated in the styles of the 17th and 18th centuries. Apart from the palace's interesting decor, there are many paintings, a collection of ceramics from the Spanish aristocracy, a display of superb leatherwork (from the 15th and 16th centuries), some tapestries based on designs by Goya, display cases full of pretty porcelain dating from the 18th century and a ceiling made from beautiful carved wood. The 'French Room' has a portrait of Franco, who once stayed here. The guided tour is interesting even though the guides only speak Spanish.

★ **El Museo Provincial de Bellas Artes** (Provincial Museum of Fine Art; C2-3 on the map): plaza del Potro. ☎ 43-33-45. Open all year round, Tuesday 3–8pm, Wednesday to Saturday 9am–8pm, Sunday and public holidays 9am–3pm. Closed on Monday. Admission is free for EU citizens, if you can show some form of identification. This museum and the Julio Romero de Torres museum are both situated in a beautiful patio shaded by orange trees and paved with tiny pebbles arranged in elegant arabesque patterns.

Housed in a beautiful building that was built as a hospital during the reign of the Catholic Monarchs in the 16th century, the museum has on display several paintings by Spanish baroque artists, some of which are from the Zurbarán school. The ground floor is dedicated to the 19th and 20th centuries and has several interesting pieces by artists from Córdoba. In one room, containing mostly sculptures by Mateo Inurria Lainosa, you can also see some beautiful paintings by Rafael Romero de Torres (brother of the famous Julio), including the moving *Últimos sacramentos* (last rites). The work of Tomás Muñoz Lucena is also very interesting. In the chapel there are more baroque paintings including works by Valdés Leal. The first floor has another collection of drawings and engravings, and some very interesting 15th- and 16th-century pictures, including *Christ with Columns*, an interesting combination of medieval and Renaissance influences.

★ **El Museo Julio Romero de Torres** (C2-3 on the map): in the same building as the Fine Arts Museum. ☎ 49-10-09. Open 10am–2pm and 5–

7pm (in summer 6–8pm), on Sunday 9.30am–3pm. Closed Monday. Admission costs about 3€ and is free at the weekend.

The 20th-century Córdoban painter Julio Romero de Torres lived all his life in this beautiful 16th-century house, which is today an art gallery. For the most part he painted romantic but erotic portraits of women. He is very popular in Córdoba and there are postcards of his work on every street corner. The gallery is definitely worth a visit. Highlights include the superb *Naranjas y Limones* (oranges and lemons), *Nieta de la Trini*, and the dark *Salomé*. The painting *Cante Hondo* – a reference to the most heartfelt and soulful of the flamenco laments – portrays the various phases of a tragic passion. Also on display is his most famous work, the superb *Chiquita piconera*.

★ **El Museo Municipal Taurino** (Municipal Bullfighting Museum; A2 on the map): plazuela de Maimonides. ☎ 20-10-56. About 150 metres west of the Mezquita. In summer it is open Tuesday to Saturday 10am–2pm, and 6–8pm, Sunday and Monday 9.30am–3pm; in winter 10am–2pm, and 5–7pm. Admission cost less than 3€, and is free on Friday. This 16th-century house, with its delightful patio, contains a collection of posters, paintings, costumes, documents and other objects associated with bullfighting. There is even a model of Manolete's mausoleum, a famous bullfighter who was gored to death in 1947. His desk and costumes are also on display.

★ **El Museo Arqueológico** (Archaeological Museum, B2 on the map): plaza Jerónimo Paez 7. Open Tuesday 3–8pm, Wednesday to Saturday 9am–8pm and Sunday from 3pm. Closed Monday. Admission is free for EU citizens, if you can show some form of identification. A very interesting museum housed in a beautiful Renaissance building. It's a shame that the information provided is only in Spanish. The rooms surrounding the patios house a rich collection of artefacts dating from prehistoric times to the Middle Ages. The most important exhibits include some noteworthy mosaics, statues, tombs and other Roman remains. There are also several beautiful pieces dating from Moorish times, with a collection of copings from Mudéjar wells.

MORE THINGS TO SEE

★ **La Plaza de la Corredera** (C2 on the map): this is a large square lined with shops and *bodega*. Above, countless windows and balconies are adorned with flower-pots. They overlook the market that is held here every morning except Sunday. A good place to get a feel of the authentic, traditional Córdoba.

★ **Los Molinos Árabes** (Arab Mills): a row of Arab mills situated along the riverside. One, the Noria de la Albolafia, has recently been restored, and was used to irrigate the gardens of the Alcázar.

WHAT TO DO

– **Swimming pools**: El Fontanar, parque Cruz Conde, about 4 kilometres (2 miles) southwest of Córdoba. Open all summer. Take the No. 5 bus going in the direction of the hospital, from opposite the Hotel Media on the avenida de la República Argentina; when you get off follow the path on your right for about 200 metres. It is more of a water park than a swimming pool. It's not too expensive, but gets packed on Sunday. The municipal campsite, on the El Brillante road, allows non-campers to use the pool, but you have to pay. It also gets very busy.

WHAT TO SEE IN THE SURROUNDING AREA

★ **Medina Azahara** (off the map from A1): about 8 kilometres (5 miles) to the west of Córdoba. ☎ 32-91-30. Take avenida Medina Azahara from where it crosses avenida de la República Argentina, carry straight on for 5 kilometres (3 miles) then take a right; and continue for 3 kilometres (2 miles). It is well signposted. By bus, take bus No. 1 from avenida de la República Argentina, just before it crosses avenida Medina Azahara. The journey takes about 45 minutes. When you get off, there is a walk of about 3 kilometres (2 miles). From 1 May to 30 September, it is open Tuesday to Saturday 10am–2pm and 6–8.30pm, and on Sunday and public holidays 10am–2pm; for the rest of the year, Tuesday to Saturday 10am–2pm and 4–6.30pm, and Sunday and public holidays 10am–2pm. Closed on Monday. Free admission. You get a map of the site and a leaflet in English at the entrance.

You can see the ruins of a former palace complex founded in the 10th century by Abd al-Rahman III for his caliphate. It used to be linked to Córdoba by a good road.

Unusually, the town had a short life. Less than a century after it had been built, it was ransacked by the Berbers who invaded from North Africa. It is difficult to imagine what the town looked like as all that remains, except for one small area, is ruins.

The town was built on three levels – the houses of the town dignitaries and the caliph were on the highest level, the vegetable and flower gardens, and the administrative offices were located on the middle one, while the houses, the barracks and the mosque were on the lower terrace. Unfortunately the boundaries of each terrace are not easy to distinguish.

One of the more interesting parts is the **dar Al-Wazara** (House of the Viziers) where civil cases and court sessions were held and where the vizier stood in government. Some of the cornices remain. Their style is in sharp contrast to the simplicity of the Moorish arches. There's not really much more to see in what used to be the residential area so go straight to the **salon d'Abd al-Rahman III**, which is the best-preserved of the remaining buildings. It has an impressive reception hall, containing a remarkable series of Moorish arches. Each one is supported by pink and black marble columns, topped with alternating red and black arches decorated with delicate floral patterns. The walls are covered with stucco chiselled into leaf designs. There are also some secular inscriptions by the architects describing how the building was constructed. This was the heart of the caliphate and the place where political meetings were held. The intricate design of the decor includes many stylized trees of life. It is very easy to imagine how it might have looked in its hey-day with carpets, cushions, dancers and music. Further along is the great mosque, but it is of relatively little interest.

The town is currently being restored. The most ambitious part of the project being to bring the gardens back to life with the reinstatement of an ancient ornamental pool.

Just before the car-park, a path on the right leads to the monastery of San Jerónimo de Valparaíso, which is about 20-minutes walk away. You can't actually go into the monastery but it is worth the walk just to admire the facade, which consists of several rows of arches with orange groves on the terraces below. In the background is the mountainside, covered with olive groves.

★ **The Castle of Almodóvar del Río**: about 25 kilometres (16 miles) to the west of Córdoba, in the village of Almodóvar del Río. As you approach the village the castle is clearly visible, perched on top of the hill. Open from 11am–7pm. The caretaker will show you round but he will expect a generous tip for his trouble. He can be contacted on ☎ 63-51-16. The main point of interest is the view of the surrounding countryside from the top of the five crenellated towers. This castle was built by the Arabs in the 12th century and is particularly well preserved. It currently belongs to Opus Dei. If you're going in this direction it's well worth a visit.

★ **La Rambla**: about 30 kilometres (19 miles) to the south of Córdoba, on the road to Málaga. Beautiful pottery and earthenware. The factory and the shop are open to the public until 6pm.

LEAVING CÓRDOBA

By Train

🚆 **RENFE** (central station; off the map from B1): avenida de las Tres Culturas. ☎ 40-02-02. This brand new station is located in the north of the city. It's the main station for inter-city services to places such as Madrid, Seville, Cádiz, Málaga or Barcelona. There's no direct service to Granada, you have to change at Seville; it's actually quicker to go by coach.

By Bus

🚌 **Bus Station** (off the map from B1): plaza de las Tres Culturas. ☎ 40-40-40. Situated behind the RENFE station. Coaches go to Granada, Seville, Almería, Cádiz, Badajoz, Cáceres, Jaén, Úbeda, Baeza, Bailen, Madrid and Mérida from here.

From Córdoba to Granada

The road through these fertile, undulating plains makes for a delightful drive – although you may well find yourself trapped behind one of the many heavy lorries that ply the route past the vast expanses of olive trees.

If you've got time, stop for a while in some of the charming old villages you'll pass through along the way. Particularly worth a look is **Alcalá la Real** (50 kilometres/30 miles south of Granada), which is crowned with a Moorish castle. Further to the west is the delightful village of **Cabra**, with its string of baroque houses. Every year, on 18 June, gypsies come from all over the country to celebrate the *Romería de Los Gitanos* (gypsy fair) on a nearby hill.

JAÉN 23000   DIALLING CODE: 953

Jaén is the capital of the province and shares its name. Situated 107 kilometres (67 miles) from Córdoba and 93 kilometres (58 miles) from Granada, it is fairly unremarkable in comparison with its illustrious neighbours. The town really only merits a day trip, but there are some wonderful panoramic views of the region from the Moorish fortress (rebuilt in the 13th century) on top of the hill. The fortress is now a *parador*, the Castillo Santa Catalina. It's worth taking time to stroll round the old town to see the few interesting churches, the cathedral and to enjoy the pleasant old streets.

USEFUL ADDRESSES

🚹 **Tourist Office**: Arquitecto Berges 1. ☎ 22-27-37.

🚌 **Bus station**: plaza Coca de la Piñera. ☎ 25-01-06.

WHERE TO STAY AND EAT

🛏 **Hostal La Española**: calle Bernardo Lopez 9, 23004 Jaén. ☎ 23-02-54. In the pedestrian quarter, near the cathedral. Go up calle Maestra (the pedestrian street to the right of the front of the cathedral), then take the second street on the right. Doubles cost 21–25€. It has a gloomy courtyard, full of artificial flowers. Some rooms have en-suites but they are all rather depressing. Expensive for what you get, so only for emergencies.

✕ **Bar Doframi**: calle de Martinez Molina 65 (at the end of the street leading away from the cathedral). ☎ 24-16-53. Closed for the last fortnight in August. Popular eatery in the liveliest area of the town, near the Moorish baths. Its location is its main selling point, but the tapas are reasonable too.

✕ **Marisquería La Gamba de Oro**: calle Nueva 5. In a narrow street between Roldán y Marin and V. de la Capilla. Open every day, lunchtime and evening. Its aluminium bar, garish neon lighting and lively atmosphere always attract plenty of customers. A good place for shellfish, prawns and fresh crabs – fried or *a la plancha* (grilled). Simple but good. Full of locals, which is always a good sign.

☆☆☆☆ Splash Out

🛏 ✕ **Parador de Jaén, Castillo de Santa Catalina**: 23003 Jaén. This is the castle on top of the hill. Well signposted. ☎ 21-91-16. Little inspiration seems to have been taken from the old fortress in constructing this luxury hotel – rather it seems to be attempting to look like something from the Middle Ages. As a consequence, this *parador* is totally lacking in charm. All is not lost, however, as the restaurant offers some particularly good cuisine. It is quite expensive, but if you opt for the à la carte menu you can try some very well-prepared local specialities such as Jaén spinach, some interesting venison dishes and a thick *gazpacho*. The tables are set out in a dining room of cathedral-like proportions, which makes the atmosphere rather cold. However, there is a breathtaking view of the valley.

WHAT TO SEE

★ **La Catedral**: calle Campanas. Open 8.30am–1pm and 4–7pm (5–8pm in summer). Dating from the 17th century, the exterior of the cathedral is a fantastic example of Renaissance splendour, but inside it is rather heavy and solemn. Of particular interest are the intricately carved choir stalls and, behind them, the altar in the style of a tabernacle with carved angels supporting it. In the chapel to the left (behind the ambulatory) is the statue which is brought out on religious holidays and paraded through the streets.

★ **El Palacio de Villardompardo** (Villardompardo Palace): plaza Santa Luis de Marillac. Open Tuesday–Friday, 9am–8pm and weekends 9.30am–2.30pm. Closed Monday and public holidays. Admission is free. These were ancient Moorish baths until they were built over to create a rather austere palace, which now houses the **Museo Provincial** (Provincial Museum).

Head straight for the superbly restored baths to see their brick cupola and carved chapters. The museum houses a modest collection of popular art, as well as an unusual collection of naïve paintings by artists from across the world. The origin of this collection was a legacy from a painter who was native to the town. The museum now enjoys international renown and plays host to some very good temporary exhibitions.

★ **Calle San Clemente** and **plaza de la Constitución**: this pedestrian street and square are the town's liveliest areas. Ideal for a wander if you've got time to kill.

BAEZA 23440   DIALLING CODE: 953

There is plenty to see on the narrow, paved streets of this small town that lies 48 kilometres (30 miles) to the northeast of Jaén. This ancient town was, by turn, in the hands of the Iberians, the Romans, the Visigoths and the Moors. It reached its zenith in the 16th and 17th centuries, when the university was founded. A visit to its main monuments could easily be combined with a trip to Úbeda en route for Granada. The only negative factor is the slightly unpleasant smell emanating from the olive oil factories that surround the town.

USEFUL ADDRESSES

❶ Tourist Office: plaza de los Leones. ☎ 74-04-44. Open Monday–Friday 9am–2.30pm and Saturday 10am–1pm. Free maps showing all the town's monuments.

■ **Torreón Puerta de Úbeda**: in the big tower of the Úbeda gate. ☎ and fax: 74-02-30 Email: RENA CIMENTO@informail.lacaixa.es. Open every day 10am–2pm and 4–7pm (8.30pm in summer). A private and very efficient organization offering guided tours, information, maps and brochures. Excellent welcome and the staff speak a number of languages. For a nominal fee you can enjoy the superb panoramic views from the top of the tower.

✉ **Post Office**: calle Julio Burell 19. ☎ 74-08-39.

🚌 **Bus station**: avenida Puche y Pardo 1. ☎ 74-04-68.

■ **Cash machine**: calle de San Pablo 3.

WHERE TO STAY

☆ Budget

♠ **Hostal El Patio**: calle Conde Romanores 13. ☎ 74-02-00. Double rooms cost from 24€ with bathroom, 18€ without. A 13th-century palace in the historic heart of the town. Fairly modern furnishings but on the whole gloomy and uninteresting. Unfortunately, there isn't much else in this price range.

♠ **Hostal Comercio**: calle San Pablo 21. ☎ 74-01-00. Its only merit lies in its central location as all in all, its rather tatty and depressing. Rooms range from 18 to 24€ depending on whether they have a sink, a shower or a bathroom. Little in the way of Andalucían charm – a shame as the house itself is quite attractive.

☆☆☆☆ Splash Out

♠ **Hotel Baeza**: calle Concepción 3. ☎ 74-81-30. Website: confcom@once.es. A 5-minute walk from the centre. Pay parking. A double room costs around 78€, breakfast included. Housed in an ancient convent that has been appallingly modernized. Having said that, the rooms are pleasant enough and perfectly comfortable, and you will get a friendly welcome.

WHERE TO EAT

☆☆ Moderate

✕ **Taberna El Pájaro**: portales Tundidores 5. ☎ 74-43-48. Snacks for around 9€. Under the arcades in plaza de la Constitución. Nothing particularly special but not a bad place to enjoy a platter of ham or cheese while soaking up the warm and lively atmosphere.

☆☆☆☆ Splash Out

✕ **Juanito**: paseo del Arca del Agua. ☎ 74-00-40. Fax: 74-23-24. On the way out of the town on the Úbeda road, next to a service station, 15-minutes walk from the centre of town. Closed Sunday evening and Monday evening. This restaurant is in the hotel of the same name, and is one of the best in the area. Good-quality, inventive cuisine with olive oil as a key ingredient. A meal will set you back a good 24€. No set menu. There are a number of interesting dishes on offer – the pheasant with mushrooms is particularly good. If you want to buy some olive oil, you will be given several to taste, in much the same way as you would choose a good wine.

WHAT TO SEE

★ **La plaza de los Leones** (Lions' Square) or **plaza del Pópulo**: a picturesque square with two interesting Renaissance monuments. The Tourist Office is housed in the Casa del Pópulo, built in 1530 with a Plateresque facade. Next to it is the crenellated Jaén gate, built to mark the passage of Carlos V on his way to Seville for his marriage. On the other side is the Antigua Carnicería – this is the former abattoir and dates from the 16th century. In the middle of the square is the Fuente de los Leones, or Fountain of the Lions, brought to this new setting from the Roman ruins in Cástulo, near Linares.

★ **La Catedral** (the cathedral): plaza Santa Maria. Open 10.30am–1pm and 4–6pm; 10.30am–1pm and 5–7pm in summer. Although the exterior is somewhat chaotic looking and lacking in a unified style, it's still very powerful. There are two particularly attractive doors, the Moorish Puerta de la Luna (door of the moon), and the Gothic Puerta del Perdón (door of the pardon). Inside it has a predominantly Renaissance style, with richly decorated, Italian-inspired chapels such as El Sagrario and La Dorada. At the far end, a small staircase leads up to the tower.

Opposite, on the walls of the former seminary (now a summer university), there are some inscriptions daubed by students in bulls' blood. There is a small Renaissance fountain in the middle of the square.

★ **El palacio de Jabalquinto** (Jabalquinto palace): plaza Santa Cruz. Open 11am–1pm and 4–6pm. Superb Isabelline facade with eight armorial crests and some elegant, magnificently carved, Gothic windows. A superb mixture of the Flamboyant Gothic and Plateresque styles. Unfortunately, much of the interior is crumbling so it's not possible to go inside and you are confined to the patio. But from here you can at least see the amazing baroque staircase.

ÚBEDA 23400

DIALLING CODE: 953

Úbeda, recaptured from the Moors in 1234 by Fernando III, is a pleasant town boasting a centre of remarkable architectural harmony. Its paved streets are lined with a number of ambitious churches and elegant palaces dating from its glory days in the 16th century. The town lies at 757 metres (2,483 feet) above sea level and overlooks a vast plain, lined with olive-tree plantations that stretch as far as the mountains of the sierra Mágina. Úbeda is a good place to stop off, especially as it does not generally feature on many tourist itineraries. There is a lovely walk round the town's ramparts and if you like pottery, don't miss calle Valencia, leading off plaza Olleros.

USEFUL ADDRESSES

🏢 Tourist Office: avenida Cristo Rey. ☎ 75-08-97. Located in the town hall, a big old building in the centre. Open Monday–Friday 8am–3pm and Saturday 8am–1pm.
🚌 Bus station: calle San José. ☎ 75-21-57.

■ **Taxis**: plaza de Andalucía. ☎ 75-12-13.
■ **Cash machines**: there are several, particularly in and around plaza de Andalucía.

WHERE TO STAY

There isn't much in the way of accommodation for budget travellers. The best you can do is try calle Ramón y Cajal, the charmless, noisy main road through the town, where there are a few ugly hotels that are far from value for money. Visitors with more money to spend will find they are only slightly better catered for.

☆☆ Moderate

⌂ Hostal Victoria: Alaminos 5. ☎ 75-29-52. The hostal is located on the first floor in a small, uninteresting building in a quiet street. Carpark. Varying sizes of double bedrooms for around 30€. Rooms are comfortable and have TV and en-suite bathroom. The owner is very friendly. Not brilliant, but the best of a bad bunch.

☆☆☆☆ Splash Out

⌂ Palacio de la Rambla: plaza del Marqués 1. ☎ 75-01-96. Fax: 75-02-67. Closed from 15 July to 15 August. Divine double rooms from 84€, large breakfasts included. In the historic centre of the town. You would be hard pushed to find a nicer place to stay. It is a stunning 16th-century palace, with a superb central patio surrounded by elegant arcades. There are only eight rooms, each of which is different. The furniture and fittings are delightful and many of them look as if they should be in a museum. Immerse yourself in a world of luxury, tranquillity and relaxation.

⌂ Parador Nacional: plaza Vásquez de Molina. ☎ 75-03-45. Fax: 75-12-59. In high season, a double costs around 111€ – at other times around 99€. Peace and serenity are the key words to describe the atmosphere of this luxury establishment that is set around an elegant patio. If you can't afford to stay here, you could enjoy the palatial surroundings by eating in the excellent restaurant (*see* 'Where to Eat').

WHERE TO EAT

☆ Budget

✕ Restaurante El Gallo Rojo: Manuel Barraca 3. ☎ 75-20-38. There is a good set menu offering large portions for around 8€. It is not the most typical of Spanish restaurants, nor is the food of the highest quality, but you are assured a friendly welcome and value for money.

☆☆ Moderate

✕ Restaurante El Seco: calle Corazón de Jesús 8. ☎ 79-14-52. Right in the centre, near the plaza del Ayuntamiento. A good little restaurant where 12€ will easily get you a good meal. Particularly good service and simple but tasty cuisine with a few local specialities on offer. There are also some tables outside in the small, quiet square.

☆☆☆☆ Splash Out

✕ Restaurant du Parador Nacional: (*see* 'Where to Stay'). It's probably better to choose something from the à la carte menu rather than opting for the set menu at around 24€. But after you've enjoyed the large portions of tapas that come free with your aperitif, you probably won't be all that hungry. Classic, perfectly executed, cuisine. Recommendations are difficult as everything is delicious, but you might try the *perdiz estafada con ciruelas* (partridge with a prune stuffing), *cabrito guisado con piñones* (goat with pine-nuts), or the *espinacas esparragadas a la moda de Jaén* (Jaén-style spinach). Perfectly trained waiting staff, an elegant setting (although beginning to get ever so slightly tatty) and reasonable prices considering the setting.

WHAT TO SEE

This is not an exhaustive list as there are numerous interesting buildings in Úbeda. You will see most of them as you stroll around the town. Many buildings are closed to the public and can only be seen from the outside.

★ **La plaza Vásquez de Molina**: the huge square is lined with some of the town's most famous buildings making up the centre of the old town. You can see immediately that the buildings are from one architectural period, giving a strong sense of how the square looked when it was first built.

★ **La Sacra Capilla del Salvador**: on the square. Open 10am–2pm and 4.30–7pm. Admission costs around 2€ for adults, and under 1€ for children, except between the hours of 6.30 and 7.30pm. The church was designed by Andrés de Vandelvira, the famous Renaissance architect. Despite their rich carvings, the facade and the porch are almost sombre in comparison with wild ornamentation of the choir and retable of multi-coloured stone. The four Evangelists, theatrically posed, form part of this animated tableau. These valuable artworks are protected by an elegant Plateresque grill from the 16th century, which is the work of Bartolomé. Along the same sumptuous lines is the sacristy, which is itself guarded by an impressive door.

★ **Santa Maria Church**: also on the square, opposite the Ayuntamiento (town hall). A lovely 13th-century church, built on the site of a mosque. Each century has made a new contribution to the church – the Plateresque grills were built in the 15th century, the Gothic cloister in the 16th, the facade was revamped in the 17th, the interior vaulting was added in the 18th century, and the 19th century saw the addition of the belltower, while the 20th century brought electricity.

★ **San Pablo Church**: on plaza del primero de Mayo. A lovely church with a mixture of styles that marry together sobriety and elegance to create an impression that is surprisingly harmonious. Access is only allowed during services. Visits to the Archives chapel are only permitted between 6 and 7pm, Monday to Friday.

★ **The City Walls**: these make for a pleasant walk in an attractive part of the town. The sloping, paved streets are lined with lime-washed houses. There are numerous pottery shops in calle Valencia.

LA SIERRA DE CAZORLA AND LA SIERRA DE SEGURA
DIALLING CODE: 953

Some distance to the east of Jaén is the sierra de Segura and the sierra de Cazorla, with its lovely natural park – the biggest in Spain. Nearby is the source of the river Guadalquivir, which provides irrigation for most of Andalucía. There are a number of attractive villages set in this rocky, rural landscape and it's a good spot if you enjoy walking. The hamlet of Torre del Vinagre (sierra de Cazorla), offers horse-riding (unaccompanied or with a guide) along the banks of the Guadalquivir. There are several campsites in the area.

The traditional cuisine of the sierras is based on game, such as partridge and hare, and locally grown fruit.

ℹ Information centre: in Torre del Vinagre.

CAZORLA 23470

Cazorla is a good starting point for exploring the sierra. It is a typical village set at the foot of a mountain and has a maze-like profusion of old streets and alleyways. At the top of the town is the castle of Yedra, offering good views of the Plateresque ruins of the Santa María church set amongst a sea of roofs and aerials and surrounded by olive plantations. Swimming is possible in the Pantano del Tranco de Reau and the Guadalquivir.

USEFUL ADDRESS

ℹ Tourist Office: paseo de Santo Cristo 17. ☎ 71-02-02.

WHERE TO STAY

Campsite

⌂ Camping-Cortijo San Isicio: camino San Isicio, Apartado 33. ☎ and fax: 72-12-80. Laid out over a terraced area that forms part of an organic farm run by a friendly Dutchman, this campsite is shaded by olive, fig and almond trees. There are various organized walks aimed at introducing visitors to the local flora and fauna.

☆☆☆ Expensive

⌂ Molina La Farraga: ☎ and fax: 72-12-49. Take the road up from plaza Santa Maria, between the ruins and the Cueva de Juan Pedro, then follow the signs for Molina La Farraga. It's about 5-minutes walk from the square. Doubles from 45€. Eight spotless, individually decorated rooms in an attractively restored building. The pretty garden is laid out in terraces with a small stream, swimming pool. A friendly welcome and peace and quiet are guaranteed. Highly recommended.

QUESADA

Slightly further to the south, Quesada is a delightfully authentic village set amid mile upon mile of olive-trees. There is a museum of paintings by Zabaleta, a painter born in the village.

SEGURA DE LA SIERRA

To the north of the sierra is the lovely and traditional village of Segura de la Sierra. It is worth visiting to see its attractive stately homes set in the centre of the village and its well restored Moorish castle.

GRANADA 18000   DIALLING CODE: 958

Granada is one of the most attractive towns in Andalucía. Set 680 metres (2,230 feet) above sea-level in the imposing mountain range of the Sierra Nevada, it benefits not only from a grandiose setting but also cooler summers than its stiflingly hot sister cities, Seville and Córdoba. Granada's most important monument is the Alhambra, a masterpiece of Moorish architecture where the last Muslims took refuge against the Catholic Monarchs as they relentlessly seized control of all the surrounding land.

Granada is a town on the move – its wide avenues are full of traffic and its narrow pavements bustle with life. There are many exciting areas to visit, including the Albaicín with its old white houses and mazes of winding streets where daily life seems to be played out publicly on its doorsteps.

Nearby is the Sierra Nevada, whose snow-capped peaks provide a magnificent backdrop to the Alhambra and the stunning scenery of the Alpujarras mountains is not far away.

A Brief History

On 2 January 1492, Boabdil, the young king of the Nasrid dynasty, surrendered the keys to the Alhambra to the Catholic Monarchs. So after 777 years of Muslim rule the Moorish era of Al-Andalus was finally over.

The city's expansion had began in 1246 when Granada was established as an independent kingdom by Ibn Ahmar. The Arab Nasrid tribe then ruled over the emirate of Granada until the end of the 15th century. The independent kingdom retained its power, culture and might for more than 250 years until the Castillians and their armies arrived at the gates. One of the reasons that Al-Ahmar and his successors had survived this long was that they paid an annual fee to the Christian king of Castilla in return for his protection. The Nasrids even fought on his side in his wars against other Muslims, for example assisting Fernando III in the capture of Seville. Excellent agricultural conditions, flourishing trade and commerce, and good organization all further aided the kingdom's resistance to invaders. But after the marriage of Fernando and Isabel, the Catholic offensive became harder and harder to resist, particularly after 1482 when Moorish strongholds were subject to pillaging and sudden attacks. After Málaga and Almería had fallen, Granada found that it was the only Moorish stronghold remaining. Dissension within the different branches of the emirate's royal family led to internal wrangling and, a few years later, cut off from all its resources and with its pleas for aid to Muslims in Morocco and Egypt going unanswered, Granada was forced to surrender to the Christians.

Despite Isabel la Católica's promises to the contrary, Muslim rights to freedom of worship and to retain their mosques were eroded and little by little they became victims of persecution and violence. Under pressure, many converted to Christianity. Meanwhile, mosques and palaces were being ransacked, and only the splendour of the Alhambra saved it from being the butt of religious grievances. In the very place where promised tolerance were made, savage vengeance was meted out. The small communities of Arabs and Jews diminished even further until, in 1526, Carlos V decreed that the *moriscos* (converted Muslims) must adopt the language, customs and dress of the Christians. This law was suspended for 40 years in exchange for a tax paid by the Muslim community, a tax that allowed Carlos to finance the building of his palace inside the Alhambra. In 1568, his son Felipe II applied the law without further ado and added measures aimed at depriving the Muslim community of both their land and commercial rights. Revolt broke out in Granada and in the Alpujarras leading to a civil war that culminated in the expulsion of all the *moriscos* who had taken part.

FEDERICO GARCÍA LORCA (1898–1936)

Born in Fuentevaqueros, near Granada, the poet published his first volume of poetry when he was just 20 years old. Concerned principally with the themes of fate and death in the lives of the Andalucían people, García Lorca's works concentrate on the most basic of human passions. He felt a strong affinity with the gypsy soul and was also inspired by bullfighting. It was his poem *Romancero gitano* (1928) on gypsy themes that first brought him into the public eye. Then came *Poeta en Nueva York* (*Poet in New York*) that he published on his return from a trip to the United States. He also wrote a number of plays, concentrating on the tragedies of rural life, the most famous of which are *Bodas de Sangre* (*Blood Wedding*), *Yerma* and *La Casa de Bernada Alba*. He returned to Granada in 1936 when the country was in the midst of the Falangist terrors. He was arrested as a Republican sympathizer and summarily executed in Viznar in the same year.

TOPOGRAPHY

Granada is a big city, but it is easy to find your way around on foot. Driving can be a nightmare as there are numerous one-way streets and a severe lack of road signs. Plaza Isabel la Católica is the main street in town and Gran Vía de Colón is the main thoroughfare leading in and out of the centre. The best option if you have come by car is to park near where you are staying and explore on foot.

– There is an area of pedestrian streets around the cathedral. In the centre is plaza Bibarrambla, and nearby plaza de la Trinidad. There are lots of hotels around this area. To get from the station to the centre, walk the short distance up avenida Andaluces to avenida de la Constitución. On the corner there is a bus stop marked Constitución 3. There are several buses from here, including Nos. 8 and 11, that go to Gran Vía de Colón.

– **The Alhambra** is on a hill to the north of the city centre and is around 25 minutes' walk away, and it's all uphill. But there are buses running from the centre to the Alhambra and you can either pay as you go or buy a one-day travel card.

– The old quarter of **Albaicín** is likewise to the north of the centre, but also on a hill, and is set to the west of the site of the Alhambra. It offers some fantastic views of the palace and town. This is where the old working-class area of Granada used to be, although today most of its residents are very much middle class.

– The **Sacromonte** district is behind the Albaicín, on the same hill.

USEFUL ADDRESSES

Tourist Information

🅷 Tourist Office (B3 on the map): in the Corral del Carbón, calle Mariana Pineda. ☎ 22-59-90. Fax: 22-39-27. Email: www.otgranada@andalucia.org. In one of the city's oldest Arab monuments, near the Ayuntamiento (town hall). Not accessible by car. Open Monday to Saturday, 9am–7pm and Sunday 10am–2pm. English-speaking staff. Documentation on the city and the whole of Andalucía. Free map. Excellent welcome.

🅷 Tourist Office (B3 on the map): plaza Mariana Pineda 10. ☎ 22-66-88. Fax: 22-89-16. Website: www.dipgra.es. In the centre. Accessible by car. Open Monday to Friday, 9.30am–7pm and Saturday 10am–2pm. Closed Sunday. Very friendly staff, most of whom speak English. Free town maps.

■ **Useful Addresses**

- 🅷 Tourist Office
- ✉ Post Office
- 🚌 Bus station
- 🚃 Railway station
- 6 Police station

🛏 **Where to Stay**

- 10 Hospedaje Almohada
- 11 Pensión Romero
- 12 Huéspedes Muñoz
- 13 Pensión Los Montes
- 14 Hostal Zacatin
- 16 Hostal Arroyo
- 17 Hostal Sevilla
- 18 Hostal Lima
- 19 Hostal Los Jeronimos
- 20 Hostal-Residencia Atlántida
- 22 Hostal Zurita
- 23 Hotel R. Niza
- 24 Hotel R. Los Tilos
- 25 Navarro Ramos
- 26 Hostal Gomérez
- 27 Hostal Venecia
- 28 Hostal R. Britz
- 29 Hotel Macia
- 30 Parador Nacional San Francisco
- 32 Hotel Navas
- 33 Hotel Reina Cristina
- 34 Hostal America
- 36 Hostal Plaza Isabel
- 37 Cuevas El Abanico

✗ **Where to Eat**

- 40 El Cepillo
- 43 León
- 45 Chikito
- 46 Jardines Zoraya
- 47 El Acebuche
- 48 Bar Aixa
- 50 La Higuera
- 51 López Mezquita Café Pastelería
- 53 Casa Juanillo
- 54 Dar Ziryab
- 55 La Veneziana, Los Italianos
- 56 Mirador de Morayma
- 57 El Boabdil

🍸 **What to Do**

- 60 El Camborio
- 61 Casa Enrique
- 62 Casa de Vinos La Brujidera
- 63 La Mancha
- 64 Bodega Castaneda
- 65 Pilar del Toro
- 66 Granada 10
- 67 Reine Mora
- 68 La Rocío
- 70 Mesón Las Murallas

GRANADA

A CÓRDOBA, MÁLAGA, SEVILLE ↘ JAÉN, MADRID ↗ B ↗ La C

Estación

NORTH

Av. de la Constitución

Severo Ochoa

Dr.

Santa Barbara

Santa

La Ventanilla

A. San Juan de Dios

Fuente Nueva

Avenida

Rector López Argüeta

Prof. Motos Guirao

Melchor

Almagro

Monasterio
San Jerónimo

Capitán ▲ 19

Gran

Homo de Haza

Homo de Abad

Cuenca Colegios

San Juan de Dios

San Juan

Mano de Hierro

Arriola

San Jerónimo

Jardines
del Triunfo

Hospital Real

Av. Hospicio

San Ildefonso

PLAZA
DEL
TRIUNFO

PLAZA
MERCEI

Puerta de Elvira

20 ▲

16 ▲

PLAZA
BOQUERÓN

Azacayas

▲ 13

Mira
del C

San Juan de Dios ✝

San Juan

San Jerónimo

PLAZA
GRAN CAPITAN

Emperatriz Eugenia

Sócrates

Carril del Picón

Calle de

Santa

Veronica

del

Obispo

Buenseceso

La Paz

Teresa

Tablas

33 ▲

PLAZA
LOBOS

Horno de Malaga

17 ▲
18 ▲

22 ▲

11 ▲

40 ✕

PLAZA
TRINIDAD

San Justo
y Pastor

Universidad

PLAZA
UNIVERSIDAD

Tendillas

Sta. Paula Marques

▲ 10

San Jerónimo

San

Capuchinas

Cárcel Baja

Catedral ✝

San Agustin

Colon

Cárcel
Caldareria

66 ▼

63 ▼

55 C

Calle Castilas

Antonio

Calle del Prats

Puentezuelas

Santa

Alhóndiga

Gracia

M. de Gerona

Los Mesones

Palacio
Arzobispal

Alcaicería

14 ▲

12 ▲

24 ▲

Pl. DE
BIBARRAMBLA

51 ✕

Zacatin

Reyes

Salamanca

PLAZA
DE ISABEL
CATÓLICA

ℹ️

Corral
del Carbón

Moral de la Magdalena

PLAZA
DE GRACIA

Calle

Avenida de Gracia

Martínez

Cruz

la

PLAZA
LINO

Magdalena

PUERTA
DEL
CARMEN

Ayuntamiento

▲ 32

de Gracia

Recogidas

Calle

PUERTA
REAL

Angel

Acera

61 ▼

✉️

Anton

del

▲ 23

San Matias

Gavinet

San

P

Campos

Tejeiro

Nueva

San

Anton

San

Darro

PLAZA
DEL CAMPILLO

PLAZA
MARIANA
PINEDA

45 ✕ ℹ️

Ronda

C. de Alhamar

de Falla

S. Vicente Ferrer

Calle

Conde

de

Cifuentes

Calle

Virgen
de las Angustias

Carretera del Genil

San Jacinto

A MOTRIL, Sierra Nevada, **Alhambra (road access)** ↘ 🚉 B

CÓRDOBA, MÁLAGA, MOTRIL ← | MÁLAGA ← | CÓRDOBA, MÁLAGA, MOTRIL ←

GRANADA

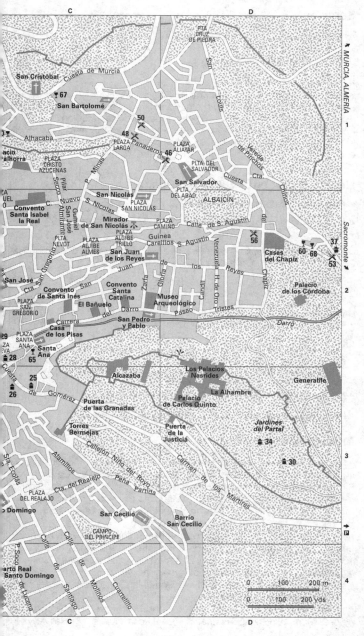

GRANADA

Services

✉ **Post Office** (B3 on the map): puerta Real. Open Monday to Friday 8.30am–8.30pm and Saturday 9.30am–2pm.

Money

■ **Banks and bureaux de change**: the big banks (Banco Central, Banco Bilbao, Banco Santander, among others) are around plaza Isabel la Católica (B3 on the map). The majority of others are on Gran Vía de Colón (B2 on the map). They all exchange foreign currency and have cash machines. Open Monday to Friday, 8.30am–2pm, as well as Saturday morning but in summer only.

Health, Emergency Services, Police

■ **Red Cross**: calle Escoriaza 8. ☎ 22-22-22.

■ **Hospital Virgen de las Niebes**: avenida de la Constitución 100. ☎ 24-11-66.

■ **Police Station** (B3, **6** on the map): plaza de los Campos. ☎ 27-83-00 or 27-80-91. Open 24 hours a day.

Taxis

– **Taxis**: ☎ 28-06-54.

Car Hire

– **Avis**: calle Recogidas 31. ☎ 25-23-58.

– **Europcar**: avenida del Sur 12. ☎ 29-50-65.

– **Gudelva**: calle Pedro Antonio de Alarcón 18. ☎ 25-14-35.

– **Hertz**: calle Luis Braill 7. ☎ 25-24-19.

Miscellaneous

– **Escuela Carmen de las Cuevas**: cuesta de los Chinos 15. ☎ 22-10-62. Fax: 22-04-76. Website: www.carmencuevas.com. In the Sacromonte district. A school offering language, art and history courses, general classes in Spanish literature and culture, and also a flamenco school for foreigners and Spaniards.

📖 **Librería Urbano La Principal** (map A-B2): calle Tablas 6. ☎ 25-11-03. This bookshop is open Monday–Saturday, 9.30am–2.30pm and 4.30–9.30pm. Wide choice of books and very good for the classics by Cervantes, Machado, García Lorca and the rest. It also sells detailed indexed maps of the town. There is another branch at calle San Juan de Dios 33.

📖 **Maps** (for walkers): Cartographic Institute, avenida D. Pastora 7. ☎ 29-04-11. These maps are also sold next to the Tourist Office in Corral del Carbón and in all the city's kiosks and bookshops.

– **Internet café**: Madar Internet, Calderería Nueva 12. Half-way up the street and surrounded by *teter-ías* (Moroccan-style tea shops). Open Monday to Saturday 10am–midnight, and Sunday and public holidays noon–midnight. It is not strictly speaking a cybercafé, but a small room full of computers with students tapping away in front of their screens. There are numerous other places where you can get on-line, mostly around Plaza del Realejo, one of the town's student areas. As a general rule, connection costs around 3€ an hour.

– **Tapichuela**: a useful website (in Spanish and English) with maps and information on the Albaicín and Sacromonte. It is also takes the form of a listings magazine with the same name, available in shops and bars all over Granada. Website: www.granadainfo.com

■ **Lost property office**: ☎ 24-81-03.

BUSES TO AND FROM THE AIRPORT

✪ The airport is around 17 kilometres (11 miles) from the town. The company Autocares J. Gonzalez operates six buses a day in both directions (only three on a Sunday). ☎ 13-13-09. The bus runs the length of Gran Vía de Colón as far as the Palacio de Congresos (conference centre), including a stop in front of the main door of the cathedral. For departure times phone the company or check with the Tourist Office.

WHERE TO STAY

The *hostales* and *pensiones* in Granada do not have the charm of those in Córdoba and Seville, nor are they as clean, particularly the ones in the centre. There are no *pensiones* in the old Albaicín district. Be on the look out for crooks at the station who will tell you certain hotels are full to get you to go elsewhere. The best idea is to phone from the station. Some hotels have parking facilities – either a private car-park or reserved places in a public one. In either case parking is rarely free and usually quite expensive. Unfortunately, though, car- parks are essential.

♠ **Albergue Juvenil (AJ)** (youth hostel): avenida Ramón y Cajal 2, 18003 Granada. ☎ 00-29-00. Fax: 28-52-85. Website: www.inturjoven.com. When you come out of the station, turn left and ask for the Estadio de la Juventud (25-minutes walk). Open all year round, 24 hours a day. As elsewhere in Andalucía, prices from April to October are just over 12€ for the under 26s and around 16€ for the over 26s (with a YHA card). It is around 2€ cheaper for the rest of the year. The hostel has little to offer – it's a long way from the centre, lacks charm and, if there are only two of you, quite expensive. Two people could get a room in a *pensión* in the centre just as cheaply.

Near the Cathedral and the Centre

▣ Budget

This is a selection of a few of the cheaper places to stay. There are others along Gran Vía de Colón, but they are usually quite noisy.

♠ **Huéspedes Muñoz** (B3, **12** on the map): calle Mesones 53, 18001 Granada. ☎ 26-38-19. In a pedestrian street. Doubles with a basin for around 19€. The entrance doesn't look too inviting, but if you dare cross the threshold and go up to the second floor it offers some simple, almost monastic rooms that are quiet and pleasant. Spotless shared bathrooms on the landing. The owner is very friendly and his son speaks a bit of English.

♨ Hospedaje Almohada (B2, **10** on the map B2): calle Postigo de Zarate 4, 18001 Granada. ☎ 20-74-46. A small unpretentious *pensión*, almost hidden at the end of a cul-de-sac, but very close to Plaza Universidad making it wonderfully central. Singles, doubles and triples from 12 to 30€, some of which have hexagonal red floor tiles. There are three spotless bathrooms per floor. The main advantage of this establishment is that it has a reasonably well-equipped communal kitchen where you can meet other travellers and cook some simple meals. It has a laidback atmosphere and guests are given a warm welcome. Advisable to book in advance.

♨ Hostal Plaza Isabel (B3, **36** on the map): calle Colcha 13, 18009 Granada. ☎ 22-30-22. A stone's throw from plaza Isabel la Católica. Small, clean, simple rooms with a basin for around 19€. The family who run the establishment are very friendly and go to a lot of effort to make their guests feel at home.

♨ Pensión Romero (B2, **11** on the map): calle Sillaría, off plaza de la Trinidad, near the cathedral, 18001 Granada. ☎ 26-60-79. Above the Flash bookshop. Small, light, clean rooms for 19€. Simple but pleasant and very centrally located. The communal bathrooms are spotless. If you have the choice, opt for one of the rooms overlooking calle Sillaría where there is a small outside area.

♨ Hostal Sevilla (A2, **17** on the map): Fabrica Vieja 18, 18002 Granada. ☎ 27-85-13. Next to plaza de los Lobos. Spotless double rooms for 20€ without bathrooms or 27€ for en-suites. With the exception of two rooms overlooking the patio, they all have a small balcony. The owners are happy to give you tips on what to see in the town and around the area. Excellent family-run establishment.

♨ Hostal Arroyo (B1, **16** on the map): Mano de Hierro 18, 18001 Granada. ☎ 20-38-28. A classic *pensión* providing just what one would expect in this price range. Rooms range from 12 to 36€ depending on whether they are en-suite, single, double or triple. They are all set around an interior courtyard. A simple, well-kept establishment with friendly owners. There is an outside area where guests can hang their washing.

♨ Pensión Los Montes (B2, **13** on the map): calle Arteaga 3, 18010 Granada. ☎ 27-79-30. In a narrow street about half-way down Gran Vía, on the first floor. Doubles from 24€ with basin, 30€ with bathroom. Simple but very clean rooms. There are two spotless communal bathrooms. Peaceful.

♨ Hostal Zacatin (B3, **14** on the map): calle Ermita 11, 18001 Granada. ☎ 22-11-55. Access via the Alcaicería, the former Arab souk that is now full of tourist shops, or directly from plaza Bibarrambla. Rooms range from 20 to 28€, depending on whether they have a basin, shower or bath. The rooms overlooking the street can be a bit noisy during the day. No. 18 has two balconies overlooking the Alcaicería. Old-fashioned and the minimum of mod cons, but the owner is charming.

☆☆ Moderate

♨ Hostal Los Jeronimos (A2, **19** on the map): Gran Capitán 1, 18002 Granada. ☎ and fax: 29-44-61. Next to the cathedral, not far from the area with all the lively bars. This hotel offers a good level of comfort and is excellent value for money Ask to see several rooms before you decide – some can be noisy, particularly those on the first floor. On the other hand, No. 501 and No. 502 have been recently revamped and offer superb views from their balconies.

🛎 **Hostal Lima** (A2, **18** on the map): Laurel de las Tablas 17, 18002 Granada. ☎ 29-50-29. Private pay parking. A double room with spotless bathroom, air-conditioning, TV and lots of ruffles costs around 33€. The kitsch decor is unforgettable. Friendly welcome and a homely atmosphere.

🛎 **Hostal Zurita** (A2, **22** on the map): plaza de la Trinidad 7, 18002 Granada. ☎ 27-50-20. Pay parking. Attractive rooms, some with balcony and bathroom for 33€, others without for 27€. Small flower-filled, covered patio overlooked by some of the rooms. The ones over the street are noisier but bigger. Friendly welcome.

🛎 **Hostal-Residencia Atlántida** (B1, **20** on the map): Gran Vía de Colón 57, 18001 Granada. ☎ 28-04-23. Fax: 20-07-52. Attractive building with a marble staircase – the hostal is on the second floor. Clean, pleasant rooms from 36 to 42€. The ones at the top, with a terrace and a view are 48 and can be noisy. Avoid the rooms which look over the road as they are very noisy, even if the view is great.

🛎 **Hotel R. Los Tilos** (B3, **24** on the map): plaza Bibarrambla 4, 18001 Granada. ☎ 26-67-12 and 26-67-51. Fax: 26-68-01. Reception on the first floor. The comfortable double rooms cost 60€, breakfast included. The hotel's location on this lively square is a definite point in its favour and the welcome is very friendly.

🛎 **Hotel R. Niza** (B3, **23** on the map): calle Navas 16, 18009 Granada. ☎ 22-54-30 and 426. Fax: 22-54-27. Private parking with attendant, 50 metres down the road. Rooms 39€, with or without air-conditioning and with shower or bath. Have a look at several rooms before you agree to stay as they vary quite a lot and can be a bit expensive for what you actually get. There is a nice dining room for breakfast. Friendly owners. The rooms over the road are noisy.

☆☆☆☆ Splash Out

🛎 **Hotel Navas** (B3, **32** on the map): calle Navas 22, 18009 Granada. ☎ 22-59-59. Fax: 22-75-23. Large, pleasant rooms with all mod cons for 84€, breakfast not included. An elegant establishment on a pedestrian street in a pleasant, central area of the city. Underground car-park nearby but rather expensive. The hotel has a restaurant where buffet meals cost around 9€, half-price for children.

🛎 **Hotel Reina Cristina** (A2, **33** on the map): calle Tablas 4, 18002 Granada. ☎ 25-32-11. Fax: 25-57-28. Private car-park. Double rooms in this central, luxury hotel cost 96€. The lobby is an attractively decorated patio with a white marble fountain and Moorish-style lounge. The rooms overlooking the courtyard are small for the price, the others are larger and lighter but calle Tablas is quite noisy.

Near The Alhambra

Strangely enough, calle Cuesta de Gomérez (C2–3 on the map), the road that leads up to the Alhambra, is lined with cheap *pensiones*. Very well located for taking a stroll in the gardens of the Generalife. Unfortunately, these hotels get booked up quickly and the road is quite noisy during the day. Also, given that these establishments enjoy what is practically a guaranteed income, they make little or no effort to make their guests feel at home.

☆ Budget

≜ **Hostal Venecia** (C2, **27** on the map): calle Cuesta de Gomérez 2, 18009 Granada. ☎ and fax: 22-39-87. On the second floor. A nice place to stay, and reasonably priced. Around 10 well-kept, tastefully decorated rooms ranging from 24 to 26€, depending on size and facilities. There are also some nice triple rooms. There is a vast communal bathroom. Friendly welcome. Free left-luggage facilities available on request.

≜ **Navarro Ramos** (C3, **25** on the map): calle Cuesta de Gomérez 21, 18009 Granada. ☎ 25-05-55. En-suite rooms cost 27€, rooms with communal bathrooms 16. The majority of rooms open onto the rear of the building and are relatively quiet. Variable welcome.

≜ **Hostal Gomérez** (C3, **26** on the map): calle Cuesta de Gomérez 10, 18009 Granada. ☎ 22-44-37. On the second floor. Rooms with basins for 24€. Not as good as the others listed in this category, but not bad if they are all full.

☆☆ Moderate

≜ **Hostal R. Britz** (C2, **28** on the map): calle Cuesta de Gomérez 1, 18009 Granada. ☎ 22-36-52. Smallish en-suite doubles for around 34€. Avoid the rooms without bathrooms for 25€, the price is ludicrous given the lack of facilities. There is a lift, and some of the rooms have small balconies overlooking plaza Nueva but even these advantages are not enough to justify the high prices. Courteous welcome.

☆☆☆ Expensive

≜ **Hotel Macia** (C2, **29** on the map): plaza Nueva 4, 18010 Granada. ☎ 22-75-36. Fax: 22-75-33. On plaza Nueva, the square from where the hike up to the Alhambra begins, and is 5 minutes from the cathedral. There is a fairly expensive public carpark 800 metres along the road. Light, comfortable rooms for 64€ with en-suite bathrooms, TV, telephone, air-conditioning and double-glazing. Breakfast not included. Ask for a room overlooking plaza Nueva, the others have rather disappointing views. Not a particularly friendly welcome and it's a touch expensive for what it has to offer.

☆☆☆☆ Splash Out

≜ **Hostal America** (D3, **34** on the map): Real de la Alhambra 53, 18009 Granada. ☎ 22-74-71. Fax: 22-74-70. In an exceptional location inside the ramparts of the Alhambra itself. This is a fabulous hotel awash with old pictures and ancient artefacts. A double room costs 102€, breakfast included It is a shame that interior design stopped at the doors to the bedrooms, which are very commonplace given the charm of the rest of the establishment. All mod cons. Reserve one to two months in advance in summer as there are only 13 rooms. Good restaurant.

≜ **Parador Nacional San Francisco** (D3, **30** on the map): Real de la Alhambra, 18009 Granada. ☎ 22-14-40. Fax: 22-22-64. E-mail: www.granada@parador.es. This four star *parador* is actually inside the Alhambra, in a former Moorish palace that was subsequently adapted to make a Franciscan monastery and is set in the middle of some beautiful gardens. Unsurprisingly, a double costs nearly 199€ in high season and 178€ in low season, with a 20 per cent reduction for

stays of two nights or more. An idyllic place, although there is no swimming pool. Good restaurant. Reserve one to two months in advance as it is very popular and there are only 35 rooms.

In the Sacromonte District

🏠 **Cuevas El Abanico** (D2, **37** on the map): verea de Enmedio 89, 18010 Granada. ☎ and fax: 22-61-99. Website: www.el-abanico.com. These tiny cave apartments are dug out of the rocky slopes of Sacromonte and set well away from the tourist hordes. Accommodation costs 55€ per night (minimum stay of two nights). and comprises a kitchenette, a bedroom, bathroom and terrace; an apartment with two bedrooms costs 85€ per night. Whitewashed walls and minimalist decor, combining authenticity with modern comforts. Not cheap but an unforgettable experience in an unusual location right in the heart of the gypsy quarter. Accommodation is limited, so it's advisable to reserve in advance.

WHERE TO STAY NEARBY

Campsites

🏕 **Reina Isabel**: on the carretera de Zubia, 4 kilometres (3 miles) from Granada, 18140 Granada. ☎ 59-00-41. Fax: 59-11-91. Website: www.campingreinaisabel.com. If you are travelling by car, take the circumvalación (ring road), then follow the signs to the Sierra Nevada. Take the Zubia exit (No. 2) and it's 2 kilometres (1 mile) further on. There is a bus every 30 minutes back into the city as far as paseo de Salón. The pitches, which are small, cost between 3 and 4€ per adult, per tent and per car. A small, well maintained site, but surrounded by walls that prevent cooling breezes from circulating. As is often the case in this region the ground is hard and dusty. It is also rather noisy, but there is a view of the Alhambra and the Sierra Nevada in the distance. The swimming pool is free and ultraclean. Restaurant. Hot showers are extra. It is also possible to hire chalets.
🏕 **Camping Granada**: 18210 Peligros. 5 kilometres (3 miles) from the

centre of Granada. ☎ 34-05-48. There are buses every 30 minutes between 7am and 10pm from plaza del Triunfo in the centre of the city. Get off at the village of Peligros and then walk the remaining kilometre. By car, take the carretera de Jaén y Madrid or circumvalación (ring road). Come off at exit No. 123 and the campsite is signposted from the first roundabout. The site is situated in an olive grove on a slight hill overlooking the plain. The pitch (tent and car) costs 4€ and there is an additional charge of 3€ or so per adult. One of the better equipped campsites – it has a recently renovated toilet and shower block, hot showers, swimming pool (admission fee), tennis courts, food shops and automatic washing machines. Quiet. Pleasant pitches but there's not a lot of shade. Friendly welcome. There is a minibus that will drop campers off at the cathedral in Granada – it leaves at 9am and returns at 6pm.
🏕 **Sierra Nevada**: avenida Madrid 107, 18014 Granada. ☎ 15-00-62. Fax: 15-09-54. The nearest to the

centre (3 kilometres/2 miles) and very close to the city's large bus station. From opposite the station, catch bus No. 3, which runs every 15 minutes. By car, head for the west of the town on carretera de Jaén y Madrid. Open from March to October. This site has a bit of a prison camp atmosphere – it is large, enclosed by walls and lacking in any particular charm. Around 4€ per adult and 10€ for the pitch. Arrive early as it gets completely full in summer and go suitably equipped to fend off the mosquitoes. There are two swimming pools (additional charge) – one is for children. The old part is fairly well shaded, elsewhere the trees are still too young. Cafeteria and restaurant (fairly expensive). Recently renovated toilet and shower blocks. Children's play area. Quite noisy because of its proximity to the main road. There is a hypermarket nearby.

â **Los Alamos**: carretera de Málaga, 18015 Grenada. 9 kilometres (5 miles) from the city. ☎ 20-84-79. On the road to Seville. Frequent buses. Open April–October. It costs 3€ per adult, and 6€ for the tent and the car. Very shady but near the *autopista*, which makes it noisy. Lovely poplar trees, planted very close together. There are only two toilet and shower blocks, which are not as clean as they could be and are insufficient for the number of campers. Hot showers cost extra. There is a big swimming pool, a small grocery, a bar and table tennis tables. There is a neighbouring village if you need other provisions. The friendly owner lives on-site in a traditional old house.

â **Las Lomas**: carretera Guejar-Sierra, at the 6.5 kilometre marker. It's 18 kilometres (11 miles) from Granada, on the Sierra Nevada road. Take the Guejar–Sierra exit and it is a further 10 kilometres (6 miles) up a steep mountain road. ☎ 48-47-42. The bus company Empresa Lioran provides a service departing from paseo del Salón. Open all year round. Arrive as early as possible in summer as it gets full very quickly. The site is spacious and as it's in the middle of the countryside it's very peaceful and there is a lovely view of the mountains. A pitch costs between 8 and 9€ for a car and a tent, and just over 3€ per adult. Free swimming pool. Well maintained toilet and shower blocks. Hot water. Decent restaurant offering a good set menu and grilled meat in the evening. Supermarket. Nice and cool at night as it is at 1,000 metres (3,281 feet) above sea-level.

WHERE TO EAT

Granada's cuisine tends to be of the good, old-fashioned, tried-and-tested variety. Some of its regional dishes are obviously Arab and Jewish in origin, the most most typical of which is perhaps *habas con jamón*, where the strong taste of the local *trevélez* ham is combined with the melt-in-the-mouth texture of broad beans. You will find this dish in nearly all the restaurants. Another one to look out for is the Sacromonte omelette (with lamb and veal offal), and *pollo al ajillo* (garlic chicken). In tapas bars, some popular favourites include stuffed peppers and *hígado de ternera* (calf's liver). Slightly more unusual, but worth keeping an eye out for, is *gallinata granadina*, chicken with spinach, potatoes and bananas. There are also a few game-based dishes. For the sweet-toothed, Granada has some wonderful cake shops – the typical doughnuts and the honey and nut pastries are especially recommended. All in all, this is an excellent city for eating well on a modest budget.

In the Centre

☆ Budget

✕ **El Cepillo** (B2, **40** on the map): plaza de la Pescadería 18. ☎ 26-70-23. Closed Saturday evening and Sunday. One of the cheapest restaurants in the city with a set menu for around 5€ (not including drinks). The restaurant overlooks a delightful little square where there is a small market in the morning. Arrive early in summer and be prepared to wait as it is very popular.

✕ **Comestibles Cristóbal**: this tiny grocery store is on the other side of the square just opposite El Cepillo. It sells good ham, excellent meat pies, high-quality cheese and fresh bread. Ideal for a snack as you wander round this area of the city. Just next door is a good *churrería* serving fresh *churros* (rather like doughnuts) from 8am to noon and from 4 to 8pm. You can eat them dipped in the thick chocolate served in the café opposite – they'll even give you a plate so you can take them away.

🛒 The local market, in calle San Augustin and calle Pescadería, sells vegetables, fruit and cold meat and has a pleasant atmosphere.

✕ **El Boabdil** (B2, **57** on the map): Hospital de Peregrinos 2. ☎ 22-81-36. From plaza Nueva take calle Elvira and it is immediately after the church. The first set menu, which is little more than 4€ a head, is very filling. Alternatively you can eat particularly generous portions of tapas at the bar, such as *la bomba* (potato stuffed with minced meat) accompanied by a glass of wine or beer. There are some tables outside on the street. If it is busy, don't choose

anything that takes time to prepare or order what the locals are having, otherwise you may have a long wait.

☆☆ Moderate

✕ **León** (C2, **43** on the map): calle Pan 1. ☎ (958) 225-143. Three minutes from the cathedral, next to plaza Nueva. Open lunchtime and evening. Closed Tuesday evening and Wednesday as well as the first fortnight in July. The cheapest set menu is around 6–7€. Popular among people working nearby who often opt for the set menu. If you're not that hungry, the *verdura* (assortment of vegetables) or fried fish, should be plenty. If you're ravenous, however, try the León's special venison.

☆☆☆ Expensive

✕ **Chikito** (B3, **45** on the map): plaza del Campillo 9. ☎ 22-33-64. Near the Tourist Office on plaza Mariana Pineda. Open noon–4pm and 7.30–11.30pm. Closed Wednesday. In the dining room you can get a good meal for 24€ or from the à la carte menu or for 18€ from the set menu, otherwise there is a big choice of tapas at the bar. A pleasant setting and historically significant as it is the old literary restaurant where the El Rinconcillo group, which included Federico García Lorca, used to meet. The walls are covered with photos of celebrities who have frequented the establishment. Excellent house wine. The only drawback is the less than brilliant service.

In the Albaicín Quarter

☆☆ Moderate

X **La Higuera** (C1, **50** on the map): calle Horno del Hoyo 17. ☎ 27-51-56. A restaurant hidden away at the far end of placeta de Fatima. Closed in the evening and on Sunday, and for the whole of February. There is an excellent set menu for between 5 and 6€, but the à la carte menu is also very tempting. The bar's dining room is built on an old Moorish *aljibe* (cistern), which the owner has filled in, although it hasn't prevented the floor from slowly sinking. There is a very pleasant patio cooled by a gurgling fountain and offering a barbecue in summer. Good traditional cooking at a reasonable price and a warm, musical welcome.

X **Jardínes Zoraya** (D1, **46** on the map): calle Panaderos del Albaicín 32. ☎ 29-35-03. Closed on Tuesday. Pleasant meal for around 15€. Depending on the season, you can eat in the dining room or the big, shady garden. Tasty, carefully prepared dishes, light wine, attentive service, all at a reasonable price. There is also a wide choice of pizzas.

X **Bar Aixa** (C1, **48** on the map): plaza Larga. Between the church of San Nicolás (giving the best panoramic views of the Alhambra) and placeta de Fatima. Open all day and every day except for Tuesday. A particularly pleasant place to eat dinner as there are tables in the small square. Set menus for around 6€, but allow around 12€ for the à la carte menu. Look out for such dishes as fried fish, prawns, *migas con tropezones* (a dish made with fried breadcrumbs and meat), excellent *gazpacho* and very good paella. Lively, popular and full of locals, especially around breakfast time. Easy-going waiting staff.

X **El Acebuche** (C2, **47** on the map): plaza San Miguel Bajo 6. Different set menus, ranging from 8 to 13€. Maria, the proprietress is an expert on olives – she combs the Andalucían countryside for the best oils and olive recipes. This is not to say that the cuisine is oily – quite the contrary in fact. An oil suited to your chosen dish is set on the table and added drop by drop, introducing a subtle flavour. There are also some delicious desserts, including a tasty pear tart.

☆☆☆ Expensive

X **Mirador de Morayma** (D2, **56** on the map): calle Pianista García Carillo 2. ☎ 22-82-90. Closed on Sunday. This restaurant has one of the best locations in Granada, on the heights of the Albaicín district, with a superb view of the terrace of the Alhambra. Set menu for 18€. A meal from the à la carte menu costs around 24€. Excellent, locally prepared cold meats and good, traditional, regional dishes. Prices are higher than you would expect, but you are probably paying for the setting as much as the food.

In the Sacromonte District

X **Casa Juanillo** (D2, **53** on the map): camino del Monte 83. ☎ 22-30-94. Simple, good dishes for around 4–5€, in a glazed dining room providing a spectacular view of the Alhambra. The specialities include the famous *tortilla de Sacromonte* (omelette made with offal). The owner will sometimes serenade diners on his guitar. Recommended, although service can sometimes be slow.

♥ Los Faroles: it would be a shame to leave the district without visiting this bar, a short distance beyond the Juanillo. Set in a cave, it is a good place to enjoy the genuine gypsy atmosphere of Sacromonte. Between noon and 1pm, you can look round the tiny Prado de Sacromonte museum, which is full of interesting things. Enjoy the atmosphere out on the terrace with a glass of *sangría* in your hand and flamenco music in your ears.

In The Campo Del Príncipe District (C3 on the map)

This is where the locals go to enjoy a night out. There are lots of bars and restaurants set around this huge square. Very pleasant, particularly on a summer's evening.

CAKES AND SWEETS

✗ López Mezquita Café Pastelería (B3, **51** on the map): calle de los Reyes Católicos 3941. ☎ 22-12-05. Closed on Sunday afternoon. This attractive pastry shop offers a wide choice of salmon, cheese, meat and chorizo pies. Highly recommended.

✗ In Granada, as elsewhere in Spain, 6pm is time for *chocolate con churros* (doughnut sticks dipped in thick chocolate). There are plenty of small cafés serving them around the cathedral.

✗ Calderería Nueva: this small, lively street is lined with a number of fantastic *teterías* (Moroccan-style tea-shops) serving delicious pastries and several varieties of tea. They are all good, but **Dar Ziryab** (B2, **54** on the map) at No. 11 (☎ 22-94-29) offers entertainment in the form of oriental groups who perform on Tuesday and Thursday evenings. The decor is in the style of the Alhambra. Just opposite is **Madar Internet** (*see* 'Useful Addresses'). A little further on is **Tetería Nazarí** (☎ 22-06-82) which is likewise very friendly and has a cocoon-like atmosphere that is very soothing after a hard day's sightseeing. Tasteful decor, nice tea and multilingual waiting staff. Affordable prices.

♥ La Veneziana, Los Italianos (B3, **55** on the map): Gran Vía de Colón 4. Open every day from 8am to midnight. A wide range of ice-creams (marron glacé, jeréz, etc.) and their speciality, *la copa Venezia*. Excellent quality but often packed out.

WHERE TO EAT TAPAS

Almost everywhere in Granada, you will be given something to eat with your glass of wine or beer. It might be a chunk of cheese, a few snails or just some olives and nuts. This is known as a *tapilla* (literally a small *tapa*). If you would like a larger portion, you should ask for a *tapa*.

♥ Bodega Castaneda (B2, **64** on the map): Almireceros 1/3. ☎ 22-32-22. Just behind plaza Nueva it offers one of the finest arrays of tapas in the area, including salami, *chorizo* (spicy sausage), *jamón de Trevélez* and *de Bellota* (ham from pigs fed on acorns), *manchego* cheese and some reliable Riojas. An irresistible choice. Helpful waiters.

♥ Behind la Castaneda, there is a narrow road that is lined with tables, all set outside the numerous bars. Packed at peak times, but very enjoyable and very Spanish.

Y Casa Enrique (B3, **61** on the map): Acera del Darro 8. Near the puerta Real. ☎ 25-50-08. Unobtrusive entrance next to the obvious facade of Solbank. Closed Sunday. Delightful old, cramped bar, famous for its *vino costa*, a smooth little wine that slips down very well with the delicious tapas. It is a charming establishment with rows of hams hanging from the ceiling and barrels lining the walls. Try the goats cheese served with anchovies. Highly recommended.

Y La Mancha (B2, **63** on the map): calle Joaquin Costa 10. ☎ 22-89-68. Between the cathedral and plaza Nueva. Open every day 8am–4pm and then from 6pm until the early hours of the morning. Ham, barrels of wine, and light tapas with less oil than elsewhere. Excellent *gazpacho*. Authentic, simple and cheap. Frequented by regulars.

Y Chikito (B3, **45** on the map): *see* 'Where to Eat, In the Centre, Splash Out'.

Y Pilar del Toro (C2, **65** on the map): plaza Santa Ana 12. ☎ 22-38-47. Near plaza Nueva. Open from 9am–3am non-stop. Once through the heavy door, you will find yourself in a trendy bar that's popular with young locals. There is a splendid covered patio, with a fountain and rattan sofas. The building dates from the 17th century and houses a bar, a restaurant (on the first floor) and a tea room in the patio during the afternoon.

Y There are plenty of good bars with tables outside in the area around plaza Bibarrambla.

Y Casa de Vinos La Brujidera (C3, **62** on the map) Monjas del Carmen 2. ☎ 22-25-95. At the end of calle Colcha, between plaza Nueva and plaza Isabel la Católica. A bar made completely from wood, it's famous for the wide choice of wines it offers from all over the country. There is a good selection of cold meats too. Tables and chairs outside, shaded by attractive white parasols. Low-key jazz or Latin music in the background. Friendly waiters and a predominantly Spanish clientele. Recommended.

WHAT TO DO

– There is a lively area along the river (río Darro), at the foot of the Alhambra. The old buildings on **carrera del Darro** (C2 on the map) now house a multitude of different sorts of bars and pubs.

– **Calle Pedro Antonio de Alarcón** is where most of the young people of Granada go out at night, particularly between plaza Albert Einstein and calle Recogidas. They come and dance in the bars before going on to a nightclub at around 3am. There is always lots of action but rarely any trouble. On Saturday evening, some bars open up flamenco rooms. Teenagers come up and dance with their friends or mothers. It is a great way to see this graceful dance in one of its most spontaneous and natural forms.

– **La plaza Nueva** (C2 on the map) and the beginning of **calle Elvira** is another area that is good for nightlife.

Y Granada 10 (B2, **66** on the map): Carcel Bája 10. ☎ 22-40-01. Open from midnight to 6am. Very near Gran Vía de Colón. The trendiest night spot and an interesting place in itself as it is actually a cinema, complete with original baroque decor (rows of seats and low tables). After evening showings, the chairs are taken away and it turns into a nightclub. It opens around midnight, but there's little point in going much before 3am at the weekend. You'll only get in if your face fits. The dress code seems to be a combination of sporty and smart.

Mesón Las Murallas (C1, **70** on the map): Cuesta Alhacaba 56. ☎ 29-13-06. In the Albaicín. Open evenings only from 9pm to the early hours of the morning. Closed Sunday. A warm, modern bar – sometimes jazzy and sometimes bluesy. There is normally a group playing Andean music on Friday and Saturday evening at around 11.30pm. The drinks are slightly more expensive at the weekend. Very trendy.

– **Palacio de la Música**: calle Arabial, near the corner of Esculptor Antonio Martinez Olalla. Music from the 1960s and 70s and a clientele of 30-somethings.

– There are a couple of clubs, **Lla** (calle Santa Barbara; B1 on the map) and **Perkusión** (plaza de Gracia; off the map from A3) that attract a younger, trendier crowd.

El Camborio (D2, **60** on the map): camino del Sacromonte, in the Sacromonte district. ☎ 22-12-15. Open every evening except Sunday and Monday. Doors open around 11pm, but things don't really get going before 2 or 3am. Entrance costs just under 4€ and includes a drink. An excellent place to round off an evening. Set in a massive cave, the music ranges from *sevillanas* to *salsa*, via techno and house. There is a lovely terrace outside with a barbecue and a great view of the Alhambra.

WHERE TO SEE FLAMENCO

Like in other big Andalucían cities, there are plenty of places in Granada where you can watch flamenco. The degree of authenticity will depend on who is playing and where. If you can find the real thing it is an unforgettable experience. The tourist shows are all around the same price, namely 21€, which includes transport, a short guided tour of the Albaicín district and free drinks. Alternatively, you can make your own way to the venues and negotiate the entrance price.

Reina Mora (C1, **67** on the map): on the edge of the Albaicín district. ☎ 40-12-65. If you go down the carretera de Murcia, it is on the small square by the mirador de San Cristóbal. It is a small venue, which means that you get an excellent view of the dancers, but the large numbers of tour groups detract from the atmosphere. The performances are always of a very high standard. In theory the shows start at 10pm and 11.30pm (the later one only takes place if there are enough people). Call in advance for information and reservations.

La Rocío (D2, **68** on the map): camino del Sacromonte 70. ☎ and fax: 22-71-29. Watch an authentic family *zambra* in a Sacromonte cave. *Zambras* are unique to Granada. In the past they were only performed at gypsies' pre-nuptial festivities, and were even forbidden under the Spanish Inquisition. Although it is largely a tourist attraction these days, the atmosphere created by the clicking heels, clapping hands, guitars and emotionally charged cries is still very powerful. There is a fantastic view of the Alhambra from the terrace.

– **La Buleria** (D2 on the map): Sacromonte, near *La Rocío* (*see above*). Demonstrations of genuine flamenco as performed by the gypsies themselves. Warm, pleasant atmosphere.

WHAT TO BUY

🔒 **Atelier A. Morales**: Cuesta de Gomérez 9. ☎ 81-43-08. In the street leading to the Alhambra. Open every day except Sunday, 9am–2pm and 5–8.30pm. A wide choice of guitars (flamenco and classical) and *bandurrias* (a Spanish instrument like a lute). The majority are handmade, but there are also a few cheaper instruments that have been made in China.

– Further up Cuesta de Gomérez are some other musical instrument workshops, including **Casa Ferrer** and **Antonio Duran**.

WHAT TO SEE

When you walk around Granada, you will have to run the gauntlet of gypsies, all thrusting buttonholes at you as 'good-luck charms' (costing 3–6€). It's up to you whether to accept any of them, though. Another annoyance is the inconsistency in opening times of major attractions. Places may be listed as being open, but these times can change at short notice, so check before you visit, or be prepared to adapt your plans or be disappointed.

If you plan to do a lot of sightseeing, you may want to buy a *bono turístico*, a pass costing 15€ that allows you access to the city's main monuments and museums (including the Alhambra, la Cartuja, the Cathedral and the San Jerónimo monastery), as well as 10 journeys on the urban bus lines. The pass is valid for a week and is on sale at the ticket offices of the Alhambra and the Capilla Real.

The Alhambra

Map reference C–D2–3, *see also* separate maps of the Alhambra and the Nasrid palaces. From April to September, open every day 8.30am–8pm (grounds open from 8am) as well as evenings, from Tuesday to Saturday, 10pm–midnight; from October to March, open every day 9am–6pm, as well as evenings on Friday and Saturday only, 8pm–10pm. Website: www.alhambra-patronato.es (in Spanish only).

To avoid overcrowding, the authorities limit access to 8,800 visitors per day. When the quota is reached, whatever time of day it is, no more tickets are sold.

You are advised to buy your ticket from Banco Bilbao Vizcaya (BBV bank), either in Granada or at any other branch in Spain. The ticket costs just under 7€ and it must be used on the day and at the time printed on it. You can also collect tickets that have been reserved in advance at the entrance to the Alhambra 2 hours before your allotted visiting time. While you wait, you can wander round the gardens of the Generalife.

You can also make reservations by phone: ☎ (902) 22-44-60 from Spain, ☎ (913) 46-59-36 from abroad using a credit card. A small fee is added to the normal entrance fee to cover costs. These tickets can be collected from BBV banks or from the Alhambra.

If you haven't booked in advance, you will probably have to queue for 1–2 hours at the ticket office (at the entrance to the Generalife, or the BBV branch in plaza Isabel la Católica), and there is no guarantee that you will get a ticket as 75 per cent of the allocation is sold in advance. Arrive very early if you intend to turn up without a pre-booked ticket. You cannot buy a ticket for the following day at the Alhambra itself – they only sell tickets for the same day, another reason for booking in advance or through the BBV.

As you would expect, the Alhambra is extremely busy on Saturday, Sunday and public holidays. You will be allocated a 30-minute or 1-hour time-slot in which you can visit the Nasrid palaces and you may not enter before or after this time, although once in, you can stay as long as you like. The entrance ticket consists of three tear-off slips for each part of the Alhambra – the Alcazaba, the Palacios Nasrides and the Generalife. Once again, bear in mind that the ticket office closes when the daily fixed quota of visitors has been reached.

Getting There
– Getting to the Alhambra on foot is fairly easy. It is around 25-minutes walk up the steep calle Cuesta de Gomérez. On the way down you can take the wide path on the right (Cuesta de los Chinos), which runs along the bottom of the ramparts and under the footbridge at the entrance then down into the Albaicín district.

– Alternatively, you can catch the minibus up to the Alhambra and then walk back down afterwards. The red minibuses (lines 30 and 32) leave every 10 minutes between 7.45am and 10.15pm from plaza Nueva. Line 32 links the Alhambra to the Albaicín district.

– Private cars are not allowed on calle Cuesta de Gomérez (the road leading up to the Alhambra). To get to the official car-park you need to get on to the Sierra Nevada road leading out of the town centre, and then follow the signs. However, the car-park is extremely expensive and sometimes full. You might also find a space near the cemetery, but many other people will have the same idea.

The Visit
Built on a promontory overlooking the city, this enormous fortress attracts thousands of visitors a year. The Alhambra, which means 'the red castle' in Arabic, owes its name to the colour that its stones assume in the sun. Far more than a mere palace, the Alhambra is a whole citadel, enclosed by high walls. Within them lie palaces, baths, a mosque, a fortress (the Alcazaba) and some stunningly beautiful gardens.

The Alhambra isn't just pretty to look at, however, but is of paramount historic importance as it is the only Moorish palace built in the Middle Ages that has remained intact. Indeed, instead of sacking it, the Catholics actually restored it.

Originally, the Arab people lived on the neighbouring hill, the Albaicín (a sort of medina). In 1238, the first king of the Nasrid dynasty decided to move to the hill where the Alhambra is now located and built a palace to which

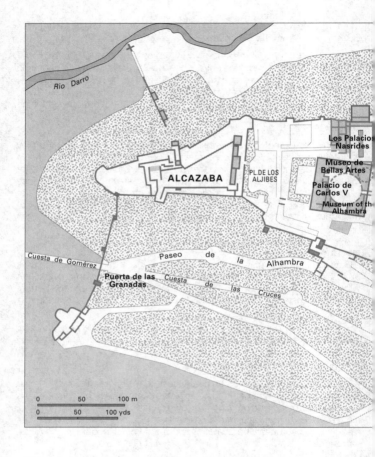

additions were made continually right up to the 14th century. All the main buildings date from the Middle Ages, apart from the Casa Real, which was built by Carlos V – notorious in history for his capacity for interfering with places of classic architectural beauty.

– **The Alcazaba**: the oldest part and the least interesting, apart from the comprehensive view that it affords of the town from the Torre de la Vela. The Alcazaba was a fortress and watchtower from where it was also possible to regulate the irrigation of the valley. The ruins of the old barracks are still visible in the central part of the Alcazaba.

– **Los Palacios Nasrides** or **Casa Real** (the Nasrid Palaces or Royal Palace): these were the main rooms of the emirs' palace. Significant

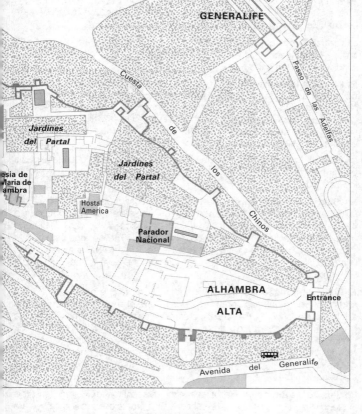

THE ALHAMBRA

rebuilding and renovation work has been carried out by successive generations so it is difficult to date many of the main features with precision, but architectural unity has been retained. The palace consists of a series of rooms, patios, corridors and alcoves. The main points of interest are given below.

El Mexuar (Council Chamber): this is where the sultan received his supplicants and emissaries, and had meetings with his ministers. The walls are beautifully decorated with star-shaped *azulejos*. Note how the floor has been worn away by the millions of visitors to the palace. The delicacy of the pillars is offset by the highly decorative cornices. A balustrade indicates where the mezzanine would once have been. This was the nucleus of a chapel that was built to mark the occasion of a visit from King Felipe IV of France in the 18th century but the ceiling has long since crumbled away. This is followed by the elegant Mexuar patio, its walls covered with delicate ceramic designs.

El Cuarto Dorado (Golden Room): a gallery whose walls are covered with ornamentation and inscriptions. Fantastic view of the city from the tall windows. Carved, golden ceiling.

El Patio de los Arrayanes (Court of Myrtles): this patio is one of the most delightful parts of the Alhambra. The harmonious interplay of light, water and space is accentuated by the large rectangular pool. The sun reflects off the water, creating dancing patterns of light on the patio's walls, animating the carved plaster decorations. The broad arcades with their decorated, semi-circular arches add to the feeling of light and space.

La Sala de la Barca (the Hall of the Boat): the waiting room outside the Sala de Ambajadores. The ceiling is exquisitely decorated and shaped like an inverted boat.

La Sala de Ambajadores (the Hall of Ambassadors): this is where the sultan held receptions and met with foreign emissaries. It is decorated with the most splendid Nasrid art – a wealth of stucco and ceramic tiles and ornamental apertures completely cover the walls. The designs incorporate geometric patterns with verses from the Koran. It is said to have been in this very room that the sultan Boabdil handed over the keys to the town to the Catholic Monarchs.

El Patio de los Leones (the Court of Lions): this is one of the best known and most photographed spots in the Alhambra. The patio is endowed with additional elegance by its double and sometimes triple pillars, maximizing the height of the finely-worked arcades. The arabesques, which initially look identical, are all different. The ornamentation includes verses from the Koran. Narrow canals carry water to an attractive fountain, supported by 12 lions whose origins are unknown. There is a pavilion at each end with decorated alcoves.

La Sala de los Reyes (the Hall of the Kings): adjacent to the Court of Lions, this is a long room divided into several sections. The ornate ceilings and arches are richly decorated. Unusually, the vaults of the arches are pointed rather than smoothly curved. The ceiling vaults are lined with leather and painted with scenes featuring the sultans of the Nasrid dynasty and horsemanship.

La Sala de los Mocárabes (the Hall of the Mocárabes): now a ruin, destroyed by an explosion in the 16th century. The original ceiling (*mozár-abes*) was subsequently replaced by one in the baroque style.

La Sala de las Dos Hermanas (the Hall of the Two Sisters): was the official quarters of the sultan's wives. Once again, the walls and ceiling are intricately decorated with arabesques and *azulejos*.

There are a number of other rooms you can visit before going on to the baths. In particular, there is an attractive patio with a gallery that gives excellent views of the Albaicín.

Los Baños (the Baths): consisting of three rooms – a hot room and a cold room used for washing, and a rest room where bathers could recline while

THE ALHAMBRA – LOS PALACIOS NASRIDES

being pampered and chatting to friends. Look for the ornamental apertures in the vaulting.

Before completing your visit to the Nasrid palace, wander through the large, green and peaceful **Daraxa**, a patio-garden, before heading to the **Jardines del Partal**, elegantly organized into avenues.

– **The palace of Carlos V**: built in the 16th century, its massive, austere architecture may at first seem totally out of place. The bulky, square buildings surround a huge but surprisingly elegant circular courtyard consisting of a two storey of gallery. The first is supported by Doric columns and the second by Ionic columns. From here you can enter the octagonal chapel. Inside, there are two caryatids and, strangely, some statues of satyrs and nymphs. The palace is often used as a venue for temporary exhibitions and also houses the Fine Arts Museum (Museo de Bellas Artes) and Museum of the Alhambra (Museo de la Alhambra).

– **Museo de Bellas Artes**: on the first floor of the palace. ☎ 24-48-43. Open Tuesday 2.30–6pm (8pm in summer), Wednesday to Saturday 9am–6pm (8pm in summer) and Sunday 9am–2.30pm. Free entrance for citizens of the EU. Contains a very attractive collection of paintings and sculptures by Granadine artists, mostly from the 16th century.

In the first room is a magnificent 16th-century triptych in brightly coloured enamel. The next contains some canvases by Juan S. Cotan who is said to

GRANADA

have inspired Zurbarán. Further down, on the left, is a Flemish scene showing the Flight from Egypt, set in 17th-century Holland. There are also numerous sculptures by Alonso Cano, the 17th-century painter and sculptor whose realist works are simple and expressive. Room 5 contains a *Christ* by José de Mora. There are also some poignant works by Pedro A. Bocanegra created in the style of Alonso Cano, including carved scenes of Jesus carrying the cross and depictions of the Nativity. The final rooms contain furniture and pictures from the 19th century. Of particular note are the works by José Maria López Mezquita and Gabriel Morcillo. All in all, this is an excellent museum, there may not be a huge number of artworks to see, but the ones that are there are impressive.

– **Museo de la Alhambra**: on the lower floor of the palace. Open Tuesday to Saturday, 9am–2.30pm. Closed Sunday and public holidays. Some lovely stucco and carved wood including an incredibly beautiful door with delicate marquetry. There are also artworks in polychrome marble and *azulejos* that date from the 9th to the 14th centuries.

– **El Generalife** (D2-3 on the map): a place of relaxation for the emirs. The buildings are relatively simple from an architectural point of view but in contrast, the gardens are absolutely magnificent. In typical Moorish style, there is a perfect harmony between the enclosed gardens, the water features and the patios. The pavilions are set around pools and fountains. At the far end is a tiny palace with a wonderful view of Granada and the Alhambra below. Higher up are the hanging gardens.

– **La Iglesia de Santa Maria de Alhambra**: this little church is behind the palace of Carlos V. Admission costs around 2€, except during services on Sunday morning, but the museum is then closed. Printed guides are available in English at the entrance. It was built at the beginning of the 17th century on the site of the former royal mosque. Things to look out for include the baroque *retablo* (altarpiece) and the fine *Christ on the Cross* above. Right at the top, there is an interesting bas-relief *Trinity*. There is also a small museum of religious art.

Other Places to Visit

★ **The Albaicín** (D2 on the map): one of the most interesting areas of Granada. You can get there on minibuses Nos. 31 and 32 from plaza Nueva. Until a few years ago, the Albaicín had a very bad reputation for crime, with regular muggings and thefts. Gradually, however, the area has become safer as the wealthy middle classes and young professionals have invaded the area – even the Mayor lives there now. Today, tourists are more likely to have their bags snatched near the cathedral than in the Albaicín or Sacromonte districts. Having said that, you should of course take sensible precautions wherever you are.

Built in Islamic style, it is a place that has retained its medina-like appearance through several centuries of architectural change. In the mid-13th century, the district underwent a sudden growth spurt following the exodus of the Muslims as they fled Córdoba. It was also here that the Moors took refuge after the Reconquest of Granada. Many of them were killed in the massacres that took place on Christmas Eve 1568, the rest were finally driven out in 1609. It is a maze of narrow streets and alleyways with unexpected flights of steps, dead-ends and small, paved squares. The patios overflow with flowers and the streets are lined with ancient villas known as *cármenes*.

The Albaicín is on a hillside overlooking the town. Conservationists are fighting tooth and nail to safeguard the area now that it has been rediscovered and repopulated by the well-to-do. These efforts have largely been successful as UNESCO classified the Albaicín as a Human Heritage site in December 1994.

It is difficult to recommend an itinerary for this maze of streets. You could spend 2 hours visiting the main points of interest, or simply pass the day just wandering around. It is probably best to start from the plaza Nueva in the centre of the city and walk along the river. In **calle Banuelo** (the fourth street on the left), you will find the Moorish baths, open Tuesday to Saturday, 10am–2pm. Two or three attractive rooms with vaulted ceilings still remain intact. You could then continue as far as **paseo Tristes** and at the end, on the left, start the climb up the **cuesta del Chapiz**, passing through the **plaza San Salvador** en route. The church of the same name in this square was built on the site of a former mosque, as is nearly always the case round here. Not far off is **plaza Aliatar**, and the lively and attractive **plaza Larga**. A little further away is the 16th-century church of **San Bartolomé**, one of the only ones not to have had its original ochre brickwork rendered over and whitewashed. From the *mirador* (viewing point) on **plaza San Nicolás**, you can enjoy the most photographed view of the Alhambra, Granada and the Sierra Nevada. You could then continue on to **San Miguel Bajo**, from where you can get to **calderería Nueva**, the street where all the *teterías* (Moroccan-style tea-shops) can be found.

Note that the streets are cobbled, so make sure you wear suitable footwear.

★ **Sacromonte** (off the map from D2): the gypsy quarter, above the Albaicín. Only the No. 6 bus provides a direct link from plaza Nueva to Sacromonte. You can also walk there following the same directions as for the Albaicín as far as Peso la Harina. When you get to the statue, take the street to the right, which leads to Sacromonte. A 5-minute walk will take you into a completely different world – the landscape is more arid, cactuses and agaves are the only plants to adorn the rocky ground and the only houses are caves dug out of the chalky hillside.

These caves provide the venues for many of the flamenco clubs, where you can watch *zambra* (*see* 'Where to See Flamenco'). The views of the Alhambra are almost as good as from the Albaicín but here you will be able to enjoy them without being surrounded by crowds of people.

★ **La Catedral** (the cathedral; B2 on the map): in the city centre. The entrance is at the bottom of Gran Vía de Colón, to the right of No. 3, through a cast iron gateway. ☎ 22-29-59. On summer weekdays and Saturdays it is open 10.30am–1.30pm and 4–7pm (3.30–6.30pm in winter); on Sundays in summer it is open 4–7pm and 3.30–6.30pm in winter. Admission is around 3€. On your left you will see the entrance to the Capilla Real (the Chapel Royal). This has the same opening hours and the same admission fee. There have recently been pick-pockets operating in the area, so be careful.

– **La Capilla Mayor**: building began in the 16th century and was in the Gothic style. It was finally finished two centuries later, but in a very elaborate

Renaissance style. It is a stark but unwieldy building, whose main feature is its five naves. The Capilla Mayor (Great Chapel), is 45 metres (148 feet) high and is adorned with statues of the apostles and paintings by Alonso Cano. At the end of the nave, in the chapter house, are collections of religious silver and gold artefacts, and Flemish tapestries and sculptures. There is a superb bust of San Pablo by Alonso Cano. If you're short of time head straight for the Capilla Real.

– **La Capilla Real**: right next to the cathedral. The Gothic-style Chapel Royal is protected by a delightful wrought-iron grill in the Isabeline style. The chapel was built as a mausoleum for the Catholic Monarchs (Isabel de Castilla and Fernando de Aragón). Next to the marble tombs lie the remains of their daughter Joana La Loca (Joana the Mad) and her husband, Felipe el Hermoso (Felipe the Handsome). The tombs on the right are slightly lower than those on the left and are a fine example of the Mannerist style. In the crypt, under the mausoleum, are the monarchs' sarcophagi. However, they are empty, apparently sacked by Napoleonic troops.

There is a delightful *retablo* (altarpiece), depicting the conquest of Granada and the mass conversion of the Moors. In the transept to the left is a beautiful triptych of the Passion. On the right is the sacristy and a small museum. This is well worth a visit as it contains Queen Isabel's private collection of Flemish art. The central exhibition case displays Fernando's sword and Isabel's sceptre. The walls are covered with masterpieces ranging from tiny 15th-century paintings to vast, impressive works like the finely executed triptych by Bouts. There are further paintings by Flemish masters such as Hans Memling (a series of pictures depicting the Descent from the Cross) and Rogier Van der Weyden. There is even a Botticelli, though you may be hard-pushed to find it amongst everything else.

★ Opposite the Capilla Real is an attractive doorway to the **Medersa**, the former Arab university that was built during the reign of Yuzuf I. If it is open, take a look at the Mudéjar-style hall at the far end of the small patio.

★ **La Plaza Bibarrambla**, just next door, is a great place for a quite drink and is a good vantage point to watch the world go by. There are also a number of other bars with places to sit outside.

★ Right next to the cathedral is the **Alcaicería** (B3 on the map), which was the Arab silk bazaar in the Middle Ages. Although the architecture is stunning, the souvenir shops that surround it are definitely not.

Cross over calle de los Reyes Católicos to **corral del Carbón**, a former caravanserai where travellers would have rested in the 14th century. The architecture isn't particularly interesting though as its brick pillars are bulky and unsophisticated.

★ **El Monasterio de San Jerónimo** (San Jerónimo Monastery: A2 on the map): calle Rector López Argüeta 9. ☎ 27-93-37. In summer it is open every day 10am–1.30pm and 4–7.30pm; in winter it is open 10am–1.30pm and 3–6.30pm. Admission costs around 3€. You can buy a booklet with information in English.

There are still 16 nuns living in the convent. Founded at the end of the 15th century and abandoned in the mid-19th century, it was recently revived in the 1980s. The whole building, including the church, the refectory, the chapels and living quarters are arranged around a large courtyard planted with orange trees. Visitors can only see round the ground floor of the superb cloisters that consist of two galleries of arcades.

At 6pm in winter and 7pm in summer it is possible to attend sung vespers, but if you go remember that talking is forbidden. The perimeter of the cloisters is paved with simple stone slabs marking the final resting place of some of the nuns. There are several Renaissance and Plateresque doors under the arcades. The focus of the visit is the church (entrance via the cloisters), which is a mixture of Gothic and Renaissance styles. It's staggeringly ornate – not a square inch seems to have escaped the artist's brush. The coffered ceiling is decorated with busts of dignitaries, angels, cherubim and monsters. There is a stunning *retablo* (altarpiece), dating from the end of the 16th century that was the work of a group of Spanish artists. A series of images recount the holy sacrament, the birth of Christ and the Adoration, among other events. Each successive storey of arches is supported by pillars – at the bottom they are Doric, in the middle they are Ionic and at the top they are Corinthian. Right at the top, in the centre, is a statue of God with Jesus on the cross below.

★ If you are interested in church architecture, it is worth having a look round the **Iglesia de San Juan de Dios** (A-B1 on the map), a fine example of the Granadine-baroque style (richly carved pillars, choir decorated with gold-leaf). This is in fact the chapel of the former hospital. There are also two interior courtyards, separated by a stairway that has a beautiful coffered ceiling.

★ On the left of the river Darro, at the foot of the Albaicín, is the old working-class district. Although it is less typical than other areas, the old streets and timeless stones are pleasant enough for a quiet wander. To get into this district just walk along the river and turn in anywhere you like down one of the side streets.

★ **Casa de Castril** (the Archaeological Museum; C-D2 on the map): carrera del Darro 43. ☎ 22-56-40. On the corner of Zafra, next to the river Darro, at the foot of the Alhambra. Open Tuesday 3–8pm, Wednesday to Saturday 9am–8pm and Sunday 9am–2.30pm. Closed Monday. Free for citizens of the EU (show your passport). Historical relics from Andalucía's past – including Neolithic, Palaeolithic, Roman, Bronze-Age items – are on display in a delightful patio. There are also some attractive funerary urns and Roman statues worth seeing. Many of the finds were made in the course of digs at the Almuñecar necropolis.

★ **El Bañuelo** (Moorish baths; C2 on the map): carrera del Darro. ☎ 22-23-39. Open Tuesday to Saturday, 10am–2pm. Free entry for EU citizens, on presentation of identity cards or passports. Entrance to the 11th-century Moorish baths is through a flower-filled courtyard, which leads to a series of vaulted rooms. The largest has some beautiful ceilings that have small holes that let in star-like pin-pricks of light. It must have been a delightful place to take the waters.

★ **La Cartuja** (the Carthusian monastery; off the map from B1): real de la Cartuja. ☎ 16-19-32. On a hill to the northwest of the centre. To get there, take bus No. 8 from the centre of Granada. Open in summer 10am–1pm and 4–8pm (3.30–6pm in winter). Admission costs around 3€. The exuberant baroque style of the presbytery, the sacristy and the Sagrario makes for quite a contrast with the Moorish beauty of the Alhambra.

The simple entrance to the monastery leads directly onto a patio that is planted with orange trees. Some of the rooms that lead off it house significant works by Sanchez Cotán. This artist monk joined the Carthusian order and entered the monastery in Granada at the beginning of the 17th century. The many art works on display here were painted specifically to decorate these rooms. An exaggerated darkness of spirit is evident in several of these works. The one in the refectory is an especially harsh depiction of the life and martyrdom of St Bruno. The apparent simplicity of the works makes them all the more violent – the monks must have had strong stomachs indeed. The other rooms display scenes along the same lines.

The church is exuberantly decorated with baroque stucco, with a multitude of cherubim and seraphim. Note the magnificent door inlaid with marble, gold-leaf, mother-of-pearl and silver. There are paintings by Bocanegra and Sanchez Cotán in the nave. A canopy surmounts a depiction of the Ascension.

Beyond the church is the **Sagrario**, the small chapel of the Holiest of Holies, dating from the 18th century. Once again it boasts a truly exuberant baroque style with the use of multicoloured marble, an excess of gold-leaf and outrageous relief-work. At the four corners of the chapel stand statues of saints – the cloth that covers them, including the fringes, is made of carved, painted wood. In the centre of the chapel stands an enormous tabernacle made of multicoloured marble, set under an extravagant *trompe l'oeil* cupola.

To the left is the Churrigueresque-style sacristy. The walls are covered in marble and extremely detailed stucco decoration. Some of the furniture is made of ebony and inlaid with tortoise shell – it took a single monk 34 years to make it.

WHAT TO SEE NEARBY

★ **Fuentevaqueros**: some 20 kilometres (13 miles) to the west of Granada, in the direction of Loja. By car, follow the *autopista* towards Málaga and then take the Fuentevaqueros exit immediately after the airport. You can also catch a bus from near the railway station in Granada, from avenida Andaluces.

This is the village where the famous poet, Federico García Lorca, was born. The house that he lived in has now been turned into a museum at calle Poeta Federico García Lorca 4. ☎ 51-64-53. Fax: 51-67-80. Officially open 10am–1pm and 5–7pm, but it is advisable to call first to check. Closed Monday. Admission costs around 1€. Items on display include photos, manuscripts, letters and a video featuring some rare film of Lorca. The collection includes the correspondence that Lorca maintained with Dalí. On the patio, there is a lovingly-tended white geranium, planted in the artist's memory.

LEAVING GRANADA

By Train

🚂 **Railway station** (A1 on the map): avenida Andaluces, to the west of the city. ☎ 27-12-72. Bus No. 11 goes to the station from Gran Vía de Colón.

– Trains to Seville, Madrid, Almería, Barcelona, Valencia and Alicante. As a rule, it is quicker to go by coach.

By Coach

🚌 **Estación de Autobuses de Granada** (off the map from A1): carretera de Jaén, 2 kilometres (1 mile) to the west of the centre. Bus No. 3 goes to the coach station from Gran Vía de Colón. All the companies use this same station. A few of the major ones are listed below:

– **Alsina Graells**: ☎ 18-54-80. There are several buses a day for Málaga, Córdoba, Jaén, Seville, Almería, Cádiz, Huelva, Úbeda, Murcia and many other destinations. Check with the relevant bus company for departure times.

– **Bacoma**: ☎ 15-75-57. Coaches to Alicante, Valencia, Tarragona, Barcelona and Madrid.

– **Autocares Bonal**: ☎ 27-31-00. Coaches to the Sierra Nevada. Three or four departures a day in high season.

LA SIERRA NEVADA 18196   DIALLING CODE: 958

The mountains of the Sierra Nevada swoop skyward to the southwest of Granada, peaking at 3,481 metres (11,412 feet). The Sierra is sparsely populated – there are very few villages – but it is blighted by one vast, ugly ski resort. If you have time, you could spend a day in the national park which incorporates most of the Sierra Nevada, but if you have a car, it is probably better to push on to the Alpujarras. There are plenty of nice walks in the park, but it's not really a place you'd want to stay.

GETTING THERE

– **By Bus**: the Bonal bus company operates two buses a day (three at weekends) between Granada and the Sierra Nevada. The buses go from in front of the *El Ventorrillo* bar, on paseo del Violón (next to the *palacio de congresos*, or convention centre). ☎ 27-31-00. The first bus generally leaves at 9am (phone to check) and the journey lasts 1 hour. The bus stops at the big car-park in the Prado Llano ski resort. There is one bus back in the morning (for visitors who have spent the night there) and another in the late afternoon. It would be perfectly possible to go and come back in a day (the bus leaves at around 6pm from plaza Solynieve). Phone to check as times change frequently. You buy your ticket on the bus.

– **By Car**: a motorway, built in honour of the 1995 world ski championships, carves an ugly scar across the landscape, but makes it an easy drive to the Sierra from Granada.

WHERE TO STAY AND EAT

The resort is particularly unappealing – ranks of uninteresting concrete hotels and a hotchpotch of modern restaurants. Prado Llano underwent massive development for the 1995 ski championships. Much of the resort is closed in summer, giving it an even more desolate air.

🛏 ✕ **Albergue Juvenil Sierra Nevada**: just under 2 kilometres (1 mile) beyond the Prado Llano resort. ☎ 48-03-05. Fax: 48-13-77. Website: www.inturjoven.com. Open all year round. Very modern and ultra clean. An excellent place to stay if you're there for the skiing. Rooms with two, three or four beds. Single set menu, lunchtime and evening.

WHAT TO SEE AND DO

★ If you've got a car, you can go up to **Velata**, at 3,470 metres (1,138 feet) the highest peak in the range. The road that runs past it is likewise the highest in Europe. You have to continue on foot from the *albergue universitario*. From there, there is a delightful trek up to **Mount Mulhacén** – 3,481 metres (1,142 feet) above sea-level and the highest point on the Iberian peninsula. Lots of people come in summer but in winter it's entirely snow-bound and of little interest unless you want to ski.

From Granada To Guadix

A mountainous *autopista* (motorway), the A92, passes through a variety of beautiful landscapes.

PURULLENA 18519   DIALLING CODE: 958

A small village 58 kilometres (36 miles) to the east of Granada, a short distance off the Almería road. Its main attraction is its proximity to the troglodyte caves that have been carved into its chalky hillsides. To get a good view of the caves, you need to come off the main road onto one of the smaller roads and up to the left of the village (if you are coming from the west). In the inhabited parts, the ochre rock has generally been white-washed. Television aerials sprout incongruously from the top of these strange dwelling places and one of the caverns even houses a disco.

Pottery is one of Purullena's specialities. There are shops all along the main street but they aren't necessarily cheaper than anything you would find in the major towns.

WHERE TO STAY AND EAT

The village doesn't really offer enough to warrant staying the night and none of the hotels are particularly enticing.

☆☆ Moderate

â ✕ **Ruta del Sur**: avenida Andalucía 51. ☎ 69-01-67. On the right as you come into the village from Granada. The best available. Its ultra-clean, cold atmosphere makes it feel a bit like a hospital. En-suite rooms. Ask for one at the back with a view of the countryside.

Good restaurant-bar on the ground floor.

â **Hostal El Caminero**: avenida Andalucía 30. ☎ 69-01-54. A double room costs 21–24€, depending on facilities (washbasin or bath). A fairly modern, two-storey building completely lacking in any sort of charm. Nothing much to distinguish it from the Ruta del Sur.

GUADIX 18500　　　　　　　　DIALLING CODE: 958

This town, 6 kilometres (4 miles) from Purullena, is bigger and much more appealing. Similarly surrounded by chalky hillsides, the place has a certain charm. The easy-going, lively streets in the centre make it a nice place for a wander, even if it is not exceptionally picturesque. The cathedral is the only real building of note. The troglodyte area of caves (Las Cuevas) is quite interesting and much less touristy than in Purullena.

The region's culinary speciality is *la cuña de San Antón*, stewed pigs trotters with carrots, dates, dried fruit, all cooked in the local wine.

WHERE TO STAY AND EAT

â ✕ **Hotel-restaurante Comercio**: calle Mira de Amezcua 3. ☎ 66-05-00. Fax: 66-50-72. En-suite rooms for around 57€, set menu for 9€. Right in the centre of town, 5 minutes from the cathedral. A very well-kept hotel with a warm welcome. Reasonably priced meals. Reservations recommended as it is popular with groups.

WHAT TO SEE

★ **La Barriada de Cuevas** (the Cave District): up the hill from the centre of town. Well signposted. Most of them are inhabited by gypsies. A pleasant, quiet place to take a stroll.

★ **Cueva Museo:** the Cave Museum stands on the small village square. Open 10am–2pm (1pm on Saturday and Sunday). There are a few household and peasant artefacts dating from the early 20th century but nothing particularly noteworthy. One interesting fact is that the temperature in the caves remains constant at 20°C (68°F), throughout summer and winter.

★ **The Alcazaba**: open in theory 9am–2pm and 4–7pm, but times tend to vary. The fortress, with its square, crenellated towers was built by the Moors in the 9th century on a manmade hill. Entrance is through a religious college. From the Alcazaba's terrace, overgrown with weeds, there is a fantastic view of the town, the cathedral and the cave district. Nothing of particular note, but a good atmosphere.

★ **El Palacio de Peñaflor**: a brick palace dating from the 16th century to the left of the Alcazaba.

★ **Cathedral**: built in a mix of Gothic and Renaissance styles. Its broad, low, angular facade features protruding columns. Inside, the only real points of interest are the highly decorated stalls and the marble pulpits. As a whole it is rather hefty and lacking in delicacy. Through the porch outside the cathedral is a pretty square surrounded by arcades.

La Costa de la Luz

The Costa de la Luz stretches from the Gulf of Cádiz to the Straits of Gibraltar. The sea on this part of the coast is rougher and the climate cooler than on the Mediterranean and the beaches are ravaged by Atlantic storms from time to time. As a result there are fewer tourists and the area is less crowded.

HUELVA 21000 — DIALLING CODE: 959

This sprawling town is a not the most exciting place to visit, caught as it is between its industrial past and its modern-day present. Huelva doesn't really have a historical centre to rival Seville, Granada or even Cádiz but survives because of its links with Christopher Columbus. According to the city signposts, it boasts several *lugares colombinos* (places associated with Columbus).

It was from the port of the nearby Palos de la Frontera that Columbus set sail to find a new route to Asia and, in one of the best documented adventures in history, ended up in the Caribbean, discovering the Americas. History aside, Huelva offers an excellent escape from the bustle of Seville – although it is just as hot. The wonderful beaches just outside the town are almost always deserted. Another of Huelva's assets is its proximity to the Doñana nature reserve and, of course, Portugal is just across the border should you fancy nipping over for a drop of *vinho verde*.

USEFUL ADDRESSES

🄳 **Tourist Information Office** (A2 on the map): avenida de Alemania 12. ☎ 25-74-03. Open Monday to Friday 9am–7pm and Saturday 10am–2pm. The staff are not especially friendly or helpful.

✉ **Post Office** (A2 on the map): avenida Tomás Domínguez 1. ☎ 24-91-84.

🚌 **Bus station** (A2 on the map): avenida de Alemania or avenida Doctor Rubio. *See* 'Leaving Huelva'.

🚆 **Train station RENFE** (B2 on the map): avenida de Italia. *See* 'Leaving Huelva'.

WHERE TO STAY

It has to be said that staying in places at the lower end of the accommodation scale in Huelva is not much fun. Most of what is on offer is poor and you would be better off paying a little more to get some decent accommodation.

☆ Budget

🛏 **Albergue Juvenil Huelva** (youth hostel, B2, **10** on the map): avenida Marchena Colombo 14, 21004 Huelva. ☎ 25-37-93. Fax: 25-34- 99. Website: www.inturjoven.com. The pricing policy at this youth hostel is a bit confusing, but basically one night will set you back about 6€ or around 20€ for the 'all in' package (bed and board for over 26s). It is well located, right in the centre of town and is a good place to stay if you are looking for somewhere cheap but reasonably decent. It has a pretty salmon-pink patio that is slightly spoilt by its metal framework. Rooms sleep two or four people and have clean, shared bathrooms. The cost depends on whether you are over or under 26 and whether it is high or low season. From April through to October the prices rise with the temperature. You can also go full board, half board or *solo dormir* (bed only).

â **Pensión Residencia Calvo** (A2, **11** on the map): Rascón 31, 21001 Huelva. ☎ 24-90-16. On the second floor of a rather ramshackle building. The rooms cost about 13€ and have obviously been decorated by someone with a marked preference for green. This place offers communal washing facilities, and you get a kind, albeit weary, welcome from the proprietress.

☆☆ Moderate

â **Hotel Los Condes** (B2, **12** on the map): avenida Alameda Sundheim 14, 21003 Huelva. ☎ 28-24-00. Fax: 28-50-41. A room costs around 36€. This is a pleasant, well-situated and comfortable hotel where a certain flashiness hides the fact that it has got a bit tatty. The staff are very welcoming. Ask for one of the top-floor rooms as they are lighter, or a room overlooking the courtyard, as there is a noisy club immediately opposite the hotel. The rooms are spacious and there is a lift.

â **Hotel Costa de la Luz** (A2, **13** on the map): José Maria Amo 8, 21001 Huelva. ☎ 25-64-22 or 25-32-14. This hotel is very pricey for the level of service offered, as a night here costs about 45€. The rooms are huge, but that is the only point in their favour and the welcome is rather indifferent, as if the staff seem to have given up all hope.

☆☆☆ Expensive

â **Hotel Monteconquero** (B1, **14** on the map): Pablo Rada 10, 21003 Huelva. ☎ 28-55-00. Fax: 28-39-12. Very ordinary rooms for about 78€ for a double and 63€ for a single. It's worth noting there's also a weekend rate of about 54€. Mainly used by businessmen, this hotel stands because of its impeccable service. It is extremely well run, the staff at the reception desk are very efficient and parking facilities are available 24 hours a day. You'll either love or hate the decor – ivy hanging from red banisters and a Hilton-style glass bubble lift. One small criticism for a hotel of this category is that there is no cable television. It's also in an area that's full of students making it rather noisy at night.

Campsites

â **Camping Playa La Bota** (**15** off the map from A1): apartado 580, 21080 Huelva. ☎ 31-45-37. Fax: 31-45-46. Well signposted from Punta Umbría. The reception is open 8am–midnight. It costs 4€ per person, 4€ per tent and about 3€ for a car. This large campsite with over 1,000 pitches manages to avoid being too impersonal. The plots are set among bushes and dunes, and some are on a nature reserve. The very eco-orientated staff keep a watchful eye on how much water is used, as it is a precious commodity in these parts. You have to buy tokens for the showers, but they are reasonably priced at less than 1€. There are three spotless toilet and shower blocks, all decorated in colours that are sympathetic to the surroundings

LA COSTA
DE LA LUZ

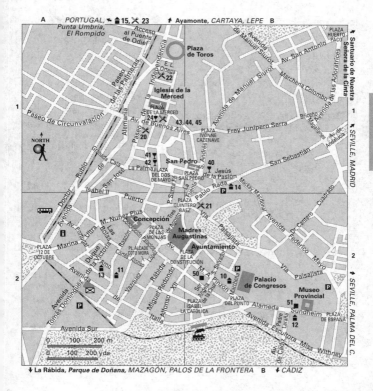

HUELVA

- **Useful Addresses**

  🅸 Tourist Office
  ✉ Post Office
  🚂 Train station RENFE
  🚌 Bus station

- **Where to Stay**

  10 Albergue Juvenil Huelva (AJ)
  11 Pensión Residencia Calvo
  12 Hotel Los Condes
  13 Hotel Costa de la Luz
  14 Hotel Monteconquero
  15 Camping Playa La Bota

- **Where to Eat**

  20 Bar Lisboa

  21 El Rincón de Pablo
  22 Tendito 4
  23 El Paraíso
  24 El Burger de la Merced

- **Where to Have a Drink**

  40 Confitería de Pasión
  41 Moe's Bar
  42 Docklands
  43 Ocho
  44 El Meridiano Cero
  45 El Saxo

- **Where to Dance**

  50 Cochabamba
  51 Alameda G

(pine green and pale ochre). This is a good place to stay if you want to make the most of the great beaches in this part of Spain.

WHERE TO EAT

☆ Budget

✕ **Bar Lisboa** (A1, **20** on the map): this is a good bar for budget travellers or if you're counting cash at the end of your holiday. You get a starter, main course, dessert, coffee and a glass of wine or a beer for under 8€. The downside is the food's a bit bland and the decor is really tacky: an odd assortment of formica chairs on a sticky tiled floor, and a refrigerator cabinet misty with condensation. There's also a parrot, which the owner encourages to wolf-whistle at girls in short skirts when he's feeling bored – you have been warned.

✕ **El Rincón de Pablo** (B2, **21** on the map): Pablo Rada 2. ☎ 26-20-02. Here, 4–5€ will get you a plate of tapas. At first glance this place seems like any other bar. Only its small tree-shaded terrace tucked down below street level, encourages you to look closer. Follow your nose and you will find a good selection of *montaditos* (miniature open sandwiches) with toppings such as anchovies in condensed milk, smoked cod pâté, and prawns and aioli.

✕ **Tendito 4** (A1, **22** on the map): paseo Independencia 50. ☎ 24-25-91. A bar serving refreshingly generous portions of dishes such as *espinacas con garbanzos* (spinach and chick peas) for about 5€. This is a small family-run restaurant decorated with numerous posters advertising fights that have taken place in the nearby *plaza de toros* (bullring).

✕ **El Burger de la Merced** (A1, **24** on the map): *see* 'Where to Go for a Drink' and 'Where to Go Out'.

WHERE TO EAT IN THE SURROUNDING AREA

☆☆☆ Expensive

✕ **El Paraíso** (**23** off the map from A1): on the road from Huelva to El Portil, El Rompido, 21100 Punta Umbría. ☎ and fax: 31-27-56. If you are careful, a meal here won't set you back more than about 30€. Take the road to Punta Umbría, crossing a large bridge over the River Odiel. Continue to follow the signs for Punta Umbría (not for Portugal) and continue until you have passed under two bridges. After the second bridge turn right and carry on for about 1 kilometre. The restaurant is not much to look at from the outside and looks like a large straw hut. It's set opposite an unattractive high-voltage transformer and its large neon sign seems to act as little more than a focal point for insects. But there's a delicious fish menu – especially recommended is the *lubina a la sal* (seabass in salt) at 30€ for two. There are several other fish dishes where the seafood is served in a sauce, which makes a pleasant change from the ubiquitous *a la brasa* (grilled) or *al ajillo* (in garlic). As for meat dishes, the steaks are always good. The dessert menu is excellent – all the sweets are homemade, including the chocolate and pine-nut cheesecake. There is a well-chosen selection of wines that even includes a half bottle of viña Aranza (about 14€).

WHERE TO HAVE A DRINK

As in many student towns, going for a drink in the *marcha onubense* (Huelva style) doesn't include much in the way of comfort. For the most part, the young crowd (mainly teenagers) meet up at Pablo Rada, buy a bottle of spirits from **Confitería de Pasión** (calle Jesus de la Pasión, next to Ermite; B1, **40** on the map) and a bottle of cola or orange juice, and then take it in turns drinking from the various bottles. The police keep a careful watch from a distance and occasionally pick up those who are the worse for wear. A word of advice – don't drive to Pablo Rada and avoid the narrow streets leading to plaza de la Merced as you'll have difficulty in parking and end up spending the evening cooped up in your car rather than out enjoying yourself.

🍸 **Moe's Bar** (A1, **41** on the map): Aragón 17. This is a themed bar based on the Simpsons – but if you're not familiar with the meaning of the expression 'Doh!' and don't know much about what goes on in the fictional town of Springfield, it probably won't mean much to you. It's quite a fun place, however, and worth a visit, as there is nowhere else quite like it, even in the States.

🍸 **Docklands** (A1, **42** on the map): Aragón 7. ☎ 25-82-70. Closed on Monday and in August. The coffee here costs less than 1€, but it's not the drink most in demand on a Saturday night. This tiny Irish bar with its smoked glass windows and yellowing walls is right next door to Moe's. It's quite low-key but not boring and has a clientele to match.

🍸 **Ocho** (A1, **43** on the map): plaza de la Merced 7. The owner of this pleasant bar has made a collection of things related to Huelva. It is rather an eclectic mix of T-shirts, faded student posters and model helicopters, which hang from the ceiling. It is very popular with students and 20-something professionals. Unfortunately, the more people there are the louder the music gets.

🍸 **El Meridiano Cero** (A1, **44** on the map) and **El Saxo** (A1, **45** on the map): both on plaza de la Merced. These two bars get quite crowded, so it's best to take your drink outside and sit in the plaza de la Merced. If you get peckish you can head for **El Burger de la Merced** (A1, **24** on the map), a *chiringuito* (mobile snack bar).

WHERE TO DANCE

■ **Cochabamba** (B2, **50** on the map): between plaza de la Constitución and plaza del Punto, on avenida Martín Alonso Pinzón. It opens at midnight but things don't really get going before 2–2.30am. Admission costs about 6€ and includes one drink. It would be difficult to miss with its mauve facade and its name written in Hawaiian garlands. There are two dance floors and two bars – on the ground floor there is a mixture of soul and funk with a slight euro trash edge and most of the crowd seem to be in their late 20s; in the basement the music is basically hard-core techno. The bar staff all seem to be body-conscious and fit, and are friendly enough.

■ **Alameda G** (B2, **51** on the map): on alameda Sundheim in a pretty park, opposite Los Condes hotel and next to the museum.

WHAT TO SEE

★ **La Iglesia de la Merced** (A1 on the map): the church in the square of the same name.

★ **Museo Provincial** (Huelva Museum; B2 on the map): alameda Sundheim 13. ☎ 25-93-00. Open Tuesday to Saturday 9am–8pm and Sunday 9am–3pm. Free admission. There is an interesting archaeology section that focuses on the town's past, but everything seems a bit tatty and in need of a dust. It would have been nice to learn a bit more about the ancient town of Tartessos, one of the principal towns of antiquity. The museum is definitely in need of a revamp.

WHAT TO SEE IN THE SURROUNDING AREA

★ **The monastery of Santa Maria de la Rábida**: ☎ 35-04-11. Open Tuesday to Sunday 10am–1pm and 4–7pm (6.15pm in winter). Guided tours every 45 minutes. This is the monastery where Christopher Columbus found his faithful ally Diego de Marchena. This Franciscan monk helped Columbus in numerous ways – he brought up Fernando, Columbus's son, and introduced Columbus to Antonio Marchena, another Franciscan monk who was interested in cosmography. Antonio Marchena made use of his network of contacts in Seville to help Columbus get his plans off the ground. He also introduced him to countless other powerful people.

The simplicity of this monastery, built on a small pine-covered hill overlooking the río Tinto, makes it a natural place for meditation. It is set around a pretty brick-paved Moorish patio. Upstairs is a gallery with a display of all the known pictures of Columbus. Seeing all these different portraits of him (especially Chantal Goya's red canopied '*Admiral of the Ocean*') makes it difficult to work out what he really looked like. The Chapter House is also on this floor.

The following rooms display copies of various documents, such as the famous Capitulation of Santa Fe. This legal document contains two sections – one part deals with the surrender of the Nasrid kingdom of Granada and the other with the fine details of the contract between Fernando and Isabel, and Columbus. The terms put forward by Columbus were only included after bitter negotiation. By asking for the title 'Admiral of the Ocean' Columbus, ever the social climber, was asking to be ranked as highly as the king's uncle and the Admiral of Castilla. He also had the effrontery to ask for the title of 'Viceroy and Governor of all the New World' (a direct encroachment on the sovereignty of the Catholic Monarchs), a tenth of the gold, pearls and spices and all the other precious commodities acquired during the voyage, as well as a hereditary peerage placing him among the nobility of Castilla. After a lot of wrangling, terms were finally agreed on 30 April 1492.

There is also an unusual but interesting collection of soil from all the different countries of South America, and a beautiful chapel.

★ **El Muelle de las Carabelas** (The Caravels of Colombus): open Tuesday to Sunday 10am–2pm and 5–9pm (10am–7pm in winter). ☎ 53-05-97. Admission costs less than 3€ (with a reduction for under 18s and over

65s). It is worth visiting the replicas of the three ships (caravels) particularly if you've got children who might enjoy scrambling over them. The boats are very small and it's hard to believe they were home to a crew of 90 and 30 administrators for two months and ten days, but they were. There is also a small display of maps related to Columbus and his discoveries. There's a 20-minute film that might also entertain the kids. Concerts are sometimes held in the Hispano-American forum. For further information call ☎ 53-02-54.

★ **Iglesia de Palos de la Frontera**: open 10.30am–1pm and 7–8pm. The church is dedicated to San Jorge Martir (St George the Martyr). Its Gothic Mudéjar architecture is particularly striking at sunset. It was in this small church that Columbus received the blessing for his enterprise.

★ **The National Park of Doñana**: about 50 kilometres (31 miles) from Huelva in the direction of Cádiz. First mentioned in records from Roman times, the area of Doñana covers an area of over 300,000 hectares (741,300 acres). West of the mouth of the Guadalquivir and to the south-west of Seville, it basically consists of several overlapping nature reserves. In 1969 UNESCO classified it a Biosphere Reserve and a World Heritage Site on the basis of its rich diversity of bird life. The heart of the protected area includes a beautiful coastal region where the dunes shift in response to wind direction. As it is a national park you have to be accompanied by a guide if you want to get in. All in all the national park incorporates 54,250 hectares (134,000 acres) of nature reserve, surrounded by a vast tract of land that has also been left wild.

Groves of pine trees, salt marshes, swampy plains, white sand dunes, rosemary, thyme, and cork oak create a wilderness landscape where the only noises are the birds and the wind. There are several pairs of imperial eagles nesting here, and a number of lynx – both of which are used as the park's symbols.

Unfortunately, the park suffered a major ecological disaster in April 1998. A waste water tank at a mine about 28 kilometres (18 miles) from Seville burst and 5 million cubic metres of liquid chemicals including pyrite, arsenic, copper, lead, zinc, cadmium, mercury and thallium flooded over 10,000 hectares (24,700 acres) of land. It spread around the banks of the Guadiamar, a tributary of the Guadalquivir, which runs along the edge of the Doñana park. Aided by torrential rain, this concoction filtered into the soil and lakes, and rivers were contaminated – 37 tonnes of fish died in the Guadiamar and at least 30,000 birds were poisoned by the heavy metals.

You can take a trip around the park in a jeep or by boat. Excursions start from Sanlúcar de Barrameda and Seville.

LEAVING HUELVA

By Bus

🚌 **Bus station** (A2 on the map): avenida de Alemania or avenida Doctor Rubio. ☎ 25-69-00 or 25-62-24. The ticket offices are open 9.15am–1.30pm and 4.30–8.45pm. There are left luggage facilities at the station – it costs about 2€, to leave a bag overnight (until 7am) irrespective of the size of the luggage.

– **To Punta Umbría**: many daily services operated by the Damas bus company, at 15 minutes past the hour. Either direct or via Aljarque.

– **To the Rompido beaches**: five services a day, departing every 2 hours.

– **To Moguer**: 31 buses a day during the week from 7am onwards, 14 services a day at weekends from 9.30am onwards.

– **To Madrid**: three services a day run by the Socibus company. Services leave at just before 10am, 4pm and 11pm, check exact times before travelling. Tickets for daytime travel cost the same as overnight journeys.

– **To Málaga**: daily service departing at 8am operated by the Damas bus company.

– **To Cádiz**: daily service departing at 10am operated by the Damas bus company.

By Train

🚂 **Train Station RENFE** (B2 on the map): avenida de Italia. ☎ 24-66-66 or 24-56-14. The ticket office is open 7.30am–9.30pm. The left luggage office is between the bar and the newspaper kiosk. It costs about 2€ for 24 hours. You can fit two small bags or one large one in the lockers, but no more.

Note that there is no train service to Portugal. All services from Huelva go through Seville. The train service links with large towns only.

– **To Cádiz**: note that you may have to make several connections.

– **To Seville**: on the Andalucía Express. There are three services a day. They leave just after 7am, just after 2am and just before 8pm. Check the exact times before travelling. You can make reservations for this serivce up to a fortnight in advance.

– **To Málaga**: change at Seville.

PUNTA UMBRÍA 21100 — DIALLING CODE: 959

This quite little fishing village is separated from the port and industrial areas of Huelva by a long stretch of land known as Espigon. Punta Umbría was used to defend the port of Huelva in the Middle Ages. Several of the old towers remain, interspersed with the more recent constructions of both pre- and post-Franco eras. Despite its long history, Punta Umbría is still little more than a fishing village even at the beginning of the 21st century. You can still watch fisherman mending their nets on the shore as the sun goes down. Punta Umbría has some wonderful long sandy beaches, and it's a dream place for campers who want to escape the bustle of Seville.

USEFUL ADDRESSES

🛈 **Tourist Office**: avenida Ciudad de Huelva. ☎ 31-46-19. In a large beach cabin built on stilts under the pine trees in the town centre.

🚌 **Bus station**: behind the Tourist Office. You buy your tickets from the driver.

WHERE TO STAY

🛏 **Albergue Juvenil Punta Umbría**: avenida Océano 13. ☎ 31-16-50. Fax: 31-42-29. Website: www.inturjoven.com. On arrival at Punta Umbría, take a right turn towards the beach, walking away from the town centre. Reception is open 8.30am–10pm. Prices vary according to season. In November, December and January there are discount prices of 5–16€; from mid-June to mid-September it is full price, although this is still low at 8–20€ depending on whether you are under or over 26. At all other times it is 6–17€ depending on whether you go for the room only, bed and breakfast, half board or full board option. Credit cards are accepted. A series of beautiful buildings faces out on to the Atlantic. Make sure you ask for one of the rooms on the first floor that opens onto the long wooden balcony. Rooms sleep two or four people, with shared bathroom facilities. There are several activities on offer, including a large basketball pitch. The beach is no more than a stone's throw away.

LA COSTA DE LA LUZ

WHERE TO STAY IN THE SURROUNDING AREA

🛏 **Camping Catapum**: off the road from El Rompido to Punta Umbría, about 3 kilometres (2 miles) in the Cartaya direction. ☎ 39-91-65. A pitch costs 3–4€ per person plus 3–4€ per tent. The site is situated just 50 metres from the very busy road to Portugal, which makes it rather noisy, but it is close to the superb San Miguel beach. The wilderness area of the sand dunes protects the beach itself. The campsite is shady but most of the plots are for caravans. The toilet and shower blocks are clean and the staff are friendly.

WHERE TO EAT AND DRINK

There is a multitude of bars on offer where you can get something to eat, including *pescaditos fritos* (whitebait). Punta Umbría is a small town, however, so don't expect haute cuisine.

✗ **Freiduría Los Manueles**: río Odiel 3. In a street at right angles to calle Ancha. At the bar you can order *una ración de langostinos* (a portion of prawns) for less than 3€ a kilo and crab claws for about 9€. It has all been caught the night before, so it is very fresh. Prices can vary depending on availability and season.

🍷 **El Refugio**: plaza de los Marineros – a pleasant little square where the children from the nearby flats play. El Refugio has pretty shutters and a thatched roof in keeping with its surroundings. It pipes unobtrusive rock music into the bar and there is a pool table. It is frequented by sailors and young locals. The *mahou* (beer) is a bit more expensive than elsewhere.

🍷 **Bar La Pequeña Alhambra**: on calle Ancha 82 and plaza 26 de Abril 1963. As the name suggests, it's decorated to resemble the Alhambra – but although the imitation stucco facade might have something of the famous monument about it, it is predominately blue and white concrete. Inside, however, there are *azulejos*, low tables, subdued lighting and cosy little cubicles. A nice place for a cup of tea in spite of its pretensions.

WHERE TO EAT IN THE SURROUNDING AREA

✕ **El Bosque**: on the road from Punta Umbría to El Rompido. ☎ 50-40-99. This is a small *chiringuito* (refreshment van) camped out on the Culata point under the pine trees. It is only open at weekend lunchtimes. A plate of seafood or a *ración de pescadito frito* (a portion of fried fish) – *chocos* (cuttlefish), *pijotas* (codling) or *acedias* (plaice) – costs less than 6€. You can also get excellent *moules marinières* here. The cockles and *almejas* (mussels) are delicious and it's no exaggeration to say that the fish is as fresh as it comes.

THE BEACHES

– **Playa de los Enebrales**: this is a beautiful beach separated from the road by a lovely pine grove teeming with rabbits. It is well signposted and easy to find with entrances just before a service station on the road to Punta Umbría. It is in fact a protected area so it is somewhat surprising to see a large notice board proclaiming the merits of a project to build dream homes nearby. The little path alongside the road is good for jogging or cycling. The beach is protected by a grove of pine trees that runs just behind it. The shore is about 4 or 5 metres (13 to 15 feet) below but the sound of the waves breaking is muffled by the dunes. There is an unofficial naturist area on the left-hand side of the beach. There aren't any showers, but in any case they would rather spoil the effect on such a beautiful wild beach.

– **Playa El Espigon**: turn off at Corrales and follow the signs. Not quite as nice as Playa de los Enebrales, but a bit quieter.

JEREZ DE LA FRONTERA 11405 DIALLING CODE: 956

This is a fairly major town – well known for its vineyards, but rather nondescript to look at. The modern part of the town is quite badly planned and it is easy to get lost, especially if you are driving. The different areas of the town have spread rather haphazardly, and it is riddled with one-way streets. If you have to stay here, get yourself a map and stick to exploring on foot.

One of the main reasons for coming to Jerez is to visit the *bodegas* (wine cellars) and try the famous sherry. The town is also well known for its horses and its traditional flamenco.

The names of several of the towns in the region end with 'la Frontera' referring to the border that divided the territory into that occupied by the Moors and that controlled by the Catholics.

THE JEREZ VINEYARD

This is claimed to be the oldest working vineyard in the world. In fact the Phoenicians planted the first vines in 1000 BC. Then the Romans intensified the culture of wines and named the town Ceret. The climatic conditions are truly exceptional, with 295 days of sunshine a year and a wine production of over 100 million litres. The soil is made up of chalky clay from the Tertiary period; it absorbs rain in winter and hardens in summer to form a pale surface that reflects the sun but still retains the precious moisture.

Today, sherry production still begins with the treading of the grapes by men wearing leather boots. The grape pulp is then fermented in casks of American oak until it reaches an alcohol level of between 11.5 and 13.5 per cent proof. Unlike other wines, sherry is exposed to the air after a year of fermentation. The barrels, which are three quarters full, are opened in the cellars. A yeast forms on the surface, making a thick protective layer so the sherry can oxidize without turning sour. Depending on the type of yeast used, the end result will produce a wine that is *fino* or *oloroso*.

Another unusual part of the sherry-making process is the use of the *solera*. This is the name of the highest cask (they are stacked in pyramids). The sherry in the barrels on the bottom row is decanted and bottled. Half the sherry in the upper barrels is decanted into the lower barrels, and so on to the bottom of the pyramid. The empty barrel at the top is refilled with the new wine (*crianza*). In this way the old sherry 'educates' the younger wine. Due to this wise mix of generations, sherry cannot be categorized by year.

Credit must be given to the British for the success of sherry, as they consume 43 per cent of the exported wine, which is about 85 per cent of the total production. It was also the British who re-named it – unable to get their tongues round the Spanish word *jerez* they settled on the simpler 'sherry'. The great sherry makers such as Williams and Humbert, John Harvey and Sons, and Osborne are of British descent but the most famous sherry house is still Domecq (of Béarnaise origin), which owns some 70 hectares (173 acres) of cellars. Some of their barrels are over 300 years old. Sixteen members of the family manage the Domecq vineyard but as there are now over 400 family descendants, the hiring process must be pretty tough. Sherry production is the livelihood of three quarters of the population of Jerez.

TYPES OF SHERRY

– *Amontillado*: between 8 and 16 per cent proof but can be over 21 per cent after it has been aged. It goes very well with seafood or ham, and has a beautiful aroma.

– *Manzanilla*: a fine, light, amber liquor, often drunk as an aperitif. Its colour ranges from pale green to gold. It has a sweet bouquet of ripe apples, hence its name (*manzana* is apple in Spanish). Between 18 and 20 per cent proof.

– *Fino*: very dry, with a scented bouquet and flowery flavour. It is less alcoholic than the *amontillado* and *manzanilla* at 15–17 per cent proof. It is drunk chilled as an aperitif or with seafood. It is almost transparent in colour and may be too dry for those unaccustomed to drinking sherry.

– *Oloroso*: this is a stronger wine at 18–20 per cent proof. It can be drunk as an aperitif or as a digestif at the end of a meal. It's slightly less dry than the others listed here and is amber in colour. Due to contact with the air it is slightly oxidized.

– *Cream*: this is a mixture of *Pedro Jimenez* and *oloroso*. The mixing process takes place just before bottling. It is an attractive reddish colour and is fairly sweet.

– *Muscatel*: this is made by mixing Muscat with *Pedro Jimenez*. It is very sweet and almost plum-coloured. On occasions the sweetness can overpower the bouquet.

USEFUL ADDRESSES

🛈 Tourist Office: calle Larga 39. ☎ 33-11-50. Open Monday to Friday 9am–3pm and 5–7pm. Closed on Sunday. The staff here are charming and very generous with leaflets and information.

✉ Post Office: calle Cerrón 1. ☎ 34-22-95.

■ Banks: there are several banks on calle Larga, and most of them have cash machines.

■ Taxis: ☎ 34-48-60.

WHERE TO STAY

This is a good place to visit for a day out, but not really worth spending the night in unless this is a stopover on the way to somewhere else. If you're touring, you're probably better off heading on to Arcos de la Frontera.

⬗ Albergue Juvenil (youth hostel): avenida Carrero Blanco 30. ☎ 34-28-90. Fax: 14-32-63. Website: www.inturjoven.com. This large modern youth hostel is unfortunately quite a distance from the town centre. It has a nice swimming pool, however. The rooms sleep two or four, with a communal bathroom.

☆ Budget

⬗ Hostal Las Palomas: calle Higueras 17 (overlooking plaza de los Angustias). ☎ 34-37-73. A double room with a washbasin costs 21€. There is a shower along the corridor. It is a clean, quiet, unassuming place and not too far from the town centre. The patio is pleasantly decorated with *azulejos* and plants.

☆☆ Moderate

⬗ Hotel San Andres: 12 and 14 calle Morenos. ☎ 34-09-83. Fax: 34-31-96. An en-suite room costs 31€; a room with a washbasin and shared washing facilities 22€. This is a lovely little *pensión* with a patio full of flowers. The rooms are clean, simply furnished, and well cared for. No. 14 calle Morenos is owned by the same people as No.12 but it is smarter and slightly more expensive, as all the rooms are en-suite.

☆☆☆ Expensive

⬗ Hotel El Coloso: calle Pedro Alonso 13. ☎ 34-90-08. A double room costs 45€. The hotel is smart, but a bit depressing. All the rooms have en-suite bathrooms and a TV.

⬗ Hostal Serit: calle Higueras 7. ☎ 34-07-00. Fax: 34-07-16. Email: hotelserit@redicom.es Double rooms cost about 55€. This hotel has a beautiful lounge, 30 double rooms and 8 single. All rooms have an en-suite bathroom, telephone, TV and air-conditioning. The hotel is spotless and the service impeccable.

WHERE TO EAT

The restaurants are fairly expensive in Jerez, so it is probably better to eat in tapas bars. All along calle Larga there are café-bars with tables outside on the pavement.

☆ Budget

✗ **El Colmado**: calle Arcos (calle Alvar Nuñez) 1. ☎ 33-76-74. The restaurant is on the first floor above a bar. The decor is very drab, but the food is good. There is a good-value set menu – generous portions, served lunchtimes and evenings every day. If you are just peckish, the *sopa de garbanzos* (chick pea soup) or *sopa de cebollas* (onion soup) will be more than enough. The *cordero* (lamb) is also very tasty.

☆☆☆ Expensive

✗ **Restaurante Gaitan**: Gaitan 3. ☎ 34-58-59. Open 1–4.30pm and 8.30–11.30pm. Closed Wednesday evening. A little bit touristy, but there are a number of traditional dishes available and the food is excellent. The set menu is good, but rather pricey. The dining area is decorated with pictures and photos of important customers.

WHAT TO SEE

★ **The *bodegas***: these are the principle attraction of the town. Many of the *bodegas* offer guided tours, although not at the weekend. Several are closed in August. The best time to go is in September at harvest time. Discover the secrets of sherry – a 'civilized drink' in the words of Somerset Maugham.

– **Bodega Domecq**: calle San Idefonso 3. ☎ 15-15-00. Probably not the best one to visit even if it is the most famous as the staff seem particularly unfriendly.

– **Bodega Gonzalez Byaz**: calle Manuel Ma. Gonzalez. ☎ 35-70-00. There are guided tours Monday to Friday at 11am, noon, 1pm, 5pm and 6pm. On Saturday the tours are at 10am, 11am and noon. You need to reserve in advance and pay on arrival.

– **Bodega Williams Humbert**: calle Nuño de Cañas. ☎ 34-65-39. Guided tour at 1.30pm.

– **Bodega Maestro Sierra**: plaza de Silos 5. ☎ 34-24-33. There are two tours a day Monday to Friday at noon and 2pm. Pay on arrival.

– **Bodega Harvey's**: calle Arcos 53. ☎ 15-10-02. There are two tours a day at 10am and noon. No need to reserve in advance, pay on arrival.

– **Bodega Wisdom**: calle Pizarro. ☎ 37-50-90. Guided tour on Thursday at 1.15pm and 2pm. No need to reserve in advance, pay on arrival.

★ **Real Escuela Andaluza del Arte Ecuestre** (Royal School of Equestrian Art of Andalucía): to the north of the town on avenida Duque de Abrantes. ☎ 31-96-35. Jerez is the equestrian centre of Andalucía and this riding school is similar to the ones in Vienna and Saumur. Every year at the beginning of May they hold the Feria del Caballo (Horse Festival), which is a fantastic spectacle featuring splendidly decked out horses and a series of races and processions.

If you're not coming to Jerez for the festival, it is still worth going to see the training sessions, which are open to the public. They are held on Monday, Wednesday and Friday at 11am and 1pm. You can turn up when you like as each session lasts two hours. On Thursday at noon there is a spectacular show entitled *Cómo bailan los caballos andaluces* (the dance of the Andalucían horses), for which you need to book tickets at least two months in advance – if you just turn up you may find that it's sold out. This excellent dressage show was first put on in 1973. The soundtrack used is by the Royal Philharmonic Orchestra. The best seats cost three times the standard admission price, but there is a wide range of prices and tickets in the stands are cheaper. You are not allowed to take videos or photos during the show.

You can also visit the stables, tack rooms and gardens. The horses are pedigrees – the name of the breed is *cartujaño* and in addition there are 20 *caballeros* (horse men) and three *amazonas* (horse women). The palace and the gardens at the school were designed by Garnier, the architect of the Opéra in Paris.

★ **El museo de los Relojes** (Clock Museum): calle Cervantes 3. ☎ 18-21-00. Open Monday to Saturday, 10am–2pm. Admission fee. The museum is housed in a 19th-century palace set in beautiful gardens. It contains more than 300 exquisite clocks from all over Europe. If you are there at 10am, 11am, noon, 1pm or 2pm you can hear all the clocks chiming in unison.

★ **San Miguel Church**: in calle San Miguel. Usually open in the evening. This stunning facade is in the heavily ornate, classical, Isabelline style. The supporting walls are 16th-century baroque and the doorway on the left-hand side of the church has attractive baroque carving. Inside there are heavy columns and a Gothic vault. The detailed, elegant *retablo* (altarpiece) depicts scenes carved by Martinez Montañéz and José de Arce.

★ **Estación de Ferrocarril** (railway station): this is probably the most beautiful building in the whole town, but the majority of guidebooks don't even give it a mention. It was built very much in the style of the French Belle Époque and is decorated with *azulejos*.

★ **Centro Andaluz de Flamenco**: palacio Pemartin, plaza de San Juan 1. ☎ 34-92-65. Open Monday 10am–2pm, Tuesday 10am–2pm and 5–7pm, and Wednesday to Friday 10am–2pm. The flamenco centre is housed in a lovely building dating from the 18th century. The main patio features carved vaulting and *azulejos*. The centre is a mine of information on anything to do with flamenco and reference works include books, paintings, documentation and old recordings. The sound and video library provides a fascinating collection of aural and film records of the art.

★ **Flea Market**: Alameda Vieja, alongside the Alcázar mosque. Every Sunday morning, in the summer.

★ The **Banda municipal de Jerez** plays paso dobles, waltzes and marches every Sunday at noon on plaza del Banco in the town centre, right next to the Tourist Office. Tips are always gratefully received.

WHERE TO SEE AND LISTEN TO FLAMENCO

As flamenco originated in this part of Andalucía, it isn't surprising to learn that it remains very popular with the local people right up to today. It's hard to get away from the tourist shows, but here are some of the better places to go:

– **Ellaga**: plaza del Mercado. ☎ 33-83-34. Go by car or taxi as it is in quite a rough part of town. There is a bar and restaurant. The show is free between 10.30pm and 12.30am. You only have to pay for drinks (although these are on the expensive side) and the meal.

– **El Rincón del Duende**: calle Velázquez 20. Flamenco shows on Friday and Saturday evening. Don't arrive before 10.30pm.

– **Camino del Rocio**: urbanización Divina Pastora. You can see a show here and even join in the *sevillanas* yourself. It's not worth arriving before 11pm. At midnight they turn off all the lights, and the owner and all the regulars sing *Ave Maria Flamenca* – a very moving scene that is not to be missed.

– **Viernes Flamencos** (Flamenco Friday): this authentic flamenco festival is held in August and has a great following among *aficionados*.

FIESTAS

– **Semana Santa**: Jerez is not particularly well known for its Holy Week celebrations, but this has had the benefit of keeping tourists away, allowing the events to retain much of their authenticity.

– **La Feria del Caballo** (Horse Festival): held at the beginning of May, this festival includes parades of beautiful Andalucían horses and a competition for the best festooned horse. Most of the participants dress in traditional costume, which makes for an interesting spectacle, and even better, it is relatively easy to get hold of tickets for the shows.

– **Fiesta de San Antón**: held on the last Sunday in January, to bless the horses.

– **Fiestas de Otoño**: this very colourful autumn festival celebrates the new vintage and is held at the end of September.

WHAT TO SEE IN THE SURROUNDING AREA

★ **La Cartuja**: a beautiful chapter house located some 7 kilometres (5 miles) from Jerez, on the right-hand side of the road to Cádiz. Only men are allowed inside the monastery itself, although women may visit the gardens. This is a splendid example of flamboyant 15th-century Gothic architecture, with a richly ornate facade. It was here in the 16th century that horses from Naples, Andalucía and Germany were first cross-bred to create the local thoroughbred horse, the *cartujaño*.

LEAVING JEREZ

By Train

🚃 **RENFE**: plaza Estación. ☎ 34-23-19. Tickets can also be bought in the town centre at calle Larga 34. ☎ 33-48-13.

– Services to Seville, Cádiz, Madrid and Barcelona.

By Bus

🚌 **Bus Station**: calle Cartuja. All companies are based at the same station.

– **Compañía Comes**: ☎ 34-21-74. Services to Málaga and Ronda, as well as all over the Costa del Sol.

– **Sevibus**: ☎ 33-50-05. Services to Madrid.

– **Linesur**: ☎ 34-10-63. Services to Sanlúcar and Chipiona.

– **Amarillos**: services across the whole province.

By Air

➊ **Airport:** about 7 kilometres (4 miles) out of town, on the main road, RN4. ☎ 33-43-00 and 15-00-00. There is no bus service to the airport, so taxis are the only option.

– There are two airlines running services to Madrid, Barcelona and Valencia.

ARCOS DE LA FRONTERA 11630

DIALLING CODE: 956

Arcos de la Frontera lies about 33 kilometres (21 miles) east of Jerez de la Frontera. This delightful little Andalucían village is perched on a rocky promontory overlooking the río Guadalete.

USEFUL ADDRESSES

🛈 **Tourist Office**: on plaza de Cabildo, at the top of the village.

🚌 **Bus station**: Bus Comes. ☎ 70-20-15.

WHERE TO STAY

Avoid the campsite if possible as it is too far away from the village. The village itself is not the cheapest of places, but the surrounding countryside more than compensates for the price of being there.

☆☆ Moderate

🛏 **Hostal San Marcos**: calle Marqués de Torresoto 6. ☎ 70-07-21. This *hostal* is set in a narrow street in the old part of the village about two minutes from plaza de Cabildo, where there is parking. A double room with en-suite bathroom costs 33€. There are only four rooms – all very clean, but rather lacking in character. Avoid the room on the corridor. The rooms sleep either two or three people. There is a bar and small restaurant on the ground floor and a roof terrace. The set menu costs about 5€. The owners are not especially friendly.

♠ **Pensión Callejón de Las Monjas**: callejón de las Monjas 6. ☎ 70-23-02. In a narrow street running alongside the Santa Maria church, just beneath the flying buttress that straddles the street. A double room costs between 30 and 36€ and an apartment costs 15€ per person. This *pensión* has six small, clean rooms, some en-suite. Room 4 is very small but has a lovely balcony that overlooks the mossy roofs and has a great view of the countryside. The two apartments have equally stunning views. The friendly owner is called Nickel – he runs the hairdressers on the ground floor, as well as the restaurant next door.

☆☆☆ Expensive

♠ **Hotel Marqués de Torresoto**: calle Marqués de Torresoto 4. ☎ 70-07-17. Fax: 70-42-05. Website: www.tugasa.com/arcos.html. This is a luxurious but still affordable place to stay – a double room costs about 60€, but prices rise by around 15 per cent over Easter and Christmas. This 17th-century building once belonging to the Marquis of Torresoto and has an elegant patio and some very comfortable rooms, all are of a decent size and pleasantly decorated. They either overlook the patio or the street. Avoid the ground floor rooms, as they are rather dark. This is a lovely place, located right in the heart of the old village. It also has a restaurant and although the cooking is nothing to

write home about, the staff are very friendly.

♠ **Hotel El Convento**: Maldonado 2 ☎ 70-23-33. Fax: 70-41-28. Website: www.turismoalsur.com. (in Spanish). As you come in to the village, it is next to the post office. Double rooms cost from 42 to 54€ in low season, and 72€ for a double room with a bathroom in high season. The hotel is better known by the name of *Los Olivos*. It is quite smart with some beautiful rooms looking out on to the valley. There is a small patio with cane tables and chairs. It is a shame that the welcome is not as warm as it could be.

♠ **Parador Casa del Corregidor**: plaza de Cabildo. ☎ 70-05-00. Fax: 70-11-16. Website:www.parador. es. A double room with an en-suite bathroom costs 105€, and the rooms with a view are an additional 6€. In the restaurant the set meals start at 22€. This parador has a three-star rating, although it really merits a five-star award. Some of the rooms have balconies that overhang the cliffs although unfortunately you can't reserve them in advance as they are allocated on a first-come, first-served basis. The other rooms overlook the square. There is an impressive view over the valley of the río Guadalete. The parador has been totally renovated – the lovely Moorish patio has been revamped in salmon pink with a cast-iron gate and there are *azulejos* decorating the bar which also features a reading corner. For travellers with a bit of money left over at the end of their trip this is the place to splash out. In July and August you get a 20 per cent reduction if you stay more than two nights on a half-board basis. If you are over 60 you get a further 35 per cent reduction. Even if you can't afford to stay here it's still worth visiting just to have a look round.

WHERE TO EAT

✗ **Bar Típico Alcavarán**: calle Nueva 1, on the street leading off plaza de Cabildo. ☎ 70-33-97. Closed on Monday and at the end of September. If you're facing the clock tower of the church it is on the left-hand side of the square, housed in a vaulted, T-shaped cellar underneath the old castle. You can eat for less than 9€. The old tables are very low.

The good hot tapas include *salchichas picantes* (spicy sausages), *riñones al Jerez* (kidneys in sherry), *solomillo a la brasa* (barbecued sirloin chops), *queso de cabra* (goat's cheese), *estofado de cordero* (lamb stew), *pimientos rellenos* (stuffed peppers) as well as many more – definitely a place worth visiting.

✗ **Hostal San Marcos**: *see* 'Where to Stay'. There is a set menu for less than 6€. Very down to earth with its large TV and neon lighting.

✗ **Mesón Murales**: in calle Boticas, behind the church. Set menu from about 6€. It is quite touristy but they serve good, traditional food that is filling.

✗ **Resto du parador Casa del Corregidor**: *see* 'Where to Stay – Expensive'. As you would expect, the food at this restaurant is very good, in keeping with the style of the parador.

– **Mercedarías Descalzas**: plazuela de Botica 2. A good selection of delicious cakes.

WHERE TO HAVE A DRINK

❢ **Taberna de los Jóvenes Flamencos**: in calle Julio Mariscal opposite calle Boliche. The beer costs less than 1€. This bar is popular with the locals and the walls are covered with photos of bullfights. There is a particularly good atmosphere in the evening.

WHAT TO SEE

★ **La plaza de Cabildo**: at the top of the village with a marvellous view of the plain below. The *parador* and the Plateresque church of Santa Maria de la Asunción are both in this square. The church has a square clock tower with balconies and baroque ornamentation. The interior features a Renaissance *retablo* (altarpiece), beautiful vaults and heavy columns that are made to seem more slender than they really are by the clever use of fluting and ribbing.

★ **La Ciudad Vieja** (the old city): take a stroll along the small, quiet streets around the plaza de España – there are some interesting medieval houses with secluded patios and some splendid architectural features.

CÁDIZ 11000 DIALLING CODE: 956

Cádiz is a sprawling city and quite disappointing on first view. It is primarily a large port, providing trade links with Africa. You have to pass through the modern suburbs to reach the old part of the town which is built on a rocky peninsula surrounded by the sea. The old town has a lively but gentle hospitality and the streets are very attractive, although there is not a great deal to see here in terms of monuments. There are several beautiful beaches, although much of the coast has been subjected to over-development. Cádiz has a reputation for social tolerance that is unmatched elsewhere in Andalucía.

A Brief History

Cádiz, known locally as the *tacita de plata* ('silver bowl') has been the epicentre of numerous conflicts, feuds and historical events.

Legend has it that Cádiz was founded by Hercules about 3,000 years ago and was then known as Gadir. More certain is that the Phoenicians settled here in about 1100 BC, on territory that had previously been occupied by the Tartesians. Cádiz can thus lay claim to the title of the oldest town in the Western world. In about 501 BC the Carthaginians landed, followed by the Romans in 206 BC – Julius Caesar was here from 69 BC until 61 BC. Then came the Visigoths and the Moors, who ruled until 1262, when Alfonso X prised Cádiz from the grasp of the invaders.

Two centuries later the town played an important part in the conquest of the Americas, because it was from here that Columbus departed for his second voyage to the New World in 1493. At the end of the 16th century the English seized the port, which had become the gateway to the Americas. Cádiz reached its zenith in the 18th century, when trade was flourishing and the town's reputation knew no bounds. It was then Napoleon's turn to invade and occupy the town at which point Cádiz became the capital of occupied Spain. Much later, during the Civil War, the people of the town valiantly resisted the Fascists, consolidating its reputation for liberalism.

USEFUL ADDRESSES

Tourist Information

🛈 Tourist Office (C3 on the map): plaza San Juan de Dios 11, DP 11005. ☎ (956) 24-10-01. Fax: (956) 24-10-05. Website: www.infocadiz.com. Open Monday to Friday 9am–2pm and 5pm–8pm, and Saturday 10am–1pm.

🛈 Tourist Office (C1 on the map): calderón de la Barca. ☎ (956) 21-13-13. Same opening times as above.

Services

✉ Post Office (C2 on the map): plaza de las Flores (its actual name is plaza Topete). Open Monday to Friday 8.30am–8.30pm, and Saturday 9.30am–2pm. Poste restante 9am–3pm.

■ Banks: there are several banks on calle Nueva (C2–3 on the map), off plaza San Juan de Dios, as well as on calle San Francisco (C2 on the map).

Transport

🚆 RENFE (D3 on the map): *see* 'Leaving Cádiz'. Left-luggage facilities.

🚌 Bus stations (D1–2 and C2 on the map): there are several companies serving different destinations. *See* 'Leaving Cádiz'.

⚓ **Trasmediterranea dock** (D2, **1** on the map): ☎ (902) 45-46-45 (free phone). Website: www.trasmediterranea.es

⚓ **Vaporcito landing stage**: (D2, **3** on the map): ☎ 22-74-21 or 22-74-22.

■ **Taxis**: ☎ 22-10-06, 22-15-03 and 28-69-69.

Health and Emergencies

■ **Chemist** (C1, **2** on the map): plaza de la Mina, on the corner of San José and Enrique de Las Marinas.

■ **Red Cross**: Santa Maria de la Soledad 10. ☎ 25-42-70.

■ **National Police**: avenida Andalucía 28. ☎ 28-61-11.

■ **Local Police**: campo del Sur. ☎ 092.

WHERE TO STAY

Take note that the places to stay listed below do not accept reservations either by phone or in writing. You have to turn up and hope for the best. They are all in the old part of the town around plaza San Juan de Dios (C3 on the map).

⌂ Budget

⚑ **Albergue Juvenil Quo Qádis** (B2, **10** on the map): calle Diego Arias 1, 11002 Cádiz; on the corner of calle de Solano. ☎ and fax: 22-19-39. Email: quoqadis@infoCadiz. com. Open all year round. This is a charming place in an old building that has recently been revamped. The *albergue* is a cross between a youth hostel and a *pensión* and is the best value for money in the whole town. For those travelling on a shoestring budget there are dormitories with three to ten beds for 6€ a night, otherwise, rooms with two to three beds cost 24€. The rooms are pleasant and all have washbasins. Some of them overlook calle Diego Arias and are consequently fairly noisy. The price includes breakfast (not to be sniffed at) served in the bar which is decorated with *azulejos*. There is a family atmosphere but the owner could put a bit more effort into making his guests feel welcome. You can sunbathe on the terrace in summer. There are excursions on offer to nearby places of interest and also courses in *sevillanas*. Highly recommended.

⌂⌂ Moderate

⚑ **Pensión Fantoni** (C3, **11** on the map): calle Flamenco 5, 11005 Cádiz. ☎ (956) 28-27-04. About 100 metres from the port. This friendly, family-run *pensión* is by far the best place to stay in this category, but it quickly gets booked up. In season, rooms with a washbasin start at about 24€, and rooms with bathrooms are about 36€. The rooms are ultra-clean. Lots of flowers and pot-plants.

⚑ **Pensión Las Cuatro Naciones** (C–D3, **12** on the map): Plocia 3, 11005 Cádiz. ☎ 25-55-39. On the first floor. A good place to stay, as it is right in the town centre and you'll get a friendly welcome. Drop by in the morning to reserve your room. The simply-furnished rooms cost about 18€ out of season – they are reasonable enough but fairly small. Good for a short stay but not ideal if you are in Cádiz for several days.

≙ Hostal Colón (C3, **13** on the map): calle Marqués de Cádiz 6, 11005 Cádiz. ☎ 28-53-51. Set in a tangle of little streets behind the Archivo Municipal. Most rooms sleep two or three people and have a washbasin and a communal bathroom down the corridor. The rooms are clean and spacious, and cost about 24€. The welcome might seem curt, but it is well-meant.

≙ Pensión Marqués (C3, **14** on the map): calle Marqués de Cádiz 1, 11005 Cádiz. ☎ 28-58-54. This place is clean and perfectly reasonable if you're only looking for a place to sleep. Rooms with a washbasin cost about 21€ – a bit on the expensive side, but the rooms are

nice enough. There are some en-suite rooms but they don't really represent value for money.

≙ Pensión Cádiz (C2, **15** on the map): calle Feduchy 20, 11005 Cádiz. ☎ 28-58-01. Reception is on the first floor. A double room costs between 26 and 32€, but note that they don't accept credit cards. The hotel is closed in July, August and September. The entrance hall leads on to an old three-storey glazed interior patio. However the rooms are plain and dark, and some even have a window looking out onto the corridor. Ask for a room with an external window and a shower. As a whole, the hotel is a bit noisy and needs smartening up. The welcome isn't that great either.

≙ Hostal San Francisco (C2, **16** on the map): calle San Francisco 12,

CÁDIZ

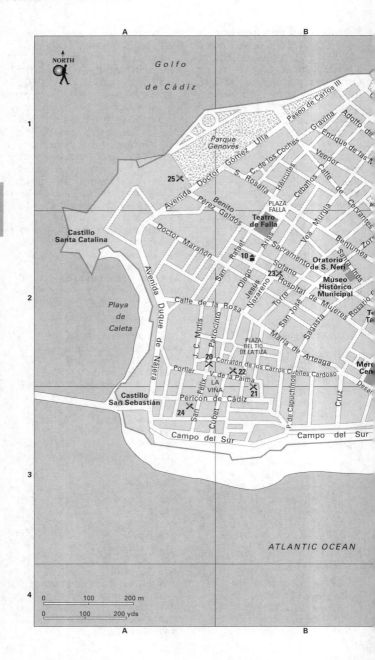

NORTH

Golfo de Cádiz

Paseo de Carlos III

Gravina

Adolfo de

Enrique de las M.

Veedor

Calle de

Cervantes

Parque Genovés

Ulía

C. de los Coches

Hércules

Ceballos

Doctor Gómez

S. Rosalía

Vea Murgía

Benjumea

PLAZA FALLA

Teatro de Falla

Avenida Pérez Galdós

Benito

Arias

Sacramento de

Sor. Inés

Zor

Castillo Santa Catalina

Doctor Marañón

San Rafael

Diego

10

Solano

23

Oratorio de S. Neri

Museo Histórico Municipal

Jesús Nazareno

Hospital de Mujeres

Rosario

Playa de Caleta

Calle de la Rosa

Torre

San José

Sagasta

Te

Ta

J. C. Mutis

Patrocinio

PLAZA DEL TÍO DE LA TIZA

María de Arteaga

Avenida Duque de Nájera

20

Corralón de los Carros Cubiles Cardoso

Mer

Cen

Portier

22

V. de la Palma

LA VIÑA

21

P. de Capuchinos

Cruz

Desa

Castillo San Sebastián

Pericón de Cádiz

24

San Felix

Cubet

Campo del Sur

Campo del Sur

ATLANTIC OCEAN

0   100   200 m

0   100   200 yds

CÁDIZ

11005 Cádiz. ☎ 22-18-42. This hotel is markedly more expensive than Pensión Cádiz – a disproportionate 29€ a night out of season. It is clean with a tiled foyer. The hotel is situated in a busy street so the rooms on the upper floor are preferable as they are less noisy.

☆☆☆ Expensive

⚓ **Hotel Francia y Paris** (C2, **17** on the map): plaza San Francisco 2,

11005 Cádiz. ☎ 21-23-19. Fax: 22-24-31. Website: www.hotelfrancia.com. The rooms here are rather expensive, starting at 60€ for en-suites and prices seem to undergo regular increases. This is a very smart hotel, in the heart of the old part of town. Some of the rooms look out on to a nice little square lined with orange trees – you can almost pick the fruit from your window. The staff are not especially friendly.

WHERE TO EAT

In the Viña Area

This is the nicest part of town. It is here where all the *peñas flamencas* (flamenco aficionados) meet up. Children play in the streets and their parents sit outside their houses drinking *fino*. If you are lucky you may hear someone singing a spontaneous *siguirya* or *bolero*. Admittedly this may not be the safest of areas, but it is not setting itself out to attract tourists. The best time to go is definitely in the evening.

☆ Budget

✗ **Taberna Casa Manteca** (A2, **20** on the map): corralón de los Carros 66. ☎ 21-36-03. Open 12.30–4.30pm and 9pm–1.30am. Closed on Sunday evening and all day Monday. José Ruiz Manteca was a bullfighter who came a little too close to a bull's horn for comfort and decided to hang up his cape for good. Now he cherishes his memories in this traditional *taberna*. Its *azulejos*, photos of famous people, blaring TV, litter on the floor around the bar, and large dusty barrels combine to give it an authentic charm. If José Ruiz himself isn't here to pour you a *manzanilla* or a *fino Pavon* (less than 1€) with a *tapita*, one of his sons will be. Otherwise there are plenty of other local characters, such as Piti de Cádiz, the flamenco singer. This taberna is very popular with local dignitaries and professionals, including doctors, lawyers and academics.

✗ **Mesón Ca' Felipe** (B2, **21** on the map): Virgen de la Palma 2. Same type of set up as the previous bar, but not quite so engaging. There is a good value set menu at lunchtime that is served in a dining room. Alternatively you could enjoy a *tortilla de camarones* (prawn omelette) and a *caña* (beer) at the bar for less than 4€. The olives are also particularly tasty.

✗ **Mesón La Palma** (B2, **22** on the map): Virgen de la Palma. A nice place to come and prop up the bar, watch the other customers and admire the montages of bullfighting memorabilia. Prices are much the same as in the previous bars in this category.

✗ **Freiduría Europa** (B2, **23** on the map): Hospital de Mujeres 51. Set menus for 7–15€. This is the place to come if you're starving. It's a fast food grill – you can have a *surtido de pescadito frito* (selection of fried fish) or *empanada* (meat pasty) for starters followed by half a roast chicken.

The food's a bit greasy but it's very filling.

☆☆☆ Expensive

✕ **El Faro de Cádiz** (A3, **24** on the map): San Félix 15. ☎ 21-10-68. Fax: 21-21-88. There is a set menu here at lunchtime and in the evening for about 18€, but it is rarely advertised. Don't hesitate to ask, as you get salad or soup, a main meal and a dessert, which works out very reasonably. Inside it is remarkably similar to an English club, with old-style crockery, tinted glassware and waitresses dressed in traditional black and white with crisp white napkins folded professionally over their arms. There are some tasty fish dishes and a generous paella. You can buy wine by the glass which can help reduce the cost of having a drink with your meal.

✕ **Hotel Atlántico Restaurant** (A1, **25** on the map): on avenida Duque de Nájera 9. ☎ 22-69-05. Fax: 21-45-82. As hotels go this is very smart, but it's far from being the flagship of this national chain of beautiful *paradores*. In fact, it is actually a great lump of yellow and white concrete opposite the barracks. It does look onto the sea, however, and the magnificent view at dawn combined with the reasonably priced food (set menu for about 21€) make it worth visiting. They serve two really tasty cold soups – *gazpacho* and *sopa de ajo blanco* (white garlic soup) as well as *cazuela de mariscos* (seafood casserole). You should have just enough room left for the homemade tart. The service here is excellent, as it should be for such an establishment.

Around Plaza San Francisco

✕ **Taberna La Manzanilla** (C2, **26** on the map): Feduchy 19. ☎ 28-54-01. Website: www.infoCádiz.com/lamanzanilla. It would be hard to find a place which is more authentic and characteristic of the region. You can get all types of sherry here, starting from about 1€ a glass. There are numerous *olorosos*, *amontilladas*, *finos* and *viejas*. They even sell vinegar from Sanlúcar de Barrameda and mend sherry casks!

✕ **El Fogón de Mariana** (B2, **27** on the map): Sacramento 39; on the corner of Rosario Cepeda. ☎ 22-06-00. Open from noon–5pm and 8pm–midnight. Meat is priced by weight or you can opt for a mixed platter (*asado especial*) costing about 11€. This small bar is just the way it should be – there are lots of hams hanging from the ceiling, and countless *embutidos* (cold sausages). If you've had enough of fried

fish (and you're not a vegetarian) this is the place for you. *Solomillo de ternera* (veal chops), *asado especial* (a selection of *chuleta de buey* – steak, *solomillo* – sirloin chops, *chorizo* and *chuleta de cordero* – lamb chops) with a jug of wine. If you feel daunted by such a display of meat, there are also small *montaditos* (open sandwiches) that are a bit lighter.

✕ **Bodegón de Paco** (C2, **28** on the map): Beato Diego de Cádiz. Open noon–4pm and 8pm–midnight. There's a large bar with the traditional garlands of garlic and half-barrels that serve as tables. This is where the locals come for their mid-day constitutional and a glass of white wine, known as here as *tierra blanca*. It costs about 2€ a glass.

✕ **Mesón Miguel Angel** (C1, **29** on the map): plaza de Mina 1. ☎ 21-35-00. Open every day. A variety of tapas and you can get a good meal for less than 6€. There is a long narrow bar and several wooden tables in the room at the end. You can also eat outside. A good place for a late-night snack.

✕ **Cervezas La Cruz Blanca** (C1, **30** on the map): calle Zorilla 4. ☎ 22-71-10. Open every day, at lunchtime and in the evening. This lively bar is almost 150 years old and serves wine and tapas.

Around Plaza de las Flores

✕ **Freiduría de las Flores** (C2, **31** on the map): plaza de las Flores. Open every day until 3.30pm. The fish is sold by the kilo – it costs 12–18€ per kilo and 2–3€ per portion. The shop is tiled from floor to ceiling so it can easily be kept spotlessly clean. You can buy fish and sea-food, both fresh and fried, wrapped in big wads of paper to take away. Most people eat with their fingers, sitting on one of the benches in the magnificent Plaza de las Flores.

✕ **Bar Terraza** (C3, **32** on the map): plaza de la Catedral. Open lunchtime and in the evening. Closed on Sunday. The tapas here are truly excellent. You can eat outside, in the large square in front of the cathedral, where the local kids play football in the evenings. The place has a very authentic feel about it.

At the Harbour

✕ **Joselito** (C2, **33** on the map): calle San Francisco 38. ☎ 25-45-57. Closed on Sunday in summer. About 5€ a dish. The set menu costs 11€ and the house specialities are seafood and fish. The place doesn't look much, and it can be fairly noisy, but the *calamares* (fried squid) and the *boquerones* (white anchovies in vinegar) are excellent.

In the Surrounding Areas

✕ **Romerijo** (**34** off the map from D3): Ribera del Marisco, 11500 El Puerto Santa Maria. ☎ 54-16-62 or 54-22-90. Website: www.romerijo.-com. Open 10am–1.30pm. It costs 15€ for a *parillada* (platter of grilled fish) for two people. This is not the sort of place where you go on your own – *Romerijo* is *the* place for a simple family lunch, especially on Sundays. This renowned restaurant (one of the landmarks of Puerto Santa Maria) employs some 125 people, and the posters boast that it has been in the business for 40 years.

Seafood is bought by the kilo and is priced according to market rates. The friendly staff cook it while you wait and wrap it up in greaseproof paper emblazoned with the name of the restaurant, and you can tuck in on the canopied terrace. There's nothing particularly special about the restaurant's surroundings, in fact the cars and the mopeds are a bit of an annoyance, but you can't claim to have 'done' Cádiz without having eaten *pescadito frito* (fried fish) at the Puerto. To make a day of it take the morning *vaporcito* from Cádiz harbour to the restaurant and return in the afternoon (*see* 'Leaving Cádiz') after your fine lunch.

Tasty Treats

🚪 **Dulcería del Pópulo** (C3, **60** on the map): there is a small market on the corner of calle Pelota and calle Marqués de Cádiz selling an assortment of sweets, souvenirs and old bottles. You can buy *turrones de Cádiz*, the town's speciality, which is made from almond paste, egg yolk and fruit. It's delicious and is perfect to take home as a present.

GOING OUT

Around Plaza de San Francisco

As in the rest of Spain, young people in Cádiz buy bottles of beer from bars and drink them with friends in the local plaza; in Cádiz, they meet in plaza San Francisco. The better-off students meet up in the numerous bars in the historical centre of town.

🍸 **Cervezas La Cruz Blanca** (C1, **30** on the map): *see* 'Where to Eat'. This is definitely the nicest bar in town and the most traditional.

🍸 **Disparate** (C2, **40** on the map): Beato Diego de Cádiz 11. You can get a beer here for less than 2€ if you can cope with sitting in a place that is unremittingly decorated in bright white.

🍸 **Woodstock Bar** (C2, **41** on the map): on the corner of calle San Antonio López and calle Manuel Rances. A pint here costs the best part of 2€. This is a great Irish bar where they sometimes have live bagpipe music. It has a lively atmosphere and is particularly popular with the student crowd.

🍸 **Bazar Inglés** (C2, **42** on the map): Sagasta 18. This black and burgundy fronted bar resembles a family-run chemist. Look out for the bottles of 12-year-old whisky displayed in the beautiful wooden window.

🍸 **Sala Central Lechera** (C1, **43** on the map): plaza de Argüelles. ☎ 22-06-28. You see several bands performing for an admission price that rarely exceeds 6€. This bar considers itself to be the town's 'alternative' venue, but do bear in mind that it is Cádiz not London or New York.

🍸 **Club Ajo** (C2, **44** on the map): plaza de España. It can be a bit tricky to find as it doesn't have a sign outside. Look out for the *Centro Medical de la Bahia de Cádiz*. On either side of the sign are white cast iron railings – head for the ones on the right, go down a short flight of steps and you will find yourself in *Club Ajo*. This is an open-mike venue, where young local musicians often perform on bass, acoustic and electric guitars.

🍸 **Tribal Club** (C2, **45** on the map): Canova del Castillo 29. This bar has great wallpaper made from fake cowhide. There are also some wonderful logos in frosted steel and laser holograms that set the tone of the place, which is drum'n'bass, hip hop and a few mixes. Things don't really get going before 1.30–2am.

Around the Plaza de las Flores

🍸 **Bar Taberna de los vinos finos de Chiclana** (C3, **46** on the map): plaza de la Catedral. This traditional bar is the perfect place to go for a quick drink after visiting the cathedral. The locals come here on Sunday for a glass of Muscat or *fino* – good value at less than 1€.

Towards Punta San Felipe

There are several clubs, cheek by jowl in this smart complex. **Zona 10** (D1, **47** on the map), **Blues** (D1, **48** on the map) and **Kim** (D1, **49** on the map) are all worth a visit.

WHAT TO SEE

Even if you're short of time, you should at least take a stroll around the historical part of the town, which is the most interesting area of Cádiz. There are several old buildings that have a lot of character.

★ **La Torre Tavira** (B2 on the map): on the corner of calle Sacramento and calle de Marqués del Real Tesoro. ☎ 21-29-10. Open daily (except Christmas Day and New Year's Day) 10am–6pm (8pm from June to end of August). Admission costs about 3€ with a reduction for students. This tall baroque tower (one of the oldest in Cádiz) houses an ingenious dark room on the top floor. Due to a special optical effect you get a complete panoramic view of Cádiz, projected on to a white concave screen. A guide recounts the history of the town through its monuments (occasionally in English). Entry is restricted to 20 people at a time, and there is a showing every 30 minutes. If it's too crowded, make your way to the top terrace, where you get a fantastic view of Cádiz. There are also art exhibitions in some of the other rooms, as well as video shows (documentaries on the region), and an interactive computer console that gives further information on the province and its whitewashed villages. This is a well-crafted cultural centre providing a careful balance between the past and the present, and it has to be the town's most interesting attraction.

★ **La Catedral de San Salvador** (C3 on the map): plaza de la Catedral. ☎ 28-61-54. In a never-ending state of restoration, as it is continually under assault from the weather, sea spray and the damp. Construction began in 1720, and ended in 1853. The building is a none-too-successful mix of Renaissance, baroque and neoclassical architecture with an imposing facade, crowned with an immense golden dome. Inside there is *Christ* by Juan de Arce and *Sleeping Virgin Mary* by Zurbarán. In the crypt lie the remains of the famous composer Manuel de Falla. On the right-hand side of the building is a small museum, open Tuesday to Saturday, 10am–noon (small admission fee). Behind the cathedral and right beside the sea are the recently excavated ruins of a large Roman theatre.

★ Between the cathedral and plaza San Juan de Dios is an attractive old part of town where the houses are festooned with flowers and the patios beautifully decorated. There is a particularly interesting house with a lovely baroque facade and balcony on calle San Martín.

★ **El Oratorio de la Santa Cueva** (C2 on the map): calle Rosario, just to the left of No. 10 D. ☎ 28-76-76. Open Monday to Friday, 10am–1pm. There is an 18th-century chapel in the basement. The main points of interest are the works of Goya and Cavallini painted under the dome of the cupola, including a depiction of *The Last Supper* and the *Miracle of the Loaves and the Fishes*.

★ **El Oratorio de San Felipe Neri** (B2 on the map): calle Santa Ines 9. ☎ 21-16-12. Open daily 8.30–10am and 7.30–10pm. This national monument (inaugurated in 1719) contains an *Immaculate Conception* by Murillo. It was here that the constitution of Spain was signed.

★ **El Museo Histórico Municipal** (B2 on the map): calle Santa Ines 9. ☎ 22-17-88. Open Tuesday to Friday 9am–1pm and 5–8pm (7pm in winter); Saturday and Sunday 9am–1pm. Closed Monday. This little museum contains an excellent model of the town, made in the 18th century, as well as a collection of pictures and various documents relating to Cádiz. Worth a visit for anyone interested in Spanish history.

★ **El Museo de Bellas Artes** (fine arts museum; C1 on the map): plaza de la Mina. ☎ 21-22-81. Open 10am–2pm. Closed on Monday. This small museum is very modern and well lit. On the ground floor is a collection of archaeological artefacts and statues dating from Phoenician and Carthaginian times, a period when Cádiz was known as Gadir. Upstairs is a gallery showing contemporary Spanish art, including a few works by the landscape painter Carlos de Haes. There are also works by Murillo, Zurbarán and Rubens. The last room houses a collection of puppet theatres.

THE BEACHES

The old town's only beach is to the far southwest, alongside avenida Duque de Nájera. Another beach worth visiting, playa de la Victoria, is near the new town and is flanked by ugly buildings. Go along avenida de Andalucía or take bus No.1.

FIESTAS

– **Cádiz Carnival** is famous throughout Spain. It usually takes place in the second week of February, about 40 days before Semana Santa. The musical festivities brighten up the dark days of winter with guitars, mandolins, tambourines and whistles, and everyone parades through the streets in fancy dress. Some of the costumes are exquisite. There is dancing, singing and general hilarity all night long. It usually winds up at sunrise with freshly cooked *churros* (similar to doughnut sticks) dipped in hot chocolate.

– A wonderful three-day International **folk dancing festival** takes place at the beginning of July.

LEAVING CÁDIZ

By Train

🚂 **RENFE** (D3 on the map): plaza de Sevilla and avenida del Puerto. ☎ 25-43-01. Left luggage facilities.

– Rail services to Jerez de la Frontera, Seville, Madrid, Barcelona.

– For Málaga and Granada change at Bobadilla.

By Bus

🚌 **Compañía Comes** (D1-2 on the map): plaza de la Hispanidad 1. ☎ 21-17-63. Buses to Tarifa and Algeciras (10 buses a day from 7am to 8pm), Jerez (15 services a day from 7am to 9pm), Murcia (one), Almería (two services a day, mornings only), Córdoba (one), Seville (every hour on the hour), Málaga (three), Arcos (six), Granada (two, morning and afternoon), Ronda (three) and Tarifa (seven).

🚌 **Los Amarillos** (C2 on the map): avenida Ramón de Carranza 31. ☎ 28-58-52. Open 10am–2pm and 5–8.30pm. This bus company mainly covers the Cádiz region – Puerto Santa Maria, Sanlúcar, Chipiona (10 buses a day), Arcos (three buses a day) and the various villages of the province. If the ticket office is closed, you can buy your ticket from the driver.

By Boat

⛴ **To El Puerto Santa María**: this is a great trip around the gulf of Cádiz – it makes for a much more interesting journey than going by car. Boats go from Cádiz harbour at 10am, noon, 2pm and 6.30pm (8.30pm in summer). Return journey from Puerto Santa María at 9am, 11am, 1pm and 3.30pm (7.30pm in summer). No service on Monday in winter. Tickets are bought from the crew as you board the boat.

⛴ **To the Canary Islands**: sailings every Tuesday at 7pm to Santa Cruz de Tenerife, to Las Palmas on Thursday and Santa Cruz de la Palma on Friday. You can buy tickets from the offices of Trasmediterranea (open daily, 9am–2pm and 5–7pm) or from any travel agency. It works out cheaper if you share a four-berth cabin.

LA SIERRA GADITANA   DIALLING CODE: 956

The landscapes and views in the region around Cádiz are beautiful and eminent Spanish families often farm these vast tracts of land. This is prime bull-breeding territory and the large *cortijos* (ranches) are generally only found well off the beaten track. The *cortijos* and *ganaderías* (cattle ranches) can often be recognized by the ensign of the bull that appears on the gate.

Grazalema 11610

About 33 kilometres (20 miles) west of Ronda and situated at 900 metres (2,953 feet) above sea level, this village is the perfect place to stop if you want to enjoy a day out of the heat. The roads that lead here meander their way between the cork oaks with cows peacefully grazing on the lower slopes. Then suddenly you come to an immense green prairie that resembles a glacial cirque. There is a type of fir that grows in Grazalema that is unique to the region and is the only one of its kind in Europe: *Abies pinsapo* grows at altitudes in excess of 1,000 metres (3,281 feet) and has been around since the Tertiary period. The small village of Grazalema huddles at the bottom of the cirque.

The village name is of Berber origin. The Saddina tribe had inhabited this area for over eight centuries when a relation of the caliph of Córdoba gave these lands to his daughter Zalema at the same time renaming the village Villa Ben Zalema. Ben Zalema was then corrupted to Cçagrazalema, and this is how it was recorded on Catholic maps.

The village hardly seems to have changed since the Middle Ages. The houses along the delightful cobbled streets have been painted brilliant white and great cast-iron grills protect their windows. There is some hope that the nature reserve in the Sierra of Grazalema will indirectly help to attract jobs and people back to the village.

USEFUL ADDRESSES

B Tourist Office: plaza de España 11 (in the main square). ☎ 13-22-25. The staff are fairly friendly, but if you want information on walks you are better off going to the address listed below.

■ **Pinzapo**: Las Piedras 11. ☎ and fax: 13-21-66. Open 10am–2pm and 5–7pm. There are several walks through the nature reserve of the Grazalema sierra. However, four of the routes can only be undertaken if you are accompanied by a guide. The walks are graded according to length (between 3 and 5 hours) and difficulty. They cost between 7 and 9€.

WHERE TO STAY AND EAT

☆ Budget

🛏 Camping El Tajo Rodillo: ☎ 23-42-21. Fax: 31-79-77. Not too far from the town centre, although it's very badly signposted. Leave the town centre, driving past the tourist office on the right-hand side of the church. Carry on past the municipal swimming pool when you get to the bend in the road. Keep going until you get to where the road heads up the side of the mountain beneath a rocky promontory – the campsite is on the left. Open from 1 April to the end of November. It costs less than 3€ per person and 3€ for a tent, no charge is made for hot water. It is in a nice spot on a small wooded slope. Bring something warm to wear if you are here in spring or autumn as it soon gets chilly in the evenings. A perfect place for ramblers, with friendly staff.
✕ There are several *bodegas* and cafés with outside tables around plaza de España.

☆☆ Moderate

🛏 ✕ Hostal-Restaurante Casa de Las Piedras: calle Las Piedras 32. ☎ and fax: 13-20-14. In a small street leading off the plaza de España to the right of a Unicaja. A double room with en-suite bathroom costs 39€. This is the only proper *hostal* in the centre of town. It has a few dozen rooms, all immaculate but somewhat lacking in character. Some have shared bathrooms. There is a great restaurant with checked tablecloths serving up tasty local specialities. The young owner is very friendly. Set menus from 8€ and an à la carte meal costs around 21€.
✕ **El Torreón**: Agua 4. ☎ 13-23-13. The set menu costs about 9€ and includes a starter, main course, dessert, wine and coffee. This place is popular with the locals – it is nice enough but nothing special.

☆☆☆ Expensive

♠ **Villa Turística de Grazalema**: as you come into the village take the right turn just before the garage and follow the signs. ☎ 13-21-36. Fax: 13-22-13. Website: www.tugasa.com/grazalema.html. A double room costs 45€ in low season and 51€ over Semana Santa and Christmas. There are also apartments for 102€, which sleep four people. This *villa turística* is set out like a small village. It is decorated in a modern style and is fairly luxurious, but is still in keeping with the local architecture. The rooms have TV, telephone and en-suite bathroom and all open out on to a lovely swimming pool. There is also a splendid view of the town and the valley. Reasonably priced, although a few corners have been cut with the decor of the rooms. The welcome is not as friendly as it could be.

WHAT TO DO

– There are a number of walks through the national park, which has one of the largest vulture colonies in Europe, as well as some Royal eagles.

– In the summer the outdoor swimming pool is open.

From Ronda to Algeciras Via Castellar De La Frontera

This short itinerary starts off on the C341 from Ronda until Jimena de la Frontera, and then follows the C3331 to Castellar de la Frontera. You pass several attractive and remote villages along the way, all of which are worth stopping to explore.

BENADALID

A small mountain village about 35 kilometres (22 miles) from Ronda. The white streets and cemetery with its striking truncated towers give it a slightly eerie charm.

JIMENA DE LA FRONTERA

Another small traditional village only a few kilometres from the sprawling coastal towns.

WHERE TO STAY

Campsites

♠ **Camping Los Alcornocales**: ☎ 64-00-60. Fax: 64-12-90. A pitch costs about 3€ per person and per car. This is a pleasant campsite set on a hill close to the village. You'll get a friendly welcome from the staff. There's a large restaurant in the style of a country club.

☆☆ Moderate

♠ **Posada La Casa Grande**: Fuentenueva 42. ☎ 64-05-78. Fax: 64-04-91. A double room costs 30€. The owner Tom has abandoned the Norwegian fjords for the *cortijos* – the bull-breeding farms. He has worked hard on his small establishment and the end result is striking. The rooms are cosy with beautifully polished floor tiles. Other special touches include the library, the lounge and the maritime-theme bar where the guests are left to serve themselves. This is a friendly place that's worth enjoying for a few nights.

CASTELLAR DE LA FRONTERA 11350

By the early 1970s, most of the population of Castellar de la Frontera had left to live and work in the town of Castellar further down the mountain. Their place was quickly taken by a band of hippies who fixed the holes in the roofs, repaved the narrow streets and whitewashed the buildings. Over the years, this newly re-colonized mountain village has gradually become more and more upmarket – the weed-strewn cobbles have been covered with tarmac and a variety of shops as well as three hotels have opened. It is a beautiful place, particularly at dusk as the sun casts its last rays on the speckled grey-green of the olive trees and the tree frogs strike up their chorus.

WHERE TO STAY AND EAT

☆☆ Moderate

🛏 **Antigua Posada Castillo de Castellar**: on the main square through the castle gates. ☎ 23-60-87. A double room costs 36€, breakfast included. Manuel and Javier let two beautifully furnished rooms, which are both cosy and plush. There is one upstairs and another on the ground floor.

🛏 **Casas Rurales Castillo de Castellar**: ☎ 23-66-20. Fax: 23-66-24. Website: www.tugasa.com/castellar.html. After going through the castle gates, turn right and continue until you get to the crossroads, turn right again and the *Casas rurales* are further up the street on the right. Double rooms cost 53€. The apartments are like miniature country houses and are fitted with every gadget and mod con. They are attractively priced for family groups ranging from 53 to 87€ for two people but there is a 15 per cent supplement over Semana Santa and Christmas. This is the latest development by the Tugasa chain whose staff are always welcoming and professional.

☆☆☆ Expensive

🛏 ✕ **The Convento Almoraima**: ☎ 69-30-02. Fax: 69-32-14. Double rooms for about 87€, breakfast costs 6€. Set menu for 18€. Situated at the foot of Castellar, this convent lies in the beautiful surroundings of the Alcornocales park. Previously a refuge for the Sisters of Mercy (it still has its delightful chapel and golden *retablo* from this period), this elegant hotel is in one of the largest hunting areas in the region. The patio, with its small gurgling fountain, is a favourite location for fashion photographers. The rooms are all on the first floor, set on a gallery around the patio, and although they are luxurious, they lack the cosiness of the rooms in the *paradores*. There are free tennis courts and a swimming pool and, for a small supplement, you can go horse-riding or hire a jeep. There is a good restaurant.

VEJER DE LA FRONTERA 11150 DIALLING CODE: 956

A lovely Andalucían village perched on a hilltop 50 kilometres (31 miles) north east of Tarifa and about 12 kilometres (7 miles) from the sea. With its white houses, narrow winding streets and labyrinth of steep steps Vejer is the perfect example of an Andalucían village as it sits basking in the heat. It is a good place to make a stop as it's remote enough to be free from large numbers of tourists.

The Romans realized the strategic importance of the location and founded a small town here. This was then developed further by the Moors, but it has undergone little change since then.

USEFUL INFORMATION AND ADDRESSES

fl Tourist Office: Marqués de Tamarón 10. ☎ 45-01-91. In the market place, right in the centre of town. Open 10.30am–2pm and 6–9pm. The staff here are fairly friendly and can provide lots of useful information.

⊠ Post Office: calle Juan Bueno 10.
🚌 Bus Station: in the main square. **Bus Comes** ☎ 45-00-30.
– **Mercado** (market): every day except Sunday, in the town centre, behind the small square.

WHERE TO STAY

☆☆ Moderate

🛏 Hotel La Posada: calle Los Remedios 21. ☎ 45-01-11. Nice, recently decorated rooms for 24€, with a pleasant view.

☆☆☆ Expensive

🛏 Hotel Convento de San Francisco: on the small square in the centre. ☎ 45-10-01. Fax: 45-10-04. Website: www.tugasa.com/vejer.html. Rooms cost 55€ in low season, with a 15 per cent supplement charged during Semana Santa and Christmas. A flagship of the Tugasa chain, this former Franciscan convent in the heart of the old village has been converted into a hotel, but has managed to retain a certain hint of asceticism. Ask for rooms 24, 25 or 26, as they have more character – you can still trace the ancient arches in the stonework. The beds are made of unpolished wood, and the wardrobes are massive. You still get the usual mod cons, however – TV, telephone, fully fitted bathroom. It is very popular so it's best to reserve in advance. The staff are welcoming and there is a great bar right next door, which means it is only a short trip to bed at the end of the evening.

WHERE TO EAT AND DRINK

✕ Cafeteria Restaurante La Posada: calle Los Remedios 19. ☎ 45-01-11. Fairly pleasant setting, and the set menu featuring fish or meat in sauce is good value at less than 8€.
🍸 Bar Chirino: on the main square. Beer here is a whole 1€ cheaper

than in most other places. This bar is popular with the old folk of the village. The tables are made of formica and there is a 1940s fridge that wheezes away. The walls are covered with photos of bullfights – see if you can spot the one where a man is being gored by a wild bull on the loose in the village streets.

♪ Several **bars** near the church and the ramparts play music in the evenings.

WHAT TO SEE

★ Wander around the maze of steep narrow streets, past patios and iron-grilled windows, and up the steps to the **Iglesia del Divino Salvador** (Church of the Divine Saviour). The church is a curious mix of Mudéjar and Gothic styles with some beautiful archways. The ruins of a Moorish fortress are nearby.

★ The **plaza de España** is the square where the old folk of the village gather, taking a rest on the polished tiled benches surrounding the pretty fountain. There are some pleasant little cafés on the square, in particular No. 27, next to the ramparts and the tower, where old men come to play dominoes on a Sunday.

★ At every turn you will come across crumbling crenellations and sections of the thick fortified walls of the medieval town.

★ Another nice route for a stroll takes you round the palm-shaded *corredera* (track) that circles the village. There is a great view of the surrounding hills.

WHAT TO SEE IN THE SURROUNDING AREA

★ **Playa de la Palmera**: 10 kilometres (6 miles) from Vejer – a large, undeveloped beach with a row of small, reasonably priced, fish restaurants.

CAÑOS DE LA MECA 11150   DIALLING CODE: 956

Not quite as lovely as the neighbouring village of Tarifa, but definitely more authentic. The main reasons for visiting Caños de la Meca are the delightful protected pine forests and the windsurfing, but not much else.

WHERE TO STAY

Campsite

⛺ **Camping Caños de la Meca**: 10 kilometres (6 miles) along the road from Vejer to los Caños, at Barbate. ☎ 43-71-20. Fax: 43-71-37. In low season about 3€ per person and 3€ per tent, in high season the cost rises to 4€. Good facilities, including a swimming pool. Quiet and shady with a friendly welcome, especially from the mosquitoes . . . The plots are marked by stone borders.

☆☆ Moderate

⛺ **Hostal Miramar**: Trafalgar 112. ☎ 43-70-24. In high season a room with a balcony costs 42€, or 36€ for a room without (note that it probably isn't worth paying the extra). Out of season prices drop to 25€ and 22€ respectively. The name means 'sea view' – a bit of an exaggeration as there is a large building in the way of anything interesting. This small hotel is very pleasant and welcoming, however, and the rooms are clean and simply furnished. You can't go wrong spending a couple of nights here.

WHERE TO EAT

☆ Budget

✕ **Venta Curo**: Zahora, Barbate. ☎ 43-70-64. Tasty fish, fried or *a la plancha* (grilled), for about 6€. To get there follow the signs to the *Caños de la Meca* campsite. Skirt round the left-hand side of the campsite, then turn right as if you were heading for the sea. This is a traditional *venta* (country inn) with a thatched roof and adobe walls. It is also *bien de precio* (good value), and service is speedy. Open daily and popular with Sevillian families spending a weekend at the beach.

☆☆☆ Expensive

✕ **El Rezón de la Fontanilla**: Hijuela de Lojo 27, in Conil de la Frontera. ☎ 44-27-55. A meal costs between 24 and 30€. Good selection of fish on the menu with plenty of seafood – some dishes are flavoured with saffron. They serve a good *revuelto de setas con bacalao* (wild-mushroom omelette with salt cod) and a tasty paella. Friendly service without being too chummy. Definitely worth a try, and probably worth booking in advance.

BEACHES

★ Travel down through the pine forest from Barbate, then take a left turn when you get to the beach. Carry on to the end of the road and leave your car here. Continue on foot to the right of the small wall surrounding a house with gardens stretching down to the sea. This takes you to the **nudist beach** at Caños. If the tide is in and you can't get round via the beach, go back round the house and up the road to the pine forest. When you get to the unsurfaced part of the road slip off your shoes and make your way down to the sea. Small paths lead down between the coves and the promontories. Choose your spot on the beach carefully, as the further you go from the sandy part the more likely you are to be disturbed – there are some scruffy-looking Romeos whose attentions can be a bit of a nuisance.

This beach has also become home to a number of hippies, who have set up camp between the two promontories. You'll notice that there are several small rivulets (*caños*) running down from the cliffs. This fresh water comes from springs located somewhere beneath the pine forest. When the Moors first discovered this water, they saw it as a gift from Allah, and as a mark of gratitude they named the spot *Caños de la Meca*.

Further along there are great lumps of rock strewn all over the shore. They have fallen off the cliff face as a result of the combined action of the wind, rain and the force of the sea. They come from fossilized dunes from the Quaternary period. The sand slowly piled up and became partially compacted, which is why at a later period parts of it came loose from the cliff. At the base of the cliffs you can still see embedded shells of sea creatures that became trapped in the sandy mire and were unable to escape. Further evidence of the sandiness of the soil is the presence of *doncel* pine trees in the forest at Barbate. These are pioneer pines that only grow on very sandy ground. They help to break up an otherwise flat and monotonous country-side.

TARIFA 11380   DIALLING CODE: 956

Tarifa is a small town at the extreme southern tip of Spain, some 22 kilometres (14 miles) from Algeciras, enclosed within high walls. There are some beautiful views from the approach road that snakes its way through a hilly landscape sprinkled with windmills. There is a tangible feel of North Africa about the town – the houses are white like those of a Kasbah and the *mercado central* (town market) bears evident Moorish influences.

Tarifa is the first really pleasant town on this part of the coast, and very welcome after the horrors of the Costa del Sol. The modern part of the town encircles the historic centre but has developed in such away as not to engulf it. The new buildings have been constructed in accordance with stringent height restrictions and are of similar colours to the old. Of course it goes without saying that it is busy here, but not in comparison with places like Marbella or Torremolinos. Tarifa has adapted to the rhythm of tourism without losing its soul, and is the kind of place you could fall in love with. The old town is an endless maze of narrow pedestrian streets and passageways leading to tiny squares and is a lovely place to wander around.

The town isn't confined to the limits of its old walls, but extends to the outskirts of Algeciras and Zahara de los Atunes. Zahara is so named because the current flowing along the nearby coast attracts tuna fish (*atún*).

The main reason that so many people flock to Tarifa, however, is for its beautiful, long, deserted beaches, which have become a target for wind-surfers. This is one of the windiest spots in Europe, with winds sometimes reaching speeds of 120 kilometres per hour (75 miles per hour). The consistently strong wind and sheltered waters create the perfect conditions for the pros to zip backwards and forwards performing feats of daring to their hearts' content. There are several windsurfing centres along the length of the coast where you can hire a board, have lessons, practise your technique or simply watch the acrobatics.

A Brief History

Tarifa used to be a busy fishing port and was initially settled by the Romans. In 711, Tarik's Moorish forces seized the town and renamed it Yebel Tarik. In 1292 the Christians, led by Sancho IV recaptured the town, but the Muslims quickly returned to seize it back. Around the same time a dramatic event took place that earned Tarifa a place in the history books for ever. The Christian, Guzmán el Bueno (the Good), offered the life of his nine-year old son to stop the Moors from advancing on the town. His son had been captured by the Muslims and they threatened to kill the boy if the Christians didn't release the captured territories. Guzmán was quick to respond – from the top of the Castle he threw them his dagger to use for the deed and watched as they cut his son's throat before his eyes. This dubious act of faith made Guzmán el Bueno the patron saint of Tarifa.

USEFUL ADDRESSES

🛈 Tourist Office (A-B2 on the map): paseo de la Alameda, in a small park that runs the length of the old part of town. ☎ 68-09-93. Website: www.tarifa.net. The opening times are a little erratic, although in theory they are 11am–2pm and 5–7pm. Don't expect much help here, but try to get hold of the leaflet *Tarifa Alternativa*, which maps the various paths for walking, cycling and horse-riding. It also tells you how long each walk should take and the level of difficulty.

✉ Post Office (B2 on the map): calle Coronel Moscardó on the corner with calle Melo, in the old part of town.

■ Taxis: avenida de Andalucía. ☎ 68-42-41.

■ Police: plaza de Santa Maria 3. ☎ 68-41-86. The police in Tarifa are very friendly.

■ Red Cross (A2, **1** on the map): calle Juan Nuñez. ☎ 68-48-96.

■ Windsurf Emergency: ☎ 20-22-02 (free phone).

■ Supermercado Syp (A1, **2** on the map): on the corner of calle Callao and calle San José.

■ Cycle hire (A1, **3** on the map A1): agencia de ocio Aky Oaky Tarifa, Batalla del Salado 37. ☎ 68-53-56. Fax: 68-41-85. Website: www.akyoaky.com. You can hire bikes for 18€ for a whole day or 12€ for half a day.

WHERE TO STAY

There aren't really any cheap places to stay in Tarifa during the high season, although prices drop considerably at other times of year.

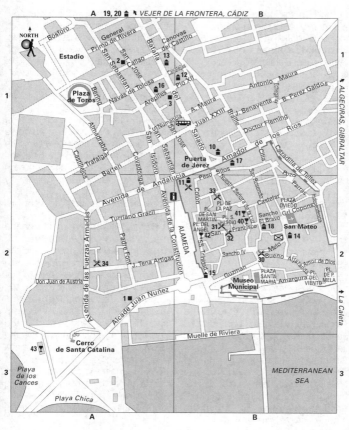

TARIFA

☆ Budget

â Casa de Huéspedes Eusebio
(B1, **10** on the map): Amador de los Ríos. Facing puerta Jerez, in a small house opposite the traffic lights. There's no phone and you can't make a reservation. Not the greatest of luxury, but what can you expect at this price? A double room costs 15€. Prices may rise in high season, but the owner (who is a seasoned traveller) tends to charge what he

feels like, so don't be afraid to haggle. The rooms can be a bit dirty and all the bathroom facilities are communal.

☆☆ Moderate

â Hotel Avenida (B1, **12** on the map): at the junction of Pio XII and Batalla del Salado. ☎ 68-48-18. A room costs 24€ which is in line with what you get for your money. Clean rooms tiled from top to bottom. Ask for one on the ground floor – they are more spacious and open out on to a small patio.

â **Facundo Camas** (A1, **13** on the map): calle Batalla del Salado 47. ☎ 68-42-98 or 68-45-36. This well-kept *hostal* is 100 metres from the bus stop in the Cádiz direction and about 5-minute-walk from the old part of town. There is a large neon sign outside. It costs 24€ for a room with a bathroom and 18€ without – the rooms are slightly disappointing for a place of this size. The *hostal* has no particular attraction, but has a friendly family atmosphere. There are facilities for storing surf-boards.

â **Pensión Correos** (B2, **14** on the map): calle Coronel Moscardó 8. ☎ 68-02-06. Opposite the post office as its name would suggest. A delightful little *pensión* that has recently been redecorated. Double rooms cost 24€ with a shower or 21€ without. Some rooms sleep three to five people for 30€. The rooms are pleasant and simple, although the ones on the ground floor are a bit dark. There are rooms for three to five people on the top floor and there is a delightful view over the town. There's also a roof terrace enclosed by low white walls.

â **Hostal Alameda** (B2, **15** on the map): paseo Alameda 4. ☎ 68-02-64 or 68-11-81. Set on the outskirts of the old town in a lovely spot at the end of the main promenade. Rooms cost between 30 and 42€ depending on season. There are about a dozen spotless rooms, with all mod cons (including a TV) and pine furniture. The building itself has quite a bit of character. Breakfast is available.

â **Hostal Alborada** (A1, **16** on the map): calle San José 52. ☎ 68-11-40. Fax: (959) 68-19-35. In a fairly central location, behind the main street with all the surf shops. Housed in a large white building offering some lovely rooms at 24€

out of season and 45€ in season. Each room has a well-equipped bathroom. There is a large patio overlooked by several balconies, *azulejos* decorating the walls, cable TV in the rooms and friendly welcoming staff.

â **Hostal El Asturiano** (B1, **17** on the map): Amador de los Ríos 8. ☎ 68-06-19. Pretty much market rates – out of season a room costs 24€ and in season 42–45€. The rooms on the second floor have a wonderful view of Morocco and the town's rooftops. Try and get one of these rooms if you can. One drawback is that the staff are very unfriendly.

â **Hostal Villanueva** (B2, **11** on the map): avenida de Andalucía 11. ☎ 68-41-49. At the entrance to the old part of town alongside the taxi rank. Closed from the beginning of January to mid-February. Fairly expensive in summer, with rooms costing 60€. Half price in low season. There is a terrace on the top floor with a rooftop view. All the rooms have bathrooms and have been tastefully redecorated. This hotel is almost too clean for comfort and is owned by a lovely lady who is always willing to help if needed. Good family restaurant (*see* 'Where to Eat').

Apartments

â **La Casa Amarilla** (B2, **18** on the map): Sancho IV El Bravo 9. ☎ 68-19-93 or (929) 97-50-88. Fax: 62-71-30. Website: www.tarifa.net/lacasaamarilla. Set in the heart of the old town, this recently renovated establishment has lovely apartments for two, three or four people, each with a kitchen, living room, bedrooms and bathroom. Compared to a luxury hotel, which is the next best alternative, prices are extremely reasonable. Prices vary according to the season and the number of tourists, starting at 36€ in low season for two and rising to 90€ for four in high season. Apartment No. 1 is particularly lovely with its flowery tiles, central archway, slatted blinds and bow window opening on to the lively street. Apartment No. 6 is completely different with a plaster mosque-style double archway. The bathrooms are especially beautiful, with colourful earthenware tiling. You also get a very warm welcome.

WHERE TO STAY IN THE SURROUNDING AREA

Campsites

There are a number of campsites by the long beach, where all the windsurfers hang out. Prices only tend to vary by tiny amounts. What really distinguishes them are the facilities and the amount of shade they offer as the sun can be quite hot in spite of the wind. The following selection of campsites is listed in the order in which they appear as you travel along the N340 from Tarifa in the direction of Cádiz.

⬧ **Tarifa**: 5 kilometres (3 miles) northwest of the town. ☎ and fax: 68-47-78. Email: camping.tarifa@ globalmail.net. This is definitely the best of the campsites on offer. A pitch costs about 3€ per person, although you get a discount if you pay in cash or stay for more than 10 days in low season. This new campsite extends over three hectares (almost seven and a half acres) and is well shaded and quiet. The toilet and shower blocks are clean – although a bit of a trek from some of the plots – and there are free hot showers. There is also a swimming pool, bar and restaurant. The site is dotted with beautiful pine trees and offers direct access to the beach. It also has its own water purification plant, so no waste is pumped into the sea. The staff are friendly and professional.

⬧ **Torre de la Peña I**: about 6 kilometres (4 miles) out of town. ☎ 68-49-03. Fax: 68-14-73. This campsite costs the same as Torre de la Peña II (*see below*) as they are owned by the same person. There are two sections to the site, one next to the beach and the other on the hillside at the foot of the old tower. The beach side is the nicest, although it does get very busy. The hill side is nearer the road, and therefore noisier. It is less crowded, but the hot water is more unreliable.

⬧ **Torre de la Peña II**: about 8 kilometres (5 miles) out of town, on the opposite side of the road to the beach. ☎ 68-41-74. Fax: 68-18-98. A pitch costs about 3€ with an additional 4€ per person. It is more expensive for camper vans – about 5€ a night. There are three seasons with three different price bands and you can also get a range of discounts for stays between three and seven days up to longer than a month. Swimming pool and tennis courts. Unfortunately the site is not very shady, and the ground is quite uneven. It is also quite a distance from the beach. Friendly welcome.

⬧ **Paloma**: CN340, at the 74 kilometre-marker, 11380 Tarifa. About 10 kilometres (6 miles) northwest of Tarifa on the road to Vejer de la Frontera, on the left-hand side. ☎ 68-42-03. Fax: 68-18-80. Website: www.tarifa.net/paloma. About one kilometre from the beach, set in a magnificent bay and very popular with windsurfers. The reception is open 9am–10pm. A pitch costs 4€ per person and 3€ per tent and per car. This spacious site is well shaded by pine and palm trees, with a lovely green lawn. The plots are well separated by pine hedges and wooden fences. The campsite is clean and quiet – apart from the tinkling of cowbells, although there are quite a few mosquitoes, attracted by the little stream. There is a small supermarket, swimming pool and restaurant.

🛏 **Camping El Jardín de las Dunas**: right opposite playa de Valdevaqueros. ☎ 23-64-36. About 4€ per person, 3€ per tent and 5€ for a camper van. Out of season prices drop to 2€ per person and per tent, and 3€ for a camper van. This site is better equipped than the preceding one (it has a bar, reception and baths) but it's not as shaded and offers less privacy.

☆☆☆ Expensive

🛏 **Hurricane Hotel** (**19** off the map from A1): on the seafront about 4 kilometres (2 miles) from the town. ☎ 68-49-19. Fax: 68-45-08. Website: www.andalucia.com/hurricane. This is the hotel of the rich and famous, so in order to secure a room you must book early – it is so popular that it can be full as much as a year in advance. Out of season a room costs between 72 and 90€ and in season between 102 and 108€, with prices depending on whether there is a sea view. Beautiful architecture with an array of white arches, lots of plants and a swimming pool; there are even steps leading directly onto the beach. The rooms are light, and furnished in a colonial style (cane furniture and natural-cotton-coloured sheets). Avoid the rooms at the front as they are rather near the road, the ones by the swimming pool are better. Breakfast is a rather scanty affair and it is a shame that the service and the welcome are only average. They offer the opportunity to go pony-trekking, although the horses tend to be quite high-spirited and will certainly put your riding skills to the test.

🛏 **Hotel 100% Fun** (**20** off the map from A1): on the Cádiz–Tarifa road. ☎ 68-03-30. Fax: 68-00-13. Alongside Valdevaqueros beach. Closed from the beginning of January to the beginning of March. Double rooms with breakfast cost between 54 and 66€ depending on the season. The rooms are sparsely furnished and a bit expensive. However the owners manage to fill them and even raise their prices on a regular basis. This hotel complex, set in its own attractive gardens, is owned by an Englishman and consists of a collection of squat buildings the colour of faded red brick with a large hut decorated with Hawaiian masks, which is where they serve breakfast. The rooms open onto a beautiful kidney-shaped pool and narrow paved pathways cross the freshly mown lawn. There's a fountain, waterlilies and croaking frogs. It's a lovely place and quite fun too with friendly staff. The hotel has a surf shop and some gym equipment.

WHERE TO EAT

☆ Budget

✕ **Restaurante Villanueva** (B2, **11** on the map): avenida de Andalucía 11. ☎ 68-41-49. See 'Where to Stay'. Closed Monday and the beginning of January to mid-February. Set menu costs 7€. Good food served in a pleasant family setting. If the decor is slightly reminiscent of a works' canteen, at least the vases of fresh flowers brighten it up a little. Good choice of fish bought locally at the market and cooked *a la plancha* (grilled), *al ajillo* (in garlic) or in a sauce. There is also tasty Tarifan tuna on the menu. For dessert, the tempting selection may include *arroz con leche* (rice pudding) and *natilla* (custard) – maybe not the most inventive cuisine, but all home-made. Definitely a restaurant worth visiting, and also a favourite among the locals at lunchtime.

✕ **El Pasillo** (B2, **30** on the map): Guzmán el Bueno 14. Closed on Monday. *Montaditos* (pâté, kebabs, snails and shellfish) as well as a selection of *bocadillos* for 1–2€. The bar's name means 'passage-way' and the premises are indeed very small. The tapas here are good – in addition to those already mentioned you can also get razor clams, weather permitting. Every glass of beer is served with a *tapita* of olives. You get a polite welcome here, and it's so tightly packed that you soon get to know everyone.

✕ **La Cabaña de Ana** (B2, **31** on the map): calle Lorito 3. This restaurant in the old part of town is open evenings only, every night of the week. A snack costs about 4€. There is a bar, but when the owner's family's there, the place gets full with any more than five customers. You do get a genuinely warm welcome though and the tapas (mostly small sandwiches) are delicious and filling. It also serves a good tortilla and a selection of pork-based tapas.

✕ **Casa Juan Luis** (B2, **32** on the map): San Francisco 15. ☎ 68-12-65 or 68-48-03. Similar set-up to the preceding place. House specialities are *jamón jabugo* (*jabugo* ham), *bellotas* (sea urchins), and a good selection of cheese with the very drinkable local wine.

✕ **Cervecería J. J. Lopez** (B2, **33** on the map): Maria Antonia Toledo 5. Only open in the evening. *Montaditos* for less than 1€ and *raciónes* (larger portions of tapas) for 5–9€. Slightly more up-market than the previous places, but just as nice.

✕ **Pizzería La Tabla** (A2, **34** on the map): on a tree-lined avenue between two blocks of flats, very close to the old town. ☎ 68-04-42. Traditional pizzas from 9€. Popular with the local youth who usually turn up after 10pm. They also do take-away pizzas.

WHERE TO EAT ON THE OUTSKIRTS

✕ **Restaurant Las Rejas**: in Bolonia. ☎ 68-85-46. A meal costs about 12€ per person. As you come into Bolonia, take the first left, so the archaeological site is on your right. The restaurant is a little way along the seafront. The owner, a friendly young hippy-type buys all the fish directly from local fishermen or sometimes catches them himself. The fish soup is particularly recommended.

WHERE TO HAVE A DRINK

The nicest bars are all in the old part of town. It is hard to say which is the best as bar-hopping is generally the norm. Try any of the ones along calle Coronel Moscardó, calle Melo, calle Bravo and calle de La Luz.

🍸 **Moby Dick** (B2, **40** on the map) and especially **O Baïano** (B2, **41** on the map): calle de la Luz.

🍸 **Bistrot Point** (B2, **42** on the map): calle San Francisco 18. Trendy older clientele.

♟ El Balneario (A3, **43** on the map): a club run by the municipal authorities. Open in summer only at playa Chica (go past the Red Cross building in the direction of the *Puerto Pesquero* – fishing port).

WHAT TO SEE

★ **Old part of Tarifa**: take a pleasant stroll along the narrow white streets. The light changes at different times of day as the sun moves and there is always something to look at.

★ **El Castillo de Guzmán el Bueno**: next to the sea, by the old part of the town. Open Tuesday to Friday, 10am–1.30pm and at weekends 10am–1.30pm and 6–7pm. Tickets can be bought at the *Europa* bookshop right opposite the castle and cost about 1€. Enjoy a pleasant stroll through the ruins of this well-restored old castle. This is where Guzmán el Bueno's son was killed (*see* 'A Brief History'). There are ramparts and a circular path leading to the Torre de Guzmán. From the top of the tower you can clearly see the Moroccan coast, the kasbah and the port.

★ **The City Gates**: avenida de Andalucía.

WHAT TO SEE IN THE SURROUNDING AREA

★ **The Ruins of Baelo Claudia**: about 14 kilometres (9 miles) from Tarifa in the Vejer direction take a left turn towards El Chaparol and continue for another 7 kilometres (about 4 miles). The ruins are by the beach. Closed on Monday. In summer, opening times are 10am–1.30pm and 5–6.30pm, the rest of the year 10am–2.30pm and 4–6.30pm. This is an unassuming Roman site with a forum, marketplace, baths, temples and fish-salting works. There are a few columns still standing. If archaeology isn't your thing it's worth coming here for the wonderful beach.

WINDSURFING

Tarifa is an great place for windsurfers of all levels. Not only is the wind here stronger than many other places but the Atlantic waves that break on the south coast are ideal for speed surfing and wave jumping. There are several bays between Tarifa and Conil de la Frontera. The main spot is about 7 kilometres (4 miles) west of the town towards playa de Valdevaqueros. There is a small car-park here for camper vans, where the windsurfers relax while waiting for the wind to get up.

The best tubes are to be found in the area to the west of the foot of the Trafalgar lighthouse (take the Caños road towards Conil and turn left at the sign for *faro de Trafalgar*). Even if you're not particularly sporty the view from this point is amazing.

When the wind is *ponente* (blowing from the west) the best spot is playa de Valdevaqueros. Otherwise, if the wind is *levante* (blowing from the east) the windiest place will be Tarifa.

– There are a number of surf clubs, boutiques and repair shops in town. It's hard to say which are the best, as the 'in' places change regularly. Your best

COLOUR MAPS

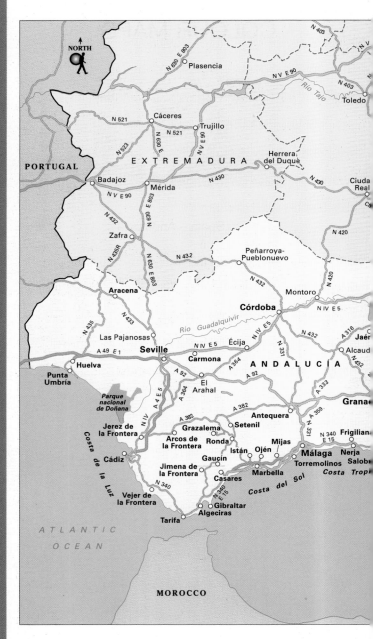

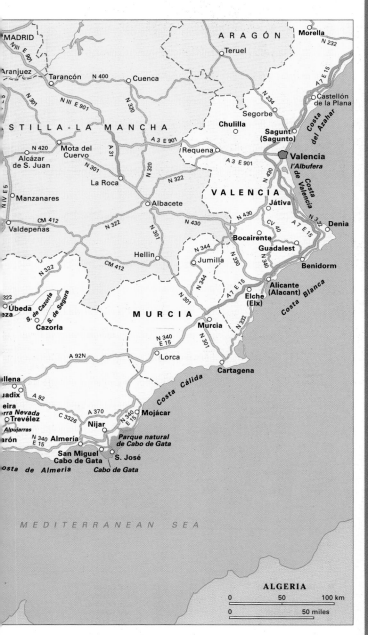

SOUTHERN SPAIN – ANDALUCÍA

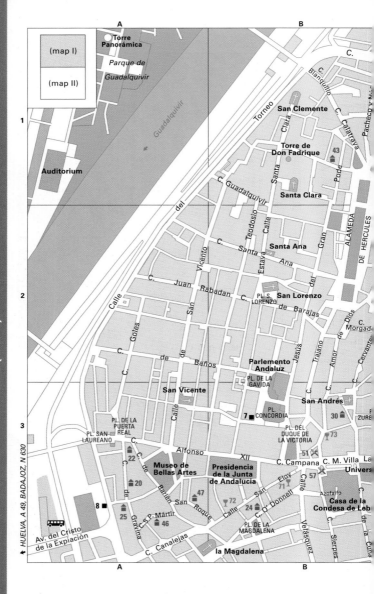

SEVILLE (MAP I)

Torre Panorámica

Parque de Guadalquivir

(map I)

(map II)

Guadalquivir

Auditorium

← HUELVA, A 49, BADAJOZ, N 630

San Clemente

Torre de Don Fadrique

Santa Clara

C. Guadalquivir

Santa Ana

C. Juan Rabadan

San Lorenzo

PL S. LORENZO

de Barajas

Parlemento Andaluz

PL DE LA GAVIDA

San Vicente

San Andrés

7 ■ PL. CONCORDIA

30

PL DE LA PUERTA REAL

PL SAN LAUREANO

PL DEL DUQUE DE LA VICTORIA

73

51

Alfonso

C. Campana C. M. Villa

Univers

22

Museo de Bellas Artes

Presidencia de la Junta de Andalucía

72

47

57

71

24

8 ■

20

25

46

PL DE LA MAGDALENA

Casa de la Condesa de Leb

Av. del Cristo de la Explación

la Magdalena

DE HERCULES

ALAMEDA

Torneo

Santa Clara

ALAMEDA

	Useful Addresses	22	Hostal Bailén
🚌	Bus Station	24	Hostal-Residencia Lis II
7	Police Station	25	Hostal Gravina
8	Underground Parking	30	Hostal Sevilla
		43	Patio de la Cartuja
🛏	Where to Stay	46	Hostal Paris
		47	Hostal Zaida
20	Hostal Romero		

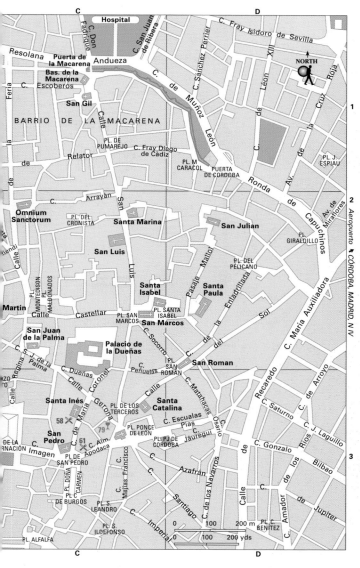

SEVILLE (MAP I)

✕	**Where to Eat**		▼	**Where to Eat Tapas and Have a Drink**
51	Mesón Los Gallegos		**71**	Patio San Eloy
57	Confitería La Campana		**72**	La Bodega
58	Convento de Santa Inés		**73**	El Caserón
61	Rayas		**79**	El Rinconcillo

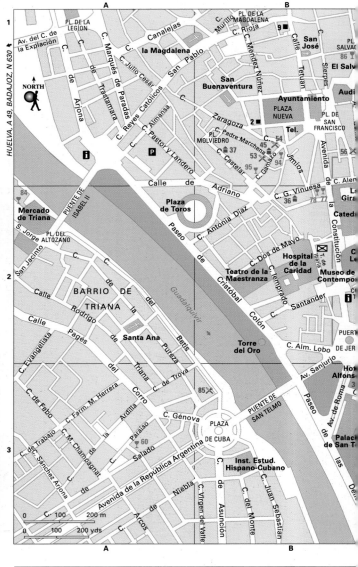
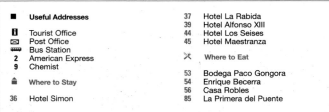

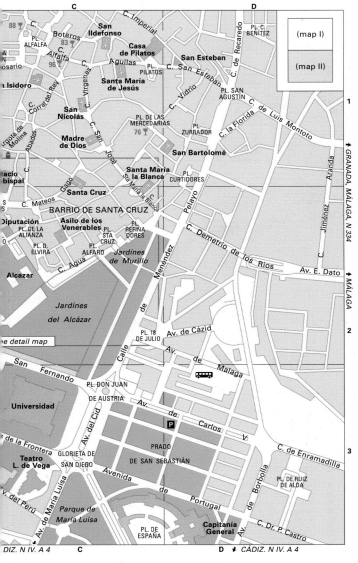

SEVILLE (MAP II)

☖	**Where to Eat Tapas and Have a Drink**	84	Cervecería Casa Cuesta
		86	La Antigua Bodeguita
60	Hostería Las Cuevas	87	La Alicantina
76	La Carbonería	88	Calle Perez Caldos
77	Horno San Buenaventura	94	Cervecería Internacional
78	Hijos de Morales	95	Bodeguita Antonio Romero II
83	Bar Garlochi	96	Bodega Extremaña

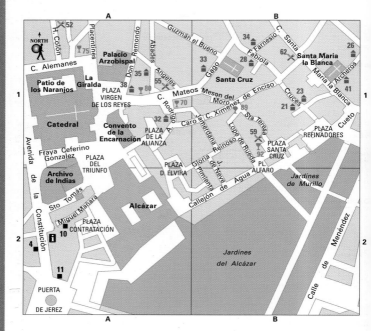

SEVILLE – SANTA CRUZ DISTRICT (MAP III)

■	**Useful Addresses**
ℹ	Tourist Office
4	Banks and Cash Machines
10	Bike Hire
11	Cybercafé

Where to Stay

21	Pensión Cruces El Patio
23	Pensión San Pancrasio
26	Hostal Bienvenido
28	Pensión Fabiola
32	Hostal Monreal
33	Hostal Goya
34	Hostal Córdoba
35	Hostal Marco de la Giralda
38	Hostal Doña Maria
41	Pensión Archeros

✕ **Where to Eat**

52	Restaurante Las Escobas
55	Restaurante A. Donaire El Tenorio
59	La Albahaca
62	Confitería-bar Cáceres

Where to Eat Tapas and Have a Drink

70	Bodega Santa Cruz
75	Antigüedades
80	Cervecería Giralda
89	Café-bar Las Teresas
92	Los Gallos

bet is to ask other surfers on the beach, in the campsites or in the bars around town.

THE BEACHES

There are many types of beach at Tarifa, from the tame parasol-and-lounger type to long stretches of wild deserted sands. The Valdevaqueros bay, surrounded by a chain of sand dunes, is much favoured by windsurfers. Naturists should walk right to the end of the bay, through two rocky outcrops and along a pathway that leads to the Punta Paloma bay. It takes about 15 minutes on foot from the small car-park opposite Camping de las Dunas. Don't leave any valuables in your car as thefts are common.

LEAVING TARIFA

By Bus

Transportes General Comes (B1 on the map): Batalla del Salado 13. ☎ 68-40-38. Services to Algeciras (ten a day), Cádiz (nine), Málaga (three), Seville (three), Jerez (one) and Almería (one). There are fewer services on a Sunday.

TARIFA

The Costa del Sol and Inland

The evocative and aptly named Costa del Sol has a summer season of almost-guaranteed sun and blue skies and has barely 40 days of bad weather a year. Add to this its 600 kilometres (375 miles) of coastline, stretching from Algeciras to Almería, the backdrop of the mountains, picturesque fishing villages, avenues of palm-trees and as much seafood as you can eat and you'll soon see why the Costa del Sol has been the top holiday destination for northern Europeans since the 1960s.

It wasn't long before a period of unchecked hotel development started. Responding to the influx of holidaymakers, locals decided to cash in on the tourist peseta. Local authorities happily turned a blind eye to the rash of developments keen to bring money into an area that had previously suffered high levels of unemployment.

Unspoilt fishing villages soon became marinas, patios were turned into parking spaces and idyllic beaches were flanked by concrete blocks of flats and hotels. Things are not much better today – the coastline to the south of Málaga, which in the 1980s sprouted tower blocks like mushrooms, is still popular with developers, keen to throw up yet more holiday accommodation. But there is much more to this area of Spain than the miles of bronzing bodies. If you venture inland and away from the coast, you will find towns and villages that have survived the tourist era where you can gain an insight into an older, more traditional way of life.

If you are keen to enjoy the pleasures of the Costa del Sol it is preferable to come outside the summer season when the weather is still pleasant but the atmosphere less frenetic. If you must come in July or August, make sure you book well in advance as despite the rate of construction of new hotels, accommodation fills up fast.

ALGECIRAS 11200   DIALLING CODE: 956

A Roman settlement in ancient times and then Muslim for six centuries –the name comes from the Arab *Al-Yazirat-al-Jadra*, which means 'the green island' – Algeciras has seen its fair share of trouble. In the 14th century, the sultan of Granada, Mohamed V, tried to seize control of the town by burning it down.

Today, Algeciras is strikingly unappealing – much of the town is derelict and it is dominated by the docks, which are heavily polluted. The port and the neighbouring streets create a somewhat desolate image of people in transit (although it is seen by some as darkly romantic).

Despite its lack of tourist appeal, Algeciras is a bustling place, mainly due to its many ferry crossings to Morocco. At the far side of the bay is the imposing Rock of Gibraltar. If you are taking a boat from here there is little point in

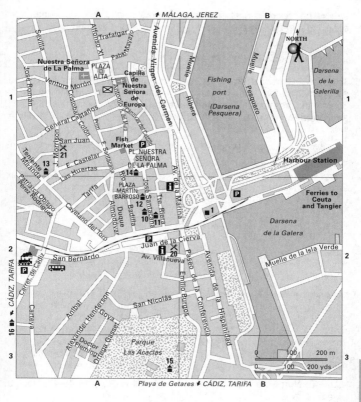

ALGECIRAS

- **Useful Addresses**

  - 🅸 Tourist Office
  - ✉ Post Office
  - 1 Trasmediterranea
  - 🚃 RENFE station
  - 🚌 Bus station

🏠 **Where to Stay**

  - 10 Nuestra Señora del Carmen
  - 11 Hostal Gonzalez

  - 12 Hostal España
  - 13 Hostal-Residencia Carymar
  - 14 Hostal Nuestra Señora de la Palma
  - 15 Hotel Reina Cristina
  - 16 Albergue Juvenil Algeciras

✕ **Where to Eat**

  - 20 Casa Blanca Restaurante
  - 21 Restaurante Montes

arriving before the day of departure as there's nothing to be gained from spending the night here.

CONNECTIONS WITH MOROCCO

There are numerous crossings every day in summer. Don't forget your passport. The two destinations are Ceuta and Tangier. Two companies operate the crossings – **Trasmediterranea** (B2, **1** on the map) ☎ 66-52-00 and **Buquebus**, ☎ (93) 443-98-20 or ☎ (90) 241-42-42 (based in Barcelona).

All travel agents and ticket-sellers offer the same tickets at the same prices.

– **By Hydrofoil** (does not take cars): faster than the ferry, but more expensive, noisier and altogether a less pleasant experience. There are two crossings a day in summer to Tangier, but only one during the rest of the year (the crossing takes 1 hour). A ticket costs around 19€ per person. To Ceuta, there are between 12 and 18 crossings a day depending on season (the crossing takes about 30 minutes).

– **By Ferry**: to Tangier, a dozen ferries a day (the journey takes 2 hours 30 minutes). To Ceuta, six ferries on weekdays and an average of two on Saturday and Sunday (the journey takes 1 hour 30 minutes).

– **Reservations**: if you are a foot passenger, there will be no problem boarding without a reservation in summer. If you are travelling with a car, you will generally have a wait of around 24 hours. If this is the case it is better to make your reservation from home. This system is for crossings with Trasmediterranea and works out slightly more expensive, but at least if you have already got an open ticket you can be sure of getting on. (Free for animals and bicycles, tickets required per person and for vehicles.)

– **Useful Numbers**: Ferries: general enquiries ☎ (902) 45-46-45; Dock at Algeciras: ☎ (956) 66-69-09.

USEFUL ADDRESSES

目 Tourist Office (A2 on the map): close to the port, in calle Juan de la Cierva. ☎ 57-26-36. A pink and red office. Open Monday to Friday 9am–2pm, and Saturday 10am–1pm. Closed Sunday. Variable welcome from the staff.

目 In summer a small **kiosk** (A2 on the map) is also open on avenida de la Marina.

⊠ Post Office: calle Ruiz Zorrilla (A1 on the map). There is another on calle José Antonio.

■ Foreign exchange: several banks at the port. Avoid changing money at the travel agencies, except in an emergency.

■ Bank: BBV, Virgen del Carmen 17.

■ Municipal Police: ☎ 092.

■ Left-luggage facilities: at the dock and the RENFE station.

WHERE TO STAY

The hotels listed are all in the same part of the town, facing the port. The standard of accommodation here is pretty poor and sometimes downright awful. Don't hesitate to ask to see several rooms before taking one.

Note that in hotels run by Moroccans – a *choukrane* ('thank you' in Arabic) sometimes smoothes the way to securing a good deal.

⊡ Budget

⚏ **Nuestra Señora del Carmen** (A2, **10** on the map): calle José Santacana 14a. ☎ 65-63-01. Rooms with or without en-suite facilities for less than 24€. A small, well kept and impeccably clean hotel with flower-filled window boxes. Suspicious landlady who is a little reluctant to open her door. By far the best value for money, especially given its central location.

⚏ **Hostal Gonzalez** (A2, **11** on the map): calle José Santacana 7. ☎ 65-28-43. Same prices as the Nuestra Señora del Carmen. A recently built, clean *hostal* with a welcoming landlady. Rooms with or without shower.

⚏ **Hostal España** (A2, **12** on the map): calle José Santacana 4. ☎ 66-82-62. Clean, decent, if rather small rooms with washbasins, at 12€ for a double. The rooms overlooking the road are very noisy from around 6am onwards. The cheapest accommodation in town, but the welcome is only just the right side of downright rude. No telephone reservations.

⚏ **Hostal-Residencia Carymar** (A1, **13** on the map): calle Emilio Castellan 46. ☎ (956) 656-506. A double room costs around 18€. A bit tatty, although generally well-kept. Some way from the town centre. Less impersonal than elsewhere, with a bit more of a family atmosphere, but nothing of any great interest. Avoid the ground floor rooms, as they can be noisy.

⊡⊡ Moderate

⚏ **Hostal Nuestra Señora de la Palma** (A1, **14** on the map): plaza Palma 12. ☎ 63-24-81. Rooms with bathrooms for around 23€ out of season, less than 30€ in season. The rooms are dark and cheerless and although they look out over an interesting market, the noise is obtrusive from the early hours of the morning. Slightly more acceptable than the small *hostales* in the neighbouring streets, however.

⊡⊡⊡⊡ Splash Out

⚏ **Hotel Reina Cristina** (A3, **15** on the map): paseo de la Conferencia. ☎ 60-26-22. Fax: 60-33-23. A double room costs a good 132€, including breakfast. The Moorish-style hotel, set in the middle of a lavish park has managed to preserve its old-world charm despite a recent revamp. Very nice swimming pool surrounded by palm trees. All rooms have en-suite bathrooms and air-conditioning. Delightful interior patio reminiscent of the ones in North African buildings. Unfortunately, the service is deplorable and the hotel caters essentially for groups. It is worth having a drink here, but it's not really recommended as a place to stay. If you are still tempted, go through an agency rather than booking direct as you will get a better price (up to 30 per cent off in the low season). This is an important place in the history of the country – in 1906, the signatories at the Algeciras conference stayed here. Under the agreement reached, 12 European countries and the United States divided up the cake that was Morocco. However, its fate was already sealed, and Morocco was on the point of being completely occupied by Spain and France.

WHERE TO STAY NEARBY

Campsite

⚑ **Bahia**: playa Rinconcillo, to the north, a few kilometres from the centre. ☎ 66-19-58. Buses to and from the centre of Algeciras. Close to the sea, but also near some rather unattractive port buildings. Reasonably green grass and canopies shading the pitches. Hot showers for an additional fee. Nothing special and quite noisy.

Youth Hostel

⚑ **Albergue Juvenil Algeciras (16** off the map from A2): in the village of Pelayo (postcode 11390), just on the way out of Algeciras. ☎ 67-90-60. Fax: 67-90-17. Website: www.inturjoven.com. 8 kilometres (5 miles) from the town and 12 kilo-metres (8 miles) from Tarifa. There are buses from Algeciras or Tarifa that can drop you off on the N340, just next to the youth hostel – the last bus is at around 9pm. Open all year round (except Christmas), 24 hours a day. For the under 26s, accommodation only costs 8€ in low season and 12€ in high season; for the over 26s, 11 and 16€ respectively. About 100 beds in all. Rooms sleeping two to four people with big windows or a small balcony. Each room shares a bathroom on the landing with one other. Nice modern building in the hills, local-style architecture. Very well-equipped. Nice swimming pool open from June to September. Lovely view of the sea.

WHERE TO EAT

The cheapest option is buy food from the market in the town centre. The restaurants are all fairly functional and have little to recommend them.

☆ Budget

✕ **Casa Blanca Restaurante** (A2, **20** on the map): Juan de la Cierva. ☎ 60-31-21. Open every day. Set menu for less than 6€. Green building beside the tourist office, near the port. This is the canteen for the port workers and is set on a large veranda. Quick service and good portions. Not the place for a quiet tête-à-tête dinner, but perfect if you are ravenous and on a shoestring budget.

☆☆ Moderate

✕ **Restaurante Montes** (A1, **21** on the map): Morrisson 27, the road at right angles to calle Castelar. ☎ 65-42-07. Open every day 12.30–5pm and 7pm–1am. The set lunch menu costs around 7€. The restaurant is under the same ownership as the bar of the same name, but this is a proper restaurant and prices are reasonable despite its smart appearance. People come here for the fish, which is very fresh and well-prepared. Excellent *sopa de pescado* (fish soup).

WHAT TO SEE AND DO

★ Most of the town's restaurants (except the Casa Blanca, *see above*) are in the **old part** of Algeciras – this area has a pleasant atmosphere, although it doesn't have any particular charm. It is a nice enough place to wander around if you need to kill an hour or so and will certainly leave you with a better impression of the place than if you just confined yourself to the area around the port.

★ **La plaza Alta** (A1 on the map): an attractive square with palm trees and a fountain in the centre, built in 1807. It has two churches – the Capilla de Nuestra Señora de Europa (18th century) and the Iglesia de Nuestra Señora de La Palma (built in 1723).

– If you want to spend some time on the beach, head for **playa de Getares,** around 5 kilometres (3 miles) south of Algeciras. The golden sands stretches for 3 kilometres (2 miles) and although it is fairly built up, it has not yet been spoilt. Lots of small villas but fortunately no tower blocks.

LEAVING ALGECIRAS

By Train

🚂 **RENFE Station** (A2 on the map): carretera de Cádiz. ☎ 63-02-02. 5 minutes from the port.

– Direct trains every day to Ronda and Granada. For Córdoba, Seville, Málaga and many others, change at Bobadilla.

By Bus

🚌 **Bus Station** (A2 on the map): calle Juan de la Cierva, opposite the station, beside hotel Octavio.

– **Compañia Comes**: ☎ 65-34-56. Buses to Huelva at 7.30am every day, to Seville (four a day), Jerez (two in the morning), Cádiz (10), Madrid (two departures – one before 11am and the other just before 11pm), to various towns in the Basque country (every evening after 8pm) and Tarifa (11 departures, every 30 minutes during peak periods).

GIBRALTAR 73220   DIALLING CODE: 350

Gibraltar is a place that seems to provoke strong reactions. Although there is much about this enclave that is British – the police, the pubs, the pictures of the Queen, and so on – the Spanish spirit is in evidence wherever you go. Gibraltar's population of 30,000 has grown out of a complex intermingling of Spanish, Portuguese, Maltese, British, Jewish and Genoese nationalities. Although the official language is English, most residents switch effortlessly between this and a Spanish dialect called *Llanito*, very similar to the Spanish spoken in Andalucía.

The town is singularly unattractive but still has a certain charisma. The fact that this historical anachronism still survives on this lump of rock renders it a curiosity in itself.

Physically, life in Gibraltar is not easy. Only the area around the base of the Rock is inhabitable, and it is here that the few streets that make up the town are concentrated. The Rock is battered by strong winds and fog frequently settles over the town.

On the positive side, there are a number of places of interest – the Rock itself of course, but also a nature reserve that is home to a number of rare plants, a large number of birds and a colony of wild apes.

A Brief History

Gibraltar was well known to ancient civilizations like the Phoenicians, the Carthaginians and the Romans. And not without good reason as this is a place where Africa and Europe meet, where two seas mingle and where trade routes from every direction cross. It was allegedly the home of Heracles, who was left there by his parents Zeus and Alcmena to guard the columns that bore his name. However, the first traces of habitation were left by the Moors, who established themselves here in 711 under the command of Tarik ibn Zyad. It was the Moors who gave the Rock its Arabic name, Gibel Tarik – the mountain of Tarik – from which its present-day name is derived. In 1309, after six centuries of peaceful existence under the Muslims, the Spanish Christians launched a surprise attack on the Rock. But despite their eviction, the Muslims refused to admit defeat. In 1333, the sultan of Fez recaptured the town after a siege lasting four and a half months. He was responsible for most of the Muslim monuments that remain today – the castle, the baths and the mosque. In 1462, San Bernardo de Claraval (still the patron saint of Gibraltar) liberated the peninsula and made it into a strategic naval base.

Two and a half centuries later, Carlos II died without leaving an heir and Spain was plunged into a war of succession. It is not clear exactly what happened next, but it was the English who, in 1704, won the day, under the leadership of Admiral Rooke. The treaty of Utrecht was signed in 1713 and Spain handed over the Rock 'absolutely and for all time' to His Gracious Majesty. During World War II, Gibraltar was one of the key British military bases and the Allies gathered their fleet here in preparation for the attack on North Africa.

In 1969, John Lennon and Yoko Ono got married in Gibraltar. In the same year, Franco closed the frontier, prohibiting all contact between Spain and Gibraltar in the vain hope of forcing the inhabitants to vote for a return to Spanish control. It was not until 4 February 1985 that the frontier was re-opened, after 16 years of negotiation, resistance and isolation.

The truce was short-lived, however, and the Spanish began to feel that they had made concessions without any gain. In 1973, when Britain joined the EC, the conditions of the Utrecht treaty were applied *de facto* to the Rock except in relation to fiscal legislation which remained totally autonomous – no taxes on company profits, no transfer tax, no wealth tax. This is now a thorn in the side of the Spanish authorities, who claim that drugs-traffickers come here to launder money with total impunity. The Spanish finance minister has even heightened the tension by estimating that 2 per cent of Spain's GNP leaks away via Gibraltar.

Despite the sunshine and the blue-edged slopes of El Peñon (the Rock in Spanish), there is a great deal of unrest about Gibraltar's continuing role as a strategic military and naval base. Nuclear submarines could well be concealed somewhere in the seas around it, and it is even claimed that there is a stock of biological and chemical weapons lurking inside the Rock. Fishing rights are another bone of contention – in 1999, Gibraltan fishermen boarded over a dozen Spanish boats. Madrid responded instantly and insults flew with both parties refusing to give an inch.

GETTING THERE

At all costs, try to avoid taking your car across the border – you will find yourself in a queue for several hours and parking is a nightmare even if you do make it into the town. Leave your car in a secure car-park in Spain and walk or catch the bus to the border. You will need to show your passport at customs which is open 24 hours a day.

– **By Bus**: from Algeciras. Compañía Comes operates a bus that leaves from in front of the hotel Octavio and runs regularly to La Línea, the border town on the Spanish side. From there, you walk over the border.

– **By Car**: if you really cannot avoid taking your car across, the best option is to arrive at Customs as early as possible in the morning and leave in the early afternoon. You should just about be able to see the sights in half a day. If you are coming from Algeciras or Marbella, follow the signs to La Línea – the Spanish highways authorities keep signposts for Gibraltar to the minimum. The advantage of coming by car is that you can make your way up the Rock independently (although entry to the park is expensive). On the other hand, it is very difficult to park in the town of Gibraltar itself and many of the streets are pedestrianized.

Note that it has been known for crooks to try and persuade drivers to part with 2,000 pesetas before arriving at customs, in exchange for a 'visa' – on no account part with your money.

– **On Foot**: Gibraltar is small enough to make exploring it on foot easy. There are regular red double-decker buses (inexpensive) to take tourists from the border into the town centre. You can then take the cable car up to the top of the Rock.

TOPOGRAPHY

The town of Gibraltar stretches along the foot of the gently sloping sides of the Rock. Main Street is 2–3 kilometres (1–2 miles) long and runs the full length of the town. It is along Main Street that most of the shops can be found. Tiny streets and alleyways lead off Main Street, which is always the reference point for getting your bearings. One road leads to the top of the Rock, and provides some superb views of the coast. On the other side, the Rock falls vertically into the sea, and no access is possible.

ALGECIRAS AND GIBRALTAR

TELEPHONE

To call Spain from Gibraltar: proceed as for an international call. Dial **00** then **34** (the code for Spain) then the required number.

To call Gibraltar from Spain: dial **00** then **350** (the code for Gibraltar) before the required number.

USEFUL ADDRESSES

Tourist Information

🛈 Tourist Office (**Gibraltar Information Centre**; A3 on the map): in the Piazza building on Main Street (just before the cathedral). ☎ 74982. Open Monday to Friday 10am–6pm, and Saturday 10am–2pm. Closed on Sunday. Friendly staff and plenty of information available.

🛈 Tourist Office (A3 on the map): 18–28 Bomb House Lane; in Gibraltar's local museum. ☎ 74805. Open Monday to Friday 10am–6pm and Saturday 10am–2pm. Closed on Sunday. Very friendly.

🛈 Tourist Office (A3 on the map) on the little cathedral square. ☎ 74950. Open Monday to Friday 9.30am–5.30pm.

Services

✉ Post Office (A–B2 on the map): 102 Main Street. Open Monday to Friday 8.45am–5pm, and Saturday 10am–1pm.

Money

■ Foreign exchange: several bureaux de change on Main Street. The banks are open Monday to Friday, until 1.30pm only. Note that the local currency, the Gibraltan pound, is not accepted in Spain.

■ Useful Addresses

🛈	Tourist Office
✉	Post Office
🚌	Bus station
✈	Airport
1	Bicycle hire
2	Ferry

🛏 Where to Stay

10	Toc H Hostel
11	Miss Serruya
12	Emile Youth Hostel

13	Bristol Hotel
14	Continental Hotel

✕ Where to Eat

20	Truly British Fish and Chips
21	The House of Sacarello
22	Kesyton's Café
23	The Angry Friar

🍷 Where to Have a Drink

30	Bull and Bush Bar
31	The Star Bar

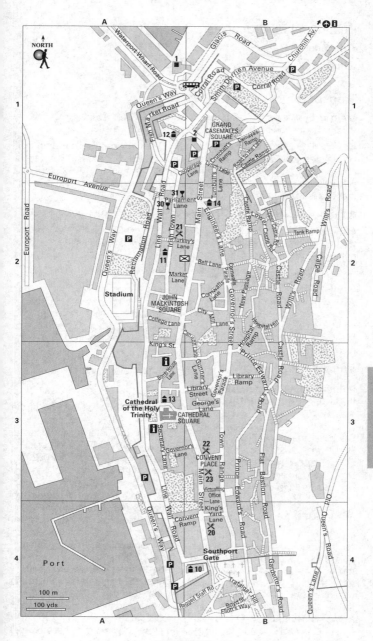

Health and Emergencies

■ **Hospital**: St Bernard's Hospital. ☎ 79700.

■ **Police**: 120 Irish Town Street. ☎ 72500.

Transport

➌ **Airport** (off the map from B1): Winston Churchill Avenue. ☎ 45000 or 73026. Some flights to Tangier and Tetouan, and to the UK.

■ **Ferry** (B1, **2** on the map): to Tangier, **Tour Africa International**, ICC Casemates, 2a Main Street, PO Box 355, Gibraltar. ☎ 77666. This company runs a 'guided tour', several times a week. It is quite pricey at £35 (56€) but this includes lunch in a 'typical' restaurant. It is probably preferable to catch the Spanish ferry from Algeciras.

■ **Taxis**: ☎ 70027 and 70052. Ranks are on the Waterport wharf.

■ **Bicycle hire** (A1, **1** on the map): 36B Waterport Circle. ☎ 70420. Behind the Ford dealer on the marina. Telephone before you set off as they are often not there.

WHERE TO STAY

You can get a list of accommodation from the tourist office. Hotels are few and far between, expensive and on the whole unappealing. If you do decide to stay the night here, make sure you phone well in advance to make a reservation.

Youth Hostel

â **Emile Youth Hostel** (A1, **12** on the map): Montagu Bastion, Line Wall Road. ☎ 51106 or 75020 or (576) 86000 (mobile). Fax: 78581. Opposite the Shell petrol station. Bed and breakfast costs around £12 (19€) per night. Accommodation is in dormitories. The staff are particularly unfriendly.

☆ Budget

You would be hard pushed to find accommodation much less desirable than the two places listed below, but they have been around for so long that Gibraltar just wouldn't be the same without them . . .

â **Toc H Hostel** (B4, **10** on the map): Line Wall Road. ☎ 73431.

Turn right at the end of Main Street, just before you reach the stone archway (Southport Gate); there is a Hambros Bank at the end of the road and the well-concealed entrance to the hotel is just opposite, built into the wall. A bed costs £5 per night (less than 8€) and £20 for the week (32€). The hostel contains an incredible hotchpotch of uninviting rooms like garden sheds, on various levels. The toilets are at the end of the garden which is completely overgrown. Cleaning seems to be kept to an absolute minimum. Incomprehensibly, this extraordinary establishment is nearly always full.

â **Miss Serruya** (A2, **11** on the map): 92/1A Irish Town. ☎ 73220. Another strange place, offering 'rooms' from £8 to £16 (13 to 26€). The owner appears to have divided up his flat using plywood partitions to make minuscule boxes to sleep in. Minuscule is no exaggeration – No. 5 is definitely the biggest, but it is still no more than a cupboard. Really sordid but when you are desperate a bed is a bed (although sleeping outside almost seems a better option). Ring the bell and shout, and sooner or later someone will generally come to the door.

☆☆☆ Expensive

♠ **Bristol Hotel** (A3, **13** on the map): 10 Cathedral Square, PO Box 56. ☎ 76800. Fax: 77613. Website: www.gibraltar.gi/bristol hotel. Email: brishtl@gibnet.gi. A double room costs around £61 (100€), breakfast included. The entrance hall is promising, with the pillars in the lounge giving it a very

colonial feel. The rooms are comfortable enough although they have seen better days. Small, lead windows look out over Algeciras Bay. All rooms are en-suite. There is a tiny swimming/paddling pool in the small garden. Friendly welcome from the owner and his wife, who speak Llanito.

☆☆☆ Splash Out

♠ **Continental Hotel** (B2, **14** on the map): 1 Engineer Lane. ☎ 76900. Fax: 41702. Doubles cost £55 (89€). The hotel has been completely renovated, and as a result is undoubtedly the best value for money, especially given its central location. Spacious rooms (a rarity in Gibraltar) with wooden beds and floral decor including thick patchwork bedspreads. Good service.

WHERE TO EAT

There is an excess of cafeterias and fast-food joints, all serving pretty much what you would expect. The food tends to be pricey and unremarkable.

✗ **Truly British Fish and Chips** (B4, **20** on the map): 295 Main Street. ☎ 74254. Open Monday to Friday, 11am–4pm and 6–9pm, and Saturday 12 noon–3pm. A satisfying meal is a reasonable £3.50 (6€), and you can completely gorge yourself for £5 (8€). It is a nice enough place – very small and narrow with a few wooden tables. People call in for typical English fish and chips (cod, haddock, plaice, and so on) which are fried as you wait by Phil, the friendly owner and his Portuguese partner. Phil likes to have a chat, so ask him how he came to be on the Rock, and you'll see why he features in the guide.

✗ **The House of Sacarello** (A2, **21** on the map): 57 Irish Town, on the corner of Irish Town and Turkey's Lane. ☎ 70625. Open Monday to Friday 9am–7.30pm, and Saturday 9am–3pm. A good place for tea with homemade scones. Excellent tea and coffee, but the meals are rather mediocre.

✗ **Kesyton's Café** (B3, **22** on the map): 1 Covent Place. ☎ 75654. You can eat outside under the flowery canopy. It is amusing to watch the guards do their exercises just opposite in front of the Governor's residence (clicking of heels, brandishing of batons and the like). There are some reasonable salads and a few Spanish-style dishes. On the whole the food is decent, but nothing special.

✗ **The Angry Friar** (B3, **23** on the map): opposite Kesyton's Café. ☎ 71570. Parasols outside to shade punters on sunny days.

ALGECIRAS AND GIBRALTAR

WHERE TO HAVE A DRINK

You will find pubs all over the place – here are a couple which are particularly recommended.

♥ Bull and Bush Bar (A2, **30** on the map): Parliament Lane. ☎ 72951. Its antiquated, smoky atmosphere, old-fashioned fan, portraits of the Queen and TV on the bar all serve to give it a very British feel. The bull's head on the wall, with its phenomenal horns, makes it worth a visit.

♥ The Star Bar (A2, **31** on the map): 10 Parliament Lane. ☎ 75924. By 50 Main Street. Claims to be the oldest bar in Gibraltar. Pleasant atmosphere, but lacking the character of the Bull and Bush.

♥ Several other pubs around town.

WHAT TO SEE AND DO

There is not a great deal to see.

★ **The Cathedral**: near the Bristol Hotel. Built in Moorish style.

★ **The Rock**: this is why you are here! You can either drive or go up to the top of the Rock by cable car (less than £5 – 8€) which you catch at the end of Main Street. The cable car operates from 9.30am to 6pm. The ticket price includes entry to the various sites on the Rock. It does not run on Sunday. There are two stops – one is halfway up at the Apes' Den (where you can also get off on the way back). The Apes' Den is inhabited by a colony of Barbary apes introduced to the peninsula by the Arabs in the 9th century. They are the only apes living in the wild in Europe. There is an old saying that while the apes are here, the British will never leave – apparently this is why Churchill ordered that there should always be at least 35 of them. Today there are 190. At one time they were fed by the army but nowadays there are special wardens to look after them. It is an odd thing, but no-one knows what happens when they die. No corpses have ever been found. Anyway, be careful – these monkeys are thieves and are not slow to swipe anything left in a half-open bag or in cars with the windows open.

There is a series of footpaths leading to the various sites, among them a 14th-century Moorish castle that has little to offer. You can also visit the stalactite-decked St Michael's Cave, which has now been turned into an auditorium where there is the occasional concert.

The second stop on the cable-car leads to the top of the rock. There is an excellent view from here and the strategic importance of the place is particularly evident.

– If you go up the Rock by car, you pay on entering the park. Follow the route marked 'Nature Reserve' which takes you to the top. The ticket price includes entrance to the various sites of interest on the Rock.

★ **Gibraltar Museum**: 18–20 Bomb House Lane. ☎ 42400. Open Monday to Friday 10am–6pm and Saturday 10am–2pm. Closed Sunday. Entrance costs £2 (3€). There is a 15-minute film (in English) on the history of the Rock, documents, engravings, black and white photographs, weapons, costumes and prehistoric finds all on show. There is a bit of everything in this museum, which aims to illuminate Gibraltar's history from the earliest times. There is even an Egyptian mummy that apparently came from a boat that was shipwrecked on its way from Thebes. There is a small café in the courtyard.

★ Also worth seeing is the **Lighthouse**, constructed in 1841, which stands 49 metres above sea level, and the church, the **Shrine of Our Lady of Europa**. Open Monday to Friday 10am–7pm and weekends 11am–7pm. It is, in fact, a former mosque converted by the Christians in 1462.

– **Beaches:** there are three, all very close to each other on the other side of the Rock. The are packed out and not very clean. To get to them, catch the No. 4 bus which goes from Line Wall Road.

LEAVING GIBRALTAR

By Bus

🚌 **Bus station:** buses go from the Línea de la Concepción bus station on the Spanish side of the border. ☎ (956) 17-00-93.

– **To Málaga**: two buses in the morning, two in the evening.

– **To Marbella**: eight buses a day.

– **To Cádiz**: five buses a day.

– **To Seville**: three buses a day.

CASARES 29690   DIALLING CODE: 952

A large mountain village, clinging to a rocky outcrop and crowned by the ruins of an Arab castle. Impressive panorama of the sea with the Rock of Gibraltar in the distance. In fine weather you can even see the coast of Africa. One of the most authentic whitewashed villages. All the action takes place around the plaza de España.

USEFUL ADDRESSES

🛈 **Tourist Office:** calle Fuente, in the centre of the village, going down to the right of the Ayuntamiento (Town Hall). Unpredictable opening hours.

■ **Foreign exchange**: Caja Rural de Málaga, just next to the plaza de España.

WHERE TO STAY

🛏 **Hostal Plaza**: on the plaza de España, opposite the fountain. ☎ 89-50-60. A bit noisy in the evenings. Rooms have a balcony from which you can watch the comings and goings in the square. The only hotel in the village.

WHERE TO EAT

✕ **Casa Benilda**: Juan Cerón 9. ☎ 89-40-69. A small restaurant near the plaza de España, opposite the post office The set menu costs around 6€.

Home cooking in small dining-rooms with tables covered in waxed cloth. A good place – but phone to make sure that it is open during the week.

RONDA 29400   DIALLING CODE: 952

The attractive town of Ronda is perched on a rocky promontory 740 metres (2,428 feet) above sea-level and is definitely worth a detour. It is one of the oldest towns in Spain, and even if only a few traces of its glorious past remain, the evidence of its history is still visible. This eyrie, standing proudly on a cliff that plunges vertically down to the Guadalevin river, is split in two by an impressive ravine linked by an 18th-century bridge with three arches – el puente Nuevo. The town's bullring, built in 1785, is the oldest in the country.

In order to really soak up the atmosphere of the town, you will need to stay at least one night. More and more tourists are discovering Ronda, but in general they don't tend to come for more than a day trip. The main street is Calle Espinel, in the modern part of the town, and is where most eating, drinking, socializing and nightlife takes place. The old part of the town is on the other side of the bridge but oddly enough is not very busy at night. Its quiet charm makes it a lovely place to visit during the day but there are very few restaurants and bars so you need to cross to the new town for food and refreshments. The ideal time to visit Ronda is in May and June or September, when the annual Feria takes place and jubilant crowds turn out to watch the splendidly Goya-esque *corridas*. If you want to stay at this time of year, you will have to book at least three months in advance.

A Brief History

The hill-top site of Ronda has been coveted and conquered by countless armies. First the Romans, who made it an important trading centre and then the Arabs, who gave it the status of an emirate. In 1485, Fernando el Católico succeeded in dislodging the Muslims after 20 days of epic and chivalrous combat and in 1808 Napoleon's troops arrived. The cathedral still bears witness to this succession of occupying forces. It was also at Ronda that Pedro Romero set out the rules for *la corrida* (the bullfight). Over 5,000 beasts fell as a result of his bullfighting mania and the art owes him a huge debt of gratitude. The *corrida* is so important in Ronda that the cellars beneath the attractive *plaza de toros* have been made into a museum.

The other celebrity from the town is none other than Carmen. This was where her very real tragedy took place, long before Bizet composed his opera, which he set in Seville. When the film-maker Francesco Rosi filmed his version of Carmen in 1984, the location shots were made in Ronda for authenticity. Hemingway stayed here in 1925, the year when *In Our Time* was published. An incident in Ronda's history inspired his novel *For Whom the Bell Tolls*. Orson Welles also visited these parts in order to pay homage to the bullfighter Antonio Ordóñez. He even asked that his ashes be scattered in the sand of the bullring so they could mix with the blood of the bulls and the toreadors! His request was refused and they were finally scattered on Antonio Ordóñez's private estate.

GETTING THERE

By Car

By car, from San Pedro de Alcántara, about 10 kilometres (6 miles) west of Marbella. Take the C339, a broad, winding, well-maintained road that climbs through beautiful countryside where pine forests cling to the red rock of the Serranía de Ronda. Finally, you come to a dry flat, rocky plateau where a few ancient sheep farmers still eke out a living.

Parking in Ronda is not easy. Try parking in the courtyard of the Monastery of the Salesian Brothers. This is authorized until 8pm and is free of charge. The entrance is off plaza Duquesa de Parcent (B4 on the map), opposite the Ayuntamiento.

By Train

– From Seville: an average of six trains a day. The journey takes 2 hours 30 minutes.

– From Algeciras: an average of seven trains a day. The journey takes 1 hour 30 minutes.

By Bus

Buses to and from Marbella (1 hour 30 minutes) and Jerez (3 hours), an average of four times a day.

USEFUL ADDRESSES

Tourist Information

🄸 **Tourist Office** (A2 on the map): plaza de España. ☎ and fax: 87-12-72. A small office open Monday to Friday 10am–2pm and 4–7pm, Saturday 10am–3pm. Closed Sunday. Unpredictable welcome. The other office is better.

🄸 **Oficina Municipal de Turismo** (A2 on the map): paseo Blas Infante (opposite the bullring). ☎ 18-71-19. Open Monday to Friday 9.30am–7.30pm; Saturday, Sunday and public holidays 10am–6.30pm. Very friendly staff.

Services

✉ **Post Office** (A2 on the map): calle Virgen de la Paz. Open 9am–2.30pm.

Money

■ **Banks** (A2 and B1 on the map): most of the banks are on carrera Espinel.

Health and Emergencies

■ **Farmacía Gimena** (pharmacy; A2, **1** on the map): carrera Espinel 38. ☎ (95) 287-13-98.

■ **Red Cross**: calle Jerez. ☎ 287-14-64.

■ **General Hospital**: carretera El Burgo. ☎ 87-15-40 and 287-31-40.

■ **Attended car-park**: under the plaza de Socorro. Underground car-park right in the centre.

■ **National Police**: avenida de Jaén. ☎ 87-10-01.

■ **Municipal Police**: plaza de la Duquesa de Parcent. ☎ 87-13-69.

Transport

🚌 **Bus station** (off the map from A1): plaza Concepción García Redondo. There are several companies:

– **Bus Comes**: ☎ 87-19-92. This company goes to Cádiz (three buses a day), Jerez (four), La Línea and Gibraltar (two buses, one very early in the morning, another in the afternoon).

– **Bus Los Amarillos**: to Málaga (three buses every day) and Seville (five).

🚆 **RENFE station**: (off the map from B1): in the north of the town. avenida de Andalucía.

Leisure

■ **Librería Hispania** (A2, **2** on the map): carrera Espinel 9. For walkers, this bookshop sells 1:50,000 maps of the region.

■ **Swimming pools**: carretera Málaga in the north of the town. Open summer only. Large open-air pool. Quite expensive. There is a new swimming pool at the Complejo Deportivo El Fuerte (sports' complex). ☎ 87-05-07. Open Monday to Saturday 8am–2pm and 4–10pm. Admission costs around 3€.

CASARES AND RONDA

■ **Useful Addresses**

🛈	Tourist Office
✉	Post Office
🚌	Bus station
🚆	Railway station
1	Farmacía Gimena (pharmacy)
2	Librería Hispania

🛏 **Where to Stay**

10 Hostal Ronda Sol
11 Pensión Biarritz
12 Pensión La Purísima
13 Hostal Virgen del Rocío

14 Hotel El Tajo
15 Hotel Polo
16 Camping El Sur
17 Hotel Maestranza

🍴 **Where to Eat**

20 Alimentación Francisco Beccera
24 Cafetería Cervecería Doña Pepa
25 Doña Pepa
26 Restaurante Macias
27 Pedro Romero
28 Confitería Harillo
29 Heladería Rico

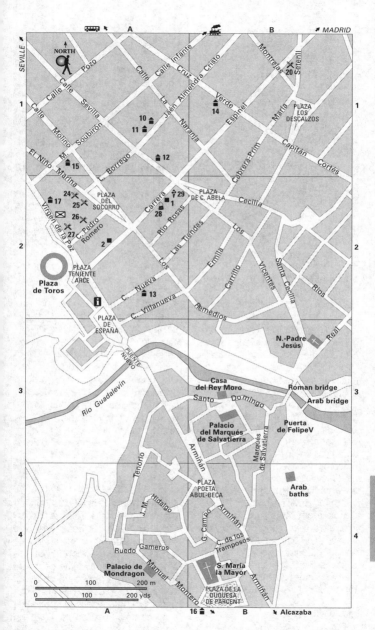

RONDA

WHERE TO STAY

Campsite

⛺ **Camping El Sur** (**16**, off the map from B4): apartado 127. 1.5 kilometres outside town on the road to Algeciras. ☎ 87-59-39. Fax: 87-70-54. A pitch costs 3€ per person, per car and per tent. An excellent place with a delightful owner who is happy to suggest walks in the vicinity. All new and planted with young olive-trees. The ground is quite hard. Swimming pool, chalets, mini-golf, beautiful view, shop and very affordable restaurant. You can also rent log cabins quite cheaply.

⌂ Budget

⛨ **Hostal Ronda Sol** (A1, **10** on the map): Almendra 11. ☎ 87-44-97. Less than 17€ for a double room. A small hotel run by a charming landlady. Comfortable, clean rooms, some of which are on the small side, with communal bathrooms. Avoid the two looking out onto the patio. Very reasonably priced for three people.

⛨ **Pensión Biarritz** (A1, **11** on the map): Almendra 7. ☎ 87-29-10. Less than 21€ for a double room, between 24 and 30€ for a triple. The rooms are a bit gloomy and some are en-suite. Once again very reasonably priced. Same owner as the Hostal Ronda Sol.

⛨ **Pensión La Purísima** (A1, **12** on the map): Sevilla 10. ☎ 87-10-50. A double room costs 27€. Pot plants in the corridors and on the small terrace. The owners spent 30 years living in Lourdes, which probably explains the religious images in the lounge. Rather quaint but perhaps a touch on the expensive side.

✩✩ Moderate

⛨ **Hotel El Tajo** (B1, **14** on the map): Cruz Verde 7. ☎ 87-62-36.

Fax: 87-24-49. Located right in the centre of town. This place is functional and lacking any particular charm. Rooms at 48€ are quite expensive for what is on offer but there is a covered car-park. The hall is an interesting mixture of neo-Arabic and mock medieval kitsch. Over 100 rooms in all.

⛨ **Hostal Virgen del Rocío** (A2, **13** on the map): Nueva 18. ☎ 287-74-25. Spotlessly clean but lacking in character. A double room costs around 39€. All the rooms are equipped with washing facilities. The decor is nothing exciting. Average welcome.

✩✩✩ Expensive

⛨ **Hotel Polo** (A1, **15** on the map): Mariano Soubirón 8. ☎ 87-24-47 and 87-24-48. Fax: 87-24-49. Right in the centre. An excellent hotel with that extra bit of luxury and all mod cons. A double room with bath costs around 63€. Blue and white rooms with bathrooms (particularly nice in the newly revamped rooms), TV and telephone. Welcoming, but a lot of groups come here. Breakfast available.

✩✩✩✩ Splash Out

⛨ **Hotel Maestranza** (A2, **17** on the map): Virgen de la Paz 24. ☎ 18-70-72. Fax: 19-01-70. Email: reservas @hotelmaestranza.com. If your budget allows, this is a lovely hotel to stay in and is right in the centre of the new town opposite the bullring. A double room costs 93–114€ depending on the season, breakfast not included. Luxuries include a big comfortable lounge, friendly staff and porters.

WHERE TO EAT

☆ Budget

– **Alimentación Francisco Beccera** (B1, **20** on the map): Espinel 90. A popular little shop on this busy street. Slices of cheese, sausages and ham. Perfect for a cheap, filling snack.

✕ As the centre of Ronda has become very touristy, hard-up travellers will have to head for the road leading to the station to find a set menu for less than 6€, such as at the **Cafetería Andalucía**.

✕ **Cafetería Cervecería Doña Pepa** (A2, **24** on the map): Marina 1. ☎ 287-26-83. A working-class cafeteria offering well cooked, typical dishes. Set menu for around 8€. Friendly welcome.

☆☆ Moderate

✕ **Doña Pepa** (A2, **25** on the map): plaza del Socorro 10. ☎ 87-47-77. Open every day, lunchtime and evening. This is an attractive restaurant with several rooms inside as well as tables outside in the square. Affordable set menus for around 12€, not including bread and drinks. If you choose from the à la carte menu, a meal will come to

about 24€. Quiet atmosphere and attentive service. The *gazpacho* is particularly delicious. Most other dishes are good but unremarkable.

✕ **Restaurante Macias** (A2, **26** on the map): Pedro Romero 3. ☎ 87-42-38. In a narrow street leading to the plaza del Socorro. You can easily get away with spending less than 12€. A pleasant bar that is typical of the region, it's usually full of tourists and locals eating tapas and drinking wine from the barrel. It also does reasonably priced breakfasts.

☆☆☆ Expensive

✕ **Pedro Romero** (A2, **27** on the map): Virgen de la Paz 18. ☎ 87-11-10 or 87-47-31. Just opposite the plaza de Toros. Open every day, lunchtime and evening. This is an excellent restaurant with first-class service included in the admittedly rather high price. It is difficult to spend less than 24–30€ on a meal from the à la carte menu. The collection of bullfighting photographs would not embarrass a museum. Dishes are mainly based on meat and the famous *rabo de toro* (oxtail).

TASTY TREATS

🍰 **Confitería Harillo** (A2, **28** on the map): carrera Espinel 36. ☎ 87-13-60. Serves very good cakes but is better known for its fruit confectionery that uses strawberries, lemons and oranges, amongst others. These are absolutely delicious, although they are very rich so you

can't eat too many at a time. These marzipan and fruit sweets make an ideal gift.

🍦 **Heladería Rico** (A2, **29** on the map): a bit further up the road from the Harillo, near No. 40. Good ice-cream that you can eat while sunning yourself at the tables outside.

WHERE TO HAVE A DRINK

🍷 **En Frente Arte** (off the map from B4)**:** calle Espíritu Santo 9. Near the Alcazaba. An unusually trendy place in this traditionalist town. Retro furnishings from the 1950s and 60s (bar stools are mounted on the legs of film-stars), bargain rock and folk CDs, and clothes, not to mention a superb view of the Serranía de Ronda. Internet access is available for 3€ per hour. There is also a contemporary art gallery and a studio for recording CDs and filming pop videos (the Belgian owner is the manager of a pop group). Not really for the over 40s unless you are particularly young at heart. The owner also runs a hotel at calle Real 40 (off the map from B2), which falls into the expensive category.

WHAT TO SEE

The cobbled streets of the old quarter are on the far side of Puente Nuevo and are a nice place for a peaceful stroll. There are good views of the valley and some delightful buildings to look at.

★ **El Puente Nuevo** (A3 on the map): the bridge is 100 metres (328 feet) high and spans the impressive gorge that divides the town in two. From the terrace of the Campillo, a narrow track zigzags down to the bottom of the ravine. You can even see some abandoned cave dwellings built into the hillside. The little promenade on the right just before the bridge makes a good vantage point for admiring the architecture of the bridge and the ravine.

The Puente Nuevo is the town's symbol and was built in the second half of the 18th century. The architect who designed it died as he was being lowered into a cradle to inspect his work. His hat blew off and in making a grab for it he overbalanced the cradle and fell to his death.

The central part of the bridge was used as a prison and during the civil war, prisoners were thrown into the gorge to their deaths. This brutality made an impression on Hemingway, who used it in his book *For Whom the Bell Tolls.*

The lower part of the bridge is open to visitors (admission costs around 2€) and is home to an exhibition about its history and construction.

★ **La Casa del Rey Moro** (B3 on the map): after crossing the bridge, take the cobbled street immediately to the left and look out for La Casa del Rey Moro, which is a big building on the left-hand side. Open every day, 10am–8pm. Admission costs around 4€. Despite its name (the 'house of the Moorish king'), this building is entirely western and dates from the 18th century. There are elegant wooden balconies and pretty friezes of *azulejos* round the windows. The house is not open to the public, but just beside it you can visit the little Andalucían gardens designed by the French landscape gardener Forestier. From there, a flight of around 200 steps takes you to the bottom of the gorge. In the past, nearly 400 slaves used to trek up and down these steps to bring water to the town.

★ Walk down the road on the same side as Casa del Rey Moro and further down you will see an old **Roman bridge** (B3 on the map), although it is not the original, and the old **Arab baths** (*baños árabes*). Open Wednesday to Saturday 10am–2pm and 3–5.30pm, and Sunday morning. This old road passes under the Puerta de Felipe V, a gate built in the 18th century. In the distance is the **Alcazaba** (off the map from B4). All of this part of town is best explored in the morning, when the sun first strikes it.

★ **El Museo Lara** (B4 on the map): Armiñán 29. ☎ 87-12-63. Website: www.museolara.org. Open every day 10.30am–8pm. Admission costs around 2€. Housed in the superb palace of the counts of Vascos y Vargas, this newly opened museum is rather interesting. Although they have tried to endow it with some homogeneity by grouping the same sorts of objects in particular rooms, it is in fact an immense collection of curiosities collected together by a rich and enlightened family of shipbuilders. You will see enamelled watches from the 18th century, classical guitars, Napoleonic pistols and costumes worn by local bullfighters. There is a lovely collection of 19th-century scientific paraphernalia, and some photographic and cinematographic material; there is also an attractive portrait of Queen Isabel. The owner, a local entrepreneur, has a passion for antiques and attends auctions in London, Paris and Madrid in search of items to add to his collection. He has renovated several of the rooms in the palace which are now used as storage areas until the museum is expanded. He is also planning to create a restaurant and a *tablao* (flamenco-dancing venue).

★ **La Plaza de la Duquesa de Parcent** (B4 on the map): a delightful, shady, breezy square in the old quarter. The buildings on the square include the **Santa María la Mayor** church, dating from the 18th century. It is usually open 10am–8pm and admission costs less than 2€. Its belltower is of particular interest as it was formerly a minaret. At the entrance, where you buy your ticket, you can see the remains of the mihrab from the former mosque. Fortunately, neither the minaret or the mihrab were destroyed by the Catholics after the Reconquest. Overall, the building is a clever mixture of styles, including baroque and Gothic.

★ Built against the cathedral is an attractive **galleried house**, which was constructed in the 18th century so that local dignitaries could watch the *corridas* taking place in the square.

★ There are some pleasant **patios** to discover in the neighbouring streets.

★ **El Palacio de Mondragon** (municipal museum; A4 on the map): Montero. ☎ 87-84-50. Open Monday to Friday 10am–6pm, and Saturday and Sunday 10am–3pm. Admission costs 1–2€. A remarkable residence of Arab origin. The last Muslim governor lived here before Fernando himself moved in for a few days after the Reconquest. Note the beautiful Renaissance portal that is flanked by the two Mudéjar towers. Inside, the little museum that occupies the rooms turns out to be less interesting than the building itself. There are several patios in different styles, beautifully laid-out gardens and a terrace with views of the valley. The Mudéjar patio with its brick archways and inlaid gates is delightful, as are the Gothic touches such as the octagonal pillars and the decorative cornices. On the first floor there are a number of small exhibitions relating to aspects of the area, including archaeological finds and some examples of local flora and fauna.

★ **Alcazaba** (off the map from B4): an Arab fortress destroyed by the French in 1809. At the western end of the town. Nothing remains but a few sections of the old wall. Still worth a quick visit, as the fortress encloses some of the oldest streets in the town. Behind the Alcazaba, on the left is the Gothic church **Espíritu Santo,** built in 1505 during the reign of Fernando el Católico.

★ Nearby, the two gateways to the town – the **Puerta de Almocabar** (18th century) and the Renaissance **Puerta de Carlos V** (16th century).

★ Go back down into the heart of the town to see the **plaza de Toros** (A2 on the map), the oldest bullring in Spain (opened in 1785).

★ **Museo Taurino** (bullfighting museum; A2 on the map): Virgen de la Paz 15. ☎ 287-41-32. Inside the Ronda bullring, open 10am–7pm. You buy tickets from the bookshop to the right of the bullring, admission costs around 4€. Before you go in, note the gateway flanked by square columns and the wrought-iron balcony with scenes from the bullfight. The exhibits bear witness to the *corrida*'s 300 years of history and include pictures of visits to Ronda by famous people such as Hemingway and Orson Welles. See also the pictures of Manolete's last fight. Take a walk round the bullring itself, encircled by twin ranks of elegant arcades. This was the spot where Francisco Romero (father of Pedro) revived the art of bullfighting, inventing the *muleta* and paving the way for a succession of famous matadors.

★ **El Palacio del Marqués de Salvatierra** (B3 on the map): The house was closed in 2000 but visits may resume in the future. It's worth going to take a look at the outside, though. The 18th-century baroque gateway, with its colonial additions, such as the four Inca-inspired characters above the door is especially interesting. There is a man and a woman on each side, symbolizing modesty.

WHAT TO SEE NEARBY (BY CAR)

You can drive to several little mountain villages from Ronda.

CARTAJIMA

Head towards San Pedro de Alcántara for about 11 kilometres (7 miles) and then take the small road to the right that cuts through the rocky hillsides. If you are in search of peace and tranquillity, this is the place for you – there's not another tourist in sight. You can make it a round trip if you follow the road through the countryside via Júzcar, Faraján and then along the A369.

SETENIL

Around 20 kilometres (13 miles) to the north of Ronda. A village of white-washed houses crouches under an immense rock face, so much so, in fact, that some of the houses use the rock as their roof. Very interesting.

BENAOJÁN 29370

Only 10 kilometres (6 miles) from Ronda and far less busy. The village itself, which shelters under a rocky promontory of the Sierra de Juan Diego is of no particular interest, but may make a good base for exploring the area.

In particular head north as far as **Montejaque** and the **Mures pass** (870 metres/2,854 feet above sea-level). The landscape here looks as if a giant has been amusing himself by chopping up rocks with a hammer and chisel and has suddenly abandoned his work. Gigantic blocks lie at the foot of a rocky peak. Driving can be hazardous round here as there is not enough room for two cars to pass.

On the road from Ronda to Benaoján, stop and take a look at the **cueva del Gato** (the cat's cave), a gaping hole in the mountainside, from where a subterranean river gushes out to join the peaceful course of the río Guadiaro a short distance further on.

WHERE TO EAT

✪ Budget

✗ **Bar-Restaurante Acuario:** avenida Constitución. ☎ 16-74-19. Less than 11€ for a meal including bread, wine and dessert. A bar-restaurant like so many others in Spanish villages. There's a counter where regulars like to sit, a dining room where visitors eat and a blaring television. However the food is home-cooked and the portions are large. Tourists are not viewed simply as money-spinners – you are served without fuss by the owner himself who will ensure that you leave replete and happy.

WHERE TO STAY

✪✪✪ Expensive

⌂ **El Molino del Santo**: bajada de la Estación. ☎ 16-71-51. Fax: 16-73-27. Email: molino@logicontrol.es. Closed from mid-November to mid-February. A double room costs around 90€ in summer and up to 120€ at the most popular times of year. Half-board is obligatory from April to September. Not far from the course of the río Guadiaro, this mill is in fact a complex of several chalets offering about 15 well-equipped rooms with bathrooms and country-style furniture. Lovely and peaceful, especially as tour buses don't stop here, as they do in Ronda. Kidney-shaped pool under weeping willows. Delightful.

GAUCÍN 29480

Another delightful village clinging to a ridge only 30 minutes from the coast. Its perfect whiteness makes it particularly attractive. Some of the houses lining its steep little roads still bear coats of arms. If you climb right up to the top of the village, you will find the ruins of a Romano-Muslim castle, **el castillo de Aguila**. This is where many fighters took refuge at the time of the Carlist wars against the French. Nice walks along the river to **El Colmenar**, 13 kilometres (8 miles) away. There are sometimes concerts in the baroque village church in summer. It is also possible to take a boat-trip down the Guadiaro.

WHERE TO STAY

⌂ ✗ **Hotel Casablanca**: Teodoro de Molina 12. ☎ and fax: 15-10-19. Closed from mid-November to March, and restaurant closed on Mondays. A room costs 60–84€, breakfast included, and a meal in the restaurant will set you back around 18€. A delightful little hotel if you feel like pampering yourself. Note the striking heavy studded doors with the metal door-jamb at the entrance. The rooms, carefully decorated by Sue, the English manager, are all rather fussy, but two of the five rooms are particularly attractive. The first is decorated in an extravagant Moroccan style and has a wonderful view encompassing the sky, the sun, the village terraces and the distant mountain ranges. The other room is in fact a separate little apartment with lounge, kitchenette and bedroom. A little staircase leads round the whitewashed walls up to the bedroom. The shower even has a mosaic floor. There is a good restaurant decorated along the same lines as the accommodation. Palms and other tropical plants wave in the breeze above the pool.

PARQUE NATURAL DE LA SIERRA DE LAS NIEVES

DIALLING CODE: 952

This vast, relatively undeveloped tract of land lying between Ronda, Coín and Marbella, encompasses the Sierra de las Nieves. The highest point is at Torrecilla (1,918 metres/6,293 feet), so-named by the Moors, who used to collect snow in barrels so they could use it for refrigeration purposes all over Andalucía. Nowadays the area is one of the most interesting wildlife parks in Europe, designated a 'biosphere reserve' by UNESCO. There is a variety of ways to get round the park, but to see the best parts of it you should leave your car, grab your rucksack and go in search of its abundant wildlife on foot. The park is home to wild boar, foxes, mountain goats and otters, numerous birds of prey including golden eagles and tawny vultures, as well as flocks of small sparrows. The dominant feature of the vegetation is the ubiquitous Andalucían fir tree (*abies pinsapo*).

USEFUL ADDRESSES

– In general it is not particularly easy to get information about the park's opening times, access points and areas of interest. Tourist development round in the area is still very much in its infancy and although several villages are beginning to realize the enormous potential for making money on their doorstep, they lack the financial resources and business acumen of the people of the coastal regions. Neglected information kiosks with out-of-date notices are the norm, although places such as Ojén in the south (*see* 'La Sierra Blanca') and El Burgo

in the north are beginning to show some awareness of how they can meet the demands of tourism. For more information try the website www.costadelsol.net/web/sierra nieves/indice.htm (in Spanish) before you set off, or pay a visit to:

■ **Monte Aventura**: Oficina de Turismo Rural (rural tourist office), Plaza de Andalucía 1, 29610 Ojén. ☎ 88-15-19. Email: monteaventura@jet. es. Guided tours of the Sierra on mountain bike, on foot or in a four-wheel-drive. The guides are very hot on the protection of the environment.

WHERE TO STAY

⬥ **Hostal La Torrecilla**: C. Polito 23, 29109 Tolox. ☎ 48-72-15. Brand new *hostal* not yet open at time of writing, but if the dynamism and enthusiasm of its owner are

anything to go by, it will no doubt be a great success.
⬥ **Posada del Canónigo**: Mesones 24, 29420 El Burgo. ☎ 16-01-85. A double room costs 48,

breakfast included. This lovely *hostal* is in a beautiful old yellow and white house. It stands at the top of the village at the end of an extremely narrow street by the market. The 12 rooms have been decorated in different styles, but all are full of character. Common features are exposed beams and stonework, and tree stumps that have been stripped of their bark and used as

small tables. The bathrooms are newly decorated. Nos. 12 and 14 are the most appealing, as they are converted attic rooms with polished tiled floors, crocheted bedspreads and wooden shutters. In the lounge there is a beautifully carved, ornate wooden chimneypiece. The restaurant has a set menu for about 9€. You can go horse-riding nearby.

WHAT TO SEE AND DO

★ **Ruta del Puerto del Viento**: this road tour is a great way to see the landscape of the area without actually going into the park itself. The route winds over a vast plateau that was created at the same time as the Alps, and runs from Ronda to El Burgo skirting around the park. The 27-kilometre (17-mile) stretch from the A366 cuts through a landscape of sparse close-cropped vegetation that is interspersed with patches of bare, blood-red earth at the foothills of the Blanquilla and Merinos sierras. This is a stunning route reminiscent of the Scottish Highlands, although it's not for the faint-hearted as it is hair-raisingly steep in parts.

★ **El Camino del Puerto de la Mujer**: this route follows a loop of about 30 kilometres (19 miles) starting south of El Burgo on the road to Coín. There is a signpost giving directions for the route in Spanish. It will help if you have an innate sense of direction as there are lots of forks in the road. It is well worth getting hold of a detailed map of the area and ensuring that your vehicle will be able to cope with the rugged terrain. Once you are under way, these deserted tracks that run through vast expanses of wild countryside, are a real pleasure. It's hard to believe that you are only 30 kilometres (19 miles) from the tourist bustle of Marbella.

★ **El Camino del Monte Aranda**: this track links Tolox on the north side of the park to Istán in the south (*see 'Istán' below*) and Monda in the east. It is about 20 kilometres (13 miles) long and makes fairly easy driving. The track crosses expanses of uninhabited wilderness and is extremely dusty.

★ **El Sendero del Peñón de Ronda**: the walking route starts at El Burgo, and follows the river Turón for some way before it cuts through a beautiful pine forest and climbs to a height of 1,297 metres (4,255 feet).

★ **Climbing La Torrecilla**: go into the park on the A376 from Ronda in the San Pedro de Alcántara direction. About 15 kilometres (9 miles) from Ronda a rough track takes you to the Felix Rodriguez de la Fuente refuge at a place known as Cortijo de los Quejigales. If you want to spend the night at the refuge, reserve two months in advance, as preference is given to members of Spanish rambling or pot-holing associations. Not far from here is the deepest chasm in Spain (plunging to a depth of 1,000 metres/3,281 feet). There is a very basic camping area, which is handy if you intend to climb to the summit. Less hardy walkers can climb to Puerto de los Pilones, which you can get to by following the path from Cañada del Cuerno (Horn Gully). It passes through a forest of a 100-year-old Andalucían fir trees and takes about 3 hours as a round trip. From the path you see a mountainous landscape dominated by the 1,918-metre (6,293-foot) peak of La Torrecilla, and round its base the Quejigal de Tolox, a forest scattered with sessile oaks. The full walk takes a minimum of 8 hours. The end of the path gets very steep, but it is manageable. Make sure you take plenty of water with you, especially in summer when it is easy to get dehydrated, which is not only dangerous, but also makes the walk hard work too.

ISTÁN 29611 DIALLING CODE: 952

About 15 kilometres (9 miles) north of Marbella at the entrance to the Parque Natural de la Sierra de las Nieves, Istán is a village where water plays an important role. Over the centuries, its numerous springs have been tapped and used to supply nearby coastal towns, especially Marbella. Nowadays, however, the resorts have to make do with desalinated sea water and the pure waters of Istán are reserved for the town's many fountains. In the height of summer the burbling of the fountains and irrigation channels gives the air a deliciously fresh feeling. A modern fountain at the exit from the Parque Natural de la Sierra de las Nieves marks the source of the rio Verde, which is about 3-minutes walk upstream. A bit further along on the outskirts of Istán a simple picnic area offers shelter from the heat of the sun and makes a pleasant place to take a rest after trekking through the park. The village has a small attractive church with a bell-tower and a Mudéjar-style door. The fiesta of the archangel St Michael is celebrated at the end of September, with processions and colourful festivities that are well worth seeing.

GETTING THERE

From Marbella there are three buses a day on weekdays, leaving at 8am, 12.30pm and 7pm, on Sunday there are two, at 2pm and 7pm.

WHERE TO EAT

✕ **El Varón**: ☎ 86-98-66. A meal costs 15€ including a bottle of Rioja. This traditional Andalucían restaurant has hams hanging from the ceiling, strings of garlic and *azulejos*. The dining room at the rear has a view of the valley with its terraced vineyards with the mountains in the background. The decor is not bad and Dionisio, the owner, is very welcoming. The food is tasty and made entirely from local produce. The garlic soup and the lamb cutlets are especially recommended. If you know some Spanish, ask the cook if he has any recommendations not listed on the menu, such as his rabbit in garlic – delicious but only available after a successful hunting trip. The food is reasonably priced and plentiful. Credit cards not accepted.

✕ **El Rincón de Curro**: ☎ 53-23-35. An assortment of *raciónes* costs 12€ per person. The restaurant is run by a German woman who married her husband Curro, a native of Istán, some 30 years ago. She is perfectly integrated into Spanish life, and even organizes the penitents' procession at Semana Santa. She cooks Andalucían cuisine with a slight European edge while she jokes with the customers in an interesting mixture of languages. The restaurant is always full of both villagers and visitors from further afield. There is a happy atmosphere and everyone receives a cheerful welcome.

LA SIERRA BLANCA   DIALLING CODE: 952

Even though the name of this coastal range means 'the white mountains' don't expect to find any snow. The only white mark you'll see is the scar on the landscape that is the sprawling town of Ojén.

GETTING THERE

On the A355 linking Coín with Marbella.

WHERE TO STAY AND EAT

⚑ **Hostal El Solar**: Córdoba 2, 29610 Ojén. ☎ 88-11-49. Right at the end of the town. A double room with a shared bathroom costs 21–27€ and a further 6–10€ for a private bathroom. The owner is fanatical about cleaning, but very friendly. This very quiet *hostal* has 11 rooms, some with and some without bathrooms. Ask for one of the upstairs rooms, some of them have a splendid view of the valley. If you don't mind the distance from the coast, it is a pleasant place to stay that is good value for money.

⚑ **Refugio de Juanar**: Sierra Blanca, 29610 Ojén. ☎ 88-10-00. Fax: 88-10-01. Email: juanar@sopde.es. On the A355 road from Marbella to Coín take the road to the left as signposted. Depending on the season a double room costs 81–96€, breakfast included. Set in the old hunting grounds of the Marquisate de Arios, the mod cons offered by this 'refuge' put it on the same level as a *parador*. It maintains that Charles de Gaulle stayed here while he finished writing his memoirs. The restaurant serves a good selection of game.

WHAT TO SEE AND DO

★ **Ojén**: 9 kilometres (6 miles) from Marbella on the road to Coín. Buses depart from Marbella bus station at 9am and 11.45am (except on Sunday) and 1.30pm, 4.30pm and 7.30pm. Don't try exploring this lovely mountain village by car – the streets are so narrow that you run the risk of getting stuck. So it's easier to see it on foot. Standing in front of the small square is the iglesia de la Encarnación with its Mudéjar-style roof. Iron mines previously brought prosperity to Ojén, but nowadays the town lives off tourism, and it certainly knows how to pull in the crowds. The flamenco festival (last week in July and first week in August) is worth seeing, as is the fiesta de San Denis (9–12 October) when the religious processions that take place during the day are followed by heady nights of dancing *sevillanas* and *malagueñas*.

★ **El mirador de Puerto-Rico**: follow the arrows from the refugio de Juanar (*see above* 'Where to Eat, Where to Stay'). There is a barrier to

THE COSTA
DEL SOL

prevent cars from going up the track, so you have to walk the 2 kilometres to the top of the path through an olive grove and rather uneventful countryside. The reward for your trouble waits upon a rocky outcrop from which there is a magnificent view of the hilltops rising in tiers towards Marbella. Several paths lead off in different directions. If you have sufficient water reserves, any one of them makes for an enjoyable walk.

★ There are a number of marked footpaths starting at the Refugio de Juanar. The walk to Istán is very pleasant, through fern covered plains and Mediterranean woodland. Keep an eye out for wild boar, golden eagles and wild goat (*capra hispanica*).

LA SIERRA BERMEJA

The name Sierra Bermeja literally means 'red mountain', but unlike the Sierra Blanca the Sierra Bermeja actually matches up to its name. The ochre colour of the earth is very distinctive, making it easy to spot from several kilometres away.

GETTING THERE

From the centre of Estepona follow the signs to Genalguacil along the MA 557. Note that there is no access from the N340. This is a pleasant route to drive, taking you through the pine-forested red-earthed landscape of the Sierra to Puerto de Peñas Blancas (white feathers' pass).

WHAT TO SEE AND DO

★ **Las Reales**: at the pass, follow the signposts and take the road to the left. Drive carefully, keeping an eye out for the wild goats and deer as they can sometimes leap unexpectedly into your path. After 4 kilometres (2 miles) go past the refuge and the picnic area and leave your car in the parking area at the end. The red-earth track that starts from here is not particularly hard going but is rather stony, so comfortable walking shoes are recommended. About 500 metres further on there is a *mirador* with a magnificent view of the entire coast from Punta Ladrones to the Rock of Gibraltar. In the distance you can see the hills of Málaga to the east and a distant body of land to the southwest, which is Africa. The fresh breeze up here is a welcome relief from the blistering heat of the plains, and it is a good 10°C (50°F) cooler. You can go back via Ronda through Jubrique and Algatocín, two white-washed villages nestling among cork oaks that are also well worth seeing. The road is narrow and full of sharp bends so keep your eyes peeled for stray goats and other motorists.

MARBELLA 29600   DIALLING CODE: 952

Marbella is both the symbolic home of the Spanish mass tourism industry and a fashionable destination for jet-setting sunseekers who come to enjoy the exclusivity of the old town. Before the Civil War this was a sleepy Andalucían port suffering the same economic decline as the rest of the coastal region, but with the boom of the 1980s came prosperity and ugly concrete tower blocks grew up forming a hideous enclosure around the attractive old town of Marbella. The beaches were redesigned to cater for the tourist hordes and the seaside promenade was built for practicality rather than any discernible romantic charm. Fortunately the pearl in the centre of this monstrous modern oyster is old Marbella, a lovely area of white houses with flower-filled balconies. The focal point is the Plaza de los Naranjos, a cool oasis of orange trees, sparkling fountains and cafés with outside seating where you can bask in the sunshine and watch the world go by. It's definitely a place where people like to see and be seen.

Historical Background

Why has Marbella become such a chic destination? The town owes much of its prestigious cachet to the Marquis don Ricardo Soriano and his nephew Prince Alfonso Hohenlohe. They started bringing their wealthy friends and relations here in 1953, turning the sleepy coastal town into an meeting place for the crème-de-la-crème of international society in one move.

Nowadays, you are just as likely to see a member of the Rothschild family as a Saudi emir. The town's characteristic cleanliness and sense of security are the work of one extraordinary man – Jesús Gil. Founder of the eponymous GIL (Independent Liberal Group), and also president of Atlético Madrid, he is one of the primary developers of the coastal region. Epitomizing the get-rich-quick ethos, he surrounds himself with a group of business cronies dedicated to his policy of rehabilitating the region. He has recently added the towns of Ceuta and Melilla to his list of conquests and plans to turn them into tax havens (which coincidentally would fit in very nicely with his own business affairs). However, he has recently been involved in a series of scandals, including one relating to his alleged misappropriation of Atlético's funds – figures as high as 20 million pesetas (£77,000) have been suggested by the press. Gil has had several judges on his back, threatening him with prison and the loss of his civic rights for having sold state-owned land and property in Marbella to his own real estate companies. The sums involved in this particular scandal haven't yet been disclosed. The saga of his financial and political misdemeanours has fascinated and repelled Spain at the same time.

USEFUL ADDRESSES AND INFORMATION

Tourist Information

Tourist Office (off the map from A3): Glorieta de la Fontanilla. ☎ 77-14-42. Open Monday to Friday 9.30am–8pm (9pm in summer). Closed Sunday. The staff are welcoming and efficient. Basic maps of the town are available free of charge or you can buy more detailed versions.

Tourist Office (A1 on the map): plaza de los Naranjos. ☎ 82-35-50. Open Monday to Friday 9am–8pm (9pm in summer) and Saturday morning. Closed Sunday.

There is also a third tourist office on the way into the town, housed in a concrete arch overlooking the Málaga road.

Services

✉ **Post Office** (off the map from A1-2): calle Alonso de Bazán 1. Opening times 8.30am–2.30pm (1pm Saturday).

Money

■ **Banks**: all the banks are on avenida Ricardo Soriano. Opening times 9am–2pm. Closed Saturday morning in summer.

■ **American Express** (**1**, off the map from A3): on paseo Marítimo. ☎ 82-14-94. Open 9.30am–1.30pm and 4.30–7.30pm.

Health and Emergencies

■ **Public Hospital Costa del Sol**: on the CN340. ☎ 86-27-48. About 4 kilometres (2 miles) east of Marbella.

■ **National Police**: calle Arias de Velasco. ☎ 82-23-53 and 77-11-93 (emergencies).

■ **Local Police**: on the CN340. ☎ 82-74-79.

Car-Parks

It is difficult to find anywhere to park in Marbella. If you are only making a brief stop in the town and you have all your luggage in your car, it is advisable to use a private car-park.

■ The easiest and the cheapest is the Huerta Chica car-park (A1, **2** on the map) underneath the supermarket.

■ Other car-parks with attendants can be found at the beginning of avenida de la Puerta del Mar (A2, **2** on the map), on Carlos Mackintosh (A2, **2** on the map) and on Duque de Ahumada (B3, **2** on the map).

If you intend to stay for a while, don't use the car-parks as they are on the expensive side, but make sure you are legally parked, as they waste no time in towing away vehicles in Marbella.

– Note that at the beginning of calle Chorrón and on avenida Ramón y Cajal (outside No. 7) there are two small maps of the old part of town in ceramic tiling – they come in very handy if you lose your way.

– To get to the town centre from the bus station take bus No. 1. The journey costs about 1€.

WHERE TO STAY

It is better to leave your car on the outskirts of the old town and walk in. Traffic is not a problem outside the centre of town except during the rush hour. All the decent hotels are in the centre, so there is no point in staying anywhere else.

MARBELLA

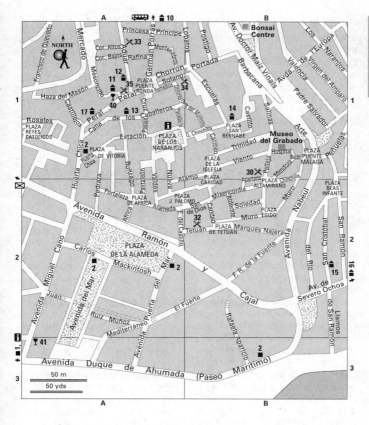

MARBELLA

☆ Budget

⚑ Albergue Juvenil Marbella (10, off the map from A1): Trapiche 2. ☎ 77-14-91. Fax: 86-32-27. Website: www.inturjoven.com. At the top of the town, slightly above the market on the outskirts of the old town. A ten-minute walk from the bus station along calle Trapiche. Open all year round with a 24-hour reception. Price depends on your age and the season you are visiting in, as is the case with all the other youth hostels in Andalucía. A night here costs 6€ per person in low season (March to mid-June and mid-September to the end of November) and 11€ in high season. This large youth hostel is housed in a former Franciscan monastery and is crowned by a tall tower resembling a minaret. It has a spacious hallway similar to a hotel foyer. There are rooms with or without bathrooms sleeping two to six people. This is a very well-kept youth hostel, suitable for both those travelling in a group or alone. Some of the rooms have a lovely view over the park surrounding the hostel. There is a swimming pool and the nearest beach is about 2 kilometres (1 mile) away.

⚑ Hostal de Pilar (A1, **11** on the map): Mesoncillo 4. ☎ 82-99-36. Email: hostal@marbella-scene.com. From 9€ per person, although a double room with a washbasin costs around 30€. Ask to look at several rooms, as some get more light than others. There are also rooms for three people, although none has its own bathroom. This is a good place for budget travellers in a pretty little street in the old part of Marbella. It is run by two friendly cousins and has a sunny terrace and a disco. There is a bar on the ground floor, which has an open fire in the winter months.

⚑ Hostal Aduar (A1, **12** on the map): Aduar 7. ☎ 77-35-78. A double room with washbasin costs 22€ and a room with bathroom costs 27€. This flowery little *hostal* is on four floors with a bathroom on each one. If there is a choice, go for one of the rooms at the top of the house. There is a little patio at the end of the corridor. It is a pity that more attention is paid to looking after the geraniums than to the cleanliness of the rooms.

⚑ There are several other small *pensiones* on Calle Aduar, which are good value, but can only accommodate a few people at a time.

☆☆ Moderate

⚑ Hostal El Castillo (B1, **14** on the map): plaza San Bernabé 2. ☎ 77-17-39. In high season a double room with a bathroom costs 35€, it is slightly cheaper in low season. This comfortable, peaceful *hostal* is in a beautiful old building with a large patio. The rooms overlooking the small square are best, as they have nicer views. They all have bathrooms. All in all, a very pleasant place to stay.

⚑ Hostal Enriqueta (A1, **13** on the map): Los Caballeros 18. ☎ 82-75-52. In a pedestrian street right in the centre of town. A double room costs 34€. This well-run *hostal* is spotlessly clean. The rooms, which sleep two to four people, are laid out over two floors and all have bathrooms. They overlook either a small quiet patio or the narrow street of Los Caballeros. The staff are very welcoming and the central location and reasonable prices make it a good place to stay.

⚑ Hostal La Pilarica (B2, **15** on the map): San Cristóbal 31. ☎ 77-42-52. Very near the town centre. A double room with a bathroom costs 27€. This is a great *pensión* in a narrow leafy street, where it seems as if the neighbours are vying with each other as to who can grow the most plants.

The establishment is peaceful and very clean. Some rooms have courtyards. The decor is characterless as nearly everything is a monastic white. Good value, although the welcome is a bit lukewarm.

⬧ Hostal La Luna (16, off the map from B2): La Luna 7. ☎ 82-57-78. About 5 minutes from the old town centre and with easy parking in an uncongested street. A double room costs about 39€ in mid-season. The rooms are spacious, light and well-equipped (with a shower or small bath and a fridge) and sleep two to four people.

⬧ Hostal Paco (A1, **17** on the map): Peral 16. ☎ 77-12-00. Fax: 82-22-65. Open from April to mid-October. A double room costs about 30€. The rooms are large, airy and light and all have washing facilities. The *hostal* is not particularly attractive, but clean, functional and spacious. The rooms at the back are quieter than those overlooking the street.

WHERE TO STAY IN THE SURROUNDING AREA

Campsites

They are all to the east of the town on the Málaga road.

⬧ Camping Marbella Playa: about 11 kilometres (7 miles) along the road to Torremolinos, on the right-hand side (if you are coming from Marbella). The campsite is on the same side of the road as the beach, next to the Coronado block of flats, which is a useful landmark from the road. ☎ 83-39-98. Fax: 83-39-99. In summer there is a bus to the town centre every 30 minutes. Open all year round. In low season it costs about 2€ per person and 4€ for a tent; in high season they charge a meagre 4€ per person and 6€ per tent. There is a discount for longer stays (over two weeks). This pleasant campsite is well laid out, tidy and peaceful, especially if you put your tent up as far away from the road as possible. This is the best of all the campsites, even though it is furthest from the town. There is a supermarket, restaurant and swimming pool. The toilet and shower blocks are spotless, although the swimming pool and beach aren't always as clean.

⬧ La Buganvilla: about 7 kilometres (4 miles) east of Marbella on a noisy coastal road and on the left-hand side if you are coming from Marbella. ☎ 83-19-73. Fax: 83-19-74. Email: buganvilla@spa.es. From Marbella take the bus for Fuengirola. Open all year round, the reception is open 9am–10pm. In high season it costs 3€ per person, 5€ per tent and about 3€ for a car. The campsite is well-equipped and shaded from the sun by the pine trees. It is separated from the beach by the road that runs along the Costa del Sol. Pitch your tent at the far end of the campsite. Although there is less shade here, it is much quieter. There is a footbridge across the road to the beach. Good facilities including swimming pool, tennis court, a reasonably priced restaurant and a small shop. There is also a small supermarket about 100 metres away on the same side of the road.

WHERE TO EAT

☆–☆☆ Budget to Moderate

✕ **El Pescador**: acera de la Marina 42. Not far from the beach. Closed on Tuesday, and over Christmas and New Year. A fish dish costs 6–9€. The house, bar and restaurant were all built at the beginning of the last century by the grandfather of the present owner, Juan. In those days the beach was 50 metres away and the fishermen would unload their catches while the old man served them drinks and his wife grilled the sea bream. When Marbella became fashionable, developers invaded the seafront and offered Juan fantastic amounts of money, but he refused to sell up. A block of flats was built in front of the restaurant cutting it off from the sea. Then another one was constructed next door and yet another sprang up behind. But Juan carried on his business just the same, with his wife working in the kitchen and his two sons waiting on the tables outside. The fish is still incredibly fresh, with small grilled cuttlefish and amazing Andalucían salads the like of which you won't find anywhere else. Of course some concessions have been made to the modern world with the formica tables and metal chairs. But while there are still people like Juan to cook traditional meals for less than 12€ (including wine) and to greet you like an old friend on your second visit, all hope is not lost. You can't reserve a table in advance (as there is no phone) and they tend to pack people in to make room for newcomers, but it's better than waiting for a table as most people come and spend the whole evening here. The only language is Spanish as nearly all the customers are locals, so you have to know what you want to order.

✕ **Bar Altamirano** (B1, **30** on the map): at No. 3 on the square of the same name. This charming restaurant is in the old part of town, behind the church. ☎ 82-49-32. Open 1–4pm and 8–11pm. Closed on Wednesday and from January to mid-February. You can get a filling meal here for about 12€. The menu appears on *azulejo* tiles on the outside of the building. The food and wine are delicious and there is a very pleasant atmosphere. They specialize in fish, including cuttlefish, squid, mullet, swordfish, skate, sea bream and many more. It is a good idea to turn up early as it gets busy quickly; sometimes you have to wait up to an hour to get a table.

✕ **Sol y Sombra** (B2, **32** on the map): Tetuán 5–7. ☎ 77-00-50. On the way into the old part of town. Open daily. The decor is a little bit tacky, but the food is good. The owners are keen football fans. If you are ravenous, start with the fortifying *sopa de mariscos* (seafood soup), which will go some way to filling you up on its own. Meat dishes are generous, and there is a wide choice of seafood. Good service and air-conditioning.

☆☆☆ Expensive

✕ **La Casa Vieja** (A1, **33** on the map): Aduar 18. ☎ 82-13-12. Closed on Sunday. Set menu served at lunchtime for about 10€. Eating the good food served here on the small patio decorated with *azulejos* is a real pleasure. The owner, a rotund man with a beard, is always keen to make sure that everything is to your liking. The service is attentive, yet discreet and the staff speak several languages. The house wine is excellent. One small criticism would be that the desserts taste a bit bland and are probably from a packet.

✗ **El Balcón de la Virgen** (A-B1, **34** on the map): Remedios 2. ☎ 77-60-92. In the old part of town and very touristy. Open 7pm–midnight. Closed Tuesday. A meal costs about 18€. The decor is lovely, with bougainvillaea covering the facade and balconies. The long dining area has a medieval air and looks as if it is built into old city walls. Outside, an illuminated statue of the Virgin Mary watches over the restaurant. The food is quite reasonably priced.

✗ **Picaros Restaurant** (A1, **35** on the map): Aduar 1, almost at the corner of Calle Peral. ☎ 82-86-50.

Email: picaros@activanet.es. Open daily in summer, but closed on Monday throughout the rest of the year. A set menu is served at lunchtime and an à la carte menu is available in the evening and costs about 24€. This is a stylish, trendy place, serving good food. There are several rooms decorated in pleasant warm colours, with a slightly baroque touch, and a lovely patio full of plants, adorned with old stones. The establishment is run by an American couple, although on the odd occasion the importance of siesta-time seems to take precedence over looking after customers, so maybe standards are slipping.

WHERE TO HAVE A DRINK

⧉ English Pub (A1, **40** on the map): Peral 6. This is a genuine pub, run by a Brit, where they have a good selection of draught beers and a dartboard. Don't turn up too early, especially on Friday and Saturday nights, as they don't usually open until after midnight.

⧉ Bodega La Venencia (A3, **41** on the map): avenida Miguel Cano 15. ☎ 82-15-57. Outside the old town centre. Open all day, every day. The high stools of the *bodega* spill over onto the pavement outside. Inside there is a pyramid of barrels (containing vermouth, *torito*, muscatel and so on), and a curved brick bar

where customers savour sweet wines and excellent tapas (marinated peppers, sardines and anchovies) for less than 1€, served as *montaditos* (on pieces of bread) and for about 9€ as *raciónes* (larger portions). The food is tasty and the wines are good.

⧉ Churrería Ramon (A1 on the map): on plaza de los Naranjos. This is one of the traditional eateries of Marbella, well known for fresh fruit juices and *churros con chocolate*. At the end of an afternoon there won't be a free table in sight – the orange juice is so good that it is worth the 10-minute wait.

WHAT TO SEE AND DO

★ If you haven't yet seen the **plaza de los Naranjos** (orange tree square, A1 on the map) take the time to visit it and maybe enjoy a drink. Good examples of Andalucían architecture in the square are the old 15th-century hermitage, el Ayuntamiento (the town hall, 16th-century) and la casa del Corregidor (the administrator's house, 17th-century). In springtime the heady scent of the orange trees and the *damas de noche* prevail well into the small hours. As to be expected there are lots of tourists in the summer. While strolling through the old town, you will come across several small attractive squares with trickling fountains and walls covered in pots of colourful flowers. In the golden glow of the afternoon sun, children play and old Andalucían women watch the world go by from behind flower-filled balconies. The streets are wonderfully clean and tidy, as the town council is wealthy and can afford to restore them tastefully without having to worry about the cost. It is lovely here, even if there are too many tourists in high season.

★ **La iglesia de Nuestra Señora de la Encarnación** (B1 on the map): plaza de la Iglesia. This 17th-century building recalls a past religious splendour. The ochre-coloured doorway makes for a delightful contrast with the white walls. Inside there is a beautiful organ (from the acoustic viewpoint, not the aesthetic). In the same square you can also see the remnants of a **tower** that used to form part of a ninth-century Muslim castle.

★ Very near plaza de los Naranjos stands the **Capilla de San Juan de Dios**. This tiny 16th-century chapel contains an attractively decorated altar. A white virgin with a golden halo stands piously above. Take a look at the elegant wooden gate with engravings of the arms of Castilla and León.

★ **El museo del Grabado Español Contemporáneo** (B1 on the map): calle Hospital Brazán 5. ☎ 82-50-35. Open 10am–2pm and 5.30–8.30pm, mornings only on Sunday and Monday. Closed Saturday. Admission costs about 2€. This former hospital dating from the 16th century contains a beautiful collection of contemporary Spanish engravings. Those interested in modern art will find it fascinating – there are lithographs, silkscreen prints, dry point art and watercolours. Almost every style of art is represented, including works by Picasso, Miró, Dalí, and Tapies among others.

★ **Bonsai Centre** (B1 on the map): in a small park on the outskirts of the old town, outside the town walls. ☎ 86-29-26. Open daily 10am–1.30pm and 4–7pm. Admission costs about 3€. A collection of bonsai trees – probably only of interest to people who are particularly keen on these miniature trees.

– **The beaches**: there are several in Marbella itself. As most of them are manmade they are not particularly enticing. If you leave Marbella and head towards the west, there are some nicer, quieter beaches. The best is playa Trocadero. Take the road to Estepona and opposite the large BP garage, walk down a narrow dead-end street that leads to the sea. The long stretch of beach with its fine sand is perfect for families – there is no obligation to hire sun-loungers, but if you do they are 6€ a day. At **Chiringuito La Pesquera** you can eat a lunch of grilled fish prepared by the old cook on a kind of barbecue set up in the hull of a beached boat (he has even planted a small herb garden on the beach so he has ready supplies for his cooking). This place is the hangout of a friendly older crowd and it happens to be the best beach bistrot in Marbella. A meal including a bottle of decent white wine should cost about 15€ per person. ☎ 77-03-38.

WHAT TO SEE IN THE SURROUNDING AREA

★ **Marbella Mosque**: 2 kilometres (1 mile) south of Marbella. In theory open daily 5–7pm, except Friday. Some say that five centuries after the success of the Catholic Monarchs in driving out the Moors, Andalucía is once more the target of a Moorish offensive, especially around Marbella. Here, Arab wealth is once more becoming increasingly evident. In Marbella, the Arabs enjoy their freedom, occasionally to excess. This wonderful mosque was financed by King Abdulaziz al-Saud, after whom it was named. Behind the brand new mosque stands King Fahd's residence, constructed on a manmade hill (so as not to be on the same level as his neighbours) and protected by ramparts topped with lookout points. The building is a copy of the White House, although on a grander scale. The king came to stay in July 1999, after an absence of 12 years. Just a simple holiday – he arrived accompanied by numerous limousines, about 200 tonnes of luggage and 400 servants. This was a godsend for the local economy as 250 suites and rooms were hired in the nearby luxury hotels and the royal purchasing staff spent a fortune in one of the local department stores.

★ **Puerto Banús**: a marina about 7 kilometres (4 miles) south of Marbella. For less than 7€ return you can catch a shuttle-boat that gets you there in 30 minutes. It is a nicer journey than travelling by bus, although more expensive. The shuttle runs from 10am–6pm. It leaves from the paseo Marítimo at Marbella harbour. Puerto Banús is the swankiest place in Spain. The Rolls Royce is the most popular car here. Dazzling white yachts crewed by sailors in equally dazzling uniforms are moored in the harbour. The boats seldom seem to leave their moorings (after all, there are no onlookers to admire these luxury toys out at sea!). On the whole the place is rather ugly and soulless but watching the rich at play is a great sport. Some of the architectural influences are clearly Islamic – domes and marble embellishments seem particularly popular. In the evening, the jet set really come into their own and can be seen out and about in the clubs, casinos and cocktail bars.

WHERE TO STAY IN THE SURROUNDING AREA

☆☆☆☆ Splash Out

⚓ **Hotel Club Santa Marta**: carretera de Cádiz at the 167-kilometre marker, 29680 Estepona (Málaga). ☎ 88-81-77. About 10 kilometres (6 miles) from Estepona and 8 kilometres (5 miles) from Puerto Banús. Open April–October. A double room costs about 67€ July–September, and 64€ the rest of the year. This three-star hotel is set in magnificent flower gardens that extend over 2 hectares (almost 5 acres) and stretch down to a sandy beach. The location and the friendly staff make it an ideal place for a holiday with the family or a group of friends. There are 25 villas and 12 rooms set round an Andalucían patio. All are equipped with bathrooms, telephones and fans. The villas have patios and the rooms have balconies. There is a wonderful swimming pool with waterfalls for both adults and children, free deck-chairs and a kids club (4–12 year olds) during the school holidays.

LEAVING MARBELLA

By Bus

🚌 **Estación de Autobuses** (off the map from A1): avenida Trapiche. ☎ 76-44-00. In a shopping centre, not far from the youth hostel.

– The bus company **Automoviles Portillo** runs services to Puerto Banús, Fuengirola and Málaga (every 30 minutes, six buses on Sunday), Ronda (four buses a day), Granada, Córdoba and Seville (two a day), Cádiz (three a day), Almería (one a day).

– There are also four buses a day to Madrid with the **Daibus** company. Ticket offices are open 9.30am–1.30pm and 5.30–9.30pm.

By Train

– There is no rail service to Marbella. The nearest station is in **Fuengirola.**

MIJAS 29649   DIALLING CODE: 952

The most enjoyable way to get to Mijas is by taking the road to 'Tívoli World' (an amusement park) on the way out of Torremolinos and to the south. This small mountain road takes you away from the coast, through pleasant but arid countryside high above the sea. Mijas is a small, whitewashed village perched among the mountains. With narrow streets, decorative wrought-ironwork and flower-filled balconies it fits the criteria for attracting tourists by the coach load. As the years go by, Mijas has become both over-exploited and overrated. It is full of donkeys, and horses and carriages, their owners touting forcefully for customers.

In the village stands an attractive little chapel (Virgen de la Peña) and a church built in the Mudéjar style – very characteristic of rural Andalucía. There is also an unusual square bullring.

During the day there are a lot of people about, but in the evenings everyone goes back to the coast and the souvenir shops close – this is the best time to see the village.

GETTING THERE

– **By bus**: frequent services from Fuengirola throughout the day.

– **By car**: a 15-minute drive from the coast. There are car-parks on the way into the village – the best way to see the village is on foot.

WHERE TO STAY AND EAT

☆ Budget

♠ Pensión Josefa Rueda: Coín 47. ☎ 48-53-10. A double room costs about 20€ with a shared bathroom. This is the only *pensión* in Mijas. Go to plaza de la Constitución and it is a 3-minute walk along the Coín road. There is no sign outside. This is a real family establishment run by two kind old ladies. Most of the rooms overlook the peaceful slopes of the valley. Prices are low considering the facilities available (hotplates in the rooms and en-suite bathrooms). It is the type of place that makes you want to stay. The owners also have several apartments to let that are likewise good value for money.

✕ Café-bar Porras: plaza Libertad 5. Small quiet bar with a few tables and chairs outside, where they serve reasonably priced, tasty tapas.

☆☆☆☆ Splash Out

✕ Restaurante El Mirlo Blanco: plaza de la Constitución. ☎ 48-57-00. Near the bullring. This restaurant, with its large expanse of tables and chairs outside, is without doubt the focal point of the village. The cuisine is of a very high standard, a fact that is reflected in the prices. If you are a bit low on funds try the *gazpacho* or the fish soup, they are both delicious. The atmosphere gets quite lively in the evenings, although it is a shame that the staff are not more friendly. It is advisable to make a reservation in advance.

WHERE TO STAY IN THE SURROUNDING AREA

⌂ **Camping La Rosaleda**: 2 kilometres (1 mile) from Fuengirola at Los Boliches, just where the Mijas road rejoins the N340 for Fuengirola. ☎ 46-01-91. Fax: 58-19-66. Open all year round. A pitch costs 4€ per tent and per person. The campsite is set back from the coast. The plots are small and campers are packed in like sardines. The swimming pool is very clean, the showers are free and there is a small shop.

WHAT TO SEE

★ The village streets are a delightful place for a stroll, especially in the morning before the tourist coaches arrive.

★ **Virgen de la Peña Chapel**: at the bottom of the village, on a small promontory. This is a small grotto-like chapel surrounded by flowers, where the people of the village leave small gifts of thanksgiving in a tiny alcove. The Virgen de la Peña is the patron saint of the village. The villagers write prayers to her and the folded slips of paper are then left in holes in the wall of the grotto. They also leave visiting cards, touching photos and amazing tresses of hair, given to the Virgen in supplication or thanksgiving. The whole scene is very moving. From the terrace in front of the chapel is a beautiful view of the coast and the ugly sprawl of Fuengirola.

TORREMOLINOS 29620   DIALLING CODE: 952

The town gets its name from the numerous towers (*torres*) and the windmills (*molinos*) that used to be such a common part of the landscape around here. Sadly, this small fishing port has become a symbol of uncontrolled property development much the same as in Benidorm. The beaches are lovely, but so packed that you can barely see the sand and all summer long a continuous stream of coaches delivers tourists from all over Europe. Unless you have a good reason for coming to Torremolinos, give it a wide berth.

USELESS ADDRESS

🄳 **Tourist Information Office**: plaza Pablo Ruiz Picasso. In the centre of town, the opening hours are supposedly 9am–2pm.

WHERE TO STAY AND EAT

⌂ ✕ **Camping Torremolinos**: to the north of the town on the Málaga road, about 2 kilometres (1 mile) from Torremolinos ☎ 38-26-02. Open all year round. Take the turning beyond the Repsol garage after the military airport.

The campsite is a 3-minute walk from the beach (about 500 metres). It costs 4€ per person, per tent and per car. It is conveniently located right next to the motorway, which can be noisy. The campsite is in a walled enclosure, with eucalyptus trees and pebbles, and the tents are packed in like sardines; you also need a pneumatic drill to get your tent-pegs into the ground. The washing facilities are rather limited. Small shop and café, but no swimming pool, cold showers in summer.

WHAT TO SEE

It has to be said that there isn't much to see in Torremolinos.

★ **La Carihuela**: in the north of the town, by the sea. This is the old part of the town, there are some historic houses, but they are few and far between and not especially interesting.

ANTEQUERA 29200   DIALLING CODE: 952

About 50 kilometres (31 miles) from Málaga, this small but pleasant town boasts a centre whose architectural wealth stems from the Renaissance and baroque periods. With the Sierra de las Cabras to the east, the Sierra de Chimenea to the west and the protective height of the Torcal and Camorro Alto mountains (1,379 metres/4,524 feet), Antequera made a good fallback position during the Reconquest of Al-Andalus. It was particularly popular with religious groups and the Carmelites (of both the shod and barefoot variety), Dominicans and Augustinians, among others, built countless monasteries and religious buildings here. This is definitely a place that will appeal to people with an interest in architecture.

USEFUL ADDRESSES

🖪 **Tourist Information Office**: plaza San Sebastián 7. ☎ and fax: 70-25-05. Open 9.30am–1.30pm and 4–7pm.
✉ **Post Office**: Najera. Behind the Santa Catalina de Siena Convent. ☎ 84-20-83.

🚌 **Bus Station**: ☎ 84-35-73. There are 11 buses a day to Málaga from paseo Real, next to the plaza de Toros.
🚃 **Train Station RENFE**: quite a distance from the town centre, in the north of the town at the end of calle Lucena and next to the Convento de la Trinidad. ☎ 84-32-26.

WHERE TO STAY

☆ Budget

🛏 **Pensión Camas Gallo**: Nueva 2. ☎ 84-21-04. The house on the left as you are facing the Tourist Office. At 16€ for a double room it would be hard to find anywhere cheaper. Run by a friendly woman called Isabel. The rooms may be a bit dark, but they are spotlessly clean. Shared bathrooms. Good value for money.
🛏 **Residencia Colón**: Infante Don Fernando 29. ☎ and fax: 84-00-10. Email: hcolon@teleline.es. Open all

year round. Rooms cost about 30€ and are slightly tatty. The well-kept establishment has two floors, and plenty of flourishing pot-plants. Most rooms only have shared bathrooms, but they all have a TV. Always ask to see several rooms before booking in.

☆☆ Moderate

🛏 **Hostal El Numero Uno**: Lucena 40. ☎ and fax: 84-31-34. The reception is in the bar on the ground floor. Open all year round. A double room costs about 27€. The *hostal* has been totally renovated with large earthenware tiles on the bottom half of the walls. All the rooms have their own bathroom. Ask for No. 8 as it is slightly larger than the other rooms,

or No. 3 as it has a wonderful view. There is nothing particularly special about this place, but it is very clean and you are made to feel welcome.

🛏 **Hotel Nuevo Infante**: Infante D. Fernando 5. ☎ and fax: 70-00-86. On the second floor. A room costs 30€. This hotel is another value-for-money establishment. It is run by a lovely woman called Mariluz (although unfortunately she is not always around). The rooms are styled as small apartments with fridges and lounge areas. They are set around a galleried patio. Fortunately they do not overlook calle Infante D. Fernando, which is one of the busiest and noisiest streets in town.

WHERE TO EAT

Try the local speciality *porra,* which is like a thick *gazpacho*. It is delicious.

☆ Budget

✕ **Bar Pañero**: cuesta Zapateros 7. There is not much to attract you to this bar apart from its set menu costing less than 6€. Good if you are short of funds, but the staff are not very friendly.

✕ **Bar Chicón**: Infante Don Fernando 1. ☎ 70-05-65. This is an excellent place to have breakfast, costing from 2€ upwards. The set meal of the day costs about 5€. Set on plaza San Sebastián, this is the bar where all the old men come for their morning coffee and to gossip about local news. As the morning

wears on, more and more cold beers are pulled and tempting tapas pile up in the refrigerator cabinet. Friendly staff.

☆☆☆ Expensive

✕ **El Angelote**: Encarnación, on plaza del Coso Viejo. ☎ 70-34-65. Closed Monday. Set menu from 8€, à la carte dishes cost 21–24€. There are generous local specialities such as the *asadura de chanfaina* (a vegetarian dish). This fine restaurant is often used as a meeting place for Antequera's local dignitaries.

WHAT TO SEE

★ **El Colegiado de San Sebastián**: on the square of the same name, next to the Tourist Office. The small angel at the top of the spire is the symbol of the Collegiate. In spite of the rows of columns with their attractive pink-stone shafts, the heaviness of the tower betrays the baroque-Mudéjar origins of this building. Inside the angel's chest are several relics of Santa Eufemia, the patron saint of Antequera. The Plaza San Sebastián, which was designed during the Renaissance, is set around a beautiful fountain built in 1545.

★ **La iglesia del Carmen**: go down calle Encarnación as far as plaza Descalzas, turn right up cuesta de los Rojas and the church is at the end of the street. Open Monday 11.30am–2pm and 4–7pm, Tuesday to Saturday 10am–2pm and 4–7pm, and Sunday 10am–2pm. Admission costs about 2€. The altar (*Altar Mayor*) is considered one of the most beautiful in Andalucía. The wealth of white cherubs and angels in the alcoves contrasts with the beautiful red brick of the capitals and the scrolled floral columns. There is a beautiful statue of the Virgen del Socorro consecrated in the 16th century and donated by the Catholic Monarchs.

★ **La iglesia de San Augustín**: near plaza San Sebastián on calle Infante Don Fernando. Open Tuesday to Sunday, 11am–1pm. Closed Monday. This 16th-century building was the work of Diego de Vergara, the architect who designed Málaga cathedral. The altar shows scenes from the life of San Augustín.

★ **La iglesia San Juan de Dios**: at the end of calle Infante Don Fernando, before you get to alameda de Andalucía. The church has a beautifully ornate plaster cupola. It was built in the 17th century and was the religious annexe to the hospital next door, which is no longer open to the public. In those days they made the most of resources and treated spiritual and physical ailments under what was practically the same roof.

★ **La plaza de Santiago, La Iglesia de Santiago and La Iglesia de Santa Eufemia**: beautiful galleried facades and a small baroque chamber containing a statue of the Virgen de la Salud. The plasterwork has recently been restored.

★ **El Convento de los Remedios**: calle Infante Don Remedios. The convent closes to visitors at 8.30pm. The *retablo* (altarpiece) practically buckles under the weight of its gilding.

★ **El Convento de Santa Catalina**: on plaza Coso Viejo. Open every morning from 7.30am on weekdays, and 8.30am at the weekend. This convent likewise has a beautiful, richly decorated *retablo*, dating from the 18th century. An unusual feature of the chapel is that it has neither a nave nor a transept. It only takes a couple of steps before you are standing in the choir. You sometimes catch a glimpse of one of the convent's few remaining nuns at prayer.

★ Antequera boasts several **palacios** and **casas solariegas** (stately homes). These luxurious residences are almost systematically designed around a patio with a fountain in the middle. The wealth of the owner is indicated by the splendour of the archways and the quantities of Torcal marble. Among those worth visiting are the following: palacio Marqués de Villadarías (calle Lucena), palacio de las Escalonias (calle Pasillas), or casa de Seraller (calle Laguna) behind casa del Conde de Colchado (calle Cantareros), in the neo-baroque style.

★ If you are spending a few days in Antequera go to the **Museo Municipal** (town museum). It is housed in the palacio de Nájera, a former palace, that has been well preserved. Open Tuesday–Friday 10am–1pm and 4–7pm. Admission costs about 2€. There is a great collection of local archaeological remains dating from the time of the first human settlement in El Torcal (*see below*) as well as a later reliquary. The show piece of the museum is the

Ephebe of Antequera, a bronze Roman statue and reputedly one of the most beautiful bronzes of the first century AD.

WHAT TO SEE IN THE SURROUNDING AREA

★ **El Torcal de Antequera**: about 13 kilometres (8 miles) from Antequera. A high karstic plateau where the combined action of wind and water has slowly worn away and smoothed down the protruding limestone outcrops, sculpting them into amazing shapes which will delight both rock climbers and photographers. It is easy to reach the **Torcal Visitor Centre** from the car park. The opening times are 10am–2pm and 3–5pm daily. There is also a stunning viewpoint from which you can see as far as the bay of Málaga and the town itself, some 30 kilometres (19 miles) away as the crow flies. The alternating olive groves and chalky hilltops speckled with clumps of trees and whitewashed villages form a very traditional Andalucían landscape. A looping path winds its way through the labyrinth of rocks. The easiest way to get onto it is to turn right at the end of the car-park. Each twist in the rock is a new surprise. These surreal rock formations lend themselves to all manner of interpretation. Keep an eye out for the diverse wildlife as this unusual habitat is home to several types of indigenous flora and fauna. Do not wander far from the path as the plateau is a nature reserve and access is forbidden.

★ **La Garganta del Chorro**: about 50 kilometres (31 miles) from Antequera. Follow the C337 road in the direction of Álora, passing through some very pastoral landscapes en route. On the way into Valle de Abdalajis, a signpost points right to El Chorro. The road winds its way through villages lost in time, where old ladies sit podding peas in doorways and children play football against the walls. If you lose your way don't hesitate to ask someone for directions, you'll find them very polite and helpful. After about 10 kilometres (6 miles) when the horizon opens out, you will find El Chorro in the valley below. Next you need to find the road that takes you over the Tajo de la Encantada weir. Once on the other side, turn right. Don't go as far as the sign for desfiladero de los Gaitanes (the Gaitan Pass), also known as Garganta del Chorro (gorge), as there are not many places to park – it is better to leave your car near the *hostal*. The desfiladero is an impressive geological fault, cleaving the rock on the other side of the narrow manmade lake. It is laced with a network of bridges, and a pathway known as the camino del Rey (path of the King). It was constructed in 1920 on the order of King Alfonso XIII but has since fallen into disrepair. You are strongly advised not to venture along this route, as it takes you along several hundred metres of the railway track between Málaga and Seville (currently in use) through a number of tunnels, then along the rock face some 60 metres (197 feet) above the river on a concrete bridge (with hardly any handrails) about 80 centimetres (30 inches) wide suspended above piles of fallen rocks and then the lake itself. By way of consolation, continue along the road in the same direction you were going in before and turn left after the chapel on the right-hand side towards the Ruinas de Bobastro. This takes you up to the plateau where there are some manmade lakes that form part of the hydraulic system of the dam. Right at the top at the end is a small car park with a splendid view of the valley and the surrounding hills, although unfortunately not of the garganta. On your left a pathway leads down to a bar run by a lovely man who welcomes children and animals with open arms. On your way down go as far as the Embalse del Conde del Guadalhorce (reservoir). The fading light of late afternoon bathes the landscape in beautiful subtle colours. If you follow the lake around to the left, you come back to Ardales and then to Álora, crowned by its citadel (only worth visiting if you are keen on grave-yards).

🛏 At Álora there is a very good hotel with an equally good restaurant: **Durán**, La Parra 9, 29500 Alora. ☎ and fax: 49-66-42. A double room with a bathroom costs about 36€. Set menu for 12€. Friendly welcome.

MÁLAGA   DIALLING CODE: 952

Founded by the Phoenicians and subsequently occupied by the Romans, Málaga has been the target of repeated attacks by invaders from the four corners of Europe. Set on the banks of the river Guadalmedina, Málaga enjoys an exceptional climate with an average of 320 days of sunshine a year.

Famous for its wine, Málaga has little in the way of attractions with the exception of a few beautiful buildings such as the cathedral, the Alcazaba and the Roman theatre. Málaga lacks the charm of Seville and Córdoba and it is only worthwhile stopping here if it happens to be on your way to somewhere more interesting. It doesn't merit a visit for its own sake. The city mourns its glory days of yesteryear. The high levels of unemployment and neglected look of its streets certainly do nothing to enhance its appeal. The outskirts of the city are especially dreary with endless rows of ugly rundown blocks of flats. You have to get right to the city centre before things start to look better – there is a certain charm about the network of streets and pedestrian alleyways tucked away in the heart of the city.

As there really isn't much to see, pass the time sitting outside one of the numerous cafés sipping sweet Málaga wine and soaking up the Andalucían way of life.

Above all else Málaga basks in its status as the birthplace of Picasso, even if he did only spend the first ten years of his life here. It is said that the impression of these early years remained with him all his life, although in fact he never set foot in the city again. A new art gallery was opened in 2001 dedicated to the painter, with more than 100 works on display (sculpture, paintings and ceramics) donated to the city by Christine Picasso, his daughter-in-law.

If you are visiting in August don't miss the Feria, a huge fun-filled celebration which takes over the whole city for a week.

Historical Background

The Phoenicians, Carthaginians and Romans all took control of the city at one time or another, even before the Moors arrived at the beginning of the eighth century. It was the Moors who developed the Alcazaba area of Málaga. Then the Catholic Monarchs seized the city and forcibly expelled them. Trade with the Americas turned Málaga into a key port and brought prosperity. This maritime importance has never declined as the port is ideally situated at the gateway between the Mediterranean and the Atlantic. The economic growth of the town has increased with the international maritime traffic. The last 25 years have particularly stimulated shipping activities in Málaga, as evidenced by the wealth of oil tankers and cargo ships.

VINO DIVINO

Málaga wine is more widely known in Britain and France than in Spain itself. It derives from a wine made by the Moors called *sharab al malaqui* which nowadays is known as *jarabe malagueño* (the syrup of Málaga). At one time it was so popular that it usurped sherry as the favourite tipple. Under the appellation 'vino de Málaga' you can find as many dry white wines and *olorosos* as you can reds. It is easy even for uninitiated wine drinkers to recognize the red *vinos de Málaga*, as they have a dense woody aroma with hints of honey and caramel. The wine growing area is about 20 kilometres (13 miles) as the crow flies from the city, in the Axarquía region, south of the small town of Riogordo. If you don't have time to go there, the next best thing is to call in at the Antigua Casa de Guardia (*see* 'Tour of the Bodegas'). Wines from López Hermanos y Gomara tend to be of a good quality.

ON ARRIVAL AT THE AIRPORT

✚**Airport**: (off map I from A3) about 9 kilometres (6 miles) from the city centre. Information: ☎ 04-88-04.

– **To the City Centre**: bus No. 19 leaves every 20 minutes from 7am to 11pm for the city centre. The bus fare costs 1€. To return to the airport, catch the bus from Paseo del Parque, next to the Hotel Marbella Palace (C2 on map II). Or you can catch it from the bus station (C2 on map II) –the service likewise runs every 20 minutes. It is advisable to have the correct money for your fare at the ready – you can get it from the change counter. There is also an RER train service to the airport.

– To get to **Torremolinos**, take the train that stops near the airport. There is a train every 30 minutes from 7am. Otherwise you can catch the bus from Portillo station (C2 on map II).

■ **Useful Addresses**

🚌 Bus station
🚂 Train station

🏠 **Where to Stay**

  17 Albergue Juvenil Málaga (youth hostel)

✗ **Where to Eat**

  26 El Tintero
  27 Marisquería Naypa

🍷 **Where to Have a Drink**

  46 El Colonial

★ **What to See**

  60 Jardín Botánico Histórico 'La Concepción'

MÁLAGA

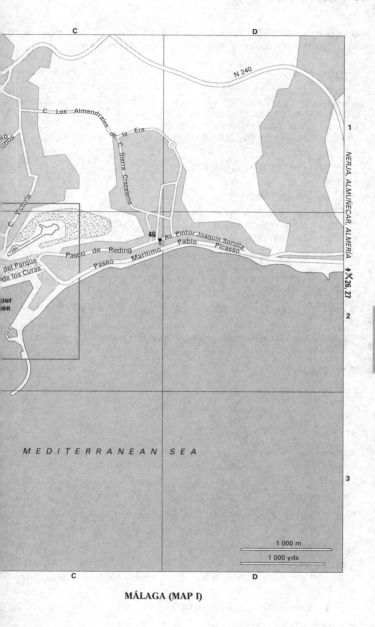

■ **Information Kiosk**: Usually open Monday to Friday 9am–9pm, and Saturday morning, useful for general information on the region.

ORIENTATION

It is easy to find your way around Málaga. The city centre lies behind paseo del Parque, a long tree-lined avenue, where you can have a drink outside one of the many pavement cafés. The hilltop which overlooks the city is crowned by the Alcazaba, a Moorish fortress built in the ninth century.

USEFUL ADDRESSES

Tourist Information

■ **Tourist Office** (C2, **1** on map II): avenida de Cervantes 1, paseo del Parque. ☎ 60-44-10. Open 9.30am–2pm and 4.30–7pm. The staff are very friendly and provide clear and detailed information.

■ **Tourist Office** (C2, **2** on map II): pasaje Chinitas 4. ☎ 21-34-45. Near the cathedral. Opening times are supposedly weekdays 9am–7pm and weekends 9am–1pm. You get a friendly welcome and there are lots of information leaflets available.

■ There is a further **tourist office** (A3, **3** on map II) at the bus station. ☎ 35-00-61.

■ There is a small **tourist office** at the airport as well. ☎ 04-84-84.

Services

✉ **Main Post Office** (B2, on map II): avenida de Andalucía. Open 9am–2pm and 4–7pm.

Money

■ **Banks** (C2, **4** on map II): there are lots of banks on calle Marqués de Larios. They all change money and have cash machines.

Embassies and Consulates

See 'Embassies and Consulates' *in* 'General Information'.

Health and Emergencies

■ **Pharmacy** (C1, **5** on map II): plaza de la Constitución 8. This is one of the most central pharmacies; there is another one in calle de Larios (C1, **5** on map II).

■ **Red Cross**: avenida José Silvela 64. ☎ 25-04-50.

■ **Guardia Civil (police)**: ☎ 091.

■ **Local police**: avenida Salvador, in the direction of the airport. ☎ 092.

Transport

🚂 **Train Station RENFE** (A3 on map II): *see* 'Leaving Málaga'. Left luggage facilities at the station. Tickets can also be bought in the city centre at calle Strachan 2 (C2, **1** on map II). ☎ 21-41-27.

🚌 **Bus Stations** (C2, **2** and A3, **1** on map II): *see* 'Leaving Málaga'.

■ **Local Bus Service**: there are about 37 lines around Málaga. Most of them have a stop on paseo del Parque (C-D2 on map II). Service information available on: ☎ 35-72-12 or 21-22-38.

■ **Taxis**: ☎ 33-33-33 and 32-30-00.

■ **Iberia** (C2, **2** on map II): Molina Larios 3. ☎ 21-37-31 or 13-61-26. Open 9am–1.30pm and 4–7.15pm.

■ **Turache Cycle Hire** (A3, **3** on map II): Roger de Flor, Unit No. 1, bus station. ☎ 31-80-69. Fax: 24-42-72. Open Monday–Saturday, 9am–9pm, and Sunday, 10am–3pm. Cycle hire costs 9€ per day and 42€ per week. Scooters are also available.

Miscellaneous

■ **El Corte Inglés** (B2, **7** on map II): avenida de Andalucía 4 and 6. ☎ 30-00-00. The department store that sells everything.

■ **Atlantes Mapas**: calle Etchegaray 7. ☎ and fax: 60-27-65. Travel shop with a good selection of maps and guidebooks.

MÁLAGA

■ **Useful Addresses**

  ℹ **1** and **2** Tourist Offices
  ✉ Main Post Office
  🚂 Train station
  🚌 **1** and **2** Bus stations
  ⛴ Trasmediterranea
  1 RENFE Booking Office
  2 Iberia
  3 Cycle Hire and Tourist Information Office
  4 Banks
  5 Pharmacies
  7 El Corte Inglés

🛏 **Where to Stay**

  10 Pensión Juanita
  11 Hospedaje Córdoba
  12 Pensión Rosa
  13 Hostal Buenos Aires
  14 Hostal El Ruedo
  15 Hostal Castilla y Guerrero

  16 Hostal Alameda
  18 Hostal La Hispanidad
  19 Parador Málaga-Gibralfaro

✕ **Where to Eat**

  20 Café Central
  21 La Cancela
  22 Lo Güeno
  23 Restaurante Tormes
  24 Yovi Restaurant
  25 Cervantes
  28 Heladería Casa Mira

🍷 **Where to Have a Drink**

  40 Antigua Casa de Guardia
  41 Quitapeñas
  42 La Tasca
  43 Mesón Las Garrafas
  44 Bar Alaska
  45 Mesón Ajo Blanco
  47 La Tetería

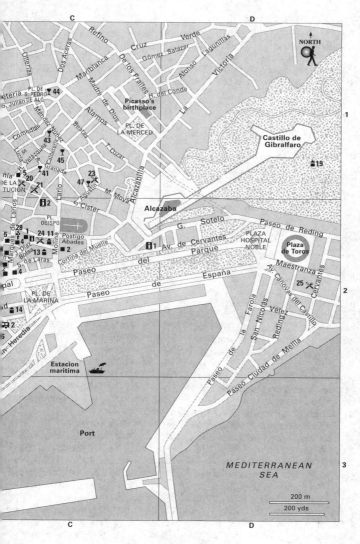

MÁLAGA

MÁLAGA (MAP II)

WHERE TO STAY

In Málaga accommodation is on the whole inexpensive but lacking in charm. This is especially true of the city centre. The *pensiónes* are all to some extent reminiscent of military barracks. The fact that this is one of the largest port towns in Spain is bound to have a knock-on effect.

Campsites

⛺ The nearest campsite is in Torremolinos (*see above*).

In the Town Centre

☆–☆☆ Budget to Moderate

⛺ **Pensión Juanita** (C2, **10** on map II): calle Alarcón Luján 8, 29005 Málaga. ☎ 21-35-86. In a street parallel to calle Martinez, at right angles to calle Marqués de Larios. The *pensión* is on the fourth floor of a block of offices (there's a lift). A double room with washbasin costs 24€ and with bathroom 30€. This is a good place to stay if you like your creature comforts. It has recently been renovated and the rooms are very clean, although not particularly light, with gleaming tiled bathrooms. There is also another set of rooms on the floor above. Good value for money considering the location and level of mod cons on offer.

⛺ **Hospedaje Córdoba** (C2, **11** on map II): calle Bolsa 11, 29015 Málaga. ☎ 21-44-69. On the second floor. A double room costs 18€. The rooms are not too bad – all have a washbasin and a small balcony. The ones overlooking the street are a bit noisy. They do not accept reservations by phone.

⛺ **Pensión Rosa** (C2, **12** on map II): calle Martinez 10, 29005 Málaga. ☎ 21-27-16. Doubles cost about 27€, but they are not the most desirable of rooms. This is a large, ancient building with a certain old-world charm. It has an interior patio where guests can hang out their washing. With condensation-covered stained-glass windows, creaking floorboards and an abundance of artificial flowers this *pensión* seems to be caught in a time-warp, although it is a mite cleaner than others in the same category. Don't hesitate to haggle over the price of your room, but take care not to ask for a copy of the bill. The staff are friendly, and likewise rather old-fashioned. Reception is open until 2–2.30am, but even after this time there will always be someone about to open the door.

⛺ **Hostal Buenos Aires** (C2, **13** on map II): calle Bolsa 14, 29001 Málaga. ☎ 21-89-35. The official room rate is 25€, but if the owner likes the look of you he'll drop the price after a bit of haggling. Some of the rooms are alright but the ones set on the corridor decorated with brown plastic wallpaper are awful. Only for emergencies, if everywhere else is full.

In the Plaza Marina Quarter

This part of town might give the impression of being some distance from the centre, but is in fact only a 5-minute walk southwest of the cathedral, between alameda Principal and the port. If you aren't bothered about being right in the centre of the town, this is an excellent place to stay, especially if you have a car (there is parking here, which is not always the case in the centre). Furthermore, for a price only slightly higher than the places in the centre, the hotels are quieter, cleaner and generally pleasanter.

☆☆ Moderate

🛏 **Hostal El Ruedo** (C2, **14** on map II): Trinidad Grund 3, 29001 Málaga. ☎ 21-58-20. A double room costs 27€. A building with tall windows protected by iron bars. The basic rooms have washbasins only and can be a bit noisy. Those opening onto the corridor are quieter but less attractive. There are only two rooms with an outside view. Bathrooms are communal and can be reached via the corridor. After midnight, the owner puts out the 'full' sign so that guests are not disturbed. This is very important in Málaga because, as already mentioned, it is a town full of sailors and in many small hotels, the partying goes on all night. Here it is rather the opposite, there must be no noise after 9pm and there is trouble if anyone is caught breaking the rule.

In Other Areas

☆ Budget

🛏 **Albergue Juvenil Málaga** (A2, **17** on map I): plaza Pie XII 6, 29007 Málaga. ☎ 30-85-00. Fax: 30-85-04. Website: www.inturjoven.com. Open all year round. A bed only costs around 8€ for the under 26s and 11€ for the over 26s. At the final stop on the No. 18 bus route which serves the railway and bus stations. A large youth hostel that could easily be mistaken for an extremely old, disused barracks. Set in a pleasant little square. The clean rooms have two, three or four beds, and are inexpensive, especially if you have a YHA card. Note that you cannot book the double rooms by phone, you have to call by in person. In any case, as the hostel is some distance from the centre, it would only be of interest to people travelling alone. If

🛏 **Hostal Castilla y Guerrero** (C2, **15** on map II): Córdoba 7, 29001 Málaga. ☎ 21-86-35. Five minutes from the centre with parking nearby. Around 40€ for a double room with en-suite bathroom. Even though it is on rather a noisy main road, this is a smart place offering genuinely competitive prices. The rooms have all been revamped, with washbasin or bathroom, pine furniture, maroon velour bedspreads and TV. It is clean and smart throughout. Friendly.

🛏 **Hostal Alameda** (C2, **16** on map II): Casas de Campos 3, 29001 Málaga. ☎ 22-20-99. Around 40€ for a double with en-suite bathroom. Under the same ownership as the Castilla y Guerrero, with the same prices and exactly the same decor. Equally good value for money.

there are two of you, a hotel in the centre would work out cheaper.

☆☆ Moderate

🛏 **Hostal La Hispanidad** (A3, **18** on map II): esplanada de la Estación, 29002 Málaga. ☎ 31-11-35. Opposite the station. A double room costs around 27€. This little hotel is ever so slightly ridiculous with its over-abundance of cutesy picture frames and frills. You'll either like it or you won't. All the rooms are named after a country in South America. Ask for 'Colombia' – a triple room for the price of a double. Two small criticisms – the decor is not exactly new and the rooms aren't as well lit as they could be. Its only good point is its location, which is just opposite the station – useful if you arrive late. Don't reckon

MÁLAGA

on staying more than a couple of days.

☆☆☆☆ Splash Out

⌂ Parador   Málaga-Gibralfaro (D1, **19** on map II): in a hilltop location 3 kilometres (2 miles) north of the town. ☎ 22-19-02. Fax: 22-19-04. Website: www.parador.es. Go along calle Victoria and follow the signs from there. From 105€ out of season to 114€ in season. Surrounded by pine and eucalyptus trees. From the terrace you have a view of the whole town and the Alcazaba below, and a bird's-eye view of the plaza de toros and the port. Entirely revamped and very tastefully decorated. Beautiful attic rooms in shades of salmon pink and ochre, with a small intimate terrace. A truly excellent buffet breakfast that includes all sorts of regional products such as *manteca colorada* (coloured butter), delicious *polvorones* (shortbread) and freshly squeezed fruit juice. Beautiful terrace for sun-bathing. Swimming pool. Real luxury. One small criticism is that the staff are not particularly friendly considering the high-class of this establishment. Even if your budget doesn't stretch to staying here, the walk amid the olive groves down the hill through puerta Oscara makes it worth the detour.

WHERE TO EAT

In the Historic Centre

☆ – ☆☆ Budget to Moderate

✕ **Café Central** (C1, **20** on map II): plaza de la Constitución. Opens very early, closes very late, and has remained unchanged from one decade to the next. This is an old-fashioned working-class sort of place, with aluminium chairs outside on the pavement. It also acts as a grocery store, a newsagent's, social security office and centre for group therapy, along with a glass or two, of course. The locals come in during the morning to have coffee with *churros* (long doughnuts). Fairly grotty but interesting from a social point of view.

✕ **La Cancela** (C1, **21** on map II): Denis Belgrano 5. ☎ 22-31-25. Open lunchtime and evenings until 11pm. Closed on Monday night and all day Wednesday. Extensive, reasonably priced set menus, for a little under 7€. Opens onto a little square surrounded by flowery balconies. A lovely little family restaurant with red table-cloths, old-fashioned pictures on the walls and vaulted rooms. This is the place where local workers come for lunch. Simple, filling food. Good fish soups. Friendly welcome. It can get very busy, which means the waiters sometimes fail to keep up with demand.

✕ **Lo Güeno** (C2, **22** on map II): Marin Garcia 9. ☎ 22-30-48. Open every day. Typical and quiet. Not very big, but pretty and welcoming with its carafes, barrels of wine and old cheeses maturing. The tapas are slightly unusual and always excellent. The beer is a bit more expensive than elsewhere. Full of tourists in the evening.

✕ **Restaurante Tormes** (C1, **23** on map II): San Agustín 13. ☎ 22-20-63. Cheap set menu at lunchtime for less than 9€. Almost opposite the Museo de Bellas Artes. The room is a bit chilly, but the tables outside are pleasant enough.

☆☆☆ Expensive

✕ **Yovi Restaurant** (C2, **24** on map II): Strachan 12. ☎ 22-00-91.

Tapas from 1€. This modern, friendly place is really a classy wine bar, with racks of expensive wines, a huge selection of delicious and sophisticated tapas, as well as good cheeses and pâtés. Faultless service and well-prepared food. The less well-off will concentrate on the tapas rather than meals from the à la carte menu. Beer is a bit more expensive here than elsewhere.

In the Malagueta Area

✘ **Cervantes** (D2, **25** on map II): Cervantes 10. ☎ 13-39-96. Closed on Monday. A meal costs around 12€ and tapas are less than 2€. A lovely little place in the area near the plaza de Toros. There is a particularly good atmosphere on days when there is a *corrida*. You can either eat leaning at the bar or sitting in the dining-room. The excellent regional specialities include *almejas a lo natural* (clams), *lomo* (ribs) and *queso con aceite* (cheese with oil).

On the Beach, Near the Public Housing Area

There are several restaurants on the beach that are favourite meeting-places for families on Sundays. Very popular, although it is not very clear why, as the area has no evident charm about it. There are lots of seafood places, but the following two are particularly recommended:

✘ **El Tintero** (**26**, off map I from D2): playa del Dedo. ☎ 20-44-64. You can generally enjoy a meal, including wine, for less than 9€. At the far end of the Dedo beach, right next to the Málaga sailing club. Buses Nos. 11 and 29 stop nearby. This is a good restaurant for fish and seafood – the day's catch is displayed on a large boat serving as a stall, you choose what you want and how you want it cooked (generally over the wood fire). If you are lucky, the chef will come round with a plate of sardines or small fried fish for you to enjoy while you wait for your main course. Large terrace and efficient service by a host of waiters. Fish is obviously cheaper than in the centre but prices fluctuate depending on supply.

✘ **Marisquería Naypa** (**27**, off map I from D2): paseo Marítimo del Palo 115. ☎ 220-46-01. Closed on Monday. Also called the Barca de Paco Carrasco. Same location as above, but not as vast. A platter of seven different sorts of fried fish costs 21€.

TASTY TREATS

♱ **Heladería Casa Mira** (ice-cream parlour: C2, **28** on map II) calle Marqués de Larios 5. Open every day, 10am–11pm. Escape from the heat by buying a cornet or *granizado de limón* (similar to a lemon Slush Puppy) at the zinc counter for 1–2€.

A TOUR OF THE *BODEGAS*

Endowed with a unique bouquet and legendary sweetness, the wines from the Málaga region are very popular among locals and visitors alike. Below is a suggested route for trying a variety of wines in different places. You can walk between all the bars listed. Prices will depend on what you drink but bear in mind that if the beer is priced at much over 1€, you are in one of the pricier establishments. Any tapas you are given are generally not included in the price of the drink.

Antigua Casa de Guardia (B2, **40** on map II): alameda Principal, on the corner of calle Pastora. ☎ 21-46-80. Open 9am–10pm. A glass costs less than 1€. Very highly recommended. Founded in 1840, this narrow old bar offers dozens of different wines, poured directly from the barrels around the room (*muscatel*, *málaga quina*, *pajarete*, and many others). The clientele stand and drink, eating enormous mussels. With such an impressive choice, don't hesitate to ask the advice of the waiters who keep your tab written in chalk on the greasy wooden bar. Each glass is served with tapas (olives, roasted or salted almonds). One particular recommendation is the *seco trasañejo* (honey-coloured and demi-sec).

Quitapeñas (C1, **41** on map II): avenida Juan Sebastian Elcano 149. ☎ 29-01-29. Open until 10.30pm. Closed on Saturday evenings and all day Sunday. Less attractive than the Antigua Casa de Guardia because it is much smaller and a bit more touristy. However there is still plenty of good wine as well as some tapas and *pescadito frito* (fried fish).

La Tasca (C2, **42** on map II): Marin Garcia 12. ☎ 22-20-82. Closed on Sunday. A narrow, cosy bar offering quite elaborate tapas. Decorated with *chorizo*, hams and *azulejos*. Magnificent carved-wood counter, although it's difficult to get near it at peak times.

Mesón Las Garrafas (C1, **43** on map II): Mendez Nuñez 5. ☎ 21-91-49. Near the plaza Uncibay. Open every day, lunchtime and evening. Easily recognizable by its green wooden doors and outside lights. Big room, pyramid of barrels and wooden bar. Friendly and very popular. Try the *vino Canasta cream* or *vino de Málaga*.

Bar Alaska (C1, **44** on map II): plaza San Pedro de Alcántara 4, at the end of calle Carreteria. Open every day, lunchtime and evening. Old-fashioned little bar set on a small square. Try a *pedro* or a *muscatel* seated at the tables outside in the shade of a big old tree. If you're hungry there is plenty of seafood (crabs, scallops, prawns, mussels, octopus, etc.) to have with your wine. Very lively and popular.

Mesón Ajo Blanco (C1, **45** on map II): plaza Uncibay 2. ☎ 22-29-35. One of the new generation of bars, made from wood and brick but without the patina that only time can endow. Wine by the glass, *gazpacho* by the bowlful and platters of *chorizo*. Good tapas. Packed at weekends.

La calle Beatas (near the plaza de Uncibay), is teeming with people by about 11pm at the weekend. There are a number of popular **bars** in the area which attract young people from all over Málaga and the surrounding areas. The sheer numbers of people give it a very special atmosphere.

MÁLAGA

After Hours

El Colonial (C-D2, **46** on map I): paseo de Reding. Closes at 2am. Big, new-style bar with comfortable sofas where you can linger over a mint tea or a long *kawa*. Stylishly worn furniture and a discreetly homosexual clientele.

La Tetería (C1, **47** on map II): San Agustín 11. Designed to be romantic, so make sure you go with a loved one. Discreet, elegant decor. Big white-cloth wall-hangings decorated with painted motifs. Good range of teas and cakes.

WHAT TO SEE AND DO

As well as the historic and cultural attractions it's worth making a visit to the paseo del Parque, which is an especially pleasant place for a walk at dusk.

★ The area around the brand-new Picasso Museum (formerly the Museum of Fine Arts), which only opened in 2000, is delightful, its maze of streets lined with typical Andalucían houses and flowery patios that you can glimpse through half-open doors and wrought-iron grilles.

★ **Alcazaba** (C-D2 on map II) and the **Museum of Archaeology**: ☎ 21-60-05. Open 9.30am–8pm but check in advance as it can vary. Closed Tuesday. Under restoration at the time of writing. An imposing fortress built by the Romans in the ninth century and restored by the Arabs, but now in ruins. You climb up to the Alcazaba from the plaza de la Aduana. Follow the footpath leading to the little Archaeological Museum at the top of the Alcazaba. It is a lovely walk and takes you through the ancient fortress, where there are clumps of typical Andalucían flowering shrubs, and along verandas and arcaded walkways.

The museum is set round a large Moorish patio. It houses a collection of Roman statues, pottery, and the like. Some of the more interesting things on display include third-century mosaics, attractively ornate Hispano-Muslim archways and colourful *azulejos*. The Arabs had a real gift for ornament and symmetry of form. There is a beautiful terrace with a view of the town.

★ At the foot of the Alcazaba, lie the **ruins of a Roman amphitheatre** (D2 on map II).

★ **El castillo de Gibralfaro** (D1 on map II): Open every day, 9.30am–8pm. From the Alcazaba it is a steep walk up the path to the castle, perched on the top of the hill. You can also drive there along a road leading off calle la Victoria. The nicely restored Phoenician castle gives an idea of the military architecture of the time and the complexity of the system of defence. It was reconstructed by Yusuf I in the 14th century.

★ **Cathedral** (C2 on map II): plaza del Obispo. Admission fee. Entrance through the garden to the left, where excavations are in progress. Official opening hours are Monday to Saturday 9am–6.45pm. Closed on Sunday (except during services). This massive, unfinished, Renaissance-style building is by no means a masterpiece. It was built in 1528 on the site of a mosque and finished in 1782. It was decorated using finds (mainly the result of pillaging) from the New World, but money soon ran out and the second tower was never built. One of the building's few attractions is the detail in its finely carved vaulted ceilings. The marble pulpit is also worth a look, as are some of the tapestries you can see in the chapels off the side aisles. Finally, through the garden you can get to the Sagrario, the remains of the former mosque, now a shrine with a superb Plateresque carved *retablo* (altarpiece) dating from the 16th century, which came from a church in Castilla. On emerging into calle Santa Maria, look out for an interesting doorway in the Isabelline style, characterized by its very ornate decoration.

MÁLAGA

★ **Picasso's Birthplace** (C1 on map II): plaza de la Merced 15. ☎ 21-50-05. Open every day, 10am–2pm and 5–8pm, and Sunday morning. Only for real devotees, as there is nothing much to see. It is owned by a foundation, and none of Picasso's works is on display. Nevertheless, this is where the famous painter was born in 1881. His father, also a painter, encouraged him to draw and it quickly became clear to his family that he had an extraordinary talent. All his life, Picasso never stopped 'learning how to draw like a child'.

★ **Plaza de Toros de la Malagueta** (bullring; D2 on map II): ☎ 21-94-82. Open 8am–3pm. Built at the end of the 19th century, this bullring originally had views of the sea. It was here that Picasso sketched out his first drawings and oil paintings in what is now termed his 'bullfighting period'. It is said to have been while he was in Málaga that he was inspired by José Moreno Carbonero, a master at painting horses gored by bulls. The horses in *Guernica* are reminiscent of this period.

★ **El Paseo de Reding**: the imposing mansions and palace in the Belle Époque style make this long avenue next to the bullring an interesting place for a stroll. There are some attractive, ornate gateways and typically Andalucían facades, painted white with unusual bow-windows.

★ **Jardín Botánico Histórico 'La Concepción'** (**60** off map I from B1): well signposted from the Granada *autopista* (motorway). ☎ 25-21-48. Opens at 10am. Closing time is a bit more complicated, varying from 4pm in winter to 7.30pm from 21 June to 10 September. Closed Monday. Visits take the form of guided tours costing around 5€. Phone in advance to find out when there are tours in English. This is a delightful tropical garden with a stream, waterfalls, imitation Roman statues and lots of birds. Unfortunately, it is right in the path of the motorway to Granada, constructed in the 1980s. Happily, it has more or less survived intact and the traffic noise is not too intrusive. There are some very unusual plants, including the gigantic ficus, monkey puzzle trees, giant bird-of-paradise plants and dragon trees from the Canaries, to name but a few. In the summer it is refreshingly cool and it is even more appealing in autumn with copper and red leaves falling from the trees.

★ **El Teatro de Cervantes**: this is where the major concerts take place, from Bob Dylan to symphony orchestras. Booking opens a fortnight before the event. Information: ☎ 22-41-09. Telephone bookings: ☎ 22-41-00. Website: www.teatrocervantes.com. Ticket office open 11am–2pm and 6–9pm.

– **Beaches**: nothing particularly special but extensive and with good amenities. They are all around 20 kilometres (13 miles) to the north of Málaga.

FIESTAS

– There is a major Feria on or around 15 August.

LEAVING MÁLAGA

By Bus

Bus Station (**1**, A3 on map II): paseo de los Tilos. ☎ 35-29-56. Next to the railway station. Trains go to all the major towns:

– Marbella, Almería, Granada, Seville, Madrid, Barcelona, Córdoba, etc. Three companies (Sierra de las Nieves, Los Amarillos, Comes) cover all destinations between them. Compare prices, it is sometimes possible to save a few pesetas.

Portillo Bus Station (C2, **2** on map II): muelle Heredia, the continuation of avenida Agustin Heredia. For nearer destinations:

– Fuengirola, Torremolinos, Nerja and Rincón de la Victoria. Departures almost every hour. No telephone. Tickets can be purchased on arrival.

By Train

RENFE Station (A3 on map II): esplanada de la Estación, at the end of calle Cuarteles. ☎ 36-02-02. Website: www.renfe.es

Connections to most towns in Andalucía. Frequent departures to Barcelona (three), Madrid (three trains to Chamartín station, one to Atocha) via Córdoba, Córdoba (two trains in the afternoon – the Andalucía Express and the TRD).

By Ferry

– **Trasmediterranea** (C2 on map II): ☎ 22-43-91 or 92. One ferry a day to Melilla. The journey takes 8 hours.

By Car

There are two delightful roads to the north – both well worth exploring if you have time on your hands.

★ **The Parque dos Montes de Málaga Road**: you can only get on this road from the town itself, there is no access from the motorway bypass. Follow the signs for 'Málaga Norte', then the C345. This is a good road offering impressive views of the Málaga bay and the town, invariably crowned by its cap of pollution. The best viewing point is fortuitously right by the El Mirador restaurant. The road then skirts the park, which lies to the left. You come into the Parque dos Montes de Málaga along a maze of tracks, some of which are signposted. The terrain is very dry and the whole area is very quiet during the week. There are a number of footpaths. If you are keen to get away from it all the Hotel Humaina lies 4 kilometres (2 miles) down a dirt track. Beyond the puerto del León, the countryside becomes more hilly and is dotted with olive groves. From Colmenar, a lovely road leads to Casabermeja where you can rejoin the Granada motorway.

– You can enjoy another equally beautiful and quiet route by exiting the Granada motorway at the sign for 'Finca de la Concepción'. At the small roundabout, turn left on the MA431 (no signpost), which runs through a very sparsely inhabited area of countryside. This is the real rural Andalucía, well off most tourist tracks – olive trees, aloe plants (used for skin-care products), cork oaks, goats, pigs, bee hives and little cottage gardens abound. After winding uphill for some time, the road suddenly emerges on the other side of the ridge to reveal a panorama of ochre and green patchwork squares, which is the land below. At this point there is a signpost to the left for 'Ermita'. Despite the bumpy road, there are some wonderful spots for picnicking, all with grand views of the Guadalmedina valley, Montes de Málaga to the east, the region of Almogía to the west and Málaga and its bay to the south. The road eventually comes out at Casabermeja and the Granada *autopista*. Around 4 kilometres (2 miles) before Casabermeja there is a little restaurant on the right with a mimosa-shaded terrace and a large, cool dining room – very quiet and surrounded by hillsides covered in olive and almond trees. Good food at a very reasonable price.

FRIGILIANA 29788   DIALLING CODE: 952

This town is 8 kilometres (5 miles) north of Nerja. Follow the road to Málaga for 1 kilometre, then turn right. A little white village, full of flowers, it was once voted the most beautiful village in Andalucía. Also well known for its olive oil and aperitif wine.

If you come by car, it is advisable to park in the car-park at the entrance to the village and explore the pretty geranium-filled, whitewashed streets on foot. Although the village is expanding, serious efforts have been made to ensure that new buildings blend with the old so it has successfully managed to retain its traditional atmosphere. In the centre, there are some good pottery shops and *bodegas* (wine cellars). There are a lot of people in summer, but they tend to be day-trippers from the coast. If you stay the night in the village you will have a chance to mix with the locals and enjoy the streets when they are free of tourists.

Other places of interest include a church from the Renaissance period, the ruins of an Arab castle and two prehistoric caves. The processions at Christmas and during Semana Santa are also worth seeing.

WHERE TO STAY AND EAT

🛏 ✕ **Hotel Las Chinas**: plaza Doña Amparo Guerrero 14. ☎ and fax: 53-30-73. Spotless rooms with en-suite bathrooms for around 35€. No particular character, but the owner is friendly. All mod cons. Good, inexpensive home-cooked food in the restaurant.

NERJA 29780   DIALLING CODE: 952

A charming little town, although it has become a bit too touristy in recent years. It is, however, about the only place on the Costa del Sol to have escaped the rampant onslaught of concrete tower blocks. It boasts two particular sights of interest – the caves and the famous Balcón de Europa (balcony of Europe), a natural promontory overlooking the sea, so named by Alfonso XII when he visited the town in 1885.

Nerja manages to retain a very laidback atmosphere, something that is rare amid the frenzied holidaymaking of the rest of this stretch of the Mediterranean coastline. Needless to say, it is very busy in summer, but the attractive streets, the pleasant ambiance and the overall impression of the place soon compensate for this.

USEFUL ADDRESSES

❶ Tourist Office (B3 on the map): puerta del Mar 2. ☎ 52-15-31. Open in theory Monday to Friday 10am–2pm and 5.30–8pm, and Saturday 10am–1pm. Closed Sunday. Open in low season 9am–2pm. In practice it only opens when it sees fit, so don't expect too much in the way of useful information.

✉ Post Office (B3 on the map): calle Almirante Ferrandiz 6. Open Monday to Friday 8.30am–2.30pm, and Saturday 9.20am–1pm.

■ Banks (**1**, A3 on the map): there are a lot in the centre, especially in calle Diputación and on the plaza Cavana. Most have a cash machine and offer currency exchange facilities. Opening hours are generally Monday to Friday 9am–2pm, and Saturday until 1pm.

■ Red Cross: ☎ 52-24-50.
■ Municipal Police: ☎ 52-15-45.
■ Taxi rank: ☎ 52-05-37.
🚌 Bus station (A1 on the map): on the road from Málaga to Almería. Regular buses to Málaga, Almuñecar, Almería, Córdoba, Cádiz and Seville. Timetables available at the tourist office. Frequent bus service to the caves.

WHERE TO STAY

There are not many hotels and most are over-priced with only a few representing good value for money. There is no accommodation in the 'Budget' category. Prices vary considerably depending on season.

☆☆ Moderate

⌂ Hostal Miguel (B3, **10** on the map): calle Almirante Ferrandiz 31. ☎ 52-15-23. Fax: 52-65-35. Email: hostal-miguel@hotmail.com. Double rooms for 24–36€ depending on the season. Not to be confused with the Hostal San Miguel. An attractive house with bow-windows. Most rooms have en-suite bathrooms. Tiny terrace for breakfast or tea. A good, central little place, offering a friendly welcome.

⌂ Hostal Castillo (A-B2, **11** on the map): calle Pintada 67. ☎ 52-81-16. A double room with en-suite bathroom costs 27–39€, depending

on season. Highly recommended – marble hallway, brand-new rooms with en-suite bathrooms. Spic and span, yet retaining a homely atmosphere at the same time. Luckily nothing has changed with the arrival of the new proprietor.

⌂ Pensión Montesol (A1, **12** on the map): calle Pintada 10. ☎ 52-00-14. Closed in November. A double room costs from 30€. A pleasant little hotel, only 5-minutes walk from the centre, with all mod cons (shower, toilets, TV) and very clean. Not the most cheerful establishment in the world, however. Less character than the Miguel and the Castillo, but friendly enough all the same.

⌂ **Hostal Nerjasol** (B2, **13** on the map): calle Pintada 54. ☎ 52-21-21. Fax: 52-36-96. Double rooms with fully-fitted bathrooms from 30€. In a quiet little street, near the Balcón de Europa. It has 1950s decor, which may or may not be to your taste, but it's spotlessly clean throughout. The rooms are spacious and set over two floors with small lounges, TVs, newspapers and other small luxuries. There is a small terrace with a view over the rooftops. Cash payments only. Friendly welcome.

⌂ **Hostal Atenbeni** (**14**, A3 on the map): calle Diputación 12. ☎ 52-13-41. A double room costs 25–37€. Closed from mid-October to the end of March. Reception is on the first floor. Right in the centre of town, and rather noisy. The rooms have tiny balconies and en-suite bath-

rooms. There is little in the way of ornamentation, other than the carved wooden furniture. All in all, rather drab. Accepts Visa cards. Does not include breakfast as the others do.

☆☆☆☆ Splash Out

⌂ **Hotel Portofino** (B3, **15** on the map): puerta del Mar 2. ☎ 52-01-50. Right next to the Tourist Office. Rooms cost 54–60€. Run by a French lady. Perfect location – the rooms overlook the bay of Cala Onda and all have verandas facing the sea. Very tasteful decoration – simple furniture and pale cotton fabrics. The rooms all have en-suite bathrooms but some are smaller than others. The restaurant has a good reputation.

WHERE TO STAY IN THE SURROUNDING AREA

Campsites

⌂ **Camping El Pino** (**16**, off the map from A1-2): carretera N340 Málaga–Almería, at the 285 kilometre-marker. ☎ 53-01-54 or 53-03-42. Fax: 53-25-78. In Torrox, about 7 kilometres (4 miles) from Nerja and 1 kilometre inland from the sea. A pitch costs around 3€ per person and 3€ per car. Well

signposted, opposite a large blue boat which serves as a restaurant. Hot showers are extra. This is a very large site, with shade in parts, set out over terraces at different levels. Swimming pool. Beach nearby.

⌂ **Camping Nerja** (**17** off the map from A1): carretera N340, at the 297-kilometre marker, 29787 Maro.

FRIGILIANA AND NERJA

■ **Useful Addresses**

🄷 Tourist Office
✉ Post Office
🚌 Bus station
1 Banks

⌂ **Where to Stay**

10 Hostal Miguel
11 Hostal Castillo
12 Pensión Montesol
13 Hostal Nerjasol
14 Hostal Atenbeni

15 Hotel Portofino
16 Camping El Pino
17 Camping Nerja

✕ **Where to Eat**

20 Café-bar Las 4 Esquinas
21 El Chispa
22 Bar Los Mariscos

🍷 **Where to Have a Drink**

24 Pub Dirty Nelly
25 La Viña

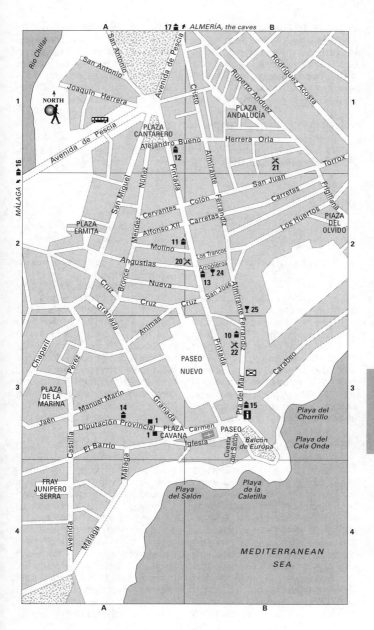

NERJA

☎ 252-97-14. Fax: 52-96-96. On the Almuñecar road, about 6 kilometres (4 miles) from Nerja. Reception is open 9am–noon. A pitch costs slightly over 3€ per person, per tent and per car, with reductions for long stays. This is its only attraction as it is a long way from the centre of the town, and on a hill. The pitches are very close together to wring as much money out of the site as possible. Central toilet and shower block. Swimming pool. Beach and the bay a few kilometres away.

WHERE TO HAVE BREAKFAST

– **Café-bar Las 4 Esquinas** (A-B2, **20** on the map): calle Pintada 55. On the corner of calle Arropiero. Fresh *churros* and toast for around 3€. The ideal way to set yourself up for the day.

WHERE TO EAT

Restaurant prices in Nerja reflect the town's popularity with tourists. Unfortunately, despite the high prices, quality has slipped over the years.

✕ **El Chispa** (B1, **21** on the map): San Pedro 12. You can eat well here for less than 9€. Fortunately, there are still a few places that continue to cater for locals, generally in parts of town well away from the tourist hordes. You choose your fish from the display window (freshly caught the night before) and decide how you want it cooked (*a la plancha* – grilled, *al ajillo* – with garlic, *al horno* – baked). You can also order shellfish cooked in white wine at the bar. A good down-to-earth place, popular with the locals.

✕ **Bar Los Mariscos** (B3, **22** on the map): calle Almirante Ferrandiz 17. ☎ 52-27-14. A meal costs 6–7€. This is a small family-run bar, that is now a bit too touristy. The food is not outstanding and prices are on the high side but it serves some good fresh tapas, grilled fish and other seafood. Good paella, although it is best to come and order it in the morning. Check your bill carefully, as errors seem to have a habit of creeping in.

WHERE TO EAT IN THE SURROUNDING AREA

This restaurant is 8 kilometres (5 miles) out of town and well worth the journey. An ugly village, with an ugly beach lined with ugly buildings – Torrox is practically a German colony – it has a German delicatessen, a German hairdresser and even a string of German restaurants. It is all the more remarkable then, that this wonderful restaurant has held firm right in the centre.

✕ **El Caballo Andaluz**: avenida del Faro, Bloque 75. ☎ 53-23-35. A meal costs a good 13€ without wine. A bottle of Rioja is 15€. The air-conditioned dining room is pleasant enough, with its Andalucían furnishings and cotton tablecloths. The service is friendly and helpful and the cuisine made with remarkably fresh, high-quality ingredients – the meat is tender, the fish perfectly cooked and the desserts irresistible (including chocolate profiteroles). There is a good choice of wine, but it adds quite a bit to the final bill.

WHERE TO HAVE A DRINK

🍷 Pub Dirty Nelly (B2, **24** on the map): calle Arropiero 8. On evenings when there's a football match, a crowd gathers in the street to watch the television in the window. A lively atmosphere guaranteed from 11pm onwards.

🍷 La Viña (B2, **25** on the map): calle Almirante Ferrandiz 40. A narrow English pub with walls covered in beer mats. Noisy and lively.

WHAT TO SEE

★ **Balcón de Europa** (B3 on the map): a huge, natural semicircular terrace in the centre of the town overhanging two popular little bays. On the left is playa de Cala Onda, and on the right playa del Salón. Steps lead down to the former. The esplanade is planted with attractive shrubs and palm trees and often lined with ice-cream sellers and small stalls. It is a delightful place for an evening stroll and the amazing panoramic view is particularly spectacular at sunset. In June and July countless swifts perform exhilarating acrobatics above the water at nightfall.

★ The streets around the church, to the left as you leave the Balcón de Europa, are all pleasant places to wander. There are some nice craft-shops – nothing too tacky or touristy. Nerja was an established village before the arrival of the tourists so it has managed to retain a certain air of authenticity.

★ **La Cueva de Nerja**: the famous caves are 2 kilometres (1 mile) to the north of the town, on the Almuñecar road. ☎ 52-95-20. There are regular buses from Nerja (approximately one an hour), exact departure times are available from the tourist office. The caves are theoretically open 10am–noon and 4–6.30pm but it is best to check before you go. Admission costs around 4€ per person. Free parking. The caves were discovered by chance in 1959 by some people out looking for bats, and have turned out to be some of the most significant in Europe.

These caves and many others are believed to have been created by a tremendous shift in the earth's crust tens of millions of years ago. Then the interior was formed through the accumulation of limestone deposits in some places and water erosion in others. It is a natural sanctuary, famous for its impressive limestone formations (one stalactite is 65 metres/213 feet long) and it is thought to have been occupied by humans about 30,000 years ago. Cave paintings dating from the late Palaeolithic period are evidence that they were inhabited thousands of years ago. New excavations and explorations are continually being undertaken. The part of the caves where the paintings are located is not open to the public for conservation reasons. Go early in the morning (or very late) to avoid the crowds. The tour (which is free) leads you through enormous caves and narrow passageways, past incredible stalactites and stalagmites. The largest cave is like a cathedral. It is a shame that the most up-to-date technology has not been brought to bear on the lighting which means that the full glory of the site has not yet been revealed.

– Every year, during the second week of July, the Cueva de Nerja vibrates with a **festival of music and dance**. Classical music is the main bill of fare with performers such as Rostropovitch and Yehudi Menuhin being among those to have broken the silence of the subterranean auditorium of the caves.

★ **Beaches**: the two delightful little beaches below the Balcón de Europa – playa de Cala Onda, with its picturesque fishermen's huts built into the rock, and playa de Caletilla on the other side – quickly become packed in summer. Further over to the left is the larger playa del Salón. All the beaches are very popular and generally quite crowded. If you prefer somewhere a bit more secluded, try heading to the north of Nerja. To get to playa Alberquillas, take the Salobreña road towards Almería. Go past the campsite and the big rock on the left with its red and white antenna. On the next bend, just after a 60-kilometres-per-hour speed-limit sign, take a little track on the right that goes down towards the coast. The beach is in a bay and is popular with the residents of Nerja. There's a small *chiringuito* (refreshment stall) where you can buy bottles of water amongst other things.

A bit further on, after a green and white gateway on the side nearest the mountains, there is a little bar called Venta de Gerardo. Carry on for a few metres and then turn left towards the sea and you will find the two beaches of Cala del Pino and Cala del Cañuelo. Carry straight on (don't take the turn to the right) down to the two coves between the rocky spurs running into the sea.

SALOBREÑA 18680   DIALLING CODE: 958

A large, attractive village of cube-shaped houses, built on a promontory near the sea. The houses are not the typical Andalucían white but light blue, which gets darker when it rains. All around are vast plains with fields of sugar cane and fruit trees extending as far as the eye can see. It is a shame that concrete tower blocks are now beginning to spoil the surrounding area. The atmosphere of the village is noticeably changing. There is a long beach of black, quite coarse-grained sand that extends as far as Velilla (playa del Tesorillo). It is packed in summer but has a great atmosphere with lots of *chiringuitos* (refreshment stalls) along the beach, set in the shade of the palm trees – it's almost like being in the Caribbean.

The ancient heart of Salobreña is typical of the Muslim villages of the former kingdom of Granada. A Phoenician-Arab castle that is open to the public (in theory 10.30am–2pm and 4–7pm, 9pm in summer) stands at the top of the town. There is nothing particular to see, but it has all been nicely restored and offers a superb panorama of the plain and the sea.

USEFUL ADDRESSES

🖪 **Tourist Office**: plaza Goya. ☎ 61-03-14. A small modern building at the bottom of the village next to the bus-stop and the taxi rank. Open Monday to Friday 9.30am–1.30pm and 4.30–7pm, and Satur-day 9.30am–1.30pm. Closed on Sunday.

■ **Taxis**: plaza Goya. ☎ 61-09-26. Very useful if you arrive by bus with lots of luggage and have to climb the twisting streets to find your hotel.

🚌 **Bus station**: beside the taxis. Destinations include Almuñecar, Granada, Málaga and Almería. Several departures every day to all these places.

WHERE TO STAY

The places listed below are in the lower part of the village – the typical streets are all higher up. There is a fantastic view of the plain and the sea from the square by the church.

🛏 **Pensión San José**: calle Cristo 68. ☎ 61-03-54. A double room costs around 21€ and a double with en-suite around 30€. Very old, picturesque house with a delightful patio. High-ceiling rooms with washbasins. Good value for money. Run by a lovely family. Breakfast and evening meals are available for around 6€.

🛏 **Pensión Maria Carmen**: calle Nueva 32. ☎ 61-09-06. A double with washbasin costs around 15€ and with bathroom around 24€. Not far from calle Hortensia, in a street leading up to the castle. Run by a delightful old lady. Very pleasant, with ultra-clean bathrooms. Inexpensive and excellent value for money. Lovely views from the terrace. Try and get one of the rooms with balconies. Excellent fortifying breakfasts and evening meals are available; there are facilities for doing your washing.

🛏 **Pensión Arnedo**: calle Fabrica Nueva 21. ☎ 61-02-27. A double room with a washbasin costs around 18€. Similar to the pensión Maria Carmen in terms of facilities and service. Very clean. Well-maintained communal toilets and bathrooms. Some rooms have small balconies (with parasol, table and chairs). Good view of the sierra. Very pleasant owner. Breakfast available.

🛏 **Pensión Palomares**: calle Fábrica Nueva 44. ☎ and fax: 61-01-81. Clean rooms with shared bathrooms for around 21€. Terrace.

WHERE TO EAT

🍴 **Bar Pesetas**: at the top of the village, just below the church, before the long vaulted passage to the right of the church. Open every day. Magnificent view of the plain and Salobreña. A good place for a drink and a few tapas. Not overly expensive. There is also a restaurant.

WHAT TO SEE IN THE SURROUNDING AREA

★ **The tropical valley of Almuñecar**: 15 kilometres (10 miles) west of Salobreña, in Otivar, in the río Verde river valley, on the tourist route to Granada via Puerta del Suspiro del Moro. Lots of avocado trees, banana trees, mango trees, papayas and medlar trees grow here. The plantations stretch for hundreds of hectares on either side of the road, but none of the fruit is ripe until winter.

– The coast between Salobreña and Nerja, has suffered some of the worst excesses of property development.

LAS ALPUJARRAS DIALLING CODE: 958

It is worth taking a couple of days to explore this semi-mountainous region, about 50 kilometres (32 miles) south of Granada. The picturesque mountain landscapes are the setting for a number of delightfully unspoilt villages at 1,000–1,500 metres (3,280–4,922 feet) above sea-level. Each has its own particular attraction and there are a number of *hostales*, good places to eat and plenty of scope for outdoor activities. If you visit outside Holy Week and the period between 15 July to 15 August, you will avoid the main tourist season and the crowds.

The road that leads towards the Alpujarras from the Granada direction starts by snaking its way through an attractive area well known for its vineyards and orange groves. Little by little it starts to climb, affording some marvellous views of the countryside below. This is ideal territory for both serious walkers (a good map is essential) and people who just want to get away from the crowds on the coast. There is an association in the village of Pampaneira that specializes in walks and mountain-bike tours and another in Bubión that organizes horse-riding (*see below* 'Useful Addresses').

Hotels and *hostales* in the mountain villages are relatively few and far between. Anyone thinking of staying for more than three days, might consider renting a house or a flat (*see* Rustic Blue under 'Useful Addresses' below).

This small region also boasts its own micro-cuisine. Trevélez is famous for its wonderful, strong-flavoured ham and all the restaurants serve *alpujarreño*, a filling traditional dish consisting of ham, small, fatty sausages, fried potatoes and a fried egg. The traditional soup has much the same ingredients. Each village has its own fiesta – check dates with the tourist office – they are often very colourful.

A Brief History

After the Reconquest of Granada by the Catholic Monarchs in 1492, many Moors took refuge in these mountains to avoid having to convert to Catholicism. It was a place of asylum but also of resistance. At the height of these troubles there are thought to have been as many as 50,000 Muslims in the region, fighting to preserve their traditions and their faith. Felipe II struggled to crush the revolts in the mid-16th century and the problems were not really resolved until the start of the next century. The descendents of the people who settled here during that time have preserved a certain spirit of independence and built their villages in keeping with their Berber culture. Consequently many villages still have certain similarities to those found in Morocco – cube-shaped houses with flat roofs, built very close together and, notably, a unique system of irrigation known as *acequias*, a network of channels for gathering water from the melting snow. The course of these *acequias* makes for a nice walk.

The Spanish writer Antonio de Alarcón played a large part in bringing the Alpujarras to a wider public. Gerald Brenan, an English travel writer who wrote *South from Granada* (*see* 'Books' in the 'General Information' section) was a regular visitor to the region in the 1920s. However, it was only in the

1960s and 70s that artists, hippies and some religious communities began to discover this haven of peace and tranquillity, just one hour from the Alhambra and the Mediterranean coast.

WALKS IN THE ALPUJARRAS

There are countless walks and treks for all abilities. If you don't know the area, join an organized walking tour (*see* 'Useful Addresses') with a guide and a set route.

Most of the villages are linked by numerous paths through the countryside dating from the time of the Moors. In some places there are springs of naturally carbonated mineral water. With its sudden changes of altitude from the coast to the high mountains, the region offers huge contrasts in vegetation and climate. Walking enthusiasts might like to try the hike to the top of the Mulhacén which at 3,481 metres (11,421 feet) is the highest peak in mainland Spain.

GETTING THERE

It is quite difficult (although possible) to visit the Alpujarras by bus, as there is usually only one bus a day between Granada and the villages. Obviously, it is much easier to get there by car. If there are a number of you, it might be worth hiring a car for a couple of days in order to explore the area in more depth.

From Granada, take the N323 south towards Motril. After about 40 kilometres (25 miles), turn towards Lanjarón. This is the start of the Alpujarras.

USEFUL ADDRESSES

■ **Rustic Blue**: barrio La Ermita, 18413 Bubión. ☎ 76-33-81. Fax: 76-31-34. Email: info@rusticblue.-com. The first building on the right when you come into the village. Built with big grey stones, it is easy to spot and well signposted. Open Monday to Friday 10am–2pm and 5–8pm, and Saturday 10.30am–1.30pm. This organization rents out apartments and houses throughout the Alpujarras. All styles and prices, old or new, in villages or in the countryside. The houses and apartments are generally of a high quality. The company has an attractive brochure with pictures of the houses available for rent. Depending on size and layout, prices per week start at 210–240€ for four or five people. Make sure you get full details of the bathroom facilities and household appliances you want, as some houses may not be fully equipped. Friendly welcome from the staff who are helpful but not over insistent.

■ **Nevadensis Guías de Natural-eza**: on the village square, in Pampaneira. ☎ 76-31-27. Fax: 76-33-01. Open Sunday, Monday and Tuesday, 10am–3pm, and Wednesday to Saturday, 10am–2pm and 4–6pm. All sorts of information about the sierra. They organize guided excursions on foot, by bike or on horseback, lasting anything from one day to a week, sleeping in *refugios* (huts) in the mountains.

■ **Cabalgar-Rutas Alternativas**: 18412 Bubión. ☎ 76-31-35. Fax: (95) 876-31-36. On the way into Bubión, on the right after Rustic Blue. Rafael Belmont organizes horse-rides in the Alpujarras and the surrounding area. Routes and excursions include a trek from Bubión to the Tabernas desert, and a swim at Cabo de Gata. Nights are spent in hotels or under canvas – after a hard day's riding and a few drinks no-one has any difficulty getting to sleep. Rafael is very friendly and also leads shorter one- or two-day rides. His horses are a mixture of small Andalucían ponies and Barbaries – all good over steep and rocky terrain. Rafael's animals come from good stock although the Cabalgar stables are not that great. Excursions cost from 60€ per day (4–6 hours' ride) but rates can be negotiated depending on the number of people and the time of year. Not suitable for beginners.

LANJARÓN

This is the first village you come to on the C333, the gateway to the Alpujarras. Not particularly attractive, but it is a spa town well known for its mineral water which is served at all the restaurants. The waters here are reputed to be a good cure for rheumatism This is where the road up to the villages of the sierra starts getting seriously steep.

– **Feria del Agua y del Jamón**: on 24 June. This is the festival of water and ham when the whole village turns out to squirt each other with water, eat ham and drink wine.

PAMPANEIRA

A delightful white, hillside village, in the Poqueira gorge. Lots of coaches stop here, so try and come at a time when the streets are not too full of tourists. The reason for its popularity is evident – whitewashed houses, cobbled streets, narrow passageways, dead-ends, promontories, terraces, all serving to endow it with a picturesque charm. There is a beautiful 16th-century church in the Gothic style. Free parking (*aparcamiento público*) on the way into the village on the left.

– **Festival of the Cross**: at the beginning of May, when they burn the *quema de la zorra*, a stuffed fox, after having trailed it all round the village streets.

USEFUL ADDRESS

■ **Nevadensis Guías de Naturaleza**: on the village square ☎ 76-31-27. Fax: 76-33-01. *See above* 'Useful Addresses' in the Alpujarras.

WHERE TO STAY

There are not many hotels in the village.

♠ **Hostal Ruta del Mulhacén**: avenida Alpujarra 6, on the left-hand side of the road. ☎ 76-30-10. Fax: 76-34-46. Email: rutamul@arrakis.es. Double rooms for 36€. A small white building without any real charm, but with a good view of the valley (from certain rooms) and good general level of comfort. Very smart but quite touristy. The rooms are decorated with typical *jarrapas alpujarreñas* (Alpujarran jars). Friendly staff.

WHERE TO EAT

Head for the delightful village square where some bars have tables outside in the shade.

WHAT TO SEE

★ **Buddhist Centre O.Sel.Ling**: apartado 99, 18400 Orgiva. ☎ and fax: 34-31-34. On the Pampaneira–Orgiva road, take a right next to a small hermitage on the bend opposite the restaurant and shop called Los Sauces. Carry straight on and after the heliport, take the right fork in the road and follow the signs. The road is wonderful (lots of picnic places) and winds over some of the foothills of the Mulhacén. Open afternoons only from 1pm onwards. Note that this is a Buddhist centre, not a monastery. Don't expect to see lots of monks busy with their prayer wheels. There is simply a *stupa* and a large hut where prayers are led. O.Sel.Ling means 'pure light', and at 1,600 metres (5,250 feet) above sea-level, the setting is quite delightful. The centre was consecrated by the Dalai Lama himself.

If you are tempted to go on a retreat, the monks, who are on the whole fairly friendly, rent out small self-contained apartments on a full-board basis for around 21€ per day. You will, of course, be expected to put in some work in terms of reflection, prayer and undertake communal work.

BUBIÓN 18412

Another quite interesting village whose flat, grey roofs are covered in slate dust. Here, the architectural style of the houses is similar to those of the Atlas mountains in Morocco – cube-shaped and set very close together. Bubión is the birth-place of Osel, a child Buddhists believe is the reincarnation of a Tibetan lama. The lama Tenzin Osel Rimpoché is now in India being educated according to his birthright.

WHERE TO STAY AND EAT

☆☆ Moderate

♨ **Alojamientos Turísticos Rural los Tinaos**: calle Parras. ☎ 76-32-17. Fax: 76-31-92. From the main road that runs through the village, turn left when you get to the centre and it is 100 metres further down. A room costs around 54€ if you are only staying one night. Peace and quiet assured along with a terrace area overlooking the valley. Good facilities, although the furniture is

getting a bit old. José, the friendly owner, grants reductions for stays of more than two nights. He also rents out apartments with a kitchen, terrace and an open fire for chilly nights.

☆☆☆☆ Splash Out

♨ ✕ **Villa Turistica de Bubión**: barrio Alto. ☎ 76-31-11. Fax: 76-31-36. A small villa for two to three people costs a good 72€, 108€ for four to five people and 120€ for four to six people. A magical place renovated by the regional authorities (la Junta de Andalucía). Perched up at 1,300 metres (4,265 feet) above sea-level, this complex is almost a village in its own right. It consists of 43 traditional-style houses, all arranged over several floors and most with their own little garden. They are furnished in the local style and set out along narrow streets and around small squares. There is an excellent restaurant serving cuisine based on local produce and accompanied by a good local white wine (viña laujar). By contrast, breakfast is not particularly special. Very friendly. All the houses have their own special characteristics, so it is difficult to recommend one in particular. The only drawback tends to be the lack of lighting in the bathrooms. It must be said that standards have started to slip over the years, so the high prices are perhaps slightly out of line with reality.

✗ **Restaurante Teide**: on the main road. ☎ 76-30-37. You can eat at the bar for around 6€, slightly more in the dining-room. This is the sort of place where visitors and locals mix together happily. Outside tables are more popular with tourists than locals, who seem to prefer the bar.

CAPILEIRA 18413

Less than a kilometre above Bubión, this lovely little village is at the end of the road that crosses the Sierra Nevada. Capileira overlooks the whole valley and offers some stunning views.

There are all sorts of wonderful walks from here, with something to suit all abilities. There are easy footpaths from Trevélez to Berchules (3 hours), Berchules to Yegen (3 hours 30 minutes) and Yegen to Urgivar (5 hours). It is worth buying a 1:150,000 map of the Sierra Nevada region or going to the Nevadensis Guías de Naturaleza information centre in Pampaneira (see above 'Useful Addresses' in the Alpujarras).

WHERE TO STAY AND EAT

☒ Budget

🛏 ✗ **Mesón Poqueira**: Doctor Castilla 11. ☎ and fax: 76-30-48. On the left-hand side of the main street, behind the Tourist Office. A double room costs around 24€. Very clean rooms with en-suite bathrooms. Most of them have a view of the valley. The ones without bathrooms are slightly cheaper but much less appealing. The owner also rents out apartments further up the village by the week. There is a bar on the ground floor that does reasonably priced food.

🛏 ✗ **Hostal Paco Lopez**: carretera de la Sierra 5. ☎ 76-30-11. Double rooms with en-suite bathrooms for around 18€. Friendly owner. A reasonable place to stay, but the view is marred by another building. In compensation, the restaurant is renowned for its local specialities – jamón serrano (local ham) and platón alpujarreño (ham, sausage and eggs), among others.

FERREIROLA 18416

If your car is up to the job, get off the main road for a while and explore some of the tiny villages on the unsurfaced roads (they are too narrow for the concrete mixers). Ferreirola is one such place, with a central fountain where the local farmers stop to give their donkey a drink or gossip with the neighbours. The wash-house is worth a quick look and the remains of a mosque lend credence to the claim that this is one of the oldest villages in the Alpujarras. Before you get to Pitres, turn right down a narrow road (on the same side as the valley) and then take the first turning on the left.

WHERE TO STAY

☎ **Sierra y Mar**: ☎ 76-61-71. Fax: 85-73-67. A double room with its own little bathroom costs around 48€ in high season, with breakfast, served on the shady terrace, included. A small establishment efficiently run by a Danish woman called Inger Norgaard, and her Italian husband from Piedmont, Giuseppe Heiss. They normally run Spanish classes for Norwegians and English people, but if they have a room available in between courses, they let it out to tourists. It is generally fully booked over the summer period. Guests have use of the owners' kitchen and library. An excellent place to stay, it's in the middle of nowhere and there's not a car in sight. Inger has been to known to wheel her shopping home in a wheelbarrow!

PORTUGOS 18415

A bigger village with some fairly modern houses. Some of them are built right over the streets creating covered passageways reminiscent of the North African kasbahs. Not as characterful as other villages and not as quiet.

WHERE TO STAY AND EAT

☎ ✕ **Hostal Mirador de Portugos**: plaza Nueva 5. ☎ 76-61-76. Some rooms have a balcony with a view. As the whole place is rather lacking in character, ask for a room overlooking the valley. If there are none left, try elsewhere. There is a bar-restaurant on the ground floor and disco in the basement. Very well kept. A bit more expensive than average.

☎ ✕ **Camping El Balcón de Pitres**: a few kilometres further on, just outside the village of Pitres (18414). ☎ 76-61-11. Less than 3€ per adult, per tent and per car. Pure air and fantastic views. Hot showers. Bar-restaurant, swimming pool. Very quiet, with good facilities and the site is terraced over various levels. Plenty of shade and very windy. Lots of walks in the area. Reception is in a little wooden hut on the way in.

WHAT TO SEE

★ About 300 metres beyond Portugos on the Trevélez road, there is a small **church** on the left. At about 7.30pm on a Saturday you can hear people singing hymns. If you head down the steps opposite the church you come to **la Fuente Agria y Chorrerón** – a delightful natural spring.

BUSQUITAR

Another traditional village, where you can avoid tourist crowds. Legend has it that at the end of a tough and bloody battle between Christians and Muslims trying to win the village, the blood of the victims refused to mingle – the blood of one army ran down the valley, while the blood of the other disappeared into the hills.

TREVÉLEZ 18417

At 1,480 metres (1,483 feet) above sea-level in the Sierra Nevada, Trevélez is the highest inhabited village in Spain. It is famous throughout the region for its mountain-cured hams, but don't go looking for pig farms, this is just where they dry the hams after they have been salted.

The village consists of three *barrios* or parts – the *baja* (low), where tourists tend to congregate, the *media* (middle) and the *alta* (high), which is more typical and generally nicer. While you are there, climb to the top of the village – there is a wonderful view and very few other people around.

WHERE TO STAY AND EAT

⚓ **Camping Trevélez**: carretera Trevélez-Orgiva, at the 1-kilometre marker. ☎ 85-87-35. Email: cam-trev@teleline.es. As you come into Trevélez, it is on the left (on the same side as the mountain). The bus that goes from Granada to the Alpujarras stops right outside. A pitch costs around 3€ per person, per tent and per car. The site is 1,500 metres (4,922 feet) above sea-level, laid out over east-facing terraces, so apart from mid-summer it gets cold quickly. It has a superb view, swimming pool and free hot showers.

⚓ ✕ **Camas y Restaurante Gonzalez**: on the village square. ☎ 85-85-31. A double room with en-suite bathroom off the hallway costs around 21€. Rooms also available with a view over the valley, with or without en-suite bathrooms. No particular character or charm so only if you arrive late and can't find anywhere else. It has a pleasant little bar.

After Trevélez, the landscape becomes gentler, the valleys between the mountains are not as steep and the terrain is less rocky.

BERCHULES

Another mountain village but with a slightly less spectacular view. The cube-shaped houses are covered in slate. No accommodation worth mentioning.

CADIAR 18440

A short distance from the Alpujarras, on the A348 going down to La Rabita and the coast. Nothing special but a nice enough place to stop off.

WHERE TO STAY

☆☆ Moderate

✗ **Centro Turístico La Alquería de Morayama**: C332 (A348) Cádiar-Torvizcón. ☎ 34-32-31 or 34-33-03. Fax: 34-32-21. A double room costs around 48€ and there are apartments for between 57€ for two people and 75€ for four. This recently opened *alquería* (village farm) is a complex of various buildings comprising eight rooms and five apartments, all well-equipped with kitchen, bathroom, a small terrace and mod cons such as TV and telephone. The apartments are perhaps the more attractive option with their slate tiles and timbered roofs, beautiful mosaic floors, mottled photographs from the 1900s and interesting door handles picked up in sales at neighbouring farms. Swimming pool and restaurant. All in all, a lovely place to stay.

YEGEN 18460

A small mountain village with a wonderful view of part of the Alpujarras mountain range. At the heart of the village is a little square that pretends to emulate the Court of Lions in the Alhambra in Granada.

WHERE TO STAY AND EAT

☆ Budget

🛏 ✗ **Bar Nuovo La Fuente**: in the centre of the village. ☎ 85-10-67. A bed costs around 8€ per person, whatever the season. They also do some reasonably priced snacks. The establishment offers around ten ultra-basic rooms with a view either over the village or the surrounding countryside. A bare light-bulb hangs from the ceiling and the picture of Christ on the Cross keeps a beady eye on guests as they toss and turn on the rock-hard mattresses. Only recommended for emergencies or for anyone on a shoe-string budget. You can leave bikes in the entrance hall. Reserve in advance in high season as the rock-bottom prices make it very popular. Very friendly welcome from Maria, the owner.

☆☆ Moderate

🛏 ✗ **El Rincón de Yegen**: camino de las Eras. ☎ 85-12-70. On the way out of Yegen, coming from the Cadiar direction. Closed on Tuesday and for three weeks in June. A few rooms for 30–36€. Set menu for around 9€. Not much to look at from the outside but the friendly owners cook up a mean partridge and lentil dish. A quiet, restful place to stay.

ALMERÍA 04000   DIALLING CODE: 950

Almería is a small port with few tourists and very limited charm. It's currently undergoing a serious face-lift in order to make itself more attractive to visitors. This task has now become especially urgent as it has been chosen to host the Mediterranean Games in the year 2005. If you scratch the surface, the town does have a few streets that have a lively atmosphere on a Friday and Saturday night and an Alcazaba with fairly well-restored ramparts. The former fishermen's quarter, el Chanco, with its colourful little houses, is a nice place for a stroll if you have time on your hands. If you are not in the town just to catch the ferry to Morocco, it is worth exploring the surrounding area where there are several interesting things to see. Despite a long sea-front to the west of the town there are no decent beaches nearby.

A Brief History

The Arabs established Almería as an extension of what is now Pechina (a village some 10 kilometres/6 miles inland). Here, on the coast, they built a fortress (the Alcazaba) and enclosed the whole citadel within fortified walls and called it 'Al Mariya', the look-out tower. When the Córdoban caliphate was dismantled, Al Mariya gained independence. Its importance was such that, throughout the 11th century, it was a more prestigious town than Seville and attracted the cream of artists and intelligentsia from across Europe.

After 40 years under the wise reign of Almotacín, during which Almariya reached its zenith, his successors abandoned the town to the greed of the Almoravides. It soon became such a notorious pirates' stronghold that the powerful Catholic naval factions agreed to forget their differences and unite in trying to bring the town back to a state of law and order. In 1147, the united forces of the Spanish, Catalans, Pisans and Genoese took control, but were forced to cede it to the Almohades just 10 years later.

The Almohades then ruled for more than three centuries, though without managing to achieve the same status for the town that it had previously enjoyed. Almería dropped into a slow decline that continued until now.

Today, though, the town is renowned for its fruit growing industry and thanks to improvements in irrigation and computerized monitoring of the land, this has made Almería a focal point as the garden of Europe. However, its rate of growth has been so rapid that Almería has struggled to keep up with the demand for facilities like car-parks or to cope with the increased number of cars on the road. In line with its expansion, offices and shops now change hands for phenomenal amounts of money.

USEFUL ADDRESSES

🄱 Tourist Office (B3 on the map): parque Nicolás Salmerón, on the corner of calle Martinez Campos. ☎ 27-43-55. Fax: 27-43-60. Open all year round, Monday to Friday 9am–7pm, and Saturday and Sunday 10am–2pm.

✉ Main Post Office (B2 on the map): calle Padre Luque, on the corner of plaza Juan Casinello 1.

■ Hospital SAS-Torrecárdenas: pasaje de Torrecárdenas. ☎ 13-48-51.

■ Emergencies: ☎ 061.

🚅 RENFE station (off the map from B1): plaza de la Estación. ☎ 25-11-35. A stone's throw from the bus station. Frequent trains to Granada (ten a day), Málaga (eight), Madrid (three).

🚌 Bus station (off the map from B1): plaza de Barcelona. ☎ 21-00-29. Two minutes' walk from the station.

✈ Iberia: at the airport. ☎ 21-37-97 or 21-37-15.

■ Laundrette: rambla de Belén 52. Open 8.30am–1.30pm and 4–8.30pm.

FERRIES TO MOROCCO

The ferries from Almería only go to Melilla and Nador. Follow signs for the Puerto (the 'Ferry Melilla' placards will show you the way).

– **Tickets**: sold at the ferry terminal. Ticket offices are usually open 7am–midnight, closed for lunch 1–3pm. Small restaurant and cash machine at the terminal.

– There are two companies:

■ **Trasmediterranea** (A3, **1** on the map): ☎ 23-69-56. In summer, there are two ferries a day to Melilla (the crossing takes 7 hours), and one to Nador. In winter there is just one ferry a day to each place. Cabins sleep four people on bunks. You pay per cabin, so obviously the more of you the better. Prices start at around 40€ for a cabin without its own toilet. Bicycles carried free of charge. All credit cards are accepted. There is no student reduction.

■ **Ferri-Maroc** (A3, **2** on the map): ☎ 27-48-00. Fax: 27-63-66. In winter, there is one ferry a day to Nador. In summer, there are two on Wednesday, Thursday and Friday, and three on the other days of the week. The set-up and fare structure is much the same as for Trasmediterranea. No student reduction.

In summer you are advised to start queuing as early as possible if you want a ticket for the same day. Otherwise, you will have to stay the night in town and travel the next day. The staff of the two companies are multilingual. Don't forget your passport, of course, and your vehicle registration document. Note that you cannot take a hire car out of Spain to Morocco or any other North African country.

WHERE TO STAY

All these hotels are fairly close to one another and are located right in the centre of town. In summer, they fill up very quickly.

Campsite

🛏 **La Garrofa Camping**: 4 kilometres (3 miles) west of Almería on the coast road, in the Motril direction, 04007 Almería. ☎ 23-57-70. From the bus station in Almería (opposite the RENFE station), ask for the bus to Aguadulce. If you are travelling by car, make sure you take the coast road from Almería and not the motorway – the campsite is 4 kilometres (3 miles) out of town on the left, in a nice shady bay. It lies between a beautiful stone aqueduct and the viaduct that carries the motorway. Relatively expensive at around 3€ per person and per tent.

The campsite is right next to an attractive, clean, pebble beach. The brightly coloured flags at the entrance make it easy to spot. Small shop. The part nearest the water is poorly shaded by artificial palm trees. Clean toilet and shower blocks.

☆ Budget

🛏 **Casa La Francesa** (A2, **10** on the map): calle Narvaez 18, 04002 Almería. ☎ 23-75-54. A double room costs 27–30€ but it gets booked up fast. Small, simply furnished rooms that are surprisingly clean and quiet for this central part of town. Shower at the end of the corridor.

⌂ **Casa Universal** (B1, **11** on the map): puerta de Purchena 3, 04001 Almería. ☎ 23-55-57. Very central, on the big crossroads. Big, high-ceilinged, rather old-looking rooms for about 23€ in an old palace that is going from dilapidated to grotty rather rapidly. Beautiful central staircase. Communal bathrooms. Avoid the rooms overlooking the road as they can be noisy. The welcome is rather off-hand. Casa La Francesa would certainly be the better option.

⌂ **Albergue Juvenil**: Isla de Fuerteventura, 04007 Almería. Ciudad Jardín. ☎ 26-97-88. Fax: 27-17-44. The youth hostel is not recommended at all as it is some distance away from the centre and there is no direct bus to the town. What is more, it is slap-bang in the middle of the red light district. Only go there if you have no other option. The nearest landmark is *el campo de fútbol*.

☆☆ Moderate

⌂ **Hostal-Residencia Nixar** (B1, **12** on the map): calle Antonio Vico 24, 04003 Almería. ☎ and fax: 23-72-55. A double room with shower costs less than 36€. Well-maintained and central, only 100 metres from the puerta Purchena. Pleasant atmosphere and courteous staff. The rooms all have a shower or bath.

⌂ **Hostal Bristol** (B1, **13** on the map): plaza San Sebastián 8, 04003 Almería. ☎ 23-15-95. A double room costs around 31€. A delightful little hotel decorated with *azulejos*. The carpets look rather tired, but the rooms are clean and bright and all have en-suite bathrooms. Friendly welcome.

WHERE TO EAT AND DRINK

☆ Budget

✕ **El Super Pollo** (B1, **20** on the map): calle Antonio Vico 2. Unsurprisingly, the speciality here is spit-roasted chicken. You can buy them whole to take away for around 7€. A great idea if you are catching a ferry.

✕ **Bodega Las Botas** (B1, **21** on the map): calle Fructuoso Perez 3. A glass of wine and a tapa of cheese or ham costs around 1€. A platter costs about 6€. Friendly, efficient waitresses, good-quality food served on barrel-shaped tables,

---

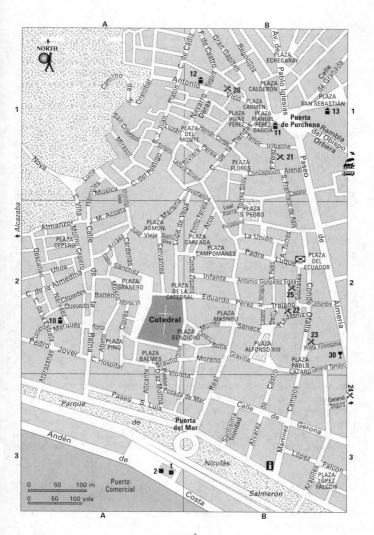

ALMERÍA

unusual red Austrian chairs and a blaring television all serve to give it a convivial atmosphere.

✗ **Cervecería La Charka** (B2, **22** on the map): calle Trajano. This *cervecería* with its rough-hewn, canopied bar is in a very narrow white street in the centre. A good meal of tapas costs less than 3€. Nothing much of interest except the plentiful beer, tasty tapas and homemade *hamburguesas*, washed down with wine.

✖ **La Bodeguilla** (B2, **23** on the map): Poeta Villaespesa 2. A meal of tapas with a small glass of wine will set you back less than 3€. Slightly more up-market that La Charka. Extensive list of tapas written in chalk on a big slate. The *patatas a lo pobre* (a kind of bubble and squeak) are particularly good. Tables and chairs in a small area outside if you want to enjoy the fresh air.

✖ **Calle Mayor** (**24**, off the map from B3): General Segura 12. Same prices as La Bodeguilla. The impressive list of tapas is displayed on the wall facing the bar. A warm atmosphere and a particularly friendly welcome from Carlos, one of the waiters. By 11pm it is packed out. Good baked potatoes with crème fraiche, *pinchos* (small portions) of salmon or cheese. A more up-market establishment, particularly popular amongst the 25–35 age group.

✖ **Taberna El Postigo** (B2, **25** on the map): on the corner of Gonzales Egea and Socrates. Closed Monday and Tuesday. A glass of wine and a tapa costs less than 2€. Traditional decor – wooden beams and shutters, hams hanging from the ceiling, paper and sawdust on the floor. Right in the heart of the old town in an area full of bars and restaurants. Good *pimientos asados* (roast peppers), grilled sausage and melted cheese. Small outdoor area.

GOING OUT

The streets of Antonio González Egea and Real in the old part of town form what everyone calls the *cuatro esquinas* (four corners). This is where all the young people meet up outside the various bars. Things don't really get going until after midnight. Teenagers prefer to hang out on the plaza de Lopez Falcón buying drinks from the various nearby bars.

♪ **Molly Malone** (B2, **30** on the map): paseo Almería 56. Open 7.30am–6am. A small beer costs less than 2€. Highly recommended even if there is nothing authentically Spanish about it. A massive, high-ceilinged room, with lots of alcoves and decoration in dark wood with gold leaf. Colourful little leaded, stained-glass windows. In short – a typical Irish bar. It stocks all sorts of whiskies, from Black Bush to Jameson, and of course it has Guinness on tap.

WHERE TO GO DANCING

♪ **Dulce Beach**: in Agua Dulce, about 10 kilometres (6 miles) from Almería in the Málaga direction. On the ground floor of the Neptuno shopping centre – its neon sign reading 'Fama Once' makes it easy to spot from a distance. Entrance costs around 6€ and a beer less than 2€. The theme is very much Bay Watch, with the waitresses in skimpy bikinis and the barmen well-toned. The decor continues the theme – fishing nets, life-belts and lots of stuff lost or forgotten by tourists on the beach. The clientele is quite wide-ranging, with locals and foreigners mingling happily. There is no particular dress code, although it is fairly trendy.

WHAT TO SEE

Not a great deal to see.

★ There are lots of refreshment stands along the boulevard near the docks, serving *limón granizado* (an iced lemon drink). If you stroll along **paseo de Almería** in the evening you can get a feel for how the Spanish used to spend their evenings before the advent of tourism.

★ **The Alcazaba** (off the map from A2): a beautiful Arab fortress overlooking the town. To get there, take calle de la Reina from the coast road, turn left into calle Almanzor and follow it to the end. Walk up the steps and slightly further on you'll find the entrance. Opening hours vary but as a general rule it is open every day 9.30am–2pm and 5.30–8pm (it closes earlier in winter). Admission is free.

There is nothing specific to see here, but this Moorish fortress still has a certain charm. The crenellated walls have been superbly restored using identical materials to the original. There are beautiful views of the town from the gardens and pathways. The picturesque ramparts run round the ochre-coloured hill. The highest points of the Alcazaba are two ancient crenellated towers. From here, you can see the strange cave-dwellings and the part of town known as El Chanco. Built into the rock, its pastel-coloured, terraced houses are reminiscent of those in North Africa. Peculiarly, there is a park with antelope. Note also the Torre de la Vela whose bell used to toll as a signal for major events and to mark the beginning and end of the working day for those working on the land.

★ **The Cathedral** (A2 on the map): in the old town. Open morning and afternoon. Access via calle Eduardo Perez. Built in Gothic and Renaissance styles on the site of a former mosque, the cathedral was fortified to protect it from pirate raids. The entrance is on the left-hand side. Beautiful choir-stalls and an unusual marble *retablo* (altarpiece) with pillars.

★ The arcades of the **plaza de la Constitución** are another nice place for a stroll.

– None of the beaches in the immediate vicinity of Almería is particularly clean or pleasant.

WHAT TO SEE IN THE SURROUNDING AREA

Film buffs may already know that many spaghetti westerns were filmed in Spain, many in this region. There are two reasons for this – the desert landscape and dried-up river beds are strangely reminiscent of the Wild West and Spanish extras cost less than American ones. Big-name producers such as Anthony Mann, Sydney Lumet, Terry Gilliam and even Steven Spielberg have used the natural scenery of the region as the backdrop for films as diverse as *The Last of the Mohicans*, *Lawrence of Arabia*, *The Adventures of Baron Münchhausen* and *Indiana Jones and the Last Crusade*.

Some location parks are still used, but most filming is now done in the *barrancos*, or ravines. The parks are all about 30 kilometres (21 miles) north of Almería on the N340. It is well signposted, just before the Murcia turn-off.

Admission fees are fairly high but it is especially worthwhile if you are taking children.

★ **Mini-Hollywood**: this is the first park you come to. ☎ 36-52-36. Entrance costs 16€ for adults and around 9€ for children. Opening hours are generally 9am–9pm in summer. Shows at noon and 5pm. Brand-new, rather artificial-looking sets.

★ **Texas-Hollywood**: 4 kilometres (2 miles) beyond Mini-Hollywood, on the left. Well signposted. ☎ 36-52-36. Same prices as above. Built over 20 years ago, the park is now completely dilapidated. All the same, the sets for Wild West towns and the Mexican village are fairly realistic. It will be of particular interest to film buffs as this is where they filmed *Once Upon a Time in the West* by Sergio Leone, *El Condor* with Lee Van Cleef (who lived in the area), *The Magnificent Seven* and some scenes for *Lawrence of Arabia*. They still make films and adverts here.

★ **Western Leone**: a third park along much the same lines as the other two but more Mexican in style. Similar attractions.

★ **The Tabernas Desert and the Sierra de Alhamilla**: This desert landscape that covers an area of land extending for 20 kilometres (13 miles) around Almería is effectively manmade. Incredible as it may seem, barely 150 years ago the Tabernas desert, the Sierra de Gador and the Sierra de Alhamilla were covered by a vast forest. In the 19th century the region's main source of income was lead mining. In order to transport the lead extracted from the mines, land was cleared and the wood used to fuel the steam engines. Since petrol has become lead free, however, the economy has suffered a rapid decline. This is now one of the most arid regions of Spain with no more than 250mm (7.5 inches) of rain per year. The desert shows no sign of retreating and temperatures regularly soar to over 40°C (well over 100°F). The 40,000 mule tracks which were gradually disappearing are now used by cross-country running fanatics or mountain bikers (there is a marked track from Pechina running towards Vietator).

To see how different things used to be, you can visit **los baños de Alhamilla** (Arabic baths) built in a crevice between two gullies – it is quite strange to see this little oasis sitting stoically on the mountainside in the middle of the desert.

WHERE TO STAY AND EAT

🛏 **Balneario de Sierra de Alhamilla**: sierra de Alhamilla, 04259 Pechina. ☎ 31-74-13. Fax: 16-02-57. There are two prices – around 63€ with a view of the Sierra and 53€ without. This spot used to be very popular with the Arabs and nowadays it still welcomes people wanting to take the waters in the heart of the Sierra. It has a wonderful patio with a double gallery of archways and a Moorish fountain burbling in the centre. Spacious rooms that are not always as up-market as they could be from the point of view of style. Ideal for a romantic break or if you want to get away from it all.

✕ **Bar Sierra**: in the centre of the village of Alhamilla. A meal costs around 6€. Go on a Sunday when it is full of Spanish families. This bar offers well-cooked delicacies such as fried calves' liver, and paella, as well as some regional specialities. Friendly waiting staff with tables outside under the shade of palm trees.

From Almería to Salobreña Along the Coast

If you don't take the route through the Alpujarras (*see above*), continue along the coast road. This area, from Almería to Motril, is the market garden of Spain and is the heart of the vegetable-growing industry. It has the greatest concentration of hothouses in the world. Indeed, the countryside round here is covered in *invernaderos* – long, blue, plastic, tunnels that protect the vegetables and speed up their growth. They are so prolific that they are even visible from the Mulhacén, and because of their colour, people often mistake them for stretches of water. These *invernaderos* are the source of the economic recovery of this area.

However, this recovery is still fairly recent – only a few decades ago this region, one of the driest in Europe, was almost uninhabited and only supported a few sheep. It was the introduction of hot-house vegetable farming that changed everything. The system involves laying down alternating layers of sand and manure to create artificial soil, covering it with plastic and irrigating it with water from the neighbouring *sierras*. Left in the baking sun, the blue hothouse tunnels produce a biannual crop of tomatoes, aubergines, peppers and asparagus, often when these crops are out of season elsewhere.

The Andalucían farmers then flood the European market with their products (a remarkable 20 per cent of green vegetables consumed in Europe come from Andalucía), contributing to the region's unprecedented increase in wealth, making it one of the richest areas in the province.

In the wake of this increased wealth, new towns are springing up while old ones develop into fine modern cities. El Ejido, some 30 kilometres (18 miles) from Almería has changed from a country village to a town with a population of over 50,000 and where banks outnumber bars. Unfortunately, it has also hit the headlines recently as a result of the racist riots that have taken place against Moroccan agricultural labourers. As the *invernaderos* require a great deal of casual labour, it attracts foreign workers who illegally make their way into the country from Morocco. This increase in racism is one of the downsides of the spectacular economic growth that the region has experienced.

This region is to agriculture what Torremolinos or Benidorm are to tourism, and it has had a similar effect on its surroundings. The 'farming' is effectively industrial agriculture. It has raised the price of land to 240,000€ per hectare, exhausted water resources and shown little regard for quality of life and the environment.

Despite all this there are a few places worth stopping off to visit. There is a beautiful beach in the village of **Castell de Ferro** (visible from the road), where fishing boats are pulled up onto the shingle beach. There is a campsite on the outskirts of the village, two kilometres (1 mile) away in the Motril direction, by a pretty little bay with very clean water.

From Salobreña as far as Málaga, the coast becomes wilder, the mountains plunge down into the sea and the road around the cliff-face offers superb views. Thankfully, this area of coastline has so far escaped the attention of the developers.

East of Almería

Much of the Spanish coastline (Costa Blanca, Costa Cálida, Costa de Almería, and so on) has been so-named by regional authorities in order to highlight the best and most attractive features of their particular area. Some of these names are quite inspired, including the Costa Tropical around Nerja where there are abundant plantations of *chirimoyas* (custard apples), and the Costa de la Luz where the land- and sea-scape is bathed in the characteristically stark but beautiful Atlantic light. Equally descriptive is the Costa Blanca or White Coast, whose name is a reference to its virgin-white sandy beaches. It lies to the east of Almería, on the perimeters of the vast plain of Valencia and starts at a rocky headland.

THE CABO DE GATA NATURE RESERVE

DIALLING CODE: 952

As a foil against the impending domination of mass tourism and the high-rise hotel, the Junta de Andalucía (the regional authorities), under pressure from ecologists designated the region of Cabo de Gata a nature reserve. It is subject to very strict restrictions on building to preserve the ecology of the area, including its beaches. The only downside to this conservation area is that its very rarity makes it extremely desirable, and this in turn makes it an expensive place to visit.

A Brief History

Little is known about the history of the Cabo de Gata reserve. It is generally agreed that gold, marble and onyx have been mined in the area since antiquity. It is likely that the name itself is a corruption of *Cabo de Agatas*, the Cape of Agate, probably named as a reference to the trade in precious stones brought through this area by the Phoenicians on their way to Tartessos (now Huelva) where they bartered them for iron. This wild, jagged coastline, where the sandy beaches are flanked by sheer cliffs, does not lend itself with ease to agriculture, nor is it an easy place for humans to settle and develop communities. The reserve is home to a succession of volcanic craters, mountains and reddish sandstone ridges that lie between outcrops of volcanic rock. Some time after the 16th century, Mexican flora became established and the terraces where they seeded produced prickly pears and cacti that in turn supported the cochineal beetles. These tiny insects were ground to produce a red dye that was very popular with the Spanish. Another feature of the landscape is the tall flowering stems of the *pitas*, the Mexican agaves whose fermented juice is the basis for *mescal*. The small, whitewashed houses of the villages, huddled around an old *noria* (water-wheel), come into view as you crest a ridge.

Until recently, almost the entire reserve belonged to the González Montoya family, who raised fighting bulls and cultivated wheat and barley with little or no concern for the world of tourism. This is particularly amazing given that the average temperature for the whole year in this area is around 20°C (around 70°F) and there are more than 3,000 hours of sun per year. All the same, the desert remained deserted and in 1987 the whole region was declared a *parque natural* (nature reserve).

The consequences of this status are far-reaching – new building is limited to existing villages and their immediate environs. Houses may not exceed two storeys and must be built in a suitable local style. There is a ban on any expansion of the fishing ports as the reserve extends to over 12,000 hectares of sea as well as 38,000 hectares of land. There are strict regulations about keeping to roads, paths and bridleways and all camping in unofficial places is forbidden (although camper vans seem to be tolerated to some degree).

This small stretch of paradise has become popular with artists and other creative people from Madrid. It has become the fashion to withdraw to Cabo de Gata to prepare for an exhibition or work on a script. The artists renovate isolated houses, secure in the knowledge that there won't be any new neighbours to bother them. It's similar to what happened in Ibiza in the 1960s, except this time everyone is safe in the knowledge that there won't be any thousand-room hotels springing up to spoil the view. As for the locals, they are split fairly evenly between those who enjoy living in such a dream location and those who would like the right to take advantage of the promise of wealth proferred by tourism.

Worth Knowing

The Cabo de Gata is separated into two very distinct parts – to the west the villages of Pujaire and San Miguel de Cabo de Gata form a fairly flat, rather unattractive area with little of interest. It is better to head for the east of the cape, to the villages of San José or Las Negras.

In August, everywhere fills up very fast and it is impossible to find anywhere to stay unless you have booked in advance. July is better but June and September are considerably cheaper and there are fewer problems finding accommodation. It is best to have a car if you want to enjoy the reserve and the beautiful, isolated beaches to the full. Hitch-hiking is next to impossible and there is only one bus route.

GETTING THERE

If you are arriving by car, the exits for Cabo de Gata are signposted from the N340, Almería–Murcia road. It is easiest to take exit 467 – if you come off on exit 471 you will find yourself on a mountain road with a succession of hair-pin bends to negotiate.

🚌 **Autocares Bernardo**: ☎ 25-04-22. There are three buses a day between Almería bus station (ticket windows Nos. 7 and 8) and San José, continuing to Isleta del Moro on Saturday and Monday.

🚌 **Autocares Becerra**: ☎ 22-13-24. There are four buses a day (two at weekends) between Almería and San Miguel de Cabo de Gata. Note that although the buses are marked 'Cabo de Gata', they only go to the west of the reserve. Do not take these buses if you want to get to San José.

USEFUL ADDRESS

■ **Centro de Interpretación de la Naturaleza** (nature studies centre): ☎ 16-04-35. On the right before the village of Ruescas if you have taken exit 467 off the road from Almería. Open 10am–3pm. Closed Monday and public holidays. Sells books and maps and provides explanatory notices in Spanish as well as lots of information, particularly about ecological matters. Temporary exhibitions by local artists.

WHERE TO STAY

■ **Camping Cabo de Gata**: carretera Cabo de Gata, Cortijo Ferron, 04150 Cabo de Gata. ☎ and fax: 16-04-43. Prices vary depending on time of year – in high season a pitch costs 12€ for a tent, two adults and a car. Student discount. This is the only campsite in the area, and it is some distance from San Miguel and Pujaire. You can see it from a distance, well-signposted on the right, just after Ruescas. There are normally spaces even in August. The drawback is obvious – it is a long way from everywhere, including the beaches and the attractive villages. All the same, it's a good place to stay while you get your bearings and look for somewhere else, or as a base to explore from, especially as it is well kept and has a swimming pool, bar and restaurant. The staff are very friendly.

To the West of Cabo de Gato

SAN MIGUEL DE CABO DE GATA

A large characterless village, known for its salt marshes and immense beach – more than 6 kilometres (4 miles) of grey, volcanic sand stretch between the village and the cape. Even in peak season, you can still escape the crowds.

SALINAS DE CABO DE GATA

On the other side of the road from the sea, between San Miguel and La Almadraba. A paradise for bird-watchers. Two easy-to-find paths lead here from the main road. Salt is still extracted from the marshes so they are covered in netting, but this does not interfere with bird-watching or photography. Look out for the white flamingos and other bird-life including avocets, ducks, and sandpipers, even in summer. In autumn and spring this is a stop-over point for numerous migratory birds. Even if you aren't much of a twitcher, you can still enjoy the wonderful landscape of grey-white salt mountains as the crystals twinkle in the sunlight. And there is a fantastic view from the lighthouse.

LA ALMADRABA DE MONTELEVA 04150

A real fishing village, with boats bobbing in the harbour and stalls where you can watch the freshly-caught fish being prepared.

■ **Hotel Las Salinas**: ☎ 37-01-03. Fax: 37-12-39. Closed in October. Double rooms with en-suite bathroom cost 90€ in high season. This hotel would be even better if it was situated somewhere else. It has been completely renovated and is spotlessly clean. There are 14 attractively decorated rooms facing the sea, a small garden-terrace and a friendly owner. Unfortunately the beach has little to recommend it, and the salt factory and main road behind it are both too close for comfort. Despite this, advance reservations are essential for July and August as it is the only decent hotel in the area.

CABO DE GATA

The road that leads to the cape and the lighthouse is narrow and breath-takingly vertiginous, offering fantastic views of the Mediterranean and the Gulf of Almería. At some points it is hewn out of the rock-face and only wide enough for one car. Do not attempt this route in a big camper van as you might scrape the overhanging rocks, wreck the suspension, or be unable to turn round. The view makes the drive worthwhile, though, especially as you can sometimes see a colony of monk seals from the *mirador* (viewpoint) near the lighthouse. Contrary to what you might be told, the small Corralete beach in the bay is not private (there are no private beaches in Spain) and the water is divine.

To the East of Cabo de Gata

POZO DE LOS FRAILES

a small village on the San José road. It is worth stopping to see the attractive, recently restored *noria* (water-wheel) and the irrigation channels that date from ancient times.

SAN JOSÉ 04118

This is the biggest village in the area and is large enough to have a pharmacy. It has undergone fairly rapid growth despite continual wrangling between the municipal authorities and people with the interests of the reserve at heart. It is true that there are too many new houses, but development remains under control and the new buildings on the sides of the hills are no more than one or two storeys high. San José is still the main base for exploring the region, especially as it offers the reserve's only youth hostel as well as its best hotel. Note that in August, all accommodation will have been booked up weeks in advance. By contrast, out of season (May, June and September) there are many rooms and apartments available and prices are lower.

USEFUL ADDRESSES

🖩 **Tourist Office**: on the central square. ☎ 61-10-55. Open 9.30am–1.30pm. Closed Tuesday and Sunday.

🖩 **Park Information Office**: calle Correos. ☎ 38-02-99. Email: grupo126@larural.es. Same opening hours as the Tourist Office. Plenty of local information and maps, particularly for walkers.

■ **Bicycle hire**: calle Carreos 14. ☎ 38-04-48. Bicycle hire costs around 12€ per bike, 21€ for two. Run by a friendly retired French

man, who will sometimes accompany his clients on cycle rides round the reserve (steep in places). He has a good knowledge of the region and can take you to places that would be inaccessible by car.
– **Alpha scuba-diving club**: on the harbour. ☎ 38-02-31.

WHERE TO STAY

⚑ **Camping Tau**: 300 metres outside the village, signposted. ☎ and fax: 38-01-66. Website: www.parquenatural.com/tau. Open from Easter to the beginning of October. Less than 4€ per person and 3–5€ for a tent, depending on size. One of the best campsites in Andalucía. Small, and ideally situated in a eucalyptus grove, family-oriented and friendly. Free hot showers. Bar (on the expensive side) and mini-market. The only downside is that the pitches are quite small.

⚑ **Albergue Juvenil de San José**: Montemar. ☎ 38-03-53. Fax: 38-02-13. Turn left when you see the sign on the way into the village. Reception is open 9–11am and 7–9pm. Beds in dormitories for around 8€ with sheets, 7€ without. Spotlessly clean, white and blue decor, with a terrace looking out towards the village, the sea and the sierra. A pleasant, quiet location. The youth hostel runs on solar electricity.

⚑ **Fonda Costa Rica**: Correos. ☎ 38-01-03. It has its own entrance from the patio, which means you don't have to walk through the bar. Central location, clean rooms with brand new pine furniture and air-conditioning at 30€ for a double room.

⚑ **Hostal San José**: Barriada San José. ☎ 38-01-16. Fax: 38-00-02. Open Easter to October. A double room with en-suite bathroom costs 90€. It has the best location in the village, facing the sea and the harbour, and is also the oldest hotel in the vicinity. Big rooms, a lovely dining room with an outside eating area, and blue and white decor that is more typical of Greece than Spain. Needless to say, prices are fairly high given the facilities but it has the sea on the doorstep and only eight rooms, which gives it a rather exclusive feel.

⚑ ✕ **Hotel Cortijo El Sotillo**: ☎ 61-11-00. Fax: 38-02-16. On the way into the village. Don't assume that its four stars put it out of your league – they are an indication of the degree of luxury, not the price. A double room costs around 84€ in high season (Easter, July, August and Christmas) and 60€ the rest of the year. In the restaurant, main dishes cost from 7€ and excellent Rioja wines 9–11€. Prices at the bar are very reasonable indeed. Brand new, very attractive and spotlessly clean. The hotel is the González Montoya family's former farm and it has been completely revamped in the style of a traditional Andalucían manor house. The buildings are low and painted white with large rooms, old furniture and *azulejos*. The main building has the reception area, dining room, lounges and bar. The rooms are beautifully decorated with private terraces, dressing-rooms and attractive bathrooms. There is a fantastic pool and great service, as you would expect for these prices.

✕ There are several restaurants along the harbour in San José. Although they aren't tourist traps they aren't particularly authentic either, but seem to be aimed at the sailors, whose yachts are moored in the harbour. Prices are reasonable – in the region of 6–12€ depending on whether you go for the set menu or à la carte.

PLAYA CALA DE HIGUERA

Follow the dirt track to the left as you come into the village of San José (signposted) and continue for 2 kilometres (1 mile) until you reach a small, quiet beach and a nice little hostel.

WHERE TO STAY AND EAT

⌂ ✕ **Refugio Mediterráneo de Gata**: Cala Higuera, 04118 San José. ☎ 52-56-25. Website: albergerar@larural.es. Prices range from 24€ for a small double room with tiny beds to more than 48€ for a functional apartment sleeping three to five people. You have to stay for a minimum of two nights. Although it is clean, a lick of paint wouldn't go amiss. Friendly staff. At the time of writing, the restaurant was closed for renovation. Highly recommended if you want to get away from it all for a few days.

PLAYA DE GENOVESES AND PLAYA DE MONSUL

Long, idyllic beaches of golden sand. Follow the signs to the right as you come into San José and continue along the attractive dirt track for 1 kilometre. After the wild-boar farm (on the right), you will see the long Genoveses beach on the right. From the tiny car-park you can get straight onto the far eastern end of the beach where there is a small eucalyptus grove. Around the trees, on the sand, there are some beach huts built of stone and woven palm leaves. Some are occupied, others vacant, or you could even build your own. The police turn a blind eye as there are no tents or caravans so it does not constitute a campsite. The second car-park, 500 metres further along, leads onto the central part of the beach. There are generally a few isolated groups of people, lots of naturists and a laidback atmosphere. If you continue slightly further still, you get to Monsul beach which is smaller and more sheltered but busier as it has the advantage of a tap which sometimes has fresh water. Although there are more people, it is hardly crowded. The footpath that leads to the other side of the cape starts from the far end of the beach (there is a gateway to stop four-wheel-drives getting through). This lovely walk takes about 1 hour. It is very easy, but make sure you take water with you in summer.

LOS ESCULLOS

A fantastic location, with a long, desolate beach overlooked by an 18th-century fort and ruined barracks that were once occupied by the Guardia Civil. The bistrot that also serves as a grocery, an open-air nightclub (but where are its clients?) and a few German hippies all contribute to the feeling that you have arrived in the back of beyond.

WHERE TO STAY

⌂ **Camping Los Escullos**: on the right before you get to the beach. ☎ and fax: 38-98-11. Reasonable prices – less than 8€ per plot for a tent or caravan and two adults in high season (July, August and Easter) and considerably less in low season (35 per cent discount for a fortnight's stay).

Reasonably priced set menus in the restaurant. A fairly recent site (built in 1994), so clean and well-kept. Friendly staff. It is medium-sized with 250 plots shaded by a system of plastic canopies. Lots of caravans are left here all year round. Big swimming pool and lots of things going on. Book at least two months in advance if you want to stay in July or August.

LA ISLETA DEL MORO

A small fishing village that has the advantage of being accessible by bus. Boats pulled up on the beach, fishing nets laid out to dry, roof terraces – a real picture-postcard spot. Signs of mass tourism are beginning to appear, but haven't yet done too much damage. There are two bars, one of which rents out rooms.

WHERE TO STAY AND EAT

🛏 ✕ **Pension-Hostal La Isleta del Moro**: next to the sea. You can't miss it as its sign can be seen from quite a distance. ☎ 38-97-13. A double room costs about 36€ (reservation necessary in July and August). A fish stew costs around 12€. The establishment itself is nothing out of the ordinary, but the setting is delightful – sit at one of the tables outside facing the sea and order a *cuajadera de pescados* (a stew of fish and shellfish) or grilled fish with a chilled bottle of white wine. Not haute cuisine, but its location is enough to make it special.

✕ **Bar La Marina**: ☎ 38-97-57. In the centre of the village. Paella costs around 6€ per person. A typical, tatty old Spanish bar-cum-grocer-cum-drinks-stall-cum-newsagents, with a gruff proprietor. Paella available if you order in advance. Tables and chairs outside. Die-hard backpackers will love it.

PLAYA DEL PEÑON BLANCO

To the north of Isleta del Moro. A large attractive sandy beach lined with camper vans from all over northern Europe. The beach is a sea of naked bodies. Naturism is not authorized but no-one seems to have objected so far.

RODALQUILAR

For a long time this village earned its livelihood from the enormous gold mine that dominates it. After it closed, the area where the workers lived was abandoned. The place now feels like a ghost town. Drive to the entrance to the mine and take a look at the enormous hoppers that the ore used to be poured from.

LAS NEGRAS

Another delightful little port that has grown considerably over the last few years. Dump your car and wander the narrow streets. Women sit mending the nets while their men folk clean the boats and dogs lie snoozing in the sun. The end of the road.

WHERE TO STAY AND EAT

⚓ ✕ **El Manteca**: at the end of the tiny promenade along the beach. ☎ 38-80-77. Antonio hires out a few apartments overlooking the port. They sleep four to six people for 601€ per fortnight in high season, 30€ per night and 150€ per week in low season; in July and August they are let for a minimum of two weeks; at other times of the year he is open to offers. To make a reservation, call Antonio at home, ☎ 38-81-20, and if he hasn't got any room, he may be able to point you in the direction of someone who has. A meal costs around 12€ and there are tables outside so you can enjoy your food in the sun. The fishermen drop off freshly-caught fish and his wife does the cooking while he indulges in a bit of banter with his guests. The menu mainly consists of fish and changes daily depending on what comes in.

AGUA AMARGA

This is the most northerly of the attractive villages within the reserve's boundaries and getting here on the tarmac road requires a major detour. The best plan is to head back towards the motorway from Las Negras and then take the track on the right when you reach the village of Fernan Perez. This is an excellent dirt track (only slightly ploughed up around the entrance to the bentonite mines, but still not too bad). When you get to the Fernan Perez windmill, the road becomes surfaced once again and swoops down to the right towards Agua Amarga. This village is painted brilliant white, with an attractive white-sand beach at the foot of a cliff. You won't be alone – there are so many Mercedes and BMWs that you wouldn't be surprised to see a showroom nearby and the boats pulled up on the sand certainly aren't used for fishing. The majority of houses are rented by the year but there is one hotel (full in August, needless to say).

WHERE TO STAY AND EAT

✕ ⚓ **Hotel-restaurant La Palmera**: ☎ 13-82-08. A double room costs 72€ and a meal in the restaurant – for example grilled angler fish – around 11€. Right next to the beach, with tables practically on the sand itself. Recently opened and spotlessly clean. There is an outside staircase decorated with *azulejos* leading up to the rooms, marble everywhere, little pink curtains and pale green bed-covers, tables with flounced covers and balconies looking out over the Mediterranean (the best view is from room No. 4). All this clearly comes at a price but the staff are very friendly and the setting superb. There's also a very good and reasonably priced fish restaurant.

MOJÁCAR 04638   DIALLING CODE: 950

A picturesque little village perched on a craggy peak 1 kilometre from the sea with wonderful views of the surrounding area. Although it has undergone a lot of recent development, it is very much in the old style – the buildings almost seem part of the rock and developers have tended to adhere to the region's traditional building techniques. It is clear evidence of the fact that even when tourism is rife, development does not have to be ugly. On the downside, the inhabitants don't seem to take particularly good care of their homes and a number of buildings have ugly brown stains marring their walls. The steep streets and dead-end alleyways all have a certain character, however. Hotels are often fully booked in summer so it may be difficult to find accommodation.

USEFUL ADDRESSES AND INFORMATION

🛈 Tourist Office: plaza Nueva, under the central square of the 'old town', in the Edificio de Servicios Multiples building. ☎ 47-51-62. Open Monday to Saturday 10am–2pm and 5–7pm. Closed on Sunday.

✉ Post Office: in the same building as the Tourist Office. In summer there is also a small office on the beach, in the parque comercial Atica. Only open 10am–noon.

▪ Banks: there are two on plaza Nueva that change currency. One has a cash machine.

▪ Police: next to the Tourist Office.
– A **shuttle bus** runs between the plaza Nueva and the beach. It leaves every hour 9.45am–9.45pm from the village, and every hour 10am–8pm from the beach.

▪ Bicycle hire: avenida del Mediterráneo 315. ☎ 47-28-23. On the beach. Hire costs less than 8€ per day and around 2€ for three days.

▪ Laundrette: to the left of the beach, opposite the Arbol supermarket. Open Monday to Saturday, 9am–5pm. Less than 1€ per kilo of laundry.

WHERE TO STAY

None of the accommodation round here is particularly cheap. If you are prepared to splash out a bit, the first two places below are right in the centre of the village on the hill. This is a delightful location and well worth paying that bit extra.

In the Village

⌂⌂ Moderate

⌂ Pensión El Torreón: calle Jazmin 4–6. ☎ and fax: 47-52-59. A double room costs 30–36€ and breakfast is less than 5€. All the locals know where it is, so if you're not sure how to find it, ask. It is a delightful little place with a well-lit hall opening onto an elegant balcony that offers an unbeatable view of the coast. The five lovely little bedrooms are decorated in pastel colours, enhanced by an attractive frieze of wild flowers. Some have a shared bathroom.

The biggest room, No. 5, has two balconies and is slightly more expensive. Cross your fingers that there will be a vacancy as this really is the best place to stay in the whole village. Reservations essential.

⌂ Hostal Casa Justa: calle Morote 5. ☎ and fax: 47-83-72. A bit more expensive than El Torreón – a good 36€ for a double. If everywhere else is full but you are determined to stay in the village, you might well find a bed here. Clean and comfortable but lacking in character.

On the Coast

All the hotels are on the coast road, but on the other side of the road from the beach. They are all characterless modern structures offering fairly pricey accommodation, extending for several kilometres on either side of the road that leads up to the village.

Campsite

⬥ **Camping El Cantal**: next to the sea – turn right onto the coast road when coming from the village, and continue for about 1 kilometre. ☎ 47-82-04. A pitch costs 3–4€ per person, per tent and per car. Well looked after and always packed. On-site supermarket. Eucalyptus trees provide a fair amount of shade but watch out for the starlings who tend to leave their calling cards all over your tent! Hot showers are extra.

☆☆ Moderate

⬥ **Hostal Bahia**: from the village, go down to the coast road and turn right. Continue for just over 1 kilometre. ☎ 47-80-10. A double costs around 27€ out of season and 33€ in season. One of the smallest and most family-oriented *hostales*. The bedrooms are simply furnished and clean. All have bathrooms but the ones opening onto the rear of the building are quieter. There are only 16 rooms which means it isn't over-run by groups. Restaurant with tables outside and a view of the beach. It is a shame that more attention hasn't been paid to the decor. Paella and sangría are the main items on the menu.

☆☆☆ Expensive

⬥ **Hotel Virgen del Mar**: from the village, go down to the coast road and turn right. Continue for around 2 kilometres (1 mile). ☎ 47-22-22. Fax: 47-22-11. Full board costs around 42€ (including parking and tax). The architecture attempts to endow it with a Moorish air but the white and blue decor and tiled walls and floors perhaps make it a tad clinical. No swimming pool. It is spotlessly clean and the beds in the bright, well-lit rooms have nicely decorated head-boards. It is popular with German groups. The breakfasts are perhaps best avoided.

WHERE TO STAY IN THE SURROUNDING AREA

☆☆ Moderate

⬥ **Cortijo El Nacimiento**: Sierra Cabrera, 04639 Turre. ☎ 52-80-90. Leave Mojácar in the Turre direction, then head for the E15. Turn left towards El Cortijo Grande and La Sierra de Cabreras, go under the high-voltage cables next to casa Williamson and casa Oxford, and you should then find yourself in a small hamlet with an avenue of eucalyptus trees and a bar by the name of Almazara. Carry straight on and you should come out at a row of small houses. Continue heading in the direction of Cabreras. You will soon see a big rock on a bend in the road – from here take the broad white track that leads down into a small valley for about 1 kilometre until you come to a dead end. The road is very steep so make sure your brakes are working! A double room with en-suite bathroom costs around 36€, breakfast included. Adolfo can also provide meals – all food is vegetarian. Dinner costs 8.5€ and reservations must be made before 4pm. This is a 150-year-old farm, huddled in a fold in the sierra, surrounded by greenery and offering a wonderful view. It has been enthusiastically restored by Adolfo and his partner. There are six double rooms decorated in a minimalist Moorish-Mediterranean style. The nicest room is the blue one, which has a mezzanine level, sponge-painted walls, a mosaic-tiled shower and small Arab-style windows filtering the rays of sun. The water is heated by solar energy and there is a swimming pool in a restored water tank, as well as a pergola and library for the use of guests. Family friendly.

WHERE TO EAT

In the Village

The village attracts more people in the evening – at lunchtime, most of the tourists stay on the beach.

✗ **El Viento del Desierto**: plaza de Abastos 4. ☎ 47-86-26. Behind the church, opposite the meat market. A meat dish costs 5–9€. The delightful Moroccan proprietor offers a choice of predominantly North African food – kebabs, grilled meat, fish soup and couscous (order in advance). Diners are soon made to feel at home.

✗ **El Antler**: calle Enmedio. Closed on Sunday. A sweet little restaurant in the street along the left-hand side of the church. Daily set menu for less than 6€ comprising main meal, soup and fruit.

On the Coast

✗ **Ristorante Piazzetta**: from the village, go down to the coast road and turn right and it is about 1.5 kilometres (1 mile) further along on the same side as the beach. ☎ 47-82-27. Prices start from around 6€. As the name suggests, this is an Italian restaurant serving good pizzas – a rarity in Spain. Prices are very reasonable and the staff attentive.

✗ **Restaurant of the hostal Bahia**: *see* 'Where to Stay'. For its paella and sangría.

THE BEACHES

There is of course the beach of Mojácar itself, which is reasonable enough if you haven't got your own transport. With a car you can get to a few others that are quieter and more isolated.

★ **Playa del Sombrerico**: as you come out of Mojácar Playa in the Sopalmo and Carboneras direction, take the road to the left in the direction of the Piruluca tower, shortly before the road heads inland. Follow the narrow dirt track along the coast, passing in front of a little yellow shack that serves as a bar. Continue along the wide, beaten-earth track, past a second look-out tower. The road comes out on Sombrerico beach. Naturists generally head for the area near the shingle over to the left.

★ **Cala de Graniletas**: in Sopalmo, take the narrow path that looks as if it leads to a vegetable garden behind the bar. The first stretch is quite hard going as the track is very rutted and full of pot-holes. You should come out on the river bed, with the bridge to your right. You are better off going by car or off-road bike than on foot as it is a fair distance. When you get to the sea, you can walk along the narrow path along the cliff to a series of quiet coves. Morning is the best time to come as the sun goes behind the tall cliffs to the west later in the day.

LEAVING MOJÁCAR

The bus stop in front of the *parque comercial* Atica, just where the road up to the village meets the coast road.

– **To Málaga**: one bus a day at noon. ☎ 22-18-88.

– **To Guadix and Granada**: two buses a day. The journey takes about 4 hours.

– **To Murcia and Madrid**: two buses a day, one in the afternoon, the other at midnight (except weekends). The journey takes 8–9 hours.

– **To Almería**: four buses a day. The journey takes approximately 1 hour 30 minutes.

La Costa Cálida and Murcia

Murcia is a curious region wedged between Valencia and Andalucía. Refreshingly untouristy, it has an allure that is very different from its more famous neighbours.

Exposed to the wind from all directions, the city of Murcia is famous for its *huerta*, a great swathe of market gardens where a large proportion of the fruit and vegetables found in supermarkets all over Europe is grown. The oft-stated view of Murcia as a place that has expanded too quickly for its own good does not hold true for the entire region and there are still some delightfully traditional spots.

Visitors eager to explore places that are off the beaten track should head for the deserted beaches of Águillas or the countryside beyond the coastal regions, where there are areas as yet undiscovered by the holidaymakers who crowd Torrevieja or San Pedro del Pinatar.

MURCIA 30000   DIALLING CODE: 968

The modern city of Murcia, capital of the autonomous community of the same name, has a mix of splendid old-style architecture, all surrounded by typical modern buildings. Its neat and tidy surface may look bland at first, but beneath this facade hide many interesting things to see and do making it is well worth spending a couple of days here.

USEFUL ADDRESSES AND INFORMATION

🛈 Tourist Office: there are several: Calle San Cristóbal (B2 on the map; open 9am–2pm and 5–7pm); calle Plano de San Francisco 8 (B3 on the map; open in summer 10am–2.30pm and 5.30–9pm) ☎ 21-98-01; and calle Maestro Alonso (B2 on the map; same opening hours)

■ Useful Addresses

- 🛈 Tourist Offices
- ✉ Post Office
- 🚂 Train station
- 🚌 Bus station

🛏 Where to Stay

- 10 Hostal El Perro Azul
- 11 Pensión Murcia
- 12 Hotel La Huertanica

✕ Where to Eat

- 20 Tasca Garrampon
- 21 Tasca El Palomo
- 23 Los Ventanales
- 24 La Tapa
- 25 El Señorio de Jomelsu
- 26 El Mesón del Corral de José Luis

✕ Where to Have Breakfast

- 27 Drexco Café
- 28 El Arco

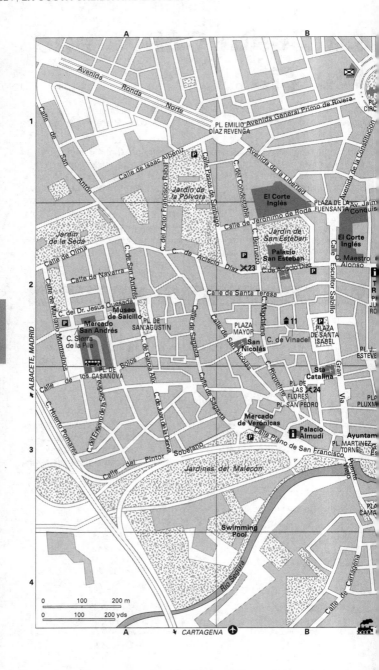

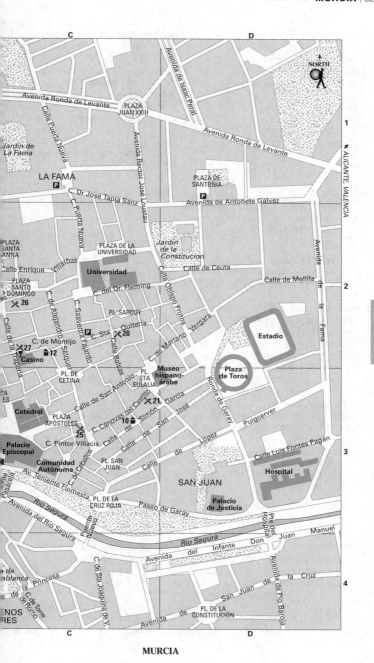

MURCIA

☎ 22-06-59. The staff in all the offices are very efficient and friendly.
✉ **Post Office** (B1 on the map): plaza Circular 8. ☎ 24-12-43.
🚂 **RENFE Train Station** (off the map from B4): Barrionuevo 4. ☎ 25-21-54. Bus No. 9 is the most direct route to the town centre, but you have to change at plaza de Camachos for buses 1-AB, 1-C and 1-DE or your best option, the No. 5.

🚌 **Bus Station** (A2 on the map): Sierra de la Pila 1. ☎ 29-22-11 or 29-22-90. Plaza San Agustín, from where many of the buses go, is a few streets away from the bus station.
➊ **San Javier Airport** (off the map from A4): ☎ 17-20-00.
– To get around Murcia on the LAT buses you can buy a *Bonobus* (a strip of 10 tickets costing around 9€), available from the bus terminal or ticket kiosks.

WHERE TO STAY

Unfortunately, there is no youth hostel in Murcia.

☆ Budget

🏨 **Hostal El Perro Azul** (C3, **10** on the map): calle Simón García 19; on the corner of Mariano Padilla, 30003 Murcia. ☎ 91-13-84. This *hostal* gives the impression of having been knocked together in a hurry, but it is well-located on the edge of the part of town with all the bars. A double room or small apartment with a kitchenette costs 24–42€. The staff are open and friendly, and you can come and go as you please.
🏨 **Pensión Murcia** (B2, **11** on the map): calle Vinadel 6. Edificio Monte Ulía, 30004 Murcia. ☎ 21-99-63 or 90-54-47. Opposite the Inem (Spanish employment) offices. A double room with shared bathroom costs 30€. Not exactly the kind of

place you would want to lounge around in bed all day. The prices charged are still quite high even allowing for the pleasantly decorated rooms and the comfortable beds. Good for one night only.

☆☆☆☆ Splash Out

🏨 **Hotel La Huertanica** (C2, **12** on the map): calle Infantes 3–5, 30001 Murcia. ☎ 21-76-68 or 21-76-69. Fax: 21-25-04. This centrally located hotel is in a quiet street on the corner of Calle de Montijo. A double room costs about 48€, not including breakfast. Pleasant decor in brick and mahogany with subdued lighting provided by small blue lamps. The staff are very friendly. Private car-park.

WHERE TO EAT

☆ Budget

There is nothing particularly novel about Murcian cuisine, the tapas here are much the same as in the rest of Spain. There is a tendency to use a lot of *habas* (white beans) in their cooking, removing the husk and serving with a chunk of dried *bonito* or maybe a sliver of *morcilla* (black pudding). Very tasty indeed with a swig of draught vermouth.

✕ **Tasca Garrampon** (C2, **20** on the map): on the corner of calle de Santa Quiteria and calle de Mese-

gueres. Closed 4–8pm and Sunday lunchtime. A selection of tapas costs about 3€ and the *chorizo* melts in the mouth. This is a popular little place that soon gets packed.

✕ **Tasca El Palomo** (C3, **21** on the map): calle Cánovas del Castillo, 28. Open evenings only. A selection of tapas and a drink cost about 3€. Rather plain decor with paper tablecloths and the air of a roadside café. However, it offers a huge selection of tapas and has not yet been taken over by tourists.

✕ **Los Ventanales** (B2, **23** on the map): on the corner of calle Arcisclo Díaz and calle García Martínez. This classic place is a bit more upmarket than the previous bars. A meal costs about 6€. Los Ventanales has revisited traditional decor and cuisine and done it very well. The mashed potatoes and *patatas a lo pobre* (a kind of bubble and squeak) are excellent, as are the various other potato-based dishes, all served with Iberian ham and *patas negras* ('black legs', in reference to the colour of the pigs from which they traditionally come). They serve either a very nice Rioja or a local wine by the glass. A good place to come just for a drink or for a meal with friends.

✕ **La Tapa** (B3, **24** on the map): plaza de las Flores 13. ☎ 21-13-17.

A quick snack at the *barra* will set you back about 6€. Open daily until 2am. It is packed at Sunday lunchtime both inside and out. Expect to wait at least 30 minutes to get served. Litter covers the floor and the locals laugh heartily and converse at the tops of their voices in a wonderfully characteristic Spanish way.

☆☆ Moderate

✕ **El Señorio de Jomelsu** (C3, **25** on the map): Isidoro de la Cierva. ☎ 21-21-33. Open 11am–4pm and from 7pm until the last customer leaves. A meal costs 9–12€. Chorizo (spicy sausage), *jamón serrano* (fine slices of cured ham), *jabugo* ham and good wine (Jumilla del Duero, Rioja, Navarra) are all reasonably priced.

✕ **El Mesón del Corral de José Luis** (C2, **26** on the map): plaza Santo Domingo 23-24. ☎ 21-45-97. A stone's throw from the Argentaria building (which you can't miss). A lot of Murcia's local dignitaries meet up here. It probably won't be within everyone's means, but it is not prohibitively expensive either. Good selection of wines, served at just the right temperature.

WHERE TO HAVE BREAKFAST

Nowhere particularly worth recommending but a couple of pleasant cafés where you can browse through the daily papers:

▮ ✕ **Drexco Café** (C2, **27** on the map): calle de la Traperia 26. ☎ 21-95-95. They serve seven different types of coffee in this warmly decorated bar with its pink marble counter and expensive wooden tables and chairs. Quite upmarket but affordable if you sit at the bar.

✕ **El Arco** (C2, **28** on the map): calle del Arco de Santo Domingo. ☎ 21-97-67. Next door to Teatro Romea. Good coffee, abstract art on the walls and more tables on the mezzanine level.

MURCIA

WHAT TO SEE AND DO

★ **El Casino** (C2 on the map): calle de la Traperia 22. ☎ 21-53-99. This is a wonderful building with a luxurious interior and is a good example of Islamic-style decor. A stairway on the left leads up to a small room where there are various art exhibitions, some better than others. Note that this is a private building and you will have to ask permission to go in and look round.

★ **La Catedral** (C3 on the map): plaza Hernández Amores 2. ☎ 21-63-44. Open daily 10am–1pm and 5–8pm. The baroque facade is rather impressive. Even if you are not a big fan of religious architecture, the interior of the cathedral is worth a visit. On one side of the aisle there is the Vélez chapel, commissioned by Don Juan Chacón, major-domo of Isabel Queen of Castilla, and Lord of Cartagena. It is built in a beautiful Gothic style and dates from the second half of the 15th century. Also worth seeing are the carved pews and the beautiful altar. There is a great view of the city from the tower.

★ **El Tetablo Mayor de Santa Ana** (C2 on the map): in the church of the Convent of Santa Ana on plaza Santa Ana. ☎ 23-92-37. In the usual style, the *retablo* (altarpiece) is groaning under the weight of its gold ornamentation – probably originating from the New World.

★ **El Monasterio de Santa Clara de la Real** (B2 on the map): Santa Clara de la Real, via Alfonso X, El Sabio 1. ☎ 23-35-19. The monastery is often referred to as 'Las Claras' after the nuns who live here. The monastery was built in medieval times on the ruins of Alcázar Seguir, a 13th-century Moorish palace. There is also an 18th-century baroque church and Gothic-Mudéjar cloisters that are also worth visiting.

★ **Centro Cultural Las Claras** (B2 on the map): ☎ 23-46-47. Open Monday to Saturday 10am–1pm and 4–9pm, and Sunday 10am–1pm. Free admission. These beautiful galleries are next to the monastery of the same name. A few stones remain from the original Roman and medieval walls. They regularly hold exhibitions here, which are usually of a high standard.

★ **Museo de Salcillo** (A2 on the map): plaza San Agustín 3. ☎ 29-18-93. Open Tuesday to Saturday 9.30am–1pm and 4–7pm, and Sunday and public holidays 11am–7pm. Admission costs 3€. A bit of a con because Salzillo's sculptures are displayed in the Church of Jesus, so you are effectively paying to enter the church. The style of the exhibition is slightly pretentious, with a glut of trompe-l'oeil paintings and huge quantities of marble. Each chapel contains a statue by the master sculptor. A fine *Last Supper*, with the Apostles sitting face to face. Another work depicts a long-haired Christ – this is one of the figures carried round the streets during the Holy Week processions. The statues of religious figures are extremely lifelike.

★ **El Palacio Episcopal** (the Archbishop's palace: C3 on the map): plaza Cardenal Belluga 1. ☎ 21-42-04.

★ **The University** (C2 on the map) with its sugar-pink facade.

– The **markets** are worth investigating if you have time on your hands. The one in calle Verónicas (B3 on the map) is more spacious and better stocked than the San Andrés market (A2 on the map). The fruit and veg stalls are on the first floor, and meat and fish on the ground floor.

– There is a path along the banks of the río Segura which makes for a pleasant stroll; for the less energetic the **Botanical Gardens** are a good place for a siesta. If you are passing, take a look at the bridge at Malecón, it has a resin and reinforced concrete structure that curves over the river. A steel pole attached to thick cables acts as a counterbalance.

WHAT TO DO

– **Climbing**: Murcia is popular with rock climbers, and there are numerous places to practise the sport. They cater for all levels of experience. To find out the best places to climb, call El Refugio, Salitre 14 ☎ 22-08-48; or Bazar La Tierra, in Alcantarilla ☎ 80-04-63. For further information you can contact the Federación de Montañismo de la Región de Murcia, Francisco Martinez Garcia 4, 30003 Murcia. ☎ 34-02-70.

WHAT TO SEE IN THE SURROUNDING AREA

To the South of Murcia

★ At the weekend many Murcianos head for the wooded foothills of the Sierra de los Villares to get some fresh air. One place that is worth visiting is the **Iglesia de la Fuentesanta.** Open 9am–1pm and occasionally in the evening. To get there take the 301 in the Cartagena direction, leave the motorway at El Palmar (but don't go into the town itself) and follow the signs to the church. Some 14 kilometres (9 miles) from the centre of Murcia, a small road starts its winding journey from the village of La Alberca. Shaded by eucalyptus trees it picks its way through a maze of blocks of stone covered with dust from the red-brick soil. This spot is popular with courting couples and picnicking families (there are several picnic areas on the hillside with play areas for children). The road leads to the Benedictine Sanctuary of **Fuentesanta** – definitely worth a visit if only for its magnificent *retablo* (altarpiece), which is highly ornamented and dripping with gold leaf.

A tip for mountain bikers and other walkers – don't bother following the road there and back as it is all boring tarmac with a constant stream of passing cars. Instead, go along as far as the **Casa Forestal el Sequen** (nature centre) and past the former youth hostel. If the car-park is open leave your car here and start cycling. If the car-park is closed, carry on along the road until you get to the radio masts. From the top there is a view of the marvellous but unexpected lunar landscape that is Murcia – eroded rocks stand against the sky-line in silhouette, bare peaks rise up and steep ridges drop into deep valleys. In Spain this landscape is only matched by la ruta de Valdemossa (in the Balearics) and the Cabo de Gata (in the area surrounding Mojácar). If you want to avoid the worst heat of the day and other visitors, it is best to come after 3.30pm or very early in the morning. Note that there is nowhere to fill your water flasks, so bring plenty with you. All the roads in the area are accessible by car and are very well surfaced. If the Casa Forestal is open don't hesitate to ask for a map as it is easy to get lost here. Climbers might also be able to get information on organized climbing trips if there is someone around who knows about it.

To the North of Murcia

★ **Los Baños de Archena**: on the way into Archena, take a right turn after the bridge. You can also reach the Baños by bus (seven a day from Murcia during the week, four on Saturday and one on Sunday). Open Monday to Friday, 10am–10pm (24 hours in summer). Admission costs 6€ before 6pm and 4€ after. This small oasis set amid palms and lemon trees has springs where the water temperature reaches 52°C (126°F). The spa buildings are not particularly special, but a quick dip in the waters can be very refreshing.

FIESTAS

– Each year 3 million people come to Murcia for the **Fiesta de la Primavera** (Spring Festival) also known as the **Entierro de la Sardina** (the Burial of the Sardine). It is held the weekend following Easter Monday. More than 80 groups (known as *sardineros*) take part from places as far afield as Barcelona, Cartagena and even Brazil. The huge variety of musical parades is followed by firework displays.

The *tunas* (traditional groups of musicians, generally students) play outside the bars long into the night and tables are set up outside especially for the occasion.

LEAVING MURCIA

By Bus

The **Graells** bus company links Murcia to nearby towns. The ticket office is open 9.30am–2pm and 4.30–9pm, outside these hours you can buy your ticket directly from the driver.

– **To Granada and Córdoba**: regular services run 8.30am–10pm.

– **To Seville**: three buses a day leave at 11.30am, 4pm and 10pm. The 11.30am service continues to Cádiz.

– **To Cartagena**: three buses a day. A single ticket costs about 3€.

VILLAGES OF THE SIERRAS   DIALLING CODE: 968

To the west of Murcia a few roads wind their way through the low hills of the sierras that look like a series of upturned dinner plates (Sierra de Espuña, Sierra de Ponce or Cambrón, Sierra de Lavía, Sierra de Ceperos, Sierra de Quipar, among others). The lack of vegetation and the relentless sun make it a fairly inhospitable area on the whole.

LOS BAÑOS DE MULA

The whole village is built around these baths, alongside a major road. Admission is a bit expensive at 6€ per person.

WHERE TO EAT

✗ **Venta Magdalena**: carretera de Caravaca, at the 17-kilometre marker. ☎ 66-05-68. A meal costs about 9€. Normally, you probably wouldn't look twice at this place, which has the appearance of a roadside café. However, according to the Murcianos, this is where you can find some of the best rice dishes in the whole region. This is country cooking at its best, rich in flavour and served in generous portions, and set amid the noisy hubbub of the regulars. Try the hare and rice, wickedly spiced with an unforgettable *pimiento morrón* (sweet pepper). Advance reservations recommended.

CARAVACA DE LA CRUZ

As the name suggests ('*de la cruz*' means 'of the cross'), this is a place with a significant religious history. In 1232, the bishop of the region, Chirinos, proclaimed that he had seen the Holy Cross (or more precisely, the Lignum Crucis, which is a cross made from the actual wood of the cross on which Christ died). Since this time, the help of the Cross has been invoked for a wide range of causes. In the days of the Reconquest it was used as the symbol in the fight against the Moors; and then became the emblem of people giving medical aid. In 1588 a procession was held under the banner of the Cross to send positive vibes to the Invincible Armada and in 1677 the town of Murcia called upon the miraculous Cross to protect them against an epidemic of the plague.

WHERE TO STAY AND EAT

Casa Rural

🛏 ✗ **El Molino del Río**: Camino Viejo de Archivel, 30400 Caravaca de la Cruz. ☎ (606) 30-14-09. ☎ and fax: 43-33-81 Website: www.molinodelrio.-com. About 11 kilometres (7 miles) from Caravaca de la Cruz, on the road to Granada. A small 16th-century windmill tucked away in the hollow of a sandy *barranco* (dry river bed). Double rooms with a bathroom cost 45–64€, and an apartment sleeping four with a kitchen costs about 83€ including tax. The rooms are lovely – exposed wooden beams and simple furnishings, yet very cosy, a feeling enhanced by the soft duvets. The welcoming dining area is ideal for lingering over dinner and a few drinks. The set menu ranges from 15€ to 30€. Swimming pool and barbecue. The friendly owner, Carmen, is always keen to make her guests feel as welcome as possible. Highly recommended.

WHAT TO SEE

★ The Cross is kept in the large **Sanctuary**, a church made from pink and grey marble. Open 8am–2pm and 4–7pm. A magnificent baroque-style, marble gateway, likewise pink and grey in colour, marks the entrance to the church. To the left of the gateway is a secular building, which was used as a safe haven during the War of Succession (1700–13) and again in the War of Independence against the French in 1812. The interior of the sanctuary has been meticulously maintained. The altar suggests Orthodox influences and is framed by two lamp-carrying cherubs. There is a small museum in the cloisters.

★ After visiting the sanctuary take a look at the unusual red and white facade of the **plaza de toros** (bullring) built in 1926. Striking in its neo-Mudéjar style, the facade gives the impression of having been washed with bull's blood. It was constructed on the site of a Franciscan monastery but abandoned by the monks around the middle of 19th century.

★ The **Iglesia del Salvador** in the centre of town, and notable for the profusion of religious trinkets on sale, is also worth a visit. This church was built in the second half of the 16th century on the site of a former hospital of the Knights Templar and is almost as interesting as the Sanctuary itself. Part of the bishopric and seat of the Order of Santiago, it was never actually completed. The *retablo* (altarpiece), which is covered in gold-leaf, is some 8 metres (26 feet) tall. The church has no transept and is only supported by four thick Ionic columns on which the fluting only starts half way up. There are seven small chapels, some in a better state of repair than others. Mass is held at 7am and noon on Sunday and at 8pm during the week.

★ Another building worth seeing is the **ayuntamiento** (town hall), which is built in the form of a beautiful archway.

MORATALLA

Another small village clinging to a rocky outcrop, crowned by a medieval castle.

WHERE TO STAY

Casas Rurales

🛏 **El Molino de Benízar**: 02438 Benízar. ☎ 73-60-06. About 20 kilometres (13 miles) from Moratalla, along a quiet road that snakes over a dry, broom- and rock-covered landscape, interspersed here and there by olive trees and grazing sheep. El Molino is well signposted from Socovos. This small windmill has been lovingly restored. It is perched on rocky ground in the shadow of an enormous boulder and a small stream flows past it. It is an ideal place for nature lovers and travellers in search of a bit of peace and quiet. Ask for directions when you make your reservation. A double room with a view costs 33€, and a standard double room 30€,

while an apartment costs 210€ per week in high season.

🛏 **El Cortijo Rojas**: ☎ 16-50-16 or 70-82-89. About 4 kilometres (2 miles) from Moratalla. To get there, leave Moratalla on the Calasparra and Elche de la Sierra road. Take a left turn as you come out of the village, then turn right along a narrow road across agricultural land and through a ford in a *barranco* (dried-up river bed). Then follow the signposts. This large property with its ochre facade backs onto a farm and is set around a central patio. There are several *viviendas* (apartments) with lounge and TV, brand new bathroom, fitted kitchen and shared use of the communal areas (barbecue, terrace and so on). Each apartment has direct access to the communal areas. An apartment for four people costs 78€ per day, 158€ for a weekend, and 379€ for a week, including tax. Slightly on the expensive side.

There is a swimming pool, tennis court and above all splendid silence – only disturbed after nightfall by the noise of the crickets.

CARTAGENA 30200   DIALLING CODE: 968

Sprawled along the coastline of the Mar Menor, there is a certain lack of refinement to this Spanish Carthage. Like its famous namesake, which mocked the power of the Roman Empire, the town has a seafaring history. Numerous ships from the Spanish navy lie at anchor in the harbour. Even if it were to receive a lick of paint, have its Punic city walls unearthed and the ancient amphitheatre reopened it would still seem a strange old place. This is a city of many faces – a sea port where the produce of the Murcian *huerta* (market gardens) is exported, the second town of the autonomous community of Murcia, an industrial town, a university and a garrison town. Its population is a mixture of sailors, seasonal labourers, well-intentioned dignitaries and students. Cartagena is a difficult place to fall in love with, but its multi-faceted personality is one that can be fascinating to explore.

USEFUL ADDRESS

🛈 Tourist Office: opposite the exit to the bus station. From the RENFE train station go up the leafy avenue immediately in front of the exit, the office is on the other side of the first roundabout. Open Monday to Friday 10am–1.30pm and 2–7pm, and Saturday morning.

WHERE TO STAY

☆ Budget

⌂ Pensión-Hospedaje Oriente: calle Jara 27, 30201 Cartagena. ☎ 50-24-69. A three-storey *pensión* immediately opposite the Citibank building. Decent rooms for 21€. The rooms are small with washbasins and shared bathrooms and all have been rejuvenated with a lick of mauve paint. A friendly welcome from Luis, the kind old gentleman who runs the place.

WHERE TO EAT

☆☆ Moderate

✗ La Tartana: calle Mayor 5. Immediately opposite McDonald's. A good selection of tapas costs about 6€. Popular with families, work parties and groups of friends. Note that prices are higher if you sit at a table rather than at the bar.

✗ Asadorio Cartagena: on the corner of paseo Alfonso XIII and calle Juan de la Cosa. Opposite the university. This kind of bar is the embodiment of traditional Spain. Strings of garlic and peppers hang above the bar; and customers eat *caldos* (thick broth), *pimientos de piquillos* (small, preserved peppers) and other tapas from huge terracotta bowls. A snack costs about 6€. Definitely worth a visit.

WHERE TO EAT IN THE SURROUNDING AREA

✗ **Restaurante El Mosqui**: carretera del Faro, 30370 Cabo de Palos. ☎ 56-45-63. Book in advance for the weekend. Easy to spot as it is shaped like a boat. The lunchtime set menu costs 8€, allow for around twice this if you go à la carte. The main attraction of this odd little restaurant is its *caldero* (stew), traditionally a dish that local fisherman used to cook over coal fires directly on the beach. To make a good *caldero* you need rice from Calasparra, 'rock' fish, grey mullet and a generous sprinkling of paprika. This is how it is made at El Mosqui. There is also a good selection of fish from the teeming waters of the nearby Mar Menor, which are often cooked in a salt crust.

WHERE TO HAVE A DRINK

♟ **La Uva de Jumilla**: calle de Jara. Small wine bar, as indicated by the name (*uva* means grape). The old men of the neighbourhood come here for their 10am intake of *manzanilla* (sherry). You can buy a selection of *montaditos* (open sandwiches) to take away.

♟ **Pub Trastera**: plaza del Rey. Near the military arsenal and on one of the quietest plazas in the whole town. The bar seems to go on for ever, which is probably why it is the most popular place in town to come for a drink. Very dim lighting.

– When all the bars in the city centre close everyone migrates to calle Principe de Asturias and calle Pintor Ballaca.

WHAT TO SEE

★ **Iglesia Santa María de Gracia**: on the corner of calle del Aire and calle San Miguel. Built in the 18th century, and renovated in the 19th and 20th there would be little of interest here but for the richly decorated chapels at the side. The chapel at the end of the church on the left-hand side is dedicated to Bernadette Soubirous – an 18th-century French visionary.

★ **Iglesia Santo Domingo**: calle Mayor. This is a strange church without a proper altar. The bizarre alternative is several planks of wood draped with the Spanish flag. The size of the church is rather daunting and it has a distinct lack of elegance. One redeeming feature is the small baroque chapel of Marraja, which has been beautifully restored and houses a number of religious paintings and an abundance of gold.

★ **El Palacio consistorial** (town hall): at the beginning of the main street. A beautiful modernist building with a watchtower that looks authoritatively out to sea. Despite its grey marble the Soviet-style gallery accentuates its ponderous character giving it a certain sophistication. As you walk round the building, note how each side of the exterior is different.

★ There are a number of modernist-style houses, in particular **Casa Llagostera** (opposite Iglesia Santo Domingo), **Casa Clares** (on the corner of calle del Aire and calle Cuatro Santos), with elegant bow-windows, cornices and other architectural embellishments.

★ **Roman Amphitheatre**: built in 100 BC, but only discovered in 1987. An army of archaeologists is still trying to uncover its terraces. They have already come across a house built in the main arena. Walk round the amphitheatre as there is a lovely view of the bay and the red tiles of Iglesia Santa María la Vieja (known as 'La Catedral') from the top.

WHERE TO SWIM

Steer clear of the area around Mar Menor, where there is a proliferation of building sites. The most deserted beaches are in the Aguilas region.

LEAVING CARTAGENA

By Bus

– **To Seville**: three buses a day with the Alsina Graells bus company. Single fare costs about 33€.

– **To Málaga**: one bus a day in the afternoon. Single fare costs about 29€.

ELCHE 03200   DIALLING CODE: 965

This is rather an ordinary town with one main attraction – the palm forest, which is one of the most beautiful in Europe, perhaps even the world. The Carthaginians planted the palm trees, but it was the Moors and their inventive irrigation methods who really cultivated them. It is a shame that the palm grove isn't better looked after, but this could change as UNESCO has afforded it 'world heritage' status.

Elche supplies churches all over Spain with palm leaves for Palm Sunday processions and decorations, and is nicknamed the 'Spanish Jerusalem'.

USEFUL ADDRESSES

🛈 **Tourist Information Office** (A1 on the map): plaza del Parque. ☎ 45-38-31. Fax: 45-78-94 Email: touristinfo.elx@turisme.m400.gva.es
✉ **Post Office** (A2 on the map): Camilo Flammarion. Closed on Saturday morning.
🚂 **RENFE Train Station** (A-B1, on the map): avenida de la Libertad, Elx-Parc. ☎ 45-62-54.

🚌 **Bus Station** (B1 on the map): avenida de la Libertad. ☎ 42-42-42.
■ **Policía Municipal** (**1**, off the map from B1): antigua fabrica de Messalina, carretera de Alicante (Altabix). ☎ 45-25-00. Bear in mind a policy of zero tolerance exists for illegally parked vehicles.

WHERE TO STAY

☆☆ Moderate

🛏 **Pensión Faro** (**11**, off the map from A1): cami dels Magros 24, 03206 Elche. ☎ 46-62-63 or 60-

85-88. A double room without breakfast costs 22€. This small *pensión* has only a few rooms, all recently redecorated in pine. The

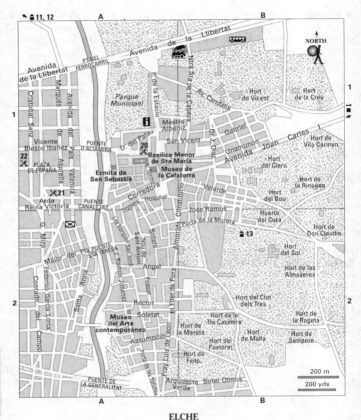

ELCHE

| **■ Useful Addresses** | **12** Hostal la Callosina |
| | **13** Hotel Huerto del Cura |

❶ Tourist Office
✉ Post Office
🚆 RENFE Train station
🚌 Bus station
1 Policía Municipal

✕ Where to Eat

🛏 Where to Stay

20 El Arlequin de Elche
21 Mesón el Tozal
22 Mesón el Granaino

11 Pensión Faro

beds are comfortable and there are shared bathrooms. Friendly welcome. Recommended.

🛏 Hostal la Callosina (**12**, off the map from A1): calle Mario Pastor Sempere 15, 03206 Elche. ☎ 46-

00-76. A double room costs about 22€. This *hostal* above a small bar is clean and unassuming. Pensión Faro is probably the better option, though.

☆☆☆☆ Splash Out

🛏 **Hotel Huerto del Cura** (B2, **13** on the map): porta de la Morera 14, 03203 Elche. ☎ 45-80-40. Fax: 42-19-10. Website: www.huertodel cura.com. A double room costs 109€ during the week and only 72€

at weekends – a real bargain. This is a wonderful four-star hotel, with chalets set in a palm grove immediately opposite the famous *huerto del Cura* (priest's garden). The buildings as a whole are starting to look a bit dated and the fittings ever so slightly worn. The grounds are expertly tended by an army of gardeners. The staff are very professional and the buffet breakfast is enormous. Tennis courts, restaurant, bar and a fantastic swimming pool.

WHERE TO EAT

☆☆ Moderate

✖ **El Arlequin de Elche** (A1, **20** on the map): plaza Congreso Eucaristico 17. ☎ 42-01-60. A meal costs about 12€. Despite being a bit of a dive with its roughcast walls and minute bar, this place is particularly popular among the older locals who come here to go over times gone by. You can enjoy big helpings of *arroz con costra*, Elche's traditional dish, a type of paella with an omelette topping, served with a dollop of tasty garlic mayonnaise. Highly recommended and you can even get paella to take away.

✖ **Mesón el Tozal** (A1, **21** on the map): carrer dels Arbres 22. Go up avenida Reina Victoria, north of the Nou bridge, and then take the third turning on the left. Open from 2pm. A dish costs 6–9€. The food is well

presented and appetizing, and the wine good quality and reasonably priced.

☆☆☆☆ Splash Out

✖ **Mesón el Granaino** (A1, **22** on the map): José María Buck 40. ☎ (966) 66-40-80. Closed on Sunday and the last fortnight in August. This dependable restaurant has been going strong since 1964 and has the traditional decor of *azulejos*, bricks and dark wood. The cuisine is inventive and made with fresh ingredients (the cod soup and fig ice-cream are particularly recommended) and there is an extremely good selection of tapas. An à la carte meal costs 24€, but a meal of tapas at the bar will work out much more cheaply.

WHAT TO SEE

★ **El Huerto del Cura** (The Priest's Garden; B2 on the map): open 9am–7pm (8pm in summer). Not to be confused with the hotel Huerto del Cura, whose grounds are not open to non-residents. Admission costs about 2. This botanical garden set in the heart of the palm grove contains cacti, bougainvillæa, orange and lemon trees and multibranched palm trees including the Imperial Palm, which is 150 years old. It is the only one of its kind in the world – its branches come out not at the foot of the tree, as is usually the case, but about 2 metres (6 feet) above the ground, giving it the curious look of an eight-branch candelabra. It weighs at least 10 tonnes and has to be supported by a metal frame. There is a statue of the famous Dama de Elche at the entrance, which is a copy of a mysterious Phoenician-style sculpture of a priestess or Iberian princess. The original is almost 2,500 years old and was discovered in the 19th century at the archaeological site of Alcudia, on the outskirts of the town. It is now on display at the Museo Nacional de Arqueología in Madrid. A bit further along you come to a bust of Jaime I Aragón, which looks as if it has come straight out of an Asterix cartoon. The park is certainly well maintained, but a visit is perhaps not worth the admission fee charged and el parque municipal is just as nice.

Opposite the *huerto* there is a stall selling fantastic dates. One of their specialities is *pastel de higos* (fig cake) made entirely of dried figs and almonds – not recommended for anyone counting calories. Made only from natural ingredients it constitutes a healthy snack and is not as sickly as the other traditional almond-based sweet *turrón*. Nearby there is a garden centre where you can buy tropical plants and miniature palms.

★ **El parque municipal** (municipal park: A1 on the map): these extensive public gardens are well tended and are a pleasant place to stroll around or snooze under the shade of the palm trees during the hottest part of the day.

★ **Basílica Menor de Santa María** (A1 on the map): right in the centre of town. Open 10.30am–1.30pm and 5–9pm. The church has wonderful domes whose polished blue tiles are among the most beautiful in Spain. On 14 and 15 of August they hold an interesting ceremony in honour of the Virgin Mary. The actors, all men, perform a detailed reconstruction of a medieval mystery play with holy chants and period costumes. At the time of writing, the church was closed for restoration.

★ **El Mercado** (market): held every day on plaza de la Fruita, behind the Ayuntamiento (town hall). There are stalls selling fish (the sea is nearby), meat, sausages, cheese, fruit and vegetables, delicious bread made from figs, dates and fresh almonds.

★ If you have time, have a trot round the **Museo del Arte Contemporáneo** (Museum of Contemporary Art; A2 on the map). The paintings on display along the paved banks of Vinalopó are also worth a quick look.

WHAT TO SEE IN THE SURROUNDING AREA

★ **La Alcudia**: about 4 kilometres (2 miles) from Elche. Open 9am–2pm and 4–7pm. Closed on Sunday and on public holidays. Excavation of Roman archaeological remains. The museum has exhibits from the Palaeolithic to Visigoth periods. This was where the Dama de Elche was discovered.

LEAVING ELCHE

By Train

– The *Cercanías* (local) line from Alicante has regular services to the 'Elche Parque' station. There are 23 services a day in both directions between Alicante and Murcia.

By Bus

– **To Murcia**: there is a bus every hour. It is slightly cheaper than the train.

ALICANTE 03000   DIALLING CODE: 965

First impressions on arrival is that Alicante is merely a series of high-rise buildings with a one way system and summer traffic jams. The coastline is vaguely reminiscent of the Côte d'Azur with the beach in the centre of the town and a long wide esplanade lined with palm trees. In summer, restaurants put tables and chairs out on the terraces so clients can enjoy the sun and a view of the sea. If you approach the town on the road from Alcoy it is quite dramatic – a desert landscape dotted with strangely eroded rock formations. It is easy to enjoy yourself in Alicante and, in summer, crowds flock to the numerous night clubs along the San Juan beach, some 6 kilometres (4 miles) to the north of the town.

A Brief History

Despite its high-rise, mass-tourism tag, Alicante stands out from other similar resorts because of its architectural wealth. It is laid out on a grid system, similar to American cities, although the old-town is typically full of small, narrow streets.

Throughout its early history, Alicante, named by the Romans as 'the city of light', was confined within its city walls at the foot of the limestone rock (known locally as 'el Macho') upon which the castle stands.

The first stage of development outside the city walls came in the 14th century when King Alfonso El Sabio (the Wise) offered housing and financial aid to the municipal council to encourage the rational organization of the town – this was common practice and was useful in repopulating territory recently reclaimed from the Arabs. Nowadays there is little to indicate that the Santa María church was built on the site of a former mosque or that the peaceful plaza Santísima Faz was where the bustling Arab markets were held in the late Middle Ages.

For a long while the rambla de Méndez Múñez served as ramparts to the city under Moorish rule and it was here that they constructed the walls to defend the city.

From the 16th to the 18th centuries Alicante's growing prosperity and increasing trade led to many Ligurians migrating from Italy. The Italians contributed to the architecture of the city with their beautiful colonial-style buildings. After the War of Succession in the 17th century, Alicante enjoyed a period of even greater urban prosperity and this is manifested in the beautiful facade of Iglesia Santa María and the Ayuntamiento (town hall). There are still a few beautiful baroque houses on calle Maldonaldo, calle Labradores, and calle Gravina, although some have been allowed to fall into disrepair.

The 19th century was a time of highs and lows for the city. On the downside it was struck by a rampant typhoid epidemic but economically it was fortified by its connection to the railway network. Even today there is a rail company that operates independently from RENFE, namely the Ferrocarril de la Generalitat Valenciana (FGV). In response to tourist development around the San Juan area, this rail company provides a constant link between Alicante and the coastal resorts.

USEFUL ADDRESSES

🛈 Tourist Office: Avenida Mendez Nuñez (C2 on the map). ☎ 20-00-00. Fax: 20-02-43. Open Monday to Friday 10am–7pm, and Saturday 10am–2pm and 3–7pm. There is also a small office at the El Atlet airport ☎ 28-50-11; and another one at the bus station (B3 on the map).

✉ Post Office (C3 on the map): plaza Gabriel Miró.

■ **Left-luggage**: open 7am–11pm at the train station opposite platform 6.
■ **Casa de Socorro**: avenida de la Constitución 1.
■ **Policía Municipal** (local police): Fernando Madronál 2.
■ **Foreign newspapers**: behind the town hall on plaza de la Santisima Faz.
■ **Iberia**: Pedro de Soto 9. ☎ 21-86-13 or 21-85-10.

TRANSPORT

🚌 Main Bus Station (B3, on the map): ☎ 13-07-00. On the corner of calle de Portugal and calle Pintor Lorenzo Casanova. All the hotels are a 10-minute walk along avenida Maisonnave.
– Bus to the San Juan beach leaves from Aparisi Guijarro 14.
– Bus to the airport – a service runs every hour from avenida de Denia, in front of the Hotel Maya. The journey takes about 30 minutes.
– The **Iberbus Linebus** company runs services from Alicante to many European cities including London,

Brussels, Paris and Amsterdam. For further information: ☎ 22-93-36 or 22-95-04.
🚆 RENFE Train Station (A2, **1** on the map): avenida de Salamanca. It also has an office at the bus station. ☎ 22-68-40.
– five trains a day to Barcelona, four to Málaga, three to Granada, two to Algeciras. About seven trains a day to Madrid, including two direct services.
🚆 FGV Train Station (A4, **2** on the map): avenida Villajoyosa. ☎ 26-27-31. For services as far as Denia only, stopping at every beach.

WHERE TO STAY

🛏 Albergue de la Juventud (**10**, off the map from A3): avenida de Orihuela 59, 03007 Alicante. ☎ 28-09-34. >From the centre of Alicante follow the Madrid road for about 3 kilometres (2 miles) which takes you directly to avenida de Orihuela; the youth hostel is on the left. Buses No.3 and No.7 from the town centre all stop here – the first two buses of the day stop directly in front of the

hostel while the third stops behind it (ask the driver for directions), and the last bus leaves at 11pm. Open all year round, a bed costs 7€ for the over 26s and 5€ for the under 26s. It is fairly expensive but offers a good standard of accommodation. There are 220 beds in total, in several buildings with one, two, three, four or eight beds to a room. Buildings A, B, C, D or E are the better option, as they are students' halls of residence and are better maintained, although they are only available in the summer. There are washing machines and spin dryers, and a cafeteria serving very good breakfasts as well as other meals.

☆–☆☆ Budget to Moderate

🛏 **Pensión los Monges** (C2, **11** on the map): calle Monjas 2, 03002 Alicante. On the first floor. ☎ 21-50-46. Extra charge for parking. This is a good place to stay as it is in the same part of town as all the bars. The *pensión* has been totally re-decorated with pine furniture and shiny new beds; they have even had double glazing installed. A double room with a shower and toilet costs about 33€. Polite and friendly staff.

🛏 **Residencia Milagrosa** (D2, **13** on the map): Villavieja 8, 03016 Alicante. ☎ 21-69-18. Simply furnished rooms in this family house. Some of the rooms look out onto the portal of Iglesia Santa María, while others over-look streets in an area that can be busy in the evening, especially at the

weekend. A double room costs 24€. The prices are slightly expensive compared with some of the newer competition in the same league. You can have breakfast on the patio facing the castle.

☆☆☆☆ Splash Out

🛏 **Hostal Cataluña** (C2, **12** on the map): calle Gerona 11, 03001 Alicante. ☎ and fax: 14-33-57. A dou-ble room costs 29€. This *hostal* has also been renovated, but the area is not quite as nice as the ones listed above, although it has the advan-tage of easier parking. The rooms don't get much light, but you do get a very friendly welcome.

🛏 **Hotel NH Cristal** (C1, **14** on the map): Tomás López Torregrosa 11, 03002 Alicante. ☎ 14-36-59. A dou-ble room with a bathroom costs about 72€. This is the Alicante branch of a Spanish chain of mid-dle-of-the-range hotels. Fairly run of the mill, with the standard chain fixtures and fittings. If you do intend to stay here, booking through a travel agency will get you a better deal.

ALICANTE

■ **Useful Addresses**

  🛈 Tourist Offices
  ✉ Post Office
  🚌 Bus station
  🚆 **1** RENFE Train station
  🚆 **2** FGV Train station

🛏 **Where to Stay**

  10 Albergue de la Juventud
  11 Pensión los Monges
  12 Hostal Cataluña
  13 Residencia Milagrosa
  14 Hotel NH Cristal

✕ **Where to Eat**

  20 Taberna Castellana
  21 O'pote Gallego
  22 Nou Manolin
  23 Bar Luis Restaurante

🍸 **Going Out**

  30 John Mulligan's and Co
  31 Desden Café
  32 Ma non troppo
  33 El Forn
  34 100 Fuegos
  35 Baccus

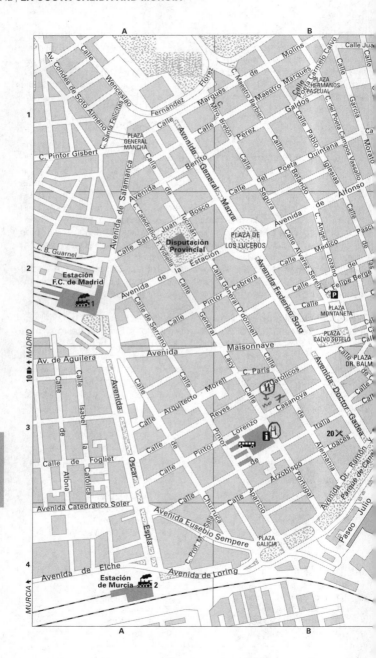

ALICANTE

ALICANTE

WHERE TO EAT

☆–☆☆ Budget to Moderate

✕ **Taberna Castellana** (B3, **20** on the map): Arzobispo Loaces 4. ☎ 22-89-31. Closed on Sunday. A meal costs about 9€. The clientele is made up of locals. A clean restaurant with good, reasonably priced food served in generous helpings.

✕ **O'pote Gallego** (C2, **21** on the map): plaza Santisima Faz 6. ☎ 20-80-84. Open 10am–4.30pm and 8pm–midnight. A main meal here costs a mere 5€. The supporters of the RCD La Coruña football team meet here for drinks on match days. On the few days when there aren't matches, this is a good place to soak up the sun at one of the tables on the small quiet square behind the Ayuntamiento.

☆☆☆ Expensive

✕ **Nou Manolin** (C2, **22** on the map): calle Villegas 3. ☎ 20-03-68. A meal costs about 18€. A smart professional clientele drink wine out of large, elegant glasses. The food might be made with the best possible ingredients but prices are still slightly too high.

✕ **Bar Luis Restaurante** (C1-2, **23** on the map): Pedro Sebastiá 7. ☎ 21-14-46. Closed on Sunday and Monday lunchtimes. A meal costs about 21€. This colonial-style restaurant offers original and stylish food including a selection of rich regional cheeses and dishes such as figs stuffed with foie gras. The setting is smart but not stuffy and the prices are reasonable for this quality of food.

GOING OUT

All the action takes place in the Santa Cruz area (known locally as El Barrio), which lies between plaza del Carmen and plaza San Cristóbal. Since the regeneration of the dock area and the building of the marina there has been a revival of activity around here. Although it is a pleasant place to stroll, there is a dearth of authentic or genuinely hip places to go. Here is a short selection of bars to be found in the streets leading away from the old town.

♟ **John Mulligan's and Co** (C2, **30** on the map): Tomás López Torregrosa 1. For several years now Spain has been gripped with a passion for Irish pubs and Alicante is no exception. The owners have spared no expense in trying to recreate the atmosphere of an authentic Irish pub – the wooden floor actually looks as if it has been polished by years of wear and strong liquor. A good place to start a night out.

♟ **Desden Café** (C2, **31** on the map): Labradores 22. ☎ 14-33-23. This café opens at 11am. The interior is decorated in glorious technicolor with exposed stonework and a mezzanine. Many of the clientele, mainly aged 25–35, seem to enjoy playing chess.

♟ **Ma non troppo** (C2, **32** on the map): Cienfuegos. Young, student clientele with decor similar to that of a barracks. Hardcore techno is very much the order of the day – if it's not your thing, give this place a miss.

♟ **El Forn** (C2, **33** on the map): Argensola. This bar has an Andalucían atmosphere with an Alicantine touch. The walls are decorated with plaster models of the facades of the typical white-washed houses, and there are lots of candles and black lace. This is the sort of place you

ALICANTE

come for a drink rather than to listen to music or dance.

❦ **100 Fuegos** (C2, **34** on the map): Cienfuegos. This bar plays a good mix of rock music and has a wide selection of spirits at the blue-neon lit, perspex bar. The establishment's slogan is bizarrely 'Rum, gold and women'.

❦ **Baccus** (C2, **35** on the map): plaza Quijano. This bar is popular with the locals, although it doesn't seem to be anything special.

In the summer months an alternative is to go to the area around playa de San Juan (bus G to playa de la Postiguet). This is an area with lots of **clubs** and **bars** that seems to be full of well-off young people out for a good time. Several are worth going to including **Voy-Voy** and its gardens.

WHAT TO SEE

★ In the oldest part of the town you can visit the small **Museo del Arte Moderno**, housed in a beautiful building with elegant arches. Open 10.30am–1.30pm and 6–9pm. Closed Monday. Free admission. Several contemporary canvasses and sculptures decorate the walls, which have recently been repainted. A random mixture of Miró, Juan Gris and other 20th-century artists. There are several works from the 'op art' movement.

★ Those with an interest in churches should take a look at the baroque facade of **Iglesia Santa María** (D2 on the map) which stands on the plaza of the same name. Not far from here is the **Ayuntamiento** (Town Hall) with its stylish facade of baroque columns. If you continue your stroll along **calle Mayor** (C-D2, on the map) you will see the town's liveliest street.

★ **El Castillo de Santa Barbara** (D1 on the map): open from 1 April to 30 September, 10am–7.30pm. The road climbs up to the fortress through a thick forest of pines, cacti and palm trees. The fortress itself is built on several levels and makes for an interesting visit, even if it is more for the views from the top – one out over the town, and the other towards the sea – than the fort itself. The castle houses the **Nace una Ciudad** (the birth of a city) museum, open Tuesday to Saturday 10am–2pm and 5–7pm, and Sunday morning. Closed Monday.

FIESTAS

– Every year, the beginning of August, the three-day **Moros y Cristianos** fiesta is celebrated. It recounts the fight between the Christians and the Moors, and ends with the Reconquest of the town by the Christians. This is celebrated with fireworks, cannon-fire, parades of horses and parades of people dressed in period costume. The fiesta is free to everyone.

– Of all the fiestas held in the Valencia region, the one with the most local colour is held between 22 and 24 April in **Alcoy.** It is held on these exact dates to tie in with St George's Day (San Jorge).

Devotion to San Jorge, the martyr of Cappadocia, probably started in Alcoy between the years 1244 and 1245 after the Christian Reconquest and the repopulation policies of Jaime I had come into force. The battle cry of the troops of the King of Aragón, Catalonia and Valencia was 'Sant Jordi, firam, firam'. Devotion to this saint became firmly rooted in this part of Spain as a result. Consequently, when Al-Açdraq tried to rebel against Jaime I, the king's troops driven by faith were able to rely on the support of San Jorge. According to the legend he appeared on the city walls dressed as a white knight. Despite many amendments to the town's bylaws the city authorities have not been able to curb the fervour of the fiesta and the commemoration of San Jorge.

The fiesta lasts for three days. On the first day they have the *entradas*, alternate processions of Moors and Christians carrying banners signalling their dedication to San Jorge or Islam. The second day is one of devotion with parades, pilgrimages and processions, while the final day is one of confrontation – the noise of the firecrackers shakes the town walls and there is a firework display on the bridge.

The fiesta has been classified as an 'event of international tourist interest' and is filmed by television crews from across the country and shown around the world.

WHAT TO SEE IN THE SURROUNDING AREA

★ The N340 which goes straight to **Alcoy** divides roughly into two parts. The countryside before you get to **Jijón**, the *turrón* (nougat) capital of Spain, is completely arid. You can visit the Turrón el Lobo factories in the town at Alcoy 62, ☎ 61-02-25, and between July and September you can watch it being made. Beyond Jijón the land gets steeper and more undulating. Here the hillsides have been cut into stepped terraces so crops can be grown on them. The land is much greener here and there are a number of good views to be enjoyed.

★ If you have time, pay a quick visit to **Novelda**, whose church looks as if it has been made from papier mâché. Little remains of the Roman towns of Petrel and Sax but ruins, which are closed to the public.

★ Finally you get to **Biar**, which has a maze of narrow streets leading up to a castle. Stop off briefly for a look round and a drink at:

L'Arc: paseo El Plátano. ☎ 81-03-73. This bar has a friendly laid-back atmosphere and is frequented by a younger crowd, a far cry from the tourist haunts of the coastal region. An unusual feature is the wide range of whiskies on offer.

BENIDORM 03500 DIALLING CODE: 965

Benidorm was the flagship of property development during the Franco era. A senseless mass of giant tower blocks, it is the capital of the mass tourist market, the destination of holidaymakers on a package deals.

Nevertheless, it is still worthwhile visiting Benidorm, even if only for a couple of hours. Most tourists come here for the beach, where they can sun themselves, usually to excess, before enjoying a night of revelry, which often consists of eating and drinking too much. Consequently it has a reputation as the capital of bad taste, bad quality, excess, tackiness, and tat. The restaurants have flashing paella-shaped signs to lure in their customers, who often don't know the difference between authentic food and cheap imitations and are often more interested in eating fish and chips. Bars compete to pump out the loudest music while karaoke and the lambada hold centre-stage as a means of entertainment. Plenty of people have fun in Benidorm and enjoy what it has to offer, but if crowded beaches, characterless bars and sangría don't appeal, move on.

Benidorm's ecological problems are even more severe than its cultural ones. Over the past few decades, water shortages have resulted in the desert reclaiming land that previous inhabitants had worked hard to make productive over many centuries. These shortages are a direct consequence of the colossal demand for water by tourists.

Water usage per capita by the tourist population is very high. There are approximately 100 tower blocks around the two beaches that make up the sea front at Benidorm. A 30-storey tower has 20 apartments on each floor, each accommodating three people. During the hot and dry Spanish summer water is a scarce commodity yet unwitting tourists take their showers (about 10 litres per person) and leave taps running regardless.

Collective needs likewise make a huge impact on the water supply. Gardens have to be watered so that they look pretty for the hordes of British, German, Danish, French and Norwegian holidaymakers who flock here every summer. To meet the demands of the gardens and especially the hotel infrastructure (kitchens, laundries and swimming pools) water is drawn from underground sources. Rivers are drained or diverted. This practice has gradually destroyed the fragile ecosystem. The earth is depleted and erosion is gradually setting in. In this way, the diversity of the countryside has slowly given way to a desert-like, dry and empty landscape.

Only recently (clear evidence of how experience does not improve decision-making), a project was given the go-ahead to reroute the Júcar river to provide further water for the tourist industry. Benidorm brings in so much revenue that its interests have been protected, whatever the cost to the local environment or long-term health of the ecology.

It is difficult to recommend any good hotels in Benidorm and in any case block bookings are already sold throughout the world several months in advance.

GOING OUT

– **Megadiscos**: Benidorm is reputed to have some of the biggest discos in Europe. If you like your music loud, head for **Penelope** or **Star Garden**. Some places include a free drink in the admission fee.

WHAT TO SEE

★ **Terra Mítica**: carretera Benidorm, Finestrat Camino de Moralet, 35000 Benidorm. ☎ (902) 02-02-20. Website: terramiticapark.com. An amusement park covering 105 hectares based on Mediterranean myths and heroes. Opened in spring 2000, the attractions and rides are divided into 15 different areas. Some three million people visited it in the first year.

WHAT TO SEE IN THE SURROUNDING AREA

★ **Villajoyosa**: about 10 kilometres (6 miles) in the direction of Alicante. This former fishing village has so far managed to avoid being engulfed by property developers. The main beach is sand (the rest are shingle), and there is a palm-fringed esplanade and a nice old town with multicoloured facades. On the outskirts of the old town is a square with many reasonably priced restaurants. The Tourist Office on plaza de Castelar 1 ☎ 89-02-50 should be able to recommend accommodation.

CASTILLO DE GUADALEST 03517

DIALLING CODE: 965

A delightful spot but as it is only some 22 kilometres (14 miles) from Benidorm it gets very crowded in summer. Coach-loads of tourists start to arrive from 10.30am onwards – a brand new road links Castillo de Guadalest to Benidorm. It is best to set off early in the morning so you can explore the town while its streets are still quiet. At this time of day you may well see mist lying at the bottom of the valley as you stand in the sun.

From Benidorm take the C3318 in the Callosa d'en Sarrià direction. Look out for the citrus trees around the Guadalest and its stark rock formations.

The car-park makes a good place for camper vans to overnight.

WHERE TO STAY AND EAT IN THE SURROUNDING AREA

There isn't anywhere to stay or eat in Castillo de Guadalest itself. This is no loss, as the size of the car-park makes the town very noisy. It is better to go on to **Benimantell**, about 2 kilometres (1 mile) away:

🛏 ✕ **Pensión El Trestellador**: ☎ 88-52-21. Fax: 88-53-71. The restaurant is closed on Tuesday. The *pensión* stands above the village. To get there, don't take the small road leading down to Benimantell, but continue for 200 metres before taking a tarmac track leading off to the left. After about 1 kilometre you come to a fork, take the left turn and carry on for a further 300 metres. The lovely *pensión* is hidden among the almond trees. A double room with a bathroom costs 36€. A huge terrace offers a marvellous view over the entire valley, which is the perfect place to take some pleasant walks along mountain paths. The owner, a kind lady with boundless energy, cooks traditional Valencian cuisine such as *arroz al horno* (rice casserole), *pilotes* (meatballs), and *olleta* (stew). There is a set menu at about 10€. This place is very clean, reasonably priced and altogether highly recommended.

🛏 A bit further on there is good spot for camping (summer only) in the grounds of the school at Benifato – note that this is not an official campsite so don't expect much in the way of facilities.

✗ **La venta de Benifato**: carretera de Alcoy, at the 15-kilometre marker. ☎ 88-52-26. The tasty set menu costs about 10€. This restaurant offers good plain fare, such as pork and maize-flour broth. It is slightly on the expensive side, but you can save a few pennies if you eat at the bar. The house wine is very good.

WHAT TO SEE

★ **El castillo**: open 10.15am–2pm and 3.15–6.45pm. This castle bears little resemblance to an impenetrable fortress, but is worth a visit nevertheless. The gently sloping pavements lead up to a small square that is set in front of the entrance to the castle. From the castle there is a spectacular view of the neighbouring region, especially the Sierra Aixorta (1,126 metres/3,693 feet high), the dam at Guadalest and the lake behind the dam.

– Avoid the tourist traps that are the natural springs at Algar and at Callosa d'en Sarrià. They are of little interest and you have to pay for admission and you will have to tackle a poorly maintained road to get there.

PLACE NAMES

Many villages in the area have Muslim-sounding names. Toponymy, or the study of place names, reveals a clan relationship between the numerous place names beginning with 'Beni'. Between Tarragona and Murcia you often come across the names of tribal groups from North Africa, for example the Masmudas – hence Benimasmut, as well as a few Arabic names.

These tribes include the Hawwaras who escaped from subjugation in Córdoba, many along the banks of the river Júcar. Interestingly this tribe was scattered all over the Mediterranean from Tripoli, Sicily and the Ebro valley to the north of Seville

JÁTIVA (XÀTIVA) 46800   DIALLING CODE: 962

Rather than taking the direct route to Játiva along a main road or motorway take the smaller back roads. They are much more enjoyable as they take you through fields of orange trees, almond groves and vineyards.

Játiva's recent expansion has not affected its historic areas and beautiful monuments, which are testament to the medieval splendour of its past. It was once part of the Moorish kingdom of Denia, and afterwards belonged in succession to the kingdoms of Valencia and Murcia. In addition, Játiva was the cradle of the Borgia family, famous for producing Pope Calixtus III and Pope Alexander VI (neither of whom was renowned for their adherence to religious virtues), yet it is a small unassuming town which those who love Spain will enjoy immensely.

COSTA CALIDA

USEFUL ADDRESSES

🛈 Tourist Office: avenida Jaume I 48. ☎ 28-23-30 and avenida Noguera 10. ☎ 27-33-46. Open Monday to Saturday 10am–1.30pm and 4–6pm, and Sunday morning.

✉ Post Office: avenida Jaume I 4. ☎ 88-25-78. Immediately opposite the Tourist Office. Open Monday to Saturday 9am–2pm.

🚆 RENFE Train Station: Ximen de Tovia. ☎ 27-16-64. This is the quickest and cheapest way to get to the larger towns. There are about three trains a day to Murcia and Cartagena on Line 1. The journey to Valencia takes about 1 hour and there are approximately eight trains a day. The journey from Valencia takes about 40 minutes and there are on average seven trains a day.

🚌 Bus Station: Ximen de Tovia. Buses to the small towns in the surrounding area and also to Gandia, Ontinyent and Valencia. This is sometimes the only way to get to the smaller towns. Check what time the buses will be running the day before you go. You can also get information from the drivers.

■ Taxis: plaza Bassa. ☎ 27-34-37. At the RENFE train station: ☎ 27-16-81.

■ Cibercafé: Cosmógrafo Ramirez 6. Between the plaza de Toros and the Guardia Civil.

WHERE TO STAY AND EAT IN THE SURROUNDING AREA

☆ Budget

🛏 ✕ Fonda El Margallonero: plaza del Mercat 42. ☎ 27-66-77. Closed on Sunday, except from April to October. Double rooms cost about 17€. A friendly welcome is given at this simply-furnished *pensión*, although the housekeeping does not stretch to removing dead flowers from the window boxes of the courtyard. The rooms are unassuming – if there is a choice, go for one with a view over the market rather than the dingy courtyard. The full-board option with home cooking is very reasonably priced.

✕ Casa Floro: plaza del Mercat 46. ☎ 27-30-20. Closed for the last fortnight in August. The set menu costs about 6€. Set under the arches of the market square immediately next to Fonda El Margallonero. Well-known for its Valencian dishes – especially paella.

☆☆ Moderate

🛏 Hotel Murta: Angel Lacalle. ☎ 27-66-11. Fax: 27-65-50. Free parking. A double room and breakfast costs 45€ including tax. A small hotel which will delight football fans – you can watch the local teams from the window as they play in the town stadium next door. Even if you're not a soccer lover, this is a decent enough hotel. The only criticism is that the breakfasts are a bit stingy. All the rooms have air-conditioning and TV.

☆☆☆ Expensive

🛏 ✕ Hostería de Mont Sant: on the hill leading up to the castle. ☎ 27-50-81. Fax: 28-19-05. Website: www.servidex.com/montsant. Open daily, but closed for a week in January. A double room with bathroom costs about 120€ excluding breakfast. The restaurant offers set menus from 24€. This is a lovely *hostería* built at the bottom of the hill crowned by the medieval castle of Játiva, formerly a Cistercian monastery. It has recently undergone a spurt of expansion – four new rooms or *cabañas* have been added with large bay windows overlooking the sleepy town. The grounds of the *hostería* – around 17,000 square metres (182,900 square feet) of almond and orange trees – have been conserved, along with the irrigation channel inherited from the Arabs, and some intimate little terraced areas have been built. The service is always very professional, the bathrooms are well-equipped and sparkling clean, and the friendly owners proudly give you oranges harvested from the gardens of the *hostería*. The decor is simple and there is a careful mix of modern avant-garde design and old traditional furnishings. This successful combination helps to create a comfortable environment that includes all mod cons (television, swimming pool, and the like). On the food front, the *hostería* has earned a reputation for high-class cuisine. The rice dishes are extraordinarily good, as is the rich foie gras flan.

WHAT TO SEE

★ From the avenida Jaume I (the main thoroughfare through the town), take calle del Porta del Lleo (next to the service station), to reach the **old town**, the most interesting part of Játiva with its Plateresque churches, and old, narrow streets. The main tourist attractions are within a short distance of the market place.

The most interesting places are the **Iglesia de Sant Francesc**, with its seven chapels built around a central nave, the **casa de Diego**, which has a wonderful collection of *azulejos*, the **Hospital Real** and the towering collegiate church of **la Seu**, which is only open in the mornings. Most of the church dates from the end of the 16th century, although the finishing touches to the facade were not completed until three hundred years later.

★ **Almodí** or **Museo Municipal**: carrer de la Corretgeria. Open Tuesday to Friday 10am–2pm and 4–6pm, and at weekends 10am–2pm. Closed Monday. Admission costs about 2€ for over 18s. This small, pleasant museum is surprisingly well-stocked for a town the size of Játiva. It is best to start at the top floor (the lift is on the right as you go in) where there is a display of archaeological finds from the region, including a few hashish pipes from the time of the Moors and a wonderful roof from an ancient Muslim palace. On the second floor there are several Murillo copies and paintings from the Velázquez School, as well as a magnificent triptych by Borbotó. Keep an eye out for the portrait of Felipe V – hung upside down as an act of rebellion by one of the Museum's curators after the king ordered that Játiva be destroyed.

★ **The Chapel of San Feliu**: on the outskirts of the town on the road leading up to the castle. Opening times are 10am–1pm and 4–7pm, public holidays 10am–1pm. This is a very attractive church, built in the Romanesque style. The canopy is supported by wonderful marble columns; inside there are some interesting works of early religious art. A white marble column-top is used as the font.

★ **The Fortress**: open 10am–6pm. Closed on Monday. Admission costs about 2€ for over 18s. The fortress is actually made up of two castles – the Castell Menor and the Castell Major, both built on the ridge. The fortress was used as a prison for a long time, and played host to many members of the nobility, from the king of Mallorca, Jaume IV, to Didac de Borgia (the brother of St Francis) who was briefly Bishop of Urgell. All that remains of the Castell Menor is a pile of stones and it is of interest today purely for its unrestricted views of the surrounding valleys. Unfortunately, Castell Major is hardly more exciting as the muddle of buildings and lack of coherent on-site information makes it difficult for visitors to gauge what was built when. Nevertheless, the chapel of St Jordi is worth a visit. A nice place for a walk with some splendid views over the Játiva plain.

WHAT TO SEE IN THE SURROUNDING AREA

Historical Background of the Region

Not far from Játiva, just next to the motorway, lie the ruins of **Castillo de Montesa**. If you are interested in Spain's medieval past then Montesa will be worth a visit.

The Knights Templar were a monastic order founded in 1112 AD to protect pilgrims on their way to the Holy Land. The Knights became very powerful in European political circles because Pope Innocent II exempted them from the influence of any other power except that of the papacy. In 1307, all the Knights Templar were simultaneouly arrested and tested for their faith and allegiance to the Catholic church.

Spain was also affected by the demise of the Order of the Templars. The kingdom of Valencia had 11 of them and they had played an important role in the Reconquest. The Templars had amassed colossal sums of money throughout medieval Europe. This was one of the reasons for their downfall as they were seen to have fallen from grace and to be living outside the laws of both state and church.

On 10 June 1317 the king and the Pope chose the Order of Montesa as successors to the now disgraced Templars. This Order, although not nearly as important as the Order of Calatrava, had its roots in Valencia. Montesa had not only defended the Aragonese Crown from the threat of the Saracen infidels but it had also been charged with the task of repopulating the region with Christians.

BOCAIRENTE 46880

This small detour is worth taking if you are in no particular hurry. Some 11 kilometres (7 miles) from Onteniente, Bocairente is a small village perched on a hillside. Famous for its plaza de toros dug into the rock. Opening times are 12 noon to 1pm only at weekends and on public holidays – details about the guided tour are available from the Tourist Office.

DENIA 03700   DIALLING CODE: 965

Set on the horn of Spain, this small seaside resort is a place of unusual peace and quiet. The pretty facades of its buildings make it a favourite tourist destination among the less well-off middle classes. The buildings on the seafront have not succumbed to the high-rise developers and most of the building are rarely taller than the tops of the umbrella pines. Add to this beautiful beaches and rocky inlets and Denia offers an ideal place to break your journey.

USEFUL ADDRESSES

🛈 **Tourist Office**: plaza Oculista Buigues 9. ☎ (966) 42-23-67. Fax: 78-09-57. Website: www.denia.net. Open Monday to Friday 9am–1.30pm and 4–7pm, and Saturday 10am–2pm and 4–7pm. You get a friendly welcome from the professional, polyglot staff. They can recommend several scuba diving clubs and even suggest itineraries for discovering the surrounding area, such as the ruta del Acuario (the Aquarium route) or the 'Cova Tallà'.

■ All the **windsurfing clubs** are north of the town centre on the beaches of Les Marines (Nova Denia ☎ (619) 53-33-95) and els Molins.

WHERE TO STAY

Campsites

⚑ **Los Pinos**: on the road to Játiva and Las Rotas, in the direction of the Marineta Cassiana and El Trampolí beaches. Go past the cemetery and then follow the signs to the left. ☎ 78-26-98. This is a lovely campsite in a small pine grove with direct access to the beach. A pitch costs 3€ per person, per tent or per car. Carla, the manager, ensures campers receive a friendly welcome.

☆ Budget

⚑ **Hostal L'Anfora**: esplanada de Cervantes 9. ☎ 78-61-19. Fax: (966) 42-16-90. On the town's main esplanade. This small hotel is well located and has recently been renovated. A double room with a bathroom, hair-dryer, toilet and air-conditioning costs 36–48€. The rooms are not very big, but it is a good place to stay nevertheless.

⚑ **Hotel Castillo**: avenida del Cid 7. ☎ (966) 42-13-20. Fax: 78-71-88. Email: tenerest@ctv.es. Go round the castle to the left and the hotel is half-way along a small street leading up to the fortress, opposite the health centre. This is a traditional family-run hotel. A double room costs 39€, breakfast included. The carpets, the decor and the surroundings are not in the best of taste, although it is very clean. A good place to stay for a couple of days.

WHERE TO EAT AND DRINK

✕ **El Jamonal de Ramonet**: passeig del Saladar 106. This small traditional Spanish bar serves good tapas, costing 5–6€. The clientele is mostly friendly locals and, typically, hams hang from the ceiling.

🍷 **Cervecería Gambrinus**: carrer marques del Campo 11. In the centre of Denia, on a small pedestrian street. A pleasant enough little drinking hole, although very different from Al Jamonal. The emphasis is on beer, mostly of German origin.

THE BEACHES

– **Nudists** tend to congregate on the beach below Torre del Gerro, right next to the Cabo de San Antonio and its underwater cave. Take the Las Rotas road and the beach is about 4.5 kilometres (3 miles) from the town centre. A bus service runs every hour 8.30am–8.30pm.

– **Windsurfers** can surf to their heart's content on the Deveses beach. From April to August the alternating *levante* (east wind) and stiff westerly breeze ensures there is always fun to be had out on the water.

The Valencia Region

VALENCIA 46000   DIALLING CODE: 963

Valencia, the third largest city in Spain in terms of population, has always tried to provide the benefits of a big city while at the same time avoiding the many downsides. Although overshadowed by its neighbour Barcelona, Valencia has the status of capital of the region of the same name.

One of the key factors in its development has been its location in a vast fertile valley, the Huerta, drained by two rivers: the Júcar – Xúquer in Valencian – and the Turia. An ingenious irrigation system introduced by the Romans and further developed by the Moors enables Valencian landowners (most of whom live in the city) to supply much of the European fruit and veg market with high-quality citrus fruits and other market garden produce.

Valencia is a surprisingly cultural city. It has a wealth of different architecture, magnificent churches, interesting museums and romantic promenades. It also has a wonderful old town with a maze of little traffic-free streets, which pedestrians enjoy at their leisure. The *Fallas* fiesta is famous throughout Spain and is, of course, the city's most important annual event, although Valencians, being especially easy-going people are always happy to indulge their festive spirit at other times of the year as well.

Valencians are proud of their identity and use two Spanish dialects: *valenciano* (Castilian Spanish) and *valencià* (Valencian Spanish). *Valencià* is the dominant language and the one that is used in the newspapers and on the regional television channel, *Canal Nou*. In common with other regions of Spain, there is a fierce pride in their *Comunidad* (regional distinctiveness).

As a city, Valencia is well worth exploring by day and revelling in by night.

A Brief History

Valencia has a rich cultural history whose diversity is a direct result of the many different civilizations that have conquered the region. It is virtually impossible to overstate the impact of the East, so greatly has it influenced the history of the area, and indeed the whole country.

Among the more significant events of Valencia's history is the period when El Cid conquered Valencia. To understand what brought this mercenary soldier to the region, you need to remember what was happening in the rest of Spain at the time. One half of the country was under Moorish and Arab rule, while the other was under the control of the Christian Visigoths. Other religious groups living in Spain and Valencia at the time were the Jews, Mozárabes and Mudéjares, all of whom were caught between the cultural extremes of the Moors and Christians.

Under the leadership of the Christian monarchy and the papacy, the Reconquest progressed gradually and following a crisis in Moorish rule, a lot of small kingdoms came into being, including Denia and Tortosa. These independent cities survived as Moorish bases only by paying taxes (*parias*) to the Christians in exchange for their continued autonomy.

El Cid was one of the king of Castille's, and by implication the Christian monarch's, army of tax collectors. However, in 1081, Rodrigo Díaz de Bivar (El Cid) was banished by the king and as a result he offered his services to anyone who could pay for them, Muslim or Christian. This great leader, extolled in writing and song, including the epic poem *El Cantar del mio Cid* (*the ballad of Mio Cid*), had basically become a mercenary. His ranks included both Muslims and Christians all of whom worked to his rules. At the same time, Alfonso VI was finding it difficult to maintain his hold over Valencia and El Cid saw an opportunity to make his fortune. In comparison with other parts of Spain, the region of Valencia was as densely populated then as it is now. Good, well-irrigated agricultural land, horse-breeding, and other cottage industries made it one of the richest territories in the peninsula, and so many other local powers were also keen to lay claim to a slice of its wealth. To win his prize, El Cid had to fight a fierce battle, flood the Huerta and finally lay siege to the city in order to overcome the Valencian Moors. Having finally taken the city he went on to rule over it as if it were his own kingdom.

Even though El Cid's motives were based on self-interest, he became one of the heroes of the Reconquest, symbolizing the spirit of the religious struggle against heresy. In the process of consolidating his position he went about restoring and propagating the Catholic faith in Valencia. One of his first acts was to construct a cathedral on the site of the mosque. Still primarily concerned with autonomy, El Cid made his church independent of a religious province. He also took the precaution of not declaring himself a vassal of the papacy, instead his church remained answerable to the Holy See.

The period of dominance of the Catholic Monarchs is not dealt with in any great detail here (*see* 'Background') but what is of most interest here is how the Moorish influence continued after the Reconquest. During the 15th century, trade with North Africa continued to be significant and the conquest of the Andalucían region and the coastal areas of North Africa bear witness to this. But it was not just the desire to increase territorial possession that drove them, they were also keen to develop areas of control and influence. Exports to Africa included dates, wheat, spices – paprika and cinnamon – dyes (such as indigo), gums and resins. Imports included slaves, leather goods, live animals, fabrics (wool, linen, cotton), canvas and crafted products.

By 1790, Valencia was one of the five most important cities in Spain, thanks to the richness of its agricultural land, commercial drive and urban industries. Economic evidence from the period and analyses of population figures show that in the 18th century Valencia underwent a major period of expansion with trade in rice, silk, wine, ceramics and rope providing Valencians with a relatively high standard of living. Communications systems were well developed and investment companies began to research potential new markets and ways to increase profits even further. This growth in trade and industry became the foundation for the economic security of the 19th and 20th centuries. Meanwhile, in the cultural arena, Valencia began to attract the intelligentsia who attended private meetings and academies; new ideas were discussed and important theories developed; a huge number of books and essays were published at around this time by the academic community.

Across the border, the French Revolution and the new Republic slowed down this commercial progress. The subsequent French occupation of Spain further exacerbated this decline resulting in rising prices and decreasing wages. Investment came to a standstill. Vagabonds and beggars became commonplace and poor general economic conditions prevented small farmers from playing the pioneering role enjoyed by those in the rest of Europe and North America. The situation was not helped by the failure to develop a good education system, which could have halted the decline in progress.

Since the 19th century, the boom in the export of citrus fruits (particularly oranges) has gradually contributed to the regeneration of Valencia's wealth. An illustration of this is the Pascual Hermanos fruit company. In 1980 (before Spain's entry into the EC), this family business sold a total of 250,000 tonnes of fruit worth 6,500 million pesetas (around £40 million), 87 per cent of which was exported. The 'brothers' have holdings all along the Levantine coast, from Tarragona to Málaga, as well as in other countries in Europe. They are a positive symbol of the driving force of the economy of the Huerta valley.

USEFUL ADDRESSES

Tourist Information

Several offices provide tourist information. Generally speaking, they are all well equipped with a range of brochures and friendly, helpful staff.

🄱 **Tourist Office** (D2, **1** on map II): calle Paz 48. ☎ 98-64-22. Fax: 98-64-21. Email: touristinfo.valencia@turisme.m400.gva.es

🄱 **Tourist Office** (C4, **2** on map II): calle Játiva 24. In the station. ☎ 52-85-73. Fax: 52-85-73. Email: touristinfo.renfe@turisme.m400.gva.es

Post Offices and Telecommunications

✉ **Main Post Office** (C3 on map II): plaza del Ayuntamiento 24. Poste restante. ☎ 51-67-50.

– In the la Seu area: plaza Conde Carlet 5 (C1 on map II). Open 8.30am–2.30pm only.

– In the Gran vía Marqués del Túria area: calle Ciscar 7 (A2 on map III). Same opening hours.

– In the Canbanyal area: calle Doctor Lluch 251 (D2 on map III). Same opening hours.

– Finally, there is a post office in the Corte Inglés, next to the bus station, Avenida Menéndez Pidal, 15 (A1 on map II). Open Monday to Friday, 8.30am–8.30pm and Saturday morning.

☎ **Telephones**: plaza del Ayuntamiento 27 (C3 on map II). Also Gran vía Germanías 34B (C4 on map II). ☎ 51-07-03. Open 9am–10.30pm.

■ **Directory Enquiries**: ☎ 1003.

■ **Telegrams by Phone**: ☎ 52-20-00.

– You can buy phone cards from tobacconists.

– Local calls (within the metropolitan area) are cheaper between 6pm and 8am. National cheap rates begin at 8pm. As in the rest of Spain, there are cheap rates at weekends for both local and national calls.

Money, Banks and Bureaux de Change

■ **American Express**: Viajes Duna, calle Cirilo Amorós 88. Open Monday to Friday 9.30am–1.30pm and 4.30–8pm.

■ **Bureaux de Change**: Caja de Ahorros, calle Xátiva 14 (**1** on map II, C4). ☎ (96) 351-78-69. Open Monday to Saturday 9am–6pm. Fenicia de Indias, calle Caballeros, on the corner of plaza de la Virgen. Open 9am–9pm.

■ **Credit Cards**: the following banks have cash machines: Argentaria (plaza del Ayuntamiento; C3 on map II), Banesto (likewise plaza del Ayuntamiento), Banco Santander (Gran Vía Marqués del Túria 29, D4 on map II; and plaza Porta de la Mar 4, A1 on map III).

Embassies and Consulates

See 'Embassies and Consulates' in 'General Information'.

Emergencies

■ **Red Cross**: ☎ (902) 22-22-92 or 67-73-75.

■ **Local Police** (A1 on map III): calle Amadeo de Saboya 12. ☎ 62-10-12.

■ **Emergency calls**: ☎ 092.

■ **Duty Chemists**: ☎ (900) 50-09-52.

Airline Companies

■ **Airport Information**: ☎ 70-95-00.

■ **Iberia** (C2, **5** on map II): calle de la Paz 14. ☎ 52-06-77.

■ **Air España**: at the airport. ☎ (961) 52-27-37.

Car Hire

■ **Hertz** (C4, **9** on map II): calle Segorbe 7. ☎ 41-50-36.

■ **Avis** (A2, **6** on map III): calle Isabel la Católica 17. ☎ 51-07-34.

■ **Budget** (A2, **6** on map III): calle Isabel la Católica 19. ☎ 51-68-18.

■ **Europcar** (D4, **7** on map II): Avenida Antic Regne de Valencia 7. ☎ 74-15-12.

■ **National Atesa** (A3, **8** on map III): calle Joaquín Costa 57. ☎ 95-36-05.

■ **Lider Rent**: San Vicente Mártir 276. ☎ and fax: 77-12-06.

■ **Abirent**: paseo de la Pechina 70. ☎ 79-21-21 or 83-67-00.

Scooter Hire

■ **Eurotransac** (B3, **10** on map III): avenida del Puerto 72. ☎ 89-06-47. A 50cc scooter costs around 15€ for one to three day's hire plus tax. Refundable deposit of 60€.

Miscellaneous

■ **Internet Cafés**: Cyberdrac (D2, **12** on map II), calle de la Paz 33. ☎ 51-04-44. Fax: 51-05-96. Open Monday to Friday 10am–2pm and 5–9pm. Also in the Corte Inglés shopping centre: Quisiera Salas Internet (A1, **13** on map II). Open 10am–9.30pm. Email: Internet@quisiera.es

■ **Left Luggage Facilities**: if you're short of cash, head for the left luggage office at the bus station as it is much cheaper than the one at the RENFE train station.

■ **Laundrette** (C2, **14** on map II): plaza del Mercado 12. Open 10am–2pm and 4–8.30pm. Closed Sunday.

LOCAL TRANSPORT

The cheapest and best way to see the city is on foot. There is no road transport in the centre of the city because of the narrow streets.

Bus

The majority of the red EMT buses go through plaza de la Reina (C2 on map II), the puerta de la Mar gate (D3 on map II and A2 on map III), and stop at the bus station (A1 on map II) and the RENFE train station (C4 on map II). They are fast but inexpensive. Make sure you know where you are going or have a map to hand as the stops are not listed inside the bus itself. You can buy single tickets (less than 1€) from the driver, or buy passes that are valid for a certain number of journeys (4–5€) from metro stations and newspaper kiosks. The *bonobus* can only be used on buses, while the Bono 10, can be used on both buses and on the metro. Both types of passes are 'transferable', namely they don't have to be used exclusively by the person who bought them.

– Visitors arriving at the bus station can catch bus No. 8 or No. 79 into the centre.

Metro

Valencia has four metro lines (a fifth is on the drawing board). The blue line, TVV Dr Lluch, is handy for getting both to the conference centre and the beaches.

The Bono 10 pass can be used on the metro as well as the bus.

Taxis

All the city's taxis are metered although for longer journeys you may sometimes be able to agree a set price.

■ **Coop. Tele Taxi**: ☎ 57-13-13.

■ **Onda Taxi**: ☎ 47-52-52.

■ **Radio Taxi**: ☎ 70-33-33.

NORTH

Burjassot

Campus

San Joan

4

La Granja

1

Empalme

Canterería

Benimàmet

Palau de Congressos

Florista

Les Carolines/ Fira

1

Garbí

Benicalap

Beniferri

Trànsits

Marxa

S

Reus

Campanar

Túria

Mislata-Almassil

3

Àngel Guimerà

Mislata

Nou d'Octubre

Av. del Cid

Plaça Espanya

Patraix

Jesús

Hospital

Sant Isidre

1 3

València-Sud

VALENCIA

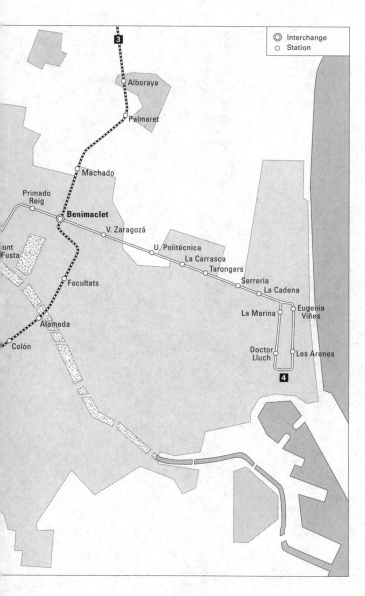

| | Interchange |
| | Station |

3

Alboraya

Palmaret

Machado

Primado
Reig

Benimaclet

V. Zaragozá

ont
Fusta

U. Politècnica

La Carrasca

Tarongers

Facultats

Serrería

La Cadena

Alameda

La Marina

Eugenia
Viñes

Colón

Doctor
Lluch

Les Arenes

4

THE METRO – VALENCIA

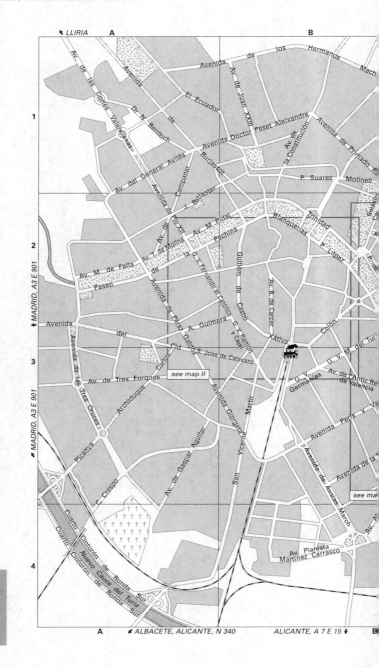

see map II

see ma

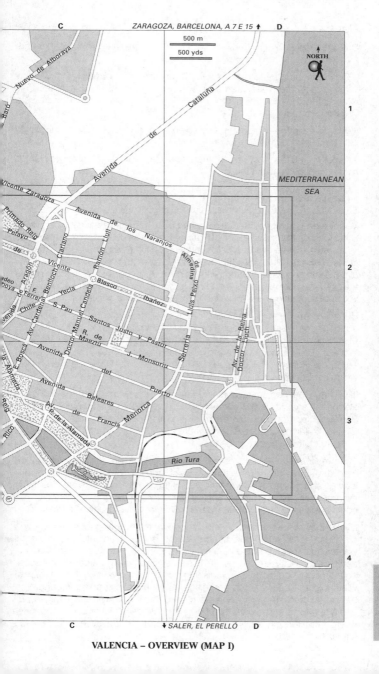

VALENCIA – OVERVIEW (MAP I)

Car

Driving in Valencia is not advised, but if you are prepared to risk it there are two things you should know:

– On no account try to park illegally. The police are very quick to tow away vehicles that break the law and can empty entire districts in 15 minutes. This is true at all times of day and night. Stick to official car-parks or make sure you buy a parking ticket.

If you do have the misfortune to have your car towed away, the number to call to retrieve your vehicle is: ☎ 69-90-34.

– If you want to avoid driving through Valencia, take the A7 motorway which acts as a bypass round the city.

THE DIFFERENT AREAS

Valencia does not have the picturesque streets of Granada, the hectic activity of Barcelona or the grandeur of the palaces in Seville but it still has plenty to recommend it. The main pedestrian area is concentrated around the Barrio del Carmen district (C1 on map II). This is the old town and with its maze of narrow streets, interspersed with crumbling old palaces, it is the most attractive part of the city. The more you explore it, the more you see, and every time you go back you spot something new. In the old town every street is different.

But there are many other contrasting areas to explore. The peace and tranquillity of the streets around La Seu (C1 on map II) contrast sharply with the hustle and bustle of the Mercado district (C2 on map II). An evening stroll in plaza Tossal is quite unlike the one you would have along the seedy calle Torno del Hospital, calle Horno del Hospital or calle Roger de Flor – all of which are best avoided.

If you can bear to tear yourself away from the worn stone paving of El Carmen, it's worth taking a look at the post-modern, shining marble of the San Francisco quarter (D3 on map II). This area finally gives way to the frightful buildings of Calle Colón, where Zara, Mango and other well-known Spanish clothes shops can be found.

The American-style blocks of the Gran Vía quarter (D4 on map II and A2 on map III) likewise offer little in the way of character, but the area is pleasantly located and borders the former course of the tree-lined river Turia. There is a riverbed park, which makes a lovely place for a walk. It is so peaceful you could easily forget that you are in the middle of one of Spain's largest cities.

If you fancy some seafood, take a walk down the heavily congested Avenida del Puerto. Its small side streets to the south, lead into old industrial wastelands. Thanks to the opening of the Ciudad de Artes y Ciencias (Arts and Sciences City; B4 on map III), this area will probably be developed soon. To the north, you reach the old fishing quarter of Malvarrosa (D1 on map III) with its long, straight roads and elegant tiled houses sporting wrought-iron balconies. Not long ago, oxen were yoked to harnesses and used to pull boats up from the sea onto the shore. This is a delightful area but it is under threat from the city's council, which plans to extend avenida de Blasco Ibáñez to the sea.

WHERE TO STAY

☆ Budget

⬧ Albergue Juvenil Las Arenas (D2, **20** on map III): calle Eugenia Viñes 24, 46011 Valencia. ☎ 56-42-88. Blue metro line: Las Arenas stop. From the RENFE train station, catch bus No. 32. A bed in a dormitory sleeping 15 costs a good 5€ per night, even with a reduction. To get the reduction you need to pick up a leaflet from the town's tourist offices. The youth hostel's name, Las Arenas, means 'sand' because it is next to the beach. This is its only advantage (albeit a major one) as it quite a long way from the city centre.

⬧ Hostal Universal (C3, **21** on map II): calle Las Barcas 5, 46002 Valencia. ☎ and fax: 51-53-84. Next to the plaza del Ayuntamiento. A double room with washbasin costs

---

■ **Useful Addresses**

  🛈 **1** and **2** Tourist Office
  ✉ Post Office
  ☎ Public telephones
  1 Bureaux de change
  5 Iberia
  7 Europcar
  9 Hertz
  12 Cyberdrac
  13 Quisiera Salas
  14 Laundrette

⬧ **Where to Stay**

  21 Hostal Universal
  22 Hostal Moratín
  23 Hostal del Rincón
  24 Hostal Alicante
  25 Hospedería del Pilar
  26 Hostal Granero
  27 Hostal Venecia
  29 Hotel Ad Hoc

✕ **Where to Eat**

  29 Restaurant Chust Godoy
  31 El Restaurante Cultural
  32 Sidrería El Molinón
  33 Bar Pilar
  34 Los Toneles
  35 Asador Pipol
  37 El Palacio de la Bellota
  38 Ca'n Bermell
  40 Ocho y medio
  41 Cervecería Villaplana
  46 La Casa Ramón

🍸 **Going Out**

  83 Ghecko
  84 Johnny Maracas
  85 Pitapeira
  86 Fox Congo
  87 Café Bolsería
  88 Café Negrito
  89 Hannase Al Babal
  90 El Carmen Sui Generis
  91 Jimmy Glass Jazz
  93 Finnegan's of Dublin
  95 Havana Club
  96 Carioca
  98 Venial
  99 La Calcatta
  100 El Gran Caimán

★ **What to See**

  110 Catedral
  111 Palacio de la Generalidad
  112 La Lonja
  113 Museo Nacional de la Cerámica González Martí
  114 Museu de Belles Arts
  115 Puente del Real
  116 Colegio del Patriarca
  117 Museo Histórico
  119 Instituto Valenciano de Arte Moderno
  121 Iglesia de Santo Domingo
  123 Torre de Serrano
  127 Parking San Agustín

A B

⊠ Corte Inglés

13

Av. de Pio XII

Túria ⊠

Ⓜ Avenida

Profesor Beltrán Báguena

Menéndez

Pidal

Pechina

C. de Na Jor

★ 119

Puente Glorias Valencianas

la

Dr. Sanchis Bergón

Castro

Corona

Calle

Guillem

de

Beneficencia

C. de Na Jor

1

Paseo

Gran

Vía

Jardín

Botánico

Museo de las Ciencias Naturales

Beato Gaspar Bono

P. Bonfil

Dr. Beltrán Bigorra

PLAZA V. IBORRA

P. Manjón

Pintor Zariñena

Calle

Turia

TORRES DE QUART

98 ♀

C. de

C. Dr. Zamenhof

C. Teruel

San

Calle Norte

Jacinto

Calle de Quart

Castro

de

Murillo

Tejedores

En Sendra

Pint. Domingo

Av. S. José de la Montaña

Calle

46 ✕

Calle

Borrul

Guillem

Carniceros

Balmes

2

Azcárraga

Fernando

Calle

Lepanto

de Mena

Viana

Carnarón

C. del

Triador

Calle Guillem

Soro

Calle del

Bany

S. Ignacio de Loyola

Miró

Juan

Gabriel

Calíxto

El

C. Espinosa

Calle

Calle EL PILAR

PLAZA DEL PILAR

Rog

S. M. Micaela

Calle

Calle

♀ 95

Oreliana

Mtro. Palau

Calle

del

Casa de Cultu

96 ♀

Juan

Católico

Ⓜ Àngel Guimerà

Guillem

de

Castr

3

Avenida

El Humano

Llorens

Erudito

Guimrà

Sívera

Gran Vía

Guardia

C. Espartero

Padre

Calle

Linares

de

Angel

Romeu

C. Dr. S.

Palleter

Cuenca

C. C. Tro

C. Lorca

C. Héroe

41 ✕

C. Buen Orden

Diego

Ramón y

Avenida del Ci

Perez

C. Alberique

S. José de Calasanz

PLAZA OBISPO

Histor.

Jesús

Pintor Benedito

PLAZA ESPAÑA

4

Ayora

Beliiver

F. Liano

C. Chiva

Galdós

C. Marqués de Zenete

C. S. F. de Borja

Calle

Plaça Espanya

C. Albacete

C. Maestro

C.

A B

0 100 200 m
0 100 200 yds

38
Carmen sw
Gertis

la Flama
(opens 10pm Thurs – Fri)

VALENCIA

around 25€, and 29€ with shower. Very big, well-kept rooms with brand new bathrooms. The ones overlooking the road are noisy. The family also owns another nearby *pensión* which is slightly cheaper: **Pensión Paris**, calle Salvá 12. ☎ 52-67-66.

☎ **Hostal Moratín** (C3, **22** on map II): calle Moratín 15, 46002 Valencia. ☎ and fax: 52-12-20. On the fifth floor but it has a lift. Doubles start at 24€. This tiny *hostal* has only 14 small rooms. The mod cons aren't extensive but breakfast and even lunch is available as long as you order it in advance from Javier, the friendly owner. He will generally cook whatever you fancy and at unbeatable prices. The five-storey car-park right next door might also be useful. Note that reservations have not always been respected in the past.

☎ **Hostal del Rincón** (C2, **23** on map II): calle Carda 11, 46001 Valencia. ☎ 91-60-83. Very close to the plaza del Mercado, in the old town. If no-one answers the door, ask at the garage next door. A double without bathroom costs around 16€, add another 6€ for an en suite. A bit tatty, but cheap, clean and well looked after. Friendly welcome.

☎ **Hostal Alicante** (C4, **24** on map II): Ribera 8 (second floor), 46002 Valencia. ☎ and fax: 51-22-96. Rooms for around 24€ with showers but without toilets, and 27€ for an en-suite with toilet. Not far from the station and the plaza del Ayuntamiento. The small but clean rooms all have washbasins.

☎ **Hospedería del Pilar** (C2, **25** on map II): plaza del Mercado 19, 46001 Valencia. ☎ 91-66-00. Open every day. Double rooms with en-suite from 23€, rooms without showers for around 14€. Slightly more expensive but otherwise much the same as the Hostal Ali-

cante, although deliveries to the market make it very noisy.

☆☆ Moderate

☎ **Hostal Granero** (D4, **26** on map II): Martínez Cubells 4, 46002 Valencia. ☎ 51-25-48. Between the station and the plaza del Ayuntamiento. On the first floor. A double room with bathroom costs 24€. In an attractive building on a quiet road. Reasonable prices. Very clean. The majority of rooms have bath or shower.

☎ **Hostal Venecia** (C3, **27** on map II): En Llop 5 (plaza del Ayuntamiento), 46002 Valencia. ☎ 52-42-67. Very central. A double room costs around 42€. Fairly impersonal. Acceptably clean. Prices vary depending on whether the rooms have a washbasin, shower or bath, and air-conditioning.

☎ **Hotel Tres Cepas** (D3, **28** on map III): paseo Neptuno 22, 46011 Valencia. ☎ 71-51-11. A double room costs a little over 48€. Decent, simply furnished rooms right next to the beach. Ideal if all you want to do is laze by the sea. The only drawback is the lack of air-conditioning – it can get very hot in mid-summer. Friendly staff.

☆☆☆ Expensive

☎ **Hotel Ad Hoc** (D1, **29** on map II): calle Boix, 4, 46003 Valencia. ☎ 91-91-40. Fax: 91-36-67. Double en-suite rooms for 57–120€. The hotel building dates from the 19th century and has been tastefully furnished by an antique dealer – a far cry from the cold, impersonal chain hotels. Restaurant. Avoid the rooms overlooking the narrow street as they are not as quiet as the ones over the courtyard. The staff are young, friendly and efficient.

WHERE TO EAT

Valencia is famous for its paella and seafood. There are a number of different types of paella – shellfish paella, *paella valenciana* with chicken, or rabbit, *paella mixta* with both seafood and meat (mainly invented for tourists, but a lot of locals like it too). Rice doesn't only appear in the form of paella, but in a dish called *arroz a banda* (a rice-based dish with seafood), or *arroz negra* (with squid cooked in its ink). *Alioli*, a garlic and oil sauce, is added to everything. Another less common condiment is *ail i pebre* – a pepper and garlic sauce that is served with a fillets of fish or seafood. More often than not you will find it drizzled over *ánguilas* (baby eels). In short, there are as many different sorts of tapas as there are types of shellfish.

In the Historical Centre

✿ Budget

If it's a snack you're after, why not try a sandwich? Valencia is enormously proud of its Mediterranean fast-food chain, **Blanc i negre**. Here, you choose your bread (baguette, roll, wholemeal, white, brown, and so on), your filling and whether you want it hot or cold. Relatively clean and fairly cheap. A basic sandwich costs 3€ with each additional filling costing an extra 1€. There are various Blanc i negre around the town, so keep an eye out for one if you're feeling peckish.

✗ **El Restaurante Cultural** (D2, **31** on map II): calle Conde Motornes 1. The set menu rarely exceeds 6€. Very cheap but the food is not always completely fresh. Don't expect enlightening discussions on recent developments in European constitutional law and other such highbrow topics – the restaurant is named after the neighbouring square, plaza de la Cultura.

✗ **Sidrería El Molinón** (C2, **32** on map II): calle Bolsería 40. ☎ 91-15-38. Open 1–4.30pm and 8pm–midnight. A meal costs less than 6€.

VALENCIA

NORTH

Jardines del Real

U. Politècni

Avenida de

Albalat dels Taro

PLAZA XÚQUER

Facultats

Estadio de Valencia CF

Alameda

Porta de la Mar

PLAZA DE AMÉRICA

PLAZA Turia

P. de Aragón

PLAZA DE SARAGOZA

PLAZA DEL CASTILLO

Avenida Antic Regne de Valencia

P. Angel Custodio

PLAZA MONTEOLIVETE

MONTE OLIVETE

VALENCIA

Av. Hermanos Maristas

You could easily walk past this tiny, narrow bar without noticing it, flanked as it is by numerous, flashier places. People mainly come for the cider, which unlike its Basque equivalent, comes in capped bottles. It is perfect accompanied by a plate of sharp Cabrales cheese.

✕ **Bar Pilar** (C2, **33** on map II): calle Moro Zeit 13. ☎ 91-04-97. Closed on Tuesday. Open 9am–11.30pm. On public holidays it closes in the afternoon. Another classic bar in an area that is busier at night than during the day. People come primarily for a *ración de clochinas* (a seafood dish). Very popular. However, if you peep into the kitchen on your way to the loos you will see that there is scant regard for European health and safety regulations here.

✕ **Los Toneles** (C4, **34** on map II): Ribera 17. ☎ 94-01-81. The bar is mounted on a row of barrels (*toneles*). Next to the station and a good place for some decent tapas.

✕ **Asador Pipol** (C3, **35** on map II): Convento de San Francisco 3. ☎ 94-11-10. Also near the station, behind the Ayuntamiento (town hall), with a big mezzanine floor overlooking the bar. Friendly staff and reasonable prices.

☆☆ **Moderate**

✕ **El Palacio de la Bellota** (C3, **37** on map II): Mosén Femades 7. ☎ 51-49-94. You could easily enjoy a meal at the bar for less than 9€. In addition to the various baskets of onions and potatoes, over 50 hams hang from the ceiling. The whole place has a delightful aroma, and the exquisite ham literally melts in the mouth. You can also buy ham by the kilo to take away. There is a selection of good-quality wine to ʻch.

☆☆☆ **Expensive**

✕ **Ca'n Bermell** (C1, **38** on map II): Sant Tomas 18. ☎ 91-02-88 or 91-89-01. Set menu for 21€. Popular among locals. The prevalent dialect is definitely Valencian here (rather than Castilian Spanish). There is a wide choice of good-quality tapas. This restaurant never disappoints.

✕ **Restaurant Chust Godoy** (D1, **29** on map II): Boix 6. ☎ 91-38-15. Closed Saturday lunchtime and Sunday during Semana Santa (Easter week) and in August. The set menu costs a good 28€. It is inside the Ad Hoc hotel, which only serves to further enhance its charm. The cooking is sophisticated and of a high quality as well as being very well presented. Carmen, the proprietress, keeps a close eye on everything that comes out of the kitchen. To ensure attention to detail, the number of tables is limited to 10. The wine cellar is the pièce de résistance and people come from far and wide just to stock up. Incredibly good value for money given the high standards in terms of quality and service. Highly recommended.

✕ **Ocho y medio** (C2, **40** on map II): plaza Lope de Vega 5. ☎ 92-20-22. Closed on Saturday lunchtime, for a fortnight over Easter and for another two weeks at the beginning of October. A selection of tapas at the bar costs around 12€ and a meal in the restaurant is about double that. Ocho y medio is one of the latest places to be opened by the owner of Gargantua. The interior decor is far less polished than the restaurant with which he made his name. There are sometimes tables outside on the little plaza de Lope de Vega. Excellent *ajoarriero* (cod with potatoes, tomatoes and garlic), and the *esgarrat* is also very good.

South of the Historical Centre

☆ Budget

✗ **Cervecería Villaplana** (A3, **41** on map II): Sanchis Sivera 24. ☎ 25-06-13. A meal costs less than 6€ per person. Closed on Sunday. Down-to-earth ambience, and packed at weekends with people of all ages, shapes and sizes. The room at the rear is very smoky. A good place for a few tapas before a night out in the area. There are also some good homemade pastries.

✗ **Taberna Andaluza El Albero** (A2–3, **42** on map III): calle Ciscar 12, bajo. ☎ 33-74-28. *Raciónes* cost 2–3€. This small bar displays the crests and badges of the farms from which it gets its supplies on its roughcast walls. Its regular clientele eat under the gaze of a small statue of the Virgin. It goes without saying that there is some excellent *jerez*.

✗ **Bar Iruña** (A3, **43** on map III): calle Salamanc, 42. ☎ 33-10-64. A meal costs less than 5€. The tiny shower-cabin style kitchen serves up an appetizing stream of *guisos* (a sort of stew) which is the house speciality. A bit tatty but definitely worth a visit.

✗ **Cervecería Maipi** (A3, **44** on map III): Maestro José Serrano 1. ☎ 73-57-09. A meal costs less than 6€. A small, family-oriented bar, with only five tables and a friendly proprietor called Gabriel (Gabi). Its size makes it an intimate place, where it is easy to meet new people. Delicious *esgarrat* and *ajoarriero* (cod with potatoes, tomatoes and garlic), and tender *solomillo* (sirloin steak). Recommended.

☆☆☆ Expensive

✗ **Gargantua** (A2, **45** on map III): Navarro Reverter 18. ☎ 34-68-49. In an avenue between the plaza de América and M. de Estella. Closed Saturday lunchtime, public holidays, a fortnight over Easter and the last two weeks of August. Set menus start at 24€ and there is a special menu that allows you to try six different dishes for around 31€. No reservations. Very friendly staff. Beautifully sophisticated decor and setting. Several nicely laid-out, pink rooms. A soothing selection of classical music plays discreetly in the background. There is a flowery terrace outside that is used when the weather is fine. The boast at the entrance is 'Imaginative Valencian cuisine' and this just about sums it up. Smooth soups and very tender meat. Try the *lubina* (seabass) with thyme. Very reasonably priced for this level of quality. Highly recommended.

✗ **La Casa Ramón** (B2, **46** on map II): Borrull 32. ☎ 91-50-24. Closed Sunday evening and Monday. One of the best shellfish places in Valencia – the seafood is delicious and very well presented. Avoid the room at the rear as it has a more formal atmosphere. The welcome is fairly warm and the waiters chat to the clients as they lean on the bar. The local *tunas* (traditional student music groups) often come here to serenade diners and earn a bit of cash.

In the Xúquer and Cabanyals Areas and By the Sea

✗ **Casa Montaña** (D3, **47** on map III): José Benlliure 69. ☎ 67-23-14. Open 10am–3pm and 7–11pm. Closed Sunday evening and Monday. A meal costs less than 9€. By far the best place to eat in this area. A delightful *bodega* full of barrels, covered in old enamelled advertising boards singing the praises of the big-name Spanish brands of anise and sherry. The wines are served by the glass and all the house specialities are written on slates that are scattered around the bar and tables.

✕ **Casa Guillermo** (D3, **48** on map III): calle José Benlliure 26. ☎ 67-38-25. Closed Saturday and Sunday lunchtime. A meal costs less than 9€. Casa Guillermo is home to a fine anchovy dish where they come served in olive oil with a few slices of garlic – a real treat.

✕ **Bar J. Flor** (D2, **49** on map III): calle Marti Grajales 21. ☎ 71-20-19. Set menu for less than 9€. If you're feeling hungry when you come out of the Cabanyals market, this little bar offering home-cooked traditional fare is a welcome sight. Reserve in advance if possible, as contrary to appearances, it gets very busy.

✕ **El Pescadito** (B3, **50** on map III): Padre Tomás Montañana 2. ☎ 60-39-48. A bit expensive considering its location – opening onto the noisy avenue along the port – and of little interest in terms of decor (white walls and neon lighting), this big canteen-style restaurant offers a wide choice of seafood. From the bar you can watch your *gambas* (prawns) being grilled (*a la plancha*) as the kitchen is right in the middle of the restaurant.

✕ **La Pepica** (D3, **51** on map III): paseo Neptuno 6. ☎ 71-03-66. Set menu for around 20€, paella for less than 7€. A big restaurant reminiscent of a ballroom with its noisy, lively ambience and mouldings lit by bright neon lights. The service is incredibly efficient, from the moment they take your order to the second the waiters pass through the swing doors leading to the ovens and the big *paelleras*. The rice dishes have a very good reputation. Reservations recommended.

✕ **El Famos** (**52**, off map III from C1): Ermita de Vera 14. ☎ 71-00-28. To get there, make your way to the Universidad Politécnica (you can get there on foot or by bus or metro), go past the departamento de Bellas Artes towards the sea and take the first on the left – if you reach the railway line you have gone too far. Closed on Monday. Paella costs just over 7€. The restaurant is set at the foot of a small church, almost hidden between the irrigation channels and market gardens. From the outside, it looks like you are going onto the veranda of a private home. Inside, there is a wide choice of seafood, *arroz a banda, ail i pebre, conill al ail* (garlic rabbit), *conill a la braza* (grilled rabbit) and Valencian paella cooked over a wood fire. The prices aren't exactly competitive but you can still get good value for money. At weekends it is best to reserve in advance.

WHERE TO EAT IN THE SURROUNDING AREA

In El Palmar (46012)

El Palmar is 15 kilometres (10 miles) from Valencia. To get there, head in the direction of El Saler (there are buses every hour with the Herca bus company; departures from Gran Vía Marqués del Túria, between calle Sueca and calle Cuba, every two hours between noon and 8pm) then continue towards Cullera. Another bus leaves from the same spot and covers the Valencia–El Perelló stretch. The bus passes through the outskirts ~ Albufera, an area that offers some attractive walks. It picks up for the ~urney at the same place it drops passengers off and runs every day, ~ every 30 minutes.

This small village, so typical of the Valencia region, offers one of the best Valencia paellas you will ever eat. The atmosphere has become a little touristy, but plenty of Valencian families come here at weekends to eat. El Palmar was once a fishing village but now makes most of its money from its restaurants. Unfortunately the local restaurateurs don't seem to buy directly from the local fishermen, who generally sell their catches to the market in Valencia.

The seafood restaurants jostle for position all the way along the two main streets, calle Sequiota and calle Recollins. Many of them are housed in typical fishermen's huts with whitewashed walls and thatched roofs.

✖ **Planta Azul**: Francisco Monleón 29. ☎ (961) 62-01-48 or (961) 62-03-25. Set menu from around 12€. A big restaurant with room for about 400 diners. The decor is nothing special – cold neon lighting and black and white mosaic tiling on the floor. On the other hand, the cuisine is fantastic. All the dishes – paella, *fideua*, *arroz a banda* and *mariscada* (seafood and grilled fish) – are plentiful and very tasty.

✖ **Bon Aire**: Caudete 41. ☎ (961) 62-03-10 or 62-01-33. Closed on Tuesday in winter. The set menu costs around 10€. The dining room is slightly more intimate that at the Planta Azul, with room for 200 diners, and is preceded by an open kitchen decorated with mosaics. Unassuming welcome from the open, friendly staff.

GOING OUT

Going out at night in Valencia is almost obligatory if you really want to get to know the city, which has the reputation for being the most party-loving in Spain. You will see crowds of people enjoying a riotous evening out. And not only at weekends, as Valencian's enjoy themselves on mid-week evenings as well. In some areas, particularly El Carmen, you may well wonder just how many people can cram themselves into such a small area. Everyone spills outside the bars and onto the pavements and the road where they mingle happily.

Timing is important if you are going out for the evening. If you arrive too early, you may well find the place completely empty. An hour too late and everything is already closed. Where the bars are concerned, things don't really get going much before 1–1.30am. The nightclubs only begin to fill up at around 3am – in fact they don't even open much before then.

Finally, even if you have your own car, take a taxi if you want to enjoy a hassle-free night out. They are cheap and avoid the trauma of searching for a parking place, only to find you are blocked in by another vehicle when you want to leave, and of worrying about drinking and driving. There are so many cars on the streets in the evening in Valencia that some park in the middle of crossroads, so forming temporary, unplanned nocturnal roundabouts.

As in most big cities, there are a number of different areas to head for. Some cater predominantly for adolescents (you can't miss the ear-splitting music), others are aimed more at business people, but most have dance floors where people salsa the night away to Latin American music.

In the Cánovas Area (A2 on map III)

This area extends either side of Gran Vía Marques de Túria. It is of little architectural interest, despite being only five minutes from the historical centre. During the day, no-one would give it a second glance. At night, however, the streets are so busy you would think they were pedestrian.

❣ Mentiroso (A2, **80** on map III): calle Serrano Morales. A long, narrow bar, with a pool table at the end, particularly lively late at night. If you've got the head for it, try the gorgeous iced champagne cocktail.
❣ El Dopo (A2, **81** on map III): calle Serrano Morales. All black and white. The ideal place to sample a *manzana* (apple) or *melocotón* (peach) liqueur.
❣ Batucada (A2, **82** on map III): calle Serrano Morales. If you love Latin American music, this is one of the best places for salsa and merengue.

In the El Carmen Area

The El Barrio del Carmen or El Carmen area, as it is known, was dismissed for a long time in favour of Cánovas. Now, however, it is beginning to fight back and is becoming very popular among Valencian yuppies, especially as other areas have been 'cleaned up'. There are a few bars that vie with each other to have the most sophisticated decor, but all serve drinks that are far from cheap. It is popular with the younger crowd, but there are also a few dodgy characters who hang out around here too. There are definite boundaries to this area, which you'll be aware of as soon as you cross them. For instance, if you head north of plaza San Jaime, the atmosphere suddenly gets a lot less fragrant. Despite this, El Carmen remains an attractive part of the city.

❣ Ghecko (C2, **83** on map II): plaza del Negrito 2. One of the area's top bars in terms of decor. The bar is named after the big lizards from the island of Kathakali, near Bali. The bars themselves are made out of two great slabs of glass with pebbles laid out beneath them. There is an immense Chinese dragon at the bar and statues of praying women on the way into the loos. The sound system is excellent and the music is predominantly soul and R'n'B. Mirrors on the walls mean you can watch people coming and going wherever you are sitting. The drinks aren't particularly cheap, but it is worth a visit just to admire the decor.
❣ Johnny Maracas (C2, **84** on map ... Caballeros 39. ☎ 91-52-66. ...ain, the bar itself is the ...raction. It is actually a 20-metre fish tank that is full of guppies and goldfish. This is the trendiest place around and if you go on a Saturday, you'll need to fight for a place at the bar so you can even order a drink. Maracas hang on the wall and Johnny gets them down from time to time to shake along to the Latin, mambo and salsa sounds. Even the loos are trendy here. As you might expect from a bar like this, it has a good collection of rum. Try the Black Death – fatal!
❣ Pitapeira (C2, **85** on map II): calle Caballeros 27. On the corner of calle Mendoza. A hot, sticky atmosphere, like a boat on the muddy waters of the Amazon. The decor consists of exposed metal beams, a mezzanine level in matt steel and un-rendered bricks. The sort of place where you ask for a beer rather than a cocktail.

Fox Congo (C2, **86** on map II): Caballeros 35. ☎ 92-55-27. Rather tacky decor but the combination of polished copper sheet and a big white marble bar lit from below makes it fairly cool all the same. Tasteful Euro-pop, disco, techno and jungle. The clientele is mainly well-dressed 30-somethings and it is popular with the gay crowd. A pleasant place for a relaxing drink.

Café Bolsería (C2, **87** on map II): Bolsería 41. ☎ 91-89-03. Wrought iron and tropical plants and small blue lamps on the mahogany-look tables. Even more chic than the others.

Café Negrito (C2, **88** on map II): plaza del Negrito. Open until 6am at the weekend. Its tables and chairs take over the whole plaza. A great place for a drink.

Hannase Al Babal (C1–2, **89** on map II): Caballeros. A section of medieval wall is still visible in this bar laid out over several levels. The place to see and be seen for the Valencian jet set. There are sometimes theme nights with drag queens and scantily clad gogo dancers, wearing multicoloured wigs. The music is deafening jungle when

it turns into a nightclub in the early hours of the morning. An excellent place that lives up to its reputation.

El Carmen Sui Generis (C1–2, **90** on map II): on the corner of calle Caballeros 38 and the plaza San Jaime 9. ☎ 92-52-73. Open from 7pm. This 18th-century palace, incorporating an 11th-century Arab wall has been the object of very careful restoration work. The bricks match the glass and the mahogany-look tables to perfection. Not the sort of venue for a night out with the lads, but the perfect place to take someone you are trying to impress.

Jimmy Glass Jazz (C1, **91** on map II): calle Baja. This jazz bar makes a change from the rest of the Valencian nightlife scene. Sometimes there are jamming sessions and live bands in this relaxing blues environment. Small pool table.

Finnegan's of Dublin (C2, **93** on map II): this bar on plaza de la Reina – crowded with buses during the day, but quiet and pleasant at night – gets packed at the weekend. As its name implies, this is an Irish bar with dark wood and glass partitions dividing the bar area. A good place for beer lovers.

In The Juan Llorens Area (A3 On Map I)

An alternative port of call for young people bored of El Carmen.

Havana Club (A3, **95** on map II): Juan Llorens 41. ☎ 84-38-40. Closed on Sunday evening and Monday. Luxurious space with live bands every Thursday evening. The ambience is cool, funky soul and acid jazz at the start of the evening, with Latin music getting everyone onto the dance floor later on. If you're a salsa fan, this is the place for you – a magazine, called *Salsa noticias*, is distributed, listing the

latest news on everything that's happening on the salsa scene in Valencia. Very friendly atmosphere.

Carioca (A3, **96** on map II): Juan Llorens 52. Whatever the case, you'll either love or hate this place. Lots of flashy colours and short pillars, decorated with masks. Regular theme nights. Music and *agua de Valencia* (a subtle mixture of orange juice, vodka, Cointreau and champagne).

In the Xúquer Area (B1 On Map II)

The area is named after the plaza Xúquer (not on the map). This square and avenida Blasco Ibáñez (not on the map) are the areas to head for to find the bars and nightclubs. This was once one of the liveliest areas, but the inhabitants started complaining about the noise and the local authorities amenably classified it an 'area of silence'. Worth a visit if you're in the area.

In the Malvarossa Area

Next door to the port and right beside the Malvarossa beach from which the area takes its name, a lot of people come here at the weekend and in summer. At other times, the nightlife is mostly confined to calle Eugenia Vines, which is lined with numerous but largely uninteresting bars. In summer, bars are set up on outdoor stands while sound systems pump enough loud music into the street to turn it into an outdoor nightclub.

Caballito de Mar and Flamingo are just a couple of the places that open on a temporary basis, mainly in summer.

NIGHTCLUBS

– **Los Jardínes del Real** (D1 on map II): home to a nightclub popular among the yuppie fraternity. As elsewhere, impromptu celebrations often turn into raves. Ask around in the record and clothes shops for information about the next party.

– **Venial** (B2, **98** on map II): calle de Quart. Admission is quite pricey at 9€. No point getting there much before 3am. The only nightclub in the centre – theoretically for the gay crowd but open to anyone who is around in the early hours of the morning.

– **La Calcatta** (C2, **99** on map II): Reloj Viejo 4. ☎ (669) 42-67-27. Closed from Sunday to Thursday in August. Don't turn up before 1am. A nice little place with its old stone staircase leading up to the first floor and a central patio. Admission is free but drinks are expensive.

– **El Gran Caimán** (B4, **100** on map II): Convento de Jerusalém 55. ☎ 42-34-62. From Wednesday to Sunday 11.30pm–6am. No point in arriving much before 2am as this is the time when people wander over from the bars in El Carmen to dance to the sound of mambo and merengue. Reasonable admission charge and packed with muscular blokes. The venue isn't great, but the ambience is hot.

– **Woody** (B1, **101** on map III): Menéndez y Pelayo 25. ☎ 61-85-61. You can't miss its two-storey pink and blue neon facade. It is a very young place and frankly nothing special on the inside where, with the exception perhaps of the small stainless steel stage, nothing seems to have changed for years.

For Techno-lovers

Valencia is renowned for its techno scene (*bacalao*). If you've done the rounds of its famed seafood restaurants during the day, why not do a '*bacalao* trail' in the evening?

– There are a dozen or so nightclubs on the way out to El Saler, the best known are perhaps **Chocolate**, **RDC** (on the Madrid road) and **Barraca**.

LEISURE

– The weekly listings magazine *Valencia Semanal* gives a good selection of what is on – from art exhibitions to concerts, without adverts or lengthy articles. *Que y Donde* comes out every Monday giving a slightly more rough and ready summary of what is happening at cinemas, theatres, concert venues and exhibition halls. *La Túria* has a more underground feel to it and gives you some good ideas about what to do and where to go in terms of Valencian nightlife.

Cinemas

■ If you prefer to see films in their original language, the **Filmoteca de la Generalidad Valenciana** (in the edificio Rialto, plaza del Ayuntamiento 17; C3 on map II) shows numerous undubbed movies, generally of the alternative, art-house variety. ☎ 51-23-36. Nominal admission fee, less than 2€.

Conventional Cinemas
■ **Babel**: calle Vicente Sancho Tello 10. ☎ 62-67-95.

■ **Albatros**: plaza Fray Luis Colomer 4. ☎ 93-26-77.

■ **Aragón**: avenida del Puerto 1. ☎ 37-12-11.

■ **Metropol**: calle Hernán Cortés 9. ☎ 51-53-38.

Some show films that are subtitled rather than dubbed. The first programme generally begins around 4pm. As a general rule, tickets costs 4–5€, concessions less than 2€.

WHAT TO SEE

★ **La Catedral** (C2, **110** on map II): shorts are forbidden, at least in theory. Work on this cathedral, which was built on the site of a mosque, was begun in the 13th century and completed in the 15th in the Gothic style. It then underwent extensive alterations in the 18th century, all of which has culminated in rather a strange exterior – on the calle Palau side, there is a Romanesque porch, in the Plaza de la Virgen a Gothic doorway, and in the Plaza de Zaragoza a superb baroque facade. To one side the Miguelete (or Micalet as the Valencians call it), a tall Gothic tower, rises up into the sky. You can climb it (open 10am–1pm and 4–7pm; reasonable admission charge) to admire the cruciform layout of the church, its elegant pinnacles with blue glazed tiles and for the view over the old town.

Inside, at the transept crossing, there is an elegant lantern tower with Gothic windows. The Capilla del Santo Cáliz (Chapel of the Holy Grail) definitely deserves a visit – an old chapter house with a magnificently rich florid Gothic relief framing the chalice from which Christ was purported to have drunk at the Last Supper. You then pass on to the cathedral museum, open 10am–2pm and 4.30–6pm; Saturday 10am–1pm. Closed Sunday and public holidays. Admission costs about 1€. It contains several early religious paintings, some beautiful statuary, highly ornate ritual vessels and monstrances, early printed books and two superb paintings by Goya.

In front of the puerta de los Apóstoles (door of the Apostles), every Thursday at 12 noon the *Tribunal de las Aguas* takes place. Since the Middle Ages, the magistrates of the eight canals of the Huerta have gathered in a small circle enclosed by a barrier, to discuss any problems or disputes arising out of the distribution of irrigation water. They wear the typical black peasant's smock of the region and are elected by their associates for a two-year term. In times of plenty, there are few conflicts but in times of drought each person can use only an amount of water proportional to the surface area of their land. Anyone (and this could be one of the magistrates too) who breaches this understanding can be reported and summoned before the Thursday tribunal. The magistrates then discuss the validity of the complaint, the magnitude of the offence and the severity of the punishment. The judgement is verbal and nothing is written down. After deliberating, the president announces the sentence, to which there is no appeal. It is important to arrive on time because there are often no cases to be heard and the session is over in a matter of minutes.

★ In the immediate vicinity of the cathedral is the chapel of **Nuestra Virgen de los Desamparados**, which houses the statue of the Virgin who is patron of the city. The chapel has a painted cupola dating from the 18th century.

Down Carrer de Palau, the **Palacio de los Almirantes de Aragón** has a magnificent patio with a gracefully constructed well. **Carrer del Cavallers** (Calle de los Caballeros) is lined with some beautiful stately homes.

La iglesia de San Nicolás, on Calle Abadia, is one of the oldest churches in Valencia. There are some paintings inside and an attractive *retablo* (altar-piece).

★ **El Palacio de la Generalidad** (C1, **111** on map II): on the other side of the Plaza de la Virgen, entrance via Calle de los Caballeros 2. As a rule, visiting hours are Monday to Friday, 9am–2pm; but in fact it is better to call and arrange a visit: ☎ 86-34-61. It has one of the most beautiful Gothic courtyards in the city. The Sala Dorada has a gilded Renaissance coffered ceiling. The Salón de Cortes is typical of 17th-century Spanish design. Opposite stands the **palacio del marqués de la Scala**.

★ **La Lonja** (C2, **112** on map II): Plaza del Mercado. Open Tuesday to Friday 9am–2pm and 4–6pm; Saturday and Sunday 9am–1.30pm. Closed Monday. Admission is free. Ancient silk-merchants' exchange, built in the 15th century in a splendidly flamboyant Gothic style. The interior architecture has an unusual elegance, with cabled columns soaring up to delicate arches. The gilded and polychrome coffered ceiling of the Consulado del Mar is also a superb sight. Opposite is the imposing Italian baroque-style facade of the **iglesia de los Santos Juanes** and the **Mercado Central** (central market), an immense steel monument to the Modernist era. This combination of architectural styles is very attractive. It is here that, in the three weeks before the Fallas that the famous exhibition of the *ninots* takes place (*see* 'Fiestas – *las Fallas*'), an admission fee is charged during the exhibition.

★ **El Museo Nacional de Cerámica González Martí** (C2, **113** on map II): Rinconada de Garcia Sanchis. ☎ 51-63-92. A small road leading off the carrer del Poeta Querol. Open Tuesday to Saturday 10am–2pm and 4–6pm, and Sunday morning. Closed Monday. Free for under 21s. The museum occupies the old palacio del marqués de dos Aguas. Splendidly exuberant facade from the height of rococo period.

Superb collections of ceramics of all kinds from the Iberian period to modern times. The graceful popular ware from Manises is particularly noteworthy. The ground floor contains 17th-century Valencian tiled friezes depicting scenes of country life. On the first floor there are some beautiful Catalan and religious ceramics, as well as depictions of craftsmen and labourers at work. You can't miss the highly kitsch piece of furniture in the corridor with its porcelain legs adorned with cherubs. On the second floor, there is an excellent reconstruction of a Valencian kitchen. If you are not too tired, wander round the last rooms at the back where there is an interesting exhibition of caricatures, cartoons, engravings and etchings.

★ **El Museo de Bellas Artes** (D1, **114** on map II): on the San Pio V embankment. ☎ 60-57-93. On the riverbank between the Puente Trinidad and the Puente del Real. Open 9am–2pm and 4–6pm; Sunday, public holidays and in August, 9am–2pm. Free with an international student card. One of the most beautiful museums in Spain, housed in an ancient monastery. The Valencian religious primitives and Renaissance works are of particular interest. There is a shaded patio on which to recuperate during very hot weather.

– Ground floor: a small archaeological section and a large sculpture department. A few of the things to look out for include a striking 16th-century alabaster statue of St Vincent with his guts hanging out; a romantic, tousle-headed statue of Vicente Domenech, a big Valencian hero who raised the first cry of revolt against the French occupation; the plaster original of the mausoleum of a bullfighter killed in the ring (of considerable expressionistic realism).

– First floor: in the cool and attractive setting of the completely renovated monastery (fine stone against a white background), a mass of retables and triptychs (with small explanatory notices to test your Spanish). Fray Bonifacio Ferrer's magnificent altarpiece, set in a room with a richly sculpted ceiling, reveals an Italian influence in Valencian art.

There is a triptych by Hieronymus Bosch depicting the Mocking of Christ; an El Greco Christ; many works by Ribalta, father of tenebrism in Spain along with Ribera, whose *Martyrdom of St Sebastian* can also be seen here, plus works by Murillo, Morales el Divino and a self-portrait of Velázquez. There is an entire room devoted to major works by Goya. Valencian Impressionists on the second floor have a tough time of it after so many masterpieces and, if it isn't more than you can take, go up to the top floor to see some good examples of modern Valencian paintings such as the heroic *Visión del Coloseo* by José Benlliure Gil.

★ As you leave the museum, note the Gothic architecture of the **Puente del Real** bridge (D1, **115** on map II), built in the 16th century. There is a beautiful perspective of all the bridges that cross the Turia riverbed from here. The river no longer flows through the city because, as a result of the dangers and problems caused by flooding in winter, it was diverted using a manmade canal to force it to by-pass the city to the south. The old river bed was drained and converted into a public park with football pitches, tennis courts and a magnificently well-integrated modern concert hall. If you are directed to the río Turia, don't expect to find any water.

Other Places of Interest

★ **El Colegio del Patriarca** (D3, **116** on map II): carrer de la Nave 1. ☎ 51-41-76. Open every day, 11am–1.30pm only. Moderate admission fee. This museum is housed in a former seminary dating from the 16th century and boasting some delicate cloisters. It contains a number of works of great value, including one of El Greco's most beautiful paintings, *The Adoration of the Shepherds*; the triptych of the *Passion* by Dieric Bouts; as well as paintings by Ribalta, Morales el Divino, Jan Gossaert (also known as Mabuse) and numerous Valencian primitives. In the chapel there are some Flemish tapestries. In the adjacent church there is a Friday Mass sung for anyone who wishes to attend. At about 10.10am, the wonderful *Last Supper* by Ribalta is removed from the high altar to make way for a crucifix. Opposite the Colegio del Patriarca is the old university.

★ **El Museo Histórico** (C3, **117** on map II): plaza del Ayuntamiento 1. In the Ayuntamiento (town hall). Open 9am–2pm. Closed on Saturday, Sunday and public holidays. Only of interest to anyone who is very keen on history. There are a few items of exceptional historical value including rare manuscripts such as the Libre del Consolat del Mar (book of the maritime tribunal of 1409) and the 'banner of the Reconquest' which flew over Valencia after the departure of the Moors in the 13th century. This is the *senyara* – the pride of Valencia – which is brought out on grand occasions and hung from the front of the town hall. This is a delicate task as the pole hangs vertically and must be completely straight – Valencian pride dictates that the *senyara* should never bow its head. Only Juan Carlos and Sofía, on a visit after their coronation, were entitled to a slight, respectful inclination.

★ **El Museo de las Fallas** (A4, **118** on map III): plaza de Monteolivete 4. Open Tuesday to Friday 10am–2pm and 4–7pm; Saturday, Sunday and public holidays 10am–2pm. Closed on Mondays; for the entire month of August and afternoons in September. The museum was supposed to move to new premises a long time ago but the provisional ones seem to have become semi-permanent. If you are not fortunate enough to be present during the Valencian *Fallas* festival, you can get an idea of what it is like at this museum. Home of the *ninots*, mock-ups of satirical scenes using giant figures (*see below* 'Fiestas – Las Fallas') that have won the annual competition for the best floats displayed during the Fallas festivities and are consequently saved from the flames. Wacky and original creations, such as the 1969 float '*Peligro de un parte multiple*', dedicated to the dangers of free love, and the 1961 float concerning the joys of family life. It also has a fine collection of posters and float designs.

★ **Instituto Valenciano de Arte Moderno, IVAM** (Museum of Modern Art; B1, **119** on map II): free admission on Sunday. A newly opened museum dedicated to recent and contemporary Spanish artists. It is divided into two sections:

– The **Julio González Centre**: calle Guillem de Castro 118. ☎ 86-30-00. Open Tuesday to Sunday, 11am–8pm. A big, very modern building, with white tiling throughout. The works of Julio González and Pinazo are permanently on show here and there are also some very fine temporary exhibitions of modern and contemporary artists (Torres García, for example).

– the **Del Carme Centre**: calle Museo 2. Open Tuesday to Sunday, noon–2.30pm and 4.30–8pm. Housed in one of the oldest cloisters in the town dating back to the 13th century. It has been completely restored and is dedicated to the promotion of local artists through temporary exhibitions. It also aims to give an insight into the current international art scene.

★ **Palau de la Música** (A3, **120** on map III): situated between the Aragón and Angel Custodio bridges, this gigantic building constructed in 1988 rightly deserves be called a palace. Built of marble and glass, and surrounded by extraordinary, lush gardens, which, when seen from outside, make it look like an exotic conservatory, the concert hall takes on the appearance of a fairy-tale palace, especially when it is lit up at night (although it is affectionately nicknamed the *micro-ondas* – the microwave – by locals!). It is equally exceptional inside. The ultra-modern main auditorium has brilliantly clear acoustics. The concerts given here are carefully planned and, as with many cultural activities in Valencia, performances by major internationally renowned artistes are alternated with those of young Spanish musicians.

★ There are several churches worth taking a look at, including **Santo Domingo** (D2, **121** on map II; plaza de Tetuán), a former royal chapel with a superb cloister and chapter house, **San Martín** (carrer San Vicente), with its 15th-century Flemish bronze facade, and **San Tomás** (plaza San Vicente Ferrer) – exuberantly baroque in style.

★ Also worth a visit is the **Las Reales Atarazanas** (D3 on map III): plaza de Juan Antonio Benlliure. Just beside the church of Santa Maria del Mar. Open Tuesday to Saturday, 9.30am–2pm and 5.30–9pm, and Sunday morning. Free entry. Beautiful building in which temporary exhibitions are held. The building itself is interesting for its *ladrillos* (brickwork) and concave roof.

★ Other museums of note include the **Museo de Etnología y Prehistoria** (Ethnology and Prehistory) in the Centro Cultural La Beneficencia (free admission), not to mention the **Museo Paleontológico** (palaeontology museum), the **Museu Taurino** (bullfighting museum) and a maritime museum, to name but a few. Further details are available from the Tourist Office.

★ There is plenty more to see if you wander the streets of the historical centre of this vibrant city. Take a look at the magnificent **Torre de Serrano** (C1, **123** on map II), the most beautiful Gothic gate in the city. To the west of the centre, you will find the **Torre de Quart**, which bears the marks of Napoleon's cannon ball fire.

★ **Ciudad de las Artes y las Ciencias** – Arts and Sciences City (B4, **125** on map III) Arzobispo Mayoral 14–2. Website: www.cac.es. On the southern outskirts of the city, near the El Saler motorway interchange. Buses 13, 14 and 15.

Santiago Calatrava

The building of the Arts and Sciences City is the most important project in the architect Santiago Calatrava's career to date. Born in 1951 in the Valencian town of Benimanet, he is known for his love of geometric design. Valencia's prodigal son took an degree in architecture in Spain then moved to Zurich to complete an engineering doctorate. He seeks inspiration from nature, combining natural forms with an almost Scandinavian simplicity. Calatrava cut his teeth on a series of spectacular bridges – in Switzerland, France, Spain and Britain – followed by increasingly important projects such as the extraordinary train station in Lyon, another train station in Zurich, the Kuwaiti Pavilion at the Seville Expo, decorative elements of the church of Saint John The Divine in New York and the Tenerife auditorium. To crown his success, Calatrava received one of Spain's most prestigious accolades in May 2000 – the Príncipe de Asturias Award for the Arts.

Setting of the Art and Sciences City

By building this City in the former riverbed of the Turia kills two birds with one stone. On the one hand it overcomes the problem of the marginalization of districts that were previously cut off from the port by disused factories, while on the other, it makes good use of the land left after the Turia was diverted away from the city. It also has a symbolic role, casting the old river bed as the new river of knowledge. It is hoped that La Ciudad de las Artes y de las Ciencias (Arts and Science City) will be to Valencia what the Guggenheim is to Bilbao; a place that puts Valencia on the map and integrates it with modern Spain (something that football is already doing). It took around four years to bring the project to fruition, from the inception of the idea to the laying of the first stone. The completed Park will not be open until 2002 when the Palacio de las Artes has finally been completed.

Calatrava's design covers an area of more than 350,000 square metres (3,766,000 square feet). It's like a futuristic city within a city. It is made up of four buildings: the Hemisfèric and the Museo de las Ciencias Príncipe Felipe (both already open), the Palacio de las Artes and the Océanográfico.

What to See

★ **L'Hemisferic**: ☎ 902-100-031. Reservations: ☎ 99-55-77. Open Monday to Friday, 10.30am–9.30pm (midnight on Friday), Saturday noon to midnight and Sunday noon–9.30pm. Admission costs about 7€ per session; reductions for students, the under 12s and various other concessions, except on Sunday and public holidays. The film programme can be found in the back pages of El País, El Mundo or El Levante.

L'Hemisfèric is the only venue in Europe capable of combining laser shows, a planetarium and Imax films. This cinema, the smallest building in the Park, is shaped like an eye. Its eyelids (quarter circles composed of glass and white steel frames) rest on an artificial lake and can fold back in twenty minutes. The illusion is very effective. As the lid pulls back, it reveals the bowl-shaped building that surrounds the main hall inside. The 900 square metres (9,684 square feet) concave screen allows spectators to enjoy the excitement of the show while sitting on banks of seats raked at a 30° angle. The films and shows have a sound-track in four different languages. Before you leave, take a look around the right-hand side of the hall where you can see the machinery. The spools of film are so large that they have to be transported by fork-lift trucks!

★ **El Museo de las Ciencias Príncipe Felipe**: Monday to Thursday 10am–8pm, and Friday to Sunday 10am–9pm. Entrance costs 6€ for the day, the usual concessions apply. The Science Museum is an imposing building covering 41,000 square metres (441,160 square feet). Although architecturally speaking it is not particularly adventurous, its white concrete honeycombed facade diffuses a gentle light throughout the interior.

★ **El Palacio de las Artes**: at the time of writing, the last steel reinforcement bars were being put into place. It may well be open to visitors by the time you visit the park.

★ **El Parque Océanográfico**: an underwater park that allows visitors to explore different marine habitats, based on the theme of 'seas of the world'. It will contain flora and fauna grouped according to their specific environments (polar, tropical, Mediterranean and Atlantic, among others).

FIESTAS – *LAS FALLAS*

This is a huge event in Valencia. Every year it attracts several million visitors and always takes place during the week preceding 19 March, which is Saint Joseph's day. If you want to stay in or near Valencia during this week, you will need to book several months in advance as everything will be full long before the festival begins. Note also, that the whole of the centre of Valencia is closed to traffic (other than buses) during this week, so arrange to come by public transport, not car. Once there, look for festival supplements in the local newspapers (*El Levante, El Mercantil Valenciano, Las Provincias* and *El País*), which publish good guides to the different *fallas* – where they are located, the category of the competition, the *fallero* artist, and so on. In addition, event sponsors publish pocket guides that are available free in bars and Tourist Offices.

Origins of the Festival

The origins of this popular festival are not clear. The popular explanation is that, in the 18th century, joiners and carpenters used to build large platforms on which to put the lamps that illuminated their workshops. In spring when the days got longer, the racks, shavings and off-cuts from the long winter months were burned on the day of their patron saint. From this came the custom of dressing up the racks, turning them into caricatures and so on. However it is not certain that this is the true origin as the custom of parading statues through the streets and lighting celebratory bonfires between the first Sunday in Lent and Easter Saturday existed elsewhere in Europe, despite the papacy's attempts to eradicate any vestiges of paganism.

In other Valencian, Catalan and Balearic towns and villages, straw effigies were burned during Lent to ward off misfortune to both people and animals, and to dispel witchcraft. There is evidence that shows that this tradition developed when people began to repopulate the region in the 13th century, after the Black Death, and continued through the generations until the end of the 19th century. The statues themselves were a result of Valencian satire, according to some historians. They argue that this was the only weapon the lower classes had against their masters and so mirth served a serious purpose – trivializing life's hardships and disparaging the people who caused them at the same time. Before long the authorities became uncomfortable with these practices and in 1885, the *concejales* of Valencia tried to suppress the festival which they claimed was 'uncultured and inappropriate in a serious and important capital city'. The dictatorship found it equally threatening and the pro-Francoists, through their archbishop, tried to suppress the festival by attempting to reduce it to the level of vulgar folklore.

Ninots and Casals

The *Fallas* is not a single festival, but several events overlapping one another. It all begins in the town's districts where people organize themselves into commissions known as *falleras*. These are set up in the 300 or so *casals* or local clubs where people gather together to watch football, dance, drink and chat. It is often on such occasions that the commissions come up with the idea for the float, which will eventually end up being burnt. The idea is mapped out on the *boceto* (sketch) and when it is approved, the *fallero* artist constructs a 1:20 model known as the *ninot*. To try and win the competition, some commissions try to raise huge sums of money, sometimes up to 32 million pesetas, to produce the best possible float. Not all of them have such high budgets, though, and those who can't afford to pay for a special artist have to design and create it themselves. For the 2000 festival, the Junta Fallera de Valencia (the organization that co-ordinates the event) recorded 456 entries. The competition is divided into seven categories, ranging from the special section (the most popular) with a prize of 3 million pesetas (18,293€), to the seventh and last category with a prize of just 20,000 pesetas (122€). It goes without saying that many do not recoup their expenses and more and more are resorting to sponsorship.

The *ninots* created by professionals are instantly distinguishable from the homemade ones, and you can easily spot the almost fanatical care that has been taken over the detail of the plastic moulding of the faces, the draping of the clothing and the intricate design of the friezes and supports. The giant effigies that are eventually built from the scale model, can reach more than 15 metres (49 feet) in height and are basically satirical, and often malicious, 3-D cartoons. Until the *plantá*, the day when all the sections of the float are put together, the *ninot* is kept in a workshop outside the town. Whereas, in days gone by, wood and plaster were the main materials used to build the full-sized *fallas*, today fibreglass, polyester and other synthetic materials are used to make the structures lighter and easier to assemble.

Fallero Artists

Traditionally, the most long-established rivalry is between the clubs of Na Jordana and El Pilar. The two districts, which are fanatical participants, fight over artists such as Julio Monterrubio, Miguel Santaeulalia, Paco López Albert and Juan Carlos Molés. There is no censorship, so the artists can really go to town. For example, one depicted the mayoress of Valencia, Rita Barberá, on all fours dressed from head to foot in sado-masochistic attire being whipped by Jordi Pujol. But not all the themes are of a sexual nature – far from it. There has been caustic criticism of anorexic girls, depictions of the mutants that might be created because of genetic engineering and even sacrilegious ideas like the one entitled the 'Jesus Harem', which came from the Jerusalem district of Valencia. Every construction is 'captioned' with short comments indicating the commission's ironic intentions. At the base of the main *fallas*, there is usually a smaller, children's *falla*, so that everyone gets to take part. *Fallero* artists are always kept very busy and their success can bring opportunities outside Spain. In the past, artists have left Spain seduced by the allure of Hollywood. Regino Mas, one of the most famous of the *fallero* artists and a native of Valencia, is one example of this. He went on to build sets for films like *The Fall of the Roman Empire* and has also been involved in designing and decorating casinos in Las Vegas, which are famed for their exotic and fantastical interiors.

Falleras

The *Fallas* would not be the same without the *falleras*. Several months before the beginning of the festival, each club enters the most attractive young woman in its area for the beauty pageant. She then surrounds herself with a throng of companions. The club also enters a young girl of around 10 years of age, to participate in a similar children's competition. An assembly made up of the presidents of the clubs then elects the *Fallera Mayor* and the *Mayor Infantil* – the Carnival Queen and Princess. These lucky girls then become the ambassadresses of the Valencian *Fallas*.

Costumed in 18th-century courtly dress, the *falleras* vie to out-dazzle and out-do each other on the parade. Considerable sums of money are spent on their finery. It is estimated that the *falleras mayores* spend between 1.5 and 2 million pesetas on material for their silk gowns, jewellery, gold combs and shawls. *Espolín*, a fine embroidered silk, is one of the biggest expenses of the budget. Less extravagant competitors may buy synthetic material but the most demanding commission a tailor to embroider one with a special motif by hand at a rate of 20 centimetres a day. On top of this, other expenses must be met by the *fallera*'s entourage, including a cameraman or photographer, and dinner for the club at one of the town's more select restaurants. These carnival queens are extremely proud of their responsibility, especially as it enables them to rub shoulders with the town's most important people. Some of them even manage to take advantage of their 'reign' to network with potential business contacts. Although the role is perhaps now beginning to lose its prestige, many end up by becoming journalists and, in the case of Sandra Clement, principal private secretary to the president of the Generalitat, the Catalan parliament.

Mascletá

The *mascletá* takes place at two o'clock in the afternoon and is definitely not the time to take a siesta. The name of the parade comes from a massive firecracker that's known as the *masclet*. All morning professional pyro-technicians, all employed by the clubs, can be seen stretching wires, tens of metres long, between trees, and attaching explosive charges (*los carcasses*), which are tied up in ribbons like sweets in coloured wrappers. Just before lunch, after a period of *broncas* (general hullabaloo) and whistling, the *fallera mayor* lights the first fuse. Three detonations warn the spectators that the explosions are about to begin. Then the town begins to shake and rattle as the fireworks explode all around. The streets become swathed in a suffocating cloud of sulphur, dust and smoke, which mingles with the smell of the traditional *buñuelos* (doughnuts). Beware, these are not like normal bangers – these fireworks let off seriously loud explosions of sound. To give you some idea of the level of noise generated by these fireworks, nearly 120 kilograms (270 lbs) of explosives are ignited during the Plaza del Ayuntamiento *mascletá*. Fans maintain that the *mascletás* can be very different from one day to the next. The technicians play with the frequency and power of the detonations, the colour of the smoke and the height of the rockets, taking the same amount of painstaking care as that used by a composer working on a rousing symphony.

Toros

If you want to see bullfights in operatic settings, check the specialist *Fallas* newspapers for details of fights. The spectacle generally starts at around noon.

There are several bullfighting taverns (El Café Gaón, El Raim, El Club Taurino) around the Plaza de Toros, where you can mingle with bullfighting *aficionados* (die-hard fans). The bullfighters themselves tend to stay in the Astoria, Valencia Palace, Rey Don Jaime and Reina Victoria hotels. Anyway, for those who want to join in discussions on the different *faenas* of *novilleros* and matadors, the people in the know can often be found at a post-mortem *tertulia* at the Astoria, the De tinto et oro association (calle Julio Antonio) and the Hotel Don Jaime.

Fireworks and *Cremà*

Every night, after midnight, there is a huge firework display on the dried-up river bed of the Turia. This is a real opportunity for firework companies, to showcase their newest and best products. The cost of these displays is usually kept quiet but an investigation has been carried out by opponents of the *Fallas* (believe it or not, there are some) who estimate the general cost at 40 thousand million pesetas, of which 222 million goes on the powder (*mascletás* and fireworks) itself.

On the night of 19 March, all the *Fallas* are set on fire (the *cremà*). This marks the end of the festival and for the *Falleras* the end of their reign. Everyone watches the pyrotechnic display – the work of the craftsmen is over in minutes, leaving nothing but vast smoking bonfires.

How to Get the Best Out of the *Fallas*

– If you can't be there during the 'big week', there are *mascletás* in the square in front of the ayuntamiento (town hall) from 1 to 19 March. Also, for one month before the *plantá*, there is an exhibition of the current year's *ninots* in the basement of the Ruzafa market.

– To get to the heart of the *Fallas*, try and get to know some *falleros*. Find a *casal* and get on friendly terms with one of its members. It is not a difficult exercise because, in general, there is a big table set up in the street where the *falleros*, the musicians and firework specialists, will dine.

– As far as the *mascletás* are concerned, don't feel you have to head for the one in the Plaza del Ayuntamiento because you think it will be the most impressive. A local neighbourhood *mascletá* makes just as much noise.

– As there have been several accidents, children should buy their bangers in authorized shops accompanied by their parents. Particular care should be taken after a local *mascletá*, regardless of whether you have children with you. Occasionally some of the *carcasses* fail to go off. Despite checks carried out by those in charge youngsters have been known to play with them.

– For the fireworks, the clearest views are from the Paseo de la Ciudadela, el Puente de Mar, la Plaza de America, el puente Aragón and el Paseo de la Alameda (A2 on map II).

– It is worth noting that the Valencian *falleras* always wear a necklace, which distinguishes them from their counterparts in Alicante, Castellón and even the Canaries.

– There is a series of free concerts every evening of the week to entertain passers-by. They are usually held in the Jardines de Viveros. Information is available from the Tourist Office.

SHOPPING

– A good thing to do in the morning is wander round the **Plaza del Mercado**, where you can admire the market itself at the same time. Built by Alejandro Soler and Francisco Guardia in the 1920s, it is apparently the biggest covered market in Europe, with an area of about 8,000 square metres (86,080 square feet). The stalls overflow with a profusion of seafood (*cigalas*, *rojos*, *almejas*, etc), fruit and vegetables, charcuterie and poultry. You will also find paella-pans up to a metre in diameter. You get a real sense here of the town's ancient Moorish influences. The tiny shops sell a wide range of products – olives, spices, gourds, hams, cheeses, and ceramics.

– On Thursday, you can also go to the **Mercado de Cabanyals** (D2, **126** on map III). Catch bus No. 32 from the Plaza del Ayuntamiento. Make sure your purse or wallet is tucked away somewhere safe from prying hands and keep a tight hold of your bag – pickpockets and unauthorized peddlers occasionally prey on tourists in this area. The market spills over into the adjacent calle Mediterraneo and calle Rosario. It is not as interesting as the Mercado Central and you won't pick up any amazing bargains but it is good for second-hand clothes.

– In calle Avellanes, calle del Mar and calle Gravador Esteve, several **antique shops** offer some unusual items for sale.

WHAT TO SEE NEARBY

★ El Palmar guides, ☎ (961) 71-07-14, provide guided excursions covering the flora and fauna of **La Albufera** and the history of their village, lasting three to four hours. In theory, it is reserved for groups but, if you give them some notice, they try to fit you in. Reasonably priced and the people leading the excursions are very friendly. Generally not available in the last fortnight in August, when they are all away on holiday. In any case, you will see more wildlife in spring and autumn.

LEAVING VALENCIA

By Bus

🚌 **Estación de Autobuses** (bus station: A1 on map II): avenida Ménendez Pidal 13. ☎ 49-72-22. To most of the country's main towns and cities. Not the fastest way to travel but a bit cheaper than the train.

– around nine buses a day to Barcelona, four to Málaga, eight to Madrid, five to Murcia and three to Seville.

By Boat

⚓ **Estación Marítima** (port: D3, **5** on map III): ☎ 67-65-12 (reservations) and 67-10-62 (information). From the bus station, catch bus No. 8 to the plaza del Ayuntamiento and change onto buses 1, 2 or 3 to the port. From the train station, you need bus No. 19 for the port.

– Boats to Ibiza (six a week), Palma (six a week) and Minorca (one a week).

By Train

🚆 **RENFE Station** (C4 on map I): calle Xátiva. ☎ 52-02-02. Night trains are a better option for shoe-string travellers as you then save on a night's accommodation (although you don't get the pleasure of seeing the landscape). The Bono City Pass means you can save up to 30 per cent on four journeys between major towns.

– two trains to **Seville** plus one night train (around 8 hour's journey).

– four trains to **Madrid Atocha** (around 3 hour 30 minutes' journey), eight from Madrid to Valencia.

– five trains to **Játiva** and **Alicante** (around 2 hour's journey).

– five trains to **Barcelona**. The most direct are the TGV Euromeds (around 3 hours).

By Air

✈ **Manises airport**: it is better to catch the train rather than the special airport bus. This is the only way of ensuring you won't get caught up in the frequent traffic jams. There are trains every hour and the station is only 2 minutes from the airport. Otherwise, bus No. 52 (yellow) leaves regularly from the bus station. It is much cheaper than a taxi. There are around 12 buses a day during the week (from 6am to 9pm), fewer on a Saturday and none on Sunday.

Hitchhiking

The best way to get to the south of Spain is to catch the bus to the beach (El Saler) and start hitching from there. Another alternative, if you are hoping to get onto the motorway towards Gandía and Alicante, is to wait in plaza Manuel Sanchis Garner. Remember to take sensible precautions when hitching, such as making sure you travel with one other person.

SAGUNTO 46500

DIALLING CODE: 962

After visiting Valencia, it would be a pity to pass Sagunto by. It's a pretty little town that is overlooked by an imposing fort called, bizarrely, the Acropolis. The fort is set on the lowest foothills of the Sierra Calderona and has a lovely view of the village, the coastline, the harbour and the beach (which has received a European 'clean beach' award).

Sagunto was the strategic centre for the control of Valencia to the north and its capture was one of the causes of the second Punic war between Rome and Carthage. Called 'Murviedro' for a long time, it only assumed its present name at the beginning of the 19th century.

USEFUL ADDRESS

🅱 Tourist Office: plaza Cronista Chabret. ☎ 46-22-13.

WHERE TO STAY AND EAT

You should definitely try to avoid staying in Sagunto itself. All the hotels are along the N340, and development of the port and local industry has led to an incessant stream of heavy lorries. Not ideal when you fancy a siesta.

🛏 There are a few cheap **pensiones** and **hostales** 4 kilometres (2 miles) away in Sagunto Puerto, but they are fairly nondescript.

✕ **Mesón Casa Felipe**: Castillo 21. ☎ 66-38-01. Right in the heart of the old Jewish quarter. Handily located on the way back down from the castle. Set menu for around 7€. Small, unassuming, family-run restaurant. The paella is not spectacular, but it is very tasty. At weekends, call in and reserve a table before you go for a stroll round the castle walls as the tables in the dining room soon fill up.

WHAT TO SEE

The whole of the old town is worth having a look at, with its medieval houses, small squares and Jewish quarter consisting of a handful of alleyways and a small cemetery. The town has quite a few major monuments that are of interest.

★ **The Castle**: open 10am–2pm and 4–6pm. Closed Sunday afternoon and Monday. Free entry. Monumental, 5-hectare (12 acre) citadel-fortress overlooking the town. The winding road that leads up to the castle is delightful in itself. It is a pity that the interior section of the fort has not been better maintained. Iberians, Moors, Romans and the architects of the Middle Ages, all modifed the Acropolis over the years. A short leaflet available at the entrance enables you to work out the different stages of the construction of the castle. In 218 BC, it was the scene of an incredible tragedy. Hannibal had laid siege to the fortress for eight months and the population of Saguntum had begun to lose strength. Rather than cede to his army, though, the men decided to build a great fire and burn everything they owned, including their wives and children, and finally themselves.

★ **The Roman Theatre**: same opening hours as the castle. The theatre has been completely rebuilt and is used to stage a number of operas in the summer. Programme available from the Tourist Office.

★ As you make your way down from the castle, in the Jewish quarter, note the **Ermita de la Sangre** with its glazed tiles.

★ **The Temple of Diana**: at the foot of the slope, behind the church of Santa María (also worth a look). The temple consists of an enormous wall, 15 metres (49 feet) in length and 4 metres (13 feet) in height, all that remains of a Roman temple built with remarkably large stones. A short distance on, to the left and beside the attractive cemetery, you can see how the Romans cut into the hill to quarry the stones for building.

★ For the conscientious, or genuine archaeology buffs, there is a small **archaeological museum** beside the theatre. It contains nothing of any particular interest.

PENÍSCOLA (PEÑISCOLA) 12598   DIALLING CODE: 964

In spite of the bleak 8 kilometres (5 miles) or so of modern flats and hotels crammed between Benicarló and Peñíscola, the town is worth a visit. A little way from the centre and perched on what is virtually its own island, is the old town. This is an interesting little place. The beach promenade is planted with palm trees, giving it an exotic and peaceful atmosphere. Remarkably, when Benedict XIII made it his chosen seat in 1411, Peñíscola became the third papal city after Rome and Avignon. Its other claim to fame is its heroic resistance, in common with so many other towns in Spain, of Napoleonic troops, especially General Suchet.

GETTING THERE

By Train and Bus

From Valencia or Barcelona: there are several trains a day. Note that the station is not in Peñíscola itself, although it does go by the same name. It is in fact 7 kilometres (4 miles) away in Benicarló, on the other side of the N340. You need to catch one of the Amsa (Autos Mediterraneo) buses to the centre of town. Out of season, the bus does not run so you will have to take a taxi: ☎ 46-05-05, 48-96-64 or (908) 66-51-95.

By Bus

– **From Benicarló and Vinarós**: with the Amsa bus company. ☎ 22-00-54.

– **From Madrid**: with the Auto Res bus company. ☎ 48-18-88.

– **From Zaragoza or Barcelona**: with the Hife bus company. ☎ (977) 44-03-00.

USEFUL ADDRESSES

🄴 Tourist Office: paseo Marítimo. ☎ 48-02-08. On the seafront. Opening hours vary, but as a general rule in summer it is open Monday to Saturday 9am–8pm, and Sunday 10am–2pm. Out of season, Monday to Friday 9.30am–1.30pm and 4–7pm; Saturday 10am–1pm and 4–7pm; closed Sunday.

✉ Post Office: calle del Río 13. ☎ 48-08-41. Open mornings only, 9am–2pm.

Banks: there are several banks on avenida José Antonio. Banesto, Banco de Valencia and Caja Rural accept all credit cards.

Rosa Marí Laundrette: calle La Cova. ☎ (989) 86-79-08.

@Internet: Bowling La Estación, in Benicarló.

RENFE Train Station: Benicarló. ☎ 46-02-12.

Bus Companies

Amsa: ☎ 22-00-54.

Auto Res: ☎ 48-18-88.

Hife: ☎ (977) 440-300.

WHERE TO STAY

☆ Budget

⌂ Camping Cactus: avenida Papa Luna 92. ☎ 47-33-38. Only 50 metres from the beach. Closes on 30 September. Quite a long way out of the town centre. Cheap, well shaded campsite. The owners are French. Good, well-maintained facilities.

⌂ Camping El Eden: avenida Papa Luna. ☎ 48-05-62 or 48-04-44. Near the centre and only 50 metres from the beach. Open all year round. Well shaded. This is the most expensive campsite in the area, but it has the best facilities – swimming pool, restaurant and supermarket.

☆☆ Moderate

⌂ Camping Ferrer: avenida Estación 27. ☎ 48-92-23 and 48-14-01. Fax: 48-92-23. The closest campsite to the centre (five minutes on foot) but also the furthest from the beach. Clean and well shaded with good facilities. Swimming pool. Supermarket nearby. Moderately priced.

⌂ Tío Pepe: avenida José Antonio 32. ☎ and fax: 48-06-40. Pension right in the centre of town, near the Tourist Office, the beach (packed) and the Casco Antiguo (old quarter). In July, doubles with en-suite bathrooms cost 30€, breakfast included. In August, the same rooms on a full board basis are 36€. Not the Ritz, but for travellers on a small budget the rooms are spacious enough and clean.

⌂ Pensión España: calle San Roque 15. ☎ 48-05-64. Doubles with shared bathrooms cost around 21€. Brightly painted, but the rooms are a bit tatty.

☆☆☆ Expensive

⌂ Mare Nostrum: avenida Primo de Rivera 13 (entrance on calle Molino). ☎ 48-16-26. Room prices range from 50€ for doubles without balconies to 58€ for double rooms with balconies and a view of Playa Norte. Breakfast is included. All mod cons and all rooms have a view of the beach or the port. Friendly welcome from the smiling owners, Manolita and Paquita. The hotel is right next to the sea and only a stone's throw from the old town. Good value for money.

🛏 **Chiki**: Mayor 3. ☎ 48-02-84. Doubles with en-suite bathrooms for 45€. If you are going to stay in Peníscola, it may as well be here in the Casco Antiguo (old quarter) – really the town's sole attraction. This is a very good hotel with well-kept rooms at reasonable prices. The only drawback is the noise of the bells that wake you in the morning.

WHERE TO EAT

🍴 **El Peñon**: calle Santos Martíres 22. ☎ 48-07-16. in the Casco Antiguo (old quarter). Lunch and evening set menus for 5–6€. A few tables, often all taken by local shopkeepers who come here for their lunch. A good restaurant serving up large portions of *comida casera* (home cooking). Debates on such important topics as how to prepare the definitive sangría rage good-naturedly between the owner and his customers.

WHAT TO SEE

★ **The Castle**: ☎ 48-00-21. Email: castillo@dipcas.es. Opening hours tend to vary, but in theory it is open 9.30am–1pm and 3.15–6pm in winter; 9.30am–2.30pm and 4.30–9.30pm in summer. Admission costs less than 2€. Concessions. Free for the disabled and accompanied children under 10 years of age.

Situated on a natural promontory, the island was turned into a peninsula by the construction of a solid, permanent causeway. This 13th-century castle, built by the Templars, has resisted several invasions over the centuries but now the only invaders are eager tourists.

The history of this fortress is particularly associated with the remarkable life of Pope Benedict XIII who made Peníscola a papal town. In 1378, on the death of Gregory XI, the great schism of the west took place. This saw one Pope being elected in Rome another deposed (Urban VI) and yet another, Clément VII, elected in Avignon. Clement VII was replaced by Pedro de Luna, who assumed the name Benedict XIII. But in the meantime, Avignon and Rome had come to an arrangement (1411), and so Benedict XIII became ostracized. Furious, he withdrew to Peníscola to create a third papal city. On Benedict's death in 1423, his replacement, Clement VIII, managed to retain his position for no more than a few months, marking the end of Peníscola's life as a papal city.

There's not a lot to see inside the castle other than several relics dating from that troubled period, but it is advisable to go in the morning before the tourist invasion begins.

★ The whole of **the old town** surrounding the fortress is very pleasant, with its steep old alleyways and well-maintained walkways along its ramparts.

★ The return of the **trawlers** to the port after fishing (about 4.30pm): the families of the fishermen leap onto the boats to sort the fish and depart as quickly as they came to sell it at auction. Fascinating.

FIESTAS

– The most important fiesta starts on 7 September in honour of the Virgin Mary. There is a big party in which the whole town participates enthusiastically and a spectacular fireworks display.

LEAVING PENÍSCOLA

By Train

– **To Tortosa, Tarragona and Barcelona**. There is also another line in the Castelló de la Plana and Valencia direction: contact RENFE in Benicarló for details of all rail services. ☎ 46-02-12.

By Bus

There is no actual bus station, but there are several bus stops in the town centre. The one you use depends on your destination. Ask in the Tourist Office for more information.

– **To Madrid, Zaragoza and Benicarló** (connection with the Valencia train) and **Barcelona** (direct in summer).

MORELLA 12300   DIALLING CODE: 964

Leaving the dreary coastline, hidden 60 kilometres (37 miles) inland from Vinarós is Morella. As you leave the coast, the road starts to climb, first through fields of cows and then over hills where the vegetation turns into scrub-land. Morella is not a place you happen upon by chance. You have to cross a landscape scorched by the sun in summer and ravaged by the wind in winter. Here and there tucked into folds in the hills, sheltered from the elements among green oaks, a few dry-stone sheep barns are the only buildings to indicate any human presence. Then, all of a sudden, the majestic citadel of Morella appears through a gap in the rocks. This is a jewel of a place, which is just begging to be included in the list of World Heritage Sites.

The walls are well preserved and the castle proudly sits in state over the village. The churches are scarcely distinguishable amongst the patchwork of curved tiles and unfortunately some nasty factories at the bottom of the village mar the general harmony. Morella seems to have expanded a little too quickly in recent years and is now living to regret it. Be that as it may, this small citadel set high up in the hills makes a wonderful change after the monotony of the coast.

PARKING

As it was built long before the invention of the internal combustion engine, the streets have little regard for the width of cars and so the historic centre is closed to traffic. Visitors with their own vehicle should park by the San Mateo or San Miguel gates. At night some people sneak their cars just inside the town walls, but this is strictly against the rules.

USEFUL ADDRESS

❚ Tourist Office: at the bottom of the Miguel tower. ☎ 17-30-32. Open 10am–2pm and 4–6pm. The staff give good information, and are especially well-informed about houses available for rent in the region.

WHERE TO STAY

☆☆ Moderate

⚑ Hostal del Cid: Porta Sant Mateu 3. ☎ 16-01-25. A double room costs around 31€. Recently revamped in the style of a motel. The exterior concrete-cube style of architecture is far from aesthetically pleasing. Inside however, the rooms are big, with natural wood furniture and modern white bathrooms.

☆☆☆☆ Splash Out

⚑ Hotel Cardenal Ram: Cuesta Suñer 1. ☎ 17-30-85. Fax: 17-32-18. A double room costs 51–54€,

breakfast not included. The opulent building that houses this hotel has the air of a *parador* about it, but unfortunately it lacks the finishing touches that would make it special. In its time, it has played host to such luminaries as Benedict XIII and the King of Aragón. The hotel has retained its country-house character, particularly evident in the large rooms. The ones with a view over the valley are often reserved for families as they have room for additional beds.

WHERE TO EAT

☆ Budget

✕ Casa Pere: Cuesta Suñer. Just opposite the hotel Cardenal Ram, under the arches. A meal costs less than 6€. Small, unassuming bar serving some excellent tapas. The ideal place for a beer before tackling the numerous steps up to the historical centre.

☆☆ Moderate

✕ Casa Roque: Segura Barreda 8. ☎ (96) 416-03-36. There is a set menu offering the opportunity to sample several different dishes for around 8€. One of the most consistently good restaurants in the town. The menu offers a good range of local dishes including *embutido*s (selection of cold sausages), *llonganissas* (long pork and beef sausages) and, season permitting, truffles.

WHAT TO SEE

★ La Iglesia de Santa María la Mayor: access to the main body of this beautiful church is through the puerta de la Virgen in the south aisle. Before you enter, take a look at the Apostles' door on the right. The interior, which according to the experts is one of the most beautiful examples of Valencian Gothic art, drips with gold ornamentation. The high altar and the retable, supported by beautiful twisted columns, was entirely financed by families living in Morella. The whole thing has been completely restored. If you want to have a really good look at the details of the architecture, take plenty of loose change to operate the time-controlled spotlights (when they were on the whole time, the original spotlights were found to be damaging the fine gold).

The central nave is divided by an unusual raised gallery and there is an interesting wooden staircase decorated with pastoral scenes and polished by the hands of the faithful.

The big, imposing organ is decorated with 18th-century motifs. There are organ concerts every Sunday and during the Morella fiesta.

★ Walk the 2.5 kilometres (1.5 miles) round the 14th-century walls to get an idea of the town's impressive defences – 10 metres (33 feet) high, interspersed with 6 gates and 14 towers.

WHAT TO SEE IF YOU HAVE A BIT MORE TIME

★ The castle (in a ruined but stable state), the church and convent of Sant Francesc (only the chapter house and cloister visible), and the church of Sant Joan.

WHAT TO SEE NEARBY

★ El Santuario de la Balma: the sanctuary, situated 10 kilometres (6 miles) or so from Morella, was built into the rock after a shepherd saw a vision of the Virgin here. It is said that not only did she appear before him in all her majesty, but she restored his amputated arm. It is a very Spanish place of devotion with bridal gowns, clanking bundles of votive offerings in the shape of artificial limbs, thousands of photographs and testimonies in thanks or supplication to the Virgin. There is a pilgrimage on 8 September every year.

SHOPPING

🔒 **Productos Artesanos José T. Guimera**: Virgen del Pilar 27. ☎ 17-31-15. Splendid display and choice of local honey and homemade charcuterie from the region.

LEAVING MORELLA

It is best to visit Morella by car. If this is not possible, there is a bus from Castellón leaving at 7.15am and 6.10pm. Buses to Castellón leave Morella very early in the morning (7.30am) and in the afternoon (4pm). The bus stop is located next door to the hotel Cid.

CHULILLA 46167   DIALLING CODE: 961

If you take the road to the Madrid, within 50 kilometres (31 miles) or so you reach the Castilian plateau and the landscape begins to get more rugged. The rich, fertile market gardens give way to olive groves and blood-red earth. This unwelcoming terrain conceals some delightful little villages and many Valencians make their escape here at weekends. Chulilla is one such retreat. It is a small town set against a cliff and overhung by a magnificent piece of rock that many rock climbers find difficult to scale. It is surprising to discover that the small stream running along the foot of the village was responsible for carving out this imposing rock-face.

GETTING THERE

Although it involves a bit of a detour, it is worth taking the 224 from Requena. The road has a series of hairpin bends that would test a grand prix driver as it weaves its way between the Tejo, Santa María and Enmedio sierras.

WHERE TO STAY, EAT AND DRINK

☺ Budget

🛏 **Refugio Albergue El Altico**: pol. 3, parcela 317. ☎ 65-70-10. The only building on the cliffs and very popular with climbers. A bed in one of the dormitories costs around 5€ per person. It is also possible to camp in the hostel's grounds. Outside bathroom facilities. All rather spartan but for these prices what can you expect? Maps of climbing routes are available in the local area and you can hire a guide to take you canyoning.
🍸 There are several small **bars** on the village's main square, beyond the traffic lights.

☆☆ Moderate

🛏 ✕ **Bar la Rueda**: calle Ermita 10. ☎ 65-70-25. On the way into the village, before you get to the service station. Closed on Tuesday and from mid-September to mid-October. There are several apartments sleeping four people from 60€ (you might be able to negotiate the price down to 30€ for two). Well equipped with pale wooden furniture, TV and wood-burning stoves. An extensive, reassuring set menu for around 11€, consisting of a starter, two main dishes and one dessert.

WHAT TO SEE AND DO

★ In the Middle Ages, the **castle** on its rocky peak was used to house prisoners of the Inquisition. The entrance is not easy to find – head uphill from the centre of village and once you are behind the church, push a small makeshift door to get in.

★ **The centre of the village**, is picturesque with a small burbling fountain to charm you.

– **El Charco Azul**: this gorge of the river Turia makes for a pleasant walk out of the village. The route is marked with an arrow. The less hardy can drive down the road to the left and past the service station. A small footpath runs along the banks of the river and past small gardens and allotments. Climbers will feel instantly at home in the El Altico refuge (*see* 'Where to Stay').

– There are several routes that will interest climbers, one is near the **Cueva del Tesoro** and the other near the **Cueva del Gollisno**. At the entrance to the village, turn left down the road that goes down to the river. Follow the road to the left and park just before the little bridge. Walk for about 15 to 20 minutes to get to the Cueva del Tesoro, a large overhang of rock that faces the castle. There are two routes to the left of the overhang, but you need to be equipped with spits to undertake them. On the way to the rock face, look out for blocks of stone painted with blue arrows pointing the way to the Cueva del Gollisno – approximately 30-minutes walk away. This second *cueva* is in fact a small gorge that you reach after crossing a couple of rather wobbly logs. There are four routes, two to the north and two to the south. They start about 50 metres (55 yards) from the log crossing. Some routes are in the process of being marked. The arrows continue at the top of the plateau where the rock is very jagged.

Index

Note: Page numbers in *italics* refer to maps/plans

Make the most of your mini-break

Great Weekend titles provide all the information you need to ensure that you really get to know a city in just a few days – from advice on what to see, where to stay and where to eat out, to exploring the city's character through its culture and lifestyle. Plus a detailed section on where to do your shopping. Full colour throughout and great value for money.

A GREAT WEEKEND *in* ....

AMSTERDAM	1 84202 002 1
BARCELONA	1 84202 170 2
BERLIN	1 84202 061 7
BRUSSELS	1 84202 017 X
DUBLIN	1 84202 096 X
FLORENCE	1 84202 010 2
LISBON	1 84202 011 0
LONDON	1 84202 168 0
MADRID	1 84202 095 1
NAPLES	1 84202 016 1
NEW YORK	1 84202 004 8
PARIS	1 84202 001 3
PRAGUE	1 84202 000 5
ROME	1 84202 169 9
VENICE	1 84202 018 8
VIENNA	1 84202 026 9

Forthcoming titles:

BUDAPEST	1 84202 160 5
SEVILLE	1 84202 162 1

Titles are available through all good booksellers, or by calling 01903 828800, quoting ref. RT2 (in the UK).

HACHETTE

HACHETTE VACANCES

A unique series of regional guides in colour that focus on the needs of families and those in search of an active holiday. Packed with hundreds of suggestions for places to visit, sights to see and things to do – as well as providing detailed information about the region's culture, heritage and history

Titles currently published:

Brittany	1 84202 007 2
Catalonia	1 84202 099 4
Corsica	1 84202 100 1
Languedoc–Roussillon	1 84202 008 0
Normandy	1 84202 097 8
Perigord & Dordogne	1 84202 098 6
Poitou–Charentes	1 84202 009 9
Provence & The Côte d'Azur	1 84202 006 4
Pyrenees & Gascony	1 84202 015 3
South West France	1 84202 014 5

Forthcoming titles:

Alsace–Vosges	1 84202 167 2
Ardeche	1 84202 161 3
Basque Country	1 84202 159 1
French Alps	1 84202 166 4

Titles are available through all good booksellers, or by calling 01903 828800, quoting ref. RT1 (in the UK).

routard

Titles in this series are available through all good booksellers, or can be ordered by calling 01903 828800, quoting ref. RT3 (in the UK).